SPSS/PC+™
Base System User's Guide
Version 5.0

Marija J. Norušis / SPSS Inc.

SPSS Inc.
444 N. Michigan Avenue
Chicago, Illinois 60611
Tel: (312) 329-2400
Fax: (312) 329-3668

SPSS Federal Systems (U.S.)
SPSS Latin America
SPSS Benelux BV
SPSS GmbH Software
SPSS UK Ltd.
SPSS UK Ltd., New Delhi
SPSS France SARL
SPSS Scandinavia AB
SPSS Asia Pacific Pte. Ltd.
SPSS Japan Inc.
SPSS Australasia Pty. Ltd.

P9-DMB-605

For more information about SPSS® software products, please write or call

Marketing Department
SPSS Inc.
444 North Michigan Avenue
Chicago, IL 60611
Tel: (312) 329-2400
Fax: (312) 329-3668

SPSS is a registered trademark and the other product names are the trademarks of SPSS Inc. for its proprietary computer software. No material describing such software may be produced or distributed without the written permission of the owners of the trademark and license rights in the software and the copyrights in the published materials.

The SOFTWARE and documentation are provided with RESTRICTED RIGHTS. Use, duplication, or disclosure by the Government is subject to restrictions as set forth in subdivision (c)(1)(ii) of The Rights in Technical Data and Computer Software clause at 52.227-7013. Contractor/manufacturer is SPSS Inc., 444 N. Michigan Avenue, Chicago, IL, 60611.

General notice: Other product names mentioned herein are used for identification purposes only and may be trademarks of their respective companies.

SPSS/PC+™ Base System User's Guide, Version 5.0
Copyright © 1992 by SPSS Inc.
All rights reserved.
Printed in the United States of America.

No part of this publication may be reproduced, stored in a retrieval system, or transmitted, in any form or by any means, electronic, mechanical, photocopying, recording, or otherwise, without the prior written permission of the publisher.

3 4 5 6 7 8 9 0   98 97 96 95 94

ISBN 0-13-177692-4

Library of Congress Catalog Card Number: 92-085164

Preface

SPSS/PC+ Version 5 continues the SPSS line of powerful statistical and information analysis systems running on a wide selection of mainframe and personal computers. As the latest product for the PC-DOS/MS-DOS operating system, it offers new facilities and enhanced flexibility in choosing the portions of the system that meet your needs. SPSS/PC+ Version 5 retains its menu system for building commands and for contextual help, as well as its command line and batch operation modes. New features in SPSS/PC+ Version 5 are described below. As in previous versions, the SPSS/PC+ Version 5 system is built around the reliable, tested routines developed for SPSS software systems over a period of more than 20 years.

This manual describes the base system of SPSS/PC+ and the base statistics procedures. The base system includes the components necessary to run statistical procedures in the base and all of the options.

Add-on enhancements that you can purchase include:

- SPSS/PC+ Professional Statistics™.
- SPSS/PC+ Advanced Statistics™.
- SPSS/PC+ Tables™ for presentation quality tabular reports.
- SPSS/PC+ Trends™ for time-series analysis.
- SPSS/PC+ Categories™ for conjoint analysis and optimal scaling.
- SPSS Data Entry II™ for data entry and validation.
- SPSS/PC+ Graphics™ from TriMetrix™.
- SPSS/PC+ Map™ from MapInfo®.

In updating the manuals for SPSS/PC+ Version 5, we have maintained the balance of operational instructions, statistical guidance, and reference material that has characterized earlier versions. Operational instructions for the system appear in the first few chapters of this manual. In each of the SPSS/PC+ manuals, including this one, statistical overviews guide the new user in the rationale behind statistical procedures, their use, and the interpretation of their output. The comprehensive Syntax Reference in each book remains an essential guide for the experienced user.

What's New?

Changes since SPSS/PC+ Version 4:

- Use of DOS extended memory.
- Quick Edit (QED), a new data-entry facility incorporated into the system.
- Repackaging of the system into units designed to be the most useful to our users— Base, Professional Statistics, and Advanced Statistics.
- New versions of Examine and T-Test procedures.
- Upgrades to Quick Cluster, Oneway, Probit, and Tables procedures.
- Menu access to products such as CHAID and DBMS/COPY.
- New LISREL 7 and PRELIS option.
- New version of the popular CHAID option.
- Mouse driver.
- Security system.
- SPSS/PC+ Graphics from TriMetrix option, with new chart types including box-plots, error bar charts, high-low-close charts, and 3-D scatterplots.
- New installation procedures.
- Trends procedures work with either SPSS/PC+ Graphics from TriMetrix or Harvard Graphics for high-resolution time-series charts.

SPSS/PC+ with the Professional Statistics option will enable you to perform many analyses on your PC that were once possible only on much larger machines. We hope that this statistical power will make SPSS/PC+ an even more useful tool in your work.

Compatibility

SPSS Inc. warrants that SPSS/PC+ and enhancements are designed for personal computers in the IBM PC and IBM PS/2™ lines with a hard disk and at least 640K of RAM. Versions of SPSS/PC+ that support extended memory require additional memory. See the installation instructions that came with your Base System for more information. These products also function on most IBM-compatible machines. Contact SPSS Inc. for details about specific IBM-compatible hardware.

Serial Numbers

Your serial number is your identification number with SPSS Inc. You will need this serial number when you call SPSS Inc. for information regarding support, payment, a defective diskette, or an upgraded system.

The serial number can be found on diskette 3 of your Base System. Before using the system, please copy this number to the **registration card.**

Registration Card

STOP! Before going on, *fill out and send us your registration card.* Until we receive your registration card, you have an unregistered system. Even if you have previously sent a card to us, please fill out and return the card enclosed in your Professional Statistics package. Registering your system entitles you to

- Technical support on our customer hotline.
- Favored customer status.
- New product announcements.

Of course, unregistered systems receive none of the above, so *don't put it off—send your registration card now!*

Replacement Policy

Call Customer Service at 1-800-521-1337 to report a defective diskette. You must provide us with the serial number of your system. (The normal installation procedure will detect any damaged diskettes.) SPSS will ship replacement diskettes the same day we receive notification from you.

Training Seminars

SPSS Inc. provides both public and onsite training seminars for SPSS/PC+. All seminars feature hands-on workshops. SPSS/PC+ seminars will be offered in major U.S. and European cities on a regular basis. For more information on these seminars, call the SPSS Inc. Training Department toll-free at 1-800-543-6607.

Technical Support

The services of SPSS Technical Support are available to registered customers of SPSS/PC+. Customers may call Technical Support for assistance in using SPSS products or for installation help for one of the warranted hardware environments.

To reach Technical Support, call 1-312-329-3410. Be prepared to identify yourself, your organization, and the serial number of your system.

If you are a Value Plus or Customer EXPress customer, use the priority 800 number you received with your materials. For information on subscribing to the Value Plus or

Customer EXPress plan, call SPSS Software Sales at 1-800-543-2185 or 1-312-329-3300.

Additional Publications

Additional copies of all SPSS product manuals may be purchased separately. To order additional manuals, just fill out the Publications insert included with your system and send it to SPSS Publications Sales, 444 N. Michigan Avenue, Chicago, IL 60611.

Note: In Europe, additional copies of publications can be purchased by site-licensed customers only. For more information, please contact your local office at the address listed at the end of this preface.

Tell Us Your Thoughts

Your comments are important. So send us a letter and let us know about your experiences with SPSS products. We especially like to hear about new and interesting applications using the SPSS/PC+ system. Write to SPSS Inc. Marketing Department, Attn: Micro Software Products Manager, 444 N. Michigan Avenue, Chicago, IL 60611.

Contacting SPSS Inc.

If you would like to be on our mailing list, write to us at one of the addresses below. We will send you a copy of our newsletter and let you know about SPSS Inc. activities in your area.

SPSS Inc.
444 North Michigan Ave.
Chicago, IL 60611
Tel: (312) 329-2400
Fax: (312) 329-3668

SPSS Federal Systems
12030 Sunrise Valley Dr.
Suite 300
Reston, VA 22091
Tel: (703) 391-6020
Fax: (703) 391-6002

SPSS Latin America
444 North Michigan Ave.
Chicago, IL 60611
Tel: (312) 329-3556
Fax: (312) 329-3668

SPSS Benelux BV
P.O. Box 115
4200 AC Gorinchem
The Netherlands
Tel: +31.1830.36711
Fax: +31.1830.35839

SPSS GmbH Software
Steinsdorfstrasse 19
D-80538 Munich
Germany
Tel: +49.89.211050
Fax: +49.89.2285413

SPSS UK Ltd.
SPSS House
5 London Street
Chertsey
Surrey KT16 8AP
United Kingdom
Tel: +44.932.566262
Fax: +44.932.567020

SPSS UK Ltd., New Delhi
c/o Ashok Business Centre
Ashok Hotel
50B Chanakyapuri
New Delhi 110 021
India
Tel: +91.11.600121 x1029
Fax: +91.11.6873216

SPSS France SARL
72-74 Avenue Edouard Vaillant
92100 Boulogne
Tel: +33.1.4684.0072
Fax: +33.1.4684.0180

SPSS Scandinavia AB
Gamla Brogatan 36-38
4th Floor
111 20 Stockholm
Sweden
Tel: +46.8.102610
Fax: +46.8.102550

SPSS Asia Pacific Pte. Ltd.
10 Anson Road, #34-07
International Plaza
Singapore 0207
Singapore
Tel: +65.221.2577
Fax: +65.221.9920

SPSS Japan Inc.
2-2-22 Jingu-mae
Shibuya-ku, Tokyo
150 Japan
Tel: +81.3.5474.0341
Fax: +81.3.5474.2678

SPSS Australasia Pty. Ltd.
121 Walker Street
North Sydney, NSW 2060
Australia
Tel: +61.2.954.5660
Fax: +61.2.954.5616

Contents

23 Establishing Order: Procedure RANK   385

24 Reporting Results: Procedure REPORT   397

Syntax Reference   425

Universals   427

Commands   444

1 About This Manual

This is a large manual, in part because it documents a large and versatile software system, and in part because it seeks to meet the differing needs of a diverse body of users. For those who have limited experience with statistics, computing, or the IBM PC environment, introductory material and statistical overviews are available. For those who are already familiar with statistical computing, a reference section presents SPSS/PC+ commands without extensive examples. You are likely to find different sections of the manual most valuable as your experience with SPSS/PC+ grows.

If you have just received the system, you should turn first to the installation instructions that accompany the system. You need to install SPSS/PC+ only once unless you remove it from your system. (You can, however, remove and reinstall portions of the SPSS/PC+ system; for information, refer to the installation booklet.)

Introduction. The introductory chapters, Chapter 2 through Chapter 4, help you become familiar with running SPSS/PC+ and using Review, the SPSS/PC+ text editor. Chapter 2 describes the system's command based operation and gives overviews of the two environments available for entering commands. This includes a discussion of the Menu and Help system, which gives you help in building commands by describing each one and guiding you through command syntax. Chapter 3 provides an example that shows you step-by-step how to edit files using the fully integrated SPSS/PC+ text editor.

Statistics Guide. The statistics chapters, Chapter 5 through Chapter 24, contain a complete user's guide to the data definition and analysis facilities of SPSS/PC+, including QED, the SPSS/PC+ data entry and editing facility. If you are new to computer data analysis, you can start at the beginning of this section and progress through introductions to coding and entering data, defining the data in SPSS/PC+, and managing it, tabulating, and analyzing data with the many statistical procedures that SPSS/PC+ makes available. If you are more experienced, you can turn to the statistics chapters whenever you want a more guided approach to certain SPSS/PC+ facilities than you find in the Syntax Reference or when you want to further your understanding of the statistics calculated by certain procedures. This section does not discuss at length the SPSS/PC+ commands that control such things as the destination of output files or the format of the output. For that information, consult Chapter 2.

Syntax Reference. The syntax reference section provides a detailed reference to the syntax and operations of each SPSS/PC+ command. The opening section, Universals, documents the general characteristics of the system. Following that section, the individual commands are presented in alphabetical order. For each command, the Syntax Reference provides complete syntax rules plus details of operations.

Editing and Data Entry Reference. The section on REVIEW in the Syntax Reference contains a complete reference to all of the editing commands and keyboard shortcuts you can use in the Review text editor, as well as tables of mouse functions. The section on QED describes all of the commands and mouse functions available for entering and editing data in QED.

Examples. The examples section following the Syntax Reference illustrates typical uses of SPSS/PC+ analytical procedures. The annotated input and output are arranged not to imitate the progress of an interactive SPSS/PC+ session but to demonstrate a set of commands that carry out a complete data analysis task. You may find that these examples, with their interpretative commentary, extend your understanding of the logic of SPSS/PC+ command structure.

Glossary. The glossary defines terms used in this manual that may be unfamiliar to many users. It does not attempt to cover the full vocabulary of DOS operating manuals or the statistical terms discussed in this manual. The SPSS/PC+ *online* glossary, which does contain statistical terms, is available from Review (press F1 and select Glossary).

Appendixes. The appendixes supply information on how to use RAM-disk software with extended or expanded memory and provide general suggestions for using data or command files created by a text editor or other software.

2 Running SPSS/PC+

Overview

SPSS/PC+ accesses and analyzes data. You communicate with SPSS/PC+ through a **command language**. Commands are simply English-like statements, using the SPSS/PC+ command vocabulary. They can be simple, like

```
LIST.
```

They can contain additional specifications, such as

```
LIST CASES FROM 1 TO 100 BY 5.
```

Or commands can contain complex combinations of subcommands, such as

```
FREQUENCIES VARIABLES = SEX JOBCAT /BARCHART /STATISTICS ALL.
```

The command language is easy to understand, and SPSS/PC+ gives you a lot of help in learning and using it.

You use commands to do three things, usually in the following order:

1. Convert data into a form that can be used by the computer and bring the data into SPSS/PC+. Your data may exist on paper, or they may already exist in some electronic form used by other software (including SPSS, the mainframe version of SPSS/PC+). **Data definition** commands like DATA LIST, TRANSLATE, and GET (among others) tell SPSS/PC+ where and how to read data. The QED facility allows you to enter data directly.

2. Modify data. Once the data are in SPSS/PC+, you might decide, for example, to convert rainfall measured in centimeters to rainfall measured in inches, for which you could use a **data manipulation** command such as

```
COMPUTE RAINFALL = RAINFALL/2.54.
```

3. Process data. When your data are in the form you want, **procedure** commands like FREQUENCIES, MEANS, and REGRESSION tell SPSS/PC+ to do something with your data, such as perform a statistical analysis; produce a report, listing, or plot; sort your cases into a different order; or save your data to a file.

For example, the following is a typical series of commands:

```
GET FILE = 'WEATHER.SYS'.
COMPUTE RAINFALL = RAINFALL/2.54.
MEANS RAINFALL BY MONTH REGION.
```

- The GET command retrieves a **system file** named *WEATHER.SYS*. (A system file is a special type of SPSS/PC+ file that contains both data and information that describes the data.)
- The COMPUTE command converts rainfall in centimeters to rainfall in inches.
- The MEANS command computes the average rainfall for each month and for each region.

SPSS/PC+ can execute these commands one at a time or as a group. The next sections tell you about ways to enter commands and have SPSS/PC+ execute them.

During the course of an SPSS/PC+ session you can repeat any of the three steps above, to use different data, arrange the data differently, or run different analyses on them. In addition to procedure and data definition and manipulation commands, SPSS/PC+ has **operation** commands such as DISPLAY and SET that you use to find out about and control the SPSS/PC+ environment. For example, notice in the example above that each command must end with a period. If you want to use a different symbol to indicate your commands are complete, you can do so using the SET command.

Table 2.1 summarizes the commands used in SPSS/PC+.

Table 2.1   SPSS/PC+ command summary

	Function	**Commands**
Operation commands	Provide assistance	SHOW, DISPLAY
	Specify options for operations and output	SET
	Submit SPSS/PC+ commands from a file	INCLUDE
	Edit a file	REVIEW
	Access DOS or other facilities	DOS, EXECUTE, DBMSCOPY[*], CODEBOOK[†], CHAID[†]

Table 2.1   SPSS/PC+ command summary

	Function	Commands
Data defini-tion and manipulation commands	Read or write data	QED, GET, SAVE, DATA LIST, BEGIN DATA, END DATA, IMPORT, EXPORT, TRANSLATE, MODIFY VARS, WRITE, DE[†]
	Modify data values	RECODE, AUTORECODE, COMPUTE, IF, COUNT, RANK, CREATE[†], RMV[†]
	Define missing data	MISSING VALUE
	Select or weight data	SELECT IF, PROCESS IF, N, SAMPLE, WEIGHT, PREDICT[†], USE[†]
	Provide labels and formats	TITLE, SUBTITLE, *(comment), VARIABLE LABELS, VALUE LABELS, ADD VALUE LABELS, FORMAT, DATE[†]
	Manipulate files	AGGREGATE, SORT, JOIN MATCH, JOIN ADD, FLIP
Procedure commands	Reports and tables	LIST, REPORT, TABLES[†], PRINT TABLES[†]
	Descriptive statistics	DESCRIPTIVES, FREQUENCIES, EXAMINE, CROSSTABS, MEANS,
	Correlation and regression	CORRELATION, REGRESSION, CURVEFIT[†], AREG[†], WLS[†], 2SLS[†], LOGISTIC REGRESSION[†], PROBIT[†], NONLINEAR REGRESSION[†]
	Comparisons of group means	T-TEST, ONEWAY, ANOVA, MANOVA[†]
	Categorical modeling	LOGLINEAR[†], HILOGLINEAR[†]
	Classification and clustering	CLUSTER[†], QUICK CLUSTER[†], FACTOR[†], DSCRIMINANT[†]
	Time series analysis[†]	ACF[†], ARIMA[†], CCF[†], EXSMOOTH[†], FIT[†], PACF[†], SPECTRA[†], SEASON[†], X11ARIMA[†]
	Optimal scaling and correspon-dence analysis[†]	ANACOR[†], HOMALS[†], PRINCALS[†] OVERALS[†], ORTHOPLAN[†], PLANCARDS[†], CONJOINT[†]
	Graphics	PLOT, GRAPH[†], MAP[†], CASEPLOT[†], TSPLOT[†], NPPLOT[†]
	Other	NPAR TESTS, RELIABILITY[†], SURVIVAL[†]

*Available only in SPSS/PC+ options.

Entering Commands into SPSS/PC+

You can enter commands into SPSS/PC+ in the Review text editor, which is integrated with the Menu and Help system, or you can enter commands at a command prompt.

- **Review text editor.** The Review system includes a **Menu and Help system** that allows you to select commands from menus and paste them into the text editor. Along with the menus are descriptions of each command to help you figure out which one to select. Another way to enter commands into the text editor is to type them directly.

  You can edit the commands, whether they were pasted or typed. When you are satisfied with the commands, you can run them and see the results on the screen. The commands remain in the text editor. After you look at the results, you can make changes or add new commands to refine the analysis.

- **SPSS/PC+ command prompt.** With this method, the system prompts you to enter a command; you enter it; the system evaluates and executes it. This method does not provide information on which command to enter; nor does it provide much opportunity to edit a command or to change your mind once you've entered it. However, if you already know exactly which commands you want to use, you may prefer to work at the command prompt.

More Information

For a tutorial session on entering and running commands, see the booklet *Getting Started with SPSS/PC+*.

For further information on all the commands available in the Review text editor, see Chapter 3 and REVIEW in the Syntax Reference.

Starting SPSS/PC+

Before you can run SPSS/PC+ for the first time, you have to install it, using the installation instructions that accompany the system. Next, you should change your current directory to the one from which you want to execute SPSS/PC+ and in which you want to keep the data and other files used by the system. You may also want to change other DOS environmental parameters. For information about DOS and directories, see Chapter 4 or your DOS manual.

To start SPSS/PC+, at the DOS prompt type:

```
spsspc
```

and press ⏎Enter. This displays the SPSS/PC+ logo screen. The system then takes you straight to the Menu and Help system, unless you have changed the starting environment. You can change the starting environment by changing the SET commands in your profile. (See SET in the Syntax Reference and the section on the *SPSSPROF.INI* file in Chapter 3.)

Working in the Review Text Editor

The menu system contains all SPSS/PC+ commands and their keywords. A help system describing the function of commands is built in. You can use the Menu and Help system together with the text editor Review to produce your commands.

The menus do not control SPSS/PC+ directly. When you select a command (or a piece of a command) from a menu, it is simply pasted into Review's scratch pad (see "The Scratch Pad" on p. 16). To run the commands, you must tell SPSS/PC+ to do so. You can do this whenever you like—you can build a lengthy set of commands and run them all at once, or you can run them one at a time.

You can take over from the Menu and Help system at any time and use Review to type in commands yourself or to modify commands that you have pasted in. Whenever you need information from the Menu and Help system, you can easily recall it. It appears at a level containing information about the command you were typing in Review, showing and explaining the appropriate options.

Using the Mouse

If a mouse is installed, you can use it for quick and easy navigation. In the following sections, after the description of an action you can perform at the keyboard, you will often find a paragraph preceded by a mouse symbol. Such a paragraph describes how to perform the same action by using the mouse. In descriptions of mouse action, the following terminology is used:

✣ **Click** means to press and release the left mouse button once.

✣ **Double-click** means to click the left mouse button twice in succession.

✣ **Click the right mouse button** means to press and release the *right* button once.

Tables of mouse functions are in the sections on REVIEW and QED in the Syntax Reference.

Parts of the Screen

When you first start SPSS/PC+, you are automatically in the Menu and Help system. The screen looks like Figure 2.1.

Figure 2.1   Review text editor with the Menu and Help system

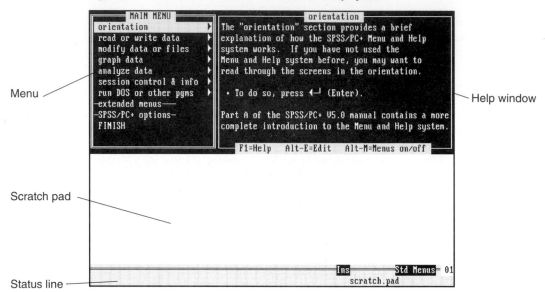

Menu

Help window

Scratch pad

Status line

Important things to notice are:

- The bottom half of the screen is the **scratch pad**, where Review works as a text editor. The cursor is initially in the scratch pad.

- The top left part of the screen is a **menu**, in this case the Main Menu, which is the "top" level of the Menu and Help system. The arrowhead character to the right of an item on any menu indicates that the item has a lower-level menu that you can access to see more detail.

- The top right part of the screen is a **Help window**. The Help window always describes the highlighted menu item, in this case orientation.

When you first enter the system, the top half of the screen—that is, the Menu and Help system—is active. If you press ⬆ or ⬇, the highlight moves up and down the menu.

Text Editor Commands

To see a list of the commands you can use to get around in the Review scratch pad and the Menu and Help system, press F1.

↜ Click in the status line.

A **mini-menu** containing several items appears in the status line at the bottom of the screen. The information you want is Review help. Since this item is highlighted, you can select it by pressing (◄Enter).

⮑ Double-click on Review help.

This displays the screen shown in Figure 2.2.

Figure 2.2   Review commands

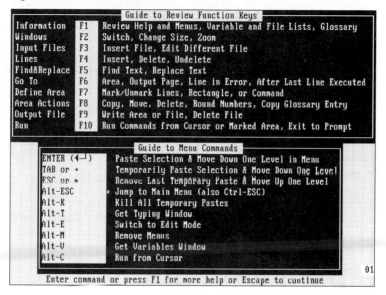

Commands at the top of the screen help you edit, review, and save files. You can run one of these commands from this screen by pressing the function key.

⮑ To run a command in the upper half of this screen, click on the command. Then look for the mini-menu in the status line below the scratch pad. Double-click on the item you want.

- When you press (F3), SPSS/PC+ asks for a filename and, depending on your selection, either inserts the file (Insert file) at the position of the cursor or replaces the current file (Edit different file). An inserted file remains in the scratch pad after you have run commands. A "different file" disappears after you run the commands.

Listed at the bottom of the screen are commands you can use to navigate in the Menu and Help system. As you can see, most of these commands use the (Alt) key, which you hold down while you press the corresponding command key.

- (Alt)-(M) clears away the Menu and Help system (leaving you in the Review environment) or brings it back if it is not on the screen.

- Alt-E allows you to edit the scratch pad but leaves the menus on screen until you press Alt-E again (or Esc) to return to the Menu system.)
- Another way to recall the menu system at any time is to press F1 followed by M.

To return from Review help to the Menu and Help system, press Esc.

Exploring the Menus

The easiest way to explore the Menu and Help system is with the cursor arrows on your keyboard or with the mouse.

- ↑ and ↓ move the highlighting up and down the menu. As each menu item is highlighted, the Help window describes what that item does, or how to use it.

↶ Click on the menu item.

- If a menu is too long to fit, up or down arrowheads at the right edge of the menu indicate the presence of items offscreen. As you move the highlighting up and down, the menu scrolls automatically to let you highlight these items. You can also use PgUp and PgDn to scroll the menus.

↶ Click on the up or down arrowhead at the right edge of the menu.

- Home and End take you to the first and last items on the menu.
- → moves you "deeper" into the menus. For example, if the item orientation is highlighted when you press →, the Orientation menu appears. You know that there is an Orientation menu because of the arrowhead beside orientation on the Main Menu.
- ← or Esc brings you back out of the menus, one level at a time, until you reach the Main Menu.

↶ Click the *right* mouse button.

- If the text in the Help window is too long to fit on the screen, an up or down arrowhead at the right edge of the Help window indicates the presence of offscreen text. Hold down Alt and use ↑, ↓, PgUp PgDn, Home, or End to scroll the text in the Help window (make sure that the Num Lock key is not active).

↶ Click on the up or down arrowhead at the right edge of the Help window.

Pasting Menu Selections

From the menus in SPSS/PC+, you can paste commands, keywords, variable names, and filenames into the scratch pad. The difference between exploring the menus with the cursor arrows, as discussed above, and pasting commands, is simple:

- To explore a menu selection without affecting the scratch pad, press →. The only thing that happens is you move to the lower-level menu associated with the current selection. (The menu selection is held for you, in case you decide to accept it after all.)

- To accept a menu selection and also (if it is part of a command that you are building) paste it into the scratch pad, press `⏎Enter`. The selection appears in the scratch pad, and again you move to the lower-level menu associated with the current selection, if there is one.

ꜱ Double-click on an item you want to paste.

Menu selections that are in upper case are either commands or parts of commands. They may be preceded on the menu by either a slash (/) or a tilde (~). The slash is a separator that SPSS/PC+ expects between different **subcommands** (parts of commands). The tilde (~) indicates a selection that is required: SPSS/PC+ cannot execute the command without that specification.

- You can always paste an uppercase menu selection into the scratch pad by pressing `⏎Enter` or double-clicking the mouse.
- Some other selections (such as the symbols +, -, *, and /) will also paste if you select them by pressing `⏎Enter` or by double-clicking the mouse.
- Selections in lower case do not paste into the scratch pad, regardless of whether you use `→` or `⏎Enter` to select them. You do move to the lower-level menu if there is one.
- When you paste a selection that needs to be "filled in," such as a pair of parentheses ( ) or apostrophes ' ', SPSS/PC+ automatically asks you to type the contents, unless the contents can be selected on a lower-level menu.

You can move the cursor to the scratch pad at any time by simply pressing `Alt`-`E`. This temporarily freezes the menus.

ꜱ Click anywhere in the scratch pad.

From there, you can do the following:
- Edit the commands you've pasted.
- Run them. We'll see below how you pass commands to SPSS/PC+ for execution.
- Save them into a file to use later. See "Saving Files" on p. 26 for an explanation of saving a list of commands.

To get back to the Menu and Help system, press `Esc`.

ꜱ Click on the Menu window.

Pasting after Exploring

If you explore a menu selection by pressing `→` and then decide to accept and paste a selection on a lower-level menu, Review goes back to fill in the intermediate steps before pasting the lower-level selection.

For example:

- You select the FREQUENCIES command and the /VARIABLES subcommand, and choose the variables for which you want frequency tables. All this is pasted into the scratch pad.

- You aren't sure whether you want to change the default format, so you explore /FORMAT by pressing ⊣. As shown in Figure 2.3, the FORMAT subcommand is not pasted into the scratch pad but is moved into a holding area or **buffer** at the bottom of the screen, in case it is needed later.

Figure 2.3   Review screen with text held in buffer

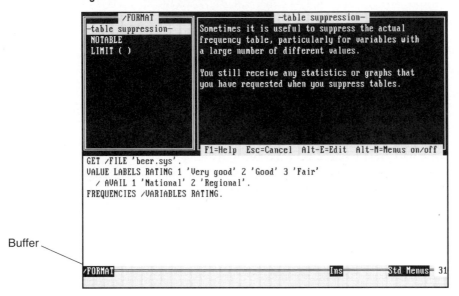

Buffer

After reading the Help windows for the various FORMAT specifications, you decide that you don't need any of them, so you "back out" by pressing ⊣ or Esc.

↪ Click the right mouse button to back out.

The buffer area and /FORMAT disappear from the bottom of the screen, and the FREQUENCIES menu reappears.

- You move the cursor to /STATISTICS and explore it by pressing ⊣. The STATISTICS menu appears, and /STATISTICS shows up in the buffer. After looking through the various choices on the STATISTICS menu, you decide that you want them all—so you highlight ALL and press ⊣Enter

↪ Double-click on ALL.

- SPSS/PC+ first pastes the subcommand /STATISTICS from the buffer, and then the keyword ALL that you explicitly pasted.

In this example, Review held the specifications that you explored (/FORMAT and /STATISTICS) in case you decided that you needed them. When you backed out of the /FORMATS menu, it discarded that specification. When you chose a statistics keyword, it filled in /STATISTICS so SPSS/PC+ would know that ALL referred to the STATISTICS subcommand.

- You can clear this holding buffer at any time by pressing (Alt)-(K).
- If you don't remember (Alt)-(K) (or any other Review command), press (F1), use the cursor arrows to highlight Review help, and press (↵Enter).

↪ Click in the status line and double-click on Review help.

Editing Pasted Commands

It's easy to add to or modify the commands you paste into the scratch pad. Press (Alt)-(E) to jump to the scratch pad or click in the scratch pad; you can also press (Alt)-(M) to clear the menus completely.

Then fix the commands. Usually the (Ins), (Del), and arrow keys will be all you need. See Chapter 3 for a discussion of more advanced editing functions.

To return to the menus, press (Alt)-(E) again or click in the Menu window; if you cleared the menus completely, press (Alt)-(M) again. (You can also press (F1), highlight Menus with the cursor arrows, and press (↵Enter).) The Menu and Help window for the specific command or subcommand you're working on in the scratch pad will be displayed. You can paste items from the menu, or you can press (Alt)-(E) to continue editing with the Help window to guide you.

Extended Menus

The standard menus do not show all of the keywords you can use to build SPSS/PC+ commands. Seldom-used keywords and options are omitted to reduce the complexity of the menus. To switch to the extended menus that show all available specifications, press (Alt)-(X). The message at the right-hand side of the bottom of the screen then changes from Std Menus to Ext Menus.

You may want to place the command

```
SET MENUS EXTENDED.
```

in your automatic profile *SPSSPROF.INI* (see the section on *SPSSPROF.INI* in Chapter 3). This will cause extended menus to be displayed automatically.

Running Commands

When you have built a command (or several commands), you can submit those lines to SPSS/PC+ for execution.

1. If you haven't done so already, press (Alt)-(E) to move the cursor to the scratch pad (or press (Alt)-(M) to clear away the menu system entirely).

2. Put the cursor on the first command you want to run.,

⤳ Click on any character in the first command you want to run.

3. Press (F10). On the mini-menu that appears at the bottom of the screen, run from Cursor is highlighted, so just press (⏎Enter). This tells SPSS/PC+ to run all the commands starting at the one containing the cursor and below.

⤳ To run the commands from the cursor on down, press the left and right mouse buttons simultaneously.

The screen clears, and your commands appear on the screen one at a time as they are executed. The word MORE appears in the corner of the screen when SPSS/PC+ is about to display something else and wants to make sure that you've had time to read what's already there. Press (Space) to continue. After all of the commands and their results have been displayed, the system returns to Review and the Menu and Help system. (You can see the results again whenever you like in the listing file; see "The Listing File" on p. 17.)

As described at the beginning of this chapter, there are three basic types of SPSS/PC+ commands:

- Operation commands.
- Data definition and manipulation commands.
- Procedure commands.

SPSS/PC+ executes an operation command as soon as you run it. As you run a data definition or manipulation command, SPSS/PC+ checks that it follows the language rules for the command. However, SPSS/PC+ does not actually execute most *data definition commands* until you run a *procedure* command, which reads the data.

The data definition and manipulation commands construct an active file of your data. The **active file** contains the data you tell SPSS/PC+ to read, the results of any transformations you request, and a dictionary of information you have provided about each variable (names, labels, missing values, and so forth), all in a format that SPSS/PC+ can understand.

As SPSS/PC+ processes cases, it displays a case counter in the status area in the upper right-hand corner of the screen.

You can specify different types of analyses for the same active file, and you can modify the active file. For example, you can use a CROSSTABS command after a FREQUENCIES command to explore the same variables with different analyses. Or you might follow a FREQUENCIES command with a RECODE command and another FRE-QUENCIES command to compare the results of the same analysis on a recoded variable.

Quitting

The FINISH command is at the bottom of the Main Menu. To leave SPSS/PC+ and return to DOS, paste and run FINISH just like any other command. Alternatively, you can type the FINISH command into the scratch pad and then run it (see "The Scratch Pad" on p. 16).

Typing Commands into the Scratch Pad

You can type commands directly into the scratch pad with the menus hidden. To clear away the Menu and Help system after you enter SPSS/PC+, press [Alt]-[M]. The menus will come back each time you run one or more commands.

Alternatively, you can turn off the menus by running the command

```
SET AUTOMENU OFF.
```

You can either put the command in your automatic profile *SPSSPROF.INI* or run it from the scratch pad at any time during your session.

If you want to paste the SET command shown above into the scratch pad, you can find it under session control & info on the Main Menu. Then select menus and paste AUTOMENU and OFF. Press [F10] and [↵Enter] to run the command. After you run the SET command, the screen looks like the one shown in Figure 2.4. In this mode of operation, the menus don't appear unless you specifically call them by pressing [Alt]-[M].

Figure 2.4   Review screen with menus off

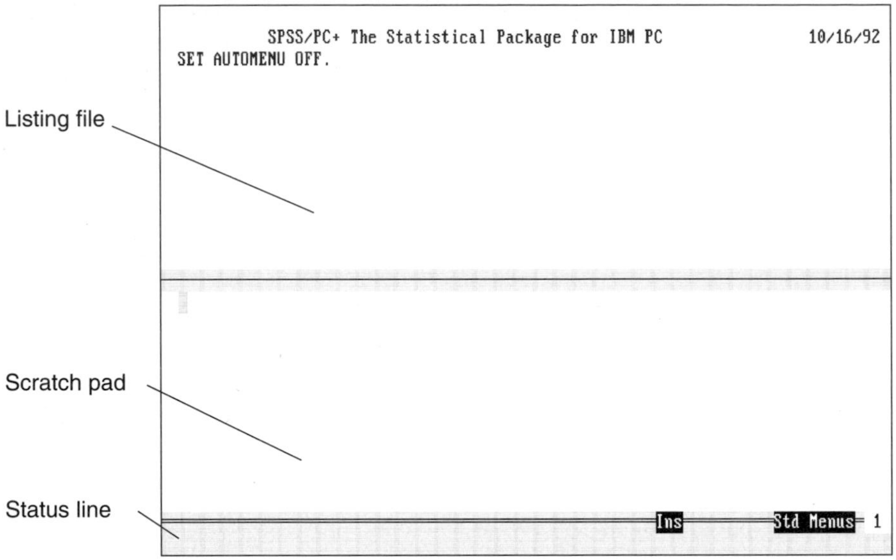

```
           SPSS/PC+ The Statistical Package for IBM PC           10/16/92
SET AUTOMENU OFF.
```

Listing file

Scratch pad

Status line

                                                          Ins   Std Menus 1

The Scratch Pad

By default, Review's bottom window contains the **scratch pad**, a place where you can play with commands until you're ready to run them. The scratch pad is identified in the bottom right corner of the screen. When you run commands, this file is saved for you, so that when you return to the scratch pad (assuming you didn't leave SPSS/PC+), all your commands are still there. If you want to run them again, perhaps with some alterations to try a different approach or correct errors, they're easy to edit (see Chapter 3).

↪ To position the cursor quickly in the scratch pad or the listing file, click at the position where you want the cursor.

To leave SPSS/PC+ when the menus are not open, type

finish.

Then press F10 and ←Enter. You will be returned to DOS.

The Listing File

The **listing file** contains a copy of all the output produced by your commands. The main use for the listing file is to review your work or to edit the output. You can save various results in separate files. When the session is over, you can print the entire listing file from DOS (it's named *SPSS.LIS* by default), or you can print any files you saved. See "Printing Files" on p. 28 for more information.

The listing file is displayed in Review's upper window, which is initially covered by the Menu and Help system. When you clear the menus by pressing Alt-M, you see the listing file in the top half of the screen. (If you haven't yet executed any commands, you won't have any output, so the top half of the screen will be blank.)

⤝ To clear menus and see the listing file, click in the Help window.

If you want to see the Menu and Help system while the cursor is in the listing file, press F1, use the cursor arrows to highlight **Menus,** and press ↵Enter (or just press F1 followed by M). The menus appear in the bottom half of your screen, as shown in Figure 2.5.

Figure 2.5   Listing file and menus

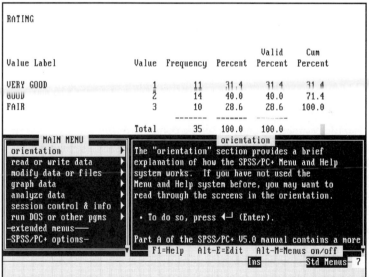

You can switch the cursor back to the bottom window by clicking in the Help window or pressing F2 and ↵Enter. The Menu and Help system reappears in the top window (if AUTOMENU is set to ON).

While you're in SPSS/PC+, it's often helpful to examine your commands against the output they produce by getting the scratch pad or the log file (described below) in the bottom window and the listing file in the top window. You can scroll whichever window is active (whichever one contains the cursor). To switch the cursor from one window to the other, press F2 and then press ↵Enter to select the highlighted item Switch from the mini-menu at the bottom of the screen.

↪ Click at a position where you want the cursor in either window.

The Log File

The **log file** contains a copy of all the commands that SPSS/PC+ has executed during your current session, in the order in which they were submitted. From within Review, it's easy to access the log file. First hide the menus and place the cursor in the scratch pad.

- Press F3, and then press ↵Enter to select the highlighted item Edit different file from the mini-menu that appears at the bottom of the screen (or just press F3 followed by E).
- Type the name of the file to edit, *SPSS.LOG*, in the box at the bottom of the screen, and press ↵Enter.

The log file is a useful record of what you've already done since, in addition to the commands you've run, it also contains

- Error messages about commands that couldn't be executed.
- Notes that direct you to the location of output in the listing file.

The log file contains a record of all the commands you submit in the session. For example, if you run a set of commands twice, the second time with modifications, the log file will contain both sets. The scratch pad, however, will only contain the modified set. By default, each command you have run also appears in the listing file, followed by its output.

Working Faster

The following features can help you work in Review more quickly:

- To select an item from a mini-menu, you can press the letter capitalized for that item, instead of using the cursor arrows to highlight the item and pressing ↵Enter. For example, to delete a line, you can just press D after pressing F4. For commonly used selections, if you know the letter for an item you want, you can bypass the mini-menu altogether by simply holding down the Alt key while pressing the letter. For example, to insert a line, you can just press Alt-I rather than pressing F4 and then selecting Insert after. For the functions for which this shortcut is available, see REVIEW in the

Syntax Reference. If you know that the selection you want is the highlighted one, you can just press the function key followed by ⏎Enter.

ᴖ To select an item from a mini-menu, double-click on your selection.

• When you press F1 and select Menus, Review identifies the command you are working on and, rather than the Main Menu, displays the menu for the command under the cursor.

• When the Menu and Help system is active, you can use incremental search to move the cursor to a menu item—just type in the first letter or letters of the item you want to select to make the cursor jump to that item.

ᴖ To move the cursor to an item, click on the item.

• When you are in the scratch pad, you can quickly place the cursor at specified locations by pressing F6 and selecting the location you want—Error line, or after executed Line. (Note: For Error line to be displayed, there must have been an error and RUNREVIEW must be set to AUTO; see SET in the Syntax Reference.)

• When the cursor is in the listing file, you can quickly move to the output page you want by pressing F6, selecting Output page from the mini-menu, and entering the number of the page you want. Output page has no effect when the cursor is in the scratch pad.

Getting Help

SPSS/PC+ provides two kinds of online assistance: a contextual help system, and an online glossary.

The Help System

Contextual help for building commands is supplied by the Menu and Help system. Any time you activate the menus, Review attempts to identify the command on which the cursor is located and displays the appropriate menu. If you are typing commands into the Review scratch pad and you want to know what the options are for the current command, activate the menus.

The Online Glossary

SPSS/PC+ contains an online glossary to help you understand the terms used in commands and in their output.

If you want to use the glossary, the cursor must be in a *file* in Review (not in the Menu and Help system).

• Place the cursor under the term you want to look up. (To look up a command or keyword from the Menu system, first paste it into the scratch pad.)

- Press ⒡, use the cursor arrows to highlight Glossary on the mini-menu, and press ⏎Enter. The system then displays a search string box at the bottom of the screen, filled in with the word at the cursor.
- ↩ Click in the status line and double-click on Glossary.
- If the displayed word isn't the one you want to look up, type the desired word over the one that appears in the box. Otherwise, just press ⏎Enter.
- ↩ To look up the term in the box, click anywhere.

If the word is in the glossary, the system then displays its definition. If the word isn't in the glossary, the system displays the closest alphabetical match.

- The bottom line of the display shows the terms that precede and follow the displayed one in the glossary. Press Ctrl PgUp or Ctrl PgDn.
- ↩ To page through the glossary, click on PgUp or PgDn at the bottom of the glossary window.
- If you don't understand a word used in the definition, you can paste the whole definition into the editing window, put the cursor on the problem word, and ask for *its* definition. ⒡8 copies the definition into the active editing window. The definition appears in the window as a marked area, so that you can easily copy or move it to another place.

You can also paste the definition into the listing file to annotate your output for later reference. (Remember to save the listing file if you make editing changes like this.)

- To close the Glossary, press Esc.
- ↩ To close the Glossary, press the right mouse button.

Special Features

Review has several special features that make your work easier. These features are available even when you aren't using the Menu and Help system:

- To see lists of files, press ⒡, move the cursor arrows to highlight File list, press ⏎Enter, and then either specify particular types of files or press ⏎Enter again to see all files in your current directory. SPSS/PC+ then displays a list of the files you requested. In the list, one of the files is highlighted; more detailed information about this file appears in the narrow box below the list. If you press ⏎Enter, the name will be pasted into the scratch pad. Or you can use the cursor arrows to highlight another file.
- ↩ To highlight a filename in the list of files, click on it. To paste a filename in the scratch pad, double-click on the filename.
- After you have brought data into SPSS/PC+ with a command like DATA LIST or GET, you can see a list of the variables in the active file by pressing ⒡, highlighting Var

list, and pressing ⏎Enter. (Alt-Ⓥ also works.) SPSS/PC+ then displays a list of the currently defined variables. In the list, one of the variables is highlighted; more detailed information about this variable appears in the narrow box below the list. If you press ⏎Enter while a variable name is highlighted, the variable name will be pasted into the scratch pad. You can also highlight a group of variables by pressing F7 at the first variable and moving the cursor arrows over the other variables you want. To paste the highlighted group into the edit window, press ⏎Enter.

⤳ To paste a variable into the scratch pad, double-click on it.

SPSS/PC+ Error Detection

As you run commands, SPSS/PC+ checks each one for proper syntax. If you misspell or improperly specify a command or subcommand, SPSS/PC+ displays an error message and positions the cursor on the command in the scratch pad that caused the error. The system also checks to make sure that you do not use variables that are not defined.

For example, the VARIABLE LABELS command in Figure 2.6 is misspelled.

Figure 2.6   Error message in the listing file

```
data list file='d:adscr.dat' /ntcpur 1-3 food 12-14 rent 23-25
 appl 34-36 service 45-47 wclothes 56-58 mclothes 67-69.
vriable labels ntcpur 'net purchasing level'

ERROR      1, Text: VRIABLE LABELS
INVALID COMMAND--Check spelling.  If it is intended as a continuation of a
previous line, the terminator must not be specified on the previous line.
If a DATA LIST is in error, in-line data can also cause this error.
This command not executed.



data list file='adscr.dat' /ntcpur 1-3 food 12-14 rent 23-25
 appl 34-36 service 45-47 wclothes 56-58 mclothes 67-69.
vriable labels ntcpur 'net purchasing level'
 /food 'Avg Food Prices'
 /rent 'Normal Rent'
 /appl 'Price of Appliances'
 /service 'Price for Services'
 /wclothes "Medium-Priced Women's Clothes"
 /mclothes "Medium-Priced Men's Clothes".
compute clothes=(wclothes + mclothes) / 2.
                                          Ins        Std Menus  2
```

The error message identifies the text where the error occurred and gives an explanation of the probable causes. Since you are allowed to abbreviate SPSS/PC+ keywords to their first three characters, you will not get an error message if you misspell a keyword after the first three characters.

Working from the Command Prompt

If you like the speed of working directly with commands and you know the commands you want to use, you can ignore Review and the Menu and Help system altogether and work from the SPSS/PC+ command prompt. To go to the command prompt upon starting SPSS/PC+, place the following command in the profile *SPSSPROF.INI*:

```
SET RUNREVIEW MANUAL.
```

To reach the command prompt when you are already in Review, press F10, use the cursor arrows to highlight Exit to prompt, and press ↵Enter.

Command Prompt Sequence

The command prompt works like this:

- SPSS/PC+ prompts for a command.
- You type a command followed by a period (command terminator) and press ↵Enter.
- SPSS/PC+ runs the command and displays a response.
- SPSS/PC+ prompts for another command.

This process continues until you end your SPSS/PC+ session.

The SPSS/PC+ Command Prompt and Terminator

SPSS/PC+ tells you it is ready for a command by displaying a command prompt. The default command prompt is SPSS/PC:. Whenever SPSS/PC+ displays the prompt, you can begin entering a command on that line.

You must end every command with a command terminator to tell SPSS/PC+ that the command is complete. The default command terminator is a period (.). *Do not type any other characters after the command terminator.*

If a command is too long to fit on one line, type whatever fits on the line and press ↵Enter. As long as you do not include a command terminator, SPSS/PC+ will respond with a continuation prompt. This signals you to continue the command on that line. The default continuation prompt is seven spaces followed by a colon. Figure 2.7 shows the default command and continuation prompts.

Figure 2.7   Command and continuation prompts

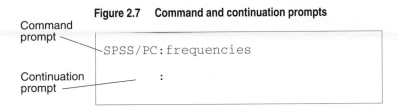

Command prompt

SPSS/PC:frequencies

Continuation prompt

:

Running a Command

When the command specifications are complete, enter the terminator and press ⏎Enter. SPSS/PC+ responds with the output for the command, if any, and prompts for another command.

If you enter a complete command and forget to include the command terminator, simply enter the terminator in response to the continuation prompt. You can also terminate the command by pressing ⏎Enter again—that is, entering a completely empty line. (Failing to end a command with a period, or whatever character you have specified as the command terminator, is a common oversight when just beginning with SPSS/PC+. Be alert for a continuation prompt when you think you have finished entering a command. Enter a period, or an empty line, to complete the command.)

You can use the SET command to change the default prompts and terminator (see SET in the Syntax Reference..

When a procedure is complete, SPSS/PC+ displays the message MORE. Press Space or click on MORE to display the procedure results.

If you make an error, SPSS/PC+ displays an appropriate error message and prompts for a new command, as shown in Figure 2.8.

Figure 2.8   Error at the command prompt

```
SPSS/PC:data list file='adscr.dat' /ntcpur 1-3 food 12-14 rent 23-35

       :appl 34-36 service 45-47 wclothes 56-58 mclothes 67-69.

SPSS/PC:vriable labels ntcpur 'Net Purchasing Level'


ERROR      1, Text: VRIABLE LABELS
INVALID COMMAND--Check spelling.  If it is intended as a continuation of a
previous line, the terminator must not be specified on the previous line.
If a DATA LIST is in error, in-line data can also cause this error.
This command not executed.

SPSS/PC:
```

Correcting Errors

Several special keys on the keyboard help you correct simple errors you make in entering commands. If you have made an error on the line you are typing, just backspace over the incorrect characters and type the rest of the line correctly before you press (↵Enter).

For information on using function keys to edit input lines, look up "Editing Keys" in the index of your DOS manual. On the IBM/PC and most compatible machines, the function keys (F1), (F2), and (F3) work at the SPSS/PC+ command prompt as described in the DOS manual.

Quitting from the Command Prompt

To go to the Review editor from the command prompt, type

`review.`

and press (←Enter). This takes you to the scratch pad.

To exit from SPSS/PC+, at the command prompt simply type

`finish.`

and press (←Enter). This returns you to the DOS prompt.

Managing Files

SPSS/PC+ writes several types of files: the scratch pad, listing files, log files, system files, portable files, and results from procedures.

Types of Files

The types of files written by SPSS/PC+ depend on what commands you give it. SPSS/PC+ writes to the scratch pad, listing file, and log file continually during a session, unless you explicitly turn off the listing or log file.

- The **scratch pad** contains the commands you type or paste into it. Its name is *SCRATCH.PAD*. This file is saved automatically whenever you leave Review, and when you leave SPSS/PC+.

- The **listing file** contains the printable output from your commands—that is, the text and plots that the computer puts out on the screen each time you run a command. By default, this output is sent to the screen and to the *SPSS.LIS* file on disk. You can specify a different disk file. You can also send this output to the printer. Some procedures, such as REPORT, allow you to send their output to a separate file by using the OUTFILE subcommand.

- The **log file** contains a log of the commands executed by SPSS/PC+, together with messages about commands that caused errors, and about the location of command output in the listing file. The default log file is *SPSS.LOG*.

- The **results file** includes special results (matrix materials, new data, etc.) from WRITE, CORRELATION, CLUSTER, QUICK CLUSTER, FACTOR, REGRESSION, ONEWAY, DSCRIMINANT, and MANOVA. (Regular output is sent to the listing file.) The default results file is *SPSS.PRC*.

SPSS/PC+ can read data from several different types of files.

- A **data file** contains only data values in ASCII format. It has no data dictionary (that is, no variable names, value labels, etc.). This type of file can be created with any text editor. You can read an ASCII data file into SPSS/PC+ by running a DATA LIST command and specifying the filename on the FILE subcommand. In this manual, we have used the extension *.DAT* to indicate a data file.

- A **system file** contains data and a data dictionary for use in SPSS/PC+. You can create or replace a system file using the SAVE command and retrieve it using the GET command. SPSS/PC+ can read this type of data file efficiently. The default system file, when you use the SAVE command without specifying another filename, is *SPSS.SYS*. A system file does *not* contain any output or other results. You cannot edit a system file with a text editor such as Review.

- A **portable file** is used to transport data and a data dictionary to another computer with a different operating system and is created by the EXPORT command. There is no default portable filename. To read a portable file, use the IMPORT command. You cannot edit a portable file with a text editor such as Review.

At the beginning of each session, the default files *SCRATCH.PAD*, *SPSS.LIS*, and *SPSS.LOG* are reinitialized. This means that the scratch pad, listing, and log files from any previous session are lost unless they were directed to a file other than the default (see SET in the Syntax Reference) or renamed. The default system file *SPSS.SYS* and results file *SPSS.PRC* are not automatically reinitialized. However, each time you write to these files, any existing contents are *replaced* by the new material.

Saving Files

To avoid overwriting any of these files, you can rename them at the DOS prompt before starting a new SPSS/PC+ session. Use the DOS RENAME command (see "DOS Commands" in your DOS manual).

Another way to avoid overwriting files is to specify names for the files using commands or function keys during an SPSS/PC+ session.

- **Scratch pad or listing window.** With the cursor in the window, press F9 and ⏎Enter. SPSS/PC+ asks for the filename. Type the filename and press ⏎Enter. This saves the current contents of the window as an ASCII file.

  If you save the contents of the scratch pad, the saved file contains a list of commands. You can run the commands contained in the saved file by running the INCLUDE command (see INCLUDE in the Syntax Reference).

- **Listing file.** To write your output to a specified file, run the following command before the commands for which you want the output:

  ```
  SET LISTING 'filename'.
  ```

  Output continues to go to this new file until you change it again with another SET LISTING command. You can specify another directory by specifying a path.

- **Log file.** To save the log record in a specified file, run the following command before the commands you want to include in the log:

  ```
  SET LOG 'filename'.
  ```

  You can specify a file in another directory by specifying a path.

- **Results file.** To save matrix output or output from the WRITE command, run the following command before running the commands that generate the output:

  ```
  SET RESULTS 'filename'.
  ```

  You *cannot* specify a path.

- **System file.** The system file contains data and a data dictionary (no commands). To save the data file in this format, run the following command after the file is defined:

  ```
  SAVE OUTFILE 'filename'.
  ```

  You can specify a file in another directory by specifying a path. You can later run a GET command to access the file quickly without having to run the data definition commands again.

- **Data file.** You can type data values into the scratch pad and then save the data file by pressing [F9] and [↵Enter], as with any scratch pad file. You can also enter data in any text editor and save the file in text or ASCII format.

- **Portable file.** To save data and a data dictionary that can be read by SPSS on other operating systems, run the following command after the file is defined and data are entered:

  ```
  EXPORT OUTFILE 'filename'.
  ```

  If you are going to use the data file on another computer running DOS, use a system file rather than a portable file.

Saving Part of a File

You may want to save only a specific part of a file in the scratch pad or the listing window. For example, if you run a FREQUENCIES command, edit it, and run the edited version, you might want to save only the final output. To save part of a file in either the scratch pad or the listing window, position the cursor on the first line you want to save and press [F7] and [↵Enter]. This marks the first line, which starts blinking. Reposition the cursor on the last line you want to save and press [F7] again. Now the whole area to be saved is marked. To save the marked area, press [F9] and then [M]. SPSS/PC+ displays a text box with the name *REVIEW.TMP*. Type a new filename right over *REVIEW.TMP*.

Printing Files

If your computer is attached to a printer, you can print files from the DOS prompt. To leave SPSS/PC+, run the FINISH command. At the DOS prompt, run the DOS PRINT command with the name of the file you want to print. For example, you can print the listing file (which contains output from commands) by running

```
PRINT SPSS.LIS
```

from the DOS prompt. (DOS commands do not end with a period.) This is the usual method of printing the file. You may have different instructions, either in your computer manual or from a system supervisor. See the DOS section of EXECUTE in the Syntax Reference for information about using the DOS PRINT command within an SPSS/PC+ session.

If a printer is attached to a single computer, you can print output as you generate it by running the command

```
SET PRINTER ON.
```

at any point in your SPSS/PC+ session. This may slow down the operation of SPSS/PC+ considerably. This command does not work for network printing.

To stop printing within a session, run the following command:

```
SET PRINTER OFF.
```

Printing Special Characters

If your printed output contains rows of question marks instead of bars for a command such as FREQUENCIES, your printer is not recognizing the extended ASCII characters. To get bars composed of X's run

```
SET SCREEN OFF.
```

before you run the procedure commands. Another way to generate printable characters is to change the characters for boxplots and histograms by using the SET command. (See SET in the Syntax Reference.)

If SET PRINTER ON is in effect, special characters are translated to standard ASCII codes by default. You can turn off the translation by specifying SET PTRANSLATE OFF.

To print plots where overprinting is specified, you must use a printer that is capable of overprinting.

3

Review: The SPSS/PC+ Editor

Review is the SPSS/PC+ text editor. As explained in the previous chapter, it is particularly designed to give you special help for entering SPSS/PC+ commands and for viewing their output, by means of the Menu and Help system, and the scratch pad, listing, and log files. But it is also very useful simply for standard editing tasks, such as creating, editing, or browsing through *any* text file. This section shows you how to perform standard text-editing tasks with Review.

Note that not all Review commands are described in this chapter. For a complete list, see REVIEW in the Syntax Reference.

Working with a Data File

A text file can serve a variety of purposes. One common use of a text file is to hold the data that you want to analyze with SPSS/PC+. For this session, we'll enter data from a fictitious survey of people's reactions to various colors for the SPSS/PC+ manual cover.

Getting into Review

When you want to use Review simply as a text editor, you can get into it directly from DOS, without using SPSS/PC+ at all. To do this, at the DOS prompt you simply type SPSSPC/RE followed by a space and the name of the file you want to edit. If you want to edit two files—one in the top window and one in the bottom—enter both filenames; the file entered first appears in the top window. (You can also get into Review from within SPSS/PC+ by typing the command REVIEW followed by the filenames *in apostrophes* at the SPSS/PC+ command prompt. This overrides the default scratch pad and listing files, and gives you the files you named.) For this example, at the DOS prompt type:

```
spsspc/re colors.dat
```

When you press (↵Enter), you see the SPSS/PC+ logo screen and then the Review screen, with the cursor positioned at the top. (The screen is initially blank, since we are creating a new file.) Since we're only editing one file, Review shows only one window, which takes up the whole screen.

Entering Data

The data we want to enter in this file consist simply of numbered codes representing colors and respondents' reactions to them. We'll put the color codes in the first column of each line, and the reaction codes in the third column of each line. Type the data shown below. Press ⏎Enter to start each new line. If you make mistakes, ignore them for now; we'll see in a minute how to make corrections.

```
1 1        2 2
1 1        2 2
1 2        2 2
1 2        3 1
1 3        3 1
1 3        3 1
2 2        3 3
2 2        3 3
2 2        3 3
```

Moving around the Screen

When you have entered the data (mistakes and all), you can experiment with moving the cursor around the screen. To do this, use the mouse or the cursor-movement keys on the right side of your keyboard: Home, End, ↑, ↓, ←, and →.

Note: If you use the cursor-movement keys located on the numeric keypad, these keys will operate correctly only when they are not locked into **numerical mode**, a mode that is indicated by the appearance of Num in the bottom-right corner of your screen. To get out of numerical mode, press Num Lock; the Num message then disappears from your screen.

As you move the cursor, notice that the column number in the lower-right corner of the screen changes to correspond to the cursor location. Notice also that the cursor will not move right of the last character in any line. If your file had lines of unequal length and you moved the cursor up or down, you would find that the cursor always tried to stay in the column in which it started—but if the line it was moving onto had fewer columns, it would move left to the last column in that line and then move back to the right when it reached a longer line.

The following keys allow quick cursor movement. (Since your file isn't very large at the moment, you won't be able to experiment with all of them now, but you'll certainly find them useful later.)

- Tab→ moves the cursor right to the next tab stop on the line. A tab stop occurs every eight characters. However, the cursor won't move to a tab stop that's beyond the last character in a line.

- ⇧Shift-Tab→ moves the cursor left to the preceding tab stop on the line.

- Ctrl-→ moves the cursor to the end of the line.

- Ctrl-← moves the cursor to the beginning of the line.
- ↵Enter moves the cursor to the start of the next line when you are in overtype mode (see "Insert Mode versus Overtype Mode" on p. 31).
- PgDn moves the cursor down one screen.
- PgUp moves the cursor up one screen.
- Ctrl-Home moves the cursor to the top of the file.
- Ctrl-End moves the cursor to the bottom of the file.

Making Changes

It's easy to make changes or corrections in your file using Review. The following section shows you a variety of ways of doing this.

Deleting Characters and Joining Lines

To delete unwanted characters, either put the cursor on the character and press Del or put the cursor immediately to the right of the character and press ←Backspace. Try this on anything you mistyped while entering the data. (If you didn't make any mistakes, type some characters at the end of the file.) You'll find that the character under or to the left of the cursor disappears and the rest of the text on the line moves over one space to fill in.

If you press Del when the cursor is on the space at the end of a line, the next line jumps up to join the line the cursor is on. Try this by putting the cursor at the end of the first line and pressing Del. (We'll see below how to split these lines again.)

Insert Mode versus Overtype Mode

There are two modes of editing in Review: insert mode and overtype mode. In **insert mode**, the text you type is inserted to the left of the current character, and the text to the right of the cursor moves over to make room for the new text. In **overtype mode**, the text you type replaces text in the current line.

When you are in insert mode, the message Ins displays in the lower-right corner of your screen. In overtype mode, the Ins message disappears. Press Ins to switch from one editing mode to the other.

It's easy to see how this works. Press Home to move to the top of the screen. Make sure you're in insert mode; then type

```
jjjj
```

The numeric codes that were already there move over to make room for the letters.

Now press Ctrl-← to get back to the beginning of the line. Press Ins to get into overtype mode; then type

```
ssss
```

Because you're in overtype mode, the s's replace the j's.

Only one editing key behaves differently depending on the mode. In overtype mode, (⏎Enter) moves the cursor to the beginning of the next line. In insert mode, (⏎Enter) splits the line the cursor is currently on, at the cursor location. To try this, make sure you're still in overtype mode, and press (⏎Enter); the cursor simply moves down to the next line. Now put the cursor under the 1 on the first line, and get into insert mode by pressing (Ins). This time when you press (⏎Enter) the line splits, with the part that was to the right of the cursor moving down to become the next line. Use this same method to split the line joined above with (Del), putting the second set of codes back on their own line.

While it is impossible to enter more than 80 characters on a line, you can create lines longer than 80 characters by joining two lines together. However, the only way to view the part of the line that extends past the 80th column is to split the line again. It is good practice to avoid such long lines. SPSS/PC+ does not read commands past the 80th column.

Editing Functions

You perform many editing functions in Review by pressing a function key and then making a selection from a mini-menu that appears at the bottom of the screen. For example, when you press (F4) you get a small menu that says:

lines: Insert after   insert Before   Delete   Undelete

- The most likely choice is highlighted. Just press (⏎Enter) to select and execute it. To select a different command on the menu, use the cursor arrows to move the highlighting, and then press (⏎Enter).

- To avoid executing any of the commands on a mini-menu, press (Esc).

- Only relevant commands appear in the mini-menu.

- One letter (usually the first) of each menu item is capitalized. Instead of selecting an item by highlighting it and pressing (⏎Enter), you can select it by just pressing its capitalized letter. For example, to insert a line after the one where the cursor is, press (I); to delete the current line, press (D), and so on.

- As alternatives to the mini-menus themselves, some commands let you use a combination of the (Alt) key and the selection key from the mini-menu. For example, to insert a line, you can hold down (Alt) and press (I), instead of pressing (F4) and selecting Insert after from the menu. See REVIEW in the Syntax Reference for these commands and key combinations.

- If you are an experienced SPSS/PC+ user, you can still use all the old key combinations if you have learned them. For example, (Ctrl)-(F4) deletes the current line without going through the mini-menu.

- Function keys that perform editing functions (such as (F4)) are not available when the Menu and Help system is active. Press (Alt)-(Esc) before using one of these function keys if you need to.

Put the cursor anywhere you like and try some editing functions. Note that if you accidentally delete a line you wanted to keep, Review gives you a chance to get it back—by pressing F4 and selecting Undelete. However, you can restore only the most recently deleted line. If you accidentally delete several lines, you can restore only the last one deleted.

Working with Areas

Some Review editing functions operate on entire areas of lines or parts of lines. In this section we'll illustrate how to perform editing tasks—copying, moving, and deleting— on areas.

To mark an area for editing, you press F7 at one boundary of the area, select the type of area you want to work with, and press F7 again at the other boundary. It doesn't matter whether you start at the beginning or ending location.

For example, let's work with an area consisting of the last six lines of your data file.

1. Press End to move the cursor to the last line.

2. Press F7 followed by ↵Enter to select the highlighted item, Lines, marking this line as one boundary of the area. The line begins to flash. On IBM PCs and some other computers, it will also be highlighted. The message

Waiting for second line mark

appears at the bottom of the screen.

3. Move the cursor up five lines to the first line that contains 3 1.

4. Press F7 to mark this as the first line of the area.

The message Area marked - 6 lines appears at the bottom of the screen. If your computer has highlighting, the entire six-line area will be highlighted. We can now invoke any of the Review commands that operate on areas.

Copying Areas. First, let's put a copy of the area at the end of the file. Move the cursor to the last line of the file by pressing Ctrl-End. To insert the copy of the area starting on the line following the cursor, press F8 followed by ↵Enter to select Copy. The copy then appears. Since the copy took more lines than were left on the screen, the screen instantly scrolls to make room for them.

Notice that the original area is still marked. Another area command would affect this original area, not the copy.

Moving Areas. Now let's move the original area to another location, at the top of the file. First move the cursor to the top of the file by pressing Ctrl Home. Then move the block to the line following the cursor by pressing F8, using the right cursor arrow to highlight Move, and pressing ↵Enter. The original marked area moves from its location and reappears just below the first line of the file. The copy that we made is still at the end of the file.

Note that the original area is still marked, even after its move to the top of the file. We can therefore continue to work with this same area in its new location.

Deleting Areas. This time, let's try deleting it: to do this, press F8, highlight Delete, and press ↵Enter. Notice that, while the original area at the top of the file disappeared, the copy that we made at the end of the file did not. The Delete Area command, like all the area commands, applies only to the currently marked area, not to copies.

Unmarking Areas. When you're done working with an area, press F7 a third time. When a marked area already exists, F7 unmarks it. You can try this by marking any area of lines you like (press F7 followed by ↵Enter at one line, and F7 again at the other line); then press F7 once again. The highlighting of the marked area disappears and the message Area cancelled appears at the bottom of the screen.

Rectangular Areas. The area that you mark does not need to consist of complete lines. Instead, it can be a rectangle made up only of selected columns within lines. Marking a rectangle is similar to marking lines—you place the cursor at one corner of the rectangle, press F7 and select Rectangle. Then place the cursor at the diagonally opposite corner of the rectangle and press F7 again.

All of the area commands work for rectangles. To copy or move a rectangle, you place the cursor at the *top left* corner of the area to which you want to copy or move it, press F8, and then select Copy or Move. If Review is in *insert* mode, copying or moving the rectangle pushes existing text to the right. If Review is in *overtype* mode, copying or moving replaces existing text. If the copy or move location is to the right of existing lines, Review adds spaces as needed to the ends of existing lines to keep the rectangle aligned.

Working with Two Files

When you are editing two files, the copy and move functions—including those for areas—can operate between the files. That is, you can copy or move an area from one file into the other. The procedure is the same as working within one file—mark the area in one file, position the cursor in the other file (by pressing F2 followed by ↵Enter to select Switch), and press the appropriate function key.

If you want to see more text in one window than in the other, you can change the size of the windows. Press F2, highlight Change window size, and press ↵Enter. Then fill in the number of lines you want to see in the upper window (the smallest number allowed is 7). After you press ↵Enter again, the system adjusts both windows accordingly.

The Help Displays

If you don't remember which function key does what, you can press F1 (or click the mouse at the bottom of the screen) and select Review help from the mini-menu to see the following help screen:

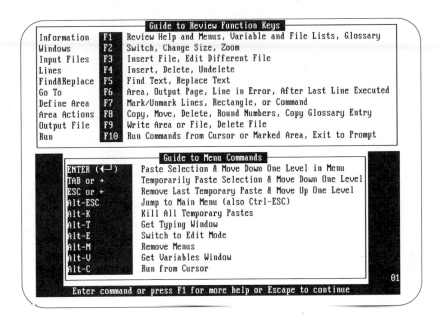

The top half of this display shows the functions associated with each key. You can call up this screen whenever you aren't sure which function key to press. (For full descriptions of all of Review's functions, see REVIEW in the Syntax Reference.)

Commands are grouped by function so that related commands are all accessed with the same function key. For example, all the line commands (inserting, deleting, and undeleting lines) are accessed with F4.

If you press F1 again while viewing the help screen, you see a second help display showing the keys that allow you to move around in Review.

A number of commands prompt you for additional information when you issue them. These prompts always appear at the bottom of your screen. You can press F1 in response to any prompt to get a fuller description of the prompt. Review will tell you exactly what information it is requesting and will list possible responses.

Entering Extended ASCII Characters

You can enter extended ASCII characters by activating NumLock and holding down Alt while you type the character's ASCII numeric code on the numeric keypad. The character appears when you release Alt.

Saving the File

After you've entered the data and made any corrections, you can save the file. (If you leave Review without saving the file, everything you've typed will be lost.) To save the file, press F9 and select write Whole file. Review asks for confirmation that you want to save the file under the same name you started with; to do so, just press ⏎Enter. (If you wanted to give the file a different name, you could just type it in.) Review then saves the file and displays a message when it's done.

Exiting Review

To exit Review, press F10 and then press ⏎Enter.

Other Files

In this session we've used Review to create and edit a data file. However, Review is also useful for editing *any* medium-sized (up to several hundred lines) file, including:

- Files that hold commands, like the scratch pad and log files, or any other file into which you've entered commands. However, when you run Review outside of SPSS/PC+ you can't *execute* commands in the file, and you can't see a variable list, since there is no active file.

- The listing file, which holds SPSS/PC+ output.

The SPSSPROF.INI File

Another file you may want to create and edit with Review is the file called *SPSSPROF.INI*, which is the **automatic profile**. This file contains commands that are automatically executed whenever you get into SPSS/PC+. Usually these are SET commands, which control the way SPSS/PC+ operates. Since these commands are executed automatically when you enter the system, they allow you to begin with the environment you prefer. You can learn about SET commands in the Syntax Reference or under the Main Menu selection session control & info.

To edit the automatic profile, specify its name as you get into Review, and then use any of Review's editing functions to add, change, or delete the commands you want.

File Limitations

In general, Review can edit ASCII files that are small enough to fit into the available memory (RAM) of your computer. Note that Review itself—and any other software currently loaded into memory—occupies some of your computer's RAM. Review *cannot* edit the following:

- Binary files. If a file has graphics characters in it when you use the DOS TYPE command to display it on your screen, it is probably a binary file. (SPSS/PC+ system files are binary files.)

- Files too large to fit in the working memory (RAM) available to Review. Review tells you if it does not have enough memory. (Operations such as scrolling may slow down noticeably as Review runs out of memory.)

4 Important DOS Concepts

SPSS/PC+ is specifically tailored to the IBM PC/XT, PC/AT, and closely compatible computers running Release 3.0 or later of DOS. To use such a computer effectively, you must acquire a basic familiarity with the concepts and commands of DOS. You should not rely on this manual for such information. Read at least the chapters in your DOS manual on files and filenames, and on using directories. Browse through the descriptions of important commands such as COPY, DEL, RENAME, TYPE, BACKUP, and DISKCOPY. After reading about directories, note how to work with them using the MKDIR (or MD) and CHDIR (or CD) commands. The CHKDSK command provides useful information about both disk space and memory (RAM).

In this chapter, you will find information on DOS as it is used with SPSS/PC+. This discussion is *not* adequate to make you proficient in the use of your computer. You do not need to be an expert on DOS to use SPSS/PC+, but a little time invested in learning basic concepts from the DOS manual will make your work easier and more efficient. If you are already familiar with DOS, you may wish to skim this section to see how the SPSS/PC+ system fits in.

DOS is an operating system, a control program that manages the hardware functions of your computer such as accepting commands from the keyboard, writing to the screen, and managing the creation and use of files on disk. When you use an application program such as SPSS/PC+, the most important concepts to understand are those involving disk files.

DOS Filenames

The files that contain information stored on your hard disk, or on floppy diskettes, are referred to by name. When you create a file yourself, you assign a name to it. When SPSS/PC+ creates a file it assigns a name, either according to your specifications or using a built-in default. A complete file specification can contain any or all of the following parts, although you rarely have to specify them all.

drive name   A single letter indicating which of the disk drives connected to your computer holds the disk on which the file is stored. When you specify this, follow it immediately by a colon (:) to show that it is a drive name. Drive names vary, but by far the most common convention is for *A:* (and perhaps *B:*) to be the names of floppy-diskette drives, and for *C:* to be the drive containing the hard disk.

pathname   A specification for the directory containing the file. Pathnames are discussed in "The Path Command" on p. 42.

filename   A name from one to eight characters that identifies the file. This is also called the "primary filename." You must also include the extension (perhaps using a wildcard) when specifying a file whose name has an extension. Letters and numbers are allowed in filenames. Blank spaces are not allowed *in the middle* of a filename. See your DOS manual for a complete discussion of the characters that are permitted in filenames.

extension   A specification from one to three characters, typically used to indicate what kind of information the file contains. The extension is always separated from the filename by a period. For example, *SPSS.LIS* has filename *SPSS* and extension *.LIS*.

In fact, most references to files use only the filename and extension. This is understood to mean that the file is on your **default drive** and in your **current directory**, as explained below.

Wildcards

You can often use DOS **wildcard** characters when specifying filenames or extensions. Use of these characters, the asterisk and the question mark, is explained in the DOS manual. Basically, the asterisk represents *any* character or characters at the end of a filename or extension, and the question mark represents any single character in a filename or extension. Thus,

```
erase *.bak
```

erases all files with the extension *.BAK* in the current directory, and

```
copy a:*.* c:
```

copies all files (any name, any extension) from the floppy diskette in the *A:* drive onto the hard disk in *C:*. Consult the DOS manual for more information on these shortcuts.

The Default Drive

When you are running DOS or a DOS program (including SPSS/PC+), a "default drive" is always assigned to you. DOS displays the letter associated with this drive in its command prompt and assumes that any file for which you do not explicitly specify a drive resides on the default drive. If your default drive is *A:*, the DOS command prompt may look like this (perhaps with some additional information):

```
A>
```

To make another drive the default, simply type in its letter followed by a colon, and DOS will confirm what you have done by using the new drive in its command prompt:

```
A> c:

C>
```

Directories and Paths

A DOS directory is simply a subset of the contents of a disk. Directories are particularly convenient on hard disks, which can contain hundreds of files. They are less often used on floppy diskettes, although they are perfectly legal. Since directories can be nested inside other directories, you have to specify a "path," *either explicitly or implicitly,* to tell DOS where to find a particular directory. Advantages of using directories include:

- A directory listing of a group of related files will often fit on a single screen, while a listing of all the files on a hard disk would be too extensive to be useful.
- You can use the same name (for example, *SPSS.LIS*) for different files as long as they are in different directories.
- Different people can share a machine without getting in each other's way by establishing individual directories to hold their files.
- Valuable software, such as SPSS/PC+, can be saved in a directory that is never used as anyone's default directory, to reduce the likelihood of accidental damage. To delete a file that is not in your default directory, you have to include a pathname on the DEL or ERASE command.

Directories can contain not only files but also other directories (which can contain other directories, and so on).

The Current Directory

Just as you always have a default drive in DOS, you always have a **current directory**. If you name a file without specifying a directory, DOS assumes that the file is in your current directory. When you start up a system that initially assigns the hard disk as your default drive, you will be in its **root directory**, which is the main directory of the whole disk. Operating from the root directory, you do not even need to be aware that directories exist. When your disk contains a large number of files, as all hard disks eventually do, you should create and work from one or more smaller directories.

It is a good idea always to be aware of your current directory. If you enter the DOS command,

```
prompt $p$g
```

then the DOS command prompt will always remind you of your current directory. See "Using Batch Files To Avoid DOS" on p. 43 to find out how to have this command entered for you automatically so that you don't have to remember it.

DOS Commands for Directories

The most important DOS commands for using directories are

MKDIR or MD   *Make directory.* Use this command to create a new directory. The short form, MD, is easier to spell and works just as well.

CHDIR or CD   *Change directory.* Use this command anytime you want to change your current directory. Unlike other directory commands, CD is typically used at least once in a session.

RMDIR or RD   *Remove directory.* This command deletes a directory. It can only be used after everything in the directory has been deleted.

Example

Here the DOS prompts are in upper case, while commands entered by the user are shown in lower case:

```
A>c:
```

```
C>prompt $p$g
```

```
C:\>md myfiles
```

```
C:\>cd myfiles
```

```
C:\MYFILES>
```

- The first command sets the default drive to *C:*
- The PROMPT command changes the command prompt to show the current directory. Since the user is still in the root directory, the current directory is simply represented by a backslash (\), as discussed in the next section.
- The MD command creates a new directory named *MYFILES*.
- The CD command establishes *MYFILES* as the current directory. Notice that the final DOS prompt displays the current directory.

Paths

A **path** specification is simply a way to indicate a particular directory. You use path specifications on the directory commands discussed above, or whenever you need to name a file that is not in your current directory. The basic rules are simple, but you should consult your DOS manual for more information.

- A path specification consists of one or more directory names, separated by backslashes (\). If you name more than one directory, they are nested, with the one named first including them all.

- The directories in a path specification must already exist (except, of course, on the MD command that creates them).

- A path specification does not include any blank spaces.

- If the first character of the path specification is a backslash, DOS understands the path to begin at the root directory.

- If the first character of the path specification is not a backslash, DOS understands the path to begin in your current directory (see the example below). This means that the path can only indicate directories *inside* your current directory. (If your current directory is the root, a backslash in the first character of a path specification is optional.)

- If you are using the path specification to identify a particular *file* rather than a directory, put a backslash after the name of the directory that contains the file and follow this immediately with the filename and the extension, if any.

Example

This example first shows the DEL (delete) command using a complete file specification, including drive, path, primary filename, and extension. As before, the DOS prompt is shown in upper case, while the command is shown in lower case. The file is in a directory named *DATA*, which in turn is in a directory named *WORK*. Since this is a complete specification, it means the same thing regardless of what your default drive or current directory is:

```
A>del c:\work\data\employ.dat
```

If the default drive is *C:* but the root is the current directory, the specification is:

```
C:\>del work\data\employ.dat
```

If, instead, the current directory is *WORK*, the same command can be entered like this:

```
C:\WORK>del data\employ.dat
```

Finally, suppose that the current directory is the *DATA* directory inside the *WORK* directory:

```
C:\WORK\DATA>del employ.dat
```

As long as you are working with files in your current directory on your default drive, you do not need to specify anything but the filename and extension. For most people, this is the typical situation.

The Path Command

The PATH command enables you to dispense with the effort of specifying (and remembering) the paths to commonly used files in other directories. Often the most convenient way to issue this command is through the *AUTOEXEC.BAT* file discussed in "Using Batch Files To Avoid DOS" on p. 43.

Normally, if you enter the name of a program, a batch file, or one of the DOS disk-based commands, DOS searches for it only in your current directory and will not find it if it is somewhere else. (The error message is Bad command or filename.)

One solution to this problem is to always specify paths; another is to copy the *SPSSPC.COM* file along with the disk-based DOS command files and other frequently used programs and batch files to your working directory so that you can access them directly.

A better solution is to use the DOS PATH command, which permits you to define other directories that should be searched to find programs, batch files, or disk-based DOS commands that do not exist in your current directory. You can enter paths to several directories, separated by semicolons, on the PATH command. (If you enter a second PATH command, the directories listed on it completely replace the list of directories on the first PATH command.) Directories are searched in the order you list them on the PATH command. For example,

```
path \;\spss;\dos
```

will permit you to execute programs, batch files, and disk-based DOS commands that are in the root directory, the *SPSS* directory, or the *DOS* directory without explicitly specifying a path.

The SPSS/PC+ System Directory

The SPSS/PC+ system must be installed in a specific directory on your system. You must specify which directory to use when you install the system. The installation procedure then creates this directory and saves the program modules into it.

Normally, you should use a directory named *SPSS*. If you choose a directory other than SPSS, you must issue the DOS command:

```
SET SPSS=path
```

to indicate where the modules can be found. (This is a DOS system environment command, not an SPSS/PC+ command.) For example, to indicate that SPSS/PC+ is installed in a directory named *PCPLUS*, specify:

```
SET SPSS=\PCPLUS
```

(You can place such a command into your *AUTOEXEC.BAT* file. You might also wish to put a path to this directory on your PATH command. See the next section.)

If the SPSS/PC+ system is on a drive other than your default drive, you must indicate this also:

```
SET SPSS=E:\PCPLUS
```

This DOS command specifies that the SPSS/PC+ system is on the *E:* drive, in a directory named *PCPLUS*.

Using Batch Files To Avoid DOS

You cannot avoid DOS entirely. The more you learn about DOS, the easier your work will be. However, there is always a point when remembering command syntax becomes more trouble than it is worth. Some people reach this point quickly when studying operating-system commands. Batch files, which contain DOS commands or groups of DOS commands that can be invoked with a single word, provide a convenient way to avoid memorizing the names or syntax of DOS commands.

You can create a batch file with any editor or word processor, for example EDLIN, which comes with DOS and is described in the DOS manual, or Review, which comes with SPSS/PC+ and is described in this manual. You simply enter some commands into a file just as you would enter them directly; or if you like, you can use some of the simple programming facilities that DOS supports in batch files.

After you have saved these commands into an ASCII file (a file containing ordinary letters, numbers, and punctuation, rather than special binary codes used only by computer programs), you can execute them simply by typing the filename. The file extension for a batch file must be *.BAT*. You do not need to type this extension when invoking a batch file.

AUTOEXEC.BAT

One batch file, *AUTOEXEC.BAT*, is particularly useful in conjunction with SPSS/PC+. If you create an *AUTOEXEC.BAT* file in the root directory of your initial default disk, it is executed automatically whenever you start up your system. As explained in the DOS manual, there are a number of useful commands you can put into this file. Two commands are especially helpful when you are running SPSS/PC+:

PROMPT PG As explained above, this command sets the DOS command prompt to include the path to your current directory. The specification PG is not particularly easy to remember, so this command is well placed in this batch file, where you do not need to remember it.

PATH \SPSS   The SPSS/PC+ system is stored in a directory that is usually named *SPSS*. If you include this directory on a PATH command in your *AUTOEXEC.BAT* file, you will be able to run both SPSS/PC+ and Review from any directory without entering a pathname to it. You may wish to define paths to other directories also; if so, enter all of the paths on the same PATH command, separated by semicolons.

Since *AUTOEXEC.BAT* is searched for and executed immediately after you start up (or "boot") your system, it must be on the startup disk from which DOS is loaded. In most systems with built-in hard disks, this is the hard disk. Systems that require a floppy diskette to be inserted at startup must have the *AUTOEXEC.BAT* file on that floppy diskette. *AUTOEXEC.BAT* must always be in the root directory, since that is the current directory at system startup.

Setting System Parameters

When you boot or reboot your system, DOS reads a special file named *CONFIG.SYS* (if it exists) to customize the system configuration. You can set a number of parameters by creating a *CONFIG.SYS* file, as explained in your DOS manual. To run SPSS/PC+, you should set up this file to include at least the following two parameters:

FILES   Specify FILES=20. This parameter controls the maximum number of open files allowed. The default number, 8, is insufficient when using SPSS/PC+.

BUFFERS   Specify BUFFERS=8 to increase the number of file buffers that the system allocates. This can significantly speed up the performance of SPSS/PC+.

Use any editor, such as EDLIN or Review, to create the *CONFIG.SYS* file. After creating it, reboot the system (hold the Ctrl and Alt keys down and press Del) so that the new parameters will take effect.

5

The SPSS/PC+ System

Many purchases come with suggestions for use. Children's blocks, microwave ovens, and woodcutting tools are all accompanied by colorful booklets describing results that can be obtained with them. What should a book accompanying a statistical software package contain? Although the results of statistical analyses are not as photogenic as block structures, gourmet meals, and fine furniture, data analysis is a creative process that can result in important contributions to many different undertakings. Increased profits in business, improved treatments for disease, as well as insights into social phenomena, are often attributable to the careful acquisition and analysis of data.

In Chapter 11 to Chapter 24, we illustrate the application of various statistical procedures to solve a variety of real problems. The problems and their solutions range from the simple—counting the number of people who die on Mondays—to the complex—searching for salary discrimination. The goal is to introduce the building blocks that can be used alone or in many combinations to analyze and display data.

Before proceeding to a detailed discussion of the hows and whys of data analysis with SPSS/PC+, let's take a quick overview of the types of analyses that can be produced. The data we will use are from a recent *Consumer Reports* evaluation of 35 beers. The beers were rated on overall quality and a variety of other attributes, such as price, calories, sodium, and alcohol content.

Preparing a Report

One of the first steps in examining the beer data may be to prepare a report that contains detailed information about each of the beers. Figure 5.1 is an excerpt from output produced by the SPSS/PC+ REPORT procedure. Reports can contain additional information, such as summary statistics. Chapter 24 describes the REPORT procedure in detail.

Figure 5.1   Excerpt from a report produced by REPORT

```
         Consumer Reports Beer Rating - July 1983

RATING      BEER                    6-Pack   Available   Price
                                    Price    in U.S.     Class

Very good   Miller High Life          2.49   National    Premium
            Budweiser                 2.59   National    Premium
            Schlitz                   2.59   National    Premium
            Lowenbrau                 2.89   National    Super-premium
            Michelob                  2.99   National    Super-premium
            Henry Weinhard            3.65   Regional    Super-premium
            Anchor Steam              7.19   Regional    Super-premium
   Mean                             $3.48

Good        Old Milwaukee             1.69   Regional    Popular
            Schmidts                  1.79   Regional    Popular
            Pabst Blue Ribbon         2.29   National    Premium
            Augsberger                2.39   Regional    Super-premium
            Strohs Bohemian Style     2.49   Regional    Premium
            Coors                     2.65   Regional    Premium
            Olympia                   2.65   Regional    Premium
   Mean                             $2.28

Fair        Blatz                     1.79   Regional    Popular
            Rolling Rock              2.15   Regional    Premium
            Hamms                     2.59   Regional    Premium
            Heilemans Old Style       2.59   Regional    Premium
            Tuborg                    2.59   Regional    Premium
   Mean                             $2.34
```

Describing the Data

A simple report just displays the data values. It does not attempt to organize or summarize the data. Several SPSS/PC+ procedures are designed especially for summarizing data. For example, a **frequency table** contains counts of the number of times a response occurs—the number of men and women in a sample, the number of children in families, or the number of visits to the dentist in a year by the head of the household. Figure 5.2, which was produced by the SPSS/PC+ FREQUENCIES procedure, is a frequency table of the number of beers rated very good, good, and fair by the *Consumer Reports* panel. Of the 35 beers, 11 (31.4%) were rated very good, 14 (40%) good, and the remaining 10 (28.6%) fair.

Figure 5.2   Frequency table from FREQUENCIES

```
RATING

                                                Valid     Cum
Value Label          Value   Frequency  Percent  Percent  Percent

Very good               1        11       31.4     31.4     31.4
Good                    2        14       40.0     40.0     71.4
Fair                    3        10       28.6     28.6    100.0
                               -------  -------  -------
                     Total       35      100.0    100.0

Valid cases     35   Missing cases       0
```

The information presented in a frequency table can also be displayed in a **bar chart**. Figure 5.3 shows a bar chart of the beer ratings. Each value in the table is represented by a bar whose length is proportional to the number of times the value occurs in the data. The FREQUENCIES procedure can also be used to produce bar charts as well as various statistics that are useful for describing data. FREQUENCIES is described in Chapter 11.

Figure 5.3   Bar chart from FREQUENCIES

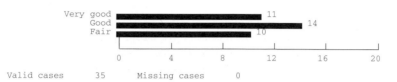

```
RATING

     Very good  ████████████████████████ 11
          Good  ████████████████████████████████ 14
          Fair  ██████████████████████ 10

               0      4      8     12     16     20

Valid cases    35    Missing cases    0
```

Counting Combinations of Responses

A frequency table just counts the number of times various responses occur to a single item. Often it is useful to count the number of times certain combinations of responses occur. For example, you might want to know how many men and how many women answered yes, no, or maybe to a survey question. Or you might want to know the number of fatal, serious, or minor accidents involving standard, compact, and subcompact cars.

Figure 5.4 shows a table that tabulates two items together—the rating of the beer and whether it was light or not. From this table, one can see that no light beers were rated as very good, 4 were rated as good, and 3 were rated as fair. This type of table, known as a **crosstabulation** or **contingency table**, is available with the CROSSTABS procedure. CROSSTABS can also compute a variety of percentages and statistics that indicate how closely two (or more) variables are related. The CROSSTABS procedure is described in Chapter 14.

Figure 5.4   Crosstabulation from CROSSTABS

```
LIGHT   by   RATING

                   RATING                    Page 1 of 1
           Count
                   Very    Good    Fair
                   Good
                      1       2       3      Row
LIGHT      ─────────────────────────────    Total
                0    11      10       7       28
     No                                      80.0

                1             4       3        7
     Yes                                     20.0

           Column  11      14      10        35
            Total  31.4    40.0    28.6     100.0

Number of Missing Observations:   0
```

Summarizing Responses

Both frequency tables and crosstabulations summarize the data by counting the number of times each response occurs. When a response can have many possible values—age, weight, or income—counting the number of times each possible individual response occurs can result in very large tables that are not very useful. Instead of looking at all responses, you might want to group values that are close to one another and see how often such groups of values (people in their twenties, individuals over 250 pounds) occur.

Figure 5.5 shows the distribution of alcohol content for the 35 beers. Each bar represents a *range* of alcohol values. As in the bar chart, the length of the bar is proportional to the number of times the values occur. For example, the longest bar corresponds to alcohol values between 4.25 and 4.75 and represents 17 beers. Such figures, called **histograms**, can be obtained from the SPSS/PC+ FREQUENCIES procedure.

Figure 5.5   Histogram of alcohol content from FREQUENCIES

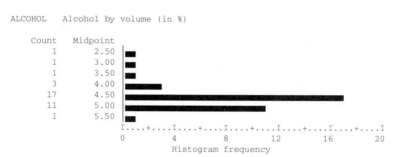

```
ALCOHOL    Alcohol by volume (in %)

     Count    Midpoint
        1       2.50
        1       3.00
        1       3.50
        3       4.00
       17       4.50
       11       5.00
        1       5.50
                     I....+....I....+....I....+....I....+....I....+....I
                     0        4        8       12       16       20
                              Histogram frequency
```

Summary Statistics

It is possible to summarize the information contained in a histogram even further by calculating single numbers that represent an average or typical value and the amount of spread or variability in the data. Figure 5.6 contains the **mean**, the **mode** (the most frequently occurring value), the **median** (the value above which half the values fall), the **variance** (a measure of how spread out the values are), and the smallest and largest values for the alcohol content of the beers in the survey. These statistics and many others are calculated in the SPSS/PC+ FREQUENCIES and MEANS procedures.

Figure 5.6   Some summary statistics available from FREQUENCIES

```
Mean        4.577    Median     4.700    Mode       4.700
Variance     .364    Minimum    2.300    Maximum    5.500
```

Although it is informative to know that the average alcohol content of all the beers is 4.58%, you may also want to see if alcohol content is similar for the three beer rating groups. Figure 5.7 shows the average alcohol content for the three ratings. Beers rated as very good had the highest alcohol content (4.9%), while those rated fair had the lowest (4.2%). The good beers were in the middle, with an average alcohol content of 4.6%. This type of table, which shows the means of a variable for subgroups of cases, can be obtained from the SPSS/PC+ MEANS procedure (see Chapter 15).

Figure 5.7   Table from MEANS

```
Summaries of    ALCOHOL      Alcohol by volume (in %)
By levels of    RATING

Variable        Value  Label                  Mean    Std Dev    Cases

For Entire Population                        4.5771    .6030        35

RATING            1   Very good              4.9000    .1789        11
RATING            2   Good                   4.5786    .4300        14
RATING            3   Fair                   4.2200    .8954        10

   Total Cases =        35
```

Plotting the Data

When you want to examine the relationship between two variables, both of which can have many values, plotting the two variables may be helpful. Figure 5.8, which was produced by the SPSS/PC+ PLOT procedure, is a plot of the price of the beer and the alcohol content. Each point is also identified by its *Consumer Reports* rating. Note that there does not appear to be a strong relationship between price and alcohol content since there are beers in various price ranges for the values of alcohol content. No "pattern" between cost and alcohol content appears to exist.

Examining plots of several variables together is a valuable step in many analyses. Plots of sales with advertising expenditures, blood pressure with weight, and birth rates with GNP all reveal interesting relationships between the two variables. The PLOT procedure produces a variety of plots that can be used to examine relationships among variables and is described in Chapter 19.

Figure 5.8   Sample output from PLOT

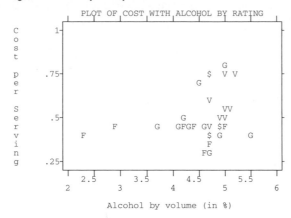

Another way to examine the strength of association between two variables is through indexes such as the **correlation coefficient**. Figure 5.9 contains correlation coefficients between price, alcohol content, and sodium content. Since these values are small (close to 0), there appears to be no **linear association** between the pairs of variables. (A linear association is one in which points cluster around a straight line.) The SPSS/PC+ COR-RELATIONS procedure can be used to calculate correlation coefficients and various associated statistics. CORRELATIONS is described in Chapter 20.

Figure 5.9   Correlation coefficients available from CORRELATIONS

```
Correlations:   PRICE       ALCOHOL     SODIUM

  PRICE        1.0000        .1961       -.0897
              (    35)      (    35)     (    35)
               P= .         P= .259      P= .608

  ALCOHOL       .1961       1.0000        .2050
              (    35)      (    35)     (    35)
               P= .259      P= .         P= .237

  SODIUM       -.0897        .2050       1.0000
              (    35)      (    35)     (    35)
               P= .608      P= .237      P= .

(Coefficient / (Cases) / 2-tailed Significance)

" . " is printed if a coefficient cannot be computed
```

Testing Hypotheses and Building Models

SPSS/PC+ also provides statistical tests for evaluating the likelihood of actual differences in a population based on observed differences in a sample. For example, we can test the hypothesis that beers rated very good and fair differ in price or alcohol content—not just for beers in the survey but for all beers. Or we may hypothesize that beers in the three rating categories differ in sodium content. The SPSS/PC+ T-TEST procedure can be used to test the hypothesis that two population means are equal, while the SPSS/PC+ procedures ONEWAY and ANOVA are useful for testing hypotheses about several population means. For a discussion of T-TEST, ONEWAY, and ANOVA, see Chapter 16, Chapter 17, and Chapter 18.

Since beers are known to vary considerably in cost, it may be interesting to try to predict the cost of a beer based on variables such as alcohol content, number of calories, availability, and origin. The SPSS/PC+ REGRESSION procedure (see Chapter 21) is used to develop a model that examines the relationship between a **dependent variable**, in this case cost, and a set of **independent variables**. Special facilities for selecting variables to be included in a model as well as testing the adequacy of fit of the model are also available.

You may want to study the associations among **categorical variables**; that is, variables whose values are categories—such as beer rating, class, and availability. The SPSS/PC+ procedure available for this type of analysis is HILOGLINEAR, a hierarchical loglinear technique. Loglinear models are a class of statistical techniques that model the number of cases in a cell of a multidimensional crosstabulation as a function of the variables used for classification.

Suppose that a number of individuals rated the beer on a number of characteristics, such as lightness, body, color, head, taste when drunk from a bottle, can, or glass, packaging, sizes available, and so on. You would expect that the responses to different items would be correlated. One explanation for the observed correlations is the idea that the items are related because they tap some of the same dimensions on which people rate beer. These dimensions may be quality, value, and accessibility. Factor analysis is one of the statistical techniques that is used to search for these underlying common dimensions, called **factors**. The SPSS/PC+ FACTOR procedure provides several methods for estimating the factors and for making their interpretation easier.

Although there are many different brands of beer in the world, one may wonder whether they are all that different from one another or whether the beers can be lumped into several fairly homogeneous categories. Since there are many attributes that can be used to describe the beers, any subset of these might serve as the basis for looking for similarities. The SPSS/PC+ CLUSTER procedure can be used to calculate "distances" between pairs of beers and then, based on these distances, group the beers into similar categories, called clusters. Several different ways of defining distances between items and forming clusters are available.

When you know in advance the number of clusters to expect, you can use the SPSS/PC+ QUICK CLUSTER procedure instead. QUICK CLUSTER is less flexible than CLUSTER. However, it can process large files efficiently, while the number of cases you can process with CLUSTER is limited by the amount of memory available.

Sometimes you already know the way your cases are grouped, but you want to know why the groupings came out that way. The beers were rated as "very good," "good," or "fair" in the *Consumer Reports* evaluation. Is there any way to predict these ratings from the other variables available? The SPSS/PC+ DSCRIMINANT procedure can be used to predict how the beers were rated in quality, on the basis of their price, alcohol content, sodium content, and so on. If the prediction works well for the beers actually rated, you could then use DSCRIMINANT to predict how other beers would have been rated if they were included in the evaluation.

Sometimes the tests available in procedures ANOVA and ONEWAY are not general enough for a complex analysis. The SPSS/PC+ MANOVA procedure lets you test a wide variety of hypotheses about the effects of categorical or continuous variables on one or more dependent variables. It can handle most types of linear models, including "repeated measures" analyses, in which dependent variables are measured on several occasions.

For more information on FACTOR, CLUSTER, DSCRIMINANT, and QUICK CLUSTER, see the *SPSS/PC+ Professional Statistics* manual. For more information on HILOGLINEAR and MANOVA, see the *SPSS/PC+ Advanced Statistics* manual.

Summary

The SPSS/PC+ product contains many facilities for analyzing and reporting data. For most problems, you will probably want to explore your data using several different techniques. Although it may be tempting to run a lot of different procedures with which you are not very familiar in the hope of making sense of the data, this is not a very good tactic. Instead, you should think about the problem you want to solve, spend some time considering the statistical techniques that may be helpful in arriving at a solution, and only then proceed with the analysis. You should also keep in mind the caveat that the most complicated procedure is not necessarily the best. A little common sense and thought will not only save time but give better results as well.

6 Preparing Data for Analysis

Before information can be analyzed by SPSS/PC+, it must be entered into a disk file. This entails two steps—arranging the data into a suitable format and entering the data into the computer.

To enter the data into the computer, you can use one of the following methods:

- QED (Quick Editor), a data entry and editing facility that is part of SPSS/PC+.
- SPSS Data Entry II, if you have purchased and installed it.
- Data entered in a spreadsheet program (such as Excel or Lotus 1-2-3), that can then be read by SPSS/PC+.

Another option for entering data is to use a text editor program to create the file and enter the data. If you are not already familiar with an editor, you may wish to use Review, which is included with your SPSS/PC+ system (see Chapter 3). It is also possible to enter data directly into an SPSS/PC+ command file or to bring in a file that already exists on a mainframe computer. This chapter describes how to prepare data for analysis when it was initially collected and stored in a format not yet ready for SPSS/PC+ analysis.

Formatting the Data

The first step, arranging the data into a suitable format, involves several decisions on how the data are to be recorded.

Cases, Variables, And Values

Consider Table 6.1 and Table 6.2, which contain an excerpt from the *Consumer Reports* report on beers discussed in Chapter 5. Each line in the tables represents a **case**, or observation, for which **values** are available for a set of **variables**. The names of the beers are listed in both tables for identification.

Table 6.1   Excerpt from uncoded data for the beer study

Rating	Beer	Origin	Avail	Price	Cost
Very good	MILLER HIGH LIFE	USA	National	2.49	.42
Very good	BUDWEISER	USA	National	2.59	.43
Very good	SCHLITZ	USA	National	2.59	.43
Very good	LOWENBRAU	USA	National	2.89	.48
Good	OLD MILWAUKEE	USA	Regional	1.69	.28
Good	DOS EQUIS	Mexico	Regional	4.22	.70
Fair	PABST EXTRA LIGHT	USA	National	2.29	.38

Table 6.2   More data from the beer study

Beer	Calories	Sodium	Alcohol	Class	Light
MILLER HIGH LIFE	149	17	4.7	Premium	Regular
BUDWEISER	144	15	4.7	Premium	Regular
SCHLITZ	151	19	4.9	Premium	Regular
LOWENBRAU	157	15	4.9	Super-premium	Regular
OLD MILWAUKEE	145	23	4.6	Popular	Regular
DOS EQUIS	145	14	4.5	Not given	Regular
PABST EXTRA LIGHT	68	15	2.3	Not given	Light

For each beer, the same variables—rating, origin, availability, price, cost, calories, sodium, alcohol content, class, and light (type of beer)—are recorded. Each case has one and only one value for each variable. "Unknown" and "missing" are acceptable values for a variable, although these values require special treatment during analysis.

The case is the basic unit for which measurements are taken. In this analysis, each case is a brand of beer. In studies of political opinion or brand preference, each case is most likely an individual respondent to a questionnaire. A case may be a larger unit, such as a school, county, or nation; it may be a time period, such as a year or month in which measurements are obtained; or it may be an event, such as an auto accident.

For any single analysis, each case must be the same type of unit. If the unit of analysis is a county, all cases are counties and the values of each variable are for individual counties. If the unit is a state, all cases are states and the values for each variable are for states.

Identifying Important Variables

A critical step in any study is the selection of variables to be included. For example, an employee can be described using many variables, such as place of residence, color of hair and eyes, years of education, work experience, and so forth. The variables that are relevant to the problem under study must be chosen from the vast array of information available. If important variables are excluded from the data file, the results will be of limited use. This point may seem obvious, but it is all too easy to overlook an important variable until you need it for analysis, when it is too late to get the information. For example, if a variable such as years of work experience is excluded from a study of salary discrimination, few—if any—correct conclusions can be drawn. All potentially relevant variables should be included in the study, since it is much easier to exclude unnecessary variables from analysis than to gather additional information.

Recording the Data

Once the variables have been selected, you must decide how they will be recorded. Do you need to record the actual date of birth, or can you simply record the age in years? Is it sufficient to know if someone is a high-school or college graduate, or do you need to know the actual number of years of education? It is usually a good idea to record the data in as much detail as possible. For example, if you record actual ages, cases can be grouped later into age categories. But if you just record each case as over 50 years or under 50 years of age, you can never analyze your data using any other age categories.

Coding the Variables

One way to simplify data entry is to assign numbers or symbols to represent responses. This is known as **coding** the data. For example, instead of typing *light* or *regular* as the values for the type of beer, the codes *1* and *0* can be used. If only numbers are included in a coding scheme for a particular variable, it is called **numeric**. If letters or a mixture of numbers, letters, and special symbols are chosen, the code is termed **alphanumeric** or **string**. By coding, you substantially decrease the number of symbols that you need to type, especially for variables whose values are originally recorded as words (such as class of beer). If you want the coded values to be labeled on the output, a few instructions in SPSS/PC+ or QED will take care of it.

Coding schemes are arbitrary by their very nature. The type of beer could also be coded *R* for regular and *L* for light. All that is necessary is that each possible response have a distinct code. For example, coding the states by their first letter is unacceptable since there are many states that begin with the same letter. Maine, Massachusetts, Michigan, Maryland, Minnesota, Mississippi, Missouri, and Montana would be indistinguishable.

It is usually helpful to have one variable that uniquely identifies each case. For the beer data, that variable is the name of the beer. Sometimes it is useful to identify cases with an ID number. This identifier can help you easily locate the data for cases with unusual values or missing information.

An Example

A possible coding scheme for the beer data is shown in Table 6.3.

Table 6.3   Coding scheme for beer data form

Variable	Description	Coding scheme
RATING		1=Very good 2=Good 3=Fair
BEER		Actual name of the beer
ORIGIN		1=USA 2=Canada 3=France 4=Holland 5=Mexico 6=Germany 7=Japan
AVAIL	Availability in the U.S.	1=National 2=Regional
PRICE	Price per six-pack of 12-ounce containers	Actual price
COST	Cost per 12 fluid ounces	Actual cost
CALORIES	Calories per 12 fluid ounces	Number of calories
SODIUM	Sodium per 12 fluid ounces in mg	Number of mg
ALCOHOL	Alcohol by volume (in %)	% of alcohol
CLASS		0=Not given 1=Super-premium 2=Premium 3=Popular
LIGHT		0=Regular 1=Light

Figure 6.1 contains data for the first three beers listed in Table 6.1 and Table 6.2 coded according to this scheme.

Figure 6.1   Coded data

```
RATING     BEER           ORIGIN AVAIL PRICE COST CALORIES SODIUM ALCOHOL CLASS LIGHT

   1   MILLER HIGH LIFE     1     1   249   42    149     17     47      2     0
   1   BUDWEISER            1     1   259   43    144     15     47      2     0
   1   SCHLITZ              1     1   259   43    151     19     49      2     0
```

Entering the Data

There are several methods of entering data into the computer in a form that SPSS/PC+ can read. The rest of this chapter gives tutorial examples of getting data into SPSS/PC+ in various ways:

- Typing data into QED (Quick Edit), which is part of the SPSS/PC+ 5.0 system.
- Reading a system file previously saved in SPSS/PC+, QED, or SPSS Data Entry II by running a GET command.
- Reading data in a file created by a spreadsheet or database program by running a TRANSLATE FROM command.
- Typing data into a text file and then reading it by using a DATA LIST command.

Entering Data with QED

An efficient method of entering data is to use QED. Complete information on the use of QED is in the Syntax Reference. To try this method, follow the numbered steps in the next sections.

🔘 Start SPSS/PC+ from the DOS prompt by typing

`spsspc`

The SPSS/PC+ Main Menu is displayed with orientation highlighted.

Shift into QED

The following steps perform the shift to QED:

🔘 Highlight read or write data on the Main Menu by pressing ⊕ or clicking the mouse. Then press ⏎Enter. This displays the next menu and highlights QED. Leave the highlight on QED.

🔘 To paste QED into the scratch pad, press ⏎Enter or double-click on QED. The command is now ready to be executed.

🔘 To run the QED command, press F10 and ⏎Enter. This transfers you to the QED facility, with no current file. (If you start QED when a file is active in SPSS/PC+, the active system file is transferred to QED, and any changes you make can be transferred back to SPSS/PC+ when you exit from QED.)

If you make a mistake, such as pasting the wrong command, you can press (Esc) several times until you get back to the Main Menu. Then start with step 1 again. SPSS/PC+ will paste the next command on a new line.

Define a New File

From the Main Menu of QED, you can perform tasks such as getting, naming, and saving files. To define a new file, follow these steps:

❶ Press (F7) and type a name for the new file such as

```
beerrpt
```

❷ Press (↵Enter). This stores the filename with default extension .*SYS* and returns to the QED Main Menu. You are now ready to define the variables.

Shift into the Dictionary Branch and Define Your Variables

In the Dictionary branch of QED, you can specify the characteristics of variables and their values, including descriptive labels.

❶ To shift into the Dictionary branch, from the Main Menu press (F4).

❷ Press (F2) to open the variable definition window. The first variable shown in Table 6.3 is *RATING*. Type

```
rating
```

and press (↵Enter). Since the meaning of *RATING* is clear, a variable label is unnecessary.

❸ Press (Ctrl)-(F10) to complete the definition of the variable. A reminder of which keys to press is at the bottom of the variable definition window, where (Ctrl)-(F10) is indicated by ^F10. When you complete a variable definition, QED displays a new variable definition window.

❹ To define the next variable, type

```
beer
```

for the variable name, and go on to the Type of Variable by pressing (↵Enter) twice. A mini-menu of variable types pops up.

❺ To select String, press (↑) and then (↵Enter).

❻ In the Variable Length space, type

```
20
```

and press (↵Enter).

This allows beer names of up to 20 characters, including spaces.

7️⃣ Press Ctrl-F10 to complete the variable definition and display a new definition window.

8️⃣ Type the name of the next variable

`origin`

and press ⏎Enter. This variable is numeric and the possible code numbers are all one digit each, making the variable length 1, which is already listed as the default.

9️⃣ Press Ctrl-F10 to complete the variable definition and display a new definition window.

🔟 Type the name of the next variable

`avail`

and press ⏎Enter.

⑪ Type the label

`Availability in the U.S.`

and press ⏎Enter.

⑫ Press Ctrl-F10 to complete the variable definition.

⑬ Continue entering variables using the information from the tables. Be sure to indicate lengths long enough for the values of each variable (including a space for a decimal point, if necessary). For example, a value of 2.49 for *PRICE* requires a total length of 4 (three digits and a decimal point).

⑭ To display a list of variables, press Esc. The variables are listed alphabetically. You can edit any variable definition by highlighting the variable in the list and pressing F3. When variables have been defined, you can enter value labels.

Add Value Labels

Value labels identify the codes in the coding scheme. To define value labels for the beer data, follow these steps:

1️⃣ Highlight *RATING* in the list of variables and press F5. A blank value label window is displayed with the name of the variable at the top.

2️⃣ The first value for *RATING* (see Table 6.3) is 1. Type 1 and press ⏎Enter.

3️⃣ Type the value label

`Very good`

and press ⏎Enter. The cursor is positioned for the next value and its label. Continue typing the other values and their labels (2=*Good*, 3=*Fair*).

4️⃣ When finished with the value labels for *RATING*, press Ctrl F10. The list of variables is displayed again.

⑤ Select another variable, press F5, and enter its values and value labels. Continue entering value labels as listed in Table 6.3. When all value labels have been entered, you are ready to enter data values.

Shift into the Data Branch and Enter Your Data

The Data branch of QED has facilities for entering and correcting data values. The data for this example are listed in Table 6.1 and Table 6.2.

❶ Press ⇧Shift-F5, which allows you to go to the Data branch directly from the Dictionary branch. Alternatively, you could press Esc to get back to the Main Menu and then press F5 without ⇧Shift.

❷ Press F10 to get the form for the first case. The variables you defined are listed on the left. The cursor (highlight) is in the *RATING* space for case 1. The rating for Miller High Life beer in Table 6.1 is *Very good*. The coding scheme in Table 6.3 translates this rating to code 1. Type 1 and press ↵Enter. This moves the highlight to the next variable, *BEER*.

❸ Type

```
MILLER HIGH LIFE
```

and press ↵Enter. This shifts the highlight to the *ORIGIN* space.

❹ The origin code for USA is 1. Type 1 and press ↵Enter.

❺ Enter the other data values for MILLER HIGH LIFE. When you press ↵Enter after entering the last variable in the list (*LIGHT*), a blank form for Case 2 is displayed. Continue by entering the data for BUDWEISER.

❻ Continue entering codes for the data in Table 6.1 and Table 6.2 until you have enough practice.

Return to the Files Branch and Save the File

The file was started from the Main Menu by giving it a name. Now it is time to return to the Main Menu and save the information you have entered in the file.

❶ Press Esc. This returns to the Main Menu of QED.

❷ Press F3. The filename is listed. At this point, you could type a new filename, but instead, press ↵Enter to accept the listed filename. This produces the query Do you want the file saved in compressed mode?

❸ You can press N to save the file in uncompressed mode, or Y to save the file in compressed mode. Compressed mode takes less space on the disk. After you press Y or N and press ↵Enter, a file information summary appears.

❹ To return to the Main Menu of QED, press Space. Then press F10 to return to SPSS/PC+, and press Space whenever MORE is displayed in the upper right corner, until the SPSS/PC+ Main Menu appears in the top half of your screen.

⑤ For a quick check to see that the variables in the *BEERRPT.SYS* file were transferred from QED, press [Alt] [V], which displays the Variables window. Use the arrow keys or the mouse to highlight *BEER* and read its description, which lists the type as string and the width as 20, just as you defined them earlier. Press [Esc] to close the Variables window.

The data are ready for analysis. The next section discusses a way to retrieve this data file or a similar file during another SPSS/PC+ session.

Reading Data Previously Saved in SPSS/PC+, QED, or Data Entry II

If you have previously saved data in a system file in SPSS/PC+, QED, or SPSS Data Entry II, you can read the file into SPSS/PC+ by running a command such as

```
GET FILE 'BEERRPT.SYS'.
```

As an illustration, you can retrieve the beer data file saved in the previous section by following these steps:

① Start SPSS/PC+, if it is not already started, by typing spsspc at the DOS prompt.

② On the main menu, highlight read or write data.

③ Press [↵Enter]. This displays the next menu.

④ Highlight GET.

⑤ To paste GET into the scratch pad, press [↵Enter]. The GET menu is displayed, with the FILE subcommand highlighted.

⑥ To paste the subcommand FILE, press [↵Enter] again. This pastes the subcommand into the scratch pad and opens the typing window in the middle of the screen.

⑦ Type the name of the file

```
beerrpt.sys
```

and press [↵Enter]. This pastes the filename into the command. If the file is not in the current directory, you must use the complete path.

⑧ To run the GET command, press [F10] and [↵Enter].

The file named on the GET command becomes the active file in your current SPSS/PC+ session. The data are ready for analysis. You can check the variables by pressing [Alt]-[V].

Reading Data Saved in Another Format

If you previously saved data in a spreadsheet or database program such as Lotus, Excel, or dBASE, you can use the TRANSLATE FROM command to bring your data into SPSS/PC+. A Lotus file, *INDEX.WK3*, was copied at installation into the directory where SPSS/PC+ is installed. To translate it into SPSS/PC+ follow these steps:

1 Start SPSS/PC+, if it is not already running.

2 On the Main Menu, highlight read or write data.

3 Press ⏎Enter. This displays the next menu.

4 Highlight other file formats and press ⏎Enter.

5 Highlight TRANSLATE FROM and press ⏎Enter to paste it into the scratch pad. The command is pasted and the TRANSLATE FROM menu is displayed.

6 At this point you need to enter the filename enclosed in apostrophes. To paste the apostrophes, press ⏎Enter again. This opens the typing window in the middle of the screen.

7 Type the name of the file:

```
index.wk3
```

The source program, Lotus, is indicated by the file extension *.WK3*. If you started SPSS/PC+ from another directory, use a path to indicate the directory where SPSS/PC+ is installed, as in:

```
c:\spss\index.wk3
```

8 Press ⏎Enter. This pastes the filename into the command.

9 Highlight and paste FIELDNAMES. This translates spreadsheet fieldnames into SPSS/PC+ variable names.

10 Highlight and paste MAP. SPSS/PC+ will display a list of the variables transferred from the Lotus file.

11 To run the TRANSLATE FROM command, press F10 and ⏎Enter.

The translated file becomes the active file in your current SPSS/PC+ session. You can check the variables by pressing Alt-V. You may want to define variable labels, value labels, and missing values. Chapter 7 contains information on the commands to implement such definitions, or you can use QED as described earlier in this chapter. For more information on TRANSLATE, see the Syntax Reference.

Entering the Data in a Text File

An alternative method of creating an SPSS/PC+ system file is to enter the data in a text (ASCII) file and then use the DATA LIST command to read the data into SPSS/PC+. To enter the data you can use any text editor or the Review editor described in Chapter 3 After the data are read into SPSS/PC+ with DATA LIST, you can use other SPSS/PC+ commands to define variable labels, value labels, and missing values. These commands are described in detail in Chapter 7. Alternatively, you can use QED to assign variable labels, value labels, and missing values.

Fixed Format

In a data file, each data line, also known as a **record,** contains columns in which the numbers or characters are stored. When you enter the value for each variable at the same column location for each case, the format is called **fixed format**. Two decisions that must be made are how many lines will be needed for each case and in what column location each variable will be stored.

Figure 6.2 shows a partial listing of the beer file in which one line is used for each case. Fifty column locations are also indicated by the two rows at the top of the listing.

Figure 6.2   One-record file

```
          1         2         3         4         5
12345678901234567890123456789012345678901234567890  Columns

1 MILLER HIGH LIFE     1 1 249   42 149 17 47 2 0
1 BUDWEISER            1 1 259   43 144 15 47 2 0
1 SCHLITZ              1 1 259   43 151 19 49 2 0
```

Rating is in column 1, name of the beer in columns 3–22, origin in column 25, availability in column 27, price in columns 29–31, cost in columns 33–35, calories in columns 37–39, sodium content in columns 41–42, alcohol content in columns 44–45, class in column 47, and the light or regular designation in column 49.

In any given row, the columns that are reserved for a particular variable make up a **field**. The numbers are positioned in each field so that the last digit is in the last column of the field for the variable. For example, a calorie count of 72 would have the digit 7 in column 38 and the digit 2 in column 39, the last column of the calorie field; leading blanks or zeros occupy the beginning columns of a field. The decimal points for the price, cost, and alcohol variables are not included in the file. The decimal point does not need to be included since SPSS/PC+ commands can be used to indicate its location. If the decimal point is included, it occupies a column like any other symbol.

When there are many variables for each case, more than one line may be necessary to store the information. For example, if your screen width is 80, you may prefer to enter information that requires more than 80 columns on two or more lines. It is usually recommended that you enter an identification number for each case and a record number on each line if it takes more than one line to record the data for a case. You can then easily locate missing or out-of-order data lines.

It is important to allocate a sufficient number of columns for each variable. For example, if only two columns are used to record a weight variable, only weights less than 100 pounds will fit. Always allocate the maximum number of columns that you might need. Don't worry if your observed data do not actually require that many columns.

All data files considered in this manual are *rectangular*. That is, all cases have the same variables and the same number of lines per case. Some data files are not rectangular. For instance, every case may not have the same number of lines recorded. In a study of adverse drug reactions, cases that are alive will not have a data line detailing autopsy findings. Another nonrectangular file might not define all cases as the same unit, as in a file containing some lines with data about families and some lines with data about individual members within families. Currently, SPSS/PC+ does not contain facilities for handling these kinds of files.

Freefield Format

Sometimes it is more convenient not to have to worry about arranging variables in particular column locations. Instead, for each case, variables are entered in the same order with at least one blank separating values. Figure 6.3 shows how a freefield data file for the first three cases of the beer data might look.

Figure 6.3   Beer data in freefield format

```
1 'MILLER HIGH LIFE' 1 1 2.49 .42 149 17 4.7 2 0
1 BUDWEISER 1 1 2.59 .43 144 15 4.7 2 0
1 SCHLITZ 1 1 2.59 .43 151 19 4.9 2 0
```

Figure 6.2 differs from Figure 6.3 in several ways. Whenever there is a blank within the name, the name of the beer is enclosed in apostrophes (or quotation marks). This indicates that the blanks are part of the value. Decimal points must be included in the data. For more information on freefield data, see DATA LIST: Freefield Format in the Syntax Reference.

Designing Forms

When a study is based on data already gathered, there is not much that can be done about the forms on which data reside or how the information is recorded. For example, if education is recorded in categories, the actual number of years cannot be entered into the data file. However, when a study is planned in advance, special forms can be designed that indicate both the type of information to be collected and where it will reside in the computer file. This type of form makes data entry much easier. You can enter the information directly from the form into your computer.

Sometimes data collection forms are designed with space for miscellaneous comments. These comments can be analyzed only if they are coded. For example, if undergraduate major is listed in the comments section, it must be coded into a variable. A coding scheme such as *1=physical sciences, 2=social sciences, 3=humanities, 4=engineering*, and so forth could be used. Unless the comment section has specific codable information, it cannot be analyzed in any reasonable manner.

The Data File

The data file is the most crucial component of any analysis. Unless the data have been carefully gathered, recorded, and entered, all subsequent analyses will be of limited use. Always try to obtain as much of the necessary information as possible for all of the cases that are to be included in a study. A special code standing for missing information should be reserved only for situations where it is impossible to ascertain a certain value. Once the data have been coded and entered, be sure to check the values. Any suspicious values should be confirmed. They may be the result of coding or data-entry errors. Subsequent chapters show how you can use SPSS/PC+ to help locate errors in a data file.

The SPSS/PC+ Session

After you have prepared your data, you are ready to run the SPSS/PC+ program. The SPSS/PC+ commands for carrying out analyses follow a simple progression.

- At the start of a session, you need to tell the system how to interpret (and perhaps where to find) your data. This chapter described various methods of entering data.

- You might want to add some labels and print formats to make the output more readable and identify values that stand for missing data. These commands are discussed in Chapter 7.

- Next, you might wish to make some modifications to the data file. For example, if you have recorded age in years (as you were advised to do above), you might want to create a new variable that gives age categories. The commands for this type of operation are in Chapter 8.

- For a given analysis, you might want to select a particular subset of cases or perhaps a random sample. Commands for selecting and sampling cases are discussed in Chapter 9.

- Finally, you can use one of many procedure commands to produce a report or a statistical analysis. Chapter 11 through Chapter 24 contain detailed information about the procedures available in SPSS/PC+. You can continue modifying the data and running procedures as long as you like.

- To leave SPSS/PC+, you end the session with the FINISH command.

The way in which you start the program and enter commands to read, modify, and analyze your data are described in Chapter 2.

7

Defining Data

Chapter 6 described several methods of entering data into a computer file that SPSS/PC+ can read. The data can be in an SPSS/PC+ format, in a spreadsheet or data-base file, or in a text (ASCII) file. This chapter is about the commands used to describe the data. If your data are in a text file or you are entering data along with your commands, you must use a DATA LIST command to define the variables and to indicate where the data can be found. After the data are read into SPSS/PC+, you can describe them further by adding or changing labels and formats.

The data definition commands in SPSS/PC+ answer the following questions:

- Where are the data stored on your computer?
- How many lines are there for each case?
- What are the names of the variables, and where are they located in the data file?
- What labels should be attached to variables and values?
- What values are used to represent missing information?

Describing the Data File

The SPSS/PC+ commands in Figure 7.1 define and produce a listing of the beer data (see Chapter 5) entered in a text file. Assume that the data are entered in **fixed format**. That is, variables are stored in the same column locations for all of the cases.

The first data definition command is DATA LIST, which tells SPSS/PC+ where to find the data and how to read it.

Figure 7.1   Command file for the beer data

```
DATA LIST /RATING 1 BEER 3-22(A) ORIGIN 25 AVAIL 27
   PRICE 29-31(2) COST 33-35(2) CALORIES 37-39 SODIUM 41-42
   ALCOHOL 44-45(1) CLASS 47 LIGHT 49.

VARIABLE LABELS AVAIL 'AVAILABILITY IN THE U.S.' /
   PRICE 'PRICE PER 6-PACK' /
   COST 'COST PER 12 FLUID OUNCES' /
   CALORIES 'CALORIES PER 12 FLUID OUNCES' /
   SODIUM 'SODIUM PER 12 FLUID OUNCES IN MG' /
   ALCOHOL 'ALCOHOL BY VOLUME (IN %)' /
   CLASS 'PRICE CLASS'.

VALUE LABELS RATING 1 'VERY GOOD' 2 'GOOD' 3 'FAIR' /
   ORIGIN 1 'USA' 2 'CANADA' 3 'FRANCE' 4 'HOLLAND'
   5 'MEXICO' 6 'GERMANY'  7 'JAPAN' /
   AVAIL 1 'NATIONAL' 2 'REGIONAL' /
   CLASS 0 'NOT GIVEN' 1 'SUPER-PREMIUM'
   2 'PREMIUM' 3 'POPULAR'/
   LIGHT 0 'REGULAR' 1 'LIGHT'.

MISSING VALUE CLASS(0).
BEGIN DATA.
1   MILLER HIGH LIFE      1 1 249   42 149 17 47 2 0
1   BUDWEISER             1 1 259   43 144 15 47 2 0
1   SCHLITZ               1 1 259   43 151 19 49 2 0

  .....

END DATA.

LIST VARIABLES=RATING TO PRICE CALORIES ALCOHOL /CASES=10.
FINISH.
```

Locating the Data

When data are entered as text, you can enter data along with your SPSS/PC+ commands or read data from a separate file. If the data are in a file other than the SPSS/PC+ command file, specify the file in which the data are stored with the FILE subcommand, as in:

```
DATA LIST FILE='BEER.DAT'
```

BEER.DAT is the name SPSS/PC+ uses to locate the file in which the data are stored. You specify the name of the file in apostrophes (or quotes). If the file is not stored in the current directory, you must include the path name within the apostrophes (see Chapter 4). If you enter the data in the same file as the SPSS/PC+ commands, you do not need to use a FILE subcommand (see "Inline Data" on p. 75).

Choosing Variable Names

After you have identified the data file, you assign names to each of the variables and give their location in the file. You use the assigned variable name to refer to the variable throughout the SPSS/PC+ session. For example, a variable that describes father's occupation might be named PAOCCUP. Keep in mind the following rules when you name variables:

- The name must begin with a letter or the @ symbol. The remaining characters in the name can be any letter, any digit, a period, or the symbols _, $, #, or @.
- The length of the name cannot exceed eight characters.
- Blanks and special symbols such as &, !, ?, /, ', cannot occur in a variable name.
- Each variable must have a unique name—duplication is not allowed.
- The reserved keywords in Table 7.1 cannot be used as variable names since they have special meaning in SPSS/PC+.

The following are all valid variable names: *LOCATION*, *LOC@5*, *X_1*, and *OVER$500*.

You can create a set of variable names by using keyword TO. When you are assigning new names, as in DATA LIST specifications, ITEM1 TO ITEM5 is equivalent to five names: ITEM1, ITEM2, ITEM3, ITEM4, and ITEM5. The prefix can be any valid name and the numbers can be any integers, as long as the first number is smaller than the second, and the full variable name, including the number, does not exceed eight characters.

Table 7.1   Reserved keywords

ALL	AND	BY	EQ	GE	GT	LE
LT	NE	NOT	OR	TO	WITH	

It is a good idea to assign names that help you identify the variables. You could give the names *X* and *Z* to variables for age and sex, but the names *AGE* and *SEX* give you a much better idea of the nature of each variable. The variable names assigned to the beer data include *RATING* for the rating of the beer, *ALCOHOL* for the alcohol content, *PRICE* for the price of a six-pack, and *CALORIES* for caloric content.

Indicating Column Locations

Along with a variable's name, you specify its column location on the data file. For example, the command

```
DATA LIST FILE='BEER.DAT'
 /RATING 1 BEER 3-22(A) ORIGIN 25 AVAIL 27.
```

describes four variables. Variable definition begins with the first slash. The numbers after the variable names give their column locations. For example, *RATING* is in column 1, and *BEER* is in columns 3 through 22 (and is alphanumeric; see "Types of Variables" on p. 71).

Although variables from the same data record must be defined together, they do not need to be defined in any particular sequence. That is, variables at the end of a record can be defined before those at the beginning of the same record. The order in which you define variables determines their order in the SPSS/PC+ active file, which is not necessarily their original order on your file.

If several variables are recorded in adjacent columns on the same record and have the same width and format type (numeric or string), you can use an abbreviated format to define them on DATA LIST. List all of the variable names followed by the beginning column location of the first variable in the list, a dash, and the ending column location of the last variable in the list. For example, in the command

```
DATA LIST FILE='HUB.DAT' /
  DEPT82 19 SEX 20 MOHIRED YRHIRED 12-15 /.
```

MOHIRED and *YRHIRED* form a list of variables, and 12–15 is the column specification for both. (The second slash is needed for this file to skip a second line of data not being defined; see "Specifying Data on Multiple Records" below). The DATA LIST command divides the total number of columns specified equally among the variables in the list. Thus, *MOHIRED* is in columns 12–13 and *YRHIRED* is in columns 14–15. Be careful to use variables of equal width when defining data this way. If you use variables of different widths, and SPSS/PC+ can divide the number of columns by the number of variables equally, your data will be read incorrectly. If the total number of columns is not an even multiple of the number of variables listed, SPSS/PC+ displays an error message and does not read the file.

Establishing Display Formats

Whenever you see the values of a variable displayed, SPSS/PC+ knows what format to use because it knows the variable's width and type from the DATA LIST specifications. This information, along with the variable name, labels, and missing values (see "Variable and Value Labels" on p. 72 and "Identifying Missing Values" on p. 73), forms the **dictionary** portion of your SPSS/PC+ active file. Any time that you want to change the format of a numeric variable use the FORMAT command (see the Syntax Reference). String variable formats cannot be changed.

Specifying Data on Multiple Records

Sometimes your data are located on more than one record for each case. To read more than one record for each case, enter a slash and define the variables recorded on the first record, and then enter a slash followed by the variable definitions for the next record. Repeat this procedure until you have defined all records for each case in your data file. For example, the following DATA LIST command defines a personnel file that was entered with two record s per case:

```
DATA LIST FILE='HUB.DAT'
  /DEPT82 19 SEX 20 MOHIRED YRHIRED 12-15
  /SALARY82 21-25.
```

This DATA LIST reads variables *DEPT82, SEX, MOHIRED*, and *YRHIRED* from the first record and *SALARY82* from the second record.

Freefield Data Input

With **freefield format**, successive data values are simply separated by one or more blanks or one comma. Variables must be in the same order for each of the cases, but they need not be in the same columns (see Chapter 6). If you choose this manner of entering data, specify the keyword FREE after the DATA LIST command. In this case, column locations are not specified after the variable names. However, you must indicate the length of long string variables using the A notation (see "Types of Variables" below). It is probably a good idea to also give the length of short strings so the dictionary format will be correct (the default for short strings is A8). For example,

```
DATA LIST FREE
 /RATING BEER (A20) ORIGIN AVAIL PRICE COST CALORIES
  SODIUM ALCOHOL CLASS LIGHT.
```

can be used to define the variables for the beer example. Note that if values of string variables include blanks (such as Miller High Life for the *BEER* variable), they must be enclosed within apostrophes in the data file. Otherwise, the blanks are interpreted as the beginning of a new variable.

The advantage of freefield format is obvious: data entry is much simpler since variables do not have to be put in particular locations. The major disadvantage of freefield data entry is that if you inadvertently omit a data value, all values for subsequent variables and cases are incorrect. For example, if the rating variable is omitted for the second case, the value for the type of beer is taken as the rating (which will cause an error since it is a string value), and everything that follows is wrong. A similar problem can arise if you mistakenly enter an extra value. Therefore, it is particularly important to list and check the data values after using freefield format.

Another disadvantage of freefield input is that all numeric variables are assigned a width of eight characters and two decimal places. However, you can use the FORMAT command to assign proper formats following the DATA LIST command.

Types of Variables

You can define two types of variables with SPSS/PC+: numeric and string (alphanumeric). A **numeric variable** contains only numbers. Numeric variables can be either decimals (such as 12.345) or integers (such as 1234). A **string variable** can contain a combination of letters, numbers, and special characters. There are two types of string variables—short strings and long strings. A string variable whose values contain eight characters or less is considered a short string. The variable *SEX*, coded as F or M, is a short string. In the beer data example, the name of the beer is a long string. The difference is that short strings can be used in several data transformation and procedure commands where long strings cannot. String variables are identified with the letter *A* in parentheses following the column specification on the DATA LIST command, as in:

```
DATA LIST FILE='BEER.DAT' /BEER 3-22(A).
```

When using freefield format, you should also indicate the width of the string variable, as in BEER (A20). Use the maximum length of a variable as the width. Count all characters and blanks in calculating the width. For example, "Miller High Life" has a width of 16 with blanks included.

Indicating Decimal Places

By default, DATA LIST assumes that the data format type is numeric and that the numbers are integers, or that any decimal points are explicitly coded. To indicate noninteger values when the decimal point is not actually coded in the data, specify the number of *implied* decimal places by enclosing the intended number in parentheses following the column specification. The specification

```
DATA LIST FILE='BEER.DAT' /ALCOHOL 44-45(1).
```

locates the variable that measures alcohol content in columns 44 through 45. The last digit of *ALCOHOL* is stored as a decimal position.

For example, if the number 47 is stored in columns 44–45, the specification ALCOHOL 44–45 (1) results in the number 4.7. The specification ALCOHOL 44–45 (2) results in the number 0.47. The dictionary format is also affected by the implied decimal. The two-column designation 44–45 (1) results in a three-column dictionary format in order to accommodate the decimal point. If the number is stored in the data file with the decimal point, the decimal point overrides the DATA LIST format specification (but the dictionary format might have to be adjusted). Implied decimals can only be used with fixed-format data.

Variable and Value Labels

The VARIABLE LABELS and VALUE LABELS commands supply information that is used for labeling the output of SPSS/PC+ sessions. These labels are optional, but using them often makes the output more readable. Some variables that have many values, such as age or weight, do not need value labels since the values themselves are meaningful.

The VARIABLE LABELS command assigns variables an extended descriptive label. Specify the variable name, followed by at least one comma or blank, and the label enclosed in apostrophes or quotation marks. Multiple label specifications are optionally separated by slashes, as in:

```
VARIABLE LABELS AVAIL 'AVAILABILITY IN THE U.S.'
 /PRICE 'PRICE PER 6-PACK'
 /COST 'COST PER 12 FLUID OUNCES'
 /CALORIES 'CALORIES PER 12 FLUID OUNCES'
 /SODIUM 'SODIUM PER 12 FLUID OUNCES IN MG'
 /ALCOHOL 'ALCOHOL BY VOLUME (IN %)'
 /CLASS 'PRICE CLASS'.
```

This command assigns variable labels to the variables *AVAIL* through *CLASS*. A variable label applies to only one variable. The variable must have been previously defined on a DATA LIST, GET, or IMPORT command, or on one of the transformation commands that create new variables. The label can be up to 40 characters long and can include blanks and any other characters.

To use an apostrophe as part of a label, enclose the label in quotation marks, as in:

```
VARIABLE LABELS SALARY82 "EMPLOYEE'S 1982 SALARY".
```

Quotation marks are entered in a label by enclosing the label in apostrophes.

The VALUE LABELS command assigns descriptive labels to values. The VALUE LABELS command is followed by a variable name, or variable list, and a list of values with associated labels. The command

```
VALUE LABELS RATING 1 'VERY GOOD' 2 'GOOD' 3 'FAIR'
 /ORIGIN 1 'USA' 2 'CANADA' 3 'FRANCE' 4 'HOLLAND'
  5 'MEXICO' 6 'GERMANY'  7 'JAPAN'
 /AVAIL 1 'NATIONAL' 2 'REGIONAL'
 /CLASS 0 'NOT GIVEN' 1 'SUPER-PREMIUM' 2 'PREMIUM' 3 'POPULAR'
 /LIGHT 0 'REGULAR' 1 'LIGHT'.
```

assigns labels to the values for the variables *RATING*, *ORIGIN*, *AVAIL*, *CLASS*, and *LIGHT*. The labels for each variable are separated from the labels for the preceding variable by a slash. You can assign labels for values of any variable already defined. If the variable is a string, the values themselves must also be enclosed in apostrophes. Value labels can be up to 20 characters long and can contain any characters, including blanks.

The VALUE LABELS command completely replaces all of the value labels for the variables named on it. If you want to add one or more new value labels or replace some of the existing labels without entering the whole set of labels, use the ADD VALUE LABELS command. This command leaves unchanged the labels for values that are not mentioned.

Identifying Missing Values

Sometimes information for a particular variable is not available for a case. When information about the value of a variable is unknown, a special code is used to indicate that the value is missing. For example, if a patient's age is not known, this can be indicated by a code such as −1 to indicate that the information is missing.

The MISSING VALUE command identifies the value that represents missing information. Specify the variable name or variable list and the specified missing value in parentheses, as in:

```
MISSING VALUE CLASS(0).
```

This command defines the value 0 as missing for variable *CLASS*.

Missing values specified on the MISSING VALUE command are called user-specified missing values, or just **user-missing values**. SPSS/PC+ also provides a **system-missing** value, which is indicated on output by a period. SPSS/PC+ assigns the system-missing value when it encounters a value other than a number for a variable declared as numeric on the DATA LIST command. For example, blanks are set to system-missing for numeric variables. An alternative to entering a special value, then, is to leave a field blank. However, you will find that assigning a user-missing value gives you more control in tables and other results from SPSS/PC+.

System-missing values are also assigned when new variables created with data transformation commands are undefined, as when an attempt is made to divide by 0 or when a case has a missing value for a variable used in computing the new variable.

The Active File

The DATA LIST command defines an **active file**. This is the file you work with during your session. The active file exists only temporarily unless you use the SAVE command. It consists of a dictionary of variable names and labels, value labels, and missing-value specifications; it also contains the actual data, whether you entered them interactively or read them from another file. At any time in your session, you can modify the labels (by entering new labels) or the data (with the commands discussed in the next chapter). You can use the SAVE command to write a copy of the active file to disk for later use. When saved in this way, it is called a **system file** (see "Using an SPSS/PC+ System File" on p. 76).

In addition to modifying the data values or the labels in your active file, you can completely replace it with another active file, or you can combine it with system files that you have previously saved. Any command that defines a new active file will replace the existing active file. (DATA LIST, GET, IMPORT, JOIN, and sometimes AGGREGATE do this.) Use the JOIN command to combine the active file with existing system files.

Listing Data

Once you have defined the data file, you are ready to specify an SPSS/PC+ procedure. SPSS/PC+ procedures are used to tabulate the data, to calculate statistics, and to generate reports and plots. For example, the following LIST command requests a listing of the data values for the first 10 cases in the beer data file:

```
LIST VARIABLES=RATING TO PRICE CALORIES ALCOHOL /CASES=10.
```

The subcommand VARIABLES indicates which of the variables are to be displayed (the default is to list all variables). The CASES subcommand indicates the number of observations for which the values are to be listed (the default is to list all cases). LIST uses the dictionary formats to display the variable's values. Therefore, it is a good check on whether a new variable has the proper width and number of decimal places.

Figure 7.2 shows the listing of the first 10 cases. This listing is useful for spotting errors in data entry or data definition. For example, if the wrong columns have been given for the *AVAIL* variable, strange values will probably appear in the listing. From this listing, you might decide to assign a DOLLAR format to *PRICE* (see FORMATS in the Syntax Reference).

Figure 7.2   Output from LIST

```
RATING BEER                  ORIGIN AVAIL PRICE CALORIES ALCOHOL

    1      MILLER HIGH LIFE      1     1    2.49    149     4.7
    1      BUDWEISER             1     1    2.59    144     4.7
    1      SCHLITZ               1     1    2.59    151     4.9
    1      LOWENBRAU             1     1    2.89    157     4.9
    1      MICHELOB              1     1    2.99    162     5.0
    1      LABATTS               2     2    3.15    147     5.0
    1      MOLSON                2     2    3.35    154     5.1
    1      HENRY WEINHARD        1     2    3.65    149     4.7
    1      KRONENBOURG           3     2    4.39    170     5.2
    1      HEINEKEN              4     1    4.59    152     5.0

NUMBER OF CASES READ =      10    NUMBER OF CASES LISTED =      10
```

You can use the TO keyword on a procedure command to refer to variables that are consecutive in the SPSS/PC+ active file (the order in which they were defined on the DATA LIST command). Thus, if you specify VARA TO VARD on a procedure, *VARA*, *VARD*, and any variables that have been defined between *VARA* and *VARD* are analyzed. For example, the command

```
LIST VARIABLES=RATING TO PRICE CALORIES ALCOHOL.
```

requests a listing for variables *RATING*, *BEER*, *ORIGIN*, *AVAIL*, and *PRICE*, plus variables *CALORIES* and *ALCOHOL*. See Figure 7.1 for the DATA LIST command that defines these variables.

Inline Data

Instead of keeping your data in an external file that you specify on the FILE subcommand), you may prefer to enter your data along with your SPSS/PC+ commands. Such data, known as **inline data,** are separated from the other lines in the command file with the BEGIN DATA and END DATA commands. The BEGIN DATA command follows the data-definition commands and precedes the data, and the END DATA command follows the last line of the data (see Figure 7.1).

Reading Matrices

For the SPSS/PC+ procedures REGRESSION and ONEWAY, and the FACTOR and CLUSTER procedures in SPSS/PC+ Professional Statistics, you can use certain summary statistics such as means, sample sizes, correlations, covariances, or distance coefficients instead of reading the original cases. This decreases processing time considerably.

All statistical computations are based on the summary statistics. (The results you get are the same as if you had entered the original cases, since all of the necessary information is contained in the summary statistics.)

Reading intermediate values instead of the actual cases is useful when you have used SPSS/PC+ procedures to write a file with summary results or when the summary results are available from some other source, such as journals.

When you enter summary statistics, special specifications are required on the DATA LIST command (see DATA LIST: Matrix Materials in the Syntax Reference).

Using an SPSS/PC+ System File

Once you have defined your data file in SPSS/PC+, you do not need to repeat the data definition process. Information from the data definition commands described in this chapter can be permanently saved along with the data in specially formatted files called the SPSS/PC+ **system files** and **portable files**. Variables created or altered by data transformations and the descriptive information for these variables can also be saved on these files.

A system file can be used in subsequent SPSS/PC+ sessions without requiring re-specification of variable locations, formats, missing values, or variable and value labels. You can update the system file, altering the descriptive information or modifying the data, and you can save the updated version in a new system file. See the SAVE and GET commands in the Syntax Reference for more information.

A portable file is used to transport your data plus definitions between SPSS/PC+ and SPSS on a mainframe computer without having to redefine them each time. See IMPORT and EXPORT in the Syntax Reference for more information.

Using Spreadsheet or Database Files

If your data are already in a spreadsheet or database file, you may be able to use the TRANSLATE command to read them directly into SPSS/PC+. TRANSLATE can also write your data into a spreadsheet or database file.

It is inefficient to translate the file format each time you use the data. Once the data are translated you should save the data as an SPSS/PC+ system file if you plan to analyze the same data repeatedly.

See TRANSLATE in the Syntax Reference for details on using the TRANSLATE command.

8

Transforming Data

In the beer data (see Chapter 5), 35 brands of beer are rated on a three-point scale with the categories *very good*, *good*, and *fair*. Suppose you want to compare the beers on their ratings, but are interested only in making a dichotomous distinction between ratings of *good* and *fair*. To do this, you would want to collapse the rating categories of *very good* and *good* into a single category.

Or suppose you have done a survey of political attitudes, and you have five *yes* or *no* questions on the topic of women's rights. You might want to create a new variable that counts the total number of *yes* responses to the five items.

Operations such as these, where you take existing variables and alter their values or use them to create new variables, are called **data transformations**.

There are four commands in SPSS/PC+ that allow you to perform a wide variety of data transformations:

- **RECODE.** Use this command to alter the values of an existing variable. Typical reasons for recoding variables include combining several values into one, rearranging the order of categories, or carrying out simple data checks. You would use RECODE to collapse the rating categories in the beer data.

- **COMPUTE.** This command creates new variables through numeric transformations of existing ones. For instance, the beer data contain a variable that is the number of calories in 12 ounces of beer. You might want to use COMPUTE to figure out how many calories there would be in an eight-ounce glass of each brand.

- **COUNT.** This command creates a new variable that, for each case, counts the occurrences of certain values across a list of variables. You would use COUNT to add the *yes* responses to the women's rights questions on the political survey.

- **IF.** You can use the IF command to transform data differently for subsets of cases. For example, a company may award vacation time on the basis of length of employment. The IF command could be used to calculate vacation time for employees who have been with the company for varying lengths of time.

Recoding Values of Variables

The RECODE command tells SPSS/PC+ to make specified changes in a variable's values as the data are being read. Take the availability variable from the beer data as an example. The command

```
RECODE AVAIL (1=2)(2=1).
```

reverses values 1 and 2 for variable *AVAIL* (i.e., if a case has value 1, it is changed to 2, and vice versa).

To be recoded, a variable must already exist in your data file. The variable's name precedes the list of value specifications on the RECODE command. You can create as many new values for a variable as you wish, as long as each specification is enclosed in parentheses. A single specification can be used to recode several values as one new value. Thus, the command

```
RECODE RATING (1,2=1)(3,4=2).
```

changes *RATING* values to 1 for cases with original ratings of 1 or 2, and to 2 for cases originally rated as 3 or 4.

You cannot list more than one *new* value in a single value specification. Thus, specifications like (2,3=0,1) or (1=5,6) cannot be used.

The value specifications on a RECODE command are evaluated from left to right, and the value of a case is recoded only once in a single RECODE command. For example, if a case has the value 0 for the variable *SEX*, the command

```
RECODE SEX (0=1)(1=0)(3=99).
```

recodes *SEX* as 1 for that case. This value is not recoded back to 0 by the second value specification. Values that you do not mention on a RECODE command are left unchanged.

If you want to recode several variables in the same way, you can use a single RECODE command to do so, as in the command:

```
RECODE SEX RACE SURGERY (0=1)(1=0)(3=99).
```

In addition, you can use one RECODE command to recode different variables by separating the variable names and their specifications with a slash, as in the command:

```
RECODE SODIUM (10 THRU 15=1)(15 THRU 20=2)
   /COST (.28 THRU .39=1)(.40 THRU .50=2)(.51 THRU 1.20=3).
```

You can use the TO keyword to refer to several consecutive variables in the file. For example, the command

```
RECODE SCORE1 TO SCORE5 (5=1)(6=2)(7=3).
```

recodes *SCORE1*, *SCORE5*, and all the variables between them in the file.

Recoding Numeric Variables

Several keywords are available to facilitate recoding of numeric variables. Use the keywords THRU, LOWEST, and HIGHEST to recode a range of variables. Thus, the command

```
RECODE CALORIES (68 THRU 100=1)(101 THRU 170=2).
```

recodes all the values between 68 and 100 (inclusive) to 1 and all the values between 101 and 170 (inclusive) to 2 for the *CALORIES* variable. The LOWEST (or LO) keyword specifies the lowest value of a variable, while HIGHEST (or HI) specifies the highest value, as in:

```
RECODE CALORIES (LO THRU 100=1)(101 THRU HI=2).
```

When you use LOWEST or HIGHEST to specify a range, user-missing values in the range are recoded, but system-missing values are not.

You can use the ELSE keyword to recode all values not previously mentioned into a single category. Thus, the command

```
RECODE CALORIES (LO THRU 100=1)(ELSE=2).
```

is equivalent to the previous command. ELSE should be the last specification for a variable, since RECODE will ignore subsequent specifications for that variable. ELSE does recode system-missing values.

You can also use ELSE as a data-cleaning device. For example, if the variables *SCORE1* to *SCORE5* have only 5, 6, and 7 as legitimate values, you might use the command

```
RECODE SCORE1 TO SCORE5 (5=1)(6=2)(7=3)(ELSE=SYSMIS).
```

to recode the valid values to new values and the nonvalid values to system-missing.

Recoding Missing Values

The MISSING keyword is useful for recoding all missing values (user- or system-missing) to a single value. For example, if −99 is the missing value you have declared for the *AGE* variable, the command

```
RECODE AGE (MISSING=-1).
```

recodes -99 and any system-missing values for *AGE* to −1, while leaving the other *AGE* values unchanged.

You can use the SYSMIS keyword as either an input or output specification. The command

```
RECODE AGE (SYSMIS=-1).
```

recodes the system-missing value to −1.

The SYSMIS keyword as an output specification recodes specified values to system-missing, as in the commands

```
RECODE AGE (MISSING=SYSMIS).
```

and

```
RECODE AGE (-99=SYSMIS).
```

Both commands recode the *AGE* missing values to system-missing.

You *cannot* use the MISSING keyword as an output specification on RECODE to recode values as user-missing. Thus, SPSS/PC+ does not accept a recode specification like (17=MISSING) for the variable *AGE*. To classify value 17 for *AGE* as missing, use the MISSING VALUE command, as in:

```
MISSING VALUE AGE(17).
```

When you use the MISSING and SYSMIS keywords to recode missing values to a single new value, that value is not automatically considered a missing value. The MISSING VALUE command is required to define it as such, as in the following example:

```
RECODE AGE (MISSING=-1).
MISSING VALUE AGE(-1).
```

Recoding Continuous Value Ranges

If a variable has noninteger values, some values may escape recoding unless you make certain they are included in a value range. For example, the command

```
RECODE AGE (0 THRU 17=1)(18 THRU 65=2)(66 THRU 99=3).
```

does not recode values between 17 and 18 and between 65 and 66. Thus, values like 17.2 and 65.8 would be left unchanged. You can avoid this problem by using overlapping endpoint values in the specifications, as in the command:

```
RECODE AGE (66 THRU 99=3)(18 THRU 66=2)(0 THRU 18=1).
```

Note that the order of the recode specifications has been reversed, since a value is recoded only once into the first specification it meets. Thus, the value 66 is coded as a 3 and is not altered further, even though it serves as an endpoint on the following specification.

Recoding String Variables

You can use the RECODE command to recode string variables. Only short strings (those containing eight or fewer characters) can be recoded. The keywords LOWEST or LO, HIGHEST or HI, THRU, SYSMIS and MISSING do not apply to recoding string variables.

When recoding string variables, you must enclose all values in apostrophes (or quotation marks). For example, the command

```
RECODE LIGHT ('Y'='A')('N'='B').
```

recodes Y into A and N into B for the string variable *LIGHT*.

When recoding string variables, the values in a specification must be of equal length, which must be the same as the defined length for the variable. Use blanks to specify the exact length. For example, the command

```
RECODE GRADES ('ABC '='ABCD').
```

recodes the value *ABC* into *ABCD* for the four-character string variable *GRADES*.

Automatic Recoding

Sometimes it's useful to have consecutive numbers as codes for a variable. Some statistical procedures require numeric data, and it's often more efficient if the numeric codes are consecutive numbers (1, 2, 3 rather than 152, 2002, 9314.5). If you know what all the existing codes are, you can do this with RECODE, but it might take quite a bit of typing. The AUTORECODE command is designed to do this automatically:

```
AUTORECODE CITY /INTO CITYCODE.
```

This command looks at all the existing values of *CITY* and creates a new variable named *CITYCODE*. *CITYCODE* will have the value 1 for all cases that have the first value of *CITY* (in ascending order if *CITY* is numeric, or in alphabetical order if *CITY* is string). *CITYCODE* will have the value 2 for all cases with the second value of *CITY*, and so on.

You can automatically recode several variables by naming them before the keyword INTO, and providing the same number of new names after INTO. If you'd rather assign new codes in descending numeric order, or reverse alphabetical order, use the DESCENDING subcommand after the list of new variable names. And if you want to see a table of old and new values, specify PRINT, as in:

```
AUTORECODE PRODUCT, SALESREP /INTO PRODNUM, REP
    /DESCENDING /PRINT.
```

AUTORECODE assigns value labels to the new variables that it creates. If the existing variables have value labels, they are copied to the new variables. If not, the *values* of the existing variables are converted into value labels for the new variables.

By using AUTORECODE for a long string variable, you can obtain a numeric variable that's accepted by SPSS/PC+ transformation commands.

Computing New Variables

The COMPUTE command creates new variables through numeric transformations of already existing variables. COMPUTE names the variable you want to create (the **target variable**) followed by an **expression** defining the variable. For example, the command

```
COMPUTE TOTSCORE=MIDTERM+FINAL+HOMEWORK.
```

defines the new variable *TOTSCORE* as the sum of the variables *MIDTERM*, *FINAL*, and *HOMEWORK*.

The target variable can be a variable that already exists or a new variable. If the target variable already exists, its values are replaced with those produced by the specified transformation. If it is a new variable, it is added to the end of the dictionary in your active file.

The expression on the COMPUTE command can use existing numeric variables, constants, arithmetic operators (such as + and -), numeric functions such as SQRT (square root) and TRUNC (truncate), the missing-value function (VALUE), the cross-case function (LAG), random-number functions, and the date function (YRMODA). For example, the command

```
COMPUTE GRADESCR=.35*MIDTERM+.45*FINAL+.2*HOMEWORK.
```

creates a new variable, *GRADESCR*, that is the weighted average of the variables *MIDTERM*, *FINAL*, and *HOMEWORK*.

Transforming String Variables

You can use COMPUTE to create or modify short string variables. A variable can be set equal to an existing string variable or to a string constant, as in the command

```
COMPUTE STATE='IL'.
```

which creates variable *STATE* with the value IL for all cases. String values and constants must be enclosed in apostrophes or quotation marks.

When you create a new string variable by setting a variable name equal to a string constant, the new string variable is assigned a dictionary format equal to the width of the string constant. Thus, the previous command creates *STATE* as a two-character string variable. When you create a string variable by setting a variable name equal to an existing string variable, the new variable's dictionary format is the same as that of the original variable.

Leading or trailing blanks must be specified. Once you have created a string variable, all subsequent transformations on the variable must use the defined width.

Specifying Arithmetic Operations

The following arithmetic operators are available for transforming numeric variables with COMPUTE:

+   *Addition.*

-    *Subtraction.*

*   *Multiplication.*

/   *Division.*

**   *Exponentiation.*

Arithmetic operators must be explicitly specified. You cannot, for example, write (PROPTAX)(100) instead of PROPTAX*100.

You can include blanks in an arithmetic expression to improve readability, as in the command:

```
COMPUTE TAXTOTAL = PROPTAX + FICA + STATETAX + FEDTAX.
```

Since fairly complex expressions are possible, it is important to keep in mind the order in which operations are performed. Functions are evaluated first, then exponentiation, then multiplication and division, and, finally, addition and subtraction. Thus, if you specify

```
COMPUTE NEWRATE=SQRT(RATE1)/SQRT(RATE1)+SQRT(RATE3).
```

the square roots (SQRT) are calculated first, then the division is performed, and the addition is performed last.

You can control the order in which operations are performed by enclosing the operation you want executed first in parentheses. Thus, the command

```
COMPUTE NEWRATE=SQRT(RATE1)/(SQRT(RATE1)+SQRT(RATE3)).
```

produces different results from the previous command, since addition is performed before division.

Operations at the same level are evaluated from left to right. For example, the command

```
COMPUTE SCORE=( A/B * C ).
```

results in a different value than the command

```
COMPUTE SCORE=( A/ (B * C) ).
```

In the first command *A* is divided by *B*, and the resulting quantity multiplied by *C*; the second command first multiplies *B* times *C* and then divides *A* by the resulting quantity.

If you are uncertain about the order of execution, you should use parentheses to make the order you want explicit.

Specifying Numeric Functions

You can specify numeric functions such as square roots, logarithms, and trigonometric functions in a COMPUTE expression. The quantity to be transformed by such a function is called the *argument* and is specified in parentheses after the function keyword. For example, in the command

```
COMPUTE TOTLCOST=RND(COST * 6).
```

the function RND (round to the nearest integer) acts on the argument COST * 6 to create the new variable *TOTLCOST*.

The argument can be a variable name, a number, or an expression involving several variables. A numeric function can have only one argument.

The following numeric function keywords are available:

ABS   *Absolute value.* For example, ABS(-4.7) is 4.7; ABS(4.7) is 4.7.

RND   *Argument rounded to the nearest integer.* For example, RND(-4.7) is -5.

TRUNC   *Argument truncated to its integer part.* For example, TRUNC(-4.7) is -4.

MOD10   *Remainder resulting when the argument is divided by 10.* For example, MOD(198) is 8.

SQRT   *Square root.*

EXP   *Exponential. e is raised to the power of the argument.*

LG10   *Base 10 logarithm.*

LN   *Natural or Naperian logarithm.*

ARTAN   *Arctangent.*

SIN   *Sine.* The argument must be in radians.

COS   *Cosine.* The argument must be in radians.

For example, in the command

```
COMPUTE LOGINCOM=LN(INCOME+1).
```

LOGINCOM is the natural logarithm of the expression INCOME+1.

Other Functions

Also available on COMPUTE are two random-number functions (UNIFORM and NORMAL), the cross-case function (LAG), and the date function (YRMODA).

UNIFORM(arg)   *Uniform pseudo-random number.* The number is drawn from a distribution having values uniformly distributed between zero and the value of the argument.

NORMAL(arg)   *Normal pseudo-random number.* The number is drawn from a normal distribution with a mean of zero and a standard deviation equal to the argument.

LAG(arg)   *The value of the previous case for the variable named.*

YRMODA(arg list) *Convert the year, month, and day in the argument list into a day number.* The year, month, and day are specified in that order. The number computed is the number of days since October 15, 1582 (the first day of the Gregorian calendar).

All of these functions can be used with numeric variables. Only the LAG function is available for short string variables.

The YRMODA Function

The YRMODA function converts a given date into the number of days since October 14, 1582. For example the expression YRMODA(1582,10,15) returns a value of 1. YRMODA(1800,1,1) returns 79337, indicating that January 1, 1800 is 79,336 days after the beginning of the Gregorian calendar.

The time interval between two dates can be calculated by converting each of the dates to day numbers and then subtracting the earlier day from the later one. For example, to calculate an individual's age in years on July 4, 1982, specify

```
AGE=(YRMODA(1982,7,4) - YRMODA(BYR,BMO,BDAY)) /365.25
```

where *BYR* is the year, *BMO* the month, and *BDAY* the day of birth.

The YRMODA function has three arguments, which can be variables, constants, or expressions that result in integer values.

- The first argument can be any year from 1582 to 47516. If you specify a number between 00 and 99, SPSS/PC+ will interpret it to mean 1900 to 1999.

- The second argument is the month, coded from 1 to 13. Month 13 refers to the first month of the subsequent year. For example, YRMODA(84,13,1) specifies January 1, 1985.

- The third argument is a day from 0 through 31. Day 0 specifies the last day of the previous month, regardless of whether it was 28, 29, 30, or 31. Thus, (84,2,0) refers to the last day of January in 1984. This is equivalent to (84,1,31), since January has 31 days.

Using Functions in Complex Expressions

You can specify more than one function in an argument as well as combine functions with arithmetic operators. Such arguments will be evaluated in the order described in "Specifying Arithmetic Operations" on p. 82 or in the order specified by parentheses. For example, if the command

```
COMPUTE PCTTAXES=RND((TAXES/INCOME)*100).
```

is used, *TAXES* is first divided by *INCOME*, the result is multiplied by 100, and this result is rounded off to the nearest integer to get the new variable *PCTTAXES*.

Missing Values

If a case has missing values for any of the variables used in a COMPUTE expression, the case is assigned the system-missing value for the computed variable. For example, if the command

```
COMPUTE AGECUBE=AGE**3.
```

is used, the *AGECUBE* variable will not be computed for any case with a missing value for *AGE*.

A case is also assigned the system-missing value for a computed variable when the specified operation is not defined for that case. For example, if the command

```
COMPUTE PCTTAXES=(TAXES/INCOME)*100.
```

is used, a case with the value 0 for *INCOME* is assigned the system-missing value for *PCTTAXES* because division by 0 is not defined. If the result of an expression cannot be represented on the computer (even when valid values are used in the expression itself), the system-missing value is assigned to the new variable. The following errors will result in assignment of the system-missing value:

**	A negative number to a noninteger power.
/	A divisor of 0.
SQRT	A negative argument.
EXP	An argument that produces a result too large to be represented on the computer.
LG10	A negative or 0 argument.
NORMAL	A negative or 0 argument.
YRMODA	Arguments that do not form a valid date.

SPSS/PC+ tries to evaluate a function using all the information it has, assigning the system-missing value only when there is insufficient information to compute the new variable.

Including User-Missing Values

The VALUE function on COMPUTE allows you to include user-missing values in a transformation.

VALUE *Ignore the missing value status of user-missing values for the variable specified.* The argument must be a variable name.

Thus, the command

```
COMPUTE TOTAL=VALUE(SCORE1)+VALUE(SCORE2)+VALUE(SCORE3).
```

includes user-missing values in computing TOTAL.

Counting Values Across Variables

Use the COUNT command to create a variable that records, for each case, the number of times some value or list of values occurs in a list of variables. For example, the command

```
COUNT FEMINISM=ERA JOBEQUAL POLEQUAL (1).
```

creates the variable *FEMINISM*, which indicates the number of times in each case the value 1 occurs for *ERA*, *JOBEQUAL*, and *POLEQUAL*. Thus, the value of *FEMINISM* is 0, 1, 2, or 3. You can count across more than one variable list and more than one value, as in the command

```
COUNT FEMINISM=ERA JOBEQUAL POLEQUAL(1) VOTE CAMPAIGN(3,4).
```

which counts the number of times the value 1 occurs in the variables *ERA*, *JOBEQUAL*, and *POLEQUAL*, and the values 3 or 4 in *VOTE* and *CAMPAIGN*.

The criterion variable list can include both string and numeric variables, provided they have separate value specifications. String values must be enclosed in apostrophes.

You can specify consecutive variables with the TO keyword and ranges of numeric values with the LOWEST, HIGHEST, and THRU keywords. (You cannot specify any keywords with string variables). More than one variable can be created with a single COUNT command by separating the specifications with a slash, as in the command

```
COUNT PSYCHTIC=PTEST1 TO PTEST10(51 THRU HIGHEST)
   /SCHIZPHR=STEST1 TO STEST10(LOWEST THRU 20).
```

The COUNT command counts user-missing values. For example, the command

```
COUNT RACISM=SCALE1 TO SCALE12(LOWEST THRU 5).
```

counts the value of −99 even though it has been defined by as missing.

To count missing values, specify the SYSMIS or MISSING keyword in parentheses after the numeric variable list. For example, the command

```
COUNT PHYSMISS=AGE WEIGHT HEIGHT(SYSMIS).
```

creates the new variable PHYSMISS, which records the number of system-missing values each case has for these variables. The MISSING keyword stands for both user- and system-missing values.

Specifying Conditional Transformations

The IF command allows you to transformation data contingent on logical conditions. IF consists of a **logical expression** in parentheses followed by a **target variable** and an **assignment expression**. For example, the command

```
IF (AGE GE 18) VOTER=1.
```

uses the logical expression (AGE GE 18) and the assignment expression VOTER=1 to assign the value 1 to the target variable *VOTER* for all cases with *AGE* values greater than or equal to 18. You construct the assignment expression in the same way as the expression in a COMPUTE statement (see "Computing New Variables" on p. 81). Thus, you can specify conditional operations like:

```
IF (INCOME GE 25000) TAXES=INCOME * .33.
```

SPSS/PC+ evaluates logical expressions as true or false and executes the specified assignment only when the expression is true; otherwise, the system-missing value is assigned.

You can use string variables in IF transformations, as in the command:

```
IF (AGE GE 18) AGEGRP='ADULTS'
```

The same conditions that apply to using string variables with COMPUTE (see "Transforming String Variables" on p. 82) also apply when using them with IF.

Specifying Conditions for Transformations

The logical expression on the IF command can be a complex statement involving variables, constants, functions, nested parentheses, and so on. You must include either a relational operator (such as EQ or GE) or a missing-value function (MISSING or SYSMIS) in the logical expression. Other operations and functions are optional.

Comparing Values in a Logical Expression

A **relation** is a logical expression that compares two values using a **relational operator**. For example, the command

```
IF (COST EQ .43) NEWCOST=2.
```

compares the equivalence of the variable *COST* and the value .43. The following relational operators are available:

EQ   *Equal to.* The logical expression is true if the expression on the left is equal to the expression on the right.

NE   *Not equal to.* The logical expression is true if the left and right expressions are not equal.

LT   *Less than.* The logical expression is true if the expression on the left is less than the expression on the right.

LE   *Less than or equal to.* The logical expression is true if the expression on the left is less than or equal to the expression on the right.

GT   *Greater than.* The logical expression is true if the expression on the left is greater than the expression on the right.

GE   *Greater than or equal to.* The logical expression is true if the expression on the left is greater than or equal to the expression on the right.

The expressions in a relation can be variables, constants, arithmetic expressions, or functions, as in the commands:

```
IF (SCORE1+SCORE2 GT TESTA) NEWSCORE=1.
```

and

```
IF (LOGINCOM GE 5) CLASS=1.
```

Use blanks to separate the relational operator from the expressions. You can use parentheses and extra blanks to make a command more readable, as in the command:

```
IF ( (SCORE1 + SCORE2)  GE 90) GRADE=4.
```

Parentheses are required around the logical expression.

Joining Relations

You can join two or more relations by using the logical operators AND and OR. For example, the command

```
IF (HOMEWORK GE 85 AND MIDTERM GE 90 AND FINAL GE 90) GRADE=4.
```

assigns *GRADE* the value 4 only when *HOMEWORK* is at least 85 and *MIDTERM* and *FINAL* are at least 90. When AND is used, the logical expression is true only when *all* relations joined by AND are true. When OR is used, the logical expression is true when *any* of the relations joined by OR are true. Thus, the command

```
IF ((A EQ 4 AND B EQ 3) OR (A EQ 3 AND B EQ 4)) C=1
```

assigns the value 1 to *C* for any case that has a value of 4 for *A* and 3 for *B* or to any case with the value 3 for *A* and 4 for *B*.

You must specify operators and expressions explicitly; the specification (X EQ 1 OR 2) cannot be used in place of (X EQ 1 OR X EQ 2).

Reversing the Logic of an Expression

The NOT logical operator reverses the true or false status of the expression that immediately follows it. For example, the command

```
IF (NOT RACE EQ 1 AND SEX EQ 0) GROUP=1.
```

assigns value 1 to *GROUP* for cases where *RACE* does not equal 1 and *SEX is* equal to 0. This is not equivalent to the command

```
IF (NOT(RACE EQ 1 AND SEX EQ 0)) GROUP=1.
```

which assigns value 1 to *GROUP* for cases where *RACE* does not equal 1 and *SEX* does *not* equal 0.

The Order of Evaluation

IF evaluates arithmetic operators and functions in a logical expression in the same order as does the COMPUTE command (see "Specifying Arithmetic Operations" on p. 82). Functions and arithmetic operators are evaluated first, then relational operators, then NOT, then AND, and then OR. In the expression (NOT SCORESUM/5 EQ 10), the value of *SCORESUM* is divided by 5, the result compared to 10, and the true-false status of this comparison is reversed by NOT.

If you specify both AND and OR, AND is executed before OR. For example, in the command

```
IF (HOMEWORK GE 90 AND MIDTERM GE 90 OR FINAL GE 95) GRADE=4.
```

the logical expression is true for a case with *HOMEWORK* and *MIDTERM* values of at least 90, or for a *FINAL* value of at least 95. You can use parentheses to clarify or change the order of evaluation. Thus, the command

```
IF ((HOMEWORK GE 90 AND MIDTERM GE 90) OR FINAL GE 95) GRADE=4.
```

is equivalent to the previous command. The command

```
IF (HOMEWORK GE 90 AND (MIDTERM GE 90 OR FINAL GE 95)) GRADE=4.
```

is not equivalent. In this statement, a case must have a score of at least 90 for *HOME-WORK* as well as a value of at least 90 for *MIDTERM or* 95 for *FINAL* to be assigned the grade 4.

Missing Values

If the truth of a logical expression cannot be determined because of missing values, the command is not executed. In a relation with only one relational operator, the logical expression is indeterminate if the expression on either side of the operator has a missing value. For example, if you specify

```
IF (FINAL GT MIDTERM) TEST=1.
```

and either *FINAL* or *MIDTERM* is missing for a case, SPSS/PC+ cannot tell whether one variable is greater than the other. In such a case, SPSS/PC+ leaves the target variable unchanged if it is an existing variable. If it is a new variable, it retains its initialized sytem-missing value.

When several relations are joined by AND, SPSS/PC+ automatically returns the missing value if *any* of the relations in the expression have missing values. When several relations are joined by OR, the expression is evaluated as true if any of the relations are evaluated as true, even if some of the relations in the expression have missing values.

Missing-Value Logical Functions

You can use the functions MISSING and SYSMIS to specify missing values as criteria for logical outcomes.

MISSING   *Return 1 if the value is missing and 0 otherwise.*

SYSMIS   *Return 1 if the value is system-missing and 0 otherwise.*

For example, the command

```
IF (SYSMIS(SCORE1)) GRADE=0.
```

determines if *SCORE1* is system-missing. If it is, *GRADE* is assigned the value 0.
   The command

```
IF (NOT(MISSING(GRADE))) GRAD=1.
```

evaluates whether the value of *GRADE* is not equal to the user- or system-missing values. Each case that has a valid value for *GRADE* is assigned the value 1 for *GRAD*.

   You can also use the VALUE function on an IF command to ignore the user-missing status of values. For example, the commands

```
RECODE AGE (5 THRU 20 = 1) (20 THRU 65 = 2) (65 THRU HI = 3).
MISSING VALUE AGE (3).
IF (VALUE(AGE) GT 0 ) GRPAGE=1.
```

collapse the values of *AGE* into three values and designate the value 3 as user-missing. The IF command specifies that any case with a value greater than 0 for *AGE* be given the value 1 for *GRPAGE*. Because the VALUE keyword on the IF command tells SPSS/PC+ to ignore user-missing values, cases with value 3 for *AGE* are given the value 1 for *GRPAGE*.

   The VALUE function should always be used in conjunction with a relational operator in a logical expression on the IF command.

Executing Data Transformations

When the data are read, transformation commands are evaluated and executed in the order in which they appear. Thus, the order in which you specify your commands can be important. For the commands

```
RECODE POLACT1 POLACT2 (1 THRU 2=1)(3 THRU 4=2)(ELSE=SYSMIS).
COUNT POLACT=POLACT1,POLACT2(1).
```

the order of execution is critical, since the COUNT command assumes that the RECODE command has already been executed.

   Transformations are not carried out until the data are read. You must include a procedure command (or another command that causes SPSS/PC+ to read the data) for the transformations to be executed. Additionally, unless a system file is saved or the data are written out in some way, the transformations are in effect only for a single SPSS/PC+ session.

Using Data Definitions with Transformations

You can use the data-definition commands VARIABLE LABELS, VALUE LABELS, MISS-ING VALUE, and so on, to describe any variable created or altered by transformations, as in the commands:

```
RECODE SEX RACE SURGERY (1=0)(0=1)(ELSE=SYSMIS).
COMPUTE LOGAGE=LN(AGE).
VARIABLE LABELS LOGAGE 'NATURAL LOG OF AGE'.
VALUE LABELS SEX 1 'FEMALE' 0 'MALE'
             RACE 1 'BLACK' 0 'WHITE'
             SURGERY 1 'SURGERY PERFORMED' 0'NO SURGERY'.
```

The data definition commands must follow the transformation commands that create the variable.

9 Selecting, Weighting, and Ordering Cases

Suppose you are interested in plotting the relationship between cost and alcohol content in the beer data, but you want the plot to include only domestic beers. Or you want to examine the distribution of calories only for the beers that have been assigned ratings of "very good." These are two examples of situations where you want to select a subset of cases from a file based on some particular criterion. The SELECT IF command in SPSS/PC+ selects a subset of cases for an entire SPSS/PC+ session, and the PROCESS IF command selects a subset of cases only for the next procedure.

When there are many cases in a file, you may want to select a random sample of them for processing. This decreases the time needed for analysis and may provide you with useful preliminary results. For example, if you had information on 10,000 cases, you might want to obtain plots or histograms for a random subset of them. These plots should reflect the overall trends present in the data. The SAMPLE command selects a random sample of cases from a file.

To restrict analysis to the first *n* cases in a data set, use the N command. This command is particularly useful if you want to get an idea of the output produced by a procedure without having to wait for all cases to be processed. For example, if you are preparing a report and want to make sure that you have included all the necessary information in an appropriate format, running it on a small number of "test" cases is an efficient strategy.

The WEIGHT command allows you to assign different "weights" to cases for an analysis. For example, if your sample does not reflect the true proportion of cases with particular attributes in the population, you can assign appropriate weights to adjust for this when estimating certain statistics. However, the sample sizes and significance levels associated with such weighted analyses cannot be interpreted in the usual fashion.

On occasion, you may wish to sort the observations in a file based on values of certain variables. For example, you might want to sort the beers in ascending order on the basis of alcohol content. Use the SORT CASES command to do this. You can then list the cases in this order or prepare reports using the sorted file (see Chapter 24).

Selecting Cases Permanently

The SELECT IF command selects cases for analysis if they meet criteria you specify. You specify these criteria in a logical expression that SPSS/PC+ can evaluate as true or false. For example, the command

```
SELECT IF (SEX EQ 1).
```

selects cases with the value 1 for *SEX*.

You can include the SELECT IF command anywhere in an SPSS/PC+ session, except between the BEGIN DATA and END DATA commands. Once you use SELECT IF, the selection specified is in effect for all subsequent procedures. If you use another SELECT IF command, it selects a subset of cases from the first selected subset rather than from the original data set.

Multiple SELECT IF commands should be used with caution, as you can end up selecting no cases. For example, if the commands

```
SELECT IF (SEX EQ 1).
FREQUENCIES VARIABLES=TEMP FIRSTEKG SECNDEKG.
SELECT IF (SEX EQ 2).
FREQUENCIES VARIABLES=TEMP FIRSTEKG SECNDEKG.
```

are used, there will be no cases for the second FREQUENCIES procedure to analyze, since *SEX* cannot equal both 1 and 2. If you want to select cases temporarily for one procedure, use the PROCESS IF command (see "Selecting Cases Temporarily" on p. 95).

Specifying the Logical Expression

The logical expression on SELECT IF is specified in the same way as the logical expression on the IF command (see Chapter 8). The logical expression must be enclosed in parentheses and include either a relational operator or a missing-value function. You can construct complex selection criteria by using the logical operators AND, OR, and NOT in the logical expression. If the logical expression cannot be determined for a case because of missing values, that case is not selected. In some situations, a logical expression can be evaluated even if data are missing (see "Missing Values in Logical Expressions" on p. 443).

To select cases with missing values, use the SYSMIS and MISSING functions. For example, the command

```
SELECT IF (MISSING(AGE)).
```

selects all cases with missing values for *AGE*.

You can use the VALUE function to include cases with user-missing values in a selection. A SELECT IF logical expression containing the VALUE function should also contain a relational operator. For example, the command

```
SELECT IF (VALUE(SCORE) LE 40).
```

selects all cases with *SCORE* values less than or equal to 40, including values that have been defined as missing. (See Chapter 8 for more information on missing values in logical expressions.)

Selecting Cases Temporarily

The PROCESS IF command temporarily selects cases for analysis by the next procedure. Like SELECT IF, its specification consists of a logical expression, and it can use any of the relational operators (EQ, NE, GT, GE, LT, or LE). However, the logical operators AND, OR, and NOT cannot be used with PROCESS IF. Thus, a specification like (SALES GE 10000 AND DIVISION EQ 3) is not valid on this command.

If you specify several PROCESS IF commands immediately before a procedure command, only the last one takes effect. For example, if the commands

```
PROCESS IF (SEX EQ 1).
PROCESS IF (SEX EQ 2).
FREQUENCIES VARIABLES=TEMP FIRSTEKG SECNDEKG.
```

are used, the second PROCESS IF command overrides the first, and the FREQUENCIES procedure will analyze all cases for which *SEX* equals 2. PROCESS IF does not affect any intervening transformations. To avoid problems, do not insert transformation commands between PROCESS IF and the command you want it to affect.

Drawing a Temporary Sample

The SAMPLE command draws a random subsample of cases for analysis in the next procedure. You can include SAMPLE anywhere in an SPSS/PC+ session except between the BEGIN DATA and END DATA commands.

To sample a proportion of cases, specify the proportion on the SAMPLE command, as in:

```
SAMPLE .25.
```

This command samples approximately one-fourth of the cases.

If you know the total number of cases, you can specify the number of cases to be sampled, as in:

```
SAMPLE 50 FROM 200.
```

This command draws a random sample of 50 cases only if there are exactly 200 total cases. If there are fewer than 200 cases, proportionately fewer cases are sampled. If there are more than 200 cases, the subsample is taken only from the first 200 cases.

If SAMPLE follows a SELECT IF command, the sample is drawn from the selected subset of cases. Conversely, if SAMPLE precedes SELECT IF, the specified subset of cases is selected from the sample. If you specify more than one SAMPLE command prior to a procedure, only the last SAMPLE command is executed.

Selecting the First *n* Cases

The N command selects the first *n* cases in a file. For example, if your file has 1000 cases, but you want to analyze only the first 100 cases, specify

```
N 100.
```

You can specify the N command at any point in an SPSS/PC+ session. Once specified, it limits the number of cases analyzed by all subsequent procedures. More than one N command can be used in a single session, but once you execute a procedure using a given *n*, you cannot increase the number of cases for subsequent procedures; you can only decrease the number of cases in the active file.

The commands PROCESS IF, SELECT IF, and SAMPLE are executed before N if the commands occur together (even if N is specified first). For example, if you specify

```
N 100.
SAMPLE .5.
```

approximately half of the total cases are sampled, and then the first 100 of these are selected for analysis.

Weighting Cases

You can adjust case weights by using the WEIGHT command. For example, if you have a sample in which males have been oversampled (that is, there is a much higher proportion of males in the sample than in the population), you may want to give the data for males less weight in your computations. The WEIGHT command is also useful for entering data from a crosstabulation (see Chapter 14).

The only specification on WEIGHT is keyword BY and the name of the variable to be used for weighting, as in:

```
WEIGHT BY WGHTVAR.
```

Only one weighting variable can be specified on the command, and it must be numeric. The values of the weighting variable do not need to be integers; missing or negative values are treated as zeros. When weighting is used, files that are saved retain the weighting in the system variable *$WEIGHT*.

The weighting variable can be an existing variable or a variable created through transformation commands. For example, suppose men have been oversampled by a factor of 2. To compensate for this, you can weight male cases by one half, as in:

```
COMPUTE WT=1.
IF (SEX EQ 2) WT=.5.
WEIGHT BY WT.
```

If you create a weighting variable with an IF command, it is important to first initialize its weight with a COMPUTE command. Otherwise, cases not covered by the IF command will have missing values for the weighting variable. A case weighted by 1 is unaffected when WEIGHT is executed, but a case weighted by 0 or by a missing value is eliminated.

A WEIGHT command stays in effect for the entire session unless it is followed by another WEIGHT command or turned off with the command WEIGHT OFF. Weighting is *not* cumulative. A new WEIGHT command reweights the sample rather than altering previously weighted values. For example, if the commands

```
WEIGHT BY WT1.
DESCRIPTIVES ALL.
WEIGHT BY WT2.
DESCRIPTIVES ALL.
```

are used, the first DESCRIPTIVES procedure computes summary statistics based on cases weighted by *WT1*, and the second DESCRIPTIVES procedure computes summary statistics based on cases weighted by *WT2*.

When weighting is in effect, significance tests are usually based on the weighted sample size. If the weighted number of cases exceeds the sample size, the *p* values given for these tests will be too small. If the weighted number of cases is smaller than the sample size, the *p* values calculated will be too large. You can avoid these problems by using weight factors that add up to the sample size.

Sorting Data

The SORT CASES command reorders your data according to the values of a specified variable or variables. Specify SORT CASES with keyword BY followed by the names of the variables to be used for sorting. The variables specified can be numeric or string. String variables are sorted in alphabetical order.

Cases can be sorted in ascending or descending order. Ascending order is the default. To sort cases in descending order (numeric values for the sorting variable are ordered from highest to lowest and string values are in reverse the alphabetical order), specify D in parentheses after the variable name, as in:

```
SORT CASES BY SALES(D).
```

You can specify A in parentheses after a variable name to explicitly request ascending order. The D or A specification applies to all preceding variables in the variable list that do not have a sort specification. For example, the command

```
SORT CASES BY PRODUCT DEPT SALES(D).
```

sorts *PRODUCT*, *DEPT*, and *SALES* in descending order.

When several sorting variables are listed, cases are first sorted according to the first variable named. Cases with the same value for the first sorting variable are then sorted according to the second sorting variable, and so on. For example, the command

```
SORT CASES BY PRODUCT(D) DEPT(A) SALES(D).
```

produces the following sorted values for *PRODUCT, DEPT*, and *SALES*:

```
4 1  $9,750
4 2 $18,083
4 2 $15,608
4 2 $15,132
4 2 $12,438
4 2 $11,240
4 2 $10,050
3 1 $17,051
3 2 $39,000
3 2 $19,682
3 2 $13,650
3 2  $9,777
3 2  $9,507
3 2  $8,872
3 2  $8,239
1 1 $35,750
1 1 $17,111
1 1 $13,910
```

10 Restructuring Files: JOIN, AGGREGATE, and FLIP

SPSS/PC+ provides two commands for restructuring files. JOIN combines the contents of system files and creates a new active file. AGGREGATE creates a system file containing summary measures for groups of cases. In this chapter, we will use school enrollment records to illustrate the use of JOIN and AGGREGATE to update and summarize the information in your SPSS/PC+ files.

Overview

Consider a simple class roster compiled at preregistration time. As more students join the class during the first week, their records need to be added to the existing roster. A simple addition of cases, as illustrated in Figure 10.1, is all that's needed. In SPSS/PC+, this addition of cases from one file to another file is accomplished using the JOIN command with keyword ADD. "Adding Files" on p. 102 discusses adding files together.

Figure 10.1 Adding cases to a file

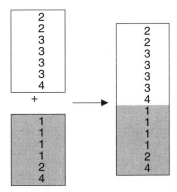

Suppose the instructor wants the new cases added according to a particular order of some variable, such as class year. He could either perform a simple addition and then sort the file or specify that the addition of cases should use the values of a key variable for interleaving, as shown in Figure 10.2. Interleaving cases from one file with cases in another file is accomplished using JOIN ADD with the BY subcommand and a key variable (see "Interleaving Cases" on p. 103).

Figure 10.2   Interleaving cases with a key

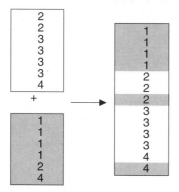

Once the instructor has a class roster, he might decide to add data related to the course to each student record. If the instructor has files that contain exactly the same cases sorted in the same order, he can perform a simple parallel match of files, as shown in Figure 10.3. Procedure JOIN with keyword MATCH combines the contents of the first record from each input file, then the contents of the second record from each input file, and so on "Parallel Files—Same Cases, Different Variables" on p. 110 describes how JOIN MATCH combines variables from parallel files.

Figure 10.3   Matching parallel data files

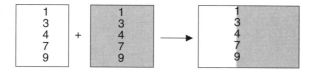

As the quarter progresses, the instructor can use the class roster as a grade book, appending test scores, grades on term papers, and so forth. By using a key variable such as student identification number, he can ensure that the correct test score is matched to the student who took the test. Figure 10.4 shows matching files with a key variable.

By using the key variable, the instructor doesn't have to worry about having test scores for each student in the roster file. For example, students who have dropped the course won't have a grade and are absent from the grade file. These students are assigned a missing value in the resulting file. In addition, each unique value of the key variable is retained in the resulting file. For example, if a student was not on the class roster but took the exam, the grade is retained in the resulting file. Matching nonparallel files with key variables is accomplished using JOIN MATCH with keyword BY and a key variable (see "Nonparallel Files—Different Cases, Different Variables" on p. 111).

Figure 10.4   Matching nonparallel data files with a key

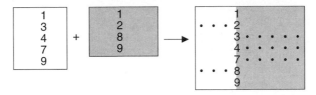

A file containing summary data can be combined with files containing case data by using JOIN MATCH with a key and designating one file a table file. For example, the instructor might build one file combining the grade files for each class he taught that year. He might also build a table file containing one case for each class, with summary information such as the number of exams, the final exam average, high and low grades, and so forth. By using the class variable as a key and designating the summary file as a table file, he can append summary variables to individual student records. Figure 10.5 shows cases from one file combined with variables from a table. A table match adds variables from the table file to cases only when there is a match on a key variable. Table matches are accomplished using JOIN MATCH with the BY and TABLE subcommands and is discussed under "Table and Case Files—Combining Group and Case Data" on p. 114.

Figure 10.5   Matching table data to a file with a key

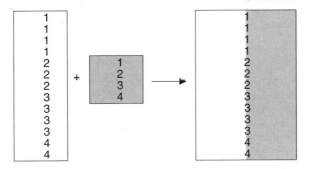

To create the table file of summary information described above, the instructor could use the SPSS/PC+ AGGREGATE procedure. AGGREGATE creates a file containing variables representing summaries (means, standard deviations, minimum value, etc.) of different groups, with one case for each group. Figure 10.6 illustrates how AGGREGATE creates cases based on common values of a grouping variable. See "Obtaining Group Data: Procedure AGGREGATE" on p. 118 for more information.

Figure 10.6   Aggregating cases

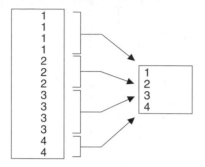

The ADD and MATCH keywords on procedure JOIN are mutually exclusive and must be specified before any other keywords or subcommands. JOIN ADD combines cases from two to five input files, and JOIN MATCH combines variables from two to five input files. The input files for JOIN are SPSS/PC+ system files or the active file. The resulting file is a new active file. Procedure AGGREGATE groups cases and creates variables from an active file and either replaces the active file or writes an SPSS/PC+ system file.

When you use JOIN to interleave cases or to match variables based on values of key variables, each input file must be sorted in ascending order of each key variable (see "Sorting Key Variables" on p. 113). AGGREGATE does not require the active file to be sorted.

Adding Files

Use JOIN with keyword ADD to combine cases from two to five system files. The input files can be SPSS/PC+ system files or the active file.

Adding Cases to the Active File

Students who register on the first day of class can be added to a previously defined system file containing students who have preregistered for a course. The *SOC100AL.DAT* file (Figure 10.7) contains data on students who registered on the first day. This file contains the same variables as the preregistration system file but different students. The commands

```
DATA LIST FILE='SOC100AL.DAT'/COURSE 1-3 SECTION 5
   (A) MEETTIME 7-10    DAYS 12-14(A) STUNUM 16-20
   LASTNAME 22-33(A) FSTNAME 35-44(A) CLASSYR 46.
VARIABLE LABELS CLASSYR 'Class'.
VALUE LABELS CLASSYR 1 'Freshman' 2 'Sophomore'
                     3 'Junior' 4 'Senior'.
TITLE 'Combined Soc100 Section A Roster'.
```

define an active file containing the data in *SOC100AL.DAT*.

Figure 10.7   Data to add to preregistration file

```
100 a 0900 mwf 10009 Atmore        Samuel     1
100 a 0900 mwf 24365 McDowell      Denise     1
100 a 0900 mwf 27111 Hutchinson    Christine  1
100 a 0900 mwf 55287 Swift         Jennifer   1
100 a 0900 mwf 62432 Jamieson      Bailey     1
100 a 0900 mwf 89765 Paulsen       Patrick    2
100 a 0900 mwf 54338 Darfler       Marleena   4
```

To combine these cases with a file containing students who preregistered for the course, issue the command:

```
JOIN ADD FILE=*
  /FILE='S100A.SYS'.
LIST.
SAVE OUTFILE='SOC100A.SYS'.
```

The JOIN ADD command adds cases from the system file *S100A.SYS* to the active file (the asterisk refers to the active file). The resulting active file contains the combined set of cases. The LIST command produces a listing of the contents of this file, shown in Figure 10.8. Note that the order of cases in the resulting active file is determined by the order in which files are named on the FILE subcommands. The SAVE command creates an SPSS/PC+ system file containing all the cases.

Figure 10.8   Listing of combined files

```
COURSE SECTION MEETTIME DAYS STUNUM LASTNAME      FSTNAME     CLASSYR

   100 a            900  mwf  10009 Atmore        Samuel         1
   100 a            900  mwf  24365 McDowell      Denise         1
   100 a            900  mwf  27111 Hutchinson    Christine      1
   100 a            900  mwf  55287 Swift         Jennifer       1
   100 a            900  mwf  62432 Jamieson      Bailey         1
   100 a            900  mwf  89765 Paulsen       Patrick        2
   100 a            900  mwf  54338 Darfler       Marleena       4
   100 a            900  mwf  43289 Sweeney       John           2
   100 a            900  mwf  23763 Baker         Catherine      2
   100 a            900  mwf  22304 Jones         Barbara        3
   100 a            900  mwf  27001 Jacobsen      Richard        3
   100 a            900  mwf  35760 Roberts       Elizabeth      3
   100 a            900  mwf  64352 Atkinson      Thomas         3
   100 a            900  mwf  79885 Klein         Janet          4

Number of cases read =     14   Number of cases listed =     14
```

Interleaving Cases

You can use JOIN ADD to interleave cases in ascending order of one or more key variables by naming the variables on the BY subcommand. You can specify up to ten variables as keys. Cases must be sorted in ascending order of the key variable before they can be interleaved. Thus, you should use SORT prior to saving system files or sort the current active file (see "Sorting Key Variables" on p. 113).

For example, you can create a combined file that contains students from the two files described on p. 102 grouped according to class year. Both the system file *S100A.SYS* and the raw data set *SOC100AL.DAT* must be sorted in ascending order of variable *CLASSYR*. To interleave cases on the basis of *CLASSYR*, use the following command:

```
JOIN ADD FILE=*
  /FILE='S100A.SYS'
  /BY=CLASSYR.

LIST.
SAVE OUTFILE='SOC100AS.SYS'.
```

Figure 10.9 shows the results of the LIST command, with all the cases interleaved in order of *CLASSYR*.

Figure 10.9   Interleaved cases on the active file

```
COURSE SECTION MEETTIME DAYS STUNUM LASTNAME      FSTNAME     CLASSYR

  100 a            900  mwf   10009 Atmore        Samuel           1
  100 a            900  mwf   24365 McDowell      Denise           1
  100 a            900  mwf   27111 Hutchinson    Christine        1
  100 a            900  mwf   55287 Swift         Jennifer         1
  100 a            900  mwf   62432 Jamieson      Bailey           1
  100 a            900  mwf   89765 Paulsen       Patrick          2
  100 a            900  mwf   43289 Sweeney       John             2
  100 a            900  mwf   23763 Baker         Catherine        2
  100 a            900  mwf   22304 Jones         Barbara          3
  100 a            900  mwf   27001 Jacobsen      Richard          3
  100 a            900  mwf   35760 Roberts       Elizabeth        3
  100 a            900  mwf   64352 Atkinson      Thomas           3
  100 a            900  mwf   54338 Darfler       Marleena         4
  100 a            900  mwf   79885 Klein         Janet            4

Number of cases read =      14    Number of cases listed =      14
```

When you combine cases from two or more files and name a BY variable for interleaving, you can expect a warning message whenever there are duplicate values of the key variable across files. The example above produces such a message because the active file and the system file, *S100A.SYS*, both contain cases with values 2 and 4 for the variable *CLASSYR*. If your input files do not contain duplicate values, no warning message is issued.

Managing Variables

Sometimes you will want to include only a subset of variables from your input files in the file you create with JOIN. Or you may have a situation where the same variable has different names on different files that you want to combine.

With the DROP and KEEP subcommands on JOIN, you can include a subset of variables in the resulting file. With the RENAME subcommand, you can supply new names for any variables in the resulting file. You can use the MAP subcommand to produce a table of the variables in all input files and in the resulting file. These subcommands are discussed on pp. 105–109.

Viewing the Active File Dictionary

The MAP subcommand produces a list of the variables in the active file, the names of each input file, and the variables from each file.

Consider the following JOIN command, which combines cases from five previously saved system files:

```
JOIN ADD FILE='SOC100AS.SYS'
   /FILE='SOC100B.SYS'
   /FILE='SOC222A.SYS'
   /FILE='SOC310A.SYS'
   /FILE='HDS444A.SYS'
   /MAP.

LIST.
SAVE OUTFILE='ALLSTU85.SYS'.
```

This example creates an active file that contains all students registered in every class and all variables that exist in any of the input files. Figure 10.10 shows the list produced by the MAP subcommand. Variables *DEPT*, *CLASSTYP*, and *PASSFAIL* from the input file *HDS444A.SYS* are present in the resulting active file. If a case comes from an input file that does not contain a particular variable, SPSS/PC+ assigns the system-missing value (numeric variables) or a blank (string variables).

Figure 10.10 Map of concatenated system files

```
RESULT        SOC100AS.SYS   SOC100B.SYS   SOC222A.SYS   SOC310A.SYS   HDS444A.SYS
------------  -------------  ------------  ------------  ------------  ------------
COURSE        COURSE         COURSE        COURSE        COURSE        COURSE
SECTION       SECTION        SECTION       SECTION       SECTION       SECTION
MEETTIME      MEETTIME       MEETTIME      MEETTIME      MEETTIME      MEETTIME
DAYS          DAYS           DAYS          DAYS          DAYS          DAYS
STUNUM        STUNUM         STUNUM        STUNUM        STUNUM        STUNUM
LASTNAME      LASTNAME       LASTNAME      LASTNAME      LASTNAME      LASTNAME
FSTNAME       FSTNAME        FSTNAME       FSTNAME       FSTNAME       FSTNAME
CLASSYR       CLASSYR        CLASSYR       CLASSYR       CLASSYR       CLASSYR
DEPT                                                                   DEPT
CLASSTYP                                                               CLASSTYP
PASSFAIL                                                               PASSFAIL
```

Figure 10.11 shows a listing of the cases in the file. Cases from *SOC100AS.SYS* come first, followed by cases from the next named file, and so on. Each case contains a value for variables *DEPT*, *CLASSTYP*, and *PASSFAIL*, even though these variables occur in only one of the five original files.

Figure 10.11 Listing of concatenated system files

COURSE	SECTION	MEETTIME	DAYS	STUNUM	LASTNAME	FSTNAME	CLASSYR	DEPT	CLASSTYP	PASSFAIL
100	a	900	mwf	10009	Atmore	Samuel	1			.
100	a	900	mwf	24365	McDowell	Denise	1			.
100	a	900	mwf	27111	Hutchinson	Christine	1			.
100	a	900	mwf	55287	Swift	Jennifer	1			.
100	a	900	mwf	62432	Jamieson	Bailey	1			.
100	a	900	mwf	89765	Paulsen	Patrick	2			.
100	a	900	mwf	43289	Sweeney	John	2			.
100	a	900	mwf	23763	Baker	Catherine	2			.
100	a	900	mwf	22304	Jones	Barbara	3			.
100	a	900	mwf	27001	Jacobsen	Richard	3			.
100	a	900	mwf	35760	Roberts	Elizabeth	3			.
100	a	900	mwf	64352	Atkinson	Thomas	3			.
100	a	900	mwf	54338	Darfler	Marleena	4			.
100	a	900	mwf	79885	Klein	Janet	4			.
100	b	1100	mwf	10229	Smithe	Peter	1			.
100	b	1100	mwf	34365	Farroro	Dennis	1			.
100	b	1100	mwf	25111	Huber	Joan	1			.
100	b	1100	mwf	55587	Westerman	David	1			.
100	b	1100	mwf	62442	Mount	Sigrid	1			.
100	b	1100	mwf	89763	Harris	Emily	4			.
100	b	1100	mwf	70395	Jones	James	2			.
100	b	1100	mwf	53763	Halley	Beth	2			.
100	b	1100	mwf	82224	Manova	Svetlana	2			.
100	b	1100	mwf	97291	Sullivan	Linda	3			.
100	b	1100	mwf	50762	Dexter	Richard	3			.
100	b	1100	mwf	62752	Colby	Jeffrey	3			.
100	b	1100	mwf	54358	Fiorello	Francis	3			.
222	a	1200	tth	12239	Smith	Patricia	1			.
222	a	1200	tth	35467	Freiberg	Gerhardt	1			.
222	a	1200	tth	65141	Mills	Charles	2			.
222	a	1200	tth	53287	West	James	2			.
222	a	1200	tth	39742	Maus	Mickey	2			.
222	a	1200	tth	9763	Herrmann	Monty	2			.
222	a	1200	tth	48364	Daveport	Joyce	2			.
222	a	1200	tth	81043	Hill	Robert	2			.
222	a	1200	tth	42524	Mason	Perry	2			.
222	a	1200	tth	95591	Evans	Linda	3			.
222	a	1200	tth	61932	Bates	Oliver	3			.
222	a	1200	tth	93132	Hughes	Olivia	3			.
222	a	1200	tth	44359	Bates	Lucy	4			.
310	a	1400	mwf	42305	O'Kane	Stanley	1			.
310	a	1400	mwf	60611	Hallet	Robin	2			.
310	a	1400	mwf	14420	Robinson	Thomas	2			.
310	a	1400	mwf	4901	Nace	Laura	3			.
310	a	1400	mwf	99999	Liebmann	Geoffrey	3			.
310	a	1400	mwf	43995	Countryman	Katharyn	3			.
310	a	1400	mwf	60618	Adams	William	3			.
310	a	1400	mwf	14520	Stephenson	Lynn	4			.
310	a	1400	mwf	22112	Jensen	Lars	4			.
444	a	1430	tth	25851	Smith	Jack	3	hds	sem	1
444	a	1430	tth	87034	Cobbleigh	Nicholas	4	hds	sem	1
444	a	1430	tth	13792	Heisenhuer	Jane	4	hds	sem	2
444	a	1430	tth	89763	Harris	Emily	4	hds	sem	1
444	a	1430	tth	91913	Chambers	Dianne	4	hds	sem	2

Number of cases read =   54   Number of cases listed =   54

Selecting a Subset of Variables

You can create an active file that contains all the variables from each input file or select a subset of variables from each file. The subcommands DROP and KEEP indicate which variables from an input file should be omitted or retained. DROP and KEEP apply only to the immediately preceding named file. For example,

```
JOIN ADD FILE='SOC100AS.SYS'/DROP=SECTION, MEETTIME, DAYS
   /FILE='SOC100B.SYS'/DROP=SECTION, MEETTIME, DAYS
   /FILE='SOC222A.SYS'/DROP=SECTION, MEETTIME, DAYS
   /FILE='SOC310A.SYS'/DROP=SECTION, MEETTIME, DAYS
   /FILE='HDS444A.SYS'
       /KEEP=COURSE STUNUM LASTNAME FSTNAME  CLASSYR
   /BY CLASSYR
   /MAP.
LIST.
```

joins five system files, interleaving cases on the basis of values of *CLASSYR*. All variables except *SECTION*, *MEETTIME*, and *DAYS* are taken from the first four system files. Only variables *COURSE*, *STUNUM*, *LASTNAME*, *FSTNAME*, and *CLASSYR* are included from the fifth system file. The output from the MAP subcommand is shown in Figure 10.12. It is placed last so that it will show the status of the resulting file. The listing of the contents of the active file from the LIST command is shown in Figure 10.13.

Figure 10.12 Map of combined system files with specific variables

```
RESULT        SOC100AS.SYS SOC100B.SYS  SOC222A.SYS  SOC310A.SYS  HDS444A.SYS
------------  ------------ ------------ ------------ ------------ ------------
COURSE        COURSE       COURSE       COURSE       COURSE       COURSE
STUNUM        STUNUM       STUNUM       STUNUM       STUNUM       STUNUM
LASTNAME      LASTNAME     LASTNAME     LASTNAME     LASTNAME     LASTNAME
FSTNAME       FSTNAME      FSTNAME      FSTNAME      FSTNAME      FSTNAME
CLASSYR       CLASSYR      CLASSYR      CLASSYR      CLASSYR      CLASSYR
```

Figure 10.13 Listing of interleaved cases after variables are dropped

COURSE	STUNUM	LASTNAME	FSTNAME	CLASSYR
100	10009	Atmore	Samuel	1
100	24365	McDowell	Denise	1
100	27111	Hutchinson	Christine	1
100	55287	Swift	Jennifer	1
100	62432	Jamieson	Bailey	1
100	10229	Smithe	Peter	1
100	34365	Farroro	Dennis	1
100	25111	Huber	Joan	1
100	55587	Westerman	David	1
100	62442	Mount	Sigrid	1
222	12239	Smith	Patricia	1
222	35467	Freiberg	Gerhardt	1
310	42305	O'Kane	Stanley	1
100	89765	Paulsen	Patrick	2
100	43289	Sweeney	John	2
100	23763	Baker	Catherine	2
100	70395	Jones	James	2
100	53763	Halley	Beth	2
100	82224	Manova	Svetlana	2
222	65141	Mills	Charles	2
222	53287	West	James	2
222	39742	Maus	Mickey	2
222	9763	Herrmann	Monty	2
222	48364	Daveport	Joyce	2
222	81043	Hill	Robert	2
222	42524	Mason	Perry	2
310	60611	Hallet	Robin	2
310	14420	Robinson	Thomas	2
100	22304	Jones	Barbara	3
100	27001	Jacobsen	Richard	3
100	35760	Roberts	Elizabeth	3
100	64352	Atkinson	Thomas	3
100	97291	Sullivan	Linda	3
100	50762	Dexter	Richard	3
100	62752	Colby	Jeffrey	3
100	54358	Fiorello	Francis	3
222	95591	Evans	Linda	3
222	61932	Bates	Oliver	3
222	93132	Hughes	Olivia	3
310	4901	Nace	Laura	3
310	99999	Liebmann	Geoffrey	3
310	43995	Countryman	Katharyn	3
310	60618	Adams	William	3
444	25851	Smith	Jack	3
100	54338	Darfler	Marleena	4
100	79885	Klein	Janet	4
100	89763	Harris	Emily	4
222	44359	Bates	Lucy	4
310	14520	Stephenson	Lynn	4
310	22112	Jensen	Lars	4
444	87034	Cobbleigh	Nicholas	4
444	13792	Heisenhuer	Jane	4
444	89763	Harris	Emily	4
444	91913	Chambers	Dianne	4

Number of cases read =   54   Number of cases listed =   54

Renaming Variables

Sometimes variables containing the same information have different variable names in different files. For example, the student's identification number might be called *STUNUM* in one file and *ID* in another. You can reconcile such differences with the RE-NAME subcommand, as in:

```
GET FILE='SOC100A.SYS'.
 JOIN ADD FILE='SOC100B.SYS'/RENAME (STUNUM=ID)
  /FILE=* /KEEP=LASTNAME FSTNAME ID CLASSYR
  /MAP.
```

The GET command retrieves the system file *SOC100A.SYS* and makes it the active file. JOIN ADD specifies *SOC100B.SYS* as the first input file. The RENAME subcommand changes the name of variable *STUNUM* in *SOC100B.SYS* to *ID* in the resulting active file. The values of *LASTNAME*, *FSTNAME*, *ID*, and *CLASSYR* for cases in the active file (*) are combined with *SOC100B.SYS*.

The MAP output is shown in Figure 10.14. If RENAME had not been specified in this example, the combined file would contain both variables *STUNUM* and *ID*. Cases from the input file *SOC100B.SYS* would have the system-missing value for *ID*, while cases from *SOC100A.SYS* would be system-missing for *STUNUM*.

Figure 10.14 Map of case additions with renamed variable

```
RESULT        SOC100B.SYS   *
------------  ------------  ------------
ID            ID            ID
LASTNAME      LASTNAME      LASTNAME
FSTNAME       FSTNAME       FSTNAME
CLASSYR       CLASSYR       CLASSYR
MAJOR         MAJOR
```

The RENAME subcommand can also be used to distinguish variables that record different attributes but have the same name on different files. For example, two files might each contain a variable called *CLASS*. In one file *CLASS* refers to course name, and in the second file it refers to the student's year in school. To avoid confusing one variable with the other, you could rename *CLASS* in the second file to *SCHLYEAR*. Cases in the second file would then have missing values for *CLASS*.

Matching Files

Once a class roster has been developed, you can use JOIN MATCH to append variables with test grades or other information to each student's record. If each input file contains corresponding cases in the same order but with different variables, the files are **parallel** (see Figure 10.3). A parallel or sequential match combines the variables for the first case in each input file, then the second case in each input file, and so on, without regard to any identifying values that may be present.

Nonparallel files have more or less overlapping sets of cases (see Figure 10.4). Often cases in one input file are missing from another, or cases may be duplicated in one or the other files. You can append variables to particular cases by specifying that cases be combined according to a common value on one or more key variables (such as an identification number) present in each input file. The BY subcommand names the key variables.

Parallel and nonparallel files contain cases with the same kinds of observations or units of analysis. For example, one file can contain a student roster while another file contains student's grades. Each file has individual students as the unit of analysis. Matching the two files results in a student grade-book file.

You can also use JOIN MATCH to combine two files containing different units of analysis. For example, one file might contain test and final grades for students enrolled in five different classes. Another file contains the number of students enrolled in each course and the average final grade for each course offered in the college. By designating the course file a *table* and using the course as a key variable, you can instruct SPSS/PC+ to "look up" the data in the table file and match values to cases in the other input file. A table file contributes variables only from cases that contain corresponding values on key variables. The table file can contain records that don't necessarily correspond to cases in the other input files.

The DROP, KEEP, RENAME, and MAP subcommands (described on pp. 105–109) can be used with JOIN MATCH. Up to five input files can be matched, one of which can be the active file. The following sections describe applications using parallel, nonparallel, and table look-up matches.

Parallel Files—Same Cases, Different Variables

After assembling a student roster, an instructor receives additional information on each student, such as the student's major and whether the course is required for graduation. The instructor can define an active file containing these variables and combine them with an existing system file containing the roster. If each input file contains corresponding cases in the same order, a parallel match can be specified.

Figure 10.15 shows a raw data file containing information on students' majors and required course status. These variables can be added to the class roster saved on p. 103 using the following commands:

```
TITLE 'Grade Book'.
DATA LIST FILE='MAJINFO.DAT'/STUNUM 7-10 LASTNAME 13-24 (A)
   FSTNAME 26-35 (A) REQUIRED 39 MAJOR 41-43 (A).
VALUE LABELS REQUIRED 1 'Must Pass'.

JOIN MATCH FILE='SOC100AS.SYS'/FILE=*.

LIST.

SAVE OUTFILE='S100AGRA.SYS'.
```

The DATA LIST command defines an active file with variables *STUNUM*, *LASTNAME*, *FSTNAME*, *REQUIRED*, and *MAJOR*. The JOIN MATCH command joins cases from the system file *SOC100AS.SYS* with the variables in the active file.

Figure 10.15 Raw data to be added to class roster

```
100 a 10009 Atmore      Samuel    1
100 a 24365 McDowell    Denise    1
100 a 27111 Hutchinson  Christine 1
100 a 55287 Swift       Jennifer  1
100 a 62432 Jamieson    Bailey    1
100 a 89765 Paulsen     Patrick   2 1 psy
100 a 43289 Sweeney     John      2 1 soc
100 a 23763 Baker       Catherine 2   adm
100 a 22304 Jones       Barbara   3 1 adm
100 a 27001 Jacobsen    Richard   3 1 pol
100 a 35760 Roberts     Elizabeth 3 1 his
100 a 64352 Atkinson    Thomas    3   csi
100 a 79885 Klein       Janet     4 1 che
100 a 54338 Darfler     Marleena  4 1 che
```

Figure 10.16 shows the listing of the active file after the parallel match has been performed. The order in which files are named determines the order of variables in the resulting active file. Variables from the first-named file are first, followed by variables from the next-named file, and so on. When two or more files have a variable with the same name, values in the resulting file are taken from the first file named on the JOIN command.

Figure 10.16 Listing of active file after parallel match

COURSE	SECTION	MEETTIME	D A Y S	STUNUM	LASTNAME	FSTNAME	CLASSYR	REQUIRED	M A J O R
100	a	900	mwf	10009	Atmore	Samuel	1	.	
100	a	900	mwf	24365	McDowell	Denise	1	.	
100	a	900	mwf	27111	Hutchinson	Christine	1	.	
100	a	900	mwf	55287	Swift	Jennifer	1	.	
100	a	900	mwf	62432	Jamieson	Bailey	1	.	
100	a	900	mwf	89765	Paulsen	Patrick	2	1	psy
100	a	900	mwf	43289	Sweeney	John	2	1	soc
100	a	900	mwf	23763	Baker	Catherine	2	.	adm
100	a	900	mwf	22304	Jones	Barbara	3	1	adm
100	a	900	mwf	27001	Jacobsen	Richard	3	1	pol
100	a	900	mwf	35760	Roberts	Eliazbeth	3	1	his
100	a	900	mwf	64352	Atkinson	Thomas	3	.	csi
100	a	900	mwf	54338	Darfler	Marleena	4	1	che
100	a	900	mwf	79885	Klein	Janet	4	1	che

```
Number of cases read =      14    Number of cases listed =      14
```

Nonparallel Files—Different Cases, Different Variables

In many circumstances input files do not contain corresponding cases. Some cases may be present in one file and not in another. For example, students are not always present in class on the day of an examination: some may have overslept, others may have dropped the class. The instructor might have one file with records for all students who registered for the class and another file with records for students who took the exam. By using a key variable such as student number, the instructor can append test scores to the appropriate student record.

Up to ten variables can be named as keys. The key variables must be present in each input file, and each file must be sorted in ascending order of the key variables. The key variables are named on the BY subcommand, which follows all other input file specifications.

For example, the raw data file containing the student identification number (*STUNUM*) and exam grades is shown in Figure 10.17. To combine this file with the student roster created on p. 110, you must first sort each file in order of the key variable:

```
GET FILE='S100AGRA.SYS'/DROP=MEETTIME DAYS.
SORT CASES BY STUNUM.

SAVE OUTFILE='SORTS100.SYS'.

DATA LIST FILE='TEST1.DAT'/STUNUM 1-5 SCORE1 7-8.
SORT CASES BY STUNUM.

TITLE 'GRADES THROUGH EXAM1'.
JOIN MATCH FILE='SORTS100.SYS'/FILE= *
   /BY STUNUM
   /MAP.
LIST.
SAVE OUTFILE='GRAS1AOS.SYS'.
```

The GET command retrieves the system file containing the roster, omitting variables *MEETTIME* and *DAYS*. The SORT command sorts cases in ascending order of *STUNUM*. The SAVE command saves the sorted version of the file for use with JOIN MATCH. The DATA LIST command defines the raw data file, *TEST1.DAT*, which contains two variables, *STUNUM* and *SCORE*. The second SORT command sorts cases in the same order as the roster file.

The FILE subcommands on the JOIN command specify system file *SORTS100.SYS* as the first file and the active file as the second file. The BY subcommand indicates that cases from the two input files are to be matched only when they have the same value for key variable *STUNUM*. The MAP subcommand requests a map of the variables contained on each file (Figure 10.18), and the LIST command shows the data saved into the system file *GRAS1AOS.SYS* (Figure 10.19). Note that students who did not take the exam have the system-missing value for variable *SCORE1*.

Figure 10.17 Student number and exam grade file

```
10009 76
24365 86
27111 68
62432 91
43289 86
23763 55
22304 76
35760 84
64352 85
79885 78
54338 80
```

Figure 10.18 Map from nonparallel match

```
RESULT          SORTS100.SYS *
------------    ------------ ------------
COURSE          COURSE
SECTION         SECTION
STUNUM          STUNUM          STUNUM
LASTNAME        LASTNAME
FSTNAME         FSTNAME
CLASSYR         CLASSYR
REQUIRED        REQUIRED
MAJOR           MAJOR
SCORE1                          SCORE1
```

Figure 10.19 Active file listing from nonparallel match

```
COURSE SECTION STUNUM LASTNAME       FSTNAME     CLASSYR REQUIRED MAJOR SCORE1

  100 a          10009 Atmore        Samuel         1        .             76
  100 a          22304 Jones         Barbara        3        1 adm         76
  100 a          23763 Baker         Catherine      2        . adm         55
  100 a          24365 McDowell      Denise         1        .             86
  100 a          27001 Jacobsen      Richard        3        1 pol          .
  100 a          27111 Hutchinson    Christine      1        .             68
  100 a          35760 Roberts       Eliazbeth      3        1 his         84
  100 a          43289 Sweeney       John           2        1 soc         86
  100 a          54338 Darfler       Marleena       4        1 che         80
  100 a          55287 Swift         Jennifer       1        .              .
  100 a          62432 Jamieson      Bailey         1        .             91
  100 a          64352 Atkinson      Thomas         3        . csi         85
  100 a          79885 Klein         Janet          4        1 che         78
  100 a          89765 Paulsen       Patrick        2        1 psy          .

Number of cases read =       14    Number of cases listed =      14
```

When you match files with the BY subcommand, the resulting active file contains values for every variable in each input file. If a variable is not a key variable but is contained in more than one input file, the value from the first-named file is used in the resulting active file. If two variables have the same name but represent different information, you can use the RENAME subcommand to ensure that no information is lost (see "Renaming Variables" on p. 109).

If an input file contains cases with the same value or combination of values for key variables, variables from the other input files are matched only to the first case. Each subsequent duplicate case is assigned system-missing values for the remaining variables from the other input files. If values should be appended to all matching cases, use a TABLE subcommand (see "Table and Case Files—Combining Group and Case Data" below).

Sorting Key Variables

When a BY subcommand is used on JOIN, all input files must be sorted in ascending order of the key variables. The best way to ensure that files are sorted in the correct order is to sort each input file with the SORT command prior to issuing the JOIN command. For all input files except the active file, you will need to resave the file as a system file after specifying SORT, as shown in the example on p. 111.

When multiple keys are used, an easy rule of thumb is to specify the variables on the SORT command in the same order as they are named on the BY subcommand. For example,

```
GET FILE='PREREG.SYS'.
SORT BY DEPT COURSE.
SAVE OUTFILE='PREREGS.SYS'.

GET FILE='LATEREG.SYS'.
SORT BY DEPT COURSE.

JOIN MATCH FILE='PREREGS.SYS'/ FILE=* /BY DEPT COURSE
```

sorts both files in ascending order of *COURSE* within categories of *DEPT*. Table 10.1 illustrates values of the variables sorted in ascending order.

Table 10.1 Sorting order for DEPT COURSE

DEPT	COURSE
hds	100
hds	101
hds	444
mat	100
mat	222
soc	100
soc	222
soc	310

Table and Case Files—Combining Group and Case Data

A **table lookup** match joins variables from one file, called a **table file**, to groups of corresponding cases based on common values of one or more key variables. The table file should contain only one case for each combination of key variables.

For example, an instructor might create a system file containing summary information on each class. Figure 10.20 shows a listing from this system file. Each case contains a unique combination of values for department, course number, and section. The instructor also has a system file containing grades for all students he taught that year. A listing of this file is shown in Figure 10.21. Each line contains individual student grades.

Figure 10.20 Listing of ALLCOURS.SYS file

```
DEPT COURSE   SECTION    EXAMS  CLASSAV

hds    272    a            4    92.02
hds    444    a            2    87.00
soc    100    a            4    86.82
soc    100    b            4    85.62
soc    222    a            6    84.92
soc    310    a            4    87.75
soc    444    a            3    94.35
```

Figure 10.21 Listing of GRADES84.SYS file

DEPT	COURSE	SECTION	STUNUM	LASTNAME	TEST1	TEST2	TEST3	TEST4	TEST5	TEST6	GRADE
hds	444	a	25851	Smith	81	93	.	.	.	.	87
hds	444	a	87034	Cobbleigh	91	96	.	.	.	.	94
hds	444	a	13792	Heisenhuer	93	94	.	.	.	.	94
hds	444	a	89763	Harris	66	85	.	.	.	.	76
hds	444	a	91913	Chambers	93	75	.	.	.	.	84
soc	100	a	10009	Atmore	97	95	95	92	.	.	95
soc	100	a	24365	McDowell	96	87	76	99	.	.	90
soc	100	a	27111	Hutchinson	73	81	91	75	.	.	80
soc	100	a	55287	Swift	.	.	.	.	.	.	.
soc	100	a	62432	Jamieson	89	84	81	87	.	.	85
soc	100	a	89765	Paulsen	.	.	.	.	.	.	.
soc	100	a	43289	Sweeney	95	75	76	82	.	.	82
soc	100	a	23763	Baker	86	79	90	99	.	.	89
soc	100	a	22304	Jones	67	95	98	78	.	.	85
soc	100	a	27001	Jacobsen	.	.	.	.	.	.	.
soc	100	a	35760	Roberts	94	88	87	95	.	.	91
soc	100	a	64352	Atkinson	68	82	90	85	.	.	81
soc	100	a	54338	Darfler	86	90	92	85	.	.	88
soc	100	a	79885	Klein	96	79	85	96	.	.	89
soc	100	b	10229	Smithe	81	71	85	86	.	.	81
soc	100	b	34365	Farroro	88	71	94	96	.	.	87
soc	100	b	25111	Huber	71	83	81	78	.	.	78
soc	100	b	55587	Westerman	76	96	91	98	.	.	90
soc	100	b	62442	Mount	87	84	77	98	.	.	87
soc	100	b	89763	Harris	95	98	84	100	.	.	94
soc	100	b	70395	Jones	68	95	98	90	.	.	88
soc	100	b	53763	Halley	91	91	92	81	.	.	89
soc	100	b	82224	Manova	92	82	97	81	.	.	88
soc	100	b	97291	Sullivan	67	80	89	80	.	.	79
soc	100	b	50762	Dexter	80	90	85	98	.	.	88
soc	100	b	62752	Colby	88	72	79	77	.	.	79
soc	100	b	54358	Fiorello	65	84	95	96	.	.	85
soc	222	a	12239	Smith	84	100	80	96	83	93	89
soc	222	a	35467	Freiberg	75	98	80	95	86	95	89
soc	222	a	65141	Mills	74	78	94	76	81	90	82
soc	222	a	53287	West	73	99	77	75	80	91	83
soc	222	a	39742	Maus	70	95	82	83	79	80	82
soc	222	a	9763	Herrmann	87	82	78	.	.	.	.
soc	222	a	48364	Daveport	84	76	94	93	97	77	87
soc	222	a	81043	Hill	71	87	87	98	91	80	86
soc	222	a	42524	Mason	69	78	84	85	82	93	82
soc	222	a	95591	Evans	80	76	92	83	93	77	84
soc	222	a	61932	Bates	93	75	86	97	82	85	86
soc	222	a	93132	Hughes	80	88	84	92	99	81	87
soc	222	a	44359	Bates	70	89	84	96	85	74	83
soc	310	a	42305	O'Kane	75	87	84	87	.	.	83
soc	310	a	60611	Hallet	75	85	91	88	.	.	85
soc	310	a	14420	Robinson	69	87	89	97	.	.	86
soc	310	a	4901	Nace	91	96	97	82	.	.	92
soc	310	a	99999	Liebmann	92	92	81	82	.	.	87
soc	310	a	43995	Countryman	80	80	85	93	.	.	85
soc	310	a	60618	Adams	72	.	.	.	.	.	.
soc	310	a	14520	Stephenson	94	90	96	87	.	.	92
soc	310	a	22112	Jensen	80	91	98	100	.	.	92

Number of cases read =   54   Number of cases listed =   54

The instructor can use JOIN MATCH with the TABLE and BY subcommands to match variables from the course file to individual student records. He can then compute a variable showing how each student did in relation to the class averages:

```
JOIN MATCH FILE='GRADES84.SYS'/TABLE='ALLCOURS.SYS'
  /BY DEPT COURSE SECTION
  /MAP.

COMPUTE GRADDIFF=GRADE-CLASSAV.

LIST VAR=DEPT COURSE SECTION STUNUM LASTNAME GRADE GRADDIFF.
```

The FILE subcommand on JOIN specifies the student file, and the TABLE subcommand specifies the course file. The BY subcommand names the three key variables, and the MAP subcommand requests a map of the variables in each file (Figure 10.22). The COMPUTE command creates a new variable based on the difference between *GRADE*, which comes from *GRADES84.SYS,* and *CLASSAV*, which comes from *ALLCOURS.SYS*.

To perform the match, JOIN reads a case in the student file and "looks up" a match of key variables in the table file. When a match is found, the values from the table file are appended to the case. Nonmatching cases from the table file are ignored. Nonmatching cases from other input files are assigned system-missing values for variables from the table file. When JOIN finds more than one case in the student file for a particular combination of *DEPT*, *COURSE*, and *SECTION*, a warning message indicating there are duplicate cases is issued. Usually this message can be ignored.

The results of the LIST command, shown in Figure 10.23, show some of the variables in the resulting active file. Note that no cases appear for courses in the table file that did not have matches in the student file.

Figure 10.22 Map from file and table match

```
RESULT         GRADES84.SYS  ALLCOURS.SYS
------------   ------------  ------------
COURSE         COURSE        COURSE
SECTION        SECTION       SECTION
STUNUM         STUNUM
LASTNAME       LASTNAME
DEPT           DEPT          DEPT
TEST1          TEST1
TEST2          TEST2
TEST3          TEST3
TEST4          TEST4
TEST5          TEST5
TEST6          TEST6
GRADE          GRADE
EXAMS                        EXAMS
CLASSAV                      CLASSAV
```

Figure 10.23 Listing of cases from table look-up match

DEPT	COURSE	SECTION	STUNUM	LASTNAME	GRADE	GRADDIFF
hds	444	a	25851	Smith	87	0.0
hds	444	a	87034	Cobbleigh	94	7.00
hds	444	a	13792	Heisenhuer	94	7.00
hds	444	a	89763	Harris	76	-11.00
hds	444	a	91913	Chambers	84	-3.00
soc	100	a	10009	Atmore	95	8.18
soc	100	a	24365	McDowell	90	3.18
soc	100	a	27111	Hutchinson	80	-6.82
soc	100	a	55287	Swift	.	.
soc	100	a	62432	Jamieson	85	-1.82
soc	100	a	89765	Paulsen	.	.
soc	100	a	43289	Sweeney	82	-4.82
soc	100	a	23763	Baker	89	2.18
soc	100	a	22304	Jones	85	-1.82
soc	100	a	27001	Jacobsen	.	.
soc	100	a	35760	Roberts	91	4.18
soc	100	a	64352	Atkinson	81	-5.82
soc	100	a	54338	Darfler	88	1.18
soc	100	a	79885	Klein	89	2.18
soc	100	b	10229	Smithe	81	-4.62
soc	100	b	34365	Farroro	87	1.38
soc	100	b	25111	Huber	78	-7.62
soc	100	b	55587	Westerman	90	4.38
soc	100	b	62442	Mount	87	1.38
soc	100	b	89763	Harris	94	8.38
soc	100	b	70395	Jones	88	2.38
soc	100	b	53763	Halley	89	3.38
soc	100	b	82224	Manova	88	2.38
soc	100	b	97291	Sullivan	79	-6.62
soc	100	b	50762	Dexter	88	2.38
soc	100	b	62752	Colby	79	-6.62
soc	100	b	54358	Fiorello	85	-.62
soc	222	a	12239	Smith	89	4.08
soc	222	a	35467	Freiberg	88	3.08
soc	222	a	65141	Mills	82	-2.92
soc	222	a	53287	West	83	-1.92
soc	222	a	39742	Maus	82	-2.92
soc	222	a	07✶✶	Hauxxxxxx	.	.
soc	222	a	48364	Daveport	87	2.08
soc	222	a	81043	Hill	86	1.08
soc	222	a	42524	Mason	82	-2.92
soc	222	a	95591	Evans	84	-.92
soc	222	a	61932	Bates	86	1.08
soc	222	a	93132	Hughes	87	2.08
soc	222	a	44359	Bates	83	-1.92
soc	310	a	42305	O'Kane	83	-4.75
soc	310	a	60611	Hallet	85	-2.75
soc	310	a	14420	Robinson	86	-1.75
soc	310	a	4901	Nace	92	4.25
soc	310	a	99999	Liebmann	87	-.75
soc	310	a	43995	Countryman	85	-2.75
soc	310	a	60618	Adams	.	.
soc	310	a	14520	Stephenson	92	4.25
soc	310	a	22112	Jensen	92	4.25

```
Number of cases read =      54    Number of cases listed =      54
```

Obtaining Group Data: Procedure AGGREGATE

Procedure AGGREGATE computes summary measures such as the sum and mean across groups of cases and produces either an SPSS/PC+ system file or a new active file containing one case per group. The variables on the resulting aggregated file are summary measures.

For example, consider a file of grades for each student enrolled in each class taught by an instructor. AGGREGATE can be used to create a class file containing such items as mean grade for each class, number of students completing the class, and percentage of students failing a class. In the new file, each case is a class and the variables contain aggregated information on students.

AGGREGATE often is used in conjunction with JOIN MATCH. For example, once you have obtained class averages with AGGREGATE, you can add the average grade for the class to each student's record and compare each student's grade to the average. The aggregated file is used as a table file on the JOIN command.

To use AGGREGATE, you must specify three sets of information: a name for the aggregated file, the variables that define groups, and the functions that create the aggregated variables. Optionally, you can specify missing-value treatments and whether the input file has been sorted according to the grouping variables.

Specifying the File Destination

AGGREGATE either produces an SPSS/PC+ system file or replaces the active file. The OUTFILE subcommand specifies a name for the aggregated file or indicates that the active file should be replaced. OUTFILE must be the first specification.

To create and save a system file, specify a DOS filename enclosed in apostrophes on the OUTFILE subcommand. For example, the commands

```
GET FILE='ALLCLASS.SYS'.
AGGREGATE OUTFILE='ENROLLN.SYS'
  /BREAK=DEPT COURSE SECTION
  /NUMSTU=NU.
```

create an aggregated file from a class roster file. The new aggregated system file is written to the file *ENROLLN.SYS*, and the active file remains unchanged. To replace the active file with the aggregated file, specify an asterisk instead of a filename on OUTFILE, as in:

```
GET FILE='ALLCLASS.SYS'.
AGGREGATE OUTFILE=*
  /BREAK=DEPT COURSE SECTION
  /NUMSTU=NU.
```

When you specify the active file on OUTFILE, the aggregated file is not permanently saved unless you use the SAVE command after the AGGREGATE procedure.

Grouping Cases

Procedure AGGREGATE summarizes groups of cases. A **break group** is a set of cases in the input file that have the same values for a variable or set of variables. Each break group defines one case in the new aggregated file.

For example, in a file of students registered for different classes, each case is a student and includes variables for class name, course number, department, student identification number, major, year in school, and other attributes. Each of these variables can be used individually or jointly to group the students. If you were to aggregate by course number, all cases with the same course number would constitute a group. If you were to aggregate by department and course number, all students taking Sociology 100 would be in one group, all students taking Sociology 200 would be in another, all students in Human Development 100 in another, and so forth. Each combination of department and course number is a break group.

The BREAK subcommand defines the break group variables and must follow the OUTFILE subcommand. You can specify as many variables as you want on the BREAK subcommand, and you can use keyword TO to refer to a set of consecutive variables in the active file. For example, to use variables *DEPT*, *COURSE*, and *SECTION* as the grouping variables, specify:

```
GET FILE='ALLCLASS.SYS'.
AGGREGATE OUTFILE=*
  /BREAK=DEPT COURSE SECTION
  /NUMSTU=NU.
LIST.
```

The GET command retrieves the *ALLCLASS.SYS* system file, which contains information on all students in all classes. The AGGREGATE command directs the aggregated file to the active file and uses values for variables *DEPT* and *COURSE* to group cases. By default, AGGREGATE arranges cases in ascending order of each variable named on the BREAK subcommand. Figure 10.24 shows the contents of the resulting active file from the LIST command. The aggregated file contains five cases, one for each unique combination of *DEPT* and *COURSE*. Note that AGGREGATE saves all variables named on the BREAK subcommand in the resulting aggregated file. Each break variable retains all dictionary information from the input file.

Figure 10.24 Aggregated file in default order

```
DEPT COURSE  SECTION   NUMSTU

hds    444  a            5
soc    100  a           14
soc    100  b           13
soc    222  a           13
soc    310  a            9


Number of cases read =        5    Number of cases listed =       5
```

You can specify the order of cases on the resulting file on the BREAK subcommand using the A and D specifications. For example, the following AGGREGATE command sorts the aggregated active file in descending order of variable *DEPT*, in ascending order of variable *COURSE*, and descending order of variable *SECTION*:

```
GET FILE='ALLCLASS.SYS'.
AGGREGATE OUTFILE=*
  /BREAK=DEPT (D) COURSE (A) SECTION (D)
  /NUMSTU=NU.
 LIST.
```

Figure 10.25 shows the sorted aggregated file.

Figure 10.25 Sorted aggregated file

```
DEPT COURSE  SECTION  NUMSTU

soc    100   b          13
soc    100   a          14
soc    222   a          13
soc    310   a           9
hds    444   a           5


Number of cases read =       5    Number of cases listed =       5
```

You can specify sort order for any variable named on the BREAK subcommand. The sort specification applies to all preceding variables without a sort specification. The default sort order is ascending. String values use the ASCII code value sequence: in ascending order numbers are first, then uppercase letters, and finally lowercase letters (see the Appendix in your IBM *BASIC Reference* manual). Sorting strings in descending order reverses the sequence, starting with lowercase letters.

Using a Presorted Active File

When your active file is already sorted in the order you want your aggregated file, you can use the PRESORTED subcommand. When you specify PRESORTED, each time a different value or combination of values is encountered on variables named on the BREAK subcommand, a new aggregate case is created. If the input file is not sorted and PRESORTED is specified, AGGREGATE produces multiple cases for combinations of the break variables.

For example, the commands

```
GET FILE='ALLCLASS.SYS'.
AGGREGATE OUTFILE=*
  /PRESORTED
  /BREAK=DEPT COURSE SECTION
  /NUMSTU=NU.
 LIST.
```

tell SPSS/PC+ that the *ALLCLASS.SYS* system file is already sorted by *DEPT*, *COURSE*, and *SECTION*.

PRESORTED is be specified between the OUTFILE and BREAK subcommands. When it is used, you cannot specify sort order for variables named on the BREAK subcommand using the A and D specifications (see "Grouping Cases" on p. 119). If the PRESORTED subcommand is used and sort order is specified on the BREAK subcommand, the aggregated file is sorted in the order of the input file and a warning is issued.

Creating Aggregated Variables

Each variable in an aggregated file is created by applying an aggregate function to a variable in the active file. The simplest specification is a *target variable list* followed by an equals sign, the function keyword, and the list of *source variables* in parentheses. The aggregate functions available are listed in "Functions" on p. 123.

For example, using the data shown in Figure 10.26, the commands

```
DATA LIST FILE='ALLGRADE.DAT'/ COURSE 2-4 SECTION 6 (A)
   STUNUM 8-12 LASTNAME 14-25 (A) DEPT 27-29 (A) EXAMS 31
   TEST1 TO TEST6 33-56.
FORMATS TEST1 TO TEST6 (F2.0).
COMPUTE
 FINGRADE=RND((TEST1+TEST2+TEST3+TEST4+TEST5+TEST6)/EXAMS).
FORMATS FINGRADE (F3).

AGGREGATE OUTFILE='CLASSAV1.SYS'
  /BREAK=DEPT COURSE SECTION
  /CLASSAV=MEAN(FINGRADE).
```

define an active file and then use it to create a new variable *CLASSAV* as the mean of variable *FINGRADE* for each section of a course within each department.

Figure 10.26 ALLGRADE.DAT data set

```
100 a 10009 Atmore      soc 4  97  95  95  92   0   0
100 a 24365 McDowell    soc 4  96  87  76  99   0   0
100 a 27111 Hutchinson  soc 4  73  81  91  75   0   0
100 a 55287 Swift       soc 4               0   0
100 a 62432 Jamieson    soc 4  89  84  81  87   0   0
100 a 89765 Paulsen     soc 4               0   0
100 a 43289 Sweeney     soc 4  95  75  76  82   0   0
100 a 23763 Baker       soc 4  86  79  90  99   0   0
100 a 22304 Jones       soc 4  67  95  98  78   0   0
100 a 27001 Jacobsen    soc 4               0   0
100 a 35760 Roberts     soc 4  94  88  87  95   0   0
100 a 64352 Atkinson    soc 4  68  82  90  85   0   0
100 a 54338 Darfler     soc 4  86  90  92  85   0   0
100 a 79885 Klein       soc 4  96  79  85  96   0   0
100 b 10229 Smithe      soc 4  81  71  85  86   0   0
100 b 34365 Farroro     soc 4  88  71  94  96   0   0
100 b 25111 Huber       soc 4  71  83  81  78   0   0
100 b 55587 Westerman   soc 4  76  96  91  98   0   0
100 b 62442 Mount       soc 4  87  84  77  98   0   0
100 b 89763 Harris      soc 4  95  98  84 100   0   0
100 b 70395 Jones       soc 4  68  95  98  90   0   0
100 b 53763 Halley      soc 4  91  91  92  81   0   0
100 b 82224 Manova      soc 4  92  82  97  81   0   0
100 b 97291 Sullivan    soc 4  67  80  89  80   0   0
100 b 50762 Dexter      soc 4  80  90  85  98   0   0
100 b 62752 Colby       soc 4  88  72  79  77   0   0
100 b 54358 Fiorello    soc 4  65  84  95  96   0   0
222 a 12239 Smith       soc 6  84 100  80  96  83  93
222 a 35467 Freiberg    soc 6  75  98  80  95  86  95
222 a 65141 Mills       soc 6  74  78  94  76  81  90
222 a 53287 West        soc 6  73  99  77  75  80  91
222 a 39742 Maus        soc 6  70  95  82  83  79  80
222 a  9763 Herrmann    soc 6  87  82  78       0   0
222 a 48364 Daveport    soc 6  84  76  94  93  97  77
222 a 81043 Hill        soc 6  71  87  87  98  91  80
222 a 42524 Mason       soc 6  69  78  84  85  82  93
222 a 95591 Evans       soc 6  80  76  92  83  93  77
222 a 61932 Bates       soc 6  93  75  86  97  82  85
222 a 93132 Hughes      soc 6  80  88  84  92  99  81
222 a 44359 Bates       soc 6  70  89  84  96  85  74
310 a 42305 O'Kane      soc 4  75  87  84  87   0   0
310 a 60611 Hallet      soc 4  75  85  91  88   0   0
310 a 14420 Robinson    soc 4  69  87  89  97   0   0
310 a  4901 Nace        soc 4  91  96  97  82   0   0
310 a 99999 Liebmann    soc 4  92  92  81  82   0   0
310 a 43995 Countryman  soc 4  80  80  85  93   0   0
310 a 60618 Adams       soc 4  72               0   0
310 a 14520 Stephenson  soc 4  94  90  96  87   0   0
310 a 22112 Jensen      soc 4  80  91  98 100   0   0
444 a 25851 Smith       hds 2  81  93   0   0   0   0
444 a 87034 Cobbleigh   hds 2  91  96   0   0   0   0
444 a 13792 Heisenhuer  hds 2  93  94   0   0   0   0
444 a 89763 Harris      hds 2  66  85   0   0   0   0
444 a 91913 Chambers    hds 2  93  75   0   0   0   0
```

The target and source variable lists must have the same number of variables, as in:

```
AGGREGATE OUTFILE='CLASSAV2.SYS'
 /BREAK=DEPT COURSE SECTION
 /CLASSAV TEST1AVE=MEAN(FINGRADE TEST1).
```

This specification creates two aggregated variables: *CLASSAV* is the mean of *FIN-GRADE*, and *TEST1AVE* is the mean of *TEST1*.

You can use keyword TO in both the target and source variable lists. For example, to create averages for each test, specify:

```
AGGREGATE OUTFILE='CLASSAV3.SYS'
  /BREAK=DEPT COURSE SECTION
  /TESTAVE1 TO TESTAVE6=MEAN(TEST1 TO TEST6).
```

Any number of functions can be used to create variables. Separate each function specification with a slash, as in:

```
AGGREGATE OUTFILE='CLASSAVE.SYS'
  /BREAK=DEPT COURSE SECTION
  /TESTAVE1 AVEFINAL=MEAN(TEST1 FINGRADE)
  /TESTSD1 SDFINAL=SD(TEST1 FINGRADE).
GET FILE='CLASSAVE.SYS'.
LIST.
```

Figure 10.27 shows the results from the LIST command.

Figure 10.27 Listing of aggregated variables and values

```
DEPT COURSE SECTION TESTAVE1 AVEFINAL  TESTSD1  SDFINAL

hds    444 a         84.80    87.00    11.63    7.55
soc    100 a         86.09    86.82    11.53    4.64
soc    100 b         80.69    85.62    10.40    4.91
soc    222 a         77.69    84.92     7.60    2.54
soc    310 a         80.89    87.75     9.28    3.69


Number of cases read =      5    Number of cases listed =      5
```

Functions

The following functions are available in procedure AGGREGATE:

SUM(varlist)

Sum across cases. The default format is F8.2.

MEAN(varlist)

Mean across cases. The default format is F8.2.

SD(varlist)

Standard deviation across cases. The default format is F8.2.

MAX(varlist)

Maximum value across cases. Complete dictionary information is copied from the source variables to the target variables.

MIN(varlist)

Minimum value across cases. Complete dictionary information is copied from the source variables to the target variables.

PGT(varlist,value)

Percentage of cases greater than the specified value. The default format is F5.1.

PLT(varlist,value)

Percentage of cases less than the specified value. The default format is F5.1.

PIN(varlist,value1,value2)

Percentage of cases between value1 and value2, inclusive. The default format is F5.1.

POUT(varlist,value1,value2)	*Percentage of cases not between value1 and value2.* Cases where the source variable equals value1 or value2 are not counted. The default format is F5.1.
FGT(varlist,value)	*Fraction of cases greater than the specified value.* The default format is F5.3.
FLT(varlist,value)	*Fraction of cases less than the specified value.* The default format is F5.3.
FIN(varlist,value1,value2)	*Fraction of cases between value1 and value2, inclusive.* The default format is F5.3.
FOUT(varlist,value1,value2)	*Fraction of cases not between value1 and value2.* Cases where the source variable equals value1 or value2 are not counted. The default format is F5.3.
N(varlist)	*Weighted number of cases in break group.* The default format is F7.0 for unweighted files and F8.2 for weighted files.
NU(varlist)	*Unweighted number of cases in break group.* The default format is F7.0.
NMISS(varlist)	*Weighted number of missing cases.* The default format is F7.0 for unweighted files and F8.2 for weighted files.
NUMISS(varlist)	*Unweighted number of missing cases.* The default format is F7.0.
FIRST(varlist)	*First nonmissing observed value in break group.* Complete dictionary information is copied from the source variables to the target variables.
LAST(varlist)	*Last nonmissing observed value in break group.* Complete dictionary information is copied from the source variables to the target variables.

The percentage functions (PGT, PLT, PIN, and POUT) return values between 0 and 100, inclusive. The fraction functions (FGT, FLT, FIN, and FOUT) return values between 0 and 1, inclusive.

Function Arguments

Only numeric variables can be used with SUM, MEAN, and SD. Both long and short string variables can be used with all other functions. For example, to obtain the percentage of females when *SEX* is coded M and F, specify either

```
PCTFEM=PLT(SEX,'M')
```

or

```
PCTFEM=PIN(SEX,'F','F')
```

Blanks and commas can be used interchangeably to separate arguments.

The argument for functions PGT, PLT, PIN, POUT, FGT, FLT, FIN, and FOUT includes values as well as a source variable. The argument for PGT, PLT, FGT, and FLT includes one value. PIN, POUT, FIN, and FOUT have two value arguments. For example, the specification

```
LOQUART1 LOFINAL=PLT(TEST1 FINGRADE,75)
```

assigns the percentage of cases with values less than 75 for *TEST1* to *LOQUART1* and for *FINGRADE* to *LOFINAL*. The specification

```
CGRADE=FIN(FINGRADE,70,79)
```

assigns the fraction of cases having final grade scores of 70 to 79 to *CGRADE*. For PIN, POUT, FIN, and FOUT, the first argument should be lower than the second argument. If the first argument is higher, AGGREGATE automatically reverses them and displays a warning message.

The N and NU functions do not require arguments. Without arguments they return the number of weighted and unweighted cases in a break group. If you supply a variable list, they return the weighted and unweighted number of nonmissing cases for the variables specified.

Labels and Formats

With the exception of the functions MAX, MIN, FIRST, and LAST, which copy complete dictionary information from the source variable, new variables created by AGGREGATE have the default dictionary formats described in "Functions" on p. 123 and no labels. To label a new variable, specify a label in apostrophes immediately following the variable name, as in:

```
AGGREGATE OUTFILE='CLASSAV2.SYS'
  /BREAK=DEPT COURSE
  /CLASSAV 'Final Average'
   TEST1AVE '1st Test Average'=MEAN(FINGRAE TEST1).
```

The label applies only to the immediately preceding variable.

If the aggregated file becomes the new active file, you could also use the VARIABLE LABELS command to add labels, as in:

```
AGGREGATE OUTFILE=*
  /BREAK=DEPT COURSE
  /CLASSAV TEST1AVE=MEAN(FINGRADE TEST1).
VARIABLE LABELS CLASSAV 'Final Average'
  /TEST1AVE '1st Test Average'.
```

Use the FORMATS command to change the format of variables in an active file created by AGGREGATE, as in:

```
AGGREGATE OUTFILE=*
  /BREAK=DEPT COURSE
  /CLASSAV TEST1AVE=MEAN(FINGRADE TEST1).
VARIABLE LABELS CLASSAV 'Final Average'
  /TEST1AVE '1st Test Average'.
FORMATS CLASSAV TEST1AVE (F4.1).
```

The formats for *CLASSAV* and *TEST1AVE* are changed from the default width of eight columns with two decimal places (F8.2) to a width of four columns with one decimal digit (F4.1).

If the aggregated file is saved as a system file, the file must be retrieved with a GET command before the FORMATS and VARIABLE LABELS commands can be issued.

Missing Data

By default, all nonmissing cases are used in the computation of aggregate variables. To force target variables to have the system-missing value if any of the cases in the group have missing values for the source variable, use the MISSING subcommand with keyword COLUMNWISE. The MISSING subcommand follows the OUTFILE subcommand, as in:

```
AGGREGATE OUTFILE='CLASSREP.SYS'
  /MISSING=COLUMNWISE
  /BREAK=DEPT COURSE
  /TESTAVE1 AVEFINAL=MEAN(TEST1 FINGRADE).
  /TESTSD1 SDFINAL=SD(TEST1 FINGRADE).
GET FILE='CLASSREP.SYS'.
LIST.
```

The results of the LIST command are shown in Figure 10.28. You can compare these values with those shown in Figure 10.27.

Figure 10.28 Listing of aggregated values with columnwise treatment

```
DEPT COURSE SECTION TESTAVE1 AVEFINAL  TESTSD1  SDFINAL

hds    444 a         84.80    87.00    11.63    7.55
soc    100 a           .         .        .       .
soc    100 b         80.69    85.62    10.40    4.91
soc    222 a         77.69       .      7.60       .
soc    310 a         80.89       .      9.28       .


Number of cases read =      5   Number of cases listed =      5
```

The MISSING subcommand has no effect on the N, NU, NMISS, or NUMISS functions. For example, N(TEST1) returns the same result if MISSING is specified or if it is not.

Including Missing Values

To treat user-missing values as valid, specify a period after the function name, as in:

```
LOFINAL=PLT.(FINGRADE,75)
```

LOFINAL will equal the percentage of cases within each group with values less than 75 for *FINGRADE* even if some of the values are defined as missing. To obtain the first value of *AGE* in a break group whether it is missing or not, specify:

```
FIRSTAGE=FIRST.(AGE)
```

If the first case in a break group has a user-missing value for *AGE*, *FIRSTAGE* is set to that value. Since variables created with *FIRST* have the same dictionary information as their source variables, the value for *FIRSTAGE* is still treated as user-missing in the aggregated file.

The period is ignored when used with N, NU, NMISS, and NUMISS if these functions have no argument. On the other hand, NMISS.(AGE) gives the number of cases for which *AGE* has the system-missing value. The effect of specifying a period on N, NU, NMISS, and NUMISS is illustrated by the following:

N = N. = N(ΛGE) ∣ NMISS(AGE) = N.(AGE)+NMISS.(AGE)

That is, the function N (the same as N. with no argument) is equal to the number of cases with valid values (N(AGE)) and with missing values (NMISS(AGE)) for *AGE*, which is also equal to the number of cases with either valid or user-missing values (N.(AGE)) and system-missing values (NMISS.(AGE)) for *AGE*. The same holds for the NU, NMISS, and NUMISS functions.

Table 10.2 demonstrates the effect of the MISSING subcommand and of including user-missing values. Each entry in the table is the number of cases used to compute the specified function for a particular break group of variable *EDUC*. The group has 10 non-missing cases, 5 user-missing cases, and 2 system-missing cases. With the exception of the MEAN function, columnwise treatment produces the same results as the default for every function.

Table 10.2   Alternative missing-value treatments

Function	Default	Columnwise
N	17	17
N.	17	17
N(EDUC)	10	10
N.(EDUC)	15	15
MEAN(EDUC)	10	0
MEAN.(EDUC)	15	0
NMISS(EDUC)	7	7
NMISS.(EDUC)	2	2

An Example of AGGREGATE with JOIN

At the end of the semester, the instructor puts together a report outlining the individual performance of each student. The commands below use JOIN and AGGREGATE to combine grade books for each class into a single file, develop summary variables of overall class performance, combine class and student variables, and then produce a listing of individual performance compared to class averages:

```
JOIN ADD FILE='SOC100A.SYS'
  /FILE='SOC100B.SYS'
  /FILE='SOC222A.SYS'
  /FILE='SOC310A.SYS'
  /FILE='HDS444A.SYS'
  /MAP.

SORT BY DEPT COURSE SECTION.

AGGREGATE OUTFILE='AVERAGE.SYS'
  /PRESORTED
  /BREAK=DEPT COURSE SECTION
  /AVEGRADE=MEAN(FINGRADE)
  /SDGRADE=SD(FINGRADE)
  /PCTFAIL=PLT(FINGRADE,65).

JOIN MATCH FILE=* /TABLE='AVERAGE.SYS'
  /BY DEPT COURSE SECTION.

COMPUTE GRADEDEV=FINGRADE-AVEGRADE.
LIST VARS=DEPT COURSE SECTION LASTNAME STUNUM FINGRADE
        GRADEDEV.
SAVE OUTFILE='YEAREND.SYS'.
```

- The JOIN ADD command combines cases from each of five system files. Variables from the files and in the resulting active file are listed with the MAP subcommand (see Figure 10.29).

- The SORT command orders cases in ascending order of *SECTION* within categories of *COURSE* within categories of *DEPT*.

- The OUTFILE subcommand on AGGREGATE directs the aggregated file to a system file named *AVERAGE.SYS*.

- The PRESORTED specification states that the active file is already sorted.

- The BREAK subcommand creates one case for each distinct combination of *DEPT*, *COURSE*, and *SECTION*. Each case contains values of the break variables as well as three variables produced with the aggregate functions, MEAN, SD, and PLT.

- The JOIN command creates a new active file that combines cases in the current active file with cases in the aggregated file, which is designated a table file. Cases are matched based on the key variables *DEPT*, *COURSE*, and *SECTION*.

- The COMPUTE command creates a variable based on the difference between the student's grade and the class average.
- The LIST command produces a simple listing of the specified variables (see Figure 10.30).
- The SAVE command saves the active file for use in subsequent sessions.

Figure 10.29 Map of variables in input and resulting files

```
RESULT        SOC100A.SYS   SOC100B.SYS   SOC222A.SYS   SOC310A.SYS   HDS444A.SYS
------------  ------------  ------------  ------------  ------------  ------------
COURSE        COURSE        COURSE        COURSE        COURSE        COURSE
SECTION       SECTION       SECTION       SECTION       SECTION       SECTION
STUNUM        STUNUM        STUNUM        STUNUM        STUNUM        STUNUM
LASTNAME      LASTNAME      LASTNAME      LASTNAME      LASTNAME      LASTNAME
DEPT          DEPT          DEPT          DEPT          DEPT          DEPT
EXAMS         EXAMS         EXAMS         EXAMS         EXAMS         EXAMS
TEST1         TEST1         TEST1         TEST1         TEST1         TEST1
TEST2         TEST2         TEST2         TEST2         TEST2         TEST2
TEST3         TEST3         TEST3         TEST3         TEST3         TEST3
TEST4         TEST4         TEST4         TEST4         TEST4         TEST4
TEST5         TEST5         TEST5         TEST5         TEST5         TEST5
TEST6         TEST6         TEST6         TEST6         TEST6         TEST6
FINGRADE      FINGRADE      FINGRADE      FINGRADE      FINGRADE      FINGRADE
```

Figure 10.30 LISTING of cases after table look-up JOIN MATCH

DEPT	COURSE	SECTION	LASTNAME	STUNUM	FINGRADE	GRADEDEV
hds	444	a	Smith	25851	87	0.0
hds	444	a	Cobbleigh	87034	94	7.00
hds	444	a	Heisenhuer	13792	94	7.00
hds	444	a	Harris	89763	76	-11.00
hds	444	a	Chambers	91913	84	-3.00
soc	100	a	Atmore	10009	95	8.18
soc	100	a	McDowell	24365	90	3.18
soc	100	a	Hutchinson	27111	80	-6.82
soc	100	a	Swift	55287	.	.
soc	100	a	Jamieson	62432	85	-1.82
soc	100	a	Paulsen	89765	.	.
soc	100	a	Sweeney	43289	82	-4.82
soc	100	a	Baker	23763	89	2.18
soc	100	a	Jones	22304	85	-1.82
soc	100	a	Jacobsen	27001	.	.
soc	100	a	Roberts	35760	91	4.18
soc	100	a	Atkinson	64352	81	-5.82
soc	100	a	Darfler	54338	88	1.18
soc	100	a	Klein	79885	89	2.18
soc	100	b	Smithe	10229	81	-4.62
soc	100	b	Farroro	34365	87	1.38
soc	100	b	Huber	25111	78	-7.62
soc	100	b	Westerman	55587	90	4.38
soc	100	b	Mount	62442	87	1.38
soc	100	b	Harris	89763	94	8.38
soc	100	b	Jones	70395	88	2.38
soc	100	b	Halley	53763	89	3.38
soc	100	b	Manova	82224	88	2.38
soc	100	b	Sullivan	97291	79	-6.62
soc	100	b	Dexter	50762	88	2.38
soc	100	b	Colby	62752	79	-6.62
soc	100	b	Fiorello	54358	85	-.62
soc	222	a	Smith	12239	89	4.08
soc	222	a	Freiberg	35467	88	3.08
soc	222	a	Mills	65141	82	-2.92
soc	222	a	West	53287	83	-1.92
soc	222	a	Maus	39742	82	-2.92
soc	222	a	Herrmann	9763	.	.
soc	222	a	Daveport	48364	87	2.08
soc	222	a	Hill	81043	86	1.08
soc	222	a	Mason	42524	82	-2.92
soc	222	a	Evans	95591	84	-.92
soc	222	a	Bates	61932	86	1.08
soc	222	a	Hughes	93132	87	2.08
soc	222	a	Bates	44359	83	-1.92
soc	310	a	O'Kane	42305	83	-4.75
soc	310	a	Hallet	60611	85	-2.75
soc	310	a	Robinson	14420	86	-1.75
soc	310	a	Nace	4901	92	4.25
soc	310	a	Liebmann	99999	87	-.75
soc	310	a	Countryman	43995	85	-2.75
soc	310	a	Adams	60618	.	.
soc	310	a	Stephenson	14520	92	4.25
soc	310	a	Jensen	22112	92	4.25

Number of cases read =   54   Number of cases listed =   54

Swapping Cases and Variables: Procedure FLIP

SPSS/PC+ assumes a file structure in which variables are the columns and cases are the rows. This is the structure required to correctly read and analyze your data. Sometimes, however, data are recorded in just the opposite fashion: the cases are the columns and each variable is a row. You might find this to be the case with spreadsheet data that you have read with TRANSLATE.

To get this kind of file into the structure required by SPSS/PC+, you need to use the FLIP command. FLIP switches the columns and rows of your data so that what was in column 1, row 2, is now in column 2, row 1. For example, suppose you have two products, each with quarterly sales, and the data are structured like this:

```
          Q1      Q2      Q3      Q4      Q5      Q6
PROD1     24      36      78      48      53      65
PROD2     39      82      31      49      22      48
```

The transposed file looks like this:

```
       PROD1   PROD2
Q1     24      39
Q2     36      82
Q3     78      31
Q4     48      49
Q5     53      22
Q6     65      48
```

If you need to use FLIP to reorganize your file, do so as soon as possible in the session, ideally right after you read the data with TRANSLATE. This is so you can be sure that any commands you issue apply to the new, corrected active file. For additional information on transposing your file, see FLIP in the Syntax Reference.

When FLIP Won't Help

A typical format for spreadsheet files containing time series data is shown in Figure 10.31. This file contains a single time series that begins in January, 1980, and ends in December, 1984.

Figure 10.31 A possible spreadsheet file structure

```
     A      B      C      D      E      F      G      H   . . .   M
1  YEAR    JAN    FEB    MAR    APR    MAY    JUN    JUL  . . .  DEC
2  1980    22     27     21     31     34     33     39   . . .   29
3  1981    31     33     33     34     41     42     44   . . .   35
4  1982    33     34     31     37     43     51     49   . . .   41
5  1983    43     49     49     55     57     62     61   . . .   54
6  1984    57     63     70     68     74     79     83   . . .   71
```

Reading this file with TRANSLATE for use with SPSS/PC+ Trends would give you 13 variables (*YEAR* through *DEC*) and five cases (1980 through 1984). However, swapping the columns and rows with FLIP would give you 5 separate series, one for each year, instead of one continuous series. To get a structure like this into the proper format, you need to read the data twice: once with TRANSLATE and once with DATA LIST. The commands that would be used for the file in Figure 10.31 are:

```
TRANSLATE FROM='SPREAD.DAT' /TYPE=WK1 /FIELDNAMES /DROP=YEAR.
WRITE.
DATA LIST FILE='SPSS.PRC' FREE /SERIES1.
DATE Y 1980 M 1.
```

- The TRANSLATE command reads the spreadsheet data from file *SPREAD.DAT*, using the first row as variable names and dropping the YEAR variable.

- The raw data are then written to an ASCII file with the WRITE command. By default, the file is named *SPSS.PRC*.

- The DATA LIST command reads the raw data in freefield format as one continuous series named *SERIES1*.

- The DATE command (available with the SPSS/PC+ Trends option) reassigns the correct year and month information to the data.

11 Data Tabulation: Procedure FREQUENCIES

Few people would dispute the effects of "rainy days and Mondays" on the body and spirit. It has long been known that more suicides occur on Mondays than other days of the week. An excess of cardiac deaths on Mondays has also been noted (Rabkin et al., 1980). In this chapter, using a study of coronary heart disease among male Western Electric employees (Paul et al.), we will examine the day of death to see if an excess of deaths occurred on Mondays.

A Frequency Table

A first step in analyzing data on day of death might be to count the number of deaths occurring on each day of the week. Figure 11.1 contains this information.

Figure 11.1 Frequency of death by day of week

```
GET FILE='ELECTRIC.SYS'.
FREQUENCIES VARIABLES=DAYOFWK.

DAYOFWK    DAY OF DEATH

                                                Valid      Cum
       Value Label           Value  Frequency  Percent  Percent  Percent
    SUNDAY                      1       19        7.9     17.3     17.3
    MONDAY                      2       11        4.6     10.0     27.3
    TUESDAY                     3       19        7.9     17.3     44.5
    WEDNESDAY                   4       17        7.1     15.5     60.0
    THURSDAY                    5       15        6.3     13.6     73.6
    FRIDAY                      6       13        5.4     11.8     85.5
    SATURDAY                    7       16        6.7     14.5    100.0
    MISSING                     9      130       54.2   Missing
                                    -------    -------  -------
                         Total      240      100.0    100.0

Valid cases     110    Missing cases    130
```

Each row of the frequency table describes a particular day of the week. The last row (labeled *Missing*) represents cases for which the day of death is not known or death has not occurred. For the table in Figure 11.1, there are 110 cases for which day of death is known. The first column (*Value Label*) gives the name of the day, while the second column contains the **value**, which is the numeric or string value given to the computer to represent the day.

133

The number of people dying on each day (the **frequency**) appears in the third column. Monday is the least-frequent day of death, with 11 deaths. These 11 deaths represent 4.6% (11/240) of all cases. This **percentage** appears in the fourth column. However, of the 240 cases, 130 are **missing cases** (cases for which day of death is unknown or death has not occurred). The 11 deaths on Monday represent 10.0% of the total deaths for which day of death is known (11/110). This **valid percentage** appears in the fifth column.

The last column of the table contains the **cumulative percentage**. For a particular day, this percentage is the sum of the valid percentages of that day and of all other days that precede it in the table. For example, the cumulative percentage for Tuesday is 44.5, which is the sum of the percentage of deaths that occurred on Sunday, Monday, and Tuesday. It is calculated as

$$\frac{19}{110} + \frac{11}{110} + \frac{19}{110} = \frac{49}{110} = 44.5\% \qquad \text{Equation 11.1}$$

Sometimes it is helpful to look at frequencies for a selected subset of cases. Figure 11.2 is a frequency table of day of death for a subset characterized by sudden cardiac death. This is a particularly interesting category, since it is thought that sudden death may be related to stressful events such as returning to the work environment. In Figure 11.2, deaths do not appear to cluster on any particular day. Twenty-two percent of deaths occurred on Sunday, while 8.3% occurred on Thursday. Since the number of sudden deaths in the table is small, the magnitude of the observed fluctuations is not very large.

Figure 11.2   Frequency of sudden cardiac death by day of week

```
SELECT IF (FIRSTCHD EQ 2).
FREQUENCIES VARIABLES=DAYOFWK.

DAYOFWK    DAY OF DEATH

                                               Valid      Cum
   Value Label          Value  Frequency  Percent  Percent  Percent
SUNDAY                     1         8      22.2     22.2     22.2
MONDAY                     2         4      11.1     11.1     33.3
TUESDAY                    3         4      11.1     11.1     44.4
WEDNESDAY                  4         7      19.4     19.4     63.9
THURSDAY                   5         3       8.3      8.3     72.2
FRIDAY                     6         6      16.7     16.7     88.9
SATURDAY                   7         4      11.1     11.1    100.0
                                  -------  -------  -------
                       Total      36     100.0    100.0

Valid cases      36    Missing cases      0
```

Visual Displays

While the numbers in the frequency table can be studied and compared, it is often useful to present results in a form that can be interpreted visually. Figure 11.3 is a pie chart of the data displayed in Figure 11.1. Each slice represents a day of the week. The size of the slice depends on the frequency of death for that day. Monday is represented by 10.0% of the pie chart, since 10.0% of the deaths for which the day is known occurred on Monday.

Figure 11.3   Pie chart of death by day of week

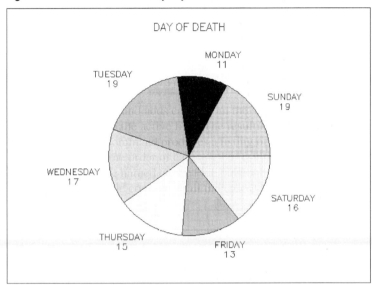

Another way to represent the data is with a bar chart, as shown in Figure 11.4. There is a bar for each day, and the length of the bar is proportional to the number of deaths observed on that day. The number of deaths, or frequency, is displayed at the end of each bar.

Figure 11.4   Bar chart of frequency of death by day of week

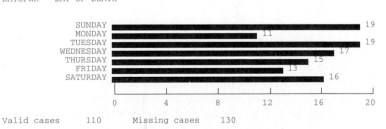

Only values that actually occur in the data are represented in the bar chart. For example, if no deaths occurred on Thursday, no space would be left for Thursday, and the bar for Wednesday would be followed by the bar for Friday. Likewise, if you charted the number of cars per family, the bar describing 6 cars might be next to the one for 25 cars if no family owned 7 to 24 cars. Therefore, you should pay attention to where categories with no cases may occur.

Although the basic information presented by frequency tables, pie charts, and bar charts is the same, the visual displays enliven the data. Differences among the days of the week are apparent at a glance, eliminating the need to pore over columns of numbers.

What Day?

Although the number of sudden cardiac deaths is small in this study, the data in Figure 11.2 indicate that the number of deaths on Mondays is not particularly large. In fact, the most deaths occurred on Sunday—slightly over 22%. A study of over a thousand sudden cardiac deaths in Rochester, Minnesota, also found a slightly increased incidence of death on weekends for men (Beard et al., 1982). The authors speculate that for men, this might mean "the home environment is more stressful than the work environment." But you should be wary of explanations that are not directly supported by data. It is only too easy to find a clever explanation for any statistical finding.

Histograms

A frequency table or bar chart of all values for a variable is a convenient way of summarizing a variable that has a relatively small number of distinct values. Variables such as sex, country, and astrological sign are necessarily limited in the number of values they can have. For variables that can take on many different values, such as income to the penny or weight in ounces, a tally of the cases with each observed value may not be very informative. In the worst situation, when all cases have different values, a frequency table is little more than an ordered list of those values.

Variables that have many values can be summarized by grouping the values of the variables into intervals and counting the number of cases with values within each interval. For example, income can be grouped into $5,000 intervals such as 0–4999, 5000–9999, 10000–14999, and so forth, and the number of observations in each group can be tabulated. Such grouping should be done when the data are analyzed by SPSS/PC+. Whenever possible, the values for variables should be entered into the data file in their original, ungrouped form.

A histogram is a convenient way to display the distribution of such grouped values. Consider Figure 11.5, which is a histogram of body weight in pounds for the sample of 240 men from the Western Electric study. The numbers below the bars indicate the midpoint, or middle value, of each interval. Each bar represents the number of cases with values in the interval. Intervals that have no observations are included in the histogram, but no bars are printed. This differs from a bar chart, which does not leave space for the empty categories.

Figure 11.5   Histogram of body weight

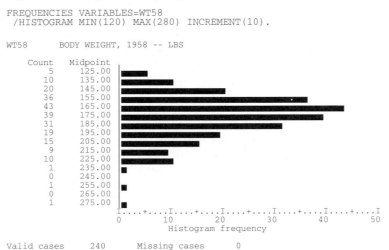

```
FREQUENCIES VARIABLES=WT58
 /HISTOGRAM MIN(120) MAX(280) INCREMENT(10).


WT58      BODY WEIGHT, 1958 -- LBS

    Count  Midpoint
        5   125.00
       10   135.00
       20   145.00
       36   155.00
       43   165.00
       39   175.00
       31   185.00
       19   195.00
       15   205.00
        9   215.00
       10   225.00
        1   235.00
        0   245.00
        1   255.00
        0   265.00
        1   275.00
            I....+....I....+....I....+....I....+....I....+....I
            0        10       20       30       40       50
                         Histogram frequency

Valid cases     240    Missing cases     0
```

A histogram can be used whenever it is reasonable to group adjacent values. Histograms should not be used to display variables when there is no underlying order to the values. For example, if 100 different religions are arbitrarily assigned codes of 1 to 100, grouping values into intervals is meaningless. Either a bar chart or a histogram in which each interval corresponds to a single value should be used to display such data.

Percentiles

The information in a histogram can be further summarized by computing values above and below which a specified percentage of cases fall. Such values are called **percentiles**. For example, the 50th percentile, or median, is the value above and below which 50% (or half) of the cases fall. The 25th percentile is the value below which 25% and above which 75% of the cases fall.

Figure 11.6 contains values for the 25th, 50th, and 75th percentiles for the weight data shown in the histogram in Figure 11.5. You see that 25% of the men weigh less than 156 pounds, 50% weigh less than 171 pounds, and 75% weigh less than 187 pounds.

Figure 11.6   Percentiles for body weight

```
FREQUENCIES VARIABLES=WT58 /FORMAT NOTABLE /PERCENTILES 25 50 75.

WT58      BODY WEIGHT -- LBS


 Percentile    Value      Percentile    Value      Percentile    Value
   25.00     156.000        50.00     171.000        75.00     187.000

Valid cases    240     Missing cases     0
```

From these three percentiles, sometimes called **quartiles** (since they divide the distribution into four parts containing the same number of cases), you can tell that 50% of the men weigh between 156 and 187 pounds. (Remember that 25% of the men weigh less than 156 and 25% weigh more than 187. That leaves 50% of the men with weights between those two values.)

Screening Data

Frequency tables, bar charts, and histograms can serve purposes other than summarizing data. Unexpected codes in the tables may indicate errors in data entry or coding. Cases with day of death coded as 0 or 8 are in error if the numbers 1 through 7 represent the days of the week and 9 stands for unknown. Since errors in the data should be eliminated as soon as possible, it is a good idea to run frequency tables as the first step in analyzing data.

Frequency tables and visual displays can also help you identify cases with values that are unusual but possibly correct. For example, a tally of the number of cars in families may show a family with 25 cars. Although such a value is possible, especially if the survey did not specify cars in working condition, it raises suspicion and should be examined to ensure that it is really correct.

Incorrect data values distort the results of statistical analyses, and correct but unusual values may require special treatment. In either case, early identification is valuable.

Running Procedure FREQUENCIES

FREQUENCIES produces frequency tables, bar charts (for discrete variables), histograms (for continuous variables), and various descriptive statistics (means, standard deviations, percentiles, and so forth). The only required subcommand is VARIABLES.

Specifying the Variables

The VARIABLES subcommand names the variables to be analyzed. Simply specify the names of the variables you want to analyze, as in:

```
FREQUENCIES VARIABLES=RAISE82 AGE DEPT.
```

No other specification or subcommand is needed when only frequency tables are desired. You can use keyword ALL to name all variables in the file, and keyword TO to refer to consecutive variables in the active file.

Format Options

You can control table formats and whether categories are sorted within a table with the FORMAT subcommand. This subcommand affects all of the variables listed on the VARIABLES subcommand. You can also use FORMAT to suppress the display of frequency tables. You can use only one FORMAT subcommand on a FREQUENCIES command, but you can specify several formatting options.

Table Formats

The following FORMAT keywords are used to control table formats:

NOLABELS   *Do not display value labels.* By default, FREQUENCIES displays the value labels defined by the VALUE LABELS command (see Chapter 7).

DOUBLE   *Double-space frequency tables.*

NEWPAGE   *Begin each table on a new page.* By default, FREQUENCIES displays as many tables on a page as it can.

CONDENSE   *Use condensed format.* Frequency counts are displayed in three columns. Value labels and percentages are not displayed, and valid and cumulative percentages are rounded off to integers.

ONEPAGE   *Use conditional condensed format.* ONEPAGE requests condensed format for tables that would require more than one page with the default format. All other tables are displayed in the default format. If CONDENSE and ONEPAGE are both specified, all tables are displayed in condensed format.

For example, the command

```
FREQUENCIES VARIABLES=RAISE82 AGE DEPT
  /FORMAT=NEWPAGE.
```

requests frequency tables for variables *RAISE82*, *AGE*, and *DEPT*. Each table begins on a new page.

Sorting Values

By default, numeric values in a frequency table are listed in ascending order and string values are listed in alphabetical order (keyword AVALUE). Three other sort sequences can be requested using one of the following keywords on the FORMAT subcommand:

DVALUE   *Sort values in descending order.*

AFREQ   *Sort values in ascending order of frequency.*

DFREQ   *Sort value in descending order of frequency.*

If more than one sorting method is requested, the last one specified is used. These keywords are ignored when HISTOGRAM, HBAR, NTILES, or PERCENTILES are requested.

Suppressing Tables

If you have a lot of variables with many values, or if you want only descriptive statistics (or histograms or bar charts), you may want to suppress the display of frequency tables. Use the following FORMAT keywords to do this:

LIMIT(n)   *Do not display tables for variables with more categories than the specified value.*

NOTABLE   *Suppress all frequency tables.*

If LIMIT and NOTABLE are both specified, no tables are displayed. When tables are suppressed, the number of cases with missing values and the number of cases with valid values are still displayed.

Requesting Bar Charts and Histograms

Both bar charts and histograms can be requested with one FREQUENCIES command. Use the BARCHART subcommand to obtain bar charts for all variables listed on the VARIABLES subcommand, and the HISTOGRAM subcommand to obtain histograms for all numeric variables. If you want only those bar charts that will fit on one page and histograms for all other numeric variables, use the HBAR subcommand.

Bar Charts

To obtain bar charts, use subcommand BARCHART. For example, the command

```
FREQUENCIES VARIABLES=DAYOFWK/BARCHART.
```

produces Figure 11.4. No further specifications are required.

By default, all tabulated values are plotted. The scale for the horizontal axis is based on frequencies and is determined by the largest frequency in the data. You can optionally specify minimum and maximum bounds for plotting, and you can base the horizontal scale on percentages. You can also specify the maximum frequency to be used for the horizontal scale.

MIN(n)   *Use the lower bound* n. Values below this minimum are not plotted.

MAX(n)   *Use the upper bound* n. Values above this maximum are not plotted.

PERCENT(n)   *Scale the horizontal axis in percentages with* n *as the maximum percentage.* If *n* is too small or not specified, SPSS/PC+ uses 5, 10, 25, 50, or 100, depending on the largest percentage in the data.

FREQ(n)   *Scale the horizontal axis in frequencies, with* n *as the maximum frequency.* If *n* is not specified, or if *n* is too small, SPSS/PC+ uses 5, 10, 20, 50, 100, 200, 500, 1000, 2000, and so on, depending on the largest frequency in the data.

These options can be entered in any order. For example, the command

```
FREQUENCIES VARIABLES=DAYOFWK/BARCHART MAX(5) MIN(2).
```

requests a bar chart for variable *DAYOFWK* for values from 2 through 5.

Histograms

To obtain histograms, specify the HISTOGRAM subcommand. No further specifications are required, although several format options are available. By default, all tabulated values are included, the horizontal axis is scaled by frequencies, and the scale is determined by the largest frequency in the data. The default number of intervals is 21 (or fewer if the range of values is less than 21).

All of the format specifications described for the BARCHART subcommand above can be used with HISTOGRAM to alter the histogram format. In addition, you can specify the interval width and superimpose a normal curve on the histogram by using the following optional specifications:

INCREMENT(n)   *Use an interval width equal to* n.

NORMAL   *Superimpose a normal curve.* A normal curve with the same mean and variance as the plotted variable is superimposed on the histogram. All valid values, including those excluded by MIN and MAX, are used in calculating the mean and variance.

HISTOGRAM specifications can be entered in any order. For example, the command

```
FREQUENCIES  VARIABLES=WT58/ FORMAT=NOTABLE
  /HISTOGRAM MIN(120) MAX(280) INCREMENT(10).
```

produces the output in Figure 11.5.

HBAR Subcommand

When the HBAR subcommand is used, bar charts are displayed for numeric variables if the chart will fit on one page; otherwise, HBAR produces a histogram. HBAR produces bar charts for short string variables and for the short-string portion of long string variables, regardless of the number of values.

All format options available for HISTOGRAM can be used with HBAR.

Requesting Percentiles and Ntiles

To obtain percentiles (the values below which given percentages of cases fall), specify PERCENTILES followed by an optional equals sign and a list of percentages. For example, the command

```
FREQUENCIES VARIABLES=VARZ/PERCENTILES=10 25 33.3 66.7 75.
```

requests the values for percentiles 10, 25, 33.3, 66.7, and 75 for variable *VARZ*. When a requested percentile cannot be calculated, a period is displayed.

To obtain ntiles (the values that divide the sample into groups with equal numbers of cases), specify NTILES followed by an optional equals sign and an integer indicating the number of subgroups. For example, the command

```
FREQUENCIES VARIABLES=VARZ /NTILES=4.
```

requests quartiles (percentiles 25, 50, and 75) for variable *VARZ*.

The PERCENTILES and NTILES subcommands produce percentiles for all variables specified on the VARIABLES subcommand. If more than one PERCENTILES or NTILES subcommand is specified, one table with the values for all requested percentiles is displayed.

Optional Statistics

To request optional statistics, use the STATISTICS subcommand. The statistics are produced for all variables listed on the VARIABLES subcommand. The following keywords are available:

MEAN	*Mean.*
SEMEAN	*Standard error of the mean.*
MEDIAN	*Median.* The median is not available if AFREQ or DFREQ is specified in the FORMAT subcommand.
MODE	*Mode.*
STDDEV	*Standard deviation.*
VARIANCE	*Variance.*

SKEWNESS   *Skewness.*

SESKEW   *Standard error of the skewness statistic.*

KURTOSIS   *Kurtosis.*

SEKURT   *Standard error of the kurtosis statistic.*

RANGE   *Range.*

MINIMUM   *Minimum.*

MAXIMUM   *Maximum.*

SUM   *Sum.*

DEFAULT   *Mean, standard deviation, minimum, and maximum.*

ALL   *All available statistics.*

NONE   *No statistics.*

You can specify as many keywords as you want on the STATISTICS subcommand. For example, the command

```
FREQUENCIES VARIABLES=RAISE82 AGE
  /STATISTICS=MEAN SKEWNESS RANGE SUM.
```

requests the mean, skewness, range, and sum for variables *RAISE82* and *AGE*.

If STATISTICS is specified without any keywords, the default statistics are displayed.

Missing Values

Both user-missing and system-missing values are included in frequency tables. They are labeled as missing and are not included in the valid or cumulative percentages. They are also not used in calculating descriptive statistics and do not appear in bar charts or histograms.

One optional missing-value treatment is available. This option is requested with the keyword INCLUDE on the MISSING subcommand.

INCLUDE   *Include cases with user-missing values.* Cases with user-missing values
            are included in the percentages, statistics, and plots.

12 Descriptive Statistics: Procedure DESCRIPTIVES

Survey data that rely on voluntary information are subject to many sources of error. People fail to recall events correctly, deliberately distort the truth, or refuse to participate. Refusals influence survey results by failing to provide information about certain types of people—those who refuse to answer surveys at all and those who avoid certain questions. For example, if college graduates tend to be unwilling to answer polls, results of surveys will be biased.

One possible way to examine the veracity of survey responses is to compare them to similar data recorded in official records. Systematic differences between actual data and self-reported responses jeopardize the usefulness of the survey. Unfortunately, in many sensitive areas illicit drug use, abortion history, or even income—official records are usually unavailable.

Wyner (1980) examined the differences between the actual and self-reported numbers of arrests obtained from 79 former heroin addicts enrolled in the Vera Institute of Justice Supported Employment Experiment. As part of their regular quarterly interviews, participants were asked about their arrest histories in New York City. The self-reported value was compared to arrest-record data coded from New York City Police Department arrest sheets. The goal of the study was not only to quantify the extent of error but also to identify factors related to inaccurate responses.

Examining the Data

Figure 12.1 shows histograms for the following three variables—actual number of arrests, self-reported number of arrests, and the difference of the two. From a histogram, it is possible to see the shape of the distribution; that is, how likely the different values are, how much spread, or **variability**, there is among the values, and where typical values are concentrated. Such characteristics are important because of the direct insight they provide into the data and because many statistical procedures are based on assumptions about the underlying distributions of variables.

Figure 12.1   Self-reported and actual arrests

```
GET FILE='ARREST.SYS'.
FREQUENCIES VARIABLES=ACTUAL /FORMAT NOTABLE
 /HISTOGRAM MIN(0) MAX (30) INCREMENT (2).
```

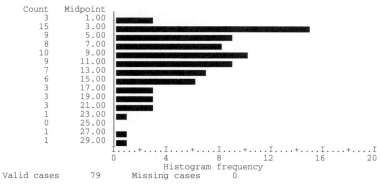

```
ACTUAL        ACTUAL NUMBER OF ARRESTS

     Count   Midpoint
         3    1.00
        15    3.00
         9    5.00
         8    7.00
        10    9.00
         9   11.00
         7   13.00
         6   15.00
         3   17.00
         3   19.00
         3   21.00
         1   23.00
         0   25.00
         1   27.00
         1   29.00
               I....+....I....+....I....+....I....+....I....+....I
               0        4        8       12       16       20
                              Histogram frequency
Valid cases      79    Missing cases       0
```

```
FREQUENCIES /VARIABLES SELF /FORMAT NOTABLE
 /HISTOGRAM MIN (0) MAX (26) INCREMENT (2).
```

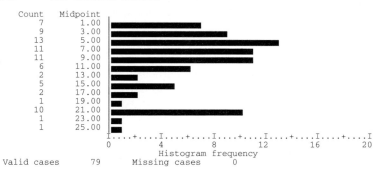

```
SELF       SELF-REPORTED ARRESTS

     Count   Midpoint
         7    1.00
         9    3.00
        13    5.00
        11    7.00
        11    9.00
         6   11.00
         2   13.00
         5   15.00
         2   17.00
         1   19.00
        10   21.00
         1   23.00
         1   25.00
               I....+....I....+....I....+....I....+....I....+....I
               0        4        8       12       16       20
                              Histogram frequency
Valid cases      79    Missing cases       0
```

```
FREQUENCIES /VARIABLES ERRORS /FORMAT NOTABLE
 /HISTOGRAM MIN (-15) MAX (17) INCREMENT (2).
```

```
ERRORS     REPORTED ARRESTS MINUS ACTUAL ARRESTS
```

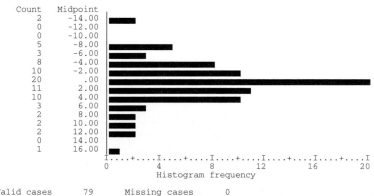

```
     Count   Midpoint
         2  -14.00
         0  -12.00
         0  -10.00
         5   -8.00
         3   -6.00
         8   -4.00
        10   -2.00
        20     .00
        11    2.00
        10    4.00
         3    6.00
         2    8.00
         2   10.00
         2   12.00
         0   14.00
         1   16.00
               I....+....I....+....I....+....I....+....I....+....I
               0        4        8       12       16       20
                              Histogram frequency

Valid cases      79    Missing cases       0
```

The distributions of the self-reported and actual number of arrests have a somewhat similar shape. Neither distribution has an obvious central value, although the self-reported values peak at 4 to 5 arrests, while the actual number of arrests peaks at 2 to 3 arrests. The distribution of self-reported arrests peaks again at 20 to 21 arrests. The peaks corresponding to intervals containing 5, 15, and 20 arrests arouse suspicion that people may be more likely to report their arrest records as round numbers. Examination of the actual number of arrests shows no corresponding peaks at multiples of five.

The distribution of the differences between reported and actual number of arrests is not as irregularly shaped as the two distributions from which it is derived. It has a peak at the interval with a midpoint of 0. Most cases cluster around the peak values, and cases far from these values are infrequent.

Summarizing the Data

Although frequency tables and bar charts are useful for summarizing and displaying data (see Chapter 11), further condensation and description is often desirable. A variety of summary measures that convey information about the data in single numbers can be computed. The choice of summary measure, or statistic, depends upon characteristics of both the data and the statistic. One important characteristic of the data that must be considered is the level of measurement of each variable being studied.

Levels of Measurement

Measurement is the assignment of numbers or codes to observations. **Levels of measurement** are distinguished by ordering and distance properties. A computer does not know what measurement underlies the values it is given. You must determine the level of measurement of your data and apply appropriate statistical techniques.

The traditional classification of levels of measurement into nominal, ordinal, interval, and ratio scales was developed by S. S. Stevens (1946). This remains the basic typology and is the one used throughout this manual. Variations exist, however, and issues concerning the statistical effect of ignoring levels of measurement have been debated (for example, see Borgatta & Bohrnstedt, 1980).

Nominal Measurement

The **nominal** level of measurement is the "lowest" in the typology because no assumptions are made about relations between values. Each value defines a distinct category and serves merely as a label or name (hence, *nominal* level) for the category. For instance, the birthplace of an individual is a nominal variable. For most purposes, there is no inherent ordering among cities or towns. Although cities can be ordered according to size, density, or air pollution, as birthplaces they cannot be ordered or ranked against other cities. When numeric values are attached to nominal categories, they are merely identifiers. None of the properties of numbers, such as relative size, addition, or multiplication, can be applied to these numerically coded categories. Therefore, statistics that assume ordering or meaningful numerical distances between the values do not ordinarily give useful information about nominal variables.

Ordinal Measurement

When it is possible to rank or order all categories according to some criterion, the **ordinal** level of measurement is achieved. For instance, classifying employees into clerical, supervisory, and managerial categories is an ordering according to responsibilities or skills. Each category has a position lower or higher than another category. Furthermore, knowing that supervisory is higher than clerical and that managerial is higher than supervisory automatically means that managerial is higher than clerical. However, nothing is known about how much higher; no distance is measured. Ordering is the sole mathematical property applicable to ordinal measurements, and the use of numeric values does not imply that any other property of numbers is applicable.

Interval Measurement

In addition to order, **interval** measurements have the property of meaningful distance between values. A thermometer, for example, measures temperature in degrees that are the same size at any point on the scale. The difference between 20°C and 21°C is the same as the difference between 5°C and 6°C. However, an interval scale does not have an inherently determined zero point. In the familiar Celsius and Fahrenheit systems, 0° is determined by an agreed-upon definition, not by the absence of heat. Consequently, interval-level measurement allows us to study differences between items but not their proportionate magnitudes. For example, it is incorrect to say that 80°F is twice as hot as 40°F.

Ratio Measurement

Ratio measurements have all the ordering and distance properties of an interval scale. In addition, a zero point can be meaningfully designated. In measuring physical distances between objects using feet or meters, a zero distance is naturally defined as the absence of any distance. The existence of a zero point means that ratio comparisons can be made. For example, it is quite meaningful to say that a 6-foot-tall adult is twice as tall as a 3-foot-tall child or that a 500-meter race is five times as long as a 100-meter race.

Because ratio measurements satisfy all the properties of the real number system, any mathematical manipulations appropriate for real numbers can be applied to ratio measures. However, the existence of a zero point is seldom critical for statistical analyses.

Summary Statistics

Figure 12.2 and Figure 12.3 contain a variety of summary statistics that are useful in describing the distributions of self-reported and actual numbers of arrests, and their difference. The statistics can be grouped into three categories according to what they quantify: central tendency, dispersion, and shape.

Figure 12.2 was obtained with the DESCRIPTIVES procedure; Figure 12.3, with the FREQUENCIES procedure. If your computer has a math coprocessor, the DESCRIPTIVES procedure is faster than the FREQUENCIES procedure. However, the median and mode are not available with DESCRIPTIVES.

Figure 12.2   Summary statistics from the DESCRIPTIVES procedure

```
DESCRIPTIVES VARIABLES=ACTUAL SELF ERRORS /STATISTICS ALL.

Variable  ACTUAL      ACTUAL NUMBER OF ARRESTS

Mean            9.253           S.E. Mean         .703
Std Dev         6.248           Variance        39.038
Kurtosis         .597           S.E. Kurt         .535
Skewness         .908           S.E. Skew         .271
Range         28.000            Minimum              1
Maximum          29             Sum           731.000

Valid observations -      79    Missing observations -        0

- - - - - - - - - - - - - - - - - - - - - - - - - - - - - - -

Variable  SELF        SELF-REPORTED ARRESTS

Mean            8.962           S.E. Mean         .727
Std Dev         6.458           Variance        41.704
Kurtosis        -.485           S.E. Kurt         .535
Skewness         .750           S.E. Skew         .271
Range         25.000            Minimum              0
Maximum          25             Sum           708.000

Valid observations -      79    Missing observations -        0

- - - - - - - - - - - - - - - - - - - - - - - - - - - - - - -

Variable  ERRORS      REPORTED ARRESTS MINUS ACTUAL ARRESTS

Mean            -.291           S.E. Mean         .587
Std Dev         5.216           Variance        27.209
Kurtosis        1.102           S.E. Kurt         .535
Skewness         .125           S.E. Skew         .271
Range         29.000            Minimum        -14.000
Maximum          15             Sum            -23.000

Valid observations -      79    Missing observations -        0
```

Figure 12.3   Summary statistics from the FREQUENCIES procedure

```
FREQUENCIES VARIABLES=ACTUAL SELF ERRORS /FORMAT NOTABLE /STATISTICS ALL.

ACTUAL     ACTUAL NUMBER OF ARRESTS


Mean          9.253    Std err        .703    Median      8.000
Mode          3.000    Std dev       6.248    Variance   39.038
Kurtosis       .597    S E Kurt       .535    Skewness     .908
S E Skew       .271    Range       28.000    Minimum     1.000
Maximum      29.000    Sum        731.000


Valid cases      79    Missing cases      0

- - - - - - - - - - - - - - - - - - - - - - - - - - - - - - - -

SELF       SELF-REPORTED ARRESTS


Mean          8.962    Std err        .727    Median      7.000
Mode          5.000    Std dev       6.458    Variance   41.704
Kurtosis      -.485    S E Kurt       .535    Skewness     .750
S E Skew       .271    Range       25.000    Minimum      .000
Maximum      25.000    Sum        708.000


Valid cases      79    Missing cases      0


ERRORS     REPORTED ARRESTS MINUS ACTUAL ARRESTS


Mean          -.291    Std err        .587    Median       .000
Mode         -1.000    Std dev       5.216    Variance   27.209
Kurtosis      1.102    S E Kurt       .535    Skewness     .125
S E Skew       .271    Range       29.000    Minimum   -14.000
Maximum      15.000    Sum        -23.000

* Multiple modes exist.  The smallest value is shown.

Valid cases      79    Missing cases      0
```

Measures of Central Tendency

The mean, median, and mode are frequently used to describe the location of a distribution. The **mode** is the most frequently occurring value (or values). For the actual number of arrests, the mode is 3; for the self-reported values, it is 5. The distribution of the difference between the actual and self-reported values is multimodal. That is, it has more than one mode since the values −1 and 0 occur with equal frequency. SPSS/PC+, however, displays only one of the modes, the smaller value, as shown in Figure 12.3. The mode can be used for data measured at any level. It is not usually the preferred measure for interval and ordinal data, since it ignores much of the available information.

The **median** is the value above and below which one half of the observations fall. For example, if there are 79 observations, the median is the 40th-largest observation. When there is an even number of observations, no unique center value exists, so the mean of the two middle observations is usually taken as the median value. For the arrest data, the median is 0 for the differences, 8 for the actual arrests, and 7 for self-reported arrests.

For ordinal data, the median is usually a good measure of central tendency, since it uses the ranking information. The median should not be used for nominal data, since ranking of the observations is not possible.

The **mean**, also called the arithmetic average, is the sum of the values of all observations divided by the number of observations. Thus

$$\bar{X} = \sum_{i=1}^{N} \frac{X_i}{N}$$

Equation 12.1

where N is the number of cases and X_i is the value of the variable for the ith case. Since the mean uses the distance between observations, the measurements should be interval or ratio. Calculating the mean race, religion, and car color provides no useful information. For dichotomous variables coded as 0 and 1, the mean has a special interpretation: it is the proportion of cases coded 1 in the data.

The three measures of central tendency need not be the same. For example, the mean number of actual arrests is 9.25, the median is 8, and the mode is 3. The arithmetic mean is greatly influenced by outlying observations, while the median is not. Adding a single case with 400 arrests would increase the mean from 9.25 to 14.1, but it would not affect the median. Therefore, if there are values far removed from the rest of the observations, the median may be a better measure of central tendency than the mean.

For symmetric distributions, the observed mean, median, and mode are usually close in value. For example, the mean of the differences between self-reported and actual arrest values is -0.291, the median is 0, and the modes are -1 and 0. All three measures give similar estimates of central tendency in this case.

Measures of Dispersion

Two distributions can have the same values for measures of central tendency and yet be very dissimilar in other respects. For example, if the actual number of arrests for five cases in two methadone clinics is 0, 1, 10, 14, 20 for clinic A, and 8, 8, 9, 10, 10 for clinic B, the mean number of arrests (9) is the same in both. However, even a cursory examination of the data indicates that the two clinics are different. In clinic B, all cases have fairly comparable arrest records, while in clinic A, the records are quite disparate. A quick and useful index of dissimilarity, or dispersion, is the **range**. It is the difference between the maximum and minimum observed values. For clinic B the range is 2, while for clinic A it is 20. Since the range is computed from only the minimum and maximum values, it is sensitive to extremes.

Although the range is a useful index of dispersion, especially for ordinal data, it does not take into account the distribution of observations between the maximum and minimum. A commonly used measure of variation that is based on all observations is the **variance**. For a sample, the variance is computed by summing the squared differences from the mean for all observations and then dividing by one less than the number of observations. In mathematical notation, this is

$$S^2 = \sum_{i=1}^{N} \frac{(X_i - \bar{X})^2}{N-1}$$

Equation 12.2

If all observations are identical—that is, if there is no variation—-the variance is 0. The more spread out they are, the greater the variance. For the methadone clinic example above, the sample variance for clinic A is 73, while for clinic B it is 1.

The square root of the variance is termed the **standard deviation**. While the variance is expressed in squared units, the standard deviation is expressed in the same units of measurement as the observations. This is an appealing property, since it is much clearer to think of variability in terms of the number of arrests rather than the number of arrests squared.

The Normal Distribution

For many variables, most observations are concentrated near the middle of the distribution. As distance from the central concentration increases, the frequency of observations decreases. Such distributions are often described as "bell-shaped." An example is the **normal distribution** (see Figure 12.4). A broad range of observed phenomena in nature and in society is approximately normally distributed. For example, the distributions of variables such as height, weight, and blood pressure are approximately normal. The normal distribution is by far the most important theoretical distribution in statistics and serves as a reference point for describing the form of many distributions of sample data.

The normal distribution is symmetric: each half is a mirror image of the other. Three measures of central tendency—the mean, median, and mode—coincide exactly. As shown in Figure 12.4, 95% of all observations fall within two standard deviations (σ) of the mean (μ) and 68% fall within one standard deviation. The exact theoretical proportion of cases falling into various regions of the normal curve can be found in tables included in most introductory statistics textbooks.

Figure 12.4   A normal curve

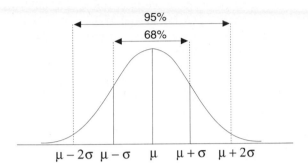

In SPSS/PC+, you can superimpose a normal distribution on a histogram. Consider Figure 12.5, a histogram of the differences in self-reported and actual arrests. The curved line indicates what the distribution of cases would be if the variable had a normal distribution with the same mean and variance. Tests for normality are available in the EXAMINE procedure (see Chapter 13).

Figure 12.5   Histogram with normal curve superimposed

```
FREQUENCIES VARIABLES=ERRORS /FORMAT=NOTABLE /HISTOGRAM=NORMAL.
```

ERRORS   REPORTED ARRESTS MINUS ACTUAL ARRESTS

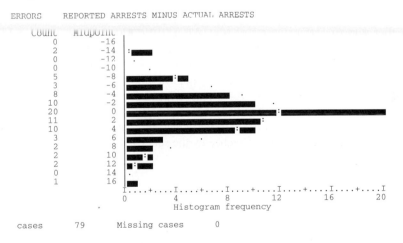

cases   79   Missing cases   0

Measures of Shape

A distribution that is not symmetric but has more cases (more of a "tail") toward one end of the distribution than the other is said to be **skewed**. If the tail is toward larger values, the distribution is positively skewed, or skewed to the right. If the tail is toward smaller values, the distribution is negatively skewed, or skewed to the left.

Another characteristic of the form of a distribution is called **kurtosis**—the extent to which, for a given standard deviation, observations cluster around a central point. If cases within a distribution cluster more than those in the normal distribution (that is, the distribution is more peaked), the distribution is called **leptokurtic**. A leptokurtic distribution also tends to have more observations straggling into the extreme tails than does a normal distribution. If cases cluster less than in the normal distribution (that is, it is flatter), the distribution is termed **platykurtic**.

Although examination of a histogram provides some indication of possible skewness and kurtosis, it is often desirable to compute formal indexes that measure these properties. Values for skewness and kurtosis are 0 if the observed distribution is exactly normal. Positive values for skewness indicate a positive skew, while positive values for kurtosis indicate a distribution that is more peaked than normal. Measures of skewness and kurtosis for samples from a normal distribution typically will not be exactly zero but will fluctuate around zero because of sampling variation.

Standard Scores

It is often desirable to describe the relative position of an observation within a distribution. Knowing that a person achieved a score of 80 in a competitive examination conveys little information about performance. Judgment of performance would depend on whether 80 was the lowest, the median, or the highest score.

One way of describing the location of a case in a distribution is to calculate its **standard score**. This score, sometimes called the **Z score**, indicates how many standard deviations above or below the mean an observation falls. It is calculated by finding the difference between the value of a particular observation X_i and the mean of the distribution, and dividing this difference by the standard deviation:

$$Z_i = \frac{X_i - \bar{X}}{S}$$

Equation 12.3

The mean of Z scores is 0 and the standard deviation is 1. For example, a participant with 5 actual arrests would have a Z score of $(5 - 9.25)/6.25$, or -0.68. Since the score is negative, the case had fewer arrests than the average for the individuals studied. Figure

12.6 shows summary statistics for Z scores based on the difference between actual and self-reported arrests.

Figure 12.6   Summary statistics for Z scores

```
DESCRIPTIVES VARIABLES=ZERRORS /STATISTICS ALL.

Variable   ZERRORS     Zscore:  REPORTED ARRESTS MINUS ACTUAL

Mean             .000         S.E. Mean        .113
Std Dev         1.000         Variance        1.000
Kurtosis        1.102         S.E. Kurt        .535
Skewness         .125         S.E. Skew        .271
Range           5.560         Minimum      -2.62812
Maximum       2.93146         Sum              .000
```

Standardization permits comparison of scores from different distributions. For example, an individual with Z scores of −0.68 for actual arrests and 1.01 for the difference between self-reported and actual arrests had fewer arrests than the average but exaggerated more than the average.

When the distribution of a variable is approximately normal and the mean and variance are known or are estimated from large samples, the Z score of an observation provides more specific information about its location. For example, if actual arrests and response error were normally distributed, 75% of cases would have more arrests than the example individual, but only 16% would have exaggerated as much as the example individual (75% of a standard normal curve lies above a Z score of −0.68, and 16% lies above a score of 1.01).

Who Lies?

The distribution of the difference between self-reported and actual arrests indicates that response error exists. Although observing a mean close to zero is comforting, misrepresentation is obvious. What, then, are the characteristics that influence willingness to be truthful?

Wyner identifies three factors that are related to inaccuracies: the number of arrests before 1960, the number of multiple-charge arrests, and the perceived desirability of being arrested. The first factor is related to a frequently encountered difficulty—the more distant an event in time, the less likely it is to be correctly recalled. The second factor, underreporting of multiple-charge arrests, is probably caused by the general social undesirability of serious arrests. Finally, persons who view arrest records as laudatory are likely to inflate their accomplishments.

Running Procedure DESCRIPTIVES

Procedure DESCRIPTIVES calculates all of the statistics provided by procedure FRE-QUENCIES, except the median and the mode, and presents them in a compact table. Because it does not sort values into a frequency table, it is an efficient procedure for computing descriptive statistics.

DESCRIPTIVES requires a list of variables for which statistics are to be computed. The optional STATISTICS subcommand indicates the statistics to be computed, and the OPTIONS subcommand specifies treatment of missing values and format options.

Descriptive statistics can be computed only for numeric variables. If a string variable is specified in the variable list, a warning is issued and no statistics are displayed for that variable.

Specifying the Variables

The VARIABLES subcommand specifies the variables for which statistics are to be calculated. For example, to calculate the default statistics (mean, standard deviation, minimum, and maximum) for variables *ACTUAL*, *SELF*, and *ERRORS*, specify

```
DESCRIPTIVES VARIABLES=ACTUAL SELF ERRORS.
```

The actual keyword VARIABLES can be omitted, as in:

```
DESCRIPTIVES ACTUAL SELF ERRORS.
```

Figure 12.7 shows the output from this command.

Figure 12.7   Default statistics available with DESCRIPTIVES

```
Number of Valid Observations (Listwise) =        79.00

Variable       Mean    Std Dev   Minimum   Maximum     N  Label

ACTUAL         9.25     6.25       1.00     29.00      79  ACTUAL NUMBER OF ARRESTS
SELF           8.96     6.46       0.0      25.00      79  SELF-REPORTED ARRESTS
ERRORS         -.29     5.22     -14.00     15.00      79  REPORTED ARRESTS MINUS
ACTUAL ARRESTS
```

You can also use keyword TO to refer to a set of consecutive variables in the active file, and keyword ALL to refer to all user-defined variables.

Optional Statistics

By default, DESCRIPTIVES calculates the mean, standard deviation, minimum, and maximum. Additional statistics can be requested with the STATISTICS subcommand:

Statistic 1   *Mean.*

Statistic 2   *Standard error of mean.*

Statistic 5 *Standard deviation.*

Statistic 6 *Variance.*

Statistic 7 *Kurtosis and the standard error of kurtosis.*

Statistic 8 *Skewness and the standard error of the skewness.*

Statistic 9 *Range.*

Statistic 10 *Minimum.*

Statistic 11 *Maximum.*

Statistic 12 *Sum.*

Statistic 13 *Mean, standard deviation, minimum, and maximum.* This is the same as the default.

ALL *All available statistics.*

If the STATISTICS subcommand is specified, only the statistics requested are displayed. If you are using the STATISTICS subcommand, you can specify Statistic 13 to get the default statistics.

Missing Values

By default, DESCRIPTIVES includes only cases with valid values for a variable in the calculation of statistics for that variable. Use one of the following options on the OPTIONS subcommand for alternative treatments of missing values.

Option 1 *Include user-missing values.* Cases that have user-missing values are included in the calculation of statistics for all variables named on the command.

Option 5 *Exclude missing values listwise.* A case with missing values for any of the variables is excluded from computations for all of the variables.

Format Options

By default, DESCRIPTIVES displays the statistics and a 40-character variable label for each variable on one line. If the statistics requested do not fit within the available width, DESCRIPTIVES first truncates the variable label and then uses serial format. (You can use the SET command to change the width of the display.)

You can request any of the following on the OPTIONS subcommand:

Option 2 *Suppress variable labels.*

Option 6   *Use serial format.* The requested statistics are displayed below each variable name, permitting larger field widths and more decimal places for very large or very small numbers.

Option 7   *Use narrow format.* The output is restricted to 79 columns, regardless of the width defined on SET.

Option 8   *Suppress variable names.* The variable name is displayed only if there is no variable label.

13 Exploring Data: Procedure EXAMINE

The first step of data analysis should always be a detailed examination of the data. Whether the problem you're solving is simple or complex, whether you're planning to do a *t* test or a multivariate repeated measures analysis of variance, you should first take a careful look at the data. In this chapter, we'll consider a variety of descriptive statistics and displays useful as a preliminary step in data analysis. Using the EXAMINE procedure, you can screen your data, visually examine the distributions of values for various groups, and test for normality and homogeneity of variance.

Reasons for Exploring Data

There are several important reasons for examining your data carefully before you begin your analysis. Let's start with the simplest.

Identifying Mistakes

Data must make a hazardous journey before finding final rest in a computer file. First, a measurement is made or a response elicited, sometimes with a faulty instrument or by a careless experimenter. The result is then recorded, often barely legibly, in a lab notebook, medical chart, or personnel record. Often this information is not actually coded and entered onto a data form until much later. From this form, the numbers must find their way into their designated slot in the computer file. Then they must be properly introduced to a computer program. Their correct location and missing values must be specified.

Errors can be introduced at any step. Some errors are easy to spot. For example, forgetting to declare a value as missing, using an invalid code, or entering the value 701 for age will be apparent from a frequency table. Other errors, such as entering an age of 54 instead of 45, may be difficult, if not impossible, to spot. Unless your first step is to carefully check your data for mistakes, errors may contaminate all of your analyses.

Exploring the Data

After completing data acquisition, entry, and checking, it's time to look at the data—not to search haphazardly for statistical significance, but to examine the data systematically using simple exploratory techniques. Why bother, you might ask? Why not just begin your analysis?

Data analysis has often been compared to detective work. Before the actual trial of a hypothesis, there is much evidence to be gathered and sifted. Based on the clues, the hypothesis itself may be altered, or the methods for testing it may have to be changed. For example, if the distribution of data values reveals a gap—that is, a range where no values occur—we must ask why. If some values are extreme (far removed from the other values), we must look for reasons. If the pattern of numbers is strange (for example, if all values are even), we must determine why. If we see unexpected variability in the data, we must look for possible explanations; perhaps there are additional variables that may explain it.

Preparing for Hypothesis Testing

Looking at the distribution of the values is also important for evaluating the appropriateness of the statistical techniques we are planning to use for hypothesis testing or model building. Perhaps the data must be transformed so that the distribution is approximately normal or so that the variances in the groups are similar; or perhaps a nonparametric technique is needed.

Ways of Displaying Data

Now that we've established why it's important to look at data, we'll consider some of the techniques available for exploring data. One technique is to create a graphical representation of the data. To illustrate, we'll use data from a study of coronary heart disease among male employees of Western Electric and salary data from a study of employees of a bank engaged in Equal Employment Opportunity litigation.

The Histogram

The **histogram** is commonly used to represent data graphically. The range of observed values is subdivided into equal intervals, and the number of cases in each interval is obtained. Each bar in the histogram represents the number of cases with values within the interval.

Figure 13.1 is a histogram of diastolic blood pressure for a sample of 239 men from the Western Electric study. The first column, labeled *Frequency*, is the number of cases with values in the intervals. The second column, *Bin Center*, is the midpoint of each of the bins. For example, the midpoint of the first bin is 67.5. The text underneath the histogram shows that the length of each bin is 5. Thus, the first interval contains cases with diastolic blood pressures between 65 and 70. Cases with diastolic blood pressure between 70 and 75 go in the next interval. The last bin center is labeled 122.5 and includes cases with values between 120 and 125.

Figure 13.1   Histogram of diastolic blood pressure

```
GET FILE 'ELECTRIC.SYS'.
EXAMINE VARIABLES=DBP58 /PLOT HISTOGRAM.

 Frequency    Bin Center

     7.00        67.5    *******
    13.00        72.5    *************
    32.00        77.5    ********************************
    44.00        82.5    ********************************************
    45.00        87.5    *********************************************
    31.00        92.5    *******************************
    27.00        97.5    ***************************
    13.00       102.5    *************
    11.00       107.5    ***********
     5.00       112.5    *****
     5.00       117.5    *****
     2.00       122.5    **
     4.00     Extremes   ****

 Bin width :      5.0
 Each star:        1 case(s)
```

The last row of the histogram is for cases whose values are much larger than the rest. These are labeled *Extremes*. The reason the histogram is not extended to accommodate these cases is to avoid having too many intervals, or intervals that are very wide. For example, if there is a person with a diastolic blood pressure of 200, the histogram would have a lot of empty bins between the bin centers of 122.5 and 202.5. Of course, we could have fewer bins and make them wider, but this would obscure potentially interesting information. That's why the histogram contains a special bin for very large and very small values.

The Stem-and-Leaf Plot

A display closely related to the histogram is the stem-and-leaf plot. The **stem-and-leaf plot** provides more information about the actual values than does a histogram. Consider Figure 13.2, which is a stem-and-leaf plot of the diastolic blood pressures. As in a histogram, the length of each row corresponds to the number of cases that fall into a particular interval. However, the stem-and-leaf plot represents each case with a numeric value that corresponds to the actual observed value. This is done by dividing observed values into two components—the leading digit or digits, called the **stem**, and a trailing digit, called the **leaf**. For example, the value 75 has a stem of 7 and a leaf of 5.

Figure 13.2   Stem-and-leaf plot of diastolic blood pressure

```
SET LENGTH=59.
EXAMINE VARIABLES=DBP58 /PLOT=STEMLEAF.


Frequency     Stem &  Leaf

      .00         6 *
     7.00         6 .  5558889
    13.00         7 *  0000111223344
    32.00         7 .  55555555566777777777777788888889999
    44.00         8 *  00000000000000000000001111122222333333334444
    45.00         8 .  555555555556666666777777777777777788888999999999
    31.00         9 *  0000000001111111122222222333334
    27.00         9 .  556666667777778888888888899999
    13.00        10 *  0000122233333
    11.00        10 .  55555577899
     5.00        11 *  00003
     5.00        11 .  55789
     2.00        12 *  01
     4.00 Extremes     (125), (133), (160)

Stem width:   10
Each leaf:     1 case(s)
```

In this example, each stem is divided into two rows. The first row of each pair has cases with leaves of 0 through 4, while the second row has cases with leaves of 5 through 9. Consider the two rows that correspond to the stem of 11. In the first row, we can see that there are four cases with diastolic blood pressure of 110 and one case with a reading of 113. In the next row, there are two cases with a value of 115 and one case each with a value of 117, 118, and 119.

The last row of the stem-and-leaf plot is for cases with extreme values (values far removed from the rest). In this row, the actual values are displayed in parentheses. In the frequency column, we see that there are four extreme cases. Their values are 125, 133, and 160. Only distinct values are listed.

To identify cases with extreme values, you can generate a table identifying cases with the largest and smallest values. Figure 13.3 shows the cases with the five largest and five smallest values for diastolic blood pressure. Values of a case-labeling variable can be used to identify cases. Otherwise, the sequence of the case in the active file is reported.

Figure 13.3   Cases with extreme values

```
EXAMINE VARIABLES=DBP58 /STATISTICS=EXTREME.


                            Extreme Values
                            ------- ------

    5    Highest     Case #        5    Lowest    Case #

         160      Case: 120             65     Case: 73
         133      Case: 56              65     Case: 156
         125      Case: 163             65     Case: 157
         125      Case: 42              68     Case: 153
         121      Case: 26              68     Case: 175
```

Other Stems

In Figure 13.2, each stem was divided into two parts—one for leaves of 0 through 4, the other for leaves of 5 through 9. When there are few stems, it is sometimes useful to subdivide each stem even further. Consider Figure 13.4, a stem-and-leaf plot of cholesterol levels for the men in the Western Electric study. In this figure, stems 2 and 3 are divided into five parts, each representing two leaf values. The first row, designated by an asterisk, is for leaves of 0 and 1; the next, designated by *t*, is for leaves of 2's and 3's; the third, designated by *f*, is for leaves of 4's and 5's; the fourth, designated by *s,* is for leaves of 6's and 7's; and the fifth, designated by a period, is for leaves of 8's and 9's. Rows without cases are not represented in the plot. For example, in Figure 13.4, the first two rows for stem 1 (corresponding to 0–1 and 2–3) are omitted.

This stem-and-leaf plot differs from the previous one in another way. Since cholesterol values have a wide range—from 106 to 515 in this example—using the first two digits for the stem would result in an unnecessarily detailed plot. Therefore, the plot uses only the hundreds digit as the stem, rather than the first two digits. The stem setting of 100 appears underneath the plot. The leaf is then the tens digit. The last digit is ignored. Thus, from this stem-and-leaf plot, it is not possible to determine the exact cholesterol level for a case. Instead, each case is classified by only its first two digits.

Figure 13.4   Stem-and-leaf plot of cholesterol levels

```
SET LENGTH=59.
EXAMINE VARIABLES=CHOL58 /PLOT=STEMLEAF.


Frequency      Stem & Leaf

     1.00  Extremes    (106)
     2.00         1  f  55
     6.00         1  s  677777
    12.00         1  .  888889999999
    23.00         2  *  00000000000001111111111
    36.00         2  t  222222222222222233333333333333333333
    35.00         2  f  44444444444444444455555555555555555
    42.00         2  s  666666666666666666666677777777777777777777
    28.00         2  .  8888888888888889999999999999
    18.00         3  *  000000011111111111
    17.00         3  t  22222222222233333
     9.00         3  f  444445555
     6.00         3  s  666777
     1.00         3  .  8
     3.00  Extremes    (393), (425), (515)

Stem width:   100
Each leaf:     1 case(s)
```

The Boxplot

Both the histogram and the stem-and-leaf plot provide useful information about the distribution of observed values. We can see how tightly cases cluster together. We can see if there is a single peak or several peaks. We can determine if there are extreme values.

A display that further summarizes information about the distribution of the values is the boxplot. Instead of plotting the actual values, a **boxplot** displays summary statistics for the distribution. It plots the median, the 25th percentile, the 75th percentile, and values that are far removed from the rest.

Figure 13.5 shows an annotated sketch of a boxplot. The lower boundary of the box is the 25th percentile and the upper boundary is the 75th percentile. (These percentiles, sometimes called Tukey's hinges, are calculated a little differently from ordinary percentiles.) The asterisk inside the box represents the median. Fifty percent of the cases have values within the box. The length of the box corresponds to the interquartile range, which is the difference between the 75th and 25th percentiles.

The boxplot includes two categories of cases with outlying values. Cases with values that are more than 3 box-lengths from the upper or lower edge of the box are called **extreme values**. On the boxplot, these are designated with the letter E. Cases with values that are between 1.5 and 3 box-lengths from the upper or lower edge of the box are called **outliers** and are designated with the letter O. The largest and smallest observed values that aren't outliers are also shown. Lines are drawn from the ends of the box to these values. (These lines are sometimes called **whiskers** and the plot is called a **box-and-whiskers plot.**

What can you tell about your data from a boxplot? From the median, you can determine the central tendency, or location. From the length of the box, you can determine the spread, or variability, of your observations. If the median is not in the center of the box, you know that the observed values are skewed. If the median is closer to the bottom of the box than to the top, the data are positively skewed. If the median is closer to the top of the box than to the bottom, the opposite is true: the distribution is negatively skewed. The length of the tail is shown by the whiskers and the outlying and extreme points.

Figure 13.5   Annotated sketch of a boxplot

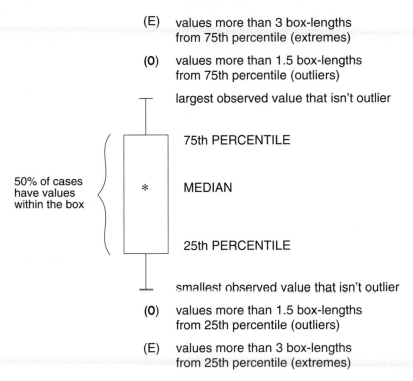

Boxplots are particularly useful for comparing the distribution of values in several groups. For example, suppose you want to compare the distribution of beginning salaries for people employed in several different positions at a bank. Figure 13.6 contains boxplots of the bank salary data. From these plots, you can see that the first two job categories have similar distributions for salary, although the first category has several extreme values. The third job category has little variability; all 27 people in this category earn similar amounts of money. The last two groups have much higher median salaries than the other groups, and a larger spread as well.

Figure 13.6   Boxplots for bank salary data

```
GET FILE 'BANK.SYS'.
SELECT IF (JOBCAT LE 5).
SET WIDTH 90 /LENGTH 59.
EXAMINE VARIABLES=SALBEG BY JOBCAT /PLOT=BOXPLOT.
```

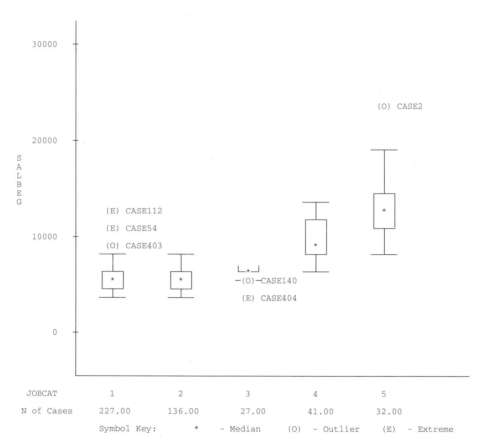

Evaluating Assumptions

Many statistical procedures, such as analysis of variance, require that all groups come from normal populations with the same variance. Therefore, before choosing a statistical hypothesis, we need to test the hypothesis that all the group variances are equal or that the samples come from normal populations. If it appears that the assumptions are violated, we may want to determine appropriate transformations.

The Levene Test

Numerous tests are available for evaluating the assumption that all groups come from populations with equal variances. Many of these tests, however, are heavily dependent on the data being from normal populations. Analysis-of-variance procedures, on the other hand, are reasonably robust to departures from normality. The **Levene test** is a homogeneity-of-variance test that is less dependent on the assumption of normality than most tests and thus is particularly useful with analysis of variance. It is obtained by computing, for each case, the absolute difference from its cell mean and performing a one-way analysis of variance on these differences.

From Figure 13.7, you can see that for the salary data, the null hypothesis that all group variances are equal is rejected. We should consider transforming the data if we plan to use a statistical procedure that requires equality of variance. Next we'll consider how to select a transformation.

Figure 13.7   The Levene test

```
SELECT IF (JOBCAT LE 5).
EXAMINE VARIABLE=SALBEG BY JOBCAT /PLOT SPREADLEVEL.

Test of homogeneity of variance             df1     df2      Significance
Levene Statistic               28.9200        4     458           .0000
```

Spread-versus-Level Plots

Often there is a relationship between the average value, or level, of a variable and the variability, or spread, associated with it. For example, we can see in Figure 13.6 that as salaries increase, so does the variability.

One way of studying the relationship between spread and level is to plot the values of spread and level for each group. If there is no relationship, the points should cluster around a horizontal line. If this is not the case, we can use the observed relationship between the two variables to choose an appropriate transformation.

Determining the Transformation

A power transformation is frequently used to stabilize variances. A power transformation raises each data value to a specified power. For example, a power transformation of 2 squares all of the data values. A transformation of 1/2 takes the square root of all the values. If the power is 0, the log of the numbers is used.

To determine an appropriate power for transforming the data, we can plot, for each group, the log of the median against the log of the interquartile range. Figure 13.8 shows such a plot for the salary data shown in Figure 13.6. You see that there is a fairly strong linear relationship between spread and level.

Figure 13.8   Spread-versus-level plot of bank data

```
SELECT IF (JOBCAT LE 5).
EXAMINE VARIABLE=SALBEG BY JOBCAT /PLOT SPREADLEVEL.
```

```
Dependent variable:    SALBEG
Factor variables:      JOBCAT
```

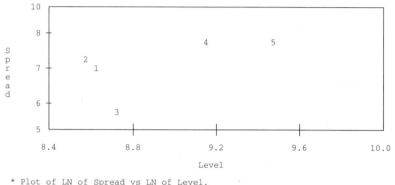

```
* Plot of LN of Spread vs LN of Level.

Slope =    1.475          Power for transformation =    -.475
```

From the slope of the line, we can estimate the power value that will eliminate or lessen this relationship. The power is obtained by subtracting the slope from 1. That is,

$$\text{Power} = 1 - \text{slope} \qquad\qquad\qquad \textbf{Equation 13.1}$$

Although this formula can result in all sorts of powers, for simplicity and clarity we usually choose the closest powers that are multiples of 1/2. Table 13.1 shows the most commonly used transformations.

Table 13.1   Commonly used transformations

Power	Transformation
3	Cube
2	Square
1	No change
1/2	Square root
0	Logarithm
−1/2	Reciprocal of the square root
−1	Reciprocal

As shown in Figure 13.8, the slope of the least-squares line for the bank data is 1.475, so the power for the transformation is −0.475. Rounding to the nearest multiple of a half, we will use the reciprocal of the square root.

After applying the power transformation, it is wise to obtain a spread-versus-level plot for the transformed data. From this plot, you can judge the success of the transformation.

Tests of Normality

Since the normal distribution is very important to statistical inference, we often want to examine the assumption that our data come from a normal distribution. One way to do this is with a normal probability plot. In a **normal probability plot**, each observed value is paired with its expected value from the normal distribution. (The expected value from the normal distribution is based on the number of cases in the sample and the rank order of the case in the sample.) If the sample is from a normal distribution, we expect that the points will fall more or less on a straight line.

The first plot in Figure 13.9 is a normal probability plot of a sample of 200 points from a normal distribution. Note how the points cluster around a straight line. You can also plot the actual deviations of the points from a straight line. This is called a detrended normal plot and is shown in the second plot in Figure 13.9. If the sample is from a normal population, the points should cluster around a horizontal line through 0, and there should be no pattern. A striking pattern suggests departure from normality.

Figure 13.9   Normal plots for a normal distribution

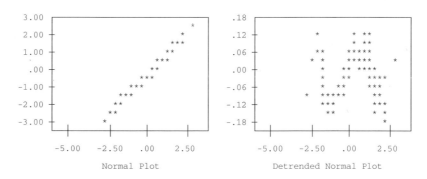

Figure 13.10 shows a normal probability plot and a detrended plot for data from a uniform distribution. The points do not cluster around a straight line, and the deviations from a straight line are not randomly distributed around 0.

Figure 13.10 Normal plots for a uniform distribution

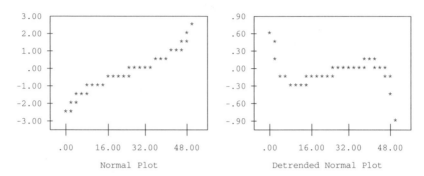

Although normal probability plots provide a visual basis for checking normality, it is often desirable to compute a statistical test of the hypothesis that the data are from a normal distribution. Two commonly used tests are the Shapiro-Wilks' test and the Lilliefors test. The **Lilliefors test**, based on a modification of the Kolmogorov-Smirnov test, is used when means and variances are not known but must be estimated from the data. The **Shapiro-Wilks' test** shows good power in many situations compared to other tests of normality (Conover, 1980).

Figure 13.11 contains normal probability plots and Figure 13.12 contains the Lilliefors test of normality for the diastolic blood pressure data. From the small observed significance levels, you see that the hypothesis of normality can be rejected. However, it is important to remember that whenever the sample size is large, almost any goodness-of-fit test will result in rejection of the null hypothesis. It is almost impossible to find data that are *exactly* normally distributed. For most statistical tests, it is sufficient that the data are approximately normally distributed. Thus, for large data sets, you should look not only at the observed significance level but also at the actual departure from normality.

Figure 13.11 Normal plots for diastolic blood pressure

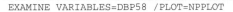

EXAMINE VARIABLES=DBP58 /PLOT=NPPLOT

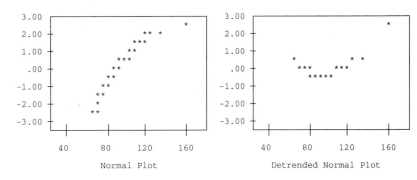

Figure 13.12 Normality test

	Statistic	df	Significance
K-S (Lilliefors)	.0974	239	.0000

Estimating Location with Robust Estimators

We often use the arithmetic mean to estimate central tendency, or location. We know, however, that the mean is heavily influenced by outliers. One very large or very small value can change the mean dramatically. The median, on the other hand, is insensitive to outliers; addition or removal of extreme values has little effect on it. The median is called a **resistant measure**, since its value depends on the main body of the data and not on outliers. The advantages of resistant measures are obvious: their values are not unduly influenced by a few observations, and they don't change much if small amounts of data are added or removed.

Although the median is an intuitive, simple measure of location, there are better estimators of location if we are willing to make some assumptions about the population from which our data originate. Estimators that depend on simple, fairly nonrestrictive assumptions about the underlying distribution and are not sensitive to these assumptions are called **robust estimators**. In the following sections, we consider some robust estimators of central tendency that depend only on the assumption that the data are from a symmetric population.

The Trimmed Mean

A simple robust estimator of location can be obtained by "trimming" the data to exclude values that are far removed from the others. For example, a 20% trimmed mean disregards the smallest 20% and the largest 20% of all observations. The estimate is based on only the 60% of data values that are in the middle. What's the advantage of a trimmed mean? Like the median, it results in an estimate that is not influenced by extreme values. However, unlike the median, it is not based solely on a single value, or two values, that are in the middle. It is based on a much larger number of middle values. (The median can be considered a 50% trimmed mean, since half of the values above and below the median are ignored.) In general, a trimmed mean makes better use of the data than does the median.

M-Estimators

When calculating a trimmed mean, we divide our cases into two groups: those included in and those excluded from the computation of the mean. A **weighted mean** is calculated by assigning a weight to each case and then using the formula $\overline{X} = (\Sigma w_i x_i) / (\Sigma w_i)$. We can consider the trimmed mean as a weighted mean in which cases have weights of 0 or 1, depending on whether they are included in or excluded from the computations. Observations that are far from most of the others are excluded altogether. A less extreme alternative is to include them but give them smaller weights than cases closer to the center, which we can do using the **M-estimator**, or generalized maximum-likelihood estimator.

Since many different schemes can be used to assign weights to cases, there are many different M-estimators. (The usual mean can be viewed as an M-estimator with all cases having a weight of 1.) All commonly used M-estimators assign weights that decrease as distance from the center of the distribution increases. Figure 13.12a through Figure 13.12d show the weights used by four common M-estimators.

Common M-Estimators

Figure 13.12a   Huber's (c = 1.339)

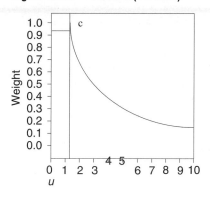

Figure 13.12b   Tukey's biweight (c = 4.685)

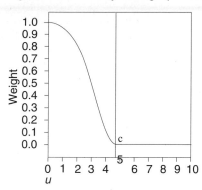

Figure 13.12c   Hampel's (a = 1.7, b = 3.4, c = 8.5)

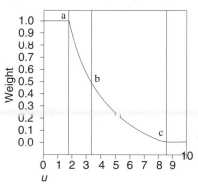

Figure 13.12d   Andrew's (c = 1.339π)

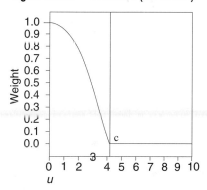

Consider Figure 13.12a, which shows Huber's M-estimator. The value on the horizontal axis is a standardized distance from the estimate of location. It is computed using the following formula:

$$u_i = \frac{|\text{value for } i\text{th case} - \text{estimate of location}|}{\text{estimate of spread}}$$

Equation 13.2

The estimate of spread used is the median of the absolute deviations from the sample median, commonly known as MAD. It is calculated by first finding the median for the sample and then computing for each case the absolute value of the deviation from the median. MAD is then the median of these absolute values. Since the weights for cases depend on the value of the estimate of central location, M-estimators must be computed iteratively.

From Figure 13.12a, you can see that cases have weights of 1 up to a certain critical point, labeled *c*. After the critical point, the weights decrease as *u*, the standardized distance from the location estimate, increases. The SPSS/PC+ values for these critical points are given in parentheses in Figure 13.12a through Figure 13.12d.

The four M-estimators in Figure 13.12a through Figure 13.12d differ from each other in the way they assign weights. The Tukey biweight (Figure 13.12b) does not have a point at which weights shift abruptly from 1. Instead, weights gradually decline to 0. Cases with values greater than *c* standardized units from the estimate are assigned weights of 0.

Hampel's three-part redescending M-estimator (Figure 13.12c) has a more complicated weighting scheme than the Huber or the Tukey biweight. It uses four schemes for assigning weights. Cases with values less than *a* receive a weight of 1, cases with values between *a* and *b* receive a weight of *a/u*, while cases between *b* and *c* receive a weight of

$$\frac{a}{u} \times \frac{c-u}{c-b}$$ **Equation 13.3**

Cases with values greater than *c* receive a weight of 0. With Andrew's M-estimator (Figure 13.12d), there is no abrupt change in the assignment of weights. A smooth function replaces the separate pieces.

Figure 13.13 contains basic descriptive statistics and values for the M-estimators for the diastolic blood pressure data. As expected, the estimates of location differ for the various methods. The mean produces the largest estimate: 88.79. That's because we have a positively skewed distribution and the mean is heavily influenced by the large values. Of the M-estimators, the Huber and Hampel estimates have the largest values. They too are influenced by the large data values. The remaining two M-estimates are fairly close in value.

Figure 13.13 M-estimators for blood pressure variable

```
EXAMINE VARIABLES=DBP58 /MESTIMATORS

    DBP58      AVERAGE DIAST BLOOD PRESS

Valid cases:       239.0  Missing cases:       1.0   Percent missing:      .4


Mean      88.7908  Std Err      .8441  Min      65.0000  Skewness   1.2557
Median    87.0000  Variance  170.3006  Max     160.0000  S E Skew    .1575
5% Trim   88.0065  Std Dev    13.0499  Range    95.0000  Kurtosis   3.5958
                                       IQR      17.0000  S E Kurt    .3137

                               M-Estimators
                               ------------

Huber  (1.339)            87.1219    Tukey  (4.685)          86.4269
```

In summary, M-estimators are good alternatives to the usual mean and median. The Huber M-estimator is good if the distribution is close to normal but is not recommended if there are extreme values. For further discussion of robust estimators, see Hogg (1979) and Hoaglin et al. (1983).

Running Procedure EXAMINE

EXAMINE provides a variety of descriptive plots and statistics, including stem-and-leaf plots, boxplots, normal probability plots, and spread-and-level plots. Also available are the Levene test for homogeneity of variance, the Shapiro-Wilks' and Lilliefors tests for normality, and several robust maximum-likelihood estimators of location. Cases can be subdivided into groups and statistics obtained for each group.

Specifying the Variables

The only required specification is the VARIABLES subcommand and a list of variables for which descriptive statistics are to be calculated. For example, to obtain descriptive statistics for the variables *SALBEG* and *EDUC*, specify:

```
EXAMINE VARIABLES=SALBEG EDUC.
```

The VARIABLES subcommand can be specified only once.

Specifying the Groups

To subdivide cases into cells based on their values for grouping (factor) variables, specify the factor variables after keyword BY. String variables can be used as factors, but only the first eight characters are used.

For example, to obtain summary statistics for *SALBEG* and *EDUC* when cases are subdivided into employment categories (*JOBCAT*), specify:

```
EXAMINE VARIABLES=SALBEG EDUC BY JOBCAT.
```

If several variables are listed after keyword BY, separate analyses are obtained for each factor variable. For example, the command

```
EXAMINE VARIABLES=SALBEG EDUC BY JOBCAT SEX.
```

will produce summary statistics for salary and education for categories of *JOBCAT* and for categories of *SEX*. To obtain summary statistics for cells based on the combination of values of *JOBCAT* and *SEX*, use keyword BY to separate the factor names. The command

```
EXAMINE VARIABLES=SALBEG EDUC BY JOBCAT BY SEX.
```

will produce descriptive statistics for cells formed by the combination of values of sex and job category. That is, there will be cells for males and females within each job category. If there are five job categories, you will obtain 11 analyses: one for all cases combined, and one for each of the ten cells formed by the combinations of *JOBCAT* and *SEX*. However, you will not obtain analyses for each individual job category and for each sex. To obtain this additional output, specify:

```
EXAMINE VARIABLES=SALBEG EDUC BY SEX JOBCAT JOBCAT BY SEX.
```

Specifying many cells will generate a large amount of output. Be sure to request only the analyses that you need.

Identifying Cases in the Output

Individual cases can be identified in the output according to their values for a selected variable specified on the ID subcommand. For example, to identify cases by their values for *EMPLNO*, specify:

```
EXAMINE VARIABLES=SALBEG BY JOBCAT /ID=EMPLNO.
```

If the ID subcommand is not specified, the system variable *$CASENUM* is used.

Obtaining Basic Descriptive Statistics

Use the STATISTICS subcommand to control the output of basic descriptive statistics. The following keywords can be specified:

DESCRIPTIVE   *Basic descriptive statistics only.* This includes the mean, median, 5% trimmed mean, standard error, variance, standard deviation, minimum, maximum, range, interquartile range, skewness, and kurtosis; standard errors are displayed for the last two. Interquartile range computations are based on the method specified with the PERCENTILES subcommand.

EXTREMES (n)   *The cases with the* n *largest and* n *smallest values.* If *n* is omitted, the cases with the five largest and five smallest values are displayed. Cases are identified by their values for the variable specified on the ID subcommand. If the ID subcommand is not used, cases are identified by their values for the system variable *$CASENUM*.

ALL   *Basic descriptive statistics and extreme values.* All statistics available with DESCRIPTIVE and EXTREMES are displayed. The default *n* of 5 is used for EXTREMES.

NONE   *Neither basic descriptive statistics nor extreme values.*

Obtaining Robust Maximum-Likelihood Estimators

Use the MESTIMATORS subcommand to obtain robust maximum-likelihood estimators of location. If the MESTIMATORS subcommand is specified without keywords, all four M-estimators are calculated. Individual estimators and values for weighting constants can be selected with the following keywords:

HUBER(c)   *Huber's M-estimator.* The value of weighting constant *c* can be specified in parentheses following the keyword. The default is *c*=1.339.

ANDREW(c)   *Andrew's wave estimator.* The value of weighting constant c can be specified in parentheses following the keyword. Constants are multiplied by π. The default constant is 1.34.

HAMPEL(a,b,c)   *Hampel's M-estimator.* The values of weighting constants a, b, and c can be specified in order in parentheses following the keyword. The default values are $a=1.7$, $b=3.4$, and $c=8.5$.

TUKEY(c)   *Tukey's biweight estimator.* The value of weighting constant c can be specified in parentheses following the keyword. The default is $c=4.685$.

ALL   *All four above M-estimators.* This is the default when MESTIMATORS is specified with no keyword. The default values for weighting constants are used.

NONE   *No M-estimators.* This is the default if MESTIMATORS is omitted.

For example, to calculate all four M-estimators for variable *DBP58*, specify:

```
EXAMINE VARIABLES=DBP58 /MESTIMATORS.
```

The output is shown in Figure 13.13. To obtain only the Andrew's estimator with a weighting constant of 2π, specify:

```
EXAMINE VARIABLES=DBP58 /MESTIMATORS ANDREW(2).
```

Obtaining Frequency Tables

Use the FREQUENCIES subcommand to obtain frequency tables. You can specify starting values and increment sizes. For example, to obtain a frequency table for *DBP58* using increments of 5 and starting at 70, specify:

```
EXAMINE VARIABLES=DBP58 /FREQUENCIES FROM (70) BY (5).
```

If you do not specify a starting value or increment, EXAMINE will select a value based on the data. If you specify an increment of 0, a frequency table for each distinct value is produced.

Obtaining Percentiles

Use the PERCENTILES subcommand to obtain percentiles. You can also select the method of estimation. For example, to calculate the 25th, 50th, and 75th percentiles using the default method of estimation, specify:

```
EXAMINE VARIABLES=DBP58 /PERCENTILES(25,50,75).
```

If you specify the PERCENTILES subcommand without percentile values in parentheses, the default percentiles are 5, 10, 25, 50, 75, 90, and 95.

The following methods are available for calculating the percentiles, where W is the sum of weights for all nonmissing cases, p is the percentile divided by 100, i is the rank of the case when cases are sorted in ascending order, and X_i is the value for the ith case.

HAVERAGE *Weighted average at* $X_{(w+1)p}$. The percentile value is the weighted average of X_i and X_{i+1} using the formula $(1-f)X_i + fX_{i+1}$, where $(w+1)p$ is decomposed into an integer part i and a fractional part f. This is the default if PERCENTILES is specified without a keyword.

WAVERAGE *Weighted average at* X_{wp}. The percentile value is the weighted average of X_i and $X_{(i+1)}$ using the formula $(1-f)X_i + fX_{i+1}$, where i is the integer part of wp and f is the fractional part of wp.

ROUND *Observation closest to* wp. The percentile value is X_i, where i is the integer part of $(wp + 0.5)$.

EMPIRICAL *Empirical distribution function.* The percentile value is X_i when the fractional part of wp is equal to 0. The percentile value is X_{i+1} when the fractional part of wp is greater than 0.

AEMPIRICAL *Empirical distribution with averaging.* The percentile value is $(X_i + X_{i+1})/2$ when the fractional part of wp equals 0. The percentile value is X_{i+1} when the fractional part of wp is greater than 0.

NONE *Suppress percentile output.* This is the default if PERCENTILES is omitted.

The keyword for the method to be used for calculating the percentiles follows the list of percentile values, as in:

```
EXAMINE  VARIABLES=DBP58 /PERCENTILES(25 50 75)=WAVERAGE.
```

To use the default percentiles with a method other than HAVERAGE, specify only a method on the PERCENTILES subcommand, as in:

```
EXAMINE VARIABLES=DBP58 /PERCENTILES EMPIRICAL.
```

Plotting the Data

EXAMINE produces boxplots, stem-and-leaf plots, histograms, normal probability plots, and spread-and-level plots. The Shapiro-Wilks' and/or Lilliefors tests of normality are calculated if normal probability plots are requested. The Levene test for homogeneity of variance is displayed if a spread-and-level plot is requested. If the PLOT subcommand is specified without any keywords or if the subcommand is omitted, stem-and-leaf plots and boxplots are produced. If any plots are specified on PLOT, only the requested plots are displayed.

The following keywords can be used with the PLOT subcommand:

BOXPLOT	*Boxplot.* The boundaries of the box are Tukey's hinges. The median is identified by an asterisk. The length of the box is the interquartile range (IQR) based on Tukey's hinges. Values more than 3 IQR's from the end of the box are labeled as extreme (E). Values more than 1.5 IQR's from the end of the box but less than 3 IQR's are labeled as outliers (O). This is produced by default.
STEMLEAF	*Stem-and-leaf plot.* Each observed value is divided into two components—the leading digits (stem) and the trailing digits (leaf). This is produced by default.
HISTOGRAM	*Histogram.*
SPREADLEVEL(n)	*Spread-and-level plot.* This type of plot requires a factor variable (after the keyword BY). If the keyword appears alone, the natural logs of the interquartile ranges are plotted against the natural logs of the medians for all cells. If a power for transforming the data (n) is given, the IQR and median of the transformed data are plotted. If 0 is specified for n, a natural log transformation of the data is done. The slope of the regression line and the Levene test for homogeneity of variance are also displayed. The Levene test is based on the original data if no transformation is specified and on the transformed data if a transformation is requested.
NPPLOT	*Normal probability and detrended probability plots.* NPPLOT calculates Shapiro-Wilks' statistic and a Kolmogorov-Smirnov statistic with a Lilliefors significance level for testing normality. Shapiro-Wilks' statistic is not calculated when the sample size exceeds 50.
ALL	*All available plots.*
NONE	*No plots.*

For example, to request stem-and-leaf plots and normal probability plots, specify:

```
EXAMINE VARIABLES=DBP58 /PLOT STEMLEAF NPPLOT.
```

To determine an appropriate transformation of the data based on a plot of the logs of the interquartile ranges against the logs of the medians, specify:

```
EXAMINE VARIABLES=DBP58 BY DAYOFWK /PLOT SPREADLEVEL.
```

To obtain a plot of interquartile ranges against medians when the data values are squared, specify:

```
EXAMINE VARIABLES=DBP58 BY DAYOFWK /PLOT SPREADLEVEL(2).
```

To obtain a plot of the interquartile ranges against the medians after the data have been log transformed, specify:

```
EXAMINE VARIABLES=DBP58 BY DAYOFWK /PLOT SPREADLEVEL(0).
```

Boxplot Display

The COMPARE subcommand controls how boxplots are displayed. Two methods are available. For each variable you can display the boxplots for all groups side by side (keyword GROUPS), or you can display all boxplots for a group together (keyword VARIABLES). You will have several boxplots for a single group only if you specify more than one dependent variable.

If you display boxplots for all groups together, you can see how the distribution of a particular variable differs for the groups. For example, suppose you have variables *SAL1*, *SAL2*, *SAL3*, and *SAL4*, containing yearly salaries for the first four years of employment. If you specify

```
EXAMINE VARIABLES=SAL1 SAL2 SAL3 SAL4 BY JOBCAT BY SEX
    /COMPARE GROUPS.
```

the distribution of *SAL1* is shown for all groups, followed by the distribution of *SAL2* for all groups, and so forth. If you specify

```
EXAMINE VARIABLES=SAL1 SAL2 SAL3 SAL4 BY JOBCAT BY SEX
    /COMPARE VARIABLES.
```

the boxplots for the four salaries for each group are grouped together. This allows you to examine salary changes over time for each group.

Controlling the Scale

By default, the scale for histograms and stem-and-leaf plots are based on the values of the cases in a particular plot. You can use the same scale for all plots for each dependent variable by specifying the SCALE subcommand. The following keywords are available:

PLOTWISE   *Scales are based on the values of cases in each plot.* This is the default.

UNIFORM   *All plots for each dependent variable use the same scale.*

For example, if you specify

```
EXAMINE VARIABLES=SAL1 BY JOCBCAT /SCALE UNIFORM.
```

the same scale is used for all stem-and-leaf plots. If histograms are requested, they will also use the same scale.

Missing Values

By default, cases with either system- or user-missing values for any variable specified on the VARIABLES subcommand are excluded from the analysis. You can specify other missing-value treatments using the MISSING subcommand. The following keywords are available:

LISTWISE   *Delete cases with missing values listwise.* A case with missing values for any dependent variable or any factor in the model specification is excluded from statistics and plots unless modified by INCLUDE. This is the default.

PAIRWISE   *Delete cases with missing values pairwise.* A case is deleted from the analysis only if it has a missing value for the dependent variable or factor being analyzed.

REPORT   *Include user- and system-missing values for factor variables.* User- and system-missing values for factors are treated as valid categories and are labeled as missing. User- and system-missing values for dependent variables are reported in frequency output and excluded from statistical computations and graphs.

INCLUDE   *Include user-missing values.* Only system-missing values are excluded from the analysis. This keyword can be used together with LISTWISE, PAIRWISE, or REPORT.

For example, the command

```
EXAMINE VARIABLES=SALBEG EDUC BY JOBCAT /MISSING PAIRWISE.
```

will exclude cases from the analysis of *SALBEG* only if they have missing values for *SALBEG* or *JOBCAT*. It doesn't matter whether the value of *EDUC* is missing or not. Only cases with missing values for *EDUC* or *JOBCAT* will be excluded from the analysis of *EDUC*.

14 Crosstabulation and Measures of Association: Procedure CROSSTABS

Unfortunately, winning the lottery is but a dream for most of us. But who hasn't pondered the consequences: paying off the mortgage, junking the old clunker, vacationing in exotic warm locations. . . And then there's the question of what to tell the boss. Although some of us have repeatedly rehearsed the parting conversation, others may delude themselves into thinking that they will continue to work.

To determine whether most people see themselves as workers or nonworkers if they should suddenly become rich, let's consider data from the 1991 General Social Survey. (Davis, et al., 1991). The General Social Survey asked a national sample of working adults 18 and older whether they would continue working if they became rich.

Crosstabulation

To see whether the hypothetical work rate is similar for males and females, the responses must be tallied separately for each sex. Figure 14.1 is a **crosstabulation** of sex and response. The number of cases with each combination of values of the two variables is displayed in a **cell** in the table, together with various percentages. These cell entries provide information about relationships between the variables.

Figure 14.1   Crosstabulation of sex by response

```
GET FILE 'GSS91.SYS'.
CROSSTABS TABLES=SEX BY RICHWORK /CELLS.

SEX   RESPONDENTS SEX  by  RICHWORK   IF RICH, CONTINUE OR STOP WORKING

                       RICHWORK        Page 1 of 1
             Count
             Row Pct CONTINUE STOP WOR
             Col Pct WORKING KING         Row
             Tot Pct    1         2      Total
      SEX
               1       234        89       323
     MALE              72.4      27.6      52.4
                       56.8      43.6
                       38.0      14.4

               2       178       115       293
     FEMALE            60.8      39.2      47.6
                       43.2      56.4
                       28.9      18.7

             Column    412       204       616
             Total     66.9      33.1     100.0

Number of Missing Observations:   901
```

In Figure 14.1, work status is called the **column variable**, since each status is displayed in a column of the table. Similarly, the sex of the respondent is called the **row variable**. With two categories of the column variable and two of the row, there are four cells in the table.

Cell Contents and Marginals

The first entry in the each cell is the number of cases, or **frequency**, in that cell. It is labeled as *Count* in the key displayed in the upper-left corner of the table. For example, 234 males would continue to work, and 89 males would stop working. The second entry in the table is the **row percentage** (*Row Pct*). It is the percentage of all cases in a row that fall into a particular cell. Of the 323 men, 72.4% would continue to work and 27.6% would not. Of the 293 women, 60.8% would continue to work and 39.2% would not.

The **column percentage** (*Col Pct*), the third item in each cell, is the percentage of all cases in a column that occur in a cell. For example, of the 412 people who would continue to work, 56.8% are men and 43.2% are women.

The last entry in the cell is the **table percentage** (*Tot Pct*). The number of cases in the cell is expressed as a percentage of the total number of cases in the table. For example, the 234 males who would continue to work represent 38% of the 616 respondents.

The numbers to the right and below the table are known as **marginals**. They are the counts and percentages for the row and column variables taken separately. In Figure 14.1, the column marginals show that 66.9% of the respondents would continue to work, while 33.1% would stop.

Choosing Percentages

Row, column, and table percentages convey different types of information, so it is important to choose carefully among them.

In this example, the column percentage indicates the distribution of males and females in each of the response categories. It conveys no direct information about whether males and females are equally likely to keep working. For example, if the number of males in the survey was twice the number of females, an identical work rate for both sexes would give column percentages of 66.7% and 33.3%. However, this does not indicate that the work rate is higher for males. There are just more of them.

The row percentage tells you the percentage of males who would continue working and the percentage of females who would continue working. By looking at row percentages, you can compare work rates for males and females. Interpretation of this comparison is not affected by unequal numbers of males and females in the study.

Since it is always possible to interchange the rows and columns of any table, general rules about when to use row and column percentages cannot be given. The percentages to use depend on the nature of the two variables. If one of the two variables is under experimental control, it is termed an **independent variable**. The independent variable is hypothesized to affect the response, or **dependent variable**. If variables can be classified as dependent and independent, the following guideline may be helpful: if the independent variable is the row variable, select row percentages; if the independent variable is the column variable, select column percentages. In this example the dependent variable is work status, whether a person would continue working or not. The sex of the respondent is the independent variable. Since the independent variable is the row variable in Figure 14.1, row percentages should be used for comparisons of work rates.

Adding a Control Variable

Figure 14.1 is an overall comparison of men's and women's responses. If you wanted to see whether particular groups of men and women differ, you would have to include additional variables in the crosstabulation table. For example, to see whether marital status affects the responses of men and women, you could crosstabulate sex and response for each of the marital status categories of interest. Figure 14.2 shows separate crosstabulations of sex and work plans for married people and for people who have never been married.

Figure 14.2 Crosstabulations of sex by response by marital status

```
CROSSTABS TABLES=SEX BY RICHWORK BY MARITAL
 /CELLS=COUNT ROW /STATISTICS=CHISQ.

SEX  RESPONDENTS SEX  by  RICHWORK  IF RICH, CONTINUE OR STOP WORKING
Controlling for..
MARITAL  MARITAL STATUS  Value = 1  MARRIED
```

		RICHWORK	Page 1 of 1	
	Count Row Pct	CONTINUE WORKING 1	STOP WOR KING 2	Row Total
SEX				
MALE	1	137 74.9	46 25.1	183 56.1
FEMALE	2	80 55.9	63 44.1	143 43.9
	Column Total	217 66.6	109 33.4	326 100.0

Chi-Square	Value	DF	Significance
Pearson	12.91011	1	.00033
Continuity Correction	12.07404	1	.00051
Likelihood Ratio	12.89133	1	.00033
Mantel-Haenszel test for linear association	12.87051	1	.00033

```
Minimum Expected Frequency -   47.813



SEX  RESPONDENTS SEX  by  RICHWORK  IF RICH, CONTINUE OR STOP WORKING
Controlling for..
MARITAL  MARITAL STATUS  Value = 5  NEVER MARRIED
```

		RICHWORK	Page 1 of 1	
	Count Row Pct	CONTINUE WORKING 1	STOP WOR KING 2	Row Total
SEX				
MALE	1	65 67.7	31 32.3	96 59.6
FEMALE	2	50 76.9	15 23.1	65 40.4
	Column Total	115 71.4	46 28.6	161 100.0

Chi-Square	Value	DF	Significance
Pearson	1.61258	1	.20413
Continuity Correction	1.19266	1	.27479
Likelihood Ratio	1.63897	1	.20047
Mantel-Haenszel test for linear association	1.60256	1	.20554

```
Minimum Expected Frequency -   18.571
```

These tables show interesting differences. Almost 75% of married men think they would continue to work, while only 56% of married women think they would continue to work. When you consider never-married respondents, however, the percentage of women who would continue to work (77%) increases substantially, surpassing the percentage of men (68%). Single women seem to be as attached to their work (or as willing to lie) as their male counterparts.

Graphical Representation of Crosstabulations

As with frequency tables, visual representation of a crosstabulation often simplifies the search for associations. Figure 14.3 is a **bar chart** of the crosstabulations shown in Figure 14.2. In a bar chart, the height of each bar represents the frequencies or percentages for each category of a variable. In Figure 14.3, the percentages plotted are the row percentages shown in Figure 14.2 for respondents who would continue to work. This chart clearly shows that the work rates differ quite a bit for married men and women, but not for those who have never married.

Figure 14.3   Bar chart

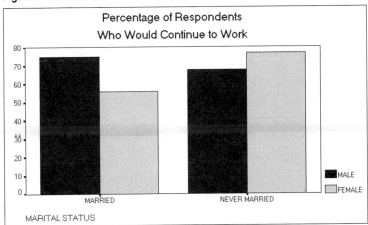

Using Crosstabulation for Data Screening

Errors and unusual values in data entry that cannot be spotted with frequency tables can sometimes be identified using crosstabulation. For example, a case coded as a male with a history of three pregnancies would not be identified as suspicious in frequency tables of sex and number of pregnancies. When considered separately, the code *male* is acceptable for sex and the value 3 is acceptable for number of pregnancies. The combination, however, is unexpected.

Whenever possible, crosstabulations of related variables should be obtained so that anomalies can be identified and corrected before further statistical analysis of the data.

Crosstabulation Statistics

Although examination of the various row and column percentages in a crosstabulation is a useful first step in studying the relationship between two variables, row and column percentages do not allow for quantification or testing of that relationship. For these purposes, it is useful to consider various indexes that measure the extent of association as well as statistical tests of the hypothesis that there is no association.

The Chi-Square Test of Independence

The hypothesis that two variables in a crosstabulation are independent of each other is often of interest. Two variables are **independent** if the probability that a case falls into a given cell is simply the product of the marginal probabilities of the two categories defining the cell.

In Figure 14.1, for example, if work status and sex are independent, the probability of a man continuing to work is the product of the probability of a male and the probability of continuing to work. From the table, 52.4% of the respondents were male and 66.9% of the respondents would continue to work. Thus, if sex and work status are independent, the probability of of a male cotinuing to work is estimated to be

$$P(\text{male})\,P(\text{continue work}) \;=\; 0.524 \times 0.669 \;=\; 0.35 \qquad \textbf{Equation 14.1}$$

The **expected** number of cases in that cell is 216, which is 35% of the 616 cases in the sample. From the table, the **observed** number of men who would continue to work is 234, 18 more than would be expected if the two variables are independent.

To construct a statistical test of the independence hypothesis, you repeat the above calculations for each cell in the table. The probability under independence of an observation falling into cell (*ij*) is estimated by

$$P(\text{row} = i \text{ and column} = j) \;=\; \left(\frac{\text{count in row } i}{N}\right)\left(\frac{\text{count in column } j}{N}\right) \qquad \textbf{Equation 14.2}$$

To obtain the expected number of observations in cell (*ij*), the probability is multiplied by the total sample size.

$$\begin{aligned} E_{ij} &= N\left(\left(\frac{\text{count in row } i}{N}\right)\left(\frac{\text{count in column } j}{N}\right)\right) \\ &= \frac{(\text{count in row } i)\,(\text{count in column } j)}{N} \end{aligned} \qquad \textbf{Equation 14.3}$$

Figure 14.4 contains the observed and expected frequencies and the **residuals**, which are the observed minus the expected frequencies for the data in Figure 14.1.

Figure 14.4   Observed, expected, and residual values

```
CROSSTABS TABLES=SEX BY RICHWORK
 /CELLS=COUNT EXPECTED RESID
 /STATISTICS=CHISQ.


SEX   RESPONDENTS SEX  by  RICHWORK   IF RICH, CONTINUE OR STOP WORKING

                    RICHWORK      Page 1 of 1
            Count
            Exp Val |CONTINUE STOP WOR
            Residual| WORKING  KING       Row
                    |    1       2      Total
SEX         --------
            1   |  234      89         323
    MALE        |  216.0   107.0      52.4%
                |   18.0   -18.0

            2   |  178      115        293
    FEMALE      |  196.0    97.0      47.6%
                |  -18.0    18.0

            Column    412      204        616
            Total    66.9%    33.1%     100.0%

        Chi-Square              Value        DF      Significance
    --------------------      ----------     ----    ------------

    Pearson                    9.48684        1        .00207
    Continuity Correction      8.96619        1        .00275
    Likelihood Ratio           9.49640        1        .00206
    Mantel-Haenszel test for   9.47144        1        .00209
        linear association

    Minimum Expected Frequency -    97.032


    Number of Missing Observations:   901
```

A statistic often used to test the hypothesis that the row and column variables are independent is the **Pearson chi-square**. It is calculated by summing over all cells the squared residuals divided by the expected frequencies.

$$\chi^2 = \sum_i \sum_j \frac{(O_{ij} - E_{ij})^2}{E_{ij}}$$

Equation 14.4

The calculated chi-square is compared to the critical points of the theoretical chi-square distribution to produce an estimate of how likely (or unlikely) this calculated value is if the two variables are in fact independent. Since the value of the chi-square depends on the number of rows and columns in the table being examined, you must know the **degrees of freedom** for the table. The degrees of freedom can be viewed as the number of cells of a table that can be arbitrarily filled when the row and column totals (marginals) are fixed. For an $r \times c$ table, the degrees of freedom are $(r - 1) \times (c - 1)$, since once $(r - 1)$ rows and $(c - 1)$ columns are filled, frequencies in the remaining row and column cells must be chosen so that marginal totals are maintained.

In this example, there is one degrees of freedom (1×1) and the Pearson chi-square value is 9.49 (see Figure 14.4). If sex and continuing to work are independent, the probability that a random sample would result in a chi-square value of at least that magnitude is 0.002. This probability is also known as the **observed significance level** of the test. If the probability is small enough (usually less than 0.05 or 0.01), the hypothesis that the two variables are independent is rejected.

Since the observed significance level in Figure 14.4 is very small, the hypothesis that sex and continuing to work are independent is rejected. When the chi-square test is calculated for married and never married persons separately (Figure 14.2), different results are obtained. The observed significance level for married respondents is 0.0003, so the independence hypothesis is rejected. For never-married people, the observed significance level is less than 0.204, and the hypothesis that sex and work status are independent is not rejected.

An alternative to the commonly used Pearson chi-square is the **likelihood-ratio chi-square** (see Figure 14.4). This test is based on maximum-likelihood theory and is often used in the analysis of categorical data. For large samples, the Pearson and likelihood-ratio chi-square statistics give very similar results. (The Mantel-Haenszel test is discussed in "Ordinal Measures" on p. 198.)

The chi-square test is a test of independence; it provides little information about the strength or form of the association between two variables. The magnitude of the observed chi-square depends not only on the goodness of fit of the independence model but also on the sample size. If the sample size for a particular table increases n-fold, so does the chi-square value. Thus, large chi-square values can arise in applications where residuals are small relative to expected frequencies but where the sample size is large.

Certain conditions must be met for the chi-square distribution to be a good approximation of the distribution of the statistic in the equation given above. The data must be random samples from multinomial distributions and the expected values must not be too small. While it has been recommended that all expected frequencies be at least 5, studies indicate that this is probably too stringent and can be relaxed (Everitt, 1977). SPSS/PC+ displays the number of cells with expected frequencies less than 5 and the minimum expected cell value.

To improve the approximation for a 2×2 table, **Yates' correction for continuity** is sometimes applied. Yates' correction for continuity involves subtracting 0.5 from positive differences between observed and expected frequencies (the residuals) and adding 0.5 to negative differences before squaring. For a discussion of the controversy over the merits of this correction, see Conover (1974) and Mantel (1974).

Fisher's exact test, based on the hypergeometric distribution, is an alternative test for the 2×2 table. It calculates exact probabilities of obtaining the observed results if the two variables are independent and the marginals are fixed. It is most useful when the total sample size and the expected values are small. SPSS/PC+ calculates Fisher's exact test if any expected cell value in a 2×2 table is less than 5.

Measures of Association

In many research situations, it is the strength and nature of the dependence of the variables that is of central concern. Indexes that attempt to quantify the relationship between variables in a crosstabulation are called **measures of association**. No single measure adequately summarizes all possible types of association. Measures vary in their interpretation and in the way they define perfect and intermediate association. These measures also differ in the way they are affected by various factors such as marginals. For example, many measures are "margin sensitive" in that they are influenced by the marginal distributions of the rows and columns. Such measures reflect information about the marginals along with information about association.

A particular measure may have a low value for a given table, not because the two variables are not related but because they are not related in the way to which the measure is sensitive. No single measure is best for all situations. The type of data, the hypothesis of interest, and the properties of the various measures must all be considered when selecting an index of association for a given table. It is not, however, reasonable to compute a large number of measures and then to report the most impressive as if it were the only one examined.

The measures of association available with crosstabulation in SPSS/PC+ are computed only from bivariate tables. For example, if three dichotomous variables are specified in the table, two sets of measures are computed, one for each subtable produced by the values of the controlling variable. In general, if relationships among more than two variables are to be studied, examination of bivariate tables is only a first step. For an extensive discussion of more sophisticated multivariate procedures for the analysis of qualitative data, see Fienberg (1977), Everitt (1977), and Haberman (1978).

Nominal Measures

Consider measures that assume only that both variables in the table are nominally measured. As such, these measures can provide only some indication of the strength of association between variables; they cannot indicate direction or anything about the nature of the relationship. The measures provided are of two types: those based on the chi-square statistic and those that follow the logic of proportional reduction in error, denoted PRE.

Chi-Square-Based Measures

As explained above, the chi-square statistic itself is not a good measure of the degree of association between two variables. But its widespread use in tests of independence has encouraged the use of measures of association based upon it. Each of these measures based on the chi-square attempts to modify the chi-square statistic to minimize the influence of sample size and degrees of freedom as well as to restrict the range of values of the measure to those between 0 and 1. Without such adjustments, comparison of chi-square values from tables with varying dimensions and sample sizes is meaningless.

The **phi coefficient** modifies the Pearson chi-square by dividing it by the sample size and taking the square root of the result:

$$\phi = \sqrt{\frac{\chi^2}{N}} \qquad \qquad \text{Equation 14.5}$$

For a 2×2 table only, the phi coefficient is equal to the Pearson correlation coefficient, so the sign of phi matches that of the correlation coefficient. For tables in which one dimension is greater than 2, phi may not lie between 0 and 1, since the chi-square value can be greater than the sample size. To obtain a measure that must lie between 0 and 1, Pearson suggested the use of

$$C = \sqrt{\frac{\chi^2}{\chi^2 + N}} \qquad \qquad \text{Equation 14.6}$$

which is called the **coefficient of contingency**. Although the value of this measure is always between 0 and 1, it cannot generally attain the upper limit of 1. The maximum value possible depends upon the number of rows and columns. For example, in a 4×4 table, the maximum value of C is 0.87.

Cramér introduced the following variant:

$$V = \sqrt{\frac{\chi^2}{N(k-1)}} \qquad \qquad \text{Equation 14.7}$$

where k is the smaller of the number of rows and columns. This statistic, known as **Cramér's V**, can attain the maximum of 1 for tables of any dimension. If one of the table dimensions is 2, V and phi are identical.

Figure 14.5 shows the values of the chi-square-based measures for the strike-it-rich data. The test of the null hypothesis that a measure is 0 is based on the Pearson chi-square probability. Since the observed significance level is very small, you can reject the null hypothesis that the chi-squared based measures are zero.

Figure 14.5   Chi-square-based measures

```
CROSSTABS TABLES=SEX BY RICHWORK
 /STATISTICS=PHI CC.
```

```
SEX   RESPONDENTS SEX  by  RICHWORK   IF RICH, CONTINUE OR STOP WORKING

                     RICHWORK        Page 1 of 1
              Count
                     CONTINUE STOP WOR
                     WORKING  KING      Row
                        1        2    Total
     SEX         ──────────────────────────
                  1     234      89     323
        MALE                            52.4

                  2     178     115     293
        FEMALE                          47.6
              Column    412     204     616
              Total    66.9    33.1   100.0
```

```
                                                        Approximate
      Statistic               Value     ASE1   Val/ASE0 Significance
  --------------------      ---------  -------- -------- ------------

  Phi                         .12410                     .00207 *1
  Cramer's V                  .12410                     .00207 *1
  Contingency Coefficient     .12315                     .00207 *1
```

```
*1 Pearson chi-square probability

Number of Missing Observations:  901
```

The chi-square-based measures are hard to interpret. Although when properly standardized they can be used to compare strength of association in several tables, the strength of association being compared is not easily related to an intuitive concept of association.

Proportional Reduction in Error

Common alternatives to chi-square-based measurements are those based on the idea of **proportional reduction in error (PRE)**, introduced by Goodman and Kruskal (1954). With PRE measures, the meaning of association is clearer. These measures are all essentially ratios of a measure of error in predicting the values of one variable based on knowledge of that variable alone and the same measure of error applied to predictions based on knowledge of an additional variable.

For example, Figure 14.6 is a crosstabulation of depth of hypnosis and success in treatment of migraine headaches by suggestion (Cedercreutz, 1978). The best guess of the results of treatment when no other information is available is the outcome category with the largest proportion of observations (the modal category).

Figure 14.6   Depth of hypnosis and success of treatment

```
GET FILE='HYPNOSIS.SYS'.
CROSSTABS TABLES=HYPNOSIS BY MIGRAINE
  /CELLS=COUNT COLUMN TOTAL
  /STATISTICS=LAMBDA.
```

```
HYPNOSIS  DEPTH OF HYPNOSIS  by  MIGRAINE  OUTCOME

                 MIGRAINE                     Page 1 of 1
          Count
          Col Pct  CURED   BETTER   NO
          Tot Pct                   CHANGE   Row
                    1.00    2.00     3.00  Total
HYPNOSIS  ───────
          1.00       13      5               18
 DEEP              56.5    15.6             18.0
                  13.0     5.0

          2.00       10      26      17      53
 MEDIUM            43.5    81.3    37.8    53.0
                  10.0    26.0    17.0

          3.00               1      28      29
 LIGHT                     3.1    62.2    29.0
                           1.0    28.0

          Column     23      32      45     100
          Total    23.0    32.0    45.0   100.0
```

```
                                             Approximate
       Statistic            Value    ASE1    T-value  Significance
    -------------------    -------  -------   -------  ------------


Lambda :
   symmetric               .35294   .11335   2.75267
   with HYPNOSIS dependent  .29787   .14702   1.72276
   with MIGRAINE dependent  .40000   .10539   3.07580
Goodman & Kruskal Tau :
   with HYPNOSIS dependent  .29435   .06304            .00000 *2
   with MIGRAINE dependent  .34508   .04863            .00000 *2

*2 Based on chi-square approximation

Number of Missing Observations:  0
```

In Figure 14.6, *no change* is the largest outcome category, with 45% of the subjects. The estimate of the probability of incorrect classification is 1 minus the probability of the modal category:

$$P(1) = 1 - 0.45 = 0.55$$

Equation 14.8

Information about the depth of hypnosis can be used to improve the classification rule. For each hypnosis category, the outcome category that occurs most frequently for that hypnosis level is predicted. Thus, *no change* is predicted for participants achieving a light level of hypnosis, *better* for those achieving a medium level, and *cured* for those achieving a deep level. The probability of error when depth of hypnosis is used to predict outcome is the sum of the probabilities of all the cells that are not row modes:

$$P(2) = 0.05 + 0.10 + 0.17 + 0.01 = 0.33$$ **Equation 14.9**

Goodman and Kruskal's **lambda**, with outcome as the predicted (dependent) variable, is calculated as

$$\lambda_{outcome} = \frac{P(1) - P(2)}{P(1)} = \frac{0.55 - 0.33}{0.55} = 0.40$$ **Equation 14.10**

Thus, a 40% reduction in error is obtained when depth of hypnosis is used to predict outcome.

Lambda always ranges between 0 and 1. A value of 0 means the independent variable is of no help in predicting the dependent variable. A value of 1 means that the independent variable perfectly specifies the categories of the dependent variable (perfection can occur only when each row has at most one nonzero cell). When the two variables are independent, lambda is 0; but a lambda of 0 does not imply statistical independence. As with all measures of association, lambda is constructed to measure association in a very specific way. In particular, lambda reflects the reduction in error when values of one variable are used to predict values of the other. If this particular type of association is absent, lambda is 0. Other measures of association may find association of a different kind even when lambda is 0. A measure of association sensitive to every imaginable type of association does not exist.

For a particular table, two different lambdas can be computed, one using the row variable as the predictor and the other using the column variable. The two do not usually have identical values, so care should be taken to specify which is the dependent variable; that is, the variable whose prediction is of primary interest. In some applications, dependent and independent variables are not clearly distinguished. In those instances, a symmetric version of lambda, which predicts the row variable and column variable with equal frequency, can be computed. When the lambda statistic is requested, SPSS/PC+ displays the symmetric lambda as well as the two asymmetric lambdas.

Goodman and Kruskal's Tau

When lambda is computed, the same prediction is made for all cases in a particular row or column. Another approach is to consider what happens if the prediction is randomly made in the same proportion as the marginal totals. For example, if you're trying to predict migraine outcome without any information about the depth of the hypnosis, you can use the marginal distributions in Figure 14.6 instead of the modal category to guess *cured* for 23% of the cases, *better* for 32% of the cases, and *no change* for 45% of the cases.

Using these marginals, you would expect to correctly classify 23% of the 23 cases in the *cured* category, 32% of the 32 cases in the *better* category, and 45% of the 45 cases in the *no change* category. This results in the correct classification of 35.78 out of 100 cases. When additional information about the depth of hypnosis is incorporated into the prediction rule, the prediction is based on the probability of the different outcomes for each depth of hypnosis. For example, for those who experienced deep hypnosis, you would predict *cure* 72% of the time (13/18) and *better* 28% of the time (5/18). Similarly, for those with light hypnosis, you would predict *better* 3% of the time and *no change* 97% of the time. This results in correct classification for about 58 of the cases.

Goodman and Kruskal's tau is computed by comparing the probability of error in the two situations. In this example, when predicting only from the column marginal totals, the probability of error is 0.64. When predicting from row information the probability of error is 0.42. Thus:

$$\text{tau (migraine} \mid \text{hypnosis)} \ = \ (0.64 - 0.42)\,/\,0.64 \ = \ 0.34 \qquad \textbf{Equation 14.11}$$

By incorporating information about the depth of hypnosis we have reduced our error of prediction by about 34%.

A test of the null hypothesis that tau is 0 can be based on the value of $(N-1)\,(c-1)$ tau (col | row), which has a chi-square distribution with $(c-1) \times (r-1)$ degrees of freedom. In this example, the observed significance level for tau is very small, and you can reject the null hypothesis that tau is 0. The asymptotic standard error for the statistic is shown in the column labeled *ASE1*. The asymptotic standard error can be used to construct confidence intervals.

Measuring Agreement

Measures of agreement allow you to compare the ratings of two observers for the same group of objects. For example, consider the data reported in Bishop et al. (1975), shown in Figure 14.7.

Two supervisors rated the classroom style of 72 teachers. You are interested in measuring the agreement between the two raters. The simplest measure that comes to mind is just the proportion of cases for which the raters agree. In this case, it is 58.3%. The disadvantage of this measure is that no correction is made for the amount of agreement expected by chance. That is, you would expect the supervisors to agree sometimes even if they were assigning ratings by tossing dice.

To correct for chance agreement, you can compute the proportion of cases that you would expect to be in agreement if the ratings are independent. For example, supervisor 1 rated 40.3% of the teachers as authoritarian, while supervisor 2 rated 44.4% of the teachers as authoritarian. If their rankings are independent, you would expect that 17.9% ($40.3\% \times 44.4\%$) of the teachers would be rated as authoritarian by both. Similarly, 6.2% ($23.6\% \times 26.4\%$) would be rated as democratic and 10.5% ($36.1\% \times 29.2\%$) as

Figure 14.7   Student teachers rated by supervisors

```
GET FILE='STUTEACH.SYS'.
CROSSTABS TABLES=SUPRVSR1 BY SUPRVSR2
 /CELLS COUNT TOTAL
 /STATISTICS=KAPPA.
```

SUPRVSR1   Supervisor 1   by   SUPRVSR2   Supervisor 2

		SUPRVSR2			Page 1 of 1
	Count Tot Pct	Authorit arian 1.00	Democrat ic 2.00	Permissi ve 3.00	Row Total
SUPRVSR1					
Authoritarian	1.00	17 23.6	4 5.6	8 11.1	29 40.3
Democratic	2.00	5 6.9	12 16.7		17 23.6
Permissive	3.00	10 13.9	3 4.2	13 18.1	26 36.1
	Column Total	32 44.4	19 26.4	21 29.2	72 100.0

Statistic	Value	ASE1	T-value	Approximate Significance
Kappa	.36227	.09075	4.32902	

Number of Missing Observations: 0

permissive. Thus, 34.6% of all the teachers would be classified the same merely by chance.

The difference between the observed proportion of cases in which the raters agree and that expected by chance is 0.237 (0.583 − 0.346). **Cohen's kappa** (Cohen, 1960) normalizes this difference by dividing it by the maximum difference possible for the marginal totals. In this example, the largest possible "non-chance" agreement is 1 − 0.346 (the chance level). Therefore:

$$\text{kappa} = 0.237 / (1 - 0.346) = 0.362 \qquad \textbf{Equation 14.12}$$

The test of the null hypothesis that kappa is 0 can be based on the ratio of the measure to its standard error, assuming that the null hypothesis is true. (See Benedetti and Brown, 1978, for further discussion of standard errors for measures of association.) This asymptotic error is not the one shown on the output. The asymptotic standard error on the output, $ASE1$, does not assume that the true value is 0.

Since the kappa statistic measures agreement between two raters, the two variables that contain the ratings must have the same range of values. If this is not true, SPSS/PC+ will not compute kappa.

Ordinal Measures

Although relationships among ordinal variables can be examined using nominal measures, other measures reflect the additional information available from ranking. Consideration of the kinds of relationships that may exist between two ordered variables leads to the notion of direction of relationship and to the concept of **correlation**. Variables are positively correlated if cases with low values for one variable also tend to have low values for the other, and cases with high values for one also tend to be high for the other. Negatively correlated variables show the opposite relationship: the higher the first variable, the lower the second tends to be.

The **Spearman correlation coefficient** is a commonly used measure of correlation between two ordinal variables. For all of the cases, the values of each of the variables are ranked from smallest to largest, and the Pearson correlation coefficient is computed on the ranks. The **Mantel-Haenszel chi-square** is another measure of linear association between the row and column variables in a crosstabulation. It is computed by multiplying the square of the Pearson correlation coefficient by the number of cases minus 1. The resulting statistic has one degree of freedom (Mantel & Haenszel, 1959). (Although the Mantel-Haenszel statistic is displayed whenever chi-square is requested, it should not be used for nominal data.)

Ordinal Measures Based on Pairs

For a table of two ordered variables, several measures of association based on a comparison of the values of both variables for all possible *pairs* of cases or observations are available. Cases are first compared to determine if they are concordant, discordant, or tied. A pair of cases is **concordant** if the values of both variables for one case are higher (or both are lower) than the corresponding values for the other case. The pair is **discordant** if the value of one variable for a case is larger than the corresponding value for the other case, and the direction is reversed for the second variable. When the two cases have identical values for one or for both variables, they are **tied**.

Thus, for any given pair of cases with measurements on variables X and Y, the pair may be concordant or discordant, or tied in one of three ways: they may be tied on X but not on Y, they may be tied on Y but not on X, or they may be tied on both variables. When data are arranged in crosstabulated form, the number of concordant, discordant, and tied pairs can be easily calculated since all possible pairs can be conveniently determined.

If the preponderance of pairs is concordant, the association is said to be positive: as ranks of variable X increase (or decrease), so do ranks of variable Y. If the majority of pairs is discordant, the association is negative: as ranks of one variable increase, those of the other tend to decrease. If concordant and discordant pairs are equally likely, no association is said to exist.

The ordinal measures presented here all have the same numerator: the number of concordant pairs (P) minus the number of discordant pairs (Q) calculated for all distinct pairs of observations. They differ primarily in the way in which $P - Q$ is normalized.

The simplest measure involves subtracting Q from P and dividing by the total number of pairs. If there are no pairs with ties, this measure (**Kendall's tau-*a***) is in the range from -1 to $+1$. If there are ties, the range of possible values is narrower; the actual range depends on the number of ties. Since all observations within the same row are tied, so also are those in the same column, and the resulting tau-*a* measures are difficult to interpret.

A measure that attempts to normalize $P - Q$ by considering ties on each variable in a pair separately but not ties on both variables in a pair is **tau-*b***

$$\tau_b = \frac{P - Q}{\sqrt{(P + Q + T_X)\ (P + Q + T_Y)}}$$

Equation 14.13

where T_X is the number of pairs tied on X but not on Y, and T_Y is the number of pairs tied on Y but not on X. If no marginal frequency is 0, tau-*b* can attain $+1$ or -1 only for a square table.

A measure that can attain, or nearly attain, $+1$ or -1 for any $r \times c$ table is **tau-*c***

$$\tau_c = \frac{2m\,(P - Q)}{N^2\,(m - 1)}$$

Equation 14.14

where m is the smaller of the number of rows and columns. The coefficients tau-*b* and tau-*c* do not differ much in value if each margin contains approximately equal frequencies.

Goodman and Kruskal's gamma is closely related to the tau statistics and is calculated as

$$G = \frac{P - Q}{P + Q}$$

Equation 14.15

Gamma can be thought of as the probability that a random pair of observations is concordant minus the probability that the pair is discordant, assuming the absence of ties. The absolute value of gamma is the proportional reduction in error between guessing the concordant and discordant ranking of each pair depending on which occurs more often and guessing the ranking according to the outcome of a fair toss of a coin. Gamma is 1 if all observations are concentrated in the upper-left to lower-right diagonal of the table. In the case of independence, gamma is 0. However, the converse (that a gamma of 0 necessarily implies independence) need not be true except in the 2×2 table.

In the computation of gamma, no distinction is made between the independent and dependent variable; the variables are treated symmetrically. Somers (1962) proposed an asymmetric extension of gamma that differs only in the inclusion of the number of pairs not tied on the independent variable (*X*) in the denominator. **Somers' *d*** is

$$d_Y = \frac{P - Q}{P + Q + T_Y}$$

Equation 14.16

The coefficient d_Y indicates the proportionate excess of concordant pairs over discordant pairs among pairs not tied on the independent variable. The symmetric variant of Somers' *d* uses for the denominator the average value of the denominators of the two asymmetric coefficients.

These ordinal measures for the migraine data are shown in Figure 14.8. All of the measures indicate that there is a fairly strong positive association between the two variables.

Figure 14.8   Ordinal measures

```
GET FILE='HYPNOSIS.SYS'.
CROSSTABS TABLES=HYPNOSIS BY MIGRAINE
 /FORMAT=NOTABLE
 /STATISTICS=CORR BTAU CTAU GAMMA D.

HYPNOSIS  DEPTH OF HYPNOSIS  by  MIGRAINE  OUTCOME

Number of valid observations = 100
```

Statistic	Value	ASE1	Val/ASE0	Approximate Significance
Kendall's Tau-b	.67901	.04445	11.96486	
Kendall's Tau-c	.63360	.05296	11.96486	
Gamma	.94034	.02720	11.96486	
Somers' D :				
symmetric	.67866	.04443	11.96486	
with HYPNOSIS dependent	.65774	.05440	11.96486	
with MIGRAINE dependent	.70096	.03996	11.96486	
Pearson's R	.71739	.04484	10.19392	.00000 *4
Spearman Correlation	.72442	.04317	10.40311	.00000 *4

```
*4 T-value and significance based on a normal approximation
```

Measures Involving Interval Data

If the two variables in the table are measured on an interval scale, various coefficients that make use of this additional information can be calculated. A useful symmetric coefficient that measures the strength of the *linear* relationship is the **Pearson correlation coefficient (*r*)**. It can take on values from −1 to +1, indicating negative or positive linear correlation.

The **eta coefficient** is appropriate for data in which the dependent variable is measured on an interval scale and the independent variable on a nominal or ordinal scale.

When squared, eta can be interpreted as the proportion of the total variability in the dependent variable that can be accounted for by knowing the values of the independent variable. The measure is asymmetric and does not assume a linear relationship between the variables.

Estimating Risk in Cohort Studies

Often you want to identify variables that are related to the occurrence of a particular event. For example, you may want to determine if smoking is related to heart disease. A commonly used index that measures the strength of the association between presence of a factor and occurrence of an event is the **relative risk ratio**. It is estimated as the ratio of two incidence rates, such as the incidence rate of heart disease in those who smoke and the incidence rate of heart disease in those who do not smoke.

For example, suppose you observe for five years 1000 smokers without a history of heart disease and 1000 nonsmokers without a history of heart disease, and you determine how many of each group develop heart disease during this time period. (Studies in which a group of disease-free people are studied to see who develops the disease are called **cohort** or **prospective studies**.) Figure 14.9 contains hypothetical results from such a cohort study

Figure 14.9 Hypothetical cohorts

```
GET FILE='HDISEASE.SYS'.
CROSSTABS TABLES=SMOKING BY HDISEASE
 /STATISTICS=RISK.
```

```
SMOKING  Smoking  by  HDISEASE  Heart Disease

                  HDISEASE       Page 1 of 1
            Count
                  Yes    No
                                    Row
                    1.00    2.00  Total
    SMOKING
            1.00   100     900    1000
      Yes                         50.0

            2.00    50     950    1000
      No                          50.0

         Column    150    1850    2000
         Total     7.5    92.5   100.0
```

```
      Statistic              Value       95% Confidence Bounds
---------------------       --------    ----------------------
Relative Risk Estimate (SMOKING 2.0 / SMOKING 1.0) :
   case control             2.11111     1.48544      3.00032
   cohort (HDISEASE 1.0 Risk)  2.00000  1.44078      2.77628
   cohort (HDISEASE 2.0 Risk)   .94737   .92390       .97143

Number of Missing Observations:  0
```

The five-year incidence rate for smokers is 100/1000, while the incidence rate for nonsmokers is 50/1000. The relative risk ratio is 2 (100/1000 divided by 50/1000). This indicates that, in the sample, smokers are twice as likely to develop heart disease as nonsmokers.

The estimated relative risk and its 95% confidence interval are in the row labeled *co-hort (HDISEASE 1.0 Risk)* in Figure 14.9. In SPSS/PC+, the ratio is always computed by taking the incidence in the first row and dividing it by the incidence in the second row. Since either column can represent the event, separate estimates are displayed for each column. The 95% confidence interval does not include the value of 1, so you can reject the null hypothesis that the two incidence rates are the same.

Estimating Risk in Case-Control Studies

In the cohort study described above, we took a group of disease-free people (the cohort) and watched what happened to them. Another type of study that is commonly used is called a retrospective, or **case-control study**. In this type of study, we take a group of people with the disease of interest (the cases) and a comparable group of people without the disease (the controls) and see how they differ. For example, we could take 100 people with documented coronary heart disease and 100 controls without heart disease and establish how many in each group smoked. The hypothetical results are shown in Figure 14.10.

Figure 14.10 Hypothetical smoking control

```
GET FILE='RETROHDIS.SYS'.
CROSSTABS TABLES=GROUP BY SMOKING
 /CELLS=COUNT ROW
 /STATISTICS=RISK.


GROUP  by   SMOKING

                     SMOKING        Page 1 of 1
              Count
              Row Pct  Yes      No
                        1.00|   2.00|  Row
                                       Total
    GROUP     _____
               1.00      30      70    100
    Cases               30.0    70.0   50.0

               2.00      10      90    100
    Control             10.0    90.0   50.0

              Column     40     160    200
              Total     20.0    80.0   100.0



        Statistic                    Value          95% Confidence Bounds
    --------------------             --------        ------------------------
    Relative Risk Estimate (GROUP 2.0 / GROUP 1.0) :
        case control                 3.85714          1.76660      8.42156
        cohort (SMOKING 1.0 Risk)    3.00000          1.55083      5.80335
        cohort (SMOKING 2.0 Risk)     .77778           .67348       .89823

    Number of Missing Observations:  0
```

From a case-control study, we cannot estimate incidence rates. Thus, we cannot compute the relative risk ratio. Instead, we estimate relative risk using what is called an **odds ratio**. We compute the odds that a case smokes and divide it by the odds that a control smokes.

For example, from Figure 14.10, the odds that a case smokes are 30/70. The odds that a control smokes are 10/90. The odds ratio is then 30/70 divided by 10/90, or 3.85. The odds ratio and its confidence interval are in the row labeled *case control* in Figure 14.10. SPSS/PC+ expects the cases to be in the first row and the controls in the second. Similarly, the event of interest must be in the first column. For further discussion of measures of risk, see Kleinbaum et al. (1982).

Running Procedure CROSSTABS

Procedure CROSSTABS produces two-way to *n*-way crosstabulations and related statistical measures for variables with numeric or string values. In addition to cell counts, you can obtain cell percentages and expected values. You can alter the handling of missing values, reorder rows, request an index of tables, and write cell frequencies to a file.

Specifying the Tables

The only required subcommand for CROSSTABS is the TABLES subcommand. The minimum specification for the TABLES subcommand is a list of one or more variables followed by the keyword BY and a second list of one or more variables, as in:

```
CROSSTABS TABLES=SEX BY RICHWORK.
```

The first variable list specifies the **row variables**, and the variable list following the first BY keyword specifies the **column variables**.

Optionally, you can specify **control variables** with additional BY keywords and variable lists, as in:

```
CROSSTABS TABLES=SEX BY RICHWOOK BY MARITAL.
```

A separate subtable is generated for each value of the control variable(s). In this example, the control variable *MARITAL* has five values, producing five subtables (two of which are shown in Figure 14.2).

You can specify more than one variable in each dimension. Use the TO keyword to imply consecutive variables in the active file, as in:

```
CROSSTABS  TABLES=CONFINAN TO CONARMY BY SEX TO REGION.
```

This command produces tables for all the variables between and including *CONFINAN* and *CONARMY* by all the variables between and including *SEX* and *REGION*.

You can specify multiple TABLES subcommands. Each subcommand should be separated by a slash.

Using Integer Mode

To run CROSSTABS in **integer mode**, use the VARIABLES subcommand. Integer mode requires more memory than general mode if the table has many empty cells, but less if the data values fall within narrow ranges. You must specify an integer value range enclosed in parentheses for each variable, as in:

```
CROSSTABS VARIABLES=SEX(1,2) RICHWORK(1,2)
 /TABLES=SEX BY RICHWORK.
```

Since only values within the specified range will be included, you can use the VARIABLES subcommand to select subsets of cases for analysis. If multiple variables have the same range, you can specify the range only once, as in:

```
CROSSTABS VARIABLES=MARITAL(1,5) SEX RICHWORK(1,2)
 /TABLES=SEX BY RICHWORK BY MARITAL.
```

This command specifies the same range for variables *SEX* and *RICHWORK*.

If used, the VARIABLES subcommand must be the first subcommand specified, and it must include all variables specified on subsequent TABLES subcommands. The TO keyword on subsequent TABLES subcommands refers to the order of variables on the VARIABLES subcommand, not the order of variables in the active file.

Specifying Cell Contents

By default, CROSSTABS displays only the number of cases in each cell. Use the CELLS subcommand to display row, column, or total percentages, expected values, and residuals. These items are calculated separately for each bivariate table or subtable.

You can specify the CELLS subcommand by itself, or with one or more keywords. If you specify the CELLS subcommand by itself, CROSSTABS displays cell counts plus row, column, and total percentages for each cell. If you specify keywords, CROSSTABS displays only the cell information you request.

The following keywords can be specified on the CELLS subcommand:

COUNT   *Cell counts.* This is the default if you omit the CELLS subcommand.

ROW   *Row percentages.* Row percentages are the number of cases in each cell in a row expressed as a percentage of all cases in that row.

COLUMN   *Column percentages.* Column percentages are the number of cases in each cell in a column expressed as a percentage of all cases in that column.

TOTAL   *Two-way table total percentages.* This is the number of cases in each cell of a subtable expressed as a percentage of all cases in that subtable.

EXPECTED   *Expected frequencies.* Expected frequencies are the number of cases expected in each cell if the two variables in the subtable are statistically independent.

RESID	*Residuals.* The residual is the value of the observed cell count minus the expected value.
SRESID	*Standardized residuals* (Haberman, 1978).
ASRESID	*Adjusted standardized residuals* (Haberman, 1978).
ALL	*All cell information.* This includes cell counts, row, column, and total percentages, expected values, residuals, standardized residuals, and adjusted standardized residuals.
NONE	*No cell information.* Use NONE to write tables to a file without displaying any tables. This has the same effect as specifying FORMAT=NOTABLES (see "Format Options" on p. 207).

For example, the command

```
CROSSTABS TABLES=SEX BY RICHWORK   /CELLS.
```

produces Figure 14.1, and the command

```
CROSSTABS TABLES=SEX BY RICHWORK
  /CELLS=COUNT EXPECTED RESID.
  /STATISTICS=CHISQ.
```

produces Figure 14.4.

Requesting Statistics

CROSSTABS can calculate a number of summary statistics for each subtable. Unless you specify otherwise, it calculates statistical measures of association for the cases with valid values included in the subtable. If you include user-missing values with the MISSING subcommand, cases with user-missing values are included in the tables as well as in the calculation of statistics.

The STATISTICS subcommand requests summary statistics. You can specify the STATISTICS subcommand by itself, or with one or more keywords. If you specify STATISTICS by itself, CROSSTABS calculates CHISQ. If you include a keyword or keywords on the STATISTICS subcommand, CROSSTABS calculates only the statistics you request.

Asymptotic standard errors (ASE1) that are not based on the assumption that the true value is 0 are also calculated. The *t* statistics displayed are the ratio of the measure to an asymptotic standard error which assumes the true coefficient is 0.

The following keywords can be specified on the STATISTICS subcommand:

CHISQ	*Chi-square.* The output includes the Pearson chi-square, likelihood-ratio chi-square, and Mantel-Haenszel linear association chi-square. For 2×2 tables, Fisher's exact test is computed when a table that does not result from missing rows or columns in a larger table has a cell with an expected frequency less

than 5; Yates' corrected chi-square is computed for all other 2×2 tables. This is the default if STATISTICS is specified without keywords.

PHI   *Phi and Cramér's V.*

CC   *Contingency coefficient.*

LAMBDA *Lambda, symmetric and asymmetric, and Goodman and Kruskal's tau.*

UC   *Uncertainty coefficient, symmetric and asymmetric.*

BTAU   *Kendall's tau*-b.

CTAU   *Kendall's tau*-c.

GAMMA   *Gamma.* Partial and zero-order gammas for 3-way to 8-way tables are available in integer mode only (see "Using Integer Mode" on p. 204). Zero-order gammas are displayed for 2-way tables and conditional gammas are displayed for 3-way to 10-way tables in general mode.

D   *Somers'* d (symmetric and asymmetric).

ETA   *Eta.* Available for numeric data only.

CORR   *Pearson's* r *and Spearman's correlation coefficient.* Available for numeric data only.

KAPPA   *Kappa coefficient.* Kappa can only be computed for square tables in which the row and column values are identical. If there is a missing row or column, use integer mode to specify the square table, since a missing column or row in general mode would keep the table from being square (see "Using Integer Mode" on p. 204). (Kraemer, 1982.)

RISK   *Relative risk.* Relative risk can be calculated only for 2×2 tables. (Kleinbaum et al., 1982).

ALL   *All available statistics.*

NONE   *No summary statistics.* This is the default if STATISTICS is omitted.

For example, the command

```
CROSSTABS TABLES=SEX BY RICHWORK
  /STATISTICS=PHI CC.
```

produces Figure 14.5.

Missing Values

By default, CROSSTABS deletes cases with missing values on a table-by-table basis. Cases with missing values for any of the variables specified for a table are not used either in the table or in the calculation of the statistics. Missing values are handled separately for each TABLES subcommand. The number of missing cases is displayed at the end of the table, following the last subtable and after any requested statistics.

The MISSING subcommand controls missing values. The following keywords can be specified on the MISSING subcommand:

TABLE   *Delete cases with missing values on a table-by-table basis.* This is the default if you omit the MISSING subcommand.

INCLUDE   *Include cases with user-missing values.*

REPORT   *Report missing values in the tables.* This option includes missing values in tables but not in the calculation of percentages or statistics. The letter *M* is used to indicate that cases within a cell are missing. REPORT is available only in integer mode (see "Using Integer Mode" on p. 204).

Format Options

Use the FORMAT subcommand to modify the default formats. The following keywords can be specified:

LABELS   *Display both variable and value labels for each table.* This is the default. The values for the row variables are displayed in order from lowest to highest. CROSSTABS uses only the first 16 characters of the value labels. Value labels for the columns are displayed on two lines with eight characters per line.

NOLABELS   *Suppress variable and value labels.*

NOVALLABS *Suppress value labels but display variable labels.*

AVALUE   *Display row variables ordered from lowest to highest.* This is the default.

DVALUE   *Display row variables ordered from highest to lowest.*

NOINDEX   *Suppress the table index.* This is the default.

INDEX   *Display an index of tables.* The index lists all tables produced by the CROSSTABS command and the page number where each table begins. The index follows the last page of tables produced by the tables list.

TABLES   *Display the tables.* This is the default.

NOTABLES   *Suppress tables.* If you use the STATISTICS subcommand (see "Requesting Statistics" on p. 205) and specify NOTABLES, only the statistics are displayed. If you do not use the STATISTICS subcommand and specify NOTABLES, the CROSSTABS command produces no output.

BOX   *Use box characters around every cell.* This is the default.

NOBOX   *Suppress box characters around each cell.* The row and column headings are still separated from the table by box characters.

Writing Cell Frequencies to a File

The WRITE subcommand writes cell frequencies to a results file (specified on the SET RESULTS command) for subsequent use by SPSS/PC+ or some other program. The output file contains one record per cell.

NONE *Do not write the cell counts to the file.* This is the default if you omit the WRITE subcommand.

CELLS *Write the cell count for nonempty cells to a file.*

ALL *Write the cell count for all cells to a file.* This is only available in integer mode.

For more information about the WRITE subcommand, see CROSSTABS in the Syntax Reference.

Entering Crosstabulated Data

You can use the CROSSTABS procedure to calculate statistics for a pre-existing crosstabulation without entering the individual case data. Each cell of the table is considered a case. The values for each case are the cell count and the values of the row, column, and control variables.

Define this file as you would any other file. Then use the WEIGHT command to count each case as many times as the value of the cell count variable. For example, Figure 14.9 was produced from a table, rather than raw data, using the following commands:

```
DATA LIST FREE /SMOKING HDISEASE COUNT.
BEGIN DATA.
1 1 100
1 2 900
2 1 50
2 2 950
END DATA.
VARIABLE LABELS
    SMOKING 'Smoking'
    HDISEASE 'Heart Disease'.
VALUE LABELS SMOKING HDISEASE 1 'Yes' 2 'No'.
WEIGHT BY COUNT.
CROSSTABS TABLES=SMOKING by HDISEASE
    /STATISTICS=RISK.
```

- The DATA LIST command names three variables: *SMOKING* is the row variable, *HDISEASE* is the column variable, and *COUNT* is the cell count.

- The optional VARIABLE LABELS and VALUE LABELS commands identify the variables and values in the tables.

- The WEIGHT command weights each case by the cell count.

- The CROSSTABS command recreates the table, and the STATISTICS subcommand provides summary statistics not provided with the original table.

15 Describing Subpopulation Differences: Procedure MEANS

The 1964 Civil Rights Act prohibits discrimination in the workplace based on sex or race; employers who violate the act can be prosecuted. Since passage of this legislation, women, blacks, and other groups have filed numerous lawsuits charging unfair hiring or advancement practices.

The courts have ruled that statistics can be used as *prima facie* evidence of discrimination, and many lawsuits depend heavily on complex statistical analyses to demonstrate that similarly qualified individuals are not treated equally. Identifying and measuring all variables that legitimately influence promotion and hiring is difficult, if not impossible, especially for nonroutine jobs. Years of schooling and prior work experience can be quantified, but what about the more intangible attributes such as enthusiasm and creativity? How are they to be objectively measured so as not to become convenient smoke screens for concealing discrimination?

Searching for Discrimination

In this chapter, we analyze employee records for 474 individuals hired between 1969 and 1971 by a bank engaged in Equal Employment Opportunity litigation. Two types of unfair employment practices are of particular interest: shunting (placing some employees in lower job categories than other employees with similar qualifications) and salary and promotion inequities.

Although extensive and intricate statistical analyses are usually involved in studies of this kind (for example, see Roberts, 1980), the discussion here is necessarily limited. The SPSS/PC+ MEANS procedure is used to calculate average salaries for groups of employees based on race and sex. Additional grouping variables are introduced to help "explain" some of the observed variability in salary.

Who Does What?

Figure 15.1 is a crosstabulation of job category at the time of hiring by sex and race characteristics. The first three job classifications contain 64% of white males (adding column percentages), 94% of both minority males and white females, and 100% of minority females. Among white males, 17% are in the college trainee program, compared to 4% of white females.

Figure 15.1   Crosstabulation of job category by sex-race

```
SET LENGTH 59.
CROSSTABS JOBCAT BY SEXRACE /CELLS COUNT COLUMN TOTAL.
JOBCAT EMPLOYMENT CATEGORY by SEXRACE SEX & RACE CLASSIFICATION
```

		SEXRACE				Page 1 of 1
	Count Col Pct Tot Pct	WHITE MALES	MINORITY MALES	WHITE FEMALES	MINORITY FEMALES	Row Total
		1	2	3	4	
JOBCAT						
CLERICAL	1	75 38.7 15.8	35 54.7 7.4	85 48.3 17.9	32 80.0 6.8	227 47.9
OFFICE TRAINEE	2	35 18.0 7.4	12 18.8 2.5	81 46.0 17.1	8 20.0 1.7	136 28.7
SECURITY OFFICER	3	14 7.2 3.0	13 20.3 2.7			27 5.7
COLLEGE TRAINEE	4	33 17.0 7.0	1 1.6 .2	7 4.0 1.5		41 8.6
EXEMPT EMPLOYEE	5	28 14.4 5.9	2 3.1 .4	2 1.1 .4		32 6.8
MBA TRAINEE	6	3 1.5 .6	1 1.6 .2	1 .6 .2		5 1.1
TECHNICAL	7	6 3.1 1.3				6 1.3
Column Total		194 40.9	64 13.5	176 37.1	40 8.4	474 100.0

```
Number of Missing Observations:   0
```

Although these observations are interesting, they do not imply discriminatory job placement because the qualifications of the various groups are not necessarily similar. If women and nonwhites are more qualified than white males in the same beginning job categories, discrimination may be suspected.

Level of Education

One easily measured employment qualification is years of education. Figure 15.2 shows the average years of education for the entire sample (labeled *For Entire Population*) and then for each of the two sexes (labeled *MALES* or *FEMALES*) and then for each of the two race categories within each sex category (labeled *WHITE* or *NONWHITE*).

Figure 15.2   Education by sex and race

```
MEANS TABLES=EDLEVEL BY SEX BY MINORITY.

                   - - Description of Subpopulations - -

Summaries of     EDLEVEL      EDUCATIONAL LEVEL
By levels of     SEX          SEX OF EMPLOYEE
                 MINORITY     MINORITY CLASSIFICATION


Variable       Value  Label                    Mean    Std Dev    Cases

For Entire Population                         13.4916    2.8848     474

SEX              0   MALES                    14.4302    2.9793     258
  MINORITY       0   WHITE                    14.9227    2.8484     194
  MINORITY       1   NONWHITE                 12.9375    2.8888      64

SEX              1   FEMALES                  12.3704    2.3192     216
  MINORITY       0   WHITE                    12.3409    2.4066     176
  MINORITY       1   NONWHITE                 12.5000    1.9081      40

  Total Cases = 474
```

The entire sample has an average of 13.49 years of education. Males have more years of education than females—an average of 14.43 years compared to 12.37. White males have the highest level of education, almost 15 years, which is 2 years more than non-white males and approximately 2.5 years more than either group of females.

In Figure 15.3, the cases are further subdivided by their combined sex-race characteristics and by their initial job category. For each cell in the table, the average years of education, the standard deviation, and number of cases are displayed. White males have the highest average years of education in all job categories except MBA trainees, where the single minority male MBA trainee has 19 years of education. From this table, it does not appear that females and minorities are overeducated when compared to white males in similar job categories. However, it is important to note that group means provide information about a particular class of employees. While discrimination may not exist for a class as a whole, some individuals within that class may be victims (or beneficiaries) of discrimination.

Figure 15.3   Education by sex-race and job category

```
MEANS TABLES=EDLEVEL BY JOBCAT BY SEXRACE.

                    - - Description of Subpopulations - -

Summaries of      EDLEVEL      EDUCATIONAL LEVEL
By levels of      JOBCAT       EMPLOYMENT CATEGORY
                  SEXRACE      SEX & RACE CLASSIFICATION


Variable          Value  Label                  Mean     Std Dev    Cases

For Entire Population                          13.4916    2.8848     474

JOBCAT              1    CLERICAL              12.7753    2.5621     227
  SEXRACE           1    WHITE MALES           13.8667    2.3035      75
  SEXRACE           2    MINORITY MALES        13.7714    2.3147      35
  SEXRACE           3    WHITE FEMALES         11.4588    2.4327      85
  SEXRACE           4    MINORITY FEMALES      12.6250    2.1213      32

JOBCAT              2    OFFICE TRAINEE        13.0221    1.8875     136
  SEXRACE           1    WHITE MALES           13.8857    1.4095      35
  SEXRACE           2    MINORITY MALES        12.5833    2.6097      12
  SEXRACE           3    WHITE FEMALES         12.8148    1.9307      81
  SEXRACE           4    MINORITY FEMALES      12.0000     .0000       8

JOBCAT              3    SECURITY OFFICER      10.1852    2.2194      27
  SEXRACE           1    WHITE MALES           10.2857    2.0542      14
  SEXRACE           2    MINORITY MALES        10.0769    2.4651      13

JOBCAT              4    COLLEGE TRAINEE       17.0000    1.2845      41
  SEXRACE           1    WHITE MALES           17.2121    1.3407      33
  SEXRACE           2    MINORITY MALES        17.0000     .           1
  SEXRACE           3    WHITE FEMALES         16.0000     .0000       7

JOBCAT              5    EXEMPT EMPLOYEE       17.2813    1.9713      32
  SEXRACE           1    WHITE MALES           17.6071    1.7709      28
  SEXRACE           2    MINORITY MALES        14.0000    2.8284       2
  SEXRACE           3    WHITE FEMALES         16.0000     .0000       2

JOBCAT              6    MBA TRAINEE           18.0000    1.4142       5
  SEXRACE           1    WHITE MALES           18.3333    1.1547       3
  SEXRACE           2    MINORITY MALES        19.0000     .           1
  SEXRACE           3    WHITE FEMALES         16.0000     .           1

JOBCAT              7    TECHNICAL             18.1667    1.4720       6
  SEXRACE           1    WHITE MALES           18.1667    1.4720       6

    Total Cases = 474
```

Beginning Salaries

The average beginning salary for the 474 persons hired between 1969 and 1971 is $6,806. The distribution by the four sex-race categories is shown in Figure 15.4.

Figure 15.4   Beginning salary by sex-race

```
MEANS TABLES=SALBEG BY SEXRACE
  /OPTIONS=6,12.
                  - - Description of Subpopulations - -

Summaries of     SALBEG     BEGINNING SALARY
By levels of     SEXRACE    SEX & RACE CLASSIFICATION


Variable        Value  Label                    Mean    Std Dev    Cases

For Entire Population                         6806.4346  3148.2553    474

SEXRACE           1    WHITE  MALES            8637.5258  3871.1017    194
SEXRACE           2    MINORITY MALES          6553.5000  2228.1436     64
SEXRACE           3    WHITE  FEMALES          5340.4886  1225.9605    176
SEXRACE           4    MINORITY FEMALES        4780.5000   771.4188     40

   Total Cases = 474
```

White males have the highest beginning salaries—an average of $8,638—followed by minority males. Since males are in higher job categories than females, this difference is not surprising.

Figure 15.5 shows beginning salaries subdivided by race, sex, and job category. For most of the job categories, white males have higher beginning salaries than the other groups. There is a $1,400 salary difference between white males and white females in the clerical jobs and a $1,000 difference in the general office trainee classification. In the college trainee program, white males averaged over $3,000 more than white females. However, Figure 15.3 shows that white females in the college trainee program had only an undergraduate degree, while white males had an average of 17.2 years of schooling.

Figure 15.5   Beginning salary by sex-race and job category

```
MEANS TABLES=SALBEG BY JOBCAT BY SEXRACE /OPTIONS 5 7.

                    - - Description of Subpopulations - -

Summaries of     SALBEG      BEGINNING SALARY
By levels of     JOBCAT      EMPLOYMENT CATEGORY
                 SEXRACE     SEX & RACE CLASSIFICATION


Variable         Value  Label                          Mean

For Entire Population                               6806.4346

JOBCAT            1  CLERICAL                        5733.9471
  SEXRACE         1  WHITE MALES                     6553.4400
  SEXRACE         2  MINORITY MALES                  6230.7429
  SEXRACE         3  WHITE FEMALES                   5147.3176
  SEXRACE         4  MINORITY FEMALES                4828.1250

JOBCAT            2  OFFICE TRAINEE                  5478.9706
  SEXRACE         1  WHITE MALES                     6262.2857
  SEXRACE         2  MINORITY MALES                  5610.0000
  SEXRACE         3  WHITE FEMALES                   5208.8889
  SEXRACE         4  MINORITY FEMALES                4590.0000

JOBCAT            3  SECURITY OFFICER                6031.1111
  SEXRACE         1  WHITE MALES                     6102.8571
  SEXRACE         2  MINORITY MALES                  5953.8462

JOBCAT            4  COLLEGE TRAINEE                 9956.4878
  SEXRACE         1  WHITE MALES                    10467.6364
  SEXRACE         2  MINORITY MALES                 11496.0000
  SEXRACE         3  WHITE FEMALES                   7326.8571

JOBCAT            5  EXEMPT EMPLOYEE                13258.8750
  SEXRACE         1  WHITE MALES                    13255.2857
  SEXRACE         2  MINORITY MALES                 15570.0000
  SEXRACE         3  WHITE FEMALES                  10998.0000

JOBCAT            6  MBA TRAINEE                    12837.6000
  SEXRACE         1  WHITE MALES                    14332.0000
  SEXRACE         2  MINORITY MALES                 13992.0000
  SEXRACE         3  WHITE FEMALES                   7200.0000

JOBCAT            7  TECHNICAL                      19996.0000
  SEXRACE         1  WHITE MALES                    19996.0000

   Total Cases = 474
```

Introducing More Variables

The differences in mean beginning salaries between males and females are somewhat suspect. It is, however, unwise to conclude that salary discrimination exists since several important variables, such as years of prior experience, have not been considered. It is necessary to **control** (or adjust statistically) for other relevant variables. **Cross-classifying** cases by the variables of interest and comparing salaries across the subgroups is one way of achieving control. However, as the number of variables increases, the number of cases in each cell rapidly diminishes, making statistically meaningful comparisons difficult. To circumvent these problems, regression methods, which achieve control by specifying certain statistical relations that may describe what is happening, are used. Regression methods are described in Chapter 21.

Running Procedure MEANS

MEANS calculates the means, sums, standard deviations, and variances of a variable for subgroups defined by other variables (the independent variables). Optional specifications on MEANS provide one-way analysis of variance and a test of linearity.

Specifying the Tables

The minimum specification required by the MEANS procedure is the TABLES subcommand with a single table list. The table list must specify at least one dependent variable, the keyword BY, and at least one independent variable, as in:

```
MEANS TABLES=SALBEG BY SEXRACE.
```

This command produces the output in Figure 15.1.

The actual keyword TABLES can be omitted. For example, Figure 15.1 could also have been obtained with the following command.

```
MEANS SALBEG BY SEXRACE.
```

Although the dependent variable must be numeric, independent variables can be numeric or string. Long strings are truncated to short strings to define categories. More than one dependent variable and independent variable can be specified, and keyword TO can be used to refer to a set of consecutive variables in the active file, as in:

```
MEANS RAISE80 TO RAISE83 BY DEPT TO AGE.
```

This command produces tables for all variables between and including *RAISE80* and *RAISE83* in the file, broken down first by *DEPT*, then by each of the variables between *DEPT* and *AGE,* and finally by *AGE.*

When several BY keywords are specified, the variable after the last *BY* changes most quickly. (This is the opposite of the CROSSTABS format, in which the last variable changes most slowly.) For example, the command

```
MEANS TABLES=SALBEG BY JOBCAT BY SEXRACE.
```

produces the table shown in Figure 15.5, which shows beginning salary (*SALBEG*) for value 1 of *JOBCAT* broken down by each of the four values of *SEXRACE*. Then beginning salary for value 2 of *JOBCAT* is shown, again broken down by the four values of *SEXRACE*, and so forth.

When you specify multiple variables in a dimension of a table, they are processed from left to right. For example, the command

```
MEANS RAISE82 RAISE83 BY DEPT AGE BY SEX RACE.
```

produces eight tables. The first is *RAISE82* by *DEPT* by *SEX*, the second is RAISE82 by *DEPT* by *RACE*, the third is *RAISE82* by *AGE* by *SEX*, and so on. The last table is *RAISE83* by *AGE* by *RACE*.

More than one table list can be specified on a single MEANS command if they are separated by a slash. For example, the command

```
MEANS TABLES=RAISE81 BY SEX/EDLEVEL BY RACE.
```

requests two tables, *RAISE81* by *SEX* and *EDLEVEL* by *RACE*.

Optional Statistics

By default, MEANS displays means, standard deviations, and the number of cases for subgroups. You can modify the display by specifying the following options on the OPTIONS subcommand:

Option 5   *Suppress group counts.* The number of cases in each group is not displayed.

Option 6   *Display group sums.*

Option 7   *Suppress group standard deviations.*

Option 11   *Suppress group means.*

Option 12   *Display group variances.*

You can also obtain a one-way analysis of variance and a test of linearity by specifying the following on the STATISTICS subcommand:

Statistic 1   *One-way analysis of variance including eta and eta^2.*

Statistic 2   *Test of linearity.* Includes the sums of squares, mean squares, and degrees of freedom associated with the linear and nonlinear components, as well as the *F* ratio, Pearson's *r*, and Pearson's r^2. The linearity test is not calculated if the independent variable is a string.

ALL   *Display all statistics.* Keyword ALL produces the same display as Statistic 2.

If a two-way or higher-order table is specified, the second and subsequent grouping variables are ignored in the analysis of variance table. For example, the command

```
MEANS SALBEG BY JOBCAT BY SEXRACE
   /STATISTICS=1.
```

produces a breakdown of *SALBEG* by *JOBCAT* within *SEXRACE*. The analysis of variance is calculated only for the *SALBEG* by *JOBCAT* table. Two-way and higher-order analyses of variance can be obtained by using the ANOVA procedure, and a more complete one-way analysis of variance can be obtained by using the ONEWAY procedure.

Missing Values

By default, MEANS deletes cases with system- or user-missing values for any of the variables specified for a table. You can specify two alternative missing-value treatments on the OPTIONS subcommand:

Option 1   *Include cases with user-missing values.* Cases with user-missing values are included in all tables and statistics.

Option 2   *Exclude cases with user-missing dependent values.* Cases with missing values for the independent variables but with a valid value for the dependent variable is included in the analysis.

Format Options

By default, MEANS displays variable names and variable labels at the beginning of each table. Within the table, groups defined by the independent variables are identified by variable name, values, and value labels. Use the OPTIONS subcommand to change these defaults.

Option 3   *Suppress all labels.* No variable or value labels are displayed.

Option 8   *Suppress value labels.* No value labels are displayed for independent variables.

Option 9   *Suppress independent variable names.*

Option 10   *Suppress independent variable values.*

16

Testing Hypotheses about Differences in Means: Procedure MEANS

Would you buy a disposable raincoat, vegetables in pop-top cans, or investment counseling via closed-circuit television? These products and 17 others were described in questionnaires administered to 100 married couples (Davis & Ragsdale, 1983). Respondents were asked to rate on a scale of 1 (definitely want to buy) to 7 (definitely do not want to buy) their likelihood of buying the product. Of the 100 couples, 50 received questionnaires with pictures of the products and 50 received questionnaires without pictures. In this chapter we will examine whether pictures affect consumer preferences and whether husbands' and wives' responses differ.

Testing Hypotheses

The first part of Figure 16.1 contains basic descriptive statistics for the buying scores of couples receiving questionnaires with and without pictures. A couple's buying score is simply the sum of all ratings assigned to products by the husband and wife individually. Low scores indicate buyers, while high scores indicate reluctance to buy. The 50 couples who received questionnaires without pictures (group 1) had a mean score of 168, while the 48 couples who received forms with pictures had an average score of 159. (Two couples did not complete the questionnaire and are not included in the analysis.) The standard deviations show that scores for the second group were somewhat more variable than those for the first.

If you are willing to restrict the conclusions to the 98 couples included in the study, it is safe to say that couples who received forms with pictures indicated a greater willingness to purchase the products than couples who received forms without pictures. However, this statement is not very satisfying. What is needed is some type of statement about the effect of the two questionnaire types for all couples—or at least some larger group of couples—not just those actually studied.

Figure 16.1   Family buying scores by questionnaire type

```
T-TEST GROUPS=VISUAL (0,1) /VARIABLES=FAMSCORE
```

Variable	Number of Cases	Mean	SD	SE of Mean
FAMSCORE Family Buying Score				
No Pictures	50	168.0000	21.787	3.081
Pictures	48	159.0833	27.564	3.979

Mean Difference = 8.9167

Levene's Test for Equality of Variances: F= 1.382   P= .243

	t-test for Equality of Means				95%
Variances	t-value	df	2-Tail Sig	SE of Diff	CI for Diff
Equal	1.78	96	.078	5.008	(-1.027, 18.860)
Unequal	1.77	89.43	.080	5.032	(-1.084, 18.918)

Samples and Populations

The totality of cases about which conclusions are desired is called the **population**, while the cases actually included in the study constitute the **sample**. The couples in this experiment can be considered a sample from the population of couples in the United States.

The field of statistics helps us draw inferences about populations based on observations obtained from **random samples**, or samples in which the characteristics and relationships of interest are independent of the probabilities of being included in the sample. The necessity of a good research design cannot be overemphasized. Unless precautions are taken to ensure that the sample is from the population of interest and that the cases are chosen and observed without bias, the results obtained from statistical analyses may be misleading. For example, if a sample contains only affluent suburban couples, conclusions about all couples may be unwarranted.

If measurements are obtained from an entire population, the population can be characterized by the various measures of central tendency, dispersion, and shape described in Chapter 12. The results describe the population exactly. If, however, you obtain information from a random sample—the usual case—the results serve as **estimates** of the unknown population values. Special notation is used to identify population values, termed **parameters**, and to distinguish them from sample values, termed **statistics**. The mean of a population is denoted by μ, and the variance by σ^2. The symbols $\bar{X}$ and S^2 are reserved for the mean and variance of samples.

Sampling Distributions

The observations actually included in a study are just one of many random samples that could have been selected from a population. For example, if the population consists of married couples in the United States, the number of different samples that could be chosen for inclusion in a study is mind-boggling. The estimated value of a population parameter depends on the particular sample chosen. Different samples usually produce different estimates.

Figure 16.2 is a histogram of 400 means produced by the FREQUENCIES procedure. Each mean is calculated from a random sample of 25 observations from a population that has a normal distribution with a mean value of 0 and a standard deviation of 1. The estimated means are not all the same. Instead, they have a distribution. Most sample means are fairly close to 0, the population mean. The mean of the 400 means is 0, and the standard deviation of these means is 0.2. In fact, the distribution of the means appears approximately normal.

Figure 16.2   Means of 400 samples of size 25 from a normal distribution

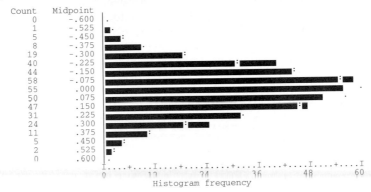

Although Figure 16.2 gives some idea of the appearance of the distribution of sample means of size 25 from a standard normal population, it is only an approximation since all possible samples of size 25 have not been taken. If the number of samples taken is increased to 1000, an even better picture of the distribution could be obtained. As the number of samples of a fixed size increases, the observed (or empirical) distribution of the means approaches the underlying (or theoretical) distribution.

The theoretical distribution of all possible values of a statistic obtained from a population is called the **sampling distribution** of the statistic. The mean of the sampling distribution is called the **expected value** of the statistic. The standard deviation is termed the **standard error**. The sampling distributions of most commonly used statistics calculated from random samples are tabulated and readily accessible. Knowing the sampling distribution of a statistic is very important for hypothesis testing, since from it you can calculate the probability of obtaining an observed sample value if a particular hypothesis is true. For example, from Figure 16.2, it appears quite unlikely that a sample mean based on a sample of size 25 from a standard normal distribution would be greater than 0.5 if the population mean were 0.

Sampling Distribution of the Mean

Since hypotheses about population means are often of interest, the sampling distribution of the mean is particularly important. If samples are taken from a normal population, the sampling distribution of the sample mean is also normal. As expected, the observed distribution of the 400 means in Figure 16.2 is approximately normal. The theoretical distribution of the sample mean, based on all possible samples of size 25, is exactly normal.

Even when samples are taken from a non-normal population, the distribution of the sample means will be approximately normal for sufficiently large samples. This is one reason for the importance of the normal distribution in statistical inference. Consider Figure 16.3, which shows a sample from a uniform distribution. In a uniform distribution, all values of a variable are equally likely; hence, the proportion of cases in each bin of the histogram is roughly the same.

Figure 16.3   Values from a uniform distribution

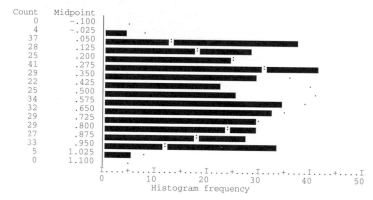

Figure 16.4 is a histogram of 400 means calculated from samples of size 25 from a uniform distribution. Note that the observed distribution is approximately normal even though the distribution from which the samples were taken is markedly non-normal.

Both the size of a sample and the shape of the distribution from which samples are taken affect the shape of the sampling distribution of the mean. If samples are small and come from distributions that are far from normal, the distribution of the means will not be even approximately normal. As the size of the sample increases, the sampling distribution of the mean will approach normality.

Figure 16.4   Distribution of 400 means from samples of size 25 from a uniform distribution

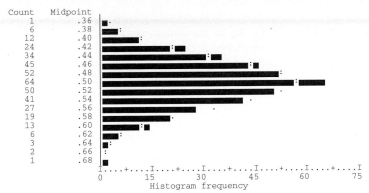

The mean of the theoretical sampling distribution of the means of samples of size N is μ, the population mean. The standard error, which is another name for the standard deviation of the sampling distribution of the mean, is

$$\sigma_{\bar{X}} = \frac{\sigma}{\sqrt{N}}$$

Equation 16.1

where σ is the standard deviation of the population and N is the sample size.

The standard deviation of the observed sampling distribution of means in Figure 16.2 is 0.20. This is the same as the value of the standard error for the theoretical distribution which, from the previous formula, is $1/5$, or 0.20.

Usually the value of the standard error is unknown and is estimated from a single sample using

$$S_{\bar{X}} = \frac{S}{\sqrt{N}}$$

Equation 16.2

where S is the *sample* standard deviation. The estimated standard error is displayed in the FREQUENCIES procedure and is also part of the output shown in Figure 16.1. For example, for group 1 the estimated standard error of the mean is

$$\frac{21.787}{\sqrt{50}} = 3.081$$

Equation 16.3

This value is displayed in the column labeled *SE of Mean* in Figure 16.1.

The standard error of the mean depends on both the sample standard deviation and the sample size. For a fixed standard deviation, as the size of a sample increases, the standard error decreases. This is intuitively clear, since the more data are gathered, the more confident you can be that the sample mean is not too far from the population mean. Also, as the standard deviation of the observations decreases, the standard error decreases as well. Small standard deviations occur when observations are fairly homogeneous. In this case, means based on different samples should also not vary much.

The Two-Sample T Test

Consider again whether there is evidence that the type of form administered influences couples' buying decisions. The question is not whether the two sample means are equal, but whether the two population means are equal.

To test the hypothesis that, in the population, buying scores for the two questionnaire types are the same, the following statistic can be calculated:

$$t = \frac{\bar{X}_1 - \bar{X}_2}{\sqrt{\dfrac{S_1^2}{N_1} + \dfrac{S_2^2}{N_2}}}$$

Equation 16.4

$\bar{X}_1$ is the sample mean of group 1, S_1^2 is the variance, and N_1 is the sample size.

Based on the sampling distribution of the above statistic, you can calculate the probability that a difference at least as large as the one observed would occur if the two population means (μ_1 and μ_2) are equal. This probability is called the **observed significance level**. If the observed significance level is small enough (usually less than 0.05, or 0.01), the hypothesis that the population means are equal is rejected.

The t value and its associated probability are given in Figure 16.1 in the row labeled *Unequal*. The t value is

$$t = \frac{168.0 - 159.08}{\sqrt{\dfrac{21.787^2}{50} + \dfrac{27.564^2}{48}}} = 1.77$$

Equation 16.5

If $\mu_1 = \mu_2$, the probability of observing a difference at least as large as the one in the sample is estimated to be about 0.08. Since this probability is greater than 0.05, the hypothesis that mean buying scores in the population are equal for the two types of forms is not rejected. The entry under *df* in Figure 16.1 is a function of the sample size in the two groups and is used together with the t value in establishing the observed significance level.

Another statistic based on the t distribution can be used to test the equality of means hypothesis. This statistic, known as the **pooled-variance t test**, is based on the assumption that the population variances in the two groups are equal and is obtained using a pooled estimate of that common variance. The test statistic is identical to the equation for t given previously except that the individual group variances are replaced by a pooled estimate, S_p^2. That is,

$$t = \frac{\bar{X}_1 - \bar{X}_2}{\sqrt{\dfrac{S_p^2}{N_1} + \dfrac{S_p^2}{N_2}}}$$

Equation 16.6

where S_p^2, the pooled variance, is a weighted average of the individual variances and is calculated as

$$S_p^2 = \frac{(N_1 - 1)\, S_1^2 + (N_2 - 1)\, S_2^2}{N_1 + N_2 - 2}$$

Equation 16.7

From the output in Figure 16.1, the pooled t-test value for the study is 1.78 (in the row labeled *Equal*). The degrees of freedom for the pooled t test are 96, the sum of the sample sizes in both groups minus 2. If the pooled-variance t test is used when the population variances are not equal, the probability level associated with the statistic may be in error. The amount of error depends on the inequality of the sample sizes and of the variances. However, using the separate-variance t value when the population variances are equal will usually result in an observed significance level somewhat larger than it should be. For large samples, the discrepancy between the two methods is small. In general, it is a good idea to use the separate-variance t test whenever you suspect that the variances are unequal.

Levene's test is used to test the hypothesis that the two population variances are equal. This test is less dependent on the assumption of normality than most tests of equality of variance. It is obtained by computing for each case the absolute difference from its group mean and then performing a one-way analysis of variance on these differences. In Figure 16.1, the value of the Levene statistic is 1.382. If the observed significance level for this test is small, the hypothesis that the population variances are equal is rejected and the separate-variance t test for means should be used. In this example, the significance level for the Levene statistic is large, and thus the pooled-variance t test is appropriate.

Significance Levels

The commonsense interpretation of a small observed significance level is straightforward: it appears unlikely that the two population means are equal. Of course, there is a possibility that the means are equal and the observed difference is due to chance. The observed significance level is the probability that a difference at least as large as the one observed would have arisen if the means were really equal.

When the observed significance level is too large to reject the equality hypothesis, the two population means may indeed be equal, or they may be unequal, but the difference cannot be detected. Failure to detect can be due to a true difference that is very small. For example, if a new cancer drug prolongs survival time by only one day when compared to the standard treatment, it is unlikely that such a difference will be detected, especially if survival times vary substantially and the additional day represents a small increment.

There are other reasons why true differences may not be found. If the sample sizes in the two groups are small or the variability large, even substantial differences may not be detected. Significant t values are obtained when the numerator of the t statistic is large compared to the denominator. The numerator is the difference between the sample means, and the denominator depends on the standard deviations and sample sizes of the two groups. For a given standard deviation, the larger the sample size, the smaller the denominator. Thus, a difference of a given magnitude may be significant if obtained with a sample size of 100 but not significant with a sample size of 25.

One-Tailed versus Two-Tailed Tests

A two-tailed test is used to detect a difference in means between two populations regardless of the direction of the difference. For example, in the study of buying scores presented in this chapter, we are interested in whether buying scores without pictures are larger *or* smaller than buying scores with pictures. In applications where you are interested in detecting a difference in one direction—such as whether a new drug is better than the current treatment—a so-called one-tailed test can be performed. The procedure is the same as for the two-tailed test, but the resulting probability value is divided by 2, adjusting for the fact that the equality hypothesis is rejected only when the difference between the two means is sufficiently large and in the direction of interest. In a two-tailed test, the equality hypothesis is rejected for large positive or negative values of the statistic.

What's the Difference?

It appears that the questionnaire type has no significant effect on couples' willingness to purchase products. Overall buying scores for the two conditions are similar. Pictures of the products do not appear to enhance their perceived desirability. In fact, the pictures actually appear to make several products somewhat less desirable. However, since the purpose of the questionnaires is to ascertain buying intent, including a picture of the actual product may help gauge true product response. Although the concept of disposable raincoats may be attractive, if they make the owner look like a walking trash bag, their appeal may diminish considerably.

Using Crosstabulation to Test Hypotheses

The T-TEST procedure is used to test hypotheses about the equality of two means for variables measured on an interval or ratio scale. Crosstabulation and the Pearson chi-square statistic can be used to test hypotheses about a dichotomous variable, such as purchase of a particular product.

Figure 16.5 is a crosstabulation showing the number of husbands who would definitely want to buy vegetables in pop-top cans when shown a picture and when not shown a picture of the product (value 1 of variable *H2S*). The vegetables in pop-top cans were chosen by 6.0% of the husbands who were tempted with pictures and 16.0% of the husbands who were not shown pictures. The chi-square statistic provides a test of the hypothesis that the proportion of husbands selecting the vegetables in pop-top cans is the same for the picture and no-picture forms.

Figure 16.5 Preference of husbands for vegetables in pop-top cans

```
CROSSTABS TABLES=H2S BY VISUAL
 /CELLS=COUNT COLUMN
 /STATISTICS=CHISQ.
```

```
H2S  Pop-Top Cans Husb Sel1  by  VISUAL  Picture Accompanied Question

                    VISUAL        Page 1 of 1
            Count
            Col Pct No Pictu Pictures
                    res
                        0        1 │  Row
                                   │  Total
H2S                 ───────────────┤
              1         8        3 │   11
    Definitely       16.0      6.0 │  11.0

              2        42       47 │   89
    Very Likely      84.0     94.0 │  89.0
                    ───────────────┘
            Column    50       50     100
            Total    50.0     50.0   100.0


        Chi-Square                Value        DF      Significance
    ──────────────────        ───────────    ────    ────────────

    Pearson                     2.55363         1          .11004
    Continuity Correction       1.63432         1          .20111
    Likelihood Ratio            2.63933         1          .10425
    Mantel-Haenszel test for    2.52809         1          .11184
        linear association

    Minimum Expected Frequency -    5.500
```

The probability of 0.11 associated with the Pearson chi-square in Figure 16.5 is the probability that a difference at least as large as the one observed would occur in the sample if in the population there were no difference in the selection of the product between the two formats. Since the probability is large, the hypothesis of no difference between the two formats is not rejected.

Independent versus Paired Samples

Several factors contribute to the observed differences in response between two groups. Part of the observed difference in scores between the picture and no-picture formats may be attributable to form type. Another component is due to differences between individuals. Not all couples have the same buying desires, so even if the type of form does not affect buying, differences between the two groups will probably be observed due to differences between the couples within the two groups. One method of minimizing the influence of individual variation is to choose the two groups so that the couples within them are comparable on characteristics that can influence buying behavior, such as income, education, family size, and so forth.

It is sometimes possible to obtain pairs of subjects, such as twins, and assign one member of each pair to each of the two treatments. Another frequently used experimental design is to expose the same individual to both types of conditions. (In this design, care must be taken to ensure that the sequential administration of treatments does not influence response by providing practice, decreasing attention span, or affecting the second treatment in other ways.) In both designs, subject-to-subject variability has substantially less effect. These designs are called **paired-samples designs**, since for each subject there is a corresponding pair in the other group. In the second design, a person is paired with himself or herself. In an **independent-samples design**, there is no pairing of cases; all observations are independent.

Analysis of Paired Data

Although the interpretation of the significance of results from paired experiments is the same as those from the two independent samples discussed previously, the actual computations are different. For each pair of cases, the difference in the responses is calculated. The statistic used to test the hypothesis that the mean difference in the population is 0 is

$$t = \frac{\overline{D}}{S_D / \sqrt{N}}$$

Equation 16.8

where $\overline{D}$ is the observed difference between the two means and S_D is the standard deviation of the differences of the paired observations. The sampling distribution of t, if the differences are normally distributed with a mean of 0, is Student's t with $N-1$ degrees of freedom, where N is the number of pairs. If the pairing is effective, the standard error of the difference will be smaller than the standard error obtained if two independent samples with N subjects each were chosen. However, if the variables chosen for pairing do not affect the responses under study, pairing may result in a test that is less powerful since true differences can be detected less frequently.

For example, to test the hypothesis that there is no difference between husbands' and wives' buying scores, a paired t test should be calculated. A paired test is appropriate since husbands and wives constitute matched observations. Including both members of a couple helps control for nuisance effects such as socioeconomic status and age. The observed differences are more likely to be attributable to differences in sex.

Figure 16.6 contains output from the paired t test. The entry under *Number of pairs* is the number of pairs of observations. The mean difference is the difference between the mean scores for males and females. The t value is the mean difference divided by the standard error of the difference $(0.55/1.73 = 0.32)$. The two-tailed probability for this test is 0.75, so there is insufficient evidence to reject the null hypothesis that married males and females have similar mean buying scores.

Figure 16.6   Husbands' versus wives' buying scores

```
T-TEST PAIRS=HSSCALE WSSCALE.

                - - - t-tests for paired samples - - -

                     Number of         2-tail
      Variable         pairs    Corr   Sig      Mean      SD     SE of Mean

      HSSCALE  Husband Self Scale               82.0918   14.352    1.490
                         98      .367   .000
      WSSCALE  Wife Self Scale                   81.5408   15.942    1.610


             Paired Differences
       Mean       SD      SE of Mean  |    t-value    df   2-tail Sig
       .5510    17.095      1.727      |      .32      97     .750
      95% CI (-2.877, 3.979)
```

The correlation coefficient between husbands' and wives' scores is 0.367. A positive correlation indicates that pairing has been effective in decreasing the variability of the mean difference. The larger the correlation coefficient, the greater the benefit of pairing.

Hypothesis Testing: A Review

The purpose of hypothesis testing is to help draw conclusions about population parameters based on results observed in a random sample. The procedure remains virtually the same for tests of most hypotheses.

- A hypothesis of no difference (called a **null hypothesis**) and its alternative are formulated.

- A test statistic is chosen to evaluate the null hypothesis.

- For the sample, the test statistic is calculated.

- The probability, if the null hypothesis is true, of obtaining a test value at least as extreme as the one observed is determined.

- If the observed significance level is judged small enough, the null hypothesis is rejected.

The Importance of Assumptions

In order to perform a statistical test of any hypothesis, it is necessary to make certain assumptions about the data. The particular assumptions depend on the statistical test being used. Some procedures require stricter assumptions than others. For parametric tests, some knowledge about the distribution from which samples are selected is required.

The assumptions are necessary to define the sampling distribution of the test statistic. Unless the distribution is defined, correct significance levels cannot be calculated. For the equal-variance t test, the assumption is that the observations are random samples from normal distributions with the same variance.

For many procedures, not all assumptions are equally important. Moderate violation of some assumptions may not always be serious. Therefore, it is important to know for each procedure not only what assumptions are needed but also how severely their violation may influence results.

The responsibility for detecting violations of assumptions rests with the researcher. Unlike the chemist who ignores laboratory safety procedures, the investigator who does not comply with good statistical practice is not threatened by explosions. However, from a research viewpoint, the consequences can be just as severe.

Wherever possible, tests of assumptions—often called diagnostic checks of the model—should be incorporated as part of the hypothesis-testing procedures. Throughout SPSS/PC+, attempts have been made to provide facilities for examining assumptions. For example, in the EXAMINE procedure there are several tests for normality. Discussions of other such diagnostics are included with the individual procedures.

Running Procedure T-TEST

The T-TEST procedure computes Student's *t* statistic for testing the equality of means of independent or paired samples. When independent samples are used, T-TEST calculates the separate-variance and pooled-variance *t* statistics, confidence intervals for the mean difference, and the Levene test for homogeneity of variances. The two-tailed observed significance level is also displayed for each *t* statistic.

Requesting Independent-Samples Tests

The variable and values that divide the sample into two independent groups are specified on the GROUPS subcommand. It is followed by the VARIABLES subcommand, which names the variable or variables to be tested.

Defining the Groups

Any of the following three methods can be used to define two groups on the GROUPS subcommand:

- If a single number in parentheses follows the grouping variable, all cases whose value for the grouping variable is greater than or equal to this number go into one group; the remaining cases go into the other group. For example, the output in Figure 16.1 could be produced by the command:

```
T-TEST GROUPS=VISUAL(1)/VARIABLES=FAMSCORE.
```

- If two values are specified in parentheses after the grouping variable, one group consists of all cases with the first value for the grouping variable and the second group consists of all cases with the second value. Thus, the output in Figure 16.1 could also have been produced by the command:

```
T-TEST GROUPS=VISUAL(0,1)/VARIABLES=FAMSCORE.
```

- If the grouping variable has only two values, 1 and 2, no value list is necessary; only the name of the grouping variable is required. If *VISUAL* had been coded 1 and 2 rather than 0 and 1, the following command could be specified:

```
T-TEST GROUPS=VISUAL /VARIABLES=FAMSCORE.
```

If the grouping variable is a string variable, you must enter each value in apostrophes, as in:

```
T-TEST GROUPS=CAPTAIN ('EVELYN  ','STEVE   ')
 /VARIABLES=GOALS ATTEMPTS.
```

Only the first eight characters of long strings are used to define the categories.

Only one variable (numeric or string) can be specified on the GROUPS subcommand, and only one GROUPS subcommand can be used per T-TEST command.

Specifying the Variables

The VARIABLES subcommand follows the GROUPS subcommand and lists the variables to be analyzed. Up to 50 variables can be specified, but they must all be numeric. The TO keyword can be used to refer to consecutive variables in the active file. Only one VARIABLES subcommand can be specified per T-TEST command.

Requesting Paired-Samples Tests

To obtain a paired *t* test, you must have two separate numeric variables that indicate the values for the two members of each pair. String variables cannot be used. The only required subcommand is PAIRS, which specifies the variables being compared. For example, the following command produces the output in Figure 16.6:

```
T-TEST PAIRS=HSSCALE WSSCALE.
```

If three or more variables are listed on PAIRS, each variable is compared with every other variable. For example, the command

```
T-TEST PAIRS=SURVEY1 SURVEY2 SURVEY3.
```

produces three paired *t* tests, one comparing *SURVEY1* and *SURVEY2*, one comparing *SURVEY1* and *SURVEY3*, and one comparing *SURVEY2* and *SURVEY3*.

The keyword WITH can be used to compare each variable to the left of WITH to every variable to the right of WITH. For example, the command

```
T-TEST PAIRS=SURVEY1 WITH SURVEY2 SURVEY3.
```

compares *SURVEY1* with *SURVEY2* and *SURVEY1* with *SURVEY3*.

You can use the PAIRED keyword in parentheses and keyword WITH to specify special pairing of variables.

PAIRED   *Special pairing for paired-samples test.* PAIRED must be used with the keyword WITH. The first variable before WITH is compared to the first variable after WITH, the second variable before WITH is compared to the second variable after WITH, and so forth. The same number of variables should be specified before and after WITH.

For example, the command

```
T-TEST SURVEY1 TO SURVEY3 WITH SURVEY4 TO SURVEY6 (PAIRED).
```

compares *SURVEY1* and *SURVEY4*, *SURVEY2* and *SURVEY5*, and *SURVEY3* and *SURVEY6*.

You can specify multiple analysis lists by separating them with a slash, as in:

```
T-TEST PAIRS=SURVEY1 SURVEY2 SURVEY3
 /PRETEST WITH POSTTST1 POSTTST2.
```

Requesting One-Sample Tests

Although T-TEST is designed to be a two-sample procedure, you can use it to calculate one-sample *t* tests by using a COMPUTE command to calculate a variable equal to the population mean. To test the null hypothesis that the mean of a population is value *m*, use the commands

```
COMPUTE MEAN=m.
T-TEST PAIRS=varname MEAN.
```

where *varname* is the name of the variable you want to test. You can give computed variable *MEAN* any name you want, as long as it conforms to the SPSS/PC+ variable-naming conventions.

Missing Values

By default, T-TEST deletes only cases with missing values for those variables necessary for a particular *t* test. For independent-samples *t* tests, T-TEST excludes cases with missing values for the grouping variable or the variable to be tested. For paired-samples *t* tests, T-TEST excludes cases with missing values for either of the variables in a given pair. Other missing-value treatments can be specified on the MISSING subcommand:

ANALYSIS   *Delete cases with missing values on an analysis-by-analysis basis.* This is the default.

LISTWISE   *Exclude missing values listwise.* Cases with missing values for any variables specified on T-TEST are excluded from the analysis.

INCLUDE   *Include user-missing values.* User-missing values are included in the analysis.

ANALYSIS and LISTWISE are mutually exclusive; however, each can be specified with INCLUDE.

Confidence Interval

You can set the value of the confidence interval by specifying the CRITERIA subcommand, the keyword CI, and a value between 0 and 1 in parentheses. CRITERIA=CI without a value restores the default 95% confidence interval.

Format Options

By default, T-TEST displays variable labels next to variable names. You can use the FORMAT subcommand to suppress these labels.

LABELS   *Display variable labels.* This is the default.

NOLABELS   *Suppress variable labels.*

17 One-Way Analysis of Variance: Procedure ONEWAY

Which of four brands of paper towels is the strongest? Do six models of midsize cars get the same average gasoline mileage? Do graduates of the top ten business schools receive the same average starting salaries? There are many situations in which you want to compare the means of several independent samples and, based on them, draw conclusions about the populations from which they were selected. Consider, for example, the following problem.

You are a manufacturer of paper used for making grocery bags. You suspect that the tensile strength of the bags depends on the pulp hardwood concentration. You currently use 10% hardwood concentration in the pulp and produce paper with an average tensile strength of about 15 pounds per square inch (psi). You want to see what happens if you vary the concentration of the pulp.

In consultation with the process engineer, you decide on four concentrations: 5%, 10%, 15%, and 20%. You measure the tensile strength of six samples at each of the four concentrations. You want to test the null hypothesis that all four concentrations result in the same average tensile strength of the paper.

Examining the Data

Before you embark on any statistical analysis, you should look at the distribution of data values to make sure that there is nothing unusual. You can use the EXAMINE command (see Chapter 13) to make a boxplot for each group.

From the plots in Figure 17.1 you see that the medians for the four groups differ. It appears that as the concentration increases, so does the tensile strength. The vertical length of the boxes, a measure of the spread or variability of the data values, also seems to differ for the concentrations, but not in any systematic fashion. There are no outlying or extreme values.

Figure 17.1   Boxplots for the four concentration groups

```
GET FILE='TENSILE.SYS'.
EXAMINE
 /VARIABLES=STRENGTH BY CONCENT
 /PLOT BOXPLOT /STATISTICS NONE.
```

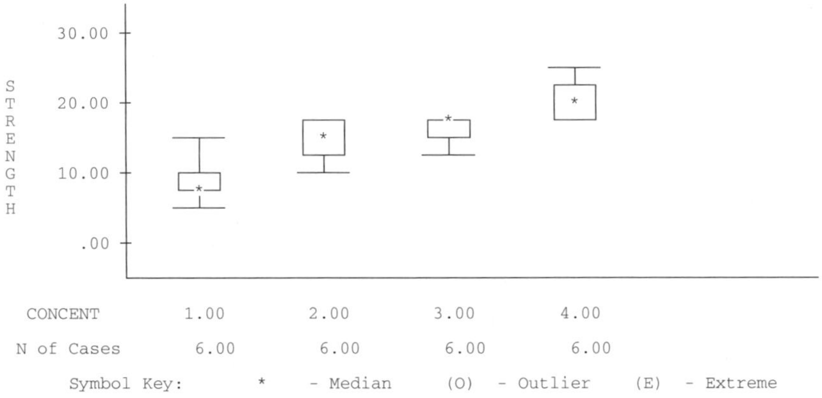

```
          30.00 ┼

S
T
R         20.00 ┼
E
N
G         10.00 ┼
T
H

           .00 ┼


    CONCENT        1.00      2.00      3.00      4.00

 N of Cases        6.00      6.00      6.00      6.00

      Symbol Key:       *   - Median    (O)  - Outlier    (E)  - Extreme
```

Sample Means and Confidence Intervals

The sample mean for a group provides the single best guess for the unknown population value μ_i. However, it is unlikely that the value of the sample mean is exactly equal to the population value. Instead, it is probably not too different. Based on the sample mean, you can calculate a range of values that, with a designated likelihood, includes the population value. Such a range is called a **confidence interval**.

As shown in Figure 17.2, the 95% confidence interval for the average tensile strength for a concentration of 10% is 12.72 to 18.61. This means that if you repeated the experiment under the same conditions and with the same sample sizes in each group, and each time calculated 95% confidence intervals, 95% of these intervals would contain the unknown population parameter value. Since the parameter value is not known, you don't know whether a particular interval contains the population value.

Figure 17.2 also shows descriptive statistics for the tensile strengths for the four concentrations. You see that as the concentration of hardwood increases, so does the mean strength. For a concentration of 5% the average tensile strength is 10, while for a concentration of 20% the average strength is 21.17. The group with a hardwood concentration of 15% has the smallest standard deviation. The others differ somewhat.

Figure 17.2   Sample means and confidence intervals for the four concentration groups

```
ONEWAY /VARIABLES STRENGTH BY CONCENT (1,4) /STATISTICS 1.
```

Group	Count	Mean	Standard Deviation	Standard Error	95 Pct Conf Int for Mean		
Grp 1	6	10.0000	2.8284	1.1547	7.0318	To	12.9682
Grp 2	6	15.6667	2.8048	1.1450	12.7233	To	18.6100
Grp 3	6	17.0000	1.7889	.7303	15.1227	To	18.8773
Grp 4	6	21.1667	2.6394	1.0775	18.3968	To	23.9366
Total	24	15.9583	4.7226	.9640	13.9642	To	17.9525

Group	Minimum	Maximum
Grp 1	7.0000	15.0000
Grp 2	12.0000	19.0000
Grp 3	14.0000	19.0000
Grp 4	18.0000	25.0000
Total	7.0000	25.0000

Testing the Null Hypothesis

The boxplots in Figure 17.1 and the means in Figure 17.2 suggest that the four concentrations result in different tensile strengths. Now you need to determine if the observed differences in the four sample means can be attributed to just the natural variability among sample means from the same population or whether it's reasonable to believe that the four concentrations come from populations that have different means. You must determine the probability of seeing results as remote as the ones you've observed when, in fact, all population means are equal.

The statistical technique you'll use to test the null hypothesis that several population means are equal is called **analysis of variance** (abbreviated ANOVA). This technique examines the variability of the observations within each group as well as the variability between the group means. Based on these two estimates of variability, you draw conclusions about the population means.

SPSS/PC+ contains two different analysis-of-variance procedures: ONEWAY and ANOVA. This chapter discusses the ONEWAY procedure. One-way analysis of variance is needed when only one variable is used to classify cases into the different groups. In the example on the tensile strength of paper, cases are assigned to groups based on their values for one variable: hardwood concentration. When two or more variables are used to form the groups, the ANOVA procedure is required (see Chapter 18).

Note that you can use the ONEWAY procedure only when your groups are independent. If you observe the same person under several conditions, you cannot use this procedure. You need a special class of procedures called *repeated measures analysis of variance*, available in the SPSS/PC+ Advanced Statistics option.

Assumptions Needed for Analysis of Variance

Analysis of variance procedures require the following assumptions:

- Each of the groups is an independent random sample from a normal population.
- In the population, the variances of the groups are equal.

One way to check these assumptions is to use the EXAMINE procedure to make stem-and-leaf plots or histograms for each group and calculate the variances. You can also use formal statistical tests to check the assumptions of normality and equal variances. See Chapter 13 for more information on stem-and-leaf plots and tests for normality.

The Levene Test

To test the null hypothesis that the groups come from populations with the same variance, you can use the **Levene test** (shown in Figure 17.3), which can be obtained with the ONEWAY procedure. If the observed significance level is small, you can reject the null hypothesis that all variances are equal. In this example, since the observed significance level (0.583) is large, you can't reject the null hypothesis. This means you don't have sufficient evidence to suspect that the variances are unequal, confirming what you saw in the plot.

Figure 17.3   Levene test

```
ONEWAY /VARIABLES STRENGTH BY CONCENT(1,4) /STATISTICS 3.

Levene Test for Homogeneity of Variances

    Statistic    df1    df2      2-tail Sig.
      .6651        3     20          .583
```

Analyzing the Variability

Now you're ready to perform the analysis-of-variance test. In analysis of variance, the observed variability in the sample is divided, or partitioned, into two parts: variability of the observations within a group (that is, the variability of the observations around their group mean) and the variability among the group means.

If the null hypothesis is true, the population means for the four groups are equal and the observed data can be considered to be four samples from the same population. In this case, you should be able to estimate how much the four sample means should vary. If your observed sample means vary more than you expect, you have evidence to reject the null hypothesis. The analysis-of-variance table is shown in Figure 17.4.

Figure 17.4   One-way analysis-of-variance table

```
ONEWAY /VARIABLES STRENGTH BY CONCENT(1,4).


        Variable   STRENGTH
     By Variable   CONCENT

                                      Analysis of Variance

                                   Sum of       Mean          F      F
          Source         D.F.      Squares      Squares     Ratio  Prob.

Between Groups            3        382.7917     127.5972    19.6052  .0000
Within Groups           20        130.1667       6.5083
Total                   23        512.9583
```

Between-Groups Variability

In Figure 17.4, the row labeled *Between Groups* contains an estimate of the variability of the observations based on the variability of the group means. To calculate the entry labeled *Sum of Squares,* start by subtracting the overall mean (the mean of all the observations) from each group mean (the overall and group means are listed in Figure 17.2). Then square each difference and multiply the square by the number of observations in its group. Finally, add the results together. For this example, the between-groups sum of squares is:

$$6 \times (10 - 15.96)^2 + 6 \times (15.67 - 15.96)^2 + 6 \times (17 - 15.96)^2$$
$$+ 6 \times (21.17 - 15.96)^2 = 382.79$$

Equation 17.1

The column labeled *DF* contains the degrees of freedom. To calculate the degrees of freedom for the between-groups sum of squares, subtract 1 from the number of groups. In this example, there are 4 concentrations, so there are 3 degrees of freedom.

To calculate the between-groups mean square, divide the between-groups sum of squares by its degrees of freedom:

$$\frac{382.79}{3} = 127.60$$

Equation 17.2

Within-Groups Variability

The row labeled *Within Groups* contains an estimate of the variability of the observations based on how much the observations vary from their group means. The within-groups sum of squares is calculated by multiplying each of the group variances (the square of the standard deviation) by the number of cases in the group minus 1 and then adding up the results. In this example, the within-groups sum of squares is

$$5 \times 8.0000 + 5 \times 7.8667 + 5 \times 3.2000 + 5 \times 6.9667 \ = \ 130.17 \qquad \text{Equation 17.3}$$

To calculate the degrees of freedom for the within-groups sums of squares, take the number of cases in all groups combined and subtract the number of groups. In this example, there are 24 cases and 4 groups, so there are 20 degrees of freedom. The mean square is then calculated by dividing the sum of squares by the degrees of freedom:

$$\frac{130.17}{20} \ = \ 6.51 \qquad \text{Equation 17.4}$$

Calculating the F Ratio

You now have two estimates of the variability in the population: the within-groups mean square and the between-groups mean square. The within-groups mean square is based on how much the observations within each group vary. The between-groups mean square is based on how much the group means vary among themselves. If the null hypothesis is true, the two numbers should be close to each other. If you divide one by the other, the ratio should be close to 1.

The statistical test for the null hypothesis that all groups have the same mean in the population is based on this ratio, called an F statistic. You take the between-groups mean square and divide it by the within-groups mean square. For this example,

$$F \ = \ \frac{127.6}{6.51} \ = \ 19.6 \qquad \text{Equation 17.5}$$

This number appears in Figure 17.4 in the column labeled *F ratio*. It certainly doesn't appear to be close to 1. What you now need to do is obtain the observed significance level. The observed significance level is obtained by comparing the calculated F value to the F distribution (the distribution of the F statistic when the null hypothesis is true). The significance level is based on both the actual F value and on the degrees of freedom for the two mean squares. In this example, the observed significance level is less than 0.00005, so you can reject the null hypothesis that the four concentrations of pulp result in paper with the same average tensile strength.

Multiple Comparison Procedures

A significant F value tells you only that the population means are probably not all equal. It doesn't tell you which pairs of groups appear to have different means. You reject the null hypothesis that all population means are equal if *any two* means are unequal. You need to use special tests called **multiple comparison procedures** to determine which means are significantly different from each other.

You might wonder why you can't just compare all possible pairs of means using a *t* test. The reason is that when you make many comparisons involving the same means, the probability that one comparison will turn out to be statistically significant increases. For example, if you have 5 groups and compare all pairs of means, you're making 10 comparisons. When the null hypothesis is true, the probability that at least one of the 10 observed significance levels will be less than 0.05 is about 0.29. The more comparisons you make, the more likely it is that you'll find one or more pairs to be statistically different, even if all population means are equal.

By adjusting for the number of comparisons you're making, multiple comparison procedures protect you from calling too many differences significant. The more comparisons you make, the larger the difference between pairs of means must be for a multiple comparison procedure to find it significant. When you use a multiple comparison procedure, you can be more confident that you are finding true differences.

Many multiple comparison procedures are available. They differ in how they adjust the observed significance level. One of the simplest is the **Bonferroni test**. It adjusts the observed significance level based on the number of comparisons you are making. For example, if you are making 5 comparisons, the observed significance level for the original comparison must be less than $0.05/5$, or 0.01, for the difference to be significant at the 0.05 significance level. For further discussion of multiple comparison techniques, see Winer et al. (1991).

Figure 17.5 shows a portion of the Bonferroni test results obtained with the ONEWAY procedure. At the bottom you see a table that orders the group means from smallest to largest in both the rows and columns. (In this example, the order happens to be the same as the order of the group code numbers.) An asterisk marks a pair of means that are different at the 0.05 level after the Bonferroni correction is made. Differences are marked only once, in the lower diagonal of the table. If the significance level is greater than 0.05, the space is left blank.

Figure 17.5   Bonferroni multiple comparisons

```
ONEWAY /VARIABLES STRENGTH BY CONCENT(1,4) /RANGES MODLSD.


Modified LSD Procedure
Ranges for the   .050 level -

        4.14    4.14    4.14

The ranges above are table ranges.
The value actually compared with Mean(J)-Mean(I) is..
      1.8039 * Range * Sqrt(1/N(I) + 1/N(J))


(*) Denotes pairs of groups significantly different at the   .050 level



      Variable  STRENGTH


                        G G G G
                        r r r r
                        p p p p

      Mean      Group   1 2 3 4

      10.0000   Grp 1
      15.6667   Grp 2   *
      17.0000   Grp 3   *
      21.1667   Grp 4   * *
```

In this example, the asterisks in the first column indicate that the mean of group 1 (5% hardwood concentration) is significantly different from every other group. In the second column, group 2 (10% concentration) is different from group 4 (20% concentration), but not from group 3 (15% concentration). There are no asterisks in the third column. Thus, you see that all pairs of means are significantly different from each other except for group 2 and group 3 and group 3 and group 4.

The line above the table indicates how large an observed difference must be for the multiple comparison procedure to call it significant. If no pairs are found to be significantly different, the table is omitted and a message is printed.

When the sample sizes in all of the groups are the same, you can also use the output of homogeneous subsets to identify subsets of means that are not different from each other. Figure 17.6 shows the homogeneous subsets output.

Figure 17.6   Homogeneous subsets

```
ONEWAY /VARIABLES STRENGTH BY CONCENT (1,4) /RANGES MODLSD.

SUBSET  1

Group       Grp 1
Mean        10.0000
- - - - - - - - - -

SUBSET  2

Group       Grp 2       Grp 3
Mean        15.6667      17.0000
- - - - - - - - - - - - - - - -

SUBSET  3

Group       Grp 3       Grp 4
Mean        17.0000      21.1667
- - - - - - - - - - - - - - - -
```

Groups that appear in the same subset are not significantly different from each other. In this example, group 2 and group 3 are in a subset together, as are group 3 and group 4. Group 1 is in a subset of its own, since it is significantly different from all of the other means.

Running Procedure ONEWAY

The ONEWAY procedure produces a one-way analysis of variance. Although ANOVA (see Chapter 18) can also produce a one-way analysis of variance, ONEWAY allows you to test for nonlinear trends, specify contrasts, and use multiple comparison tests. ONEWAY also reads and writes matrix materials.

The basic specification is a dependent variable list and an independent variable with its range of values. The optional subcommands that produce contrasts, tests for trends, and multiple comparisons appear after this specification and can be entered in any order.

Specifying the Variables

The VARIABLES subcommand is the only required specification for ONEWAY and consists of the name of at least one dependent variable, the keyword BY, and the name of the independent variable followed by its minimum and maximum values enclosed in parentheses and separated by a comma. The VARIABLES subcommand must be specified first.

The actual keyword VARIABLES can be omitted. Thus, the output in Figure 17.4 could be obtained by specifying either

```
ONEWAY /VARIABLES=STRENGTH BY CONCENT(1,4).
```

or

```
ONEWAY STRENGTH BY CONCENT(1,4).
```

The minimum and maximum values are the lowest and highest values of the independent variable to be used in the analysis. Cases with values for the independent variable outside this range are excluded from the analysis.

Only one independent variable can be used in an analysis list. When more than one dependent variable is specified, a separate one-way analysis of variance is produced for each one.

Specifying Multiple Comparison Tests

Use the RANGES subcommand to specify any of seven multiple comparison tests available in ONEWAY. You can specify multiple RANGES subcommands, and each one requests one test.

The keywords for RANGES are shown below. Each specifies a type of multiple comparison test, and some can be followed by a number in parentheses indicating the significance level. If a significance level is not specified, ONEWAY uses a 0.05 significance level.

LSD(p) *Least significant difference.* Any significance level between 0 and 1 can be specified.

DUNCAN(p) *Duncan's multiple-range test.* Only one significance level (0.01, 0.05, or 0.10) can be specified.

SNK *Student-Newman-Keuls test.* Only the default 0.05 significance level can be used.

BTUKEY *Tukey's alternate test.* Only the default 0.05 significance level can be used.

TUKEY *Honestly significant difference.* Only the default 0.05 significance level can be used.

MODLSD(p) *Modified LSD.* Any significance level between 0 and 1 can be specified.

SCHEFFE(p) *Scheffé test.* Any significance level between 0 and 1 can be specified.

For example, Figure 17.5 and Figure 17.6 were obtained by specifying

```
ONEWAY  STRENGTH BY CONCENT (1,4)
  /RANGES=MODLSD.
```

ONEWAY produces two types of output, depending on the design and multiple comparison test. Multiple comparisons for all groups are produced whenever RANGES is used. In this type of output, group means are listed in ascending order. Asterisks in the matrix of group names indicate which means are significantly different. For example, the asterisks in Figure 17.5 indicate that group 1 is significantly different from the other groups.

For balanced designs or when Option 10 (harmonic means) is specified, ONEWAY produces homogeneous subsets of means. Groups within a subset are *not* significantly different. Figure 17.6 shows output with homogeneous subsets of means for a balanced design. In this example, three subsets are produced. The first subset includes only the first group, the second subset includes groups 2 and 3, and the third subset includes groups 3 and 4.

You can specify any other type of range for multiple comparisons by listing specific range values. Up to k-1 range values can be specified in ascending order, where k is the number of groups and where the range value times the standard error of the combined subset is the critical value. If fewer than k-1 values are specified, the last value is used for the remaining values. You can specify repetitions with $n*r$, where n is the number of repetitions and r is the range value. To use a single critical value for all subsets, specify one range value. For example, the command

```
ONEWAY  VARIABLES=STRENGTH BY CONCENT(1,4)
   /RANGES=4.14.
```

produces the same results as the MODLSD test shown in Figure 17.5.

By default, the multiple comparison test uses the harmonic mean of the sizes of the two groups being compared. If you want the harmonic mean of *all* group sizes to be used, specify Option 10 on the OPTIONS subcommand. When Option 10 is specified, ONEWAY calculates homogeneous subsets.

Option 10   *Use the harmonic mean of all group sizes as the sample size for each group in range tests.* If the harmonic mean is used for unbalanced designs, ONEWAY determines homogeneous subsets for all range tests.

Partitioning Sums of Squares

The POLYNOMIAL subcommand partitions the between-groups sums of squares into linear, quadratic, cubic, and higher-order trend components. Its specification consists of a single number, which indicates the degree of the highest-order polynomial to be used. For example, the command

```
ONEWAY STRENGTH BY CONCENT (1,4)
   /POLYNOMIAL=2.
```

specifies a polynomial of order 2 (quadratic) as the highest-order polynomial. The number specified must be a positive integer less than or equal to 5 and less than the number of groups. The POLYNOMIAL subcommand follows the VARIABLES subcommand and can be used only once.

When the design is balanced and POLYNOMIAL is used, ONEWAY computes the sum of squares for each order polynomial from weighted polynomial contrasts, using the values of the independent variable as the metric. These contrasts are orthogonal, so that the sums of squares for each order polynomial are statistically independent. If the design is unbalanced but there is equal spacing between the values of the independent variable, ONEWAY computes sums of squares using the unweighted polynomial contrasts. These sums of squares are always calculated from the weighted sums of squares.

Specifying Contrasts

The CONTRAST subcommand specifies *a priori* contrasts to be tested by the *t* statistic. Its specification is simply a list of coefficients, with each coefficient corresponding to a value of the independent variable. The sequential order of the coefficients is important since it corresponds to the ascending order of the category values of the independent variable. The first coefficient in the list corresponds to the lowest group value of the independent variable, and the last coefficient corresponds to the highest value.

For example, the command

```
ONEWAY WELL BY EDUC6 (1,6)
  /CONTRAST=1 1  -2  0  0 0.
```

specifies comparison of the combined means of the first two groups with the mean for the third group. The last three groups are not included in the contrast. Fractional coefficients can also be used, as in:

```
ONEWAY WELL BY EDUC6 (1,6)
  /CONTRAST=.5  .5  -1  0  0 0.
```

For most applications, the coefficients should sum to 0. Sets of coefficients that do not sum to 0 can be specified, but a warning message is displayed.

The notation $n*c$ can be used to specify the same coefficient for n consecutive means. For example, the command

```
ONEWAY WELL BY EDUC6 (1,6)
  /CONTRAST=2*-1 2  3*0.
```

specifies a contrast coefficient of −1 for each of the first two groups, a coefficient of 2 for the third group, and a coefficient of 0 for the last three groups. You must specify a contrast coefficient for every group implied by the range given for the independent variable, even if a group has no cases. Trailing zeros need not be specified. For example, the command

```
ONEWAY WELL BY EDUC6 (1,6)
  /CONTRAST=2*-1  2.
```

is equivalent to the previous command.

Only one set of contrast coefficients can be specified per CONTRAST subcommand. However, you can specify multiple CONTRAST subcommands. Output for each contrast list includes the value of the contrast, the standard error of the contrast, the *t* statistic, the degrees of freedom for t, and the two-tailed observed significance level of t. Both pooled-variance and separate-variance estimates are displayed.

Optional Statistics

You can specify three optional sets of statistics or keyword ALL on the STATISTICS subcommand:

Statistic 1   *Group descriptive statistics.* For each group, the count, mean, standard deviation, standard error, minimum, maximum, and 95% confidence interval are displayed for each dependent variable.

Statistic 2   *Fixed- and random-effects statistics.* For the fixed-effects model, the standard deviation, standard error, and 95% confidence interval are displayed. For the random-effects model, the standard error, the 95% confidence interval, and the estimate of the between-components variance are displayed.

Statistic 3   *Homogeneity-of-variance tests.* The Levene test is displayed.

ALL   *All statistics.*

For example, the output in Figure 17.2 and Figure 17.3 was obtained by specifying

```
ONEWAY /VARIABLES STRENGTH CONCENT(1,4) /STATISTICS 1 3.
```

Missing Values

By default, cases with missing values for the dependent or independent variable for a given analysis are excluded from that analysis. Two alternative missing-value treatments are available on the OPTIONS subcommand:

Option 1   *Include cases with user-missing values.* User-missing values are treated as valid values.

Option 2   *Exclude cases with missing values listwise.* Cases with missing values for any variable in the analysis list are excluded from all analyses.

Neither option will cause ONEWAY to include cases with values for the independent value that are outside the specified range.

Format Options

By default, ONEWAY displays variable labels and identifies groups as *GRP1*, *GRP2*, and so forth. The display can be modified by specifying the following options on the OPTIONS subcommand:

Option 3   *Suppress variable labels.*

Option 6   *Display value labels for groups.* Use the first eight characters of the value labels defined for the independent variable as group labels.

Matrix Materials

ONEWAY can read and write matrix materials. It reads and writes frequencies, means, and standard deviations, and it can also read frequencies, means, and the pooled variance.

To write matrix materials to a file, specify Option 4 on the OPTIONS subcommand.

Option 4   *Write matrix materials to a file.* The matrix includes a vector of category counts, a vector of means, and a vector of standard deviations for each dependent variable. Vectors are written 80 characters per line, with each vector beginning on a new line. The format for the counts vector is F10.2, and the format for the means and standard deviations vectors is F10.4. Thus, each line has a maximum of eight values.

The file to which the material is written is controlled by the SET command (see SET in the Syntax Reference).

ONEWAY can read two types of matrix materials, specified with Options 7 and 8 on the OPTIONS subcommand:

Option 7   *Read matrix of counts, means, and standard deviations.* ONEWAY expects a vector of counts for each group, followed by a vector of group means and a vector of group standard deviations like those written by Option 4.

Option 8   *Read matrix of counts, means, pooled variance, and degrees of freedom.* ONEWAY expects a vector of counts for each group, followed by a vector of means for each group, followed by the pooled variance (the within-groups mean square) and the degrees of freedom for the pooled variance. If the degrees of freedom are omitted, $n-k$ degrees of freedom are used, where n is the number of cases and k is the number of groups. Statistics 1, 2, and 3 and the separate variance estimate for contrasts cannot be computed if Option 8 is specified.

If Option 7 or 8 is used, the MATRIX keyword must be specified on the DATA LIST command. For either option, each vector begins on a new line and can be entered in fixed or freefield format. Unless matrix materials produced by ONEWAY are to be read, it is easier to use freefield input with the FREE keyword on the DATA LIST command. For more information on reading matrix materials with ONEWAY, see DATA LIST: Matrix Materials in the Syntax Reference.

18 Analysis of Variance: Procedure ANOVA

Despite constitutional guarantees, any mirror will testify that all citizens are not created equal. The consequences of this inequity are pervasive. Physically attractive individuals are perceived as more desirable social partners, more persuasive communicators, and generally more likeable and competent. Even cute children and attractive burglars are disciplined more leniently than their homely counterparts (Sigall & Ostrove, 1975).

Anderson and Nida (1978) examined the influence of attractiveness on the evaluation of writing samples by college students. In the study, 144 male and 144 female students were asked to appraise essays purportedly written by college freshmen. As supplemental information, a slide of the "author" was projected during the evaluation. Half the slides were of authors of the same sex as the rater; the other half were of authors of the opposite sex. Each had previously been determined to be of high, medium, or low attractiveness. Each rater evaluated one essay for creativity, ideas, and style. The three scales were combined to form a composite measure of performance.

Descriptive Statistics

Figure 18.1 contains average composite scores for the essays, subdivided by the three categories of physical attractiveness and the two categories of sex similarity. The table is similar to the summary table shown for the one-way analysis of variance in Chapter 17. The difference here is that there are two independent (or grouping) variables: attractiveness and sex similarity. The first mean displayed (25.11) is for the entire sample. The number of cases (288) is shown in parentheses. Then for each of the independent variables, mean scores are displayed for each of the categories. The attractiveness categories are ordered from low (coded 1) to high (coded 3). Evaluations in which the rater and author are of the same sex are coded as 1, while opposite-sex evaluations are coded as 2. The possible combinations of the values of the two variables result in six cells. Finally, a table of means is displayed for cases classified by both grouping variables. Attractiveness is the row variable, and sex is the column variable. Each mean is based on the responses of 48 subjects.

249

Figure 18.1   Table of group means

```
ANOVA VARIABLES=SCORE BY ATTRACT(1,3) SEX(1,2) /STATISTICS 3.

                    * * * C E L L   M E A N S * * *

                  SCORE        COMPOSITE SCORE
              BY ATTRACT       ATTRACTIVENESS LEVEL
                  SEX          SEX SIMILARITY

TOTAL POPULATION

      25.11
   (    288)


ATTRACT
      1           2           3

      22.98       25.78       26.59
   (    96)   (    96)   (    96)


SEX
      1           2

      25.52       24.71
   (   144)   (   144)


         SEX
                     1           2
ATTRACT
      1      22.79       23.17
          (    48)   (    48)

      2      28.63       22.92
          (    48)   (    48)

      3      25.13       28.04
          (    48)   (    48)
```

The overall average score is 25.11. Highly attractive individuals received the highest average score (26.59), while those rated low in physical appeal had the lowest score (22.98). There doesn't appear to be much difference between the average scores (across attractiveness levels) assigned by same-sex (25.52) and opposite-sex (24.71) evaluators. However, highly attractive individuals received an average rating of 25.13 when evaluated by people of the same sex and 28.04 when evaluated by people of the opposite sex.

Analysis of Variance

Three hypotheses are of interest in the study: Does attractiveness relate to the composite scores? Does sex similarity relate to the scores? And is there an interaction between the effects of attractiveness and sex? The statistical technique used to evaluate these hypotheses is an extension of the one-way analysis of variance outlined in Chapter 17. The same assumptions are needed for correct application: the observations should be independently selected from normal populations with equal variances. Discussion here is limited to situations in which both grouping variables are considered **fixed**; that is, they constitute the populations of interest.

The total observed variation in the scores is subdivided into four components: the sums of squares due to attractiveness, sex, their interaction, and the residual. This can be expressed as

$$\text{Total SS} = \text{Attractiveness SS} + \text{Sex SS}$$
$$+ \text{Interaction SS} + \text{Residual SS}$$

Equation 18.1

Figure 18.2 is the analysis-of-variance table for this study. The first column lists the sources of variation. The sums of squares attributable to each of the components are given in the second column. The sums of squares for each independent variable alone are sometimes termed the **main effect** sums of squares. The **explained** sum of squares is the total sum of squares for the main effect and interaction terms in the model.

The degrees of freedom for sex and attractiveness, listed in the third column, are one fewer than the number of categories. For example, since there are three levels of attractiveness, there are two degrees of freedom. Similarly, sex has one degree of freedom. The interaction term (the product of the degrees of freedom of each of the individual variables) has two degrees of freedom. The degrees of freedom for the residual are $N - 1 - k$, where k equals the degrees of freedom for the explained sum of squares.

Figure 18.2 Analysis-of-variance table

ANOVA VARIABLES=SCORE BY ATTRACT(1,3) SEX(1,2).

```
            * * *   A N A L Y S I S   O F   V A R I A N C E   * * *

            SCORE     COMPOSITE SCORE
        by  ATTRACT   ATTRACTIVENESS LEVEL
            SEX       SEX SIMILARITY

                           Sum of            Mean               Sig
Source of Variation        Squares    DF     Square      F      of F

Main Effects               733.700    3      244.567    3.276   .022
    ATTRACT                686.850    2      343.425    4.600   .011
    SEX                     46.850    1       46.850    0.628   .429

2-Way Interactions         942.350    2      471.175    6.311   .002
    ATTRACT   SEX           942.350    2      471.175    6.311   .002

Explained                 1676.050    5      355.210    4.490   .000

Residual                 21053.140  282       74.656

Total                    22729.190  287       79.196
```

The mean squares shown in the fourth column in Figure 18.2 are obtained by dividing each sum of squares by its degrees of freedom. Hypothesis tests are based on the ratios of the mean squares of each source of variation to the mean square for the residual. When the assumptions are met and the true means are in fact equal, the distribution of the ratio is an F with the degrees of freedom for the numerator and denominator terms.

Testing for Interaction

The F value associated with the attractiveness and sex interaction is 6.311, as shown in Figure 18.2. The observed significance level is approximately 0.002. Therefore, it appears that there is an interaction between the two variables. What does this mean?

Consider Figure 18.3, which is a plot of the cell, or group, means in Figure 18.1. Notice how the mean scores relate not only to the attractiveness of the individual and to the sex of the rater, but also to the particular combination of the values of the variables. Opposite-sex raters assign the highest scores to highly attractive individuals. Same-sex raters assign the highest scores to individuals of medium attractiveness. Thus, the ratings for each level of attractiveness depend on the sex variable. If there were no interaction between the two variables, a plot similar to the one shown in Figure 18.4 might result, in which the difference between the two types of raters is the same for the three levels of attractiveness.

Figure 18.3   Cell means

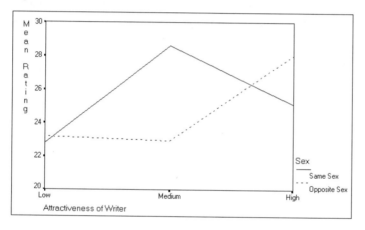

Figure 18.4   Cell means with no interaction

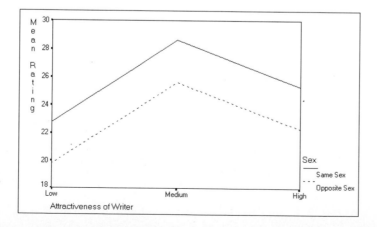

Tests for Sex and Attractiveness

Once the presence of interaction has been established, it is not particularly useful to continue hypothesis testing since the two variables *jointly* affect the dependent variable. If there is no significant interaction, the grouping variables can be tested individually. The *F* value associated with attractiveness would provide a test of the hypothesis that attractiveness does not affect the rating. Similarly, the *F* value associated with sex would test the hypothesis that sex has no main effect on evaluation.

Note that the small *F* value associated with sex does not indicate that response is unaffected by sex, since sex is included in the significant interaction term. Instead, it shows that when response is averaged over attractiveness levels, the two sex-category means are not significantly different.

Explanations

Several explanations are consistent with the results of this study. Since people generally identify with individuals most like themselves, and since most people consider themselves moderately attractive, the highest degree of identification should be with same-sex individuals of moderate attractiveness. The higher empathy may result in the higher scores. An alternate theory is that moderately attractive individuals are generally perceived as more desirable same-sex friends; they have more favorable personality profiles and don't encourage unfavorable comparisons. Their writing scores may benefit from their perceived popularity.

Although we don't want friends who outshine us, attractive dates can reflect favorably on us and enhance our status. Physical beauty is advantageous for heterosexual relationships, but not for same-sex friendships. This prejudice may affect all evaluations of highly attractive members of the opposite sex. Regardless of the explanation, certain practical conclusions are apparent. Students, choose your instructors carefully! Authors, think twice before including your photo on the book jacket!

Extensions

Analysis-of-variance techniques can be used with any number of grouping variables. For example, the data in this chapter originated from a more complicated experiment than described here. There were four factors—essay quality, physical attractiveness, sex of writer, and sex of subject. The original data were analyzed with a $3 \times 3 \times 2 \times 2$ ANOVA table. (The numbers indicate how many categories each grouping variable has.) The conclusions from our simplified analysis are the same as those from the more elaborate analysis.

Each of the cells in our experiment had the same number of subjects. This greatly simplifies the analysis and its interpretation. When unequal sample sizes occur in the cells, the total sum of squares cannot be partitioned into nice components that sum to the total. Various techniques are available for calculating sums of squares in such **nonorthogonal designs**. The methods differ in the way they adjust the sums of squares to account for other effects in the model. Each method results in different sums of squares and tests different hypotheses. However, when all cell frequencies are equal, the methods yield the same results. For discussion of various procedures for analyzing designs with unequal cell frequencies, see Kleinbaum and Kupper (1978) and Overall and Klett (1972).

Running Procedure ANOVA

The ANOVA procedure performs an *n*-way analysis of variance. Multiple factors (independent variables) and several dependent variables can be analyzed in one ANOVA procedure. Cell means and counts can be displayed in addition to the analysis of variance table.

For one-way analysis of variance, the ONEWAY procedure is often preferable (see Chapter 17). Contrasts, multiple comparisons, tests for trends, and homogeneity-of-variance statistics are produced by ONEWAY but not by ANOVA.

The default ANOVA model is the full factorial design, although other models can be analyzed. Covariates can be specified, but ANOVA does not perform a full analysis of covariance. There are three methods available for decomposing sums of squares. The order of entry for covariates and factor main effects can be specified, and you can suppress various orders of interaction effects. Multiple classification analysis tables are also available.

Specifying the Variables

The only required specification for ANOVA is the VARIABLES subcommand with a list of one or more dependent variables, the keyword BY, and one to five factors (independent variables) followed by their minimum and maximum values enclosed in parentheses and separated by a comma or space. The actual keyword VARIABLES can be omitted. For example, the analysis of variance table in Figure 18.2 could be obtained by specifying either

```
ANOVA SCORE BY ATTRACT(1,3) SEX(1,2).
```

or

```
ANOVA VARIABLES=SCORE BY ATTRACT(1,3) SEX(1,2).
```

The values of the factors are arbitrary from a statistical point of view. They are not arbitrary, however, from a computational point of view, since they define the dimensions of the table of means and variances from which the analysis of variance is obtained. If the factor variables do not have consecutive values, they should be recoded using either the RECODE or AUTORECODE command before running ANOVA. Otherwise, SPSS/PC+ may not have enough computer resources to complete the analysis.

Specifying Full Factorial Models

The full factorial model is the default. Interaction terms up to fifth order are analyzed. If two or more dependent variables are specified, separate analyses of variance are produced for each. They are not analyzed jointly.

If two or more factor variables have the same value range, the range can be listed following the last factor it applies to, as in the command

```
ANOVA CHOL BY OVERWT AGE RACE(1,4).
```

The value specification does not need to correspond exactly to a variable's actual range of values. If the specified range is smaller than the actual range, cases with values outside the specified range are excluded from the analysis. If a range larger than the actual range is specified, the memory required to process the ANOVA command is needlessly increased.

Only integer-valued variables should be used as factors. If a noninteger variable is included in the factor list, its values are truncated to integers, which may produce unexpected results. The RECODE command should be used before ANOVA to transform noninteger factor values into integers.

More than one design can be specified on an ANOVA command by using multiple analysis lists separated by slashes, as in:

```
ANOVA PRESTIGE BY INCOME(1,3) RACE SEX (1,2)
  /PRSTCHNG BY INCOME(1,3) RACE SEX (1,2) AGE (1,5).
```

Requesting Cell Means and Counts

The means and counts table is displayed when Statistic 3 is specified on the STATISTICS subcommand.

Statistic 3   *Cell means and counts for the dependent variable.* For each dependent variable a separate table is displayed, showing the means and cell counts for each combination of factor values that define the effect, ignoring all other factors. Means of covariates are not displayed.

For example, the command

```
ANOVA SCORE BY ATTRACT(1,3) SEX (1,2)
  /STATISTICS=3.
```

produces the tables in Figure 18.1. Tables for *SEX*, *ATTRACT*, and the *SEX* by *AT-TRACT* interaction effects are included.

If Option 9 is used, this table is not available (see "Decomposing Sums of Squares" on p. 257). Cell means corresponding to the suppressed interaction terms are not displayed when Options 3–6 are used (see "Suppressing Interaction Effects" on p. 256).

Suppressing Interaction Effects

By default, all interaction effects up to and including fifth-order effects are examined. You can suppress various orders of interaction effects and pool them into the error (residual) sums of squares by using the following on the OPTIONS subcommand:

Option 3   *Suppress all interaction terms.* Only main effects and covariate effects are in the ANOVA table.

Option 4   *Delete all three-way and higher-order interaction terms.*

Option 5   *Delete all four-way and higher-order interaction terms.*

Option 6   *Delete all five-way interaction terms.*

ANOVA will not examine six-way or higher-order interactions, and the sums of squares for such terms are always pooled into the error sum of squares.

Specifying Covariates

Specify covariates after the factor list, following keyword WITH, as in:

```
ANOVA SCORE BY ATTRACT(1,3) WITH SELFATRT.
```

By default, covariates are assessed first, with main effects assessed after adjusting for the covariates. You can specify the order in which blocks of covariates and factor main effects are assessed with the following options:

Option 7   *Process covariates concurrently with main effects for factors.*

Option 8   *Process covariates after main effects for factors have been included.*

The order of entry is irrelevant if Option 9 (the regression approach) is specified (see "Decomposing Sums of Squares" on p. 257).

Unstandardized regression coefficients for the covariates are displayed if Statistic 2 is specified on the STATISTICS subcommand:

Statistic 2   *Display unstandardized regression coefficients for covariates.* These regression coefficients are computed when the covariates are entered into the equation. Their values depend on the design specified by Options 7 through 10 or by default. (See "Decomposing Sums of Squares" on p. 257 for a discussion of Options 9 and 10.) These coefficients are displayed immediately below the analysis of variance table.

Decomposing Sums of Squares

Three methods are available for decomposing sums of squares. The default method is the *classical experimental approach,* in which each type of effect is assessed separately in the following order (unless Option 7 or 8 has been specified):

- Effects of covariates.
- Main effects of factors.
- Two-way interaction effects.
- Three-way interaction effects.
- Four-way interaction effects.
- Five-way interaction effects.

Each effect is adjusted for all other effects of that type and for all previously entered effects.

The following optional methods can be specified on the OPTIONS subcommand:

Option 9   *Regression approach.* All effects are assessed simultaneously, with each effect adjusted for all other effects in the model. Option 9 overrides Options 7 and 8. The MCA table (Statistic 1) and cell means and counts (Statistic 3) are not available with Option 9.

Option 10   *Hierarchical approach.* Factor main effects and covariate effects are assessed hierarchically. Factor main effects are adjusted only for factor main effects already assessed, and covariate effects are adjusted only for covariates already assessed. Factors are assessed in the order they are listed on the ANOVA command.

When Option 9 is used, the lowest specified categories of all the independent variables must have a marginal frequency of at least 1, since the lowest specified category is used as the reference category. If this rule is violated, no ANOVA table is produced and a message is displayed identifying the first offending variable. For example, specifying a range of (0,9) for a variable that actually has values of 1 through 9 results in an error, and no ANOVA table is produced.

To understand the three approaches for decomposing sums of squares, consider the following command:

```
ANOVA TESTSCOR BY SEX(1,2) MTVN(1,5) ATT(1,3).
```

Table 18.1 summarizes the way each approach analyzes the design. In the default classical experimental approach, each main effect is assessed with the two other main effects held constant. The two-way interactions are assessed with all main effects and all other two-way interactions held constant, and the three-way interaction is assessed with all main effects and two-way interactions held constant. The regression approach assesses each factor or interaction while holding all other factors and interactions constant. In the hierarchical approach, the order in which the factors are specified on the ANOVA command determines the order in which they are assessed.

Table 18.1   Terms adjusted for in each approach

Effect	Classical approach (default)	Regression approach (Option 9)	Hierarchical approach (Option 10)
SEX	MTVN, ATT	All others	None
MTVN	SEX, ATT	All others	SEX
ATTN	SEX, MTVN	All others	SEX, MTVN
SEX*MTVN	SEX, MTVN, ATT, SEX*ATT, MTVN*ATT	All others	SEX, MTVN, ATT, SEX*ATT, MTVN*ATT
SEX*ATT	SEX, MTVN, ATT, SEX*MTVN, MTVN*ATT	All others	SEX, MTVN, ATT, SEX*MTVN, MTVN*ATT
MTVN*ATT	SEX, MTVN, ATT, SEX*MTVN, SEX*ATT	All others	SEX, MTVN, ATT, SEX*MTVN, SEX*ATT
SEX*MTVN*ATT	SEX, MTVN, ATT, SEX*MTVN, SEX*ATT, MTVN*ATT	All others	SEX, MTVN, ATT, SEX*MTVN, SEX*ATT, MTVN*ATT

Summary of Analysis Methods

Table 18.2 summarizes the types of analyses produced when combinations of these methods are used.

Table 18.2   Summary of analysis methods

	Assessments between types of effects	Assessments within the same type of effect
Default	**Covariates** then **Factors** then **Interactions**	**Covariates:** adjust for all other covariates **Factors:** adjust for covariates and all other factors **Interactions:** adjust for covariates, factors, and all other interactions of the same and lower orders
Option 7	**Factors** and **Covariates** concurrently then Interactions	**Covariates:** adjust for factors and all other covariates **Factors:** adjust for covariates and all other factors **Interactions:** adjust for covariates, factors, and all other interactions of the same and lower orders

Table 18.2 Summary of analysis methods

	Assessments between types of effects	Assessments within the same type of effect
Option 8	Factors then Covariates then Interactions	**Factors**: adjust for all other factors **Covariates**: adjust for factors and all other covariates **Interactions**: adjust for covariates, factors, and all other interactions of the same and lower orders
Option 9	Covariates, Factors, and **Interactions** simultaneously	**Covariates**: adjust for factors, interactions, and all other covariates **Factors**: adjust for covariates, interactions, and all other factors **Interactions**: adjust for covariates, factors, and all other interactions
Option 10	Covariates then Factors then Interactions	**Covariates**: adjust for covariates that are preceding in the list **Factors**: adjust for covariates and factors preceding in the list **Interactions**: adjust for covariates, factors, and all other interactions of the same and lower orders
Options 7 and 10	**Factors** and **Covariates** concurrently then Interactions	**Factors**: adjust only for preceding factors **Covariates**: adjust for factors and preceding covariates **Interactions**: adjust for covariates, factors, and all other interactions of the same and lower orders
Options 8 and 10	Factors then Covariates then Interactions	**Factors**: adjust only for preceding factors **Covariates**: adjust factors and preceding covariates **Interactions**: adjust for covariates, factors, and all other interactions of the same and lower orders

Multiple Classification Analysis

Multiple classification output consists of the grand mean of the dependent variables, a table of deviations from the grand mean for each factor level (**treatment effects**), and several measures of association. The deviations indicate the magnitude of the effect of each factor level. To obtain this output, specify Statistic 1 on the STATISTICS subcommand.

Statistic 1   *Multiple classification analysis (MCA) table.* Three types of deviations are displayed: unadjusted deviations; deviations adjusted for the main effects of other factors if covariates are used; and deviations adjusted for the main effects of other factors and for covariates. The adjusted deviations show the effect of a particular factor level after variation due to other factors (or to other factors and covariates) has been taken into account.

If covariates are used, a complete table can be obtained only if Option 8, Options 8 and 10, or Options 7 and 10 are used. If a model in which factors are not assessed first is specified, deviations adjusted only for factors are not displayed in the MCA table. The MCA table is not produced if Option 9 is used. Ordinarily, this table is of interest only when no interaction terms are significant.

Several measures of association are also displayed in the MCA table. For each factor in the table, the eta statistic is calculated. Its squared value indicates the proportion of variance "explained" by a given factor. Standardized regression coefficients, called betas, multiple R, and R^2 are also displayed. R^2 indicates the proportion of variance in the dependent variable "accounted for" by all factors, covariates, and interaction terms.

Missing Values

By default, a case with a system- or user-missing value for any variable in the analysis list is excluded from all analyses specified by that list. With Option 1, cases with user-defined missing data are included in the analysis.

Option 1   *Include cases with user-missing values.*

Format Options

By default, variable and value labels (if defined) are included in the output, and the table of cell means and counts (Statistic 3) uses the available width. Two options are available for controlling the format of the output:

Option 2   *Suppress variable and value labels.*

Option 11   *Narrow format for the table of cell means and counts (Statistic 3).* The width of the table is restricted to narrow width regardless of the width defined on SET.

19 Plotting Data: Procedure PLOT

Today the quest for the Fountain of Youth has been replaced by the Search for Slimness. It's almost acceptable to grow old, as long as one remains trim and fit. Programs for weight loss are gaining ever-increasing attention, and behavioral psychologists are studying the effectiveness of many different weight-loss strategies. Black and Sherba (1983) studied the effects of two different types of behavior programs on weight loss. One group of subjects was taught behavioral weight-loss techniques, while the second was taught weight-loss techniques and problem-solving behavior. Their data set is examined in this chapter.

Describing Weight Loss

As discussed in Chapter 11, a histogram is a convenient method for displaying the distribution of a variable that can have many values. Figure 19.1 shows the percentage of excess weight actually lost during treatment for each of the twelve cases in the study. From this figure, we can see that about one third of the participants lost 20% or more of the required weight. Figure 19.2 shows the percentage of weight loss one year after treatment. It appears that subjects did not gain back the weight but maintained weight loss.

Figure 19.1 Histogram of weight loss during treatment

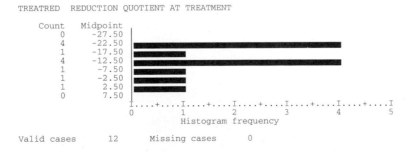

```
FREQUENCIES VARIABLES=TREATRED /FORMAT NOTABLE
  /HISTOGRAM MIN(-30) MAX(10) INC(5).

TREATRED  REDUCTION QUOTIENT AT TREATMENT

   Count   Midpoint
      0     -27.50
      4     -22.50  |
      1     -17.50  |
      4     -12.50  |
      1      -7.50  |
      1      -2.50  |
      1       2.50  |
      0       7.50  |
              I....+....I....+....I....+....I....+....I....+....I
              0         1         2         3         4         5
                         Histogram frequency

Valid cases    12    Missing cases    0
```

261

Figure 19.2   Histogram of weight loss after one year

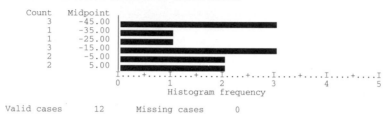

```
FREQUENCIES VARIABLES=TWELVRED /FORMAT NOTABLE
  /HISTOGRAM MIN(-50) MAX(10) INC(10).

TWELVRED   REDUCTION QUOTIENT AT TWELVE MONTHS

      Count    Midpoint
        3      -45.00
        1      -35.00
        1      -25.00
        3      -15.00
        2       -5.00
        2        5.00
                         0        1        2        3        4        5
                                     Histogram frequency

Valid cases       12    Missing cases      0
```

Although the histograms provide information about weight loss during treatment and after twelve months, they reveal nothing about the relationship between the two variables since they each describe single variables. To determine whether weight lost during treatment is maintained or replaced at twelve months, the two variables must be studied together.

Figure 19.3 is a scatterplot of the percentage of weight loss during treatment and at one year for the twelve cases. Each plot symbol (the *1*'s) represents one case and gives the values for that case for the two variables. For example, the circled point represents a case with a treatment loss of 25% and a twelve-month value of −18%.

Figure 19.3   Scatterplot for weight loss during treatment and after one year

```
PLOT PLOT TREATRED WITH TWELVRED.
```

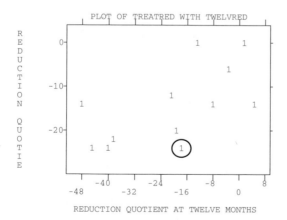

The scale of the plot depends on the minimum and maximum values for the two variables plotted. If the values for a few cases are far removed from the others, the majority of cases may appear bunched together so that outlying cases appear on the same plot.

When two or more cases with similar values fall on the same point on the scatterplot, a symbol is displayed indicating how many cases overlap at that point. Figure 19.4 contains the symbols used to represent multiple cases at each point. For example, the symbol D is used when there are 13 overlapping points.

Figure 19.4   Scatterplot symbols for multiple cases

```
Frequencies and symbols used (not applicable for control or overlay plots)

        1 -  1      11 - B      21 - L      31 - V
        2 -  2      12 - C      22 - M      32 - W
        3 -  3      13 - D      23 - N      33 - X
        4 -  4      14 - E      24 - O      34 - Y
        5 -  5      15 - F      25 - P      35 - Z
        6 -  6      16 - G      26 - Q      36 - *
        7 -  7      17 - H      27 - R
        8 -  8      18 - I      28 - S
        9 -  9      19 - J      29 - T
       10 -  A      20 - K      30 - U
```

Controlled Scatterplots

Often it is informative to identify each point on a scatterplot by its value on a third variable. For example, cases may be designated as males or females. Figure 19.5 is the same as Figure 19.3 except each case is identified as being a participant in the behavior program (value 1) or the problem-solving program (value 2). A dollar sign is displayed if cases from different groups overlap. By examining Figure 19.5, you can see if the relationship between weight-loss and weight-loss maintenance is similar for the two groups.

Figure 19.5   Scatterplot identifying the two programs

```
PLOT PLOT TREATRED WITH TWELVRED BY TREATMNT.
```

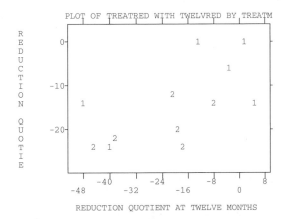

Plotting Multiple Variables

Weight-loss maintenance may be associated with many variables, including age. Figure 19.6 is a plot of age with weight loss during treatment, and Figure 19.7 is a plot of age with weight loss at twelve months. There appears to be a somewhat negative relationship between age and weight loss. Older people appear to have lost a greater percentage of weight than younger ones.

Figure 19.6 Scatterplot of age with weight loss during treatment

PLOT PLOT TREATRED WITH AGE.

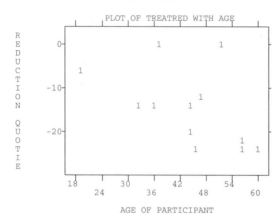

Figure 19.7 Scatterplot of age with weight loss at twelve months

PLOT PLOT TWELVRED WITH AGE.

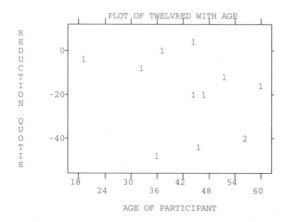

Figure 19.6 and Figure 19.7 can be combined into a single plot, as shown in Figure 19.8. Each case appears twice on Figure 19.8: once with treatment weight loss (denoted as *1*) and once with twelve-month loss (denoted as *2*). When there are several cases with similar ages, you cannot tell which are the matching points. For example, at age 36 there are four points, since there are two cases with similar ages (one is 36, one is 35). The $ represents multiple occurrences at a given location. However, we cannot tell if these are the two values for the same case or one value from one case and one from another.

Figure 19.8   Overlay plot of weight loss during treatment and at twelve months

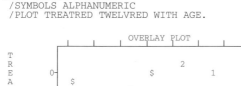

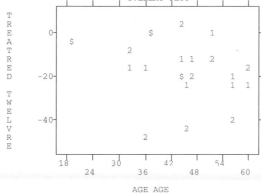

Running Procedure PLOT

The PLOT procedure produces bivariate scatterplots or regression plots (with or without control variables), contour plots, overlay plots, and some regression statistics. (For complete regression analysis, use procedure REGRESSION (see Chapter 21)). Format options enable you to control axis size and scale, the plotting symbols used, and the frequency they represent. You can also label the plot and its axes, request reference lines, and plot standardized variables.

Specifying the Variables

Use the PLOT subcommand to specify the variables to be plotted. Variables to be plotted on the vertical (*y*) axis are specified first, followed by keyword WITH and the variables to be plotted on the horizontal (*x*) axis.

By default, PLOT produces bivariate scatterplots. For example, the following command produces the output in Figure 19.3:

```
PLOT PLOT=TREATRED WITH TWELVRED.
```

You can produce multiple plots with one PLOT subcommand. For example, the command

```
PLOT PLOT=IQ GRE WITH GPA SAT.
```

produces four plots: *IQ* with *GPA*, *IQ* with *SAT*, *GRE* with *GPA*, and *GRE* with *SAT*.

You can also plot individual pairs of variables using the PAIR keyword. For example, the command

```
PLOT PLOT=IQ GRE WITH GPA SAT (PAIR).
```

produces two plots: *IQ* with *GPA* and *GRE* with *SAT*.

Multiple plot lists can be specified on the PLOT subcommand if they are separated by semicolons, as in:

```
PLOT PLOT=IQ WITH GPA EDUC;GRE WITH SAT.
```

This produces three plots: *IQ* with *GPA*, *IQ* with *EDUC*, and *GRE* with *SAT*. You can also specify multiple PLOT subcommands on one PLOT command.

A control variable or contour variable (see "Choosing the Type of Plot" below) can be specified on the PLOT subcommand by naming it after the BY keyword. For example, the command

```
PLOT PLOT=TREATRED WITH TWELVRED BY TREATMNT.
```

produces the plot in Figure 19.5. Only one control or contour variable can be specified on a plot list. PLOT uses the first character of a control variable's value label as a plotting symbol. For example, if *SEX* is the control variable with value labels *FEMALE* and *MALE*, the observations for females are represented by *F* and those for males by *M*. If a variable has no value labels, the first character of the actual value is used as the plotting symbol. When multiple control values occur in the same position on the plot, they are represented by a single dollar sign.

Choosing the Type of Plot

Use the FORMAT subcommand to specify the type of plot you want to produce. Four types of plots are available: scatterplots, regression plots, contour plots, and overlay plots. If FORMAT is not specified or is specified without keywords, scatterplots are displayed. The following keywords can be specified on FORMAT:

DEFAULT   *Bivariate scatterplot.* When there are no control variables, each symbol represents the case count at that plot position. When a control variable is specified, each symbol represents the first character of the value label of the control variable, or the first character of the value if no labels have been defined.

REGRESSION   *Regression of the* y *axis variable on the* x *axis variable.* The regression-line intercepts are marked with the letter *R*. When there is no control variable, each symbol represents the frequency of cases at that position. If a control variable is specified, regression statistics are pooled over all categories and each symbol represents the first character of the control variable's value label, or the first character of the value if no labels have been defined.

CONTOUR(n)   *Contour plot with* n *levels.* Contour plots use a continuous variable as the control variable and *n* successive symbols to represent the lowest to highest levels of the variable. The control variable is specified after BY on the PLOT subcommand and is recoded into *n* equal-width intervals. If *n* is omitted, the default of 10 is used; the maximum is 35. When more than one level of the contour variable occurs at the same position, PLOT displays the value of the highest level at that position.

OVERLAY   *Overlay plots.* All plots specified on the next PLOT subcommand are displayed in one plot frame. A unique plotting symbol is used for each overlaid plot. An additional symbol indicates multiple plot points at the same position. Control plots cannot be overlaid.

For more information on these keywords, see PLOT in the Syntax Reference.

Specify the FORMAT subcommand before the PLOT subcommand to which it refers. One FORMAT subcommand can be specified before each PLOT subcommand. For example, the command

```
PLOT FORMAT OVERLAY
 /SYMBOLS ALPHANUMERIC
 /PLOT=TREATRED TWELVRED WITH AGE.
```

produces the overlay plot in Figure 19.8.

Overlay plots are useful when several similar variables are measured or when the same variable is measured at different times. For example, the command

```
PLOT  SYMBOLS='MD'
 /VSIZE=30 /HSIZE=70
 /FORMAT=OVERLAY
 /TITLE 'MARRIAGE AND DIVORCE RATES  1900-1981'
 /VERTICAL='RATES PER 1000 POPULATION'
 /HORIZONTAL='YEAR' REFERENCE (1918,1945) MIN (1900) MAX (1983)
 /PLOT=MARRATE DIVRATE WITH YEAR.
```

produces the overlay plot of marriage and divorce rates shown in Figure 19.9 (data taken from the *Information Please Almanac,* 1983).

Figure 19.9 An overlay plot

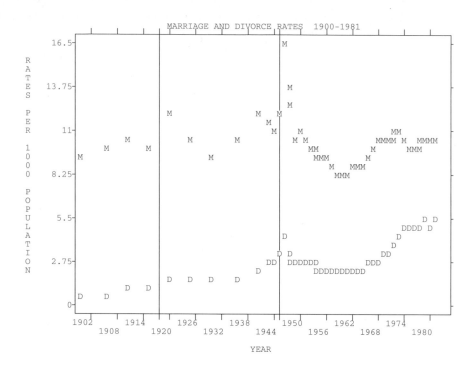

Contour plots evaluate the effect of a continuous variable as a control variable. If you use symbols with different degrees of density, you can produce a visual representation of the density of your contour variable. For example, the command

```
PLOT FORMAT=CONTOUR (10)
  /HSIZE=50/VSIZE=30
  /SYMBOLS='.-=*+%#0&X'
  /TITLE='SOLUBILITY OF AMMONIA IN WATER'
  /HORIZONTAL='ATMOSPHERIC PRESSURE'
  /VERTICAL='TEMPERATURE'
  /PLOT=TEMP WITH PRESSURE BY CONCENT.
```

produces the output in Figure 19.10, representing the concentration of ammonia in water under varying conditions of temperature and atmospheric pressure. The key to symbols is shown in Figure 19.11.

Figure 19.10 A contour plot

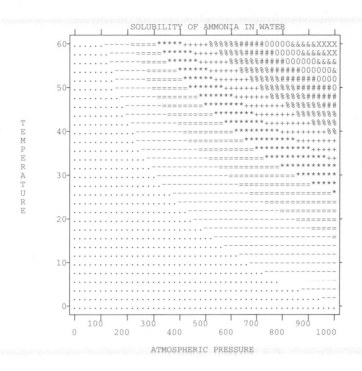

Figure 19.11 Contour plot key

```
6161 cases plotted. The bounds of CONCENT are defined as follows:
*:    .090-    .120  +:    .120-    .150  %:    .150-    .180
#:    .180-    .210  0:    .210-    .240  &:    .240-    .270
X:    .270-    .300
```

Plots with regression statistics are described and shown in Chapter 20 and in Chapter 21.

Setting Plot Symbols

A wide range of alphabetical, numeric, and special ASCII graphic characters are available as plot symbols. Use the CUTPOINT and SYMBOLS subcommands to control the display of plot symbols.

The CUTPOINT subcommand specifies the number of cases represented by each symbol. For example, the symbol 1 can represent one case at a position, the symbol 2 can represent two cases at a position, and the symbol 3 can represent three or more cases at a position. CUTPOINT can be used only once on a PLOT command and applies to all plots requested. The CUTPOINT subcommand cannot be used for control plots, overlay, or contour plots.

The following specifications are available with CUTPOINT:

EVERY(n)   *Frequency intervals of width* n. Each plot symbol represents the specified frequency interval. The default is an interval width of 1. The last symbol specified represents all frequencies greater than those for the next-to-last symbol.

(value list)   *Each value defines a cut point.* Successive plot symbols are assigned to each cut point. Up to 35 cut points can be specified. Specify values separated by blanks or commas. The number of cut points is one less than the number of intervals.

For example, if the command

```
PLOT CUTPOINT=EVERY(4)
  /PLOT=SCORE WITH ANXIETY.
```

is specified, one to four cases in the same position are represented by a 1, five to eight cases by a 2, and so on. If the command

```
PLOT CUTPOINT=(5,10,25)
  /PLOT=SCORE WITH ANXIETY.
```

is used, one to five cases in the same position are represented by a 1, six to ten cases by a 2, 11 to 25 cases by a 3, and more than 25 cases by a 4.

The SYMBOLS subcommand allows you to choose other plotting symbols to represent a plot position. For scatterplots and regression plots, each symbol represents the number of cases at a plot position. For overlay plots, each symbol represents one of the overlaid plots. For contour plots, each symbol represents one interval of the contour variable. SYMBOLS cannot be used with control plots. Instead, use the VALUE LABELS command to define appropriate labels when control plots are requested. The SYMBOLS subcommand can be used only once on a PLOT command and applies to all plots requested.

You can specify one of the following options on SYMBOLS:

ALPHANUMERIC   *Alphanumeric plotting symbols.* The characters 1 through 9, A through Z, and an asterisk (*) are used, in that order. For example, in a scatterplot, 1 indicates one case at a position, and an asterisk represents 36 or more cases at a position. This is the default if the SYMBOLS subcommand is not specified.

NUMERIC   *Numeric plotting symbols.* The characters 1 through 9 and an asterisk are used, with the asterisk indicating 10 or more cases at a position in a scatterplot.

'symbols'[,'ovprnt']	*List of plot symbols.* Up to 36 symbols can be specified. Symbols are specified without any intervening blanks or commas. Optionally, you can specify a list of overprinting symbols separated from the first list by a comma or space.
X'hexsym'[,'ovprnt']	*List of hexadecimal plot symbols.* Indicate hexadecimal symbols by specifying X before the hexadecimal representation list enclosed in apostrophes. Optionally, you can specify a list of overprinting symbols separated from the first list by a comma or space.

Symbols and their equivalents are displayed in a table like the one shown in Figure 19.4. If the SYMBOLS subcommand is omitted, the default alphanumeric symbol set is used.

For example, the command

```
PLOT CUTPOINTS=(1,2,3,4)
  /SYMBOLS='.:x*X'
  /PLOT=INCOME WITH ASTRSIGN.
```

requests a scatterplot with a period (.) representing one case at a position, a colon (:) representing two cases, x representing three cases, an asterisk (*) representing four cases, and X representing five or more cases.

Specifying Plot Titles

Use the TITLE subcommand to specify a plot title. The title can contain up to 60 characters and must be enclosed in single quotation marks, as in:

```
PLOT TITLE='CORPORATE TAKEOVERS 1975-1983'
  /PLOT=TAKEOVER WITH YEAR.
```

TITLE can be specified once before each PLOT subcommand and applies only to the following PLOT subcommand. Titles longer than the horizontal axis are truncated. If TITLE is not specified, the title consists of the names of the variables plotted for scatterplots or the type of the plot requested on FORMAT.

Scaling and Labeling Plot Axes

The VERTICAL and HORIZONTAL subcommands allow you to control the scaling and labeling of the vertical and horizontal axes, obtain reference lines at specified positions, specify minimum and maximum values, and obtain plots of standardized variables. Resetting minimum or maximum values is especially useful when you want to focus on a subset of a larger plot. Standardized plots are appropriate when you want to overlay plots of variables with very different scales.

The VERTICAL and HORIZONTAL subcommands can be used once before each PLOT subcommand and apply to all plots specified in the next PLOT subcommand. The following specifications are available:

'label'
: *Label for the axis.* The label can contain up to 40 characters. The default label is the variable label or, if there is no variable label, the variable name. Labels longer than the axis are truncated.

MIN(n)
: *Minimum axis value.* The default is the minimum observed value for the plotted variable.

MAX(n)
: *Maximum axis value.* The default is the maximum observed value for the plotted variable or a slightly larger number (to obtain equal-width integer scaling).

UNIFORM
: *Uniform axis scale.* This keyword is unnecessary when MIN and MAX are specified. If UNIFORM is specified, PLOT determines the minimum and maximum observed values across all variables on the PLOT subcommand.

REFERENCE(values)
: *Draw reference lines at the values specified.* Specify values separated by blanks or commas. The default is no reference lines.

STANDARDIZE
: *Standardized variables.* The default is to plot observed values.

Setting the Plot Size

The VSIZE and HSIZE subcommands control the height and width, respectively, of the plot. The default size of the plot depends on the current page size (for information on the defaults, see PLOT in the Syntax Reference). For example, the command

```
PLOT VSIZE=30/HSIZE=45
  /PLOT=SALES WITH REP DISTRICT.
```

requests a height of 30 lines and a width of 45 positions for the plots of *SALES* with *REP* and *SALES* with *DISTRICT*.

The VSIZE and HSIZE subcommands can be used only once: all plots requested are then drawn to the specified size.

HSIZE and VSIZE with HORIZONTAL and VERTICAL

If you specify both MIN and MAX values on the HORIZONTAL or VERTICAL subcommands, your axes may contain some fractional values, even if your data contain only integer values. You can control the axis values displayed and the interval between values by specifying HSIZE and VSIZE in conjunction with MIN and MAX values on the HORIZONTAL and VERTICAL subcommands.

The formula is

$$\frac{\text{MAX} - \text{MIN}}{\text{interval}} \times 5 = \text{VSIZE or HSIZE specification}$$

Equation 19.1

If the result of (MAX − MIN)/interval is not an integer, some of your axis values will be fractional. You can compensate by adjusting either MIN, MAX, or interval values.

For example, to display the years from 1880 to 2000 in 10-year increments on the horizontal axis, you would calculate HSIZE as

$$\frac{2000 - 1880}{10} \times 5 = 60$$

The commands and results are shown in Figure 19.12.

Figure 19.12 Overlay plot of marriage and divorce rates

```
PLOT SYMBOLS='MD'
 /FORMAT=OVERLAY
 /TITLE='MARRIAGE AND DIVORCE RATES 1900-1981'
 /VSIZE=20 /HSIZE=60
 /VERTICAL='RATES PER 1000 POPULATION' MIN(0) MAX(20)
 /HORIZONTAL='YEAR'REFERENCE(1918,1945) MIN(1880) MAX(2000)
 /PLOT=MARRATE DIVRATE WITH YEAR.
```

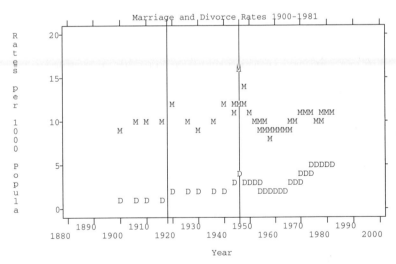

Missing Values

The MISSING subcommand controls the treatment of missing values. The subcommand can be used only once on each PLOT command. You can request the following options on the MISSING subcommand:

PLOTWISE   *Exclude cases with missing values plotwise.* Cases that have a missing value for any variable within a single plot are not included. In an overlay plot, plotwise deletion applies to each plot that is overlaid. This is the default if no missing-value treatment is specified.

LISTWISE   *Exclude cases with missing values listwise.* Cases with missing values for any variable named on the PLOT subcommand are excluded from all plots.

INCLUDE   *Include cases with user-defined missing values.* INCLUDE can be used with either PLOTWISE or LISTWISE to include cases with user-missing values. Only cases with system-missing values are excluded.

20 Measuring Linear Association: Procedure CORRELATIONS

Youthful lemonade-stand entrepreneurs and executives of billion-dollar corporations share a common concern—how to increase sales. Hand-lettered signs affixed to neighborhood trees, television campaigns, siblings canvassing local playgrounds, and international sales forces are known to be effective marketing tactics. Since it can be difficult to measure the effectiveness of specific marketing techniques, businesses routinely conduct market research to determine exactly what makes their products sell.

Churchill (1979) describes a study undertaken by the manufacturer of Click ballpoint pens to determine the effectiveness of the firm's marketing efforts. A random sample of 40 sales territories is selected, and sales, amount of advertising, and number of sales representatives are recorded. This chapter looks at the relationship between sales and these variables.

Examining Relationships

A scatterplot can reveal various types of associations between two variables. Some commonly encountered patterns are illustrated in Figure 20.1. In the first example, there appears to be no discernible relationship between the two variables. In the second example, the variables are related exponentially; that is, Y increases very rapidly for increasing values of X. In the third example, the relationship between the two variables is U-shaped. Small and large values of the X variable are associated with large values of the Y variable.

Figure 20.1   Scatterplots showing common relationships

Figure 20.2 is a scatterplot showing the amount of sales and the number of television spots in each of 40 territories from the study. From the figure, it appears there is a positive association between sales and advertising. That is, as the amount of advertising increases, so does the number of sales. The relationship between sales and advertising may be termed **linear**, since the observed points cluster more or less around a straight line.

Figure 20.2   Scatterplot showing a linear relationship

```
GET FILE='TVSALES.SYS'.
PLOT /FORMAT REGRESSION /PLOT=SALES WITH ADVERTIS
```

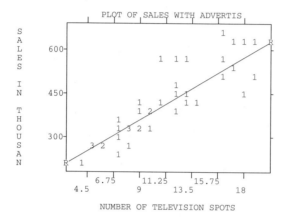

The Correlation Coefficient

Although a scatterplot is an essential first step in studying the association between two variables, it is often useful to quantify the strength of the association by calculating a summary index. One commonly used measure is the **Pearson correlation coefficient**, denoted by r. It is defined as

$$r = \frac{\sum_{i=1}^{N} (X_i - \bar{X})(Y_i - \bar{Y})}{(N-1) S_X S_Y}$$

Equation 20.1

where N is the number of cases and S_X and S_Y are the standard deviations of the two variables. The absolute value of r indicates the strength of the linear relationship. The largest possible absolute value is 1, which occurs when all points fall exactly on the line.

When the line has a positive slope, the value of r is positive, and when the slope of the line is negative, the value of r is negative (see Figure 20.3).

Figure 20.3   Scatterplots with correlation coefficients of +1 and –1

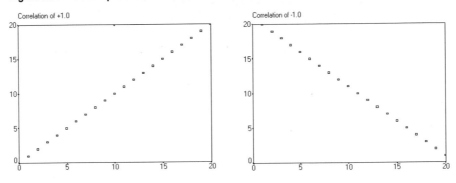

A value of 0 indicates no *linear* relationship. Two variables can have a strong association but a small correlation coefficient if the relationship is not linear. Figure 20.4 shows two plots with correlation coefficients of 0.

Figure 20.4   Scatterplots with correlation coefficients of 0

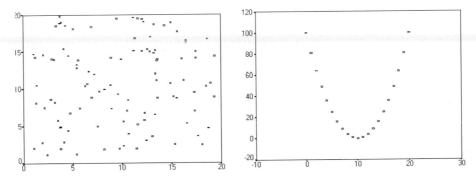

It is important to examine correlation coefficients together with scatterplots since the same coefficient can result from very different underlying relationships. The variables plotted in Figure 20.5 have a correlation coefficient greater than 0.8, as do the variables plotted in Figure 20.2. But note how different the relationships are between the two sets of variables. In Figure 20.5, there is a strong positive linear association for only part of the plot. The relationship between the two variables is basically nonlinear. The scatterplot in Figure 20.2 is very different. The points cluster more or less around a line. The correlation coefficient should be used only to summarize the strength of linear association.

Figure 20.5　Scatterplot showing nonlinear relationship

```
GET FILE 'HAIR.SYS'.
PLOT HORIZONTAL MIN(1820) MAX(1980) /HSIZE 40
/PLOT CLEAN WITH YEAR.
```

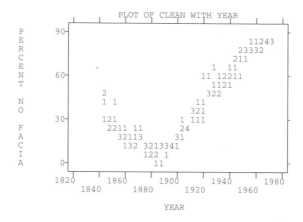

Some Properties of the Correlation Coefficient

A common mistake in interpreting the correlation coefficient is to assume that correlation implies causation. No such conclusion is automatic. While sales are highly correlated with advertising, they are also highly correlated with other variables, such as the number of sales representatives in a territory. Advertising alone does not necessarily result in increased sales. For example, territories with high sales may simply have more money to spend on TV spots, regardless of whether the spots are effective.

The correlation coefficient is a **symmetric measure**, since interchanging the two variables X and Y in the formula does not change the results. The correlation coefficient is not expressed in any units of measure, and it is not affected by linear transformations such as adding or subtracting constants or multiplying or dividing all values of a variable by a constant.

Calculating Correlation Coefficients

Figure 20.6 is a table of correlation coefficients for the number of television spots, number of sales representatives, and amount of sales. The entry in each cell is the correlation coefficient. For example, the correlation coefficient between advertising and sales is 0.8802. This value indicates that there is a fairly strong linear association between the two variables, as shown in Figure 20.2. The table is symmetric, since the correlation between X and Y is the same as the correlation between Y and X. The correlation values on the diagonal are all 1, since a variable is perfectly related to itself.

Figure 20.6   Correlation coefficients

```
CORRELATIONS VARIABLES=ADVERTIS REPS SALES

Correlations:  ADVERTIS   REPS       SALES

   ADVERTIS   1.0000     .7763**    .8802**
   REPS        .7763**   1.0000      .8818**
   SALES       .8802**    .8818**   1.0000

N of cases:   40          2-tailed Signif:  * - .01  ** - .001

" . " is printed if a coefficient cannot be computed
```

Hypothesis Tests about the Correlation Coefficient

Although the correlation coefficient is sometimes used only as a summary index to describe the observed strength of the association, in some situations description and summary are but a first step. The primary goal may be to test hypotheses about the unknown population correlation coefficient—denoted as ρ—based on its estimate, the sample correlation coefficient r. In order to test such hypotheses, certain assumptions must be made about the underlying joint distribution of the two variables. A common assumption is that independent random samples are taken from a distribution in which the two variables together are distributed normally. If this condition is satisfied, the test that the population coefficient is 0 can be based on the statistic

$$t = r\sqrt{\frac{N-2}{1-r^2}}$$

Equation 20.2

which, if $\rho = 0$, has a Student's t distribution with $N-2$ degrees of freedom. Either one- or two-tailed tests can be calculated. If nothing is known in advance, a two-tailed test is appropriate. That is, the hypothesis that the coefficient is zero is rejected for both extreme positive and extreme negative values of t. If the direction of the association can be specified in advance, the hypothesis is rejected only for t values that are of sufficient magnitude and in the direction specified.

In Figure 20.6, coefficients with two-tailed observed significance levels less than 0.01 are identified with a single asterisk and those with two-tailed significance levels less than 0.001 are identified with two asterisks. From Figure 20.6, the probability of obtaining a correlation coefficient of at least 0.88 in absolute value when there is no linear association in the population between sales and advertising is less than 0.001. Care should be exercised when examining the significance levels for large tables. Even if there is no association between the variables, if many coefficients are computed, some would be expected to be statistically significant by chance alone.

Special procedures must be employed to test more general hypotheses of the form $\rho = \rho_0$, where ρ_0 is a constant. If the assumptions of bivariate normality appear unreasonable, nonparametric measures such as Spearman's rho and Kendall's tau-*b* can be calculated. These coefficients make limited assumptions about the underlying distributions of the variables. You can compute Spearman's rho using the RANK procedure with CORRELATIONS (see Chapter 23).

Correlation Matrices and Missing Data

For a variety of reasons, data files frequently contain incomplete observations. Survey respondents scrawl illegible responses or refuse to answer certain questions. Laboratory animals die before experiments are completed. Patients fail to keep scheduled clinic appointments.

Analysis of data with missing values is troublesome. Before even considering possible strategies, you should determine whether there is evidence that the missing-value pattern is not random. That is, are there reasons to believe that missing values for a variable are related to the values of that variable or other variables? For example, people with low incomes may be less willing to report their financial status than more affluent people. This may be even more pronounced for people who are poor but highly educated.

One simple method of exploring such possibilities is to subdivide the data into two groups—those observations with missing data for a variable and those with complete data—and examine the distributions of the other variables in the file across these two groups. The SPSS/PC+ CROSSTABS and T-TEST procedures are particularly useful for this. For a discussion of more sophisticated methods for detecting nonrandomness, see Frane (1976).

If it appears that the data are not missing randomly, use great caution in attempting to analyze the data. It may be that no satisfactory analysis is possible, especially if there are only a few cases.

If you are satisfied that the missing data are random, several strategies are available. First, if the same few variables are missing for most cases, exclude those variables from the analysis. Since this luxury is not usually available, alternatively you can keep all variables but eliminate the cases with missing values. This is termed **listwise** missing-value treatment since a case is eliminated if it has a missing value for any variable in the list. If many cases have missing data for some variables, listwise missing-value treatment can eliminate too many cases and leave you with a very small sample. One common technique is to calculate the correlation coefficient between a pair of variables based on all cases with complete information for the two variables, regardless of whether the cases have missing data for any other variable. For example, if a case has values for variables 1, 3, and 5 only, it is used in computations involving only variable pairs 1 and 3, 1 and 5, and 3 and 5. This is **pairwise** missing-value treatment.

Choosing Pairwise Missing-Value Treatment

Several problems can arise with pairwise matrices, one of which is inconsistency. There are some relationships between coefficients that are clearly impossible but may seem to occur when different cases are used to estimate different coefficients. For example, if age and weight and age and height have high positive correlations, it is impossible in the same sample for height and weight to have a high negative correlation. However, if the same cases are not used to estimate all three coefficients, such an anomaly can occur.

There is no single sample size that can be associated with a pairwise matrix since each coefficient can be based on a different number of cases. Significance levels obtained from analyses based on pairwise matrices must be viewed with caution since little is known about hypothesis testing in such situations.

It should be emphasized that missing-value problems should not be treated lightly. You should base your decision on careful examination of the data and not leave the choices up to system defaults.

The Regression Line

If there is a linear relationship between two variables, a straight line can be used to summarize the data. When the correlation coefficient is +1 or −1, little thought is needed to determine the line that best describes the data: it is the line passes through all of the observations. When the observations are less highly correlated, many different lines can be drawn to represent the data.

One of the most commonly used procedures for fitting a line to the observations is the method of **least squares**. This method results in a line that minimizes the sum of squared vertical distances from the data points to the line.

The equation for the straight line that relates predicted sales to advertising is

$$\text{predicted sales} \ = \ a + b\,(\text{advertising})$$

Equation 20.3

The intercept, a, is the predicted sales when there is no advertising. The slope, b, is the change in predicted sales for a unit change in advertising. That is, it is the amount of change in sales per television spot.

The actual values of a and b calculated with the method of least squares are displayed as part of the SPSS/PC+ PLOT output (see Figure 20.7). The least-squares equation for the line is

$$\text{predicted sales} \ = \ 135.4 + 25.31\,(\text{advertising})$$

Equation 20.4

Figure 20.2 shows this regression line.

Figure 20.7   Intercept and slope from PLOT

```
40 cases plotted. Regression statistics of SALES on ADVERTIS:
Correlation  .88016 R Squared  .77467  S.E. of Est   59.56023 Sig.  .0000
Intercept(S.E.)  135.43360( 25.90649)  Slope(S.E.)   25.30770(  2.21415)
```

For each pair of variables, two different regression lines can be calculated, since the values of the slope and intercept depend on which variable is dependent (the one being predicted) and which is independent (the one used for prediction). In the SPSS/PC+ PLOT output, the variable plotted on the vertical axis is considered the dependent variable in the calculation of statistics.

Prediction

Based on the regression equation, it is possible to predict sales from advertising. For example, a territory with 10 television spots per month is expected to have sales of about $388,400 (135.4 + 25.3(10)). Note that considerable caution is needed when predictions are made for values of the independent variable that are much larger or much smaller than those used to derive the equation. A relationship that is linear for the observed range of values may not be linear everywhere. For example, estimating Y values for the beginning of Figure 20.5 based on a regression line for the latter part of the plot would result in a very poor fit.

The difference between observed sales and sales predicted by the model is called a **residual**. The residual for a territory with 10 television spots and observed sales of 403.6 is 15.2:

$$\text{residual} = \text{observed} - \text{predicted} = 403.6 - 388.4 = 15.2 \qquad \textbf{Equation 20.5}$$

Residuals can be calculated for each of the sales territories. Figure 20.8 contains the observed value (*SALES*), the predicted value (*PRED*), and the residual for the first 10 territories (*RESID*). The residuals provide an idea of how well the calculated regression line actually fits the data.

Figure 20.8   Residuals from the regression line

```
Casewise Plot of Standardized Residual

*: Selected   M: Missing

          -3.0      0.0      3.0
Case #    O:.........:.........:O    SALES      *PRED      *RESID
   1      .         *         .      260.3    261.9721    -1.6721
   2      .        *.         .      286.1    312.5875   -26.4875
   3      .         *         .      279.4    287.2798    -7.8798
   4      .          . *      .      410.8    363.2029    47.5971
   5      .         *         .      438.2    439.1260     -.9260
   6      .        *.         .      315.3    337.8952   -22.5952
   7      .         .      *  .      565.1    413.8183   151.2817
   8      .         .*        .      570.0    540.3568    29.6432
   9      .        *.         .      426.1    464.4337   -38.3337
  10      .         *         .      315.0    312.5875     2.4125
Case #    O:.........:.........:O    SALES      *PRED      *RESID
          -3.0      0.0      3.0
```

Goodness of Fit

Although the regression line is a useful summary of the relationship between two variables, the values of the slope and intercept alone do little to indicate how well the line actually fits the data. A goodness-of-fit index is needed.

The observed variation in the dependent variable can be subdivided into two components: the variation "explained" by the regression and the residual from the regression:

$$\text{total SS} = \text{regression SS} + \text{residual SS}$$ **Equation 20.6**

The **total sum of squares** is a measure of overall variation and is given by

$$\text{total sum of squares} = \sum_{i=1}^{N} (Y_i - \bar{Y})^2$$ **Equation 20.7**

The total sum of squares for sales is 598,253. (It is $N - 1$ times the variance.)

The **regression sum of squares**, or the sum of squares due to regression, is

$$\text{regression sum of squares} = \sum_{i=1}^{N} (\hat{Y}_i - \bar{Y})^2$$ **Equation 20.8**

where $\hat{Y}_i$ is the predicted value for the ith case. The regression sum of squares is a measure of how much variability in the dependent variable is attributable to the linear relationship between the two variables. For this example, the regression sum of squares is 463,451.

The **residual sum of squares**, sometimes called the error sum of squares, is obtained by squaring each of the residuals and then summing them:

$$\text{residual sum of squares} \; = \; \sum_{i=1}^{N} (Y_i - \hat{Y}_i)^2 \qquad \textbf{Equation 20.9}$$

The residual sum of squares for sales is 134,802. The standard deviation of the residuals, called the standard error of the estimate (SEE), is

$$\text{SEE} \; = \; \sqrt{\frac{\text{residual sum of squares}}{N-2}} \; = \; \sqrt{\frac{134,802}{38}} \; = \; 59.56 \qquad \textbf{Equation 20.10}$$

The standard error is displayed in Figure 20.7.

The proportion of the variation in the dependent variable that is explained by the linear regression is computed by comparing the total sum of squares and the regression sum of squares:

$$r^2 \; = \; \frac{\text{regression sum of squares}}{\text{total sum of squares}} \; = \; \frac{463,451}{598,253} \; = \; 0.775 \qquad \textbf{Equation 20.11}$$

If there is no linear association in the sample, the value of r^2 is 0, since the predicted values are just the mean of the dependent variable and the regression sum of squares is 0. If Y and X are perfectly linearly related, the residual sum of squares is 0 and r^2 is 1. The square root of r^2 is r, the Pearson correlation coefficient between the two variables.

Further Topics in Regression

In this chapter, only the most basic concepts in regression analysis are discussed. Chapter 21 contains detailed descriptions of simple two-variable regression as well as multiple regression analysis.

Running Procedure CORRELATIONS

The CORRELATIONS procedure calculates Pearson product-moment correlations for pairs of variables. The display includes the coefficient (r), an indication of significance level, and the number of cases upon which the coefficients are computed. Means, standard deviations, cross-product deviations, and covariances are available. You can also specify optional formats and methods of handling missing data. In addition, you can write out a square matrix containing correlation coefficients and the number of cases for use in other SPSS/PC+ procedures.

Specifying the Variables

The VARIABLES subcommand lists all variables to be included in the correlation matrix. For example, to produce the correlation matrix shown in Figure 20.6, specify

```
CORRELATIONS VARIABLES=ADVERTIS REPS SALES.
```

The actual keyword VARIABLES can be omitted.

The order in which you name the variables is the order in which they are displayed. Use keyword WITH to obtain the correlations of one set of variables with another set. For example, the command

```
CORRELATIONS VARIABLES=ADVERTIS WITH REPS SALES.
```

produces two correlations, *ADVERTIS* with *REPS* and *ADVERTIS* with *SALES*. You can specify several variable lists by separating them with slashes.

Only numeric variables can be specified on the VARIABLES subcommand. If long or short string variables are specified on a variable list, CORRELATIONS will not be executed.

Optional Statistics

By default, the correlation matrix and the number of valid cases on which the matrix is based are displayed. A correlation that cannot be computed is displayed as a period (.). Two-tailed probabilities of less than 0.01 are indicated by an asterisk (*) and those less than 0.001 by two asterisks (**). The output uses the width defined on the SET command (see SET in the Syntax Reference).

The following options and statistics are available using the OPTIONS and STATISTICS subcommands:

Option 3   *One-tailed probabilities.* One-tailed probabilities less than 0.01 are indicated by an asterisk (*) and those less than 0.001 by two asterisks (**). When Option 5 is also specified, exact one-tailed probabilities are given.

Option 5   *Count and probability.* The number of cases used to compute each coefficient and exact probability are displayed.

Statistic 1   *Univariate mean, standard deviation, and count.* Missing values are handled on a variable-by-variable basis, regardless of the missing-value option in effect.

Statistic 2   *Cross-product deviations and covariance.*

ALL   *All statistics.* ALL includes statistics available with Statistics 1 and 2.

For example, to obtain the statistics in Figure 20.9 (in addition to the correlation matrix) specify

```
CORRELATIONS VARIABLES=ADVERTIS REPS SALES
  /STATISTIC=1.
```

Figure 20.9   Univariate statistics with Statistic 1

```
Variable      Cases        Mean        Std Dev

ADVERTIS       40        10.9000        4.3074
REPS           40         5.0000        1.6486
SALES          40       411.2875      123.8540
```

Missing Values

By default, SPSS/PC+ excludes a case from the calculation of all correlation coefficients if it has a missing value for any variable named on the VARIABLES subcommand. This is listwise missing-value treatment. Specify Options 1 or 2 on the OPTIONS subcommand for alternative missing-value treatments.

Option 1   *Include cases with user-missing values in the computations.*

Option 2   *Exclude cases with missing values pairwise.* All cases with valid values for the pair of variables used to compute a coefficient are included in the computation of that coefficient (see "Choosing Pairwise Missing-Value Treatment" on p. 281).

Writing Matrices

By default, matrices are written only to the display file. Use Option 4 on the OPTIONS subcommand to write matrices to the results file named on the SET command for use in other procedures.

Option 4   *Write count and correlation matrix.* The correlation matrix and number of cases used to compute each coefficient for each analysis list are written to the results file named on the SET command. You cannot use the keyword WITH in the analysis list if you specify Option 4.

Multiple Linear Regression Analysis: Procedure REGRESSION

In this chapter we use the employee data set described in Chapter 15 to study discrimination in the workplace. The data contain employee records for 474 individuals hired between 1969 and 1971 by a bank engaged in Equal Employment Opportunity litigation. We will develop a mathematical model that relates beginning salary and salary progression to employee characteristics such as seniority, education, and previous work experience. One objective is to determine whether sex and race are important predictors of salary.

The technique used to build the model is linear regression analysis, one of the most versatile data analysis procedures. Regression can be used to summarize data as well as to study relations among variables.

Linear Regression

Before examining a model that relates beginning salary to several other variables, consider the relationship between beginning and current (as of March, 1977) salary. For employees hired during a similar time period, beginning salary should serve as a reasonably good predictor of salary at a later date. Although superstars and underachievers might progress differently from the group as a whole, salary progression should be similar for the others. The scatterplot of beginning salary and current salary shown in Figure 21.1 supports this hypothesis.

A scatterplot may suggest what type of mathematical functions would be appropriate for summarizing the data. Many functions, including parabolas, hyperbolas, polynomials, and trigonometric functions, are useful in fitting models to data. The scatterplot in Figure 21.1 shows that current salaries tend to increase linearly with increases in beginning salary. If the plot indicates that a straight line is not a good summary measure of the relationship, you should consider other methods of analysis, including transforming the data to achieve linearity (see "Coaxing a Nonlinear Relationship to Linearity" on p. 314).

Figure 21.1   Scatterplot of beginning and current salaries

```
PLOT VERTICAL=MIN(0)  /HORIZONTAL=MIN(0) MAX(40000)  /HSIZE=50
/CUTPOINT=EVERY(3)  /SYMBOLS='.+*#@'
/PLOT=SALNOW WITH SALBEG.
```

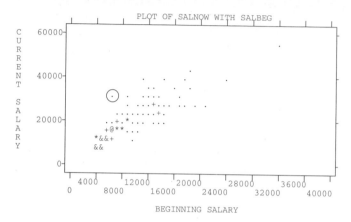

Outliers

A plot may also indicate the presence of points suspiciously different from the others. Such observations, termed **outliers**, should be examined carefully to see if they result from errors in gathering, coding, or entering data. The circled point in Figure 21.1 appears to be an outlier. Though neither the value of beginning salary ($6,300) nor the value of current salary ($32,000) is unique, jointly they are unusual.

The treatment of outliers can be difficult. If the point is incorrect due to coding or entry problems, you should correct it and rerun the analysis. If there is no apparent explanation for the outlier, consider interactions with other variables as a possible explanation. For example, the outlier may represent an employee who was hired as a low-paid clerical worker while pursuing an MBA degree. After graduation, the employee rose rapidly to a higher position; in this instance, the variable for education explains the unusual salary characteristics.

Choosing a Regression Line

Since current salary tends to increase linearly with beginning salary, a straight line can be used to summarize the relationship. The equation for the line is

$$\text{predicted current salary} = B_0 + B_1 (\text{beginning salary})$$

Equation 21.1

The **slope** (B_1) is the change (in dollars) in fitted current salary for a change in beginning salary. The **intercept** (B_0) is the theoretical estimate of current salary for a beginning salary of 0.

However, the observed data points do not all fall on a straight line, they cluster around it. Many lines can be drawn through the data points; the problem is to select among the possible lines. The method of **least squares** results in a line that minimizes the sum of squared vertical distances from the observed data points to the line. Any other line has a larger sum. Figure 21.2 shows the least-squares line superimposed on the salary scatterplot. Some vertical distances from points to the line are also shown.

Figure 21.2 Regression line for beginning and current salaries

```
PLOT FORMAT=REGRESSION
 /VERTICAL=MIN(0)  /HORIZONTAL=MIN(0)  MAN(40000)  /HSIZE 50
 /CUTPOINTS=EVERY(3)  /SYMBOLS='.+*#@'
 /PLOT SALNOW WITH SALBEG.
```

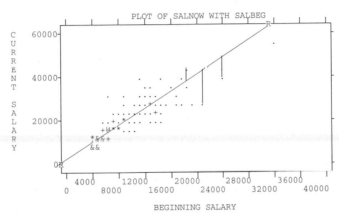

You can use SPSS/PC+ to calculate the least-squares line. For the data in Figure 21.1, that line is

predicted current salary $= 771.28 + 1.91$ (beginning salary)   **Equation 21.2**

The slope and intercept values are shown in the column labeled B in the output shown in Figure 21.3.

Figure 21.3   Statistics for variables in the equation

```
REGRESSION DEPENDENT=SALNOW
  /ENTER SALBEG.

----------------- Variables in the Equation -----------------

Variable            B        SE B       Beta         T   Sig T

SALBEG       1.909450    .047410    .880117    40.276   .0000
(Constant)  771.282303  355.471941             2.170   .0305
```

The Standardized Regression Coefficient

The **standardized regression coefficient**, labeled *Beta* in Figure 21.3, is defined as

$$\text{beta} = B_1 \frac{S_X}{S_Y}$$

Equation 21.3

Multiplying the regression coefficient (B_1) by the ratio of the standard deviation of the independent variable (S_X) to the standard deviation of the dependent variable (S_Y) results in a dimensionless coefficient. In fact, the beta coefficient is the slope of the least-squares line when both X and Y are expressed as Z scores. The beta coefficient is discussed further in "Beta Coefficients" on p. 322.

From Samples to Populations

Generally, more is sought in regression analysis than a description of observed data. You usually want to draw inferences about the relationship of the variables in the population from which the sample was taken. How are beginning and current salaries related for all employees, not just those included in the sample? Inferences about population values based on sample results are based on the following assumptions:

Normality and Equality of Variance. For any fixed value of the independent variable X, the distribution of the dependent variable Y is normal, with mean $\mu_{Y/X}$ (the mean of Y for a given X) and a constant variance of σ^2 (see Figure 21.4). This assumption specifies that not all employees with the same beginning salary have the same current salary. Instead, there is a normal distribution of current salaries for each beginning salary. Though the distributions have different means, they have the same variance: σ^2.

Figure 21.4   Regression assumptions

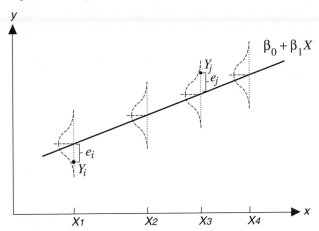

Independence. The Y's are statistically independent of each other; that is, observations are in no way influenced by other observations. For example, observations are *not* independent if they are based on repeated measurements from the same experimental unit. If three observations are taken from each of four families, the twelve observations are not independent.

Linearity. The mean values $\mu_{Y/X}$ all lie on a straight line, which is the population regression line. This is the line drawn in Figure 21.4. An alternative way of stating this assumption is that the linear model is correct.

When there is a single independent variable, the model can be summarized by

$$Y_i = \beta_0 + \beta_1 X_i + e_i \qquad \qquad \textbf{Equation 21.4}$$

The population parameters (values) for the slope and intercept are denoted by β_1 and β_0. The term e_i, usually called the **error**, is the difference between the observed value Y_i and the subpopulation mean at the point X_i. The e_i terms are assumed to be normally distributed, independent, random variables with a mean of 0 and variance of σ^2 (see Figure 21.4).

Estimating Population Parameters

Since β_0 and β_1 are unknown population parameters, they must be estimated from the sample. The least-squares coefficients B_0 and B_1, discussed in "Choosing a Regression Line" on p. 288, are used to estimate the population parameters.

However, the slope and intercept estimated from a single sample typically differ from the population values and vary from sample to sample. To use these estimates for inference about the population values, the sampling distributions of the two statistics are needed. When the assumptions of linear regression are met, the sampling distributions of B_0 and B_1 are normal, with means of β_0 and β_1.

The standard error of B_0 is

$$\sigma_{B_0} = \sigma \sqrt{\frac{1}{N} + \frac{\bar{X}^2}{(N-1)\,S_X^2}} \qquad\qquad \textbf{Equation 21.5}$$

where S_X^2 is the sample variance of the independent variable. The standard error of B_1 is

$$\sigma_{B_1} = \frac{\sigma}{\sqrt{(N-1)\,S_X^2}} \qquad\qquad \textbf{Equation 21.6}$$

Since the population variance of the errors, σ^2, is not known, it must also be estimated. The usual estimate of σ^2 is

$$S^2 = \frac{\displaystyle\sum_{i=1}^{N} (Y_i - B_0 - B_1 X_i)^2}{N-2} \qquad\qquad \textbf{Equation 21.7}$$

The positive square root of S^2 is termed the **standard error of the estimate**, or the standard deviation of the residuals. (The reason for this name is discussed in "Predicting a New Value" on p. 299.) The estimated standard errors of the slope and intercept are displayed in the third column (labeled *SE B*) in Figure 21.3.

Testing Hypotheses

A frequently tested hypothesis is that there is no linear relationship between X and Y—that the slope of the population regression line is 0. The statistic used to test this hypothesis is

$$t = \frac{B_1}{S_{B_1}} \qquad\qquad \textbf{Equation 21.8}$$

The distribution of the statistic, when the assumptions are met and the hypothesis of no linear relationship is true, is Student's t distribution with $N-2$ degrees of freedom. The statistic for testing the hypothesis that the intercept is 0 is

$$t = \frac{B_0}{S_{B_0}}$$

Equation 21.9

Its distribution is also Student's t with $N-2$ degrees of freedom.

These t statistics and their two-tailed observed significance levels are displayed in the last two columns of Figure 21.3. The small observed significance level (less than 0.00005) associated with the slope for the salary data supports the hypothesis that beginning and current salary have a linear association.

Confidence Intervals

A statistic calculated from a sample provides a point estimate of the unknown parameter. A point estimate can be thought of as the single best guess for the population value. While the estimated value from the sample is typically different from the value of the unknown population parameter, the hope is that it isn't too far away. Based on the sample estimate, it is possible to calculate a range of values that, within a designated likelihood, includes the population value. Such a range is called a **confidence interval**. For example, as shown in Figure 21.5, the 95% confidence interval for β_1, the population slope, is 1.816 to 2.003.

Figure 21.5 Confidence intervals

```
REGRESSION
 /STATISTICS=CI
 /DEPENDENT=SALNOW
 /ENTER SALBEG.

---- Variables in the Equation ---

Variable       95% Confdnce Intrvl B

SALBEG        1.816290    2.002610
(Constant)   72.778982  1469.785624
```

Ninety-five percent confidence means that if repeated samples are drawn from a population under the same conditions and 95% confidence intervals are calculated, 95% of the intervals will contain the unknown parameter β_1. Since the parameter value is unknown, it is not possible to determine whether a particular interval contains it.

Goodness of Fit

An important part of any statistical procedure that builds models from data is establishing how well the model actually fits, or its **goodness of fit**. This includes the detection of possible violations of the required assumptions in the data being analyzed.

The R-squared Coefficient

A commonly used measure of the goodness of fit of a linear model is R^2, or the **coefficient of determination**. It can be thought of in a variety of ways. Besides being the square of the correlation coefficient between variables X and Y, it is the square of the correlation coefficient between Y (the observed value of the dependent variable) and $\hat{Y}$ (the predicted value of Y from the fitted line). If you compute the predicted salary for each employee (based on the coefficients in the output in Figure 21.3) as follows

$$\text{predicted current salary} = 771.28 + 1.91\,(\text{beginning salary})$$ **Equation 21.10**

and then calculate the square of the Pearson correlation coefficient between predicted current salary and observed current salary, you will get R^2. If all the observations fall on the regression line, R^2 is 1. If there is no linear relationship between the dependent and independent variables, R^2 is 0.

Note that R^2 is a measure of the goodness of fit of a particular model and that an R^2 of 0 does not necessarily mean that there is no association between the variables. Instead, it indicates that there is no *linear* relationship.

In the output in Figure 21.6, R^2 is labeled *R Square* and its square root is labeled *Multiple R*. The sample R^2 tends to be an optimistic estimate of how well the model fits the population. The model usually does not fit the population as well as it fits the sample from which it is derived. The statistic *adjusted R^2* attempts to correct R^2 to more closely reflect the goodness of fit of the model in the population. Adjusted R^2 is given by

$$R_a^2 = R^2 - \frac{p\,(1 - R^2)}{N - p - 1}$$ **Equation 21.11**

where p is the number of independent variables in the equation (1 in the salary example).

Figure 21.6   Summary statistics for the equation

```
REGRESSION DEPENDENT=SALNOW
 /ENTER SALBEG.

Multiple R          .88012
R Square            .77461
Adjusted R Square   .77413
Standard Error   3246.14226
```

Analysis of Variance

To test the hypothesis that there is no linear relationship between X and Y, several equivalent statistics can be computed. When there is a single independent variable, the hypothesis that the population R^2 is 0 is identical to the hypothesis that the population slope is 0. The test for $R^2_{pop} = 0$ is usually obtained from the analysis-of-variance table (see Figure 21.7).

Figure 21.7   Analysis-of-variance table

```
REGRESSION DEPENDENT=SALNOW
 /ENTER SALBEG.

Analysis of Variance
                   DF      Sum of Squares       Mean Square
Regression          1   17092967800.01977   17092967800.0198
Residual          472    4973671469.79455   10537439.55465

F =    1622.11776      Signif F =   .0000
```

The total observed variability in the dependent variable is subdivided into two components—that which is attributable to the regression (labeled *Regression*) and that which is not (labeled *Residual*). Consider Figure 21.8. For a particular point, the distance from Y_i to $\bar{Y}$ (the mean of the Y's) can be subdivided into two parts:

$$Y_i - \bar{Y} = (Y_i - \hat{Y}_i) + (\hat{Y}_i - \bar{Y})$$

Equation 21.12

The distance from Y_i (the observed value) to $\hat{Y}_i$ (the value predicted by the regression line), or $\hat{Y}_i - Y_i$, is called the **residual from the regression**. It is zero if the regression line passes through the point. The second component $(\hat{Y}_i - \bar{Y})$ is the distance from the regression line to the mean of the Y's. This distance is "explained" by the regression in

Figure 21.8   Components of variability

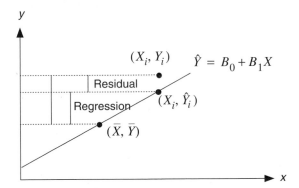

that it represents the improvement in the estimate of the dependent variable achieved by the regression. Without the regression, the mean of the dependent variable $\bar{Y}$ is used as the estimate. It can be shown that

$$\sum_{i=1}^{N} (Y_i - \bar{Y})^2 = \sum_{i=1}^{N} (Y_i - \hat{Y}_i)^2 + \sum_{i=1}^{N} (\hat{Y}_i - \bar{Y})^2 \qquad \textbf{Equation 21.13}$$

The first quantity following the equals sign is called the **residual sum of squares** and the second quantity is the **regression sum of squares**. The sum of these is called the **total sum of squares**.

The analysis-of-variance table in Figure 21.7 displays these two sums of squares under the heading *Sum of Squares*. The *Mean Square* for each entry is the sum of squares divided by the degrees of freedom (*DF*). If the regression assumptions are met, the ratio of the mean square regression to the mean square residual is distributed as an *F* statistic with p and $N - p - 1$ degrees of freedom. *F* serves to test how well the regression model fits the data. If the probability associated with the *F* statistic is small, the hypothesis that $R^2_{\text{pop}} = 0$ is rejected. For this example, the *F* statistic is

$$F = \frac{\text{mean square regression}}{\text{mean square residual}} = 1622 \qquad \textbf{Equation 21.14}$$

The observed significance level (*Signif F*) is less than 0.00005.

The square root of the *F* value (1622) is 40.28, which is the value of the *t* statistic for the slope in Figure 21.3. The square of a *t* value with k degrees of freedom is an *F* value with 1 and k degrees of freedom. Therefore, either *t* or *F* values can be computed to test that $\beta_i = 0$. Another useful summary statistic is the standard error of the estimate, *S*, which can also be calculated as the square root of the residual mean square (see "Predicting a New Value" on p. 299).

Another Interpretation of R-squared

Partitioning the sum of squares of the dependent variable allows another interpretation of R^2. It is the proportion of the variation in the dependent variable "explained" by the model.

$$R^2 = 1 - \frac{\text{residual sum of squares}}{\text{total sum of squares}} = 0.775 \qquad \textbf{Equation 21.15}$$

Similarly, adjusted R^2 is

$$R^2_a = 1 - \frac{\text{residual sum of squares} / (N - p - 1)}{\text{total sum of squares} / (N - 1)} \qquad \textbf{Equation 21.16}$$

where p is the number of independent variables in the equation (1 in the salary example).

Predicted Values and Their Standard Errors

By comparing the observed values of the dependent variable to the values predicted by the regression equation, you can learn a good deal about how well a model and the various assumptions fit the data (see the discussion of residuals beginning with "Searching for Violations of Assumptions" on p. 301). Predicted values are also of interest when the results are used to predict new data. You may wish to predict the mean Y for all cases with a given value of X (denoted X_0) or to predict the value of Y for a single case. For example, you can predict either the mean salary for all employees with a beginning salary of \$10,000 or the salary for a particular employee with a beginning salary of \$10,000. In both situations, the predicted value

$$\hat{Y}_0 = B_0 + B_1 X_0 = 771 + 1.91 \times 10,000 = 19,871 \qquad \text{Equation 21.17}$$

is the same. What differs is the standard error.

Predicting Mean Response

The estimated standard error for the predicted mean Y at X_0 is

$$S_{\hat{Y}} = S \sqrt{\frac{1}{N} + \frac{(X_0 - \bar{X})^2}{(N-1)S_X^2}} \qquad \text{Equation 21.18}$$

The equation for the standard error shows that the smallest value occurs when X_0 is equal to $\bar{X}$, the mean of X. The larger the distance from the mean, the greater the standard error. Thus, the mean of Y for a given X is better estimated for central values of the observed X's than for outlying values. Figure 21.9 is a plot of the standard errors of predicted mean salaries for different values of beginning salary (this plot is obtained by saving the standard error as a new variable in the REGRESSION procedure and then using the PLOT procedure).

Figure 21.9   Standard errors for predicted mean responses

```
REGRESSION DEPENDENT=SALNOW
 /ENTER SALBEG
 /SAVE SEPRED(SE).
PLOT /VERTICAL MIN(0) /HORIZONTAL MIN(0) MAX(40000) /HSIZE 50
 /CUTPOINTS=EVERY(20) /SYMBOLS='*'
 /PLOT SE WITH SALBEG.
```

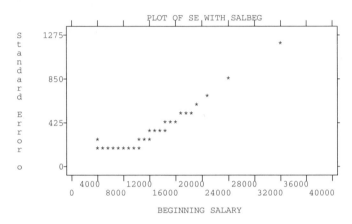

Prediction intervals for the mean predicted salary are calculated in the standard way. The 95% confidence interval at X_0 is

$$\hat{Y} \pm t_{(1-\frac{\alpha}{2}, N-2)} S_{\hat{Y}}$$

Equation 21.19

Figure 21.10 shows a typical 95% confidence band for predicted mean responses. It is narrowest at the mean of X and widens as the distance from the mean $(X_0 - \overline{X})$ increases.

Figure 21.10 95% confidence band for mean prediction

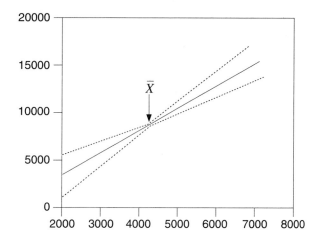

Predicting a New Value

Although the predicted value for a single new observation at X_0 is the same as the predicted value for the mean at X_0, the standard error is not. The two sources of error when predicting an individual observation are:

1. The individual value may differ from the population mean of Y for X_0.

2. The estimate of the population mean at X_0 may differ from the population mean.

The sources of error are illustrated in Figure 21.11.

Figure 21.11 Sources of error in predicting individual observations

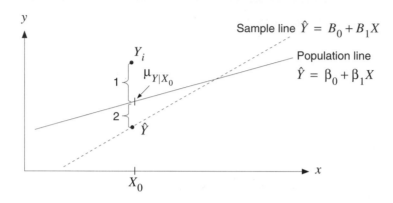

When estimating the mean response, only the second error component is considered. The variance of the individual prediction is the variance of the mean prediction plus the variance of Y_i for a given X. This can be written as

$$S^2_{\text{ind } \hat{Y}} = S^2_{\hat{Y}} + S^2 = S^2 \left(1 + \frac{1}{N} + \frac{(X_0 - \overline{X})^2}{(N-1)\, S^2_X} \right)$$

Equation 21.20

Prediction intervals for the new observation are obtained by substituting $S_{\text{ind } \hat{Y}}$ for $S_{\hat{Y}}$ in Equation 21.19. If the sample size is large, the terms $1/N$ and

$$\frac{(X_0 - \overline{X})^2}{(N-1)\, S^2_X}$$

Equation 21.21

are negligible. In that case, the standard error is simply S, which explains the name standard error of the estimate for S (see "Estimating Population Parameters" on p. 291).

Reading the Casewise Plot

You can generate predicted values and the standard errors of the mean responses in the REGRESSION procedure, and you can display both of these values for all cases or for a subset of cases along with a casewise plot. Figure 21.12 shows the output from the beginning and end of a plot of the salary data. The sequential number of the case is listed first, followed by the plot of standardized residuals, the observed (*SALNOW*), predicted (**PRED*), and residual (**RESID*) values.

Figure 21.12 Casewise plot with predicted values

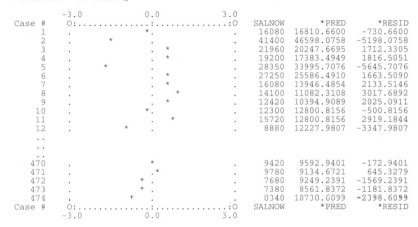

```
REGRESSION
 /DEPENDENT=SALNOW
 /ENTER SALBEG
 /CASEWISE=PLOT(ZRESID) ALL.

Casewise Plot of Standardized Residual

*: Selected   M: Missing

         -3.0            0.0            3.0
 Case #   O:...............:...............:O   SALNOW      *PRED      *RESID
    1     .           *.            .          16080   16810.6600    -730.6600
    2     .      *    .             .          41400   46598.0758   -5198.0758
    3     .           .  *          .          21960   20247.6695    1712.3305
    4     .           .  *          .          19200   17383.4949    1816.5051
    5     .      *    .             .          28350   33995.7076   -5645.7076
    6     .           . *           .          27250   25586.4910    1663.5090
    7     .           . *           .          16080   13946.4854    2133.5146
    8     .           .   *         .          14100   11082.3108    3017.6892
    9     .           .  *          .          12420   10394.9089    2025.0911
   10     .          *.             .          12300   12800.8156    -500.8156
   11     .           .   *         .          15720   12800.8156    2919.1844
   12     .       *   .             .           8880   12227.9807   -3347.9807
   ..
   ..
   ..
  470     .           *             .           9420    9592.9401    -172.9401
  471     .           .*            .           9780    9134.6721     645.3279
  472     .         * .             .           7680    9249.2391   -1569.2391
  473     .         * .             .           7380    8561.8372   -1181.8372
  474     .        *  .             .           0040   10730.6099   -2398.6099
 Case #   O:...............:...............:O   SALNOW      *PRED      *RESID
         -3.0            0.0            3.0
```

Searching for Violations of Assumptions

You usually don't know in advance whether a model such as linear regression is appropriate. Therefore, you need to conduct a search focused on residuals to look for evidence that the necessary assumptions are violated.

Residuals

In model building, a **residual** is what is left after the model is fit. It is the difference between an observed value and the value predicted by the model:

$$E_i = Y_i - B_0 - B_1 X_i = Y_i - \hat{Y}_i \qquad\qquad \textbf{Equation 21.22}$$

In regression analysis, the true errors, e_i, are assumed to be independent normal values with a mean of 0 and a constant variance of σ^2. If the model is appropriate for the data, the observed residuals, E_i, which are estimates of the true errors, e_i, should have similar characteristics.

If the intercept term is included in the equation, the mean of the residuals is always 0, so the mean provides no information about the true mean of the errors. Since the sum of the residuals is constrained to be 0, the residuals are *not* strictly independent. However, if the number of residuals is large when compared to the number of independent variables, the dependency among the residuals can be ignored for practical purposes.

The relative magnitudes of residuals are easier to judge when they are divided by estimates of their standard deviations. The resulting **standardized residuals** are expressed in standard deviation units above or below the mean. For example, the fact that a particular residual is -5198.1 provides little information. If you know that its standardized form is -3.1, you know not only that the observed value is less than the predicted value but also that the residual is larger than most in absolute value.

Residuals are sometimes adjusted in one of two ways. The standardized residual for case i is the residual divided by the sample standard deviation of the residuals. Standardized residuals have a mean of 0 and a standard deviation of 1. The **Studentized residual** is the residual divided by an estimate of its standard deviation that varies from point to point, depending on the distance of X_i from the mean of X. Usually standardized and Studentized residuals are close in value, but not always. The Studentized residual reflects more precisely differences in the true error variances from point to point.

Linearity

For the bivariate situation, a scatterplot is a good means for judging how well a straight line fits the data. Another convenient method is to plot the residuals against the predicted values. If the assumptions of linearity and homogeneity of variance are met, there should be no relationship between the predicted and residual values. You should be suspicious of any observable pattern.

For example, fitting a least-squares line to the data in the plots shown in Figure 21.13 yields the residual plots shown in Figure 21.14. The two residual plots show patterns, since straight lines do not fit the data well. Systematic patterns between the predicted values and the residuals suggest possible violations of the assumption of linearity. If the assumption were met, the residuals would be randomly distributed in a band clustered around the horizontal line through 0, as shown in Figure 21.15.

Figure 21.13 Scatterplots of cubic and quadratic relationships

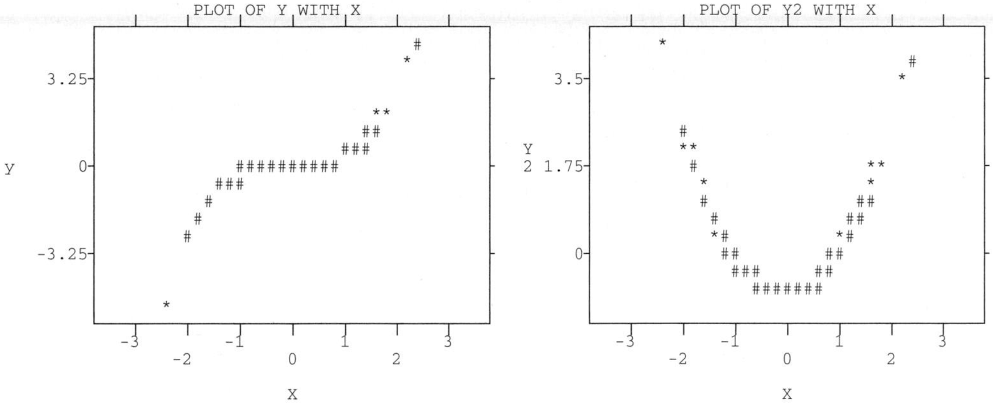

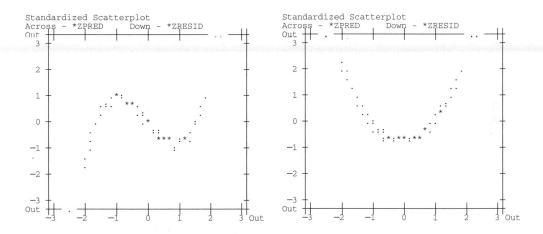

Figure 21.14 Standardized residuals scatterplots— cubic and quadratic relationships

Figure 21.15 Randomly distributed residuals

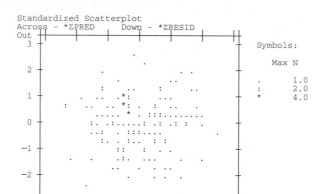

Residuals can also be plotted against individual independent variables. Again, if the assumptions are met, you should see a horizontal band of residuals. Consider as well plotting the residuals against independent variables not in the equation. If the residuals are not randomly distributed, you may want to include the variable in the equation for a multiple regression model (see "Multiple Regression Models" on p. 319).

Equality of Variance

You can also use the previously described plots to check for violations of the equality-of-variance assumption. If the spread of the residuals increases or decreases with values of the independent variables or with predicted values, you should question the assumption of constant variance of Y for all values of X.

Figure 21.16 is a plot of the Studentized residuals against the predicted values for the salary data. The spread of the residuals increases with the magnitude of the predicted values, suggesting that the variability of current salaries increases with salary level. Thus, the equality-of-variance assumption appears to be violated.

Figure 21.16 Unequal variance

```
REGRESSION
 /DEPENDENT=SALNOW
 /METHOD=ENTER SALBEG
 /SCATTERPLOT=(*SRESID,*PRED).
```

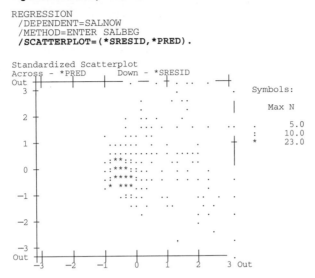

Independence of Error

Whenever the data are collected and recorded sequentially, you should plot residuals against the sequence variable. Even if time is not considered a variable in the model, it could influence the residuals. For example, suppose you are studying survival time after surgery as a function of complexity of surgery, amount of blood transfused, dosage of medication, and so forth. In addition to these variables, it is also possible that the surgeon's skill increased with each operation and that a patient's survival time is influenced by the number of prior patients treated. The plot of standardized residuals corresponding to the order in which patients received surgery shows a shorter survival time for earlier patients than for later patients (see Figure 21.17). If sequence and the residual are independent, you should not see a discernible pattern.

Figure 21.17 Casewise serial plot

```
REGRESSION /DEP LIFE /ENTER X
/RESIDUALS ID(TIME)
/CASEWISE ALL DEP PRED RESID ZRESID.

Casewise Plot of Standardized Residual

*: Selected   M: Missing

              -3.0      0.0      3.0
  Case #   TIME   O:.......:........:O   LIFE    *PRED    *RESID   *ZRESID
     1    78012   .      *   .        .   15.00   23.2217  -8.2217  -1.6426
     2    78055   .     *     .       .   13.50   19.6218  -6.1218  -1.2231
     3    78122   .      *   .        .    9.90   14.5820  -4.6820   -.9354
     4    78134   .       *   .       .   15.50   18.1819  -2.6819   -.5358
     5    78233   .         . *       .   35.00   31.1413   3.8587    .7709
     6    78298   .         *         .   14.70   15.3020   -.6020   -.1203
     7    78344   .         . *       .   34.80   31.1413   3.6587    .7310
     8    79002   .         .*        .   20.80   18.9018   1.8982    .3792
     9    79008   .         . *       .   15.90   13.1421   2.7579    .5510
    10    79039   .         .   *     .   22.00   16.7419   5.2581   1.0505
    11    79101   .         .   *     .   13.70    8.8222   4.8778    .9745
         ...
  Case #   TIME   O:.......:........:O   LIFE    *PRED    *RESID   *ZRESID
              -3.0      0.0      3.0
```

The **Durbin-Watson statistic**, a test for serial correlation of adjacent error terms, is defined as

$$d = \frac{\sum\limits_{t=2}^{N} (E_t - E_{t-1})^2}{\sum\limits_{t=1}^{N} E_t^2}$$

Equation 21.23

The possible values of the statistic range from 0 to 4. If the residuals are not correlated with each other, the value of d is close to 2. Values less than 2 indicate that adjacent residuals are positively correlated. Values greater than 2 indicate that adjacent residuals are negatively correlated. Consult tables of the d statistic for bounds upon which significance tests can be based.

Normality

The distribution of residuals may not appear to be normal for reasons other than actual non-normality: misspecification of the model, nonconstant variance, a small number of residuals actually available for analysis, and so forth. Therefore, you should pursue several lines of investigation. One of the simplest is to construct a histogram of the residuals, such as the one for the salary data shown in Figure 21.18.

Figure 21.18 Histogram of standardized residuals

```
REGRESSION
 /DEPENDENT=SALNOW
 /METHOD=ENTER SALBEG
 /RESIDUALS=HISTOGRAM(ZRESID).

Histogram - Standardized Residual

  N    Exp N       (* = 2 Cases,     . : = Normal Curve)
  7     .37   Out ****
  1     .73  3.00 *
  5    1.85  2.67 :**
  2    4.23  2.33 *.
  6    8.65  2.00 ***.
 12   15.85  1.67 ****** .
  7   26.01  1.33 ****
 18   38.23  1.00 *********
 35   50.34   .67 *****************.
 63   59.38   .33 ******************************:**
 87   62.74   .00 **********************************:*************
114   59.38  -.33 *********************************:***************************
 64   50.34  -.67 **************************:*******
 32   38.23 -1.00 ****************.
  9   26.01 -1.33 *****
  6   15.85 -1.67 ***    .
  1    8.65 -2.00 * .
  2    4.23 -2.33 *.
  1    1.85 -2.67 :
  0     .73 -3.00
  2     .37   Out *
```

The regression histogram contains a tally of the observed number of residuals (labeled *N*) in each interval and the number expected in a normal distribution with the same mean and variance as the residuals (*Exp N*). The first and last intervals (*Out*) contain residuals more than 3.16 standard deviations from the mean. Such residuals deserve examination. A histogram of expected *N*'s is superimposed on that of the observed *N*'s. Expected frequencies are indicated by a period. When observed and expected frequencies overlap, a colon is displayed. It is unreasonable to expect the observed residuals to be exactly normal—some deviation is expected because of sampling variation. Even if the errors are normally distributed in the population, sample residuals are only approximately normal.

In the histogram in Figure 21.18, the distribution does not seem normal, since there is an exaggerated clustering of residuals toward the center and a straggling tail toward large positive values. Thus, the normality assumption may be violated.

Another way to compare the observed distribution of residuals to the expected distribution under the assumption of normality is to plot the two cumulative distributions against each other for a series of points. If the two distributions are identical, a straight line results. By observing how points scatter about the expected straight line, you can compare the two distributions.

Figure 21.19 is a cumulative probability plot of the salary residuals. Initially, the observed residuals are below the "normal" line, since there is a smaller number of large negative residuals than expected. Once the greatest concentration of residuals is reached, the observed points are above the line, since the observed cumulative proportion exceeds the expected. Tests for normality are available using the EXAMINE procedure (see Chapter 13).

Figure 21.19 A normal probability (P–P) plot

```
REGRESSION
 /DEPENDENT=SALNOW
 /METHOD=ENTER SALBEG
 /RESIDUALS=NORMPROB.
```

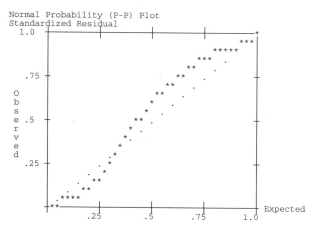

Locating Outliers

You can spot outliers readily on residual plots, since they are cases with very large positive or negative residuals. In general, standardized residual values greater than 3 in absolute value are considered outliers. Since you usually want more information about outliers, you can use the CASEWISE subcommand to display identification numbers and a variety of other statistics for cases with residuals beyond a specified cutoff point.

Figure 21.20 displays information for the nine cases with standardized residuals greater than the absolute value of 3. Only two of these nine cases have current salaries less than those predicted by the model (cases 67 and 122). The others all have salaries larger than the average for the sample (an average of $33,294 compared to $13,767 for the sample). Thus, there is some evidence that the model may not fit well for the highly paid cases.

Figure 21.20 Casewise plot of residuals outliers

```
REGRESSION
 /DEPENDENT=SALNOW
 /METHOD=ENTER SALBEG
 /CASEWISE=PLOT(ZRESID) DEPENDENT PRED RESID.

Casewise Plot of Standardized Residual

Outliers = 3.    *: Selected    M: Missing

            -6.    -3.   3.     6.
   Case #   O:.......:   :......:O    SALNOW     *PRED       *RESID
      24    .            ..*      .    28000   17383.4949   10616.5051
      60    .            ..     *.    32000   12800.8156   19199.1844
      67    .           *..      .    26400   37043.1894  -10643.1894
     114    .            .. *     .    38800   27511.2163   11288.7837
     122    .        *   ..      .    26700   40869.7266  -14169.7266
     123    .            .. *     .    36250   24639.4039   11610.5961
     129    .            ..    *  .    33500   17383.4949   16116.5051
     149    .            ..      *    41500   21782.8671   19717.1329
     177    .            ..   *   .    36500   23295.1513   13204.8487
```

Other Unusual Observations: Mahalanobis Distance

In the section "Outliers" on p. 288, one case was identified as an outlier because the combination of values for beginning and current salaries was atypical. This case (case 60) also appears in Figure 21.20, since it has a large value for the standardized residual. Another unusual case (case 56) has a beginning salary of $31,992. Since the average beginning salary for the entire sample is only $6,806 and the standard deviation is 3148, the case is eight standard deviations above the mean. But since the standardized residual is not large, this case does not appear in Figure 21.20.

However, cases that have unusual values for the independent variables can have a substantial impact on the results of analysis and should be identified. One measure of the distance of cases from average values of the independent variables is **Mahalanobis distance**. In the case of a regression equation with a single independent variable, it is the square of the standardized value of X:

$$D_i = \left(\frac{X_i - \bar{X}}{S_X}\right)^2$$

Equation 21.24

When there is more than one independent variable—where Mahalanobis distance is most valuable—the computations are more complex. As shown in Figure 21.21, the Mahalanobis distance for case 56 is 64 (8^2).

Figure 21.21 Mahalanobis distances

```
REGRESSION
 /DEPENDENT=SALNOW /METHOD=ENTER SALBEG
 /RESIDUALS=OUTLIERS(MAHAL) ID(SEXRACE).

Outliers - Mahalanobis' Distance

   Case #   SEXRACE      *MAHAL

       56        1       63.99758
        2        1       29.82579
      122        1       20.32559
       67        1       14.99121
      132        1       12.64145
       55        1       12.64145
      415        2       11.84140
        5        1       11.32255
      172        1       10.49188
       23        1       10.46720
```

Influential Cases: Deleted Residuals and Cook's Distance

Certain observations in a set of data can have a large influence on estimates of the parameters. Figure 21.22 shows such a point. The regression line obtained for the data is quite different if the point is omitted. However, the residual for the circled point is not particularly large when the case (case 8) is included in the computations and does not therefore arouse suspicion (see the column labeled *RESID* in Figure 21.23).

Figure 21.22 Influential observation

```
REGRESSION
 /STATISTICS=DEFAULTS CI
 /DEPENDENT=Y /METHOD=ENTER X
 /SCATTERPLOT=(Y,X).
```

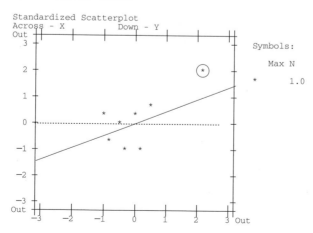

One way to identify an influential case is to compare the residuals for a case when the suspected case is included in the equation and when it is not. The **adjusted predicted value** for case i when it is not included in the computation of the regression line is

$$\hat{Y}_i^{(i)} = B_0^{(i)} + B_1^{(i)} X_i$$

Equation 21.25

where the superscript (i) indicates that the ith case is excluded. The change in the predicted value when the ith case is deleted is

$$\hat{Y}_i - \hat{Y}_i^{(i)}$$

Equation 21.26

The residual calculated for a case when it is not included is called the **deleted residual**, computed as

$$Y_i - \hat{Y}_i^{(i)}$$

Equation 21.27

The deleted residual can be divided by its standard error to produce the **Studentized deleted residual**.

Although the difference between the deleted and ordinary residual for a case is useful as an index of the influence of that case, this measure does not reflect changes in residuals of other observations when the ith case is deleted. **Cook's distance** does consider changes in all residuals when case i is omitted (Cook, 1977). It is defined as

$$C_i = \frac{\sum_{j=1}^{N} (\hat{Y}_j^{(i)} - \hat{Y}_j)^2}{(p+1) S^2}$$

Equation 21.28

The casewise plot and influence measures for the data in Figure 21.22 are shown in Figure 21.23. The measures for case 8 (the circled point) are given in the last row. The case has neither a very large Studentized residual (*SRESID*), nor a very large Studentized deleted residual (*SDRESID*). However, the deleted residual (*DRESID*), 5.86, is somewhat larger than the ordinary residual (*RESID*). The large Mahalanobis distance (*MAHAL*) identifies the case as having an X value far from the mean, while the large Cook's D (*COOK D*) identifies the case as an influential point.

Figure 21.23 Influence measures

```
REGRESSION
 /WIDTH 132
 /DEPENDENT=y /METHOD=ENTER X
 /CASEWISE ALL DEP RESID SRESID SDRESID ADJPRED DRESID MAHAL COOK.
```

```
Casewise Plot of Standardized Residual

*: Selected   M: Missing

        -3.0      0.0      3.0
Case #  O:.......:........:O   Y    *RESID   *SRESID  *SDRESID  *DRESID   *ADJPRED  *MAHAL   *COOK D
   1    .        .        *   .  7   2.9394   1.4819    1.6990    4.0904    2.9096   1.0947    .4300
   2    .        *  .         .  4   -.5758   -.2780    -.2554    -.7349    4.7349    .6401    .0107
   3    .        .*           .  6    .9091    .4262     .3951    1.0938    4.9062    .3068    .0184
   4    .     *  .            .  3  -2.6061  -1.2000   -1.2566   -3.0252    6.0252    .0947    .1158
   5    .        .*           .  7    .8788    .4016     .3717    1.0050    5.9950    .0038    .0116
   6    .   *    .            .  3  -3.6364  -1.6661   -2.0747   -4.1791    7.1791    .0341    .2071
   7    .        .*           .  8    .8485    .3937     .3641    1.0000    7.0000    .1856    .0138
   8    .        .   *        . 12   1.2425   1.1529    1.1929    5.8574    6.1426   4.6402   2.4687
Case #  O:.......:........:O   Y    *RESID   *SRESID  *SDRESID  *DRESID   *ADJPRED  *MAHAL   *COOK D
        -3.0      0.0      3.0
```

The regression coefficients with and without case 8 are shown in Figure 21.24 and Figure 21.25. Both $B_0^{(8)}$ and $B_1^{(8)}$ are far removed from B_0 and B_1, since case 8 is an influential point.

Figure 21.24 Regression coefficients from all cases

```
REGRESSION
 /STATISTICS=DEFAULTS CI
 /DEPENDENT=Y /METHOD=ENTER x.
```

```
---------------------- Variables in the Equation ----------------------

Variable               B       SE B    95% Confdnce Intrvl B      Beta

X                .515145   .217717    -.017587    1.047877     .694761
(Constant)      3.545466  1.410980     .092941    6.997990
```

```
----------- in -----------

Variable       T   Sig T

X            2.366  .0558
(Constant)   2.513  .0457
```

Figure 21.25 Regression coefficients without case 8

```
REGRESSION
 /SELECT=$CASENUM NE 8
 /STATISTICS=DEFAULTS CI
 /DEPENDENT=Y /METHOD=ENTER X.
```

```
--------------------- Variables in the Equation ----------------------

Variable              B        SE B     95% Confdnce Intrvl B      Beta

X               .071407    .427380    -1.027192    1.170005    .074513
(Constant)     5.142941   1.911317      .229818   10.056065


----------- in -----------

Variable         T    Sig T

X              .167   .8739
(Constant)    2.691   .0433
```

You can examine the change in the regression coefficients when a case is deleted from the analysis by looking at the intercept and X values for *DFBETA* in the casewise plot. In Figure 21.26, you see that the change in the intercept is -1.5975 and the change in slope is 0.4437 for case 8.

Figure 21.26 Diagnostic statistics for influential observations

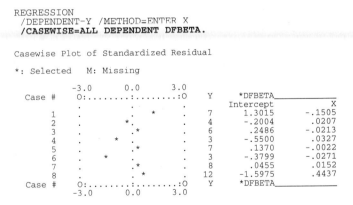

```
REGRESSION
 /DEPENDENT-Y /METHOD=ENTER X
 /CASEWISE=ALL DEPENDENT DFBETA.

Casewise Plot of Standardized Residual

*: Selected   M: Missing

           -3.0      0.0      3.0
   Case #   O:.......:........:O     Y      *DFBETA_____
            .                .               Intercept          X
        1   .          .  *   .      7        1.3015      -.1505
        2   .        *.       .      4        -.2004       .0207
        3   .          .*     .      6         .2486      -.0213
        4   .        * .      .      3        -.5500       .0327
        5   .          .*     .      7         .1370      -.0022
        6   .        * .      .      3        -.3799      -.0271
        7   .          .*     .      8         .0455       .0152
        8   .          . *    .     12       -1.5975       .4437
   Case #   O:.......:........:O     Y      *DFBETA_____
           -3.0      0.0      3.0
```

When Assumptions Appear to Be Violated

When there is evidence of a violation of assumptions, you can pursue one of two strategies. You can formulate an alternative model, such as weighted least squares, or you can transform the variables so that the current model will be more adequate. For example, taking logs, square roots, or reciprocals can stabilize the variance, achieve normality, or linearize a relationship.

Coaxing a Nonlinear Relationship to Linearity

To try to achieve linearity, you can transform either the dependent or independent variables, or both. If you alter the scale of independent variables, linearity can be achieved without any effect on the distribution of the dependent variable. Thus, if the dependent variable is normally distributed with constant variance for each value of X, it remains normally distributed.

When you transform the dependent variable, its distribution is changed. This new distribution must then satisfy the assumptions of the analysis. For example, if logs of the values of the dependent variable are taken, log Y—not the original Y—must be normally distributed with constant variance.

The choice of transformation depends on several considerations. If the form of the true model governing the relationship is known, it should dictate the choice. For instance, if it is known that $\hat{Y} = AC^X$ is an adequate model, taking logs of both sides of the equation results in

$$\log \hat{Y}_i = (\log A) + (\log C) X_i \qquad\qquad \text{Equation 21.29}$$
$$[B_0] \qquad [B_1]$$

Thus, log Y is linearly related to X.

If the true model is not known, you should choose the transformation by examining the plotted data. Frequently, a relationship appears nearly linear for part of the data but is curved for the rest (for example, Figure 21.27). Taking the log of the dependent variable results in an improved linear fit (see Figure 21.28).

Figure 21.27 A nonlinear relationship

```
REGRESSION /DEPENDENT Y /ENTER X
  /SCATTERPLOT (Y,X).
```

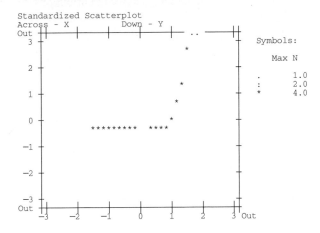

Figure 21.28 A transformed relationship

```
REGRESSION /DEPENDENT LOGY /ENTER X
  /SCATTERPLOT (LOGY,X).
```

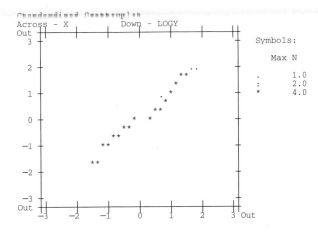

Other transformations that may diminish curvature are $-1/Y$ and the square root of Y. The choice depends, to a certain extent, on the severity of the problem.

Coping with Skewness

When the distribution of residuals is positively skewed, the log transformation of the dependent variable is often helpful. For negatively skewed distributions, the square transformation is common. It should be noted that the F tests used in regression hypothesis testing are usually quite insensitive to moderate departures from normality.

Stabilizing the Variance

If the variance of the residuals is not constant, you can try a variety of remedial measures:

- When the variance is proportional to the mean of Y for a given X, use the square root of Y if all Y_i are positive.

- When the standard deviation is proportional to the mean, try the logarithmic transformation.

- When the standard deviation is proportional to the square of the mean, use the reciprocal of Y.

- When Y is a proportion or rate, the arc sine transformation may stabilize the variance.

Transforming the Salary Data

The assumptions of constant variance and normality appear to be violated with the salary data (see Figure 21.16 and Figure 21.18). A regression equation using logs of beginning and current salary was developed to obtain a better fit to the assumptions. Figure

21.29 is a scatterplot of Studentized residuals against predicted values when logs of both variables are used in the regression equation.

Figure 21.29 Scatterplot of transformed salary data

```
COMPUTE  LOGBEG=LG10(SALBEG).
COMPUTE  LOGNOW=LG10(SALNOW).
REGRESSION
 /DEPENDENT=LOGNOW
 /METHOD=ENTER  LOGBEG
 /SCATTERPLOT=(*SRESID,*PRED).
```

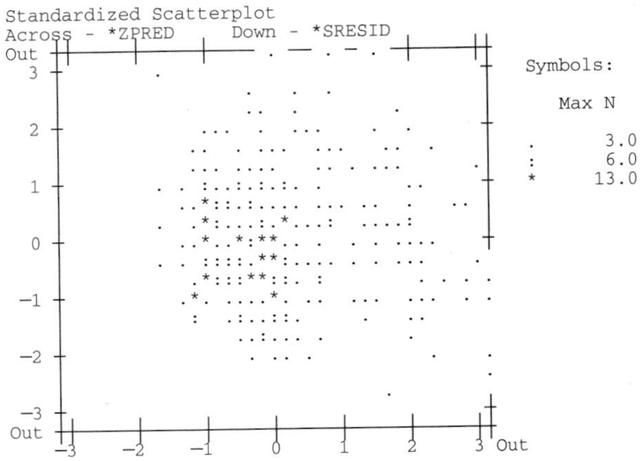

Compare Figure 21.16 and Figure 21.29, and note the improvement in the behavior of the residuals. The spread no longer increases with increasing salary level. Also compare Figure 21.18 and Figure 21.30, and note that the distribution in Figure 21.30 is nearly normal.

Figure 21.30 Histogram of transformed salary data

```
COMPUTE LOGBEG=LG10(SALBEG).
COMPUTE LOGNOW=LG10(SALNOW).
REGRESSION
 /DEPENDENT=LOGNOW
 /METHOD=ENTER LOGBEG
 /RESIDUALS=HISTOGRAM(ZRESID).


Histogram - Standardized Residual

  N  Exp N       (* = 1 Cases,     . : = Normal Curve)
  3    .37   Out ***
  1    .73  3.00 :
  3   1.85  2.67 *:*
  4   4.23  2.33 ***:
 10   8.65  2.00 ********:*
 14  15.85  1.67 ************** .
 20  26.01  1.33 ******************* .
 32  38.23  1.00 ******************************* .
 48  50.34   .67 ********************************************** .
 55  59.38   .33 ****************************************************** .
 63  62.74   .00 ************************************************************:
 64  59.38  -.33 *************************************************** :*****
 63  50.34  -.67 ***********************************************:*************
 43  38.23 -1.00 *****************************************:*****
 28  26.01 -1.33 ***********************:**
 15  15.85 -1.67 ************** .
  6   8.65 -2.00 ****** .
  1   4.23 -2.33 *  .
  1   1.85 -2.67 *.
  0    .73 -3.00 .
  0    .37   Out
```

For the transformed data, the multiple R increases slightly to 0.8864 (compare with Figure 21.6), and the outlier plot contains only four cases (compare with Figure 21.20). Thus, the transformation appears to have resulted in a better model. (For more information on transformations, see Chapter 8.)

A Final Comment on Assumptions

Rarely are assumptions not violated one way or another in regression analysis and other statistical procedures. However, this is not a justification for ignoring the assumptions. Cranking out regressions without considering possible violations of the necessary assumptions can lead to results that are difficult to interpret and apply. Significance levels, confidence intervals, and other results are sensitive to certain types of violations and cannot be interpreted in the usual fashion if serious violations exist.

By carefully examining residuals and, if need be, using transformations or other methods of analysis, you are in a much better position to pursue analyses that solve the problems you are investigating. Even if everything isn't perfect, you can at least knowledgeably gauge the potential for difficulties.

Multiple Regression Models

Beginning salary seems to be a good predictor of current salary, given the evidence shown above. Nearly 80% ($R^2 = 0.77$ from Figure 21.6) of the observed variability in current salaries can be explained by beginning salary levels. But how do variables such as education level, years of experience, race, and sex affect the salary level at which one enters the company?

Predictors of Beginning Salary

Multiple linear regression extends bivariate regression by incorporating multiple independent variables. The model can be expressed as:

$$Y_i = \beta_0 + \beta_1 X_{1i} + \beta_2 X_{2i} + \ldots + \beta_p X_{pi} + e_i$$

Equation 21.30

The notation X_{pi} indicates the value of the pth independent variable for case i. Again, the β terms are unknown parameters and the e_i terms are independent random variables that are normally distributed with mean 0 and constant variance σ^2. The model assumes that there is a normal distribution of the dependent variable for every combination of the values of the independent variables in the model. For example, if child's height is the dependent variable and age and maternal height are the independent variables, it is assumed that for every combination of age and maternal height there is a normal distribution of children's heights and, though the means of these distributions may differ, all have the same variance.

The Correlation Matrix

One of the first steps in calculating an equation with several independent variables is to calculate a correlation matrix for all variables, as shown in Figure 21.31. The variables are the log of beginning salary, years of education, sex, years of work experience, minority status (race), and age in years. Variables *SEX* and *MINORITY* are **indicator variables**, that is, variables coded as 0 or 1. *SEX* is coded 1 for female and 0 for male, and *MINORITY* is coded 1 for nonwhite and 0 for white.

Figure 21.31 The correlation matrix

```
COMPUTE LOGBEG=LG10(SALBEG).
REGRESSION
 /DESCRIPTIVES=CORR
  /VARIABLES=LOGBEG,EDLEVEL,SEX,WORK,MINORITY,AGE
  /DEPENDENT=LOGBEG
  /METHOD=ENTER EDLEVEL TO AGE.
Correlation:

            LOGBEG    EDLEVEL      SEX      WORK   MINORITY      AGE

LOGBEG      1.000       .686     -.548      .040     -.173     -.048
EDLEVEL      .686      1.000     -.356     -.252     -.133     -.281
SEX         -.548      -.356     1.000     -.165     -.076      .052
WORK         .040      -.252     -.165     1.000      .145      .804
MINORITY    -.173      -.133     -.076      .145     1.000      .111
AGE         -.048      -.281      .052      .804      .111     1.000
```

The matrix shows the correlations between the dependent variable (*LOGBEG*) and each independent variable, as well as the correlations between the independent variables. Note particularly any large intercorrelations between the independent variables, since such correlations can substantially affect the results of multiple regression analysis.

Partial Regression Coefficients

The summary output when all independent variables are included in the multiple regression equation is shown in Figure 21.32. The *F* test associated with the analysis-of-variance table is a test of the null hypothesis that

$$\beta_1 = \beta_2 = \beta_3 = \beta_4 = \beta_5 = 0$$

Equation 21.31

In other words, it is a test of whether there is a linear relationship between the dependent variable and the entire set of independent variables.

Figure 21.32 Statistics for the equation and analysis-of-variance table

```
COMPUTE LOGBEG=LOG10(SALBEG).
REGRESSION VARIABLES=SALBEG LOGBEG EDLEVEL SEX WORK MINORITY AGE
 /DEPENDENT=LOGBEG
 /METHOD=ENTER EDLEVEL TO AGE.


Multiple R          .78420
R Square            .61498
Adjusted R Square   .61086
Standard Error      .09559

Analysis of Variance
                 DF    Sum of Squares    Mean Square
Regression        5           6.83039        1.36608
Residual        468           4.27638         .00914

F =    149.50125      Signif F =   .0000
```

The statistics for the independent variables in Figure 21.33 are parallel to those obtained in regression with a single independent variable (see Figure 21.3). In multiple regres-

Figure 21.33 Statistics for variables in the equation

```
COMPUTE LOGBEG=LOG10(SALBEG).
REGRESSION VARIABLES=SALBEG LOGBEG EDLEVEL SEX WORK MINORITY AGE
 /DEPENDENT=LOGBEG
 /METHOD=ENTER EDLEVEL TO AGE.


------------------ Variables in the Equation ------------------

Variable              B        SE B      Beta        T   Sig T

AGE               .001015  6.6132E-04   .078106    1.535  .1254
SEX              -.103576    .010318   -.336987  -10.038  .0000
MINORITY         -.052366    .010837   -.141573   -4.832  .0000
EDLEVEL           .031443    .001748    .591951   17.988  .0000
WORK              .001608  9.2407E-04   .091428    1.740  .0826
(Constant)       3.385300    .033233             101.866  .0000
```

sion, the coefficients labeled B are called **partial regression coefficients**, since the coefficient for a particular variable is adjusted for other independent variables in the equation. The equation that relates the predicted log of beginning salary to the independent variables is

$$logbeg = 3.3853 + 0.00102(age) - 0.10358(sex)$$
$$- 0.05237(minority) + 0.03144(edlevel)$$
$$+ 0.00161(work)$$

Equation 21.32

Determining Important Variables

In multiple regression, you sometimes want to assign relative importance to each independent variable. For example, you might want to know whether education is more important in predicting beginning salary than previous work experience. There are two possible approaches, depending on which of the following questions is asked:

- How important are education and work experience when each one is used alone to predict beginning salary?

- How important are education and work experience when they are used to predict beginning salary along with other independent variables in the regression equation?

The first question is answered by looking at the correlation coefficients between salary and the independent variables. The larger the absolute value of the correlation coefficient, the stronger the linear association. Figure 21.31 shows that education correlates more highly with the log of salary than does previous work experience (0.686 and 0.040, respectively). Thus, you would assign more importance to education as a predictor of salary.

The answer to the second question is considerably more complicated. When the independent variables are correlated among themselves, the unique contribution of each is difficult to assess. Any statement about an independent variable is contingent upon the other variables in the equation. For example, the regression coefficient (B) for work experience is 0.0007 when it is the sole independent variable in the equation, compared to 0.00161 when the other four independent variables are also in the equation. The second coefficient is more than twice the size of the first.

Beta Coefficients

It is also inappropriate to interpret the B's as indicators of the relative importance of variables. The actual magnitude of the coefficients depends on the units in which the variables are measured. Only if all independent variables are measured in the same units—years, for example—are their coefficients directly comparable. When variables differ substantially in units of measurement, the sheer magnitude of their coefficients does not reveal anything about relative importance.

One way to make regression coefficients somewhat more comparable is to calculate beta weights, which are the coefficients of the independent variables when all variables are expressed in standardized (Z score) form (see Figure 21.33). The **beta coefficients** can be calculated directly from the regression coefficients using

$$\text{beta}_k = B_k \left(\frac{S_k}{S_Y} \right)$$

Equation 21.33

where S_k is the standard deviation of the kth independent variable.

However, the values of the beta coefficients, like the B's, are contingent on the other independent variables in the equation. They are also affected by the correlations of the independent variables and do not in any absolute sense reflect the importance of the various independent variables.

Part and Partial Coefficients

Another way of assessing the relative importance of independent variables is to consider the increase in R^2 when a variable is entered into an equation that already contains the other independent variables. This increase is

$$R^2_{\text{change}} = R^2 - R^2_{(i)}$$

Equation 21.34

where $R^2_{(i)}$ is the square of the multiple correlation coefficient when all independent variables except the ith are in the equation. A large change in R^2 indicates that a variable provides unique information about the dependent variable that is not available from the other independent variables in the equation. The signed square root of the increase is called the **part correlation coefficient**. It is the correlation between Y and X_i when the linear effects of the other independent variables have been removed from X_i. If all independent variables are uncorrelated, the change in R^2 when a variable is entered into the equation is simply the square of the correlation coefficient between that variable and the dependent variable.

The value of *RsqCh* in Figure 21.34 shows that the addition of years of education to an equation that contains the other four independent variables results in a change in R^2 of 0.266. This value tells only how much R^2 increases when a variable is added to the regression equation. It does not indicate what proportion of the unexplained variation this increase constitutes. If most of the variation had been explained by the other variables, a small change in R^2 is all that is possible for the remaining variable.

Figure 21.34 Change in R-squared

```
COMPUTE LOGBEG=LG10(SALBEG).
REGRESSION
 /STATISTICS R CHA BCOV ZPP F
 /DEPENDENT LOGBEG
 /METHOD ENTER AGE /ENTER SEX /ENTER MINORITY /ENTER WORK /ENTER EDLEVEL.

Variable(s) Entered on Step Number
    5..     EDLEVEL    EDUCATIONAL LEVEL


Multiple R              .78420
R Square                .61498      R Square Change     .26619
Adjusted R Square       .61086      F Change         323.55404
Standard Error          .09559      Signif F Change     .0000

F =      149.50125      Signif F =   .0000

------------- Variables in the Equation --------------

Variable      Correl Part Cor  Partial       F  Sig F

AGE           -.047795  .044040  .070796     2.357  .1254
SEX           -.548020 -.287918 -.420903   100.761  .0000
MINORITY      -.172836 -.138596 -.217989    23.349  .0000
WORK           .039940  .049897  .080154     3.026  .0826
EDLEVEL        .685719  .515935  .639342   323.554  .0000
(Constant)                               10376.613  .0000
```

A coefficient that measures the proportional reduction in variation is

$$Pr_i^2 = \frac{R^2 - R_{(i)}^2}{1 - R_{(i)}^2}$$

Equation 21.35

The numerator is the square of the part coefficient; the denominator is the proportion of unexplained variation when all but the ith variable are in the equation. The signed square root of Pr_i^2 is the **partial correlation coefficient**. It can be interpreted as the correlation between the ith independent variable and the dependent variable when the linear effects of the other independent variables have been removed from both X_i and Y. Since the denominator of Pr_i^2 is always less than or equal to 1, the part correlation coefficient is never larger in absolute value than the partial correlation coefficient.

Plots of the residuals of Y and X_i, when the linear effects of the other independent variables have been removed, are a useful diagnostic aid. They are discussed in "Checking for Violations of Assumptions" on p. 335.

Building a Model

Our selection of the five variables to predict beginning salary has been arbitrary to some extent. It is unlikely that all relevant variables have been identified and measured. Instead, some relevant variables have no doubt been excluded, while others that were included may not be very important determinants of salary level. This is not unusual; you must try to build a model from available data, as voluminous or scanty as the data may be. Before considering several formal procedures for model building, we will examine some of the consequences of adding and deleting variables from regression equations. The regression statistics for variables not in the equation are also described.

Adding and Deleting Variables

The first step in Figure 21.35 shows the summary statistics when years of education is the sole independent variable and log of beginning salary is the dependent variable. Consider the second step in the same figure, when another variable, *SEX*, is added. The value displayed as *R Square Change* in the second step is the change in R^2 when *SEX* is added. R^2 for *EDLEVEL* alone is 0.47021, so R_{change}^2 is $0.57598 - 0.47021$, or 0.10577.

Figure 21.35 Adding a variable to the equation

```
COMPUTE LOGBEG=LOG10(SALBEG).
REGRESSION
 /STATISTICS DEFAULTS CHA
 /DEPENDENT LOGBEG
 /METHOD ENTER EDLEVEL /ENTER SEX.
```

```
Variable(s) Entered on Step Number
   1..    EDLEVEL    EDUCATIONAL LEVEL


Multiple R             .68572
R Square               .47021        R Square Change    .47021
Adjusted R Square      .46909        F Change        418.92011
Standard Error         .11165        Signif F Change    .0000

------------------ Variables in the Equation ------------------

Variable               B       SE B      Beta        T  Sig T

EDLEVEL          .036424   .001780   .685719   20.468  .0000
(Constant)      3.310013   .024551            134.821  .0000


Variable(s) Entered on Step Number
   2..    SEX        SEX OF EMPLOYEE


Multiple R             .75893
R Square               .57598        R Square Change    .10577
Adjusted R Square      .57418        F Change        117.48552
Standard Error         .09999        Signif F Change    .0000
------------------ Variables in the Equation ------------------

Variable               B       SE B      Beta        T  Sig T

EDLEVEL          .029843   .001703   .561000   17.408  .0000
SEX             -.106966   .009869  -.348017  -10.839  .0000
(Constant)      3.447542   .025386            135.806  .0000
```

The null hypothesis that the true population value for the change in R^2 is 0 can be tested using

$$F_{change} = \frac{R^2_{change}(N-p-1)}{q(1-R^2)} = \frac{(0.1058)(474-2-1)}{1(1-0.5760)} = 117.49 \qquad \textbf{Equation 21.36}$$

where N is the number of cases in the equation, p is the total number of independent variables in the equation, and q is the number of variables entered at this step. This is also referred to as a **partial F test**. Under the hypothesis that the true change is 0, the significance of the value labeled *F Change* can be obtained from the *F* distribution with q and $N-p-1$ degrees of freedom.

The hypothesis that the real change in R^2 is 0 can also be formulated in terms of the β parameters. When only the *i*th variable is added in a step, the hypothesis that the change in R^2 is 0 is equivalent to the hypothesis that $β_i$ is 0. The *F* value displayed for the change in R^2 is the square of the *t* value for the test of the coefficient. For example, the *t* value for sex from Figure 21.35 is −10.839. This value squared is 117.48, the value displayed for *F Change*.

When q independent variables are entered in a single step, the test that R^2 is 0 is equivalent to the simultaneous test that the coefficients of all q variables are 0. For example, if sex and age were added in the same step to the regression equation that contains education, the F test for R^2 change would be the same as the F test which tests the hypothesis that $\beta_{sex} = \beta_{age} = 0$.

Entering sex into the equation with education has effects in addition to changing R^2. For example, the magnitude of the regression coefficient for education from step 1 to step 2 decreases from 0.0364 to 0.0298. This is attributable to the correlation between sex and level of education.

When highly intercorrelated independent variables are included in a regression equation, results may appear anomalous. The overall regression may be significant, while none of the individual coefficients are significant. The signs of the regression coefficients may be counterintuitive. High correlations between independent variables inflate the variances of the estimates, making individual coefficients quite unreliable without adding much to the overall fit of the model. The problem of linear relationships between independent variables is discussed further in "Measures of Collinearity" on p. 341.

Statistics for Variables Not in the Equation

When you have independent variables that have not been entered into the equation, you can examine what would happen if they were entered at the next step. Statistics describing these variables are shown in Figure 21.36. The column labeled *Beta In* is the standardized regression coefficient that would result if the variable were entered into the equation at the next step. The t test and level of significance are for the hypothesis that the coefficient is 0. (Remember that the t test and the partial F test for the hypothesis that a coefficient is 0 are equivalent.) The partial correlation coefficient with the dependent variable adjusts for the variables already in the equation.

Figure 21.36 Coefficients for variables not in the equation

```
COMPUTE LOGBEG LG10(SALBEG).
REGRESSION VARIABLES LOGBEG,EDLEVEL,SEX,WORK,MINORITY,AGE
 /STATISTICS OUTS
 /DEPENDENT LOGBEG
 /METHOD FORWARD.


------------ Variables not in the Equation -------------

Variable     Beta In  Partial  Min Toler       T  Sig T

WORK          .144245  .205668   .773818    4.556  .0000
MINORITY     -.129022 -.194642   .847583   -4.302  .0000
AGE           .139419  .205193   .804253    4.545  .0000
```

From statistics calculated for variables not in the equation, you can decide what variable should be entered next. This process is detailed in "Procedures for Selecting Variables" on p. 329.

The "Optimal" Number of Independent Variables

Having seen what happens when sex is added to the equation containing education (Figure 21.35), consider now what happens when the remaining three independent variables are entered one at a time in no particular order. Summary output is shown in Figure 21.37. Step 5 shows the statistics for the equation with all independent variables entered. Step 3 describes the model with education, sex, and work experience as the independent variables.

Figure 21.37 All independent variables in the equation

```
COMPUTE LOGBET=LG10(SALBEG).
REGRESSION /WIDTH 132
 /VARIABLES=LOGBEG,EDLEVEL,SEX,WORK,AGE,MINORITY
 /STATISTICS=HISTORY F
 /DEPENDENT LOGBEG
 /METHOD ENTER EDLEVEL /ENTER SEX /ENTER WORK /ENTER AGE
 /ENTER MINORITY.
```

Step	MultR	Rsq	AdjRsq	F(Eqn)	SigF	RsqCh	FCh	SigCh		Variable	BetaIn	Correl	
1	.6857	.4702	.4691	418.920	.000	.4702	418.920	.000	In:	EDLEVEL	.6857	.6857	EDUC
2	.7589	.5760	.5742	319.896	.000	.1058	117.486	.000	In:	SEX	-.3480	-.5480	SEX
3	.7707	.5939	.5913	229.130	.000	.0179	20.759	.000	In:	WORK	.1442	.0399	WORK
4	.7719	.5958	.5923	172.805	.000	.0019	2.149	.143	In:	AGE	.0763	-.0478	AGE
5	.7842	.6150	.6109	149.501	.000	.0192	23.349	.000	In:	MINORITY	-.1416	-.1728	MIN

Examination of Figure 21.37 shows that R^2 never decreases as independent variables are added. This is always true in regression analysis. However, this does not necessarily mean that the equation with more variables better fits the population. As the number of parameters estimated from the sample increases, so does the goodness of fit to the sample as measured by R^2. For example, if a sample contains six cases, a regression equation with six parameters fits the sample exactly, even though there may be no true statistical relationship at all between the dependent variable and the independent variables.

As indicated in "The R-squared Coefficient" on p. 294, the sample R^2 in general tends to overestimate the population value of R^2. Adjusted R^2 attempts to correct the optimistic bias of the sample R^2. Adjusted R^2 does not necessarily increase as additional variables are added to an equation and is the preferred measure of goodness of fit because it is not subject to the inflationary bias of unadjusted R^2. This statistic is shown in the column labeled *AdjRsq* in the output.

Although adding independent variables increases R^2, it does not necessarily decrease the standard error of the estimate. Each time a variable is added to the equation, a degree of freedom is lost from the residual sum of squares and one is gained for the regression sum of squares. The standard error may increase when the decrease in the residual sum of squares is very slight and not sufficient to make up for the loss of a degree of freedom for the residual sum of squares. The F value for the test of the overall regression decreases when the regression sum of squares does not increase as fast as the degrees of freedom for the regression.

Including a large number of independent variables in a regression model is never a good strategy, unless there are strong, previous reasons to suggest that they all should be included. The observed increase in R^2 does not necessarily reflect a better fit of the model in the population. Including irrelevant variables increases the standard errors of all estimates without improving prediction. A model with many variables is often difficult to interpret.

On the other hand, it is important not to exclude potentially relevant independent variables. The following sections describe various procedures for selecting variables to be included in a regression model. The goal is to build a concise model that makes good prediction possible.

Additional Statistics for Comparing Models

In addition to R^2 and adjusted R^2, many other criteria have been suggested for comparing models and selecting among them (Judge et al., 1985). One of the most commonly used alternatives to R^2 is called Mallow's C_p, which measures the standardized total mean squared error of prediction for the observed data. It is defined as

$$C_p = \frac{SSE}{\hat{\sigma}^2} + 2p - N$$

Equation 21.37

where σ^2 is an estimate of σ^2 usually obtained from the full set of variables, SSE is the error sum of squares from a model with p coefficients, including the constant, and N is the sample size.

The first part of Mallow's C_p is called the "variance" component, the second is the bias component. Subsets of variables that produce values close to p are considered good. Graphical methods for evaluation of models based on C_p are discussed in Daniel and Wood (1980) and Draper and Smith (1981).

Amemiya's prediction criteria PC is similar to adjusted R^2 with a higher penalty for adding variables. It is defined as

$$PC = \frac{N+p}{N-p} (1 - R^2)$$

Equation 21.38

Aikake's information criterion is based on an information measure of model selection. It is computed as

$$AIC = N \ ln \left(\frac{SSE}{N}\right) + 2p$$

Equation 21.39

The Schwarz Bayesian criterion is

$$SBC = N\ ln\left(\frac{SSE}{N}\right) + p\ ln\left(N\right)$$

Equation 21.40

Detailed discussions of these criteria can be found in Judge et al. (1985).

Procedures for Selecting Variables

You can construct a variety of regression models from the same set of variables. For instance, you can build seven different equations from three independent variables: three with only one independent variable, three with two independent variables, and one with all three. As the number of variables increases, so does the number of potential models (ten independent variables yield 1,023 models).

Although there are procedures for computing all possible regression equations, several other methods do not require as much computation and are more frequently used. Among these procedures are forward selection, backward elimination, and stepwise regression. None of these variable selection procedures is "best" in any absolute sense; they merely identify subsets of variables that, for the sample, are good predictors of the dependent variable.

Forward Selection

In **forward selection**, the first variable considered for entry into the equation is the one with the largest positive or negative correlation with the dependent variable. The F test for the hypothesis that the coefficient of the entered variable is 0 is then calculated. To determine whether this variable (and each succeeding variable) is entered, the F value is compared to an established criterion. You can specify one of two criteria in SPSS/PC+. One criterion is the minimum value of the F statistic that a variable must achieve in order to enter, called **F-to-enter** (FIN), with a default value of 3.84. The other criterion you can specify is the probability associated with the F statistic, called **probability of F-to-enter** (PIN), with a default of 0.05. In this case, a variable enters into the equation only if the probability associated with the F test is less than or equal to the default 0.05 or the value you specify. By default, PIN is the criterion used. (If you specify OUTS (the default) on the STATISTICS subcommand rather than F, SPSS/PC+ generally displays t values and their probabilities. These t probabilities are equivalent to those associated with F. You can obtain F values by squaring t values, since $t^2 = F$.)

The PIN and FIN criteria are not necessarily equivalent. As variables are added to the equation, the degrees of freedom associated with the residual sum of squares decrease while the regression degrees of freedom increase. Thus, a fixed F value has different significance levels depending on the number of variables currently in the equation. For large samples, the differences are negligible.

The actual significance level associated with the F-to-enter statistic is not the one usually obtained from the F distribution, since many variables are being examined and the largest F value is selected. Unfortunately, the true significance level is difficult to compute, since it depends not only on the number of cases and variables but also on the correlations between independent variables.

If the first variable selected for entry meets the criterion for inclusion, forward selection continues. Otherwise, the procedure terminates with no variables in the equation. Once one variable is entered, the statistics for variables not in the equation are used to select the next one. The partial correlations between the dependent variable and each of the independent variables not in the equation, adjusted for the independent variables in the equation, are examined. The variable with the largest partial correlation is the next candidate. Choosing the variable with the largest partial correlation in absolute value is equivalent to selecting the variable with the largest F value.

If the criterion is met, the variable is entered into the equation and the procedure is repeated. The procedure stops when there are no other variables that meet the entry criterion.

Figure 21.38 shows output generated from a forward-selection procedure using the salary data. The default entry criterion is PIN = 0.05. In the first step, education (variable *EDLEVEL*) is entered, since it has the highest correlation with beginning salary. The significance level associated with education is less than 0.0005, so it certainly meets the criterion for entry.

Figure 21.38 Summary statistics for forward selection

```
COMPUTE LOGBEG=LG10(SALBEG).
REGRESSION /WIDTH 132
 /VARIABLES LOGBEG,EDLEVEL,SEX,WORK,MINORITY,AGE
 /STATISTICS HISTORY F
 /DEPENDENT LOGBEG
 /METHOD FORWARD.


Step   MultR    Rsq    F(Eqn)   SigF         Variable  BetaIn
  1    .6857   .4702   418.920  .000   In:   EDLEVEL    .6857
  2    .7589   .5760   319.896  .000   In:   SEX       -.3480
  3    .7707   .5939   229.130  .000   In:   WORK       .1442
  4    .7830   .6130   185.750  .000   In:   MINORITY  -.1412
```

To see how the next variable, *SEX*, was selected, look at the statistics shown in Figure 21.39 for variables not in the equation when only *EDLEVEL* is in the equation. The variable with the largest partial correlation is *SEX*. If entered at the next step, it would have a *t* value of −10.839. Since the probability associated with the *t* value is less than 0.05, variable *SEX* is entered in the second step.

Figure 21.39 Status of the variables at the first step

```
COMPUTE LOGBEG=LG10(SALBEG).
REGRESSION
 /VARIABLES LOGBEG,EDLEVEL,SEX,WORK,MINORITY,AGE
 /STATISTICS OUTS
 /DEPENDENT LOGBEG
 /METHOD FORWARD.


------------------ Variables in the Equation ------------------

Variable              B        SE B      Beta         T   Sig T

EDLEVEL          .036424     .001780   .685719    20.468   .0000
(Constant)      3.310013     .024551             134.821   .0000


------------ Variables not in the Equation -------------

Variable     Beta In  Partial  Min Toler        T   Sig T

SEX         -.348017 -.446811    .873274   -10.839   .0000
WORK         .227473  .302405    .936316     6.885   .0000
MINORITY    -.083181 -.113267    .982341    -2.474   .0137
AGE          .157180  .207256    .921128     4.598   .0000
```

Once variable *SEX* enters at step 2, the statistics for variables not in the equation must be examined (see Figure 21.36). The variable with the largest absolute value for the partial correlation coefficient is now years of work experience. Its *t* value is 4.556 with a probability less than 0.05, so variable *WORK* is entered in the next step. The same process takes place with variable *MINORITY*, leaving *AGE* as the only variable out of the equation. However, as shown in Figure 21.40, the significance level associated with the *AGE* coefficient *t* value is 0.1254, which is too large for entry. Thus, forward selection yields the summary table for the four steps shown in Figure 21.38.

Figure 21.40 The last step

```
COMPUTE LOGBEG=LG10(SALBEG).
REGRESSION
 /VARIABLES LOGBEG,EDLEVEL,SEX,WORK,MINORITY,AGE
 /STATISTICS OUTS
 /DEPENDENT LOGBEG
 /METHOD FORWARD.


------------- Variables not in the Equation -------------

Variable     Beta In  Partial  Min Toler        T   Sig T

AGE          .078106  .070796    .297843     1.535   .1254
```

Backward Elimination

While forward selection starts with no independent variables in the equation and sequentially enters them, **backward elimination** starts with all variables in the equation and sequentially removes them. Instead of entry criteria, removal criteria are used.

Two removal criteria are available in SPSS/PC+. The first is the minimum F value that a variable must have in order to remain in the equation. Variables with F values less than this **F-to-remove** (FOUT) are eligible for removal. The second criterion available is the maximum **probability of F-to-remove** (POUT) that a variable can have. The default FOUT value is 2.71 and the default POUT value is 0.10. The default criterion is probability of F-to-remove.

Look at the salary example again, this time constructing the model with backward elimination. The output in Figure 21.41 is for the first step, in which all variables are entered into the equation. The variable with the smallest partial correlation coefficient in absolute value, *AGE* is examined first. Since the probability of its t (0.1254) is greater than the default POUT criterion value of 0.10, variable *AGE* is removed. (Recall that the t test and partial F test for the hypothesis that a coefficient is 0 are equivalent.)

Figure 21.41 Backward elimination at the first step

```
COMPUTE LOGBEG=LG10(SALBEG).
REGRESSION VARIABLES=LOGBEG,EDLEVEL,SEX,WORK,MINORITY,AGE
 /STATISTICS=COEFF OUTS ZPP
 /DEPENDENT=LOGBEG
 /METHOD=BACKWARD.


Variable              B        SE B      Beta    Correl Part Cor  Partial

AGE             .001015 6.61324E-04    .078106 -.047795   .044040   .070796
SEX            -.103576     .010318   -.336987 -.548020  -.287918  -.420903
MINORITY       -.052366     .010837   -.141573 -.172836  -.138596  -.217989
EDLEVEL         .031443     .001748    .591951  .685719   .515935   .639342
WORK            .001608 9.24066E-04    .091428  .039940   .049897   .080154
(Constant)     3.385300     .033233


----------- in ------------

Variable         T  Sig T

AGE           1.535  .1254
SEX         -10.038  .0000
MINORITY     -4.832  .0000
EDLEVEL      17.988  .0000
WORK          1.740  .0826
(Constant)  101.866  .0000
```

The equation is then recalculated without *AGE*, producing the statistics shown in Figure 21.42. The variable with the smallest partial correlation is *MINORITY*. However, its significance is less than the 0.10 criterion, so backward elimination stops. The equation resulting from backward elimination is the same as the one from forward selection. This is not always the case, however. Forward- and backward-selection procedures can give different results, even with comparable entry and removal criteria.

Figure 21.42 Backward elimination at the last step

```
COMPUTE LOGBEG=LG10(SALBEG).
REGRESSION VARIABLES=LOGBEG,EDLEVEL,SEX,WORK,MINORITY,AGE
 /STATISTICS=COEFF OUTS ZPP
 /DEPENDENT=LOGBEG
 /METHOD=BACKWARD.
```

```
---------------------- Variables in the Equation ----------------------

Variable              B         SE B        Beta    Correl  Part Cor   Partial

SEX           -.099042     .009901     -.322234 -.548020 -.287333 -.419331
MINORITY      -.052245     .010853     -.141248 -.172836 -.138282 -.216998
EDLEVEL        .031433     .001751      .591755  .685719  .515768  .638270
WORK           .002753 5.45823E-04      .156592  .039940  .144891  .226848
(Constant)    3.411953     .028380


----------- in -----------

Variable        T  Sig T

SEX         -10.003  .0000
MINORITY     -4.814  .0000
EDLEVEL      17.956  .0000
WORK          5.044  .0000
(Constant)  120.225  .0000


------------ Variables not in the Equation -------------

Variable   Beta In  Partial  Min Toler       T  Sig T

AGE        .078106  .070796   .297843    1.535  .1254

End Block Number   2   POUT =     .100 Limits reached.
```

Stepwise Selection

Stepwise selection of independent variables is really a combination of backward and forward procedures and is probably the most commonly used method. The first variable is selected in the same manner as in forward selection. If the variable fails to meet entry requirements (either FIN or PIN), the procedure terminates with no independent variables in the equation. If it passes the criterion, the second variable is selected based on the highest partial correlation. If it passes entry criteria, it also enters the equation.

After the first variable is entered, stepwise selection differs from forward selection: the first variable is examined to see whether it should be removed according to the removal criterion (FOUT or POUT), as in backward elimination. In the next step, variables not in the equation are examined for entry. After each step, variables already in the equation are examined for removal. Variables are removed until none remain that meet the removal criterion. To prevent the same variable from being repeatedly entered and removed, the PIN must be less than the POUT (or FIN greater than FOUT). Variable selection terminates when no more variables meet entry and removal criteria.

In the salary example, stepwise selection with the default criteria results in the same equation produced by both forward selection and backward elimination (see Figure 21.43).

Figure 21.43 Stepwise output at the last step

```
COMPUTE LOGBEG=LG10(SALBEG).
REGRESSION VARIABLES=LOGBEG EDLEVEL SEX WORK MINORITY AGE
 /STATISTICS=R COEFF OUTS ZPP
 /DEPENDENT=LOGBEG
 /METHOD=STEPWISE.

Variable(s) Entered on Step Number
   4..    MINORITY   MINORITY CLASSIFICATION


Multiple R          .78297
R Square            .61304
Adjusted R Square   .60974
Standard Error      .09573

F =     185.74958      Signif F =   .0000


---------------------- Variables in the Equation ----------------------

Variable            B          SE B      Beta    Correl Part Cor  Partial

EDLEVEL         .031433      .001751    .591755  .685719  .515768  .638270
SEX            -.099042      .009901   -.322234 -.548020 -.287333 -.419331
WORK            .002753  5.45823E-04    .156592  .039940  .144891  .226848
MINORITY       -.052245      .010853   -.141248 -.172836 -.138282 -.216998
(Constant)     3.411953      .028380

---------- in -----------

Variable          T  Sig T

EDLEVEL       17.956  .0000
SEX          -10.003  .0000
WORK           5.044  .0000
MINORITY      -4.814  .0000
(Constant)   120.225  .0000


------------ Variables not in the Equation -------------

Variable    Beta In  Partial  Min Toler      T  Sig T

AGE         .078106  .070796   .297843    1.535  .1254

End Block Number   1   PIN =     .050 Limits reached.
```

The three procedures do not always result in the same equation, though you should be encouraged when they do. The model selected by any method should be carefully studied for violations of the assumptions. It is often a good idea to develop several acceptable models and then choose among them based on interpretability, ease of variable acquisition, parsimony, and so forth.

Checking for Violations of Assumptions

The procedures for checking for violations of assumptions in bivariate regression (see "Searching for Violations of Assumptions" on p. 301) apply in multiple regression as well. Residuals should be plotted against predicted values as well as against each independent variable. The distribution of residuals should be examined for normality.

Several additional residual plots may be useful for multiple regression models. One of these is the **partial regression plot**. For the jth independent variable, it is obtained by calculating the residuals for the dependent variable when it is predicted from all the independent variables excluding the jth and by calculating the residuals for the jth independent variable when it is predicted from all of the other independent variables. This removes the linear effect of the other independent variables from both variables. For each case, these two residuals are plotted against each other.

A partial regression plot for educational level for the regression equation that contains work experience, minority, sex, and educational level as the independent variables is shown in Figure 21.44. (Summary statistics for the regression equation with all independent variables are displayed in the last step of Figure 21.43.) The partial regression plot (created by saving residuals in the REGRESSION procedure and then using the PLOT procedure to plot the residuals) shows residuals for *LOGBEG* on the y axis and residual values for *EDLEVEL* on the x axis.

Figure 21.44 Partial regression plot from PLOT

```
COMPUTE LOGBEG=LG10(SALBEG).
REGRESSION VARIABLES=LOGBEG SEX MINORITY EDLEVEL WORK
 /DEPENDENT=LOGBEG
 /METHOD=ENTER MINORITY SEX WORK
 /SAVE=RESID(RES1)
 /DEPENDENT=EDLEVEL
 /METHOD=ENTER MINORITY SEX WORK
 /SAVE=RESID(RES2)/
PLOT FORMAT=REGRESSION /HSIZE 40 /PLOT=RES1 WITH RES2.
```

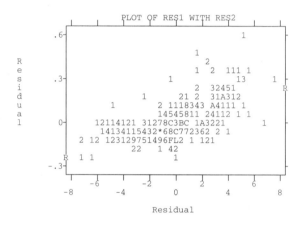

```
474 cases plotted. Regression statistics of RES1 on RES2:
Correlation  .63827 R Squared  .40739  S.E. of Est    .09542 Sig.  .0000
Intercept(S.E.)    .00000(   .00438)  Slope(S.E.)    .03143(   .00174)
```

Several characteristics of the partial regression plot make it a particularly valuable diagnostic tool. The slope of the regression line for the two residual variables (0.03143) is equal to the coefficient for the *EDLEVEL* variable in the multiple regression equation after the last step (step 4 in Figure 21.43). Thus, by examining the bivariate plot, you can conveniently identify points that are influential in the determination of the particular regression coefficient. The correlation coefficient between the two residuals, 0.638, is the partial correlation coefficient discussed in "Part and Partial Coefficients" on p. 323. The residuals from the least-squares line in Figure 21.44 are equal to the residuals from the final multiple regression equation, which includes all the independent variables.

The partial regression plot also helps you assess the inadequacies of the selected model and violations of the underlying assumptions. For example, the partial regression plot of educational level does not appear to be linear, suggesting that an additional term, such as years of education squared, might also be included in the model. This violation is much easier to spot using the partial regression plot than the plot of the independent variable against the residual from the equation with all independent variables. Figure 21.45 shows the residual scatterplot and Figure 21.46 shows the partial regression plot produced by the REGRESSION procedure. Note that the nonlinearity is much more apparent in the partial regression plot.

Figure 21.45 Residual scatterplot from REGRESSION

```
COMPUTE LOGBEG=LG10(SALBEG).
REGRESSION VARIABLES=LOGBEG SEX MINORITY EDLEVEL WORK
 /DEPENDENT=LOGBEG
 /METHOD=STEPWISE
 /SCATTERPLOT=(*RESID,EDLEVEL).
```

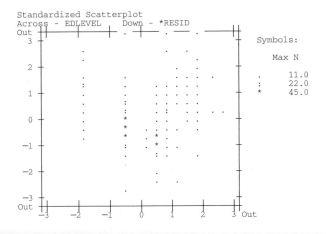

Figure 21.46 Partial regression plot from REGRESSION

```
COMPUTE LOGBEG=LG10(SALBEG).
REGRESSION VARIABLES=LOGBEG SEX MINORITY EDLEVEL WORK
 /DEPENDENT=LOGBEG
 /METHOD=STEPWISE
 /PARTIALPLOT=EDLEVEL.
```

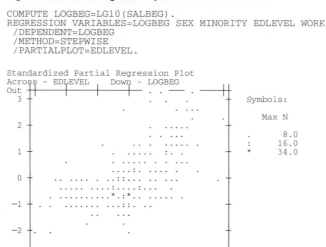

Figure 21.47 contains the summary statistics generated when the number of years of education squared is included in the multiple regression equation. The multiple R^2 increases from 0.61 (step 4 in Figure 21.43) to 0.71, a significant improvement.

Figure 21.47 The regression equation with education squared

```
COMPUTE LOGBEG=LG10(SALBEG).
COMPUTE ED2=EDLEVEL*EDLEVEL.
REGRESSION VARIABLES=LOGBEG SEX MINORITY EDLEVEL ED2 WORK
 /DEPENDENT=LOGBEG
 /METHOD=ENTER.


Multiple R             .84302
R Square               .71068
Adjusted R Square      .70759
Standard Error         .08286

Analysis of Variance
                  DF      Sum of Squares      Mean Square
Regression         5             7.89331          1.57866
Residual         468             3.21345           .00687

F =     229.91286       Signif F =   .0000
```

Looking for Influential Points

As discussed earlier, when building a regression model it is important to identify cases that are influential, or that have a disproportionately large effect on the estimated model (see "Locating Outliers" on p. 308). We can look for cases that change the values of the regression coefficients and of predicted values, cases that increase the variances of the coefficients, and cases that are poorly fitted by the model.

Among the important influence measures is the **leverage** of a case. The predicted values of the dependent variable can be expressed as

$$\hat{Y} = HY$$

Equation 21.41

The diagonal elements of the H matrix (commonly called the hat matrix) are called leverages. The leverage for a case describes the impact of the observed value of the dependent variable on the prediction of the fitted value. Leverages are important in their own right and as fundamental building blocks for other diagnostic measures. For example, the Mahalanobis distance for a point is obtained by multiplying the leverage value by $N-1$.

SPSS/PC⌐ computes centered leverages (LEVER). They range from 0 to $(N-1)/N$, where N is the number of observations. The mean value for the centered leverage is p/N, where p is the number of independent variables in the equation. A leverage of 0 identifies a point with no influence on the fit, while a point with a leverage of $(N-1)/N$ indicates that a degree of freedom has been devoted to fitting the data point. Ideally, you would like each observation to exert a roughly equal influence. That is, you want all of the leverages to be near p/N. It is a good idea to examine points with leverage values that exceed $2p/N$.

To see the effect of a case on the estimation of the regression coefficients, you can look at the change in each of the regression coefficients when the case is removed from the analysis. SPSS/PC+ can display or save the actual change in each of the coefficients, including the intercept (*DFBETA*) and the standardized change (*SDBETA*).

Figure 21.48 is a plot of standardized change values for the *MINORITY* variable on the vertical axis against case number on the horizontal axis. As expected, most of the points cluster in a horizontal band around 0. However, there are a few points far removed from the rest. Belsley et al. (1980) recommend examining standardized change values that are larger than $(2/\sqrt{N})$.

Figure 21.48 Plot of standardized changed values for minority status

```
COMPUTE LOGBEG=LG10(SALBEG).
COMPUTE ED2=EDLEVEL*EDLEVEL.
REGRESSION VARIABLES=LOGBEG SEX MINORITY EDLEVEL ED2 WORK
 /DEPENDENT=LOGBEG /METHOD=ENTER
 /SAVE SDBETA.
PLOT /HORIZONTAL MIN(0) MAX(500) /HSIZE 50 /VSIZE 35
 /PLOT=SDB2_1 WITH ID.
```

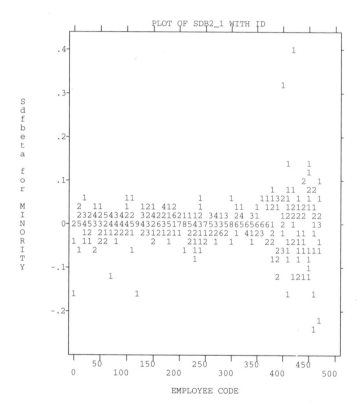

In addition to looking at the change in the regression coefficients when a case is deleted from an analysis, we can look at the change in the predicted value (*DFFIT*) or at the standardized change (*SDFFIT*). Cases with large values far removed from the rest should be examined. As a rule of thumb, you may want to look at standardized values larger than $2/\sqrt{p/N}$.

Another type of influential observation is one that influences the variance of the estimated regression coefficients. A measure of the impact of an observation on the variance-covariance matrix of the parameter estimates is called the **covariance ratio**

(COVRATIO). It is computed as the ratio of the determinant of the variance-covariance matrix computed without the case to the determinant of the variance-covariance matrix computed with all cases. If this ratio is close to 1, the case leaves the variance-covariance matrix relatively unchanged. Belsley et al. (1980) recommend examining points for which the absolute value of the ratio minus 1 is greater than $3p/N$.

You can save covariance ratios with the REGRESSION procedure and plot them using the PLOT procedure. Figure 21.49 is a plot of covariance ratios for the salary example. Note the circled point, which has a covariance ratio substantially smaller than the rest.

Figure 21.49 Plot of the covariance ratio

```
COMPUTE LOGBEG=LG10(SALBEG).
COMPUTE ED2=EDLEVEL*EDLEVEL.
REGRESSION VARIABLES=LOGBEG SEX MINORITY EDLEVEL ED2 WORK
 /DEPENDENT=LOGBEG /METHOD=ENTER
 /SAVE SDBETA.
PLOT /HORIZONTAL MIN(0) MAX(500) /HSIZE 50 /VERTICAL MIN(.6) MAX(1.1)
 /VSIZE 35
 /PLOT=COV_1 WITH ID.
```

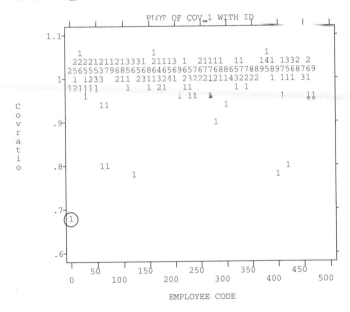

Measures of Collinearity

Collinearity refers to the situation in which there is a high multiple correlation when one of the independent variables is regressed on the others (that is, when there is a high correlation between independent variables). The problem with collinear variables is that they provide very similar information, and it is difficult to separate out the effects of the individual variables. Diagnostics are available which allow you to detect the presence of collinear data and to assess the extent to which the collinearity has degraded the estimated parameters.

The **tolerance** of a variable is a commonly used measure of collinearity. The tolerance of variable i is defined as $1 - R_i^2$, where R_i is the multiple correlation coefficient when the ith independent variable is predicted from the other independent variables. If the tolerance of a variable is small, it is almost a linear combination of the other independent variables.

The **variance inflation factor** (**VIF**) is closely related to the tolerance. In fact, it is defined as the reciprocal of the tolerance. That is, for the ith variable,

$$\text{VIF}_i = \frac{1}{(1 - R_i^2)}$$

Equation 21.42

This quantity is called the variance inflation factor, since the term is involved in the calculation of the variance of the ith regression coefficient. As the variance inflation factor increases, so does the variance of the regression coefficient.

Figure 21.50 shows the tolerances and VIF's for the variables in the final model. Note the low tolerances and high VIF's for *EDLEVEL* and *ED2* (the square of *EDLEVEL*). This is to be expected, since there is a relationship between these two variables.

Figure 21.50 Measures of collinearity—tolerance and VIF

```
COMPUTE LOGBEG=LG10(SALBEG).
COMPUTE ED2=EDLEVEL*EDLEVEL.
REGRESSION VARIABLES=LOGBEG SEX MINORITY EDLEVEL ED2 WORK
 /WIDTH 90
 /STATISTICS COEF TOL
 /DEPENDENT=LOGBEG /METHOD=ENTER.
```

```
--------------------------- Variables in the Equation ---------------------------

Variable            B        SE B       Beta  Tolerance        VIF         T  Sig T

WORK          .001794 4.78593E-04    .102038   .834367      1.199     3.749  .0002
MINORITY     -.038225     .009460   -.103342   .945107      1.058    -4.041  .0001
SEX          -.082503     .008671   -.268426   .776799      1.287    -9.515  .0000
EDLEVEL      -.089624     .009751  -1.687260   .018345     54.511    -9.191  .0000
ED2           .004562 3.63028E-04   2.312237   .018263     54.756    12.567  .0000
(Constant)   4.173910     .065417                                    63.804  .0000
```

Two useful tools for examining the collinearity of a data matrix are the eigenvalues of the scaled, uncentered cross-products matrix and the decomposition of regression variance corresponding to the eigenvalues.

Eigenvalues and Condition Indexes

We can compare the eigenvalues of the scaled, uncentered cross-products matrix to see if some are much larger than others. If this is the case, the data matrix is said to be **ill-conditioned**. If a matrix is ill-conditioned, small changes in the values of the independent or dependent variables may lead to large changes in the solution. The condition index is defined as

$$\text{condition index} = \sqrt{\frac{\text{eigenvalue}_{max}}{\text{eigenvalue}_i}}$$

Equation 21.43

There are as many near-dependencies among the variables as there are large condition indexes.

Figure 21.51 shows the eigenvalues and condition indexes for the salary example. You can see that the last two eigenvalues are much smaller than the rest. Their condition indexes are 10.29 and 88.22.

Figure 21.51 Measures of collinearity—eigenvalues and condition indexes

```
COMPUTE LOGBEG=LG10(SALBEG).
COMPUTE ED2=EDLEVEL*EDLEVEL.
REGRESSION VARIABLES=LOGBEG SEX MINORITY EDLEVEL ED2 WORK
 /STATISTICS COLLIN
 /DEPENDENT=LOGBEG /METHOD=ENTER.
```

Collinearity Diagnostics

Number	Eigenval	Cond Index	Variance Proportions Constant	SEX	MINORITY	EDLEVEL	ED2
1	4.08812	1.000	.00019	.01223	.01375	.00004	.00013
2	.79928	2.262	.00005	.08212	.65350	.00002	.00009
3	.59282	2.626	.00001	.37219	.22139	.00003	.00022
4	.48061	2.917	.00005	.14964	.05421	.00012	.00091
5	.03864	10.286	.05223	.37811	.04876	.00004	.02337
6	.00053	88.221	.94746	.00571	.00839	.99975	.97527

	WORK
1	.01466
2	.04351
3	.17437
4	.51370
5	.20721

Variance Proportions

The variances of each of the regression coefficients, including the constant, can be decomposed into a sum of components associated with each of the eigenvalues. If a high proportion of the variance of two or more coefficients is associated with the same eigenvalue, there is evidence for a near-dependency.

Consider Figure 21.51 again. Each of the columns following the condition index tells you the proportion of the variance of each of the coefficients associated with each of the eigenvalues. Consider the column for the *SEX* coefficient. You see that 1.22% of the variance of the coefficient is attributable to the first eigenvalue, 8.2% to the second, and 0.57% to the sixth (the proportions in each column sum to 1).

In this table you're looking for variables with high proportions for the same eigenvalue. For example, looking at the last eigenvalue, you see that it accounts for 95% of the variance of the constant, almost 100% of the variance of *EDLEVEL*, and 98% of the variance of *ED2*. This tells you that these three variables are highly dependent. Since the other independent variables have small variance proportions for the sixth eigenvalue, it does not appear that the observed dependencies are affecting their coefficients. (See Belsley et al., 1980, for an extensive discussion of these diagnostics.)

Interpreting the Equation

The multiple regression equation estimated above suggests several findings. Education appears to be the best predictor of beginning salary, at least among the variables included in this study (Figure 21.41). The sex of the employee also appears to be important. Women are paid less than men, since the sign of the regression coefficient is negative (men are coded 0 and women are coded 1). Years of prior work experience and race are also related to salary, but when education and sex are included in the equation, the effect of experience and race is less striking.

Do these results indicate that there is sex discrimination at the bank? Not necessarily. It is well recognized that all education is not equally profitable. Master's degrees in business administration and in political science are viewed quite differently in the marketplace. Thus, a possible explanation of the observed results is that women enter areas that are just not very well paid. Although this may suggest inequities in societal evaluation of skills, it does not necessarily imply discrimination at the bank. Further, many other potential job-related skills or qualifications are not included in the model. In addition, some of the existing variables, such as age, may make nonlinear as well as linear contributions to the fit. Such contributions can often be approximated by including new variables that are simple functions of the existing one. For example, the age values squared may improve the fit.

Statistics for Unselected Cases

As previously noted, a model usually fits the sample from which it is derived better than it fits the population. A sometimes useful strategy for obtaining an estimate of how well the model fits the population is to split the sample randomly into two parts. One part is then used to estimate the model, while the remaining cases are reserved for testing the goodness of fit.

It is also sometimes interesting to split the data on some characteristics of the sample. For example, you can develop the salary equation for males alone and then apply it to females to see how well it fits. For example, Figure 21.52 shows histograms of residuals for males (denoted as selected cases) and females (unselected cases). Note that the females' salaries are too large when predicted from the male equation since most of the residuals are negative. The multiple *R* for the females is 0.45596, which is smaller than the 0.73882 for males (stepwise selection was used).

Figure 21.52 Histograms for males (selected) and females (unselected)

```
COMPUTE LOGBEG=LG10(SALBEG)
COMPUTE ED2=EDLEVEL*EDLEVEL
REGRESSION WIDTH=90
  /SELECT SEX EQ 0
  /VARIABLES=LOGBEG,EDLEVEL,ED2,SEX,WORK,MINORITY,AGE
  /DEPENDENT=LOGBEG
  /METHOD=STEPWISE
  /RESIDUALS=HISTOGRAM.


Histogram - Standardized Residual
- Selected Cases
 N Exp N     (* = 1 Cases,    . : = Normal Curve)
 3   .20  Out ***
 3   .40  3.00 ***
 0  1.01  2.67 .
 1  2.30  2.33 *.
 2  4.71  2.00 **  .
 5  8.63  1.67 *****    .
11 14.16  1.33 **********  .
19 20.81  1.00 ******************* .
26 27.40   .67 **************************.
35 32.32   .33 *********************************.***
31 34.15   0.0 *******************************   .
30 32.32  -.33 ***************▲▲▲▲▲*▲*********
42 27.40  -.67 *****************************:***************
31 20.81 -1.00 **********************:**********
10 14.16 -1.33 **********   .
 5  8.63 -1.67 *****   .
 3  4.71 -2.00 *** .
 0  2.30 -2.33   .
 1  1.01 -2.67 :
 0   .40 ▬3.00
 0   .20  Out


Histogram - Standardized Residual
- Unselected Cases
 N Exp N     (X = 1 Cases,    . : = Normal Curve)
 0   .17  Out
 0   .33  3.00
 0   .84  2.67 .
 0  1.93  2.33 .
 0  3.94  2.00   .
 1  7.22  1.67 X    .
 1 11.85  1.33 X      .
 3 17.42  1.00 XXX        .
 4 22.94   .67 XXXX           .
10 27.06   .33 XXXXXXXXXX        .
14 28.59   0.0 XXXXXXXXXXXXXX    .
32 27.06  -.33 XXXXXXXXXXXXXXXXXXXXXXXXXX:XXXXX
32 22.94  -.67 XXXXXXXXXXXXXXXXXXXXXX:XXXXXXXX
52 17.42 -1.00 XXXXXXXXXXXXX:XXXXXXXXXXXXXXXXXXXXXXXXXXXXXX
22 11.85 -1.33 XXXXXXXXXXX:XXXXXXXXX
13  7.22 -1.67 XXXXX:XXXXX
12  3.94 -2.00 XXX:XXXXXXX
 8  1.93 -2.33 X:XXXXXX
 7   .84 -2.67 :XXXXXX
 1   .33 -3.00 X
 4   .17  Out XXXX
```

Running Procedure REGRESSION

The REGRESSION procedure provides five equation-building methods: forward selection, backward elimination, stepwise selection, forced entry, and forced removal. The subcommands for residual analysis help detect influential data points, outliers, and violations of the regression model assumptions.

Building the Equation

To build a simple regression model, you must specify three subcommands: a VARIABLES subcommand that names the variables to be analyzed, a DEPENDENT subcommand that indicates the dependent variable, and a METHOD subcommand that names the method to be used. For example, to build the simple bivariate model of beginning salary and current salary discussed earlier in the chapter, specify

```
REGRESSION   VARIABLES=SALBEG   SALNOW
   /DEPENDENT=SALNOW
   /METHOD=ENTER   SALBEG.
```

The beginning (*SALBEG*) and current (*SALNOW*) salaries are named, with the latter specified as the dependent variable. The ENTER keyword enters beginning salary into the equation. The output produced from this command is shown in Figure 21.3, Figure 21.6, and Figure 21.7.

VARIABLES Subcommand

The optional VARIABLES subcommand lists all variables to be used in the regression analysis. The order of variables on the VARIABLES subcommand determines the order of variables in the correlation matrix from which the equation is calculated. Keyword TO can be used on the VARIABLES subcommand to imply consecutive variables in the active file. On subsequent DEPENDENT and METHOD subcommands, keyword TO refers to the order variables are specified on the VARIABLES subcommand.

The VARIABLES subcommand is followed by a variable list or one of the following keywords:

ALL   *Include all user-defined variables in the active file.*

(COLLECT)   *Include all variables named on the DEPENDENT and METHOD subcommands.* This is the default if the VARIABLES subcommand is not included.

If you do not include a VARIABLES subcommand or you specify the keyword (COLLECT), the METHOD subcommands must include a variable list. If used, the VARIABLES subcommand must precede the first DEPENDENT and METHOD subcommands, as in:

```
REGRESSION   VARIABLES=SALBEG  SALNOW LOGBEG EDLEVEL SEX  WORK
             MINORITY  AGE
  /DEPENDENT=LOGBEG
  /METHOD=ENTER  EDLEVEL  TO  AGE.
```

DEPENDENT Subcommand

The DEPENDENT subcommand indicates the dependent variable for the regression analysis. The DEPENDENT subcommand is followed by a variable name or variable list. If you specify more than one variable on the DEPENDENT subcommand, SPSS/PC+ produces a separate equation for each dependent variable specified.

You can specify more than one analysis with multiple DEPENDENT and METHOD subcommands. For example, to run both a bivariate and multivariate analysis in the same REGRESSION procedure, specify

```
REGRESSION   VARIABLES=SALBEG  SALNOW  LOGBEG  EDLEVEL  SEX
             WORK MINORITY  AGE
  /DEPENDENT=SALNOW
  /METHOD=ENTER  SALBEG
  /DEPENDENT=LOGBEG
  /METHOD=ENTER EDLEVEL TO AGE.
```

The first DEPENDENT subcommand defines a single equation with *SALNOW* as the dependent variable, and the METHOD subcommand enters *SALBEG* into the equation. The second DEPENDENT subcommand defines another equation, with *LOGBEG* as the dependent variable. The associated METHOD subcommand enters variables *EDLEVEL* to *AGE* into the equation. The TO keyword in the second METHOD subcommand refers to the order in which the variables are named on the VARIABLES subcommand, not their order on the active file. See Figure 21.32 and Figure 21.33 for the output from the second equation.

METHOD Subcommand

At least one METHOD subcommand must immediately follow each DEPENDENT subcommand, specifying the method to be used in developing the regression equation. The available methods are:

FORWARD (varlist)   *Forward selection.* Variables are entered one at a time based on entry criteria (see "Forward Selection" on p. 329).

BACKWARD (varlist)   *Backward elimination.* All variables are entered and then removed one at a time based on removal criteria (see "Backward Elimination" on p. 332).

STEPWISE (varlist)   *Stepwise entry and removal.* Variables are examined at each step for entry or removal (see "Stepwise Selection" on p. 333).

ENTER (varlist)   *Forced entry.* The variables named are entered in a single step.

REMOVE (varlist)   *Forced removal.* The variables named are removed in a single step. REMOVE requires a variable list.

TEST (varlist)   *Test indicated subsets of independent variables.* TEST offers an easy way to test a variety of models using R^2 change and its test of significance as the criterion for the "best" model. TEST requires a variable list.

A variable list is required with the REMOVE and TEST keywords and is optional for the other METHOD keywords. The default variable list for methods FORWARD, BACKWARD, STEPWISE, and ENTER includes all variables named on the VARIABLES subcommand that are not named on the preceding DEPENDENT subcommand. For example, to request backward elimination using all independent variables listed on the VARIABLES subcommand, specify:

```
REGRESSION  VARIABLES=LOGBEG  EDLEVEL  SEX  WORK  MINORITY  AGE
   /DEPENDENT=LOGBEG
   /METHOD=BACKWARD.
```

The keyword METHOD is optional and can be omitted. For example, the command

```
REGRESSION  VARIABLES=LOGBEG  EDLEVEL  SEX  WORK  MINORITY  AGE
   /DEPENDENT=LOGBEG
   /BACKWARD.
```

produces the same results as the previous example.

You can specify multiple METHOD subcommands. For example, you might want to force one variable into the equation first and then enter the remaining variables using forward selection, as in:

```
REGRESSION  VARIABLES=LOGBEG  EDLEVEL  SEX  WORK  MINORITY  AGE
   /DEPENDENT=LOGBEG
   /METHOD=ENTER  EDLEVEL
   /METHOD=FORWARD  SEX  TO  AGE.
```

STATISTICS Subcommand

By default, REGRESSION displays the four sets of statistics described for keywords R, ANOVA, COEFF, and OUTS below. These statistics are shown in Figure 21.3, Figure 21.6, and Figure 21.7 for the bivariate equation, and in Figure 21.32 and Figure 21.33 for the multivariate equation. You can specify exactly which statistics you want displayed by using any of the following keywords on the STATISTICS subcommand:

DEFAULTS   *R, ANOVA, COEFF, and OUTS.* These statistics are displayed when the STATISTICS subcommand is omitted or if it is specified without keywords. If you specify keywords on STATISTICS, the default statistics are not displayed unless you specify them explicitly, either individually or with the DEFAULTS keyword.

ALL   *All statistics except F, LINE, and END.*

R   *Multiple* R. R displays multiple R, R^2, adjusted R^2, and the standard error. (See Figure 21.6.)

ANOVA   *Analysis of variance table.* This option displays degrees of freedom, sums of squares, mean squares, F value for multiple R, and the observed significance level of F. (See Figure 21.7.)

CHA   *Change in* R^2. This option includes the change in R^2 between steps, F at the end of each step and its probability, and F for the equation and its probability. (See Figure 21.35.)

BCOV   *Variance-covariance matrix.* This option displays a matrix with covariances above the diagonal, correlations below the diagonal, and variances on the diagonal.

XTX   *Sweep matrix.*

COLLIN   *Collinearity diagnostics.* COLLIN includes the variance-inflation factor (VIF), the eigenvalues of the scaled and uncentered cross-products matrix, condition indexes, and variance-decomposition proportions (Belsley et al., 1980).

SELECTION *Selection statistics.* This option includes Akaike's information criterion (AIK), Amemiya's prediction criterion (PC), Mallow's conditional mean squared error of prediction criterion (C_p), and Schwarz Bayesian criterion (SBC) (Judge et al., 1985).

COEFF   *Statistics for variables in the equation.* This option displays regression coefficient B, standard error of B, standardized coefficient Beta, t value for B, and two-tailed significance level of t.

OUTS   *Statistics for variables not in the equation that have been named on the METHOD subcommand for the equation.* OUTS displays beta if the variable were entered, t value for Beta, significance level of t, partial correlation with the dependent variable controlling for variables in the equation, and minimum tolerance. (See Figure 21.36.)

ZPP   *Zero-order, part, and partial correlation.* (See Figure 21.34.)

CI   *Confidence intervals.* CI displays the 95% confidence interval for the unstandardized regression coefficient. (See Figure 21.5.)

SES   *Approximate standard error of the standardized regression coefficients*
(Meyer and Younger, 1976).

TOL   *Tolerance.* This option displays tolerance and VIF for variables in the
equation and, for variables not in the equation, the tolerance a variable
would have if it were the only variable entered next. (See Figure 21.50.)

F   F *value for* B *and significance of* F. This is displayed instead of *t* for CO-
EFF and OUTS.

LINE   *Summary line for each step in step methods.* LINE displays a single summary line for each step in BACKWARD, FORWARD, or STEPWISE methods and the default or requested statistics at the end of each method block
(BACKWARD, FORWARD, STEPWISE, ENTER, REMOVE, or TEST).

HISTORY   *Step history.* HISTORY displays a summary report with a summary line
for each method (ENTER, REMOVE, or TEST, if the equation changes)
or step if the method involves steps (FORWARD, BACKWARD, or STEP-
WISE). If HISTORY is the only statistic requested, COEFF is displayed
for the final equation. (See Figure 21.37 and Figure 21.38.)

END   *One summary line per step or method block.* END displays a summary
line per step for BACKWARD, FORWARD, or STEPWISE, and one summary line per block for ENTER, REMOVE, or TEST, if the equation
changes.

The STATISTICS subcommand must be specified before the DEPENDENT subcommand
that initiates the equation and remains in effect until overridden by another STATISTICS
subcommand. For example, to produce the output in Figure 21.5, specify:

```
REGRESSION  VARIABLES=SALBEG  SALNOW
  /STATISTICS=CI
  /DEPENDENT=SALNOW
  /METHOD=ENTER  SALBEG.
```

CRITERIA Subcommand

You can control the statistical criteria by which REGRESSION chooses variables for entry into or removal from an equation with the CRITERIA subcommand. Place the CRI-
TERIA subcommand after the VARIABLES subcommand and before the DEPENDENT
subcommand. A CRITERIA subcommand affects any subsequent DEPENDENT and
METHOD subcommands and remains in effect until overridden with another CRITERIA
subcommand.

The CRITERIA keywords are:

DEFAULTS	*PIN(0.05), POUT(0.10), and TOLERANCE(0.0001).* These are the defaults if no CRITERIA subcommand is specified. If criteria have been changed, DEFAULTS restores the default values.
PIN(value)	*Probability of* F-*to-enter.* The default value of 0.05.
POUT(value)	*Probability of* F-*to-remove.* The default value of 0.10.
FIN(value)	F-*to-enter.* The default value is 3.84. Either PIN or FIN can be specified. If more than one is used, the last one specified is in effect.
FOUT(value)	F-*to-remove.* The default value is 2.71. Either POUT or FOUT can be specified. If more than one is used, the last one specified is in effect.
TOLERANCE(value)	*Tolerance.* The default value is 0.0001. All variables must pass both tolerance and minimum tolerance tests before entering the equation. The minimum tolerance is the smallest tolerance for that variable or any other variable in the equation if the variable is entered.
MAXSTEPS(n)	*Maximum number of steps.* For the STEPWISE method, the default is twice the number of independent variables. For the FORWARD and BACKWARD methods, the default maximum is the number of variables meeting the PIN and POUT or FIN and FOUT criteria. The MAXSTEPS value applies to the total model. The default value for the total model is the sum of the maximum number of steps for each method in the model.

For example, to change stepwise entry and removal criteria to FIN and FOUT and use their default values of 3.84 and 2.71, respectively, specify

```
REGRESSION  VARIABLES=LOGBEG  EDLEVEL  SEX  WORK  MINORITY  AGE
  /CRITERIA=FIN,FOUT
  /DEPENDENT=LOGBEG
  /METHOD=STEPWISE.
```

ORIGIN Subcommand

The regression model contains a constant term. You can use the ORIGIN subcommand to suppress this term and obtain regression through the origin. The NOORIGIN subcommand, which is the default, includes a constant term.

Place the ORIGIN or NOORIGIN subcommand between the VARIABLES subcommand and the DEPENDENT subcommand for the equation. For example,

```
REGRESSION  VARIABLES=SALBEG  SALNOW EDLEVEL
  /DEPENDENT=SALNOW
  /METHOD=ENTER  SALBEG
    /ORIGIN
    /DEPENDENT=SALBEG
    /METHOD=ENTER  EDLEVEL.
```

requests two equations, the first with a constant term (the default) and the second with regression through the origin.

There are no specifications for the ORIGIN and NOORIGIN subcommands. Once specified, the ORIGIN subcommand remains in effect until NOORIGIN is requested.

SELECT Subcommand

Use the SELECT subcommand to select a subset of cases for computing the regression equation. Only selected cases contribute to the correlation coefficients and to the regression equation. Residuals and predicted values are calculated and reported separately for both selected and unselected cases. The SELECT subcommand can precede or immediately follow the VARIABLES subcommand and is in effect for the entire REGRESSION command. The form of the SELECT subcommand is

```
/SELECT= varname relation value
```

The relation can be EQ, NE, LT, LE, GT, or GE.

For example, to generate separate residuals histograms for males and females based on the equation developed for males alone (*SEX*=0) as shown in Figure 21.52, specify

```
REGRESSION   SELECT   SEX   EQ   0
  /VARIABLES=LOGBEG   EDLEVEL   SEX   WORK   MINORITY   AGE
  /DEPENDENT=LOGBEG
  /METHOD=STEPWISE
  /RESIDUALS=HISTOGRAM.
```

MISSING Subcommand

Use the MISSING subcommand to specify the treatment of cases with missing values. If the MISSING subcommand is omitted, a case with user- or system-missing values for any variable named on the VARIABLES subcommand is excluded from the computation of the correlation matrix on which all analyses are based. The MISSING subcommand can precede or immediately follow the VARIABLES subcommand and is in effect for the entire REGRESSION command.

The available keywords are:

LISTWISE   *Delete cases with missing values listwise.* Only cases with valid values for all variables listed on the VARIABLES subcommand are included in analyses. If INCLUDE is also specified, only cases with system-missing values are deleted listwise. LISTWISE is the default.

PAIRWISE   *Delete cases with missing values pairwise.* Cases with valid values for the pair of variables being correlated are used to compute the correlation coefficient. If INCLUDE is also specified, only cases with system-missing values are deleted pairwise.

MEANSUBSTITUTION   *Replace missing values with the variable mean.* All cases are used for computations, with the mean of a variable substituted for missing observations. If INCLUDE is also specified, user-missing values are included in the computation of the means and only system-missing values are substituted.

INCLUDE   *Include all cases with user-missing values.* Only cases with system-missing values are excluded.

LISTWISE, PAIRWISE, and MEANSUBSTITUTION are alternatives. Only the last one specified on a MISSING subcommand will be in effect. INCLUDE can be used in combination with any one of these.

DESCRIPTIVES Subcommand

You can request a variety of descriptive statistics with the DESCRIPTIVES subcommand. These statistics are displayed for all variables specified on the VARIABLES subcommand, regardless of which variables you specify for computations. Descriptive statistics are based on all valid cases for each variable if you have specified PAIRWISE or MEANSUB on the MISSING subcommand. Otherwise, only cases that are included in the computation of the correlation matrix are used. If you specify the DESCRIPTIVES subcommand without any keywords, the statistics listed for keyword DEFAULTS are displayed. If you name any statistics on DESCRIPTIVES, only those explicitly requested are displayed.

The following descriptive statistics are available:

DEFAULTS   *MEAN, STDDEV, and CORR.* This is the default if DESCRIPTIVES is specified without any keywords.

MEAN   *Variable means.*

STDDEV   *Variable standard deviations.*

VARIANCE   *Variable variances.*

CORR   *Correlation matrix.*

SIG   *One-tailed significance levels for the correlation coefficients.*

BADCORR   *Correlation matrix only if some coefficients cannot be computed.*

COV   *Covariance matrix.*

XPROD   *Cross-product deviations from the mean.*

N   *Number of cases used to compute the correlation coefficients.*

ALL   *All descriptive statistics.*

For example, to produce the correlation matrix shown in Figure 21.31, specify:

```
REGRESSION  DESCRIPTIVES=CORR
  /VARIABLES=LOGBEG  EDLEVEL  SEX  WORK  MINORITY  AGE
  /DEPENDENT=LOGBEG
  /METHOD=ENTER  EDLEVEL  TO  AGE.
```

Analyzing Residuals

Once you have built an equation, REGRESSION can calculate a variety of temporary variables containing several types of residuals, predicted values, and related measures. You can use these variables to detect outliers and influential data points and to examine the regression assumptions described in "From Samples to Populations" on p. 290.

The following temporary variables are available for the analysis of residuals:

PRED   *Unstandardized predicted values.*

ZPRED   *Standardized predicted values.*

SEPRED   *Standard errors of the predicted values.*

RESID   *Unstandardized residuals.*

ZRESID   *Standardized residuals.*

SRESID   *Studentized residuals.*

MAHAL   *Mahalanobis distances.*

ADJPRED   *Adjusted predicted values.*

DRESID   *Deleted residuals.*

SDRESID   *Studentized deleted residuals.*

COOK   *Cook's distances.*

LEVER   *Centered leverage values.*

DFBETA   *Change in the regression coefficient that results from the deletion of the ith case.* A DFBETA value is computed for each case for each regression coefficient generated by a model.

SDBETA   *Standardized DFBETA.* An SDBETA value is computed for each case for each regression coefficient generated in a model. (See Belsley et al., 1980.)

DFFIT   *Change in the predicted value when the ith case is deleted.* (See Belsley et al., 1980.)

SDFIT   *Standardized DFFIT.* (See Belsley et al., 1980.)

COVRATIO   *Ratio of the determinant of the covariance matrix with the ith case delet-ed to the determinant of the covariance matrix with all cases included.* (See Belsley et al., 1980.)

MCIN   *Lower and upper bounds for the prediction interval of the mean predict-ed response.* A lower bound *LMCI_n* and an upper bound *UMCI_n* are generated. The default confidence interval is 95%. The interval can be re-set with the CIN keyword on CRITERIA. (See Dillon & Goldstein, 1984.)

ICIN   *Lower and upper bounds for the prediction interval for a single observa-tion.* (See Dillon & Goldstein, 1978.) A lowerbound *LICI_n* and an up-perbound *UICI_n* are generated. The default confidence interval is 95%. The interval can be reset with the CIN keyword on CRITERIA.

Residuals analysis is specified with four subcommands: RESIDUALS, CASEWISE, PAR-TIALPLOT, and SCATTERPLOT. You can specify these subcommands in any order, but you cannot specify more than one of each per equation, and they must immediately fol-low the last METHOD subcommand that completes an equation. The residuals subcom-mands affect only the equation they follow. Requesting any residuals analysis always produces descriptive statistics for at least four of the temporary variables (*PRED*, *ZPRED*, *RESID*, and *ZRESID*).

RESIDUALS Subcommand

Use the RESIDUALS subcommand to obtain the statistics and plots listed below. Speci-fying the RESIDUALS subcommand without any specifications produces the display de-scribed for keyword DEFAULTS. If any keywords are specified on RESIDUALS, only the displays for those keywords are produced.

DEFAULTS   *HISTOGRAM(ZRESID),   NORMPROB(ZRESID),   OUTLIERS (ZRESID), and DURBIN.* These plots are produced if RESIDUALS is specified without any specifications.

HISTOGRAM(tempvars) *Histogram of standardized temporary variables named.* The de-fault temporary variable is ZRESID. Other variables that can be plotted are *PRED*, *RESID*, *ZPRED*, *DRESID*, *ADJPRED*, *SRESID*, and *SDRESID*. (See Figure 21.18.)

NORMPROB(tempvars) *Normal probability (P-P) plot of standardized values.* The default variable is *ZRESID*. Other variables that can be plotted are *PRED*, *RESID*, *ZPRED*, *DRESID*, *ADJPRED*, *SRESID*, and *SDRESID*. (See Figure 21.19.)

SIZE(plotsize)   *Plot sizes.* The plot size can be specified as SMALL or LARGE. The default is SMALL.

OUTLIERS(tempvars)   *The ten most extreme values for the temporary variables named.* The default temporary variable is *ZRESID*. Other variables can be *RESID, DRESID, SRESID, SDRESID, MAHAL*, and *COOK*. (See Figure 21.21.)

DURBIN   *Durbin-Watson test statistic.* (See "Independence of Error" on p. 305.)

ID(varname)   *Case identifier.* Cases are labeled with values of the variable named after the ID keyword. By default, the plots are labeled with the sequential case number. ID also labels the CASEWISE list of cases. (See Figure 21.21.)

POOLED   *Pooled plots and statistics when the SELECT subcommand is in effect.* All cases in the active file are used. The default is separate reporting of residuals statistics and plots for selected and unselected cases (keyword SEPARATE).

All variables are standardized before plotting. If an unstandardized version of a variable is requested, the standardized version is plotted.

For example, to produce the output shown in Figure 21.18, Figure 21.19, and Figure 21.21, specify:

```
REGRESSION  VARIABLES=SALBEG  SALNOW
   /DEPENDENT=SALNOW
   /METHOD=ENTER  SALBEG
   /RESIDUALS=HISTOGRAM(ZRESID) NORMPROB OUTLIERS(MAHAL)
              ID(SEXRACE).
```

CASEWISE Subcommand

You can display a casewise plot of one of the temporary variables accompanied by a listing of the values of the dependent and other temporary variables. The plot can be requested for all cases or limited to outliers. Specifying the CASEWISE subcommand without keywords produces the output listed for DEFAULTS.

The following can be specified on the CASEWISE subcommand:

DEFAULTS   *OUTLIERS(3), PLOT(ZRESID), DEPENDENT, PRED, and RESID.* This is the default if CASEWISE is specified without any keywords.

OUTLIERS(value)   *Plot only cases for which the absolute standardized value of the plotted variable is at least as large as the specified value.* The default value is 3. Keyword OUTLIERS is ignored if keyword ALL is also specified.

ALL   *Include all cases in the casewise plot.* Keyword OUTLIERS is ignored when ALL is specified.

PLOT(tempvar)   *Plot the standardized values of the temporary variable named.* The default variable is *ZRESID*. The other variables that can be plotted arc *RESID*, *DRESID*, *SRESID*, and *SDRESID*. (See Figure 21.20.)

varlist   *List values of the dependent and temporary variables named.* Any temporary variable, including *LEVER*, can be listed. The defaults are DEPENDENT (the dependent variable), *PRED*, and *RESID*. (See Figure 21.12 and Figure 21.20.)

To plot outliers whose absolute values are equal to or greater than 3 based on ZRESID, you need to specify only the CASEWISE subcommand.

If you request more variables than will fit on the page width specified on the SET WIDTH command or the WIDTH subcommand in REGRESSION, your output will be truncated (see "WIDTH Subcommand" on p. 360).

SCATTERPLOT Subcommand

Use the SCATTERPLOT subcommand to generate scatterplots for the variables in the equation. You must specify at least one pair of variables on the SCATTERPLOT subcommand. You can also specify the SIZE keyword to control the size of the plots. All scatterplots are standardized.

The specifications for SCATTERPLOT are:

(varname,varname)   *The pair of variables to be plotted.* Available variables are *PRED*, *RESID*, *ZPRED*, *ZRESID*, *DRESID*, *ADJPRED*, *SRESID*, *SDRESID*, and any variable named on the VARIABLES subcommand. Temporary variables should be preceded by an asterisk on this subcommand.

SIZE(plotsize)   *Plot size.* The plot size can be SMALL or LARGE. The default is SMALL.

The first variable named inside the parentheses is plotted on the vertical (*y*) axis, and the second is plotted on the horizontal (*x*) axis. For example, to generate the scatterplot shown in Figure 21.16, specify

```
REGRESSION   VARIABLES=SALBEG   SALNOW
  /DEPENDENT=SALNOW
  /METHOD=ENTER   SALBEG
  /SCATTERPLOT=(*SRESID,*PRED).
```

To produce a scatterplot for *SRESID* and *PRED* based on the logarithmic transformation of both the dependent and independent variables, as shown in Figure 21.29, use the SCATTERPLOT subcommand along with the following transformation commands:

```
COMPUTE  LOGBEG=LG10(SALBEG).
COMPUTE  LOGNOW=LG10(SALNOW).
REGRESSION  VARIABLES=LOGBEG,LOGNOW
  /DEPENDENT=LOGNOW
  /METHOD=ENTER  LOGBEG
  /SCATTERPLOT=(*SRESID,*PRED).
```

To produce more than one scatterplot, simply add pairs of variable names in parentheses, as in:

```
  /SCATTERPLOT=(*SRESID,*PRED)(SALBEG,*PRED)
```

PARTIALPLOT Subcommand

Use the PARTIALPLOT subcommand to generate partial residual plots. Partial residual plots are scatterplots of the residuals of the dependent variable and an independent variable when both variables are regressed on the rest of the independent variables.

If no variable list is given on the PARTIALPLOT subcommand, a partial residual plot is produced for every independent variable in the equation. Plots are displayed in descending order of the standard error of *B*. All plots are standardized.

The specifications on the PARTIALPLOT subcommand are

varlist   *Independent variables to be used in partial residual plot.* At least two independent variables must be in the equation for a partial residual plot to be produced. You can specify keyword ALL to obtain the default plots for every independent variable in the equation.

SIZE(plotsize)   *Plot size.* The plot size can be SMALL or LARGE. The default plot size is SMALL.

For example, the following commands produced Figure 21.46:

```
COMPUTE  LOGBEG=LG10(SALBEG).
REGRESSION  VARIABLES=LOGBEG  SEX  MINORITY  EDLEVEL  WORK
  /DEPENDENT=LOGBEG /METHOD=STEPWISE
  /PARTIALPLOT=EDLEVEL.
```

SAVE Subcommand

Use the SAVE subcommand to save any or all of the temporary variables described in "Analyzing Residuals" on p. 354. The specification is the name of the temporary variable followed by a valid variable name in parentheses, as in:

```
GET  FILE='BANK.SYS'.
REGRESSION  VARIABLES=SALBEG, SALNOW
  /DEPENDENT=SALNOW
  /METHOD=ENTER  SALBEG
  /SAVE=SEPRED(SE).
PLOT  CUTPOINTS=EVERY(20) /SYMBOLS='.'
    /PLOT=SE  WITH  SALBEG.
```

This example saves the standard errors of the predicted values as a variable named *SE*. The PLOT procedure is used to plot the standard errors against the values of the independent variable *SALBEG*. If you don't specify a new variable name, SPSS/PC+ generates a new variable name by default.

If you specify DFBETA or SDBETA, the number of new variables saved is equal to the total number of variables in the equation, including the constant. For example, the command

```
REGRESSION  DEPENDENT=SALBEG
 /METHOD=ENTER AGE SEX
 /SAVE=DFBETA(DFBVAR).
```

will create and save three new variables with the names *DFBVAR0*, *DFBVAR1*, and *DFBVAR2*.

You can use keyword FITS to automatically save the temporary variables *DFFIT*, *SDFIT*, *DFBETA*, *SDBETA*, and *COVRATIO*, as in:

```
/SAVE=FITS.
```

If you specify FITS, you cannot specify new variable names. SPSS/PC+ automatically generates new variable names.

READ and WRITE Subcommands

Procedure REGRESSION can read and write matrix materials, which can be processed more quickly than cases. Use the WRITE subcommand to write matrix materials to a file. You can write default matrix materials or specify the materials you want to write, including variable means, standard deviations, variances, a correlation or covariance matrix, and the number of cases used to compute the correlations or covariances. You can then use the READ subcommand to read the matrix materials into REGRESSION for additional analysis.

The READ subcommand can also read matrix materials written by other procedures, such as CORRELATION, or entered as data in free or fixed format. See REGRESSION: Matrix Materials in the Syntax Reference for complete instructions on using matrix materials with REGRESSION.

REGWGT Subcommand

The REGWGT subcommand specifies a variable for estimating weighted least-squares models. The only specification on REGWGT is the name of the single variable containing the weights, as in:

```
REGRESSION  VARIABLES=IQ  TO  ACHIEVE /REGWGT=WGT1
  /DEPENDENT=VARY /METHOD=ENTER /SAVE=PRED(P) RESID(R).
```

REGWGT remains in effect for all analyses specified on the REGRESSION command. If you specify more than one REGWGT subcommand, only the last one specified will be in effect.

WIDTH Subcommand

You can use the WIDTH subcommand to control the width of the output produced by the REGRESSION procedure. The default is the width specified on the SET command. The WIDTH subcommand in REGRESSION overrides the width specified on SET.

A narrow width limits the number of statistics that can be displayed in a summary line and may also cause casewise output to be truncated (see "CASEWISE Subcommand" on p. 356). A narrow width may also reduce the size of scatterplots and normal probability plots in the residuals output. In Figure 21.23, the command

```
REGRESSION
 /WIDTH 132
 /DEPENDENT=y /METHOD=ENTER X
 /CASEWISE ALL DEP RESID SRESID SDRESID ADJPRED
  DRESID MAHAL COOK.
```

uses the WIDTH subcommand to ensure that all of the requested variables are displayed.

22 Distribution-Free or Nonparametric Tests: Procedure NPAR TESTS

Broccoli and Brussels sprouts have recently joined coffee, carrots, red meat, oat bran, saccharin, tobacco, and alcohol on the ever-expanding list of substances thought to contribute to the development or prevention of cancer. This list is necessarily tentative and complicated. The two major sources of evidence—experiments on animals and examination of the histories of people with cancer—are problematic. It is difficult to predict, based on the results of giving large doses of suspect substances to small animals, the consequences for humans of consuming small amounts over a long time span.

In studies of people, lifestyle components are difficult to isolate, and it is challenging—if not impossible—to unravel the contribution of a single factor. For example, what conclusions may be drawn about the role of caffeine, based on a sample of overweight, sedentary, coffee- and alcohol-drinking, cigarette-smoking urban dwellers?

In addition to certain lifestyle factors, dietary fat is thought to play an important role in the development and progression of cancer. Wynder (1976) showed that the per capita consumption of dietary fats is positively correlated with the incidence of breast and colon cancer in humans. In another study, King et al. (1979) examined the relationship between diet and tumor growth in rats. Three groups of animals of the same age, species, and physical condition were injected with tumor cells. The rats were divided into three groups and fed diets of either low, saturated, or unsaturated fat.

One hypothesis of interest is whether the length of time it takes for tumors to develop differs in two of the groups—rats fed saturated fats and rats fed unsaturated fats. If we assume a normal distribution of the tumor-free time, the independent-samples t test (described in Chapter 16) can be used to test the hypothesis that the population means are equal. However, if the distribution of times does not appear normal, and especially if the sample sizes are small, we should consider statistical procedures not requiring assumptions about the shape of the underlying distribution.

The Mann-Whitney Test

The **Mann-Whitney test**, also known as the Wilcoxon test, does not require assumptions about the shape of the underlying distributions. It tests the hypothesis that two independent samples come from populations having the same distribution. The form of the distribution need not be specified. The test does not require that the variable be measured on an interval scale; an ordinal scale is sufficient.

Ranking the Data

To compute the test, the observations from both samples are first combined and ranked from smallest to largest value. Consider Table 22.1, which shows a sample of the King data reported by Lee (1980). Case 4 has the shortest elapsed time to development of a tumor: 68 days. It is assigned a rank of 1. Case 3 has the next shortest time (81), so it is assigned a rank of 2. Cases 5 and 6 both exhibited tumors after 112 days. They are both assigned a rank of 3.5, the average of the ranks (3 and 4) for which they are tied. Case 2, with the next longest elapsed time (126 days), is given a rank of 5, and case 1, with the longest elapsed time (199 days), is given a rank of 6.

Table 22.1   Ranking the data

Saturated			Unsaturated		
Case	Time	Rank	Case	Time	Rank
1	199	6	4	68	1
2	126	5	5	112	3.5
3	81	2	6	112	3.5

Calculating the Test

The statistic for testing the hypothesis that the two distributions are equal is the sum of the ranks for each of the two groups. If the groups have the same distribution, their sample distributions of ranks should be similar. If one of the groups has more than its share of small or large ranks, there is reason to suspect that the two underlying distributions are different.

Figure 22.1 shows the output from the Mann-Whitney test for the complete King data. For each group, the mean rank and number of cases is given. (The mean rank is the sum of the ranks divided by the number of cases.) Note that the saturated-fats group has only 29 cases, since one rat died of causes unrelated to the experiment. The number (963) displayed under W is the sum of the ranks for the group with the smaller number of observations. If both groups have the same number of observations, W is the rank sum for the group specified first on the M-W subcommand. In this example, the value of W is 963, the sum of the ranks for the saturated-fats group.

Figure 22.1   Mann-Whitney test

```
NPAR TESTS M-W=TUMOR BY DIET(0,1).

- - - - - Mann-Whitney U - Wilcoxon Rank Sum W Test

       TUMOR
   by DIET


     Mean Rank    Cases

        26.90       30  DIET = 0  UNSATURATED
        33.21       29  DIET = 1  SATURATED
                    --
                    59  Total

                                  Corrected for Ties
           U             W           Z     2-tailed P
         342.0         963.0     -1.4112    0.1582
```

The number (342) identified in the output as U represents the number of times a value in the unsaturated-fats group precedes a value in the saturated-fats group. To understand what this means, consider again the data in Table 22.1. All three cases in the unsaturated-fats group have smaller ranks than the first case in the saturated-fats group, so they all precede case 1 in the rankings. Similarly, all three cases in the unsaturated-fats group precede case 2. Only one unsaturated-fats case (case 4) is smaller in value than case 3. Thus, the number of times the value for an unsaturated-fats case precedes the value for a saturated-fats case is $3 + 3 + 1 = 7$. The number of times the value of a saturated-fats case precedes the value of an unsaturated-fats case is 2, since case 3 has a smaller rank than both cases 5 and 6. The smaller of these two numbers is displayed in the output as U. If the two distributions are equal, values from one group should not consistently precede values in the other.

The significance levels associated with U and W are the same. They can be obtained by transforming the score to a standard normal deviate (Z). If the total sample size is less than 30, an exact probability level based on the distribution of the score is also displayed. From Figure 22.1, the observed significance level for this example is 0.158. Since the significance level is large, the hypothesis that tumor-free time has the same distribution for the two diet groups is not rejected.

Which Diet?

You should not conclude from these findings that it doesn't matter—as far as tumors are concerned—what kind of fat you (or rats) eat. King et al. found that rats fed the unsaturated diet had a total of 96 tumors at the end of the experiment, while rats fed the saturated diet had only 55 tumors. They also found that large tumors were more common in the unsaturated-diet group than in the saturated-diet group. Thus, unsaturated fats may be more hazardous than saturated fats.

Assumptions

The Mann-Whitney test requires only that the sample be random and that values can be ordered. These assumptions—especially randomness—should not be made lightly, but they are less restrictive than those for the two-sample t test for means. The t test requires further that the observations be selected from approximately normally distributed populations with equal variances.

Since the Mann-Whitney test can always be calculated instead of the t test, what determines which should be used? If the assumptions needed for the t test are met, the t test is more powerful than the Mann-Whitney test. That is, the t test will detect true differences between the two populations more often than the Mann-Whitney test will, since the t test uses more information from the data. Substituting ranks for the actual values eliminates potentially useful information. On the other hand, using the t test when its assumptions are substantially violated may result in an erroneous observed significance level.

In general, if the assumptions of the t test appear reasonable, it should be used. When the data are ordinal—or interval but from a markedly non-normal distribution—the Mann-Whitney test is the procedure of choice.

Nonparametric Tests

Like the Mann-Whitney test, many statistical procedures require limited distributional assumptions about the data. Collectively, these procedures are termed **distribution-free tests** or **nonparametric tests**. Like the Mann-Whitney test, distribution-free tests are generally less powerful than their parametric counterparts. They are most useful in situations where parametric procedures are not appropriate—for example, when the data are nominal or ordinal, or when interval data are from markedly non-normal distributions. Significance levels for certain nonparametric tests can be determined regardless of the shape of the population distribution, since they are based on ranks.

In the following sections, various nonparametric tests will be used to analyze some of the data described in previous chapters. Since the data were chosen to illustrate parametric procedures, they satisfy assumptions that are more restrictive than those required for nonparametric procedures. However, using the same data provides an opportunity to learn new procedures easily and to compare results obtained from different types of analyses.

One-Sample Tests

Various one-sample nonparametric procedures are available for testing hypotheses about the parameters of a population. These include procedures for examining differences in paired samples.

The Sign Test

In Chapter 16, the paired *t* test for means is used to test the hypothesis that mean buying scores for husbands and wives are equal. Remember that this test requires the assumption that differences are normally distributed.

The **sign test** is a nonparametric procedure used with two related samples to test the hypothesis that the distributions of two variables are the same. This test makes no assumptions about the shape of these distributions.

To compute the sign test, the difference between the buying scores of husbands and wives is calculated for each case. Next, the numbers of positive and negative differences are obtained. If the distributions of the two variables are the same, the numbers of positive and negative differences should be similar.

The output in Figure 22.2 shows that the number of negative differences is 56, while the number of positive differences is 39. The total number of cases is 98, including three with no differences. The observed significance level is 0.1007. Since this value is large, the hypothesis that the distributions are the same is not rejected.

Figure 22.2   Sign test

```
NPAR TESTS SIGN=HSSCALE WITH WSSCALE.

- - - - - Sign Test

     HSSCALE    Husband Self Scale
with WSSCALE    Wife Self Scale


     Cases
        56   - Diffs (WSSCALE Lt HSSCALE)              Z =      1.6416
        39   + Diffs (WSSCALE Gt HSSCALE)
         3     Ties                          2-tailed P =       .1007
       ---
        98     Total
```

The Wilcoxon Signed-Ranks Test

The sign test uses only the direction of the differences between the pairs and ignores the magnitude. A discrepancy of 15 between husbands' and wives' buying scores is treated in the same way as a discrepancy of 1. The **Wilcoxon signed-rank test** incorporates information about the magnitude of the differences and is therefore more powerful than the sign test.

To compute the Wilcoxon signed-rank test, the differences are ranked without considering the signs. In the case of ties, average ranks are assigned. The sums of the ranks for positive and negative differences are then calculated.

As shown in Figure 22.3, the average rank of the 56 negative differences is 45.25. The average positive rank is 51.95. In the row labeled *Ties*, there are 3 cases with the same value for both variables. The observed significance level associated with the test is large (0.3458), and once again the hypothesis of no difference is not rejected.

Figure 22.3   Wilcoxon signed-ranks test

```
NPAR TESTS WILCOXON=HSSCALE WITH WSSCALE.

- - - - - Wilcoxon Matched-pairs Signed-ranks Test

     HSSCALE    Husband Self Scale
with WSSCALE    Wife Self Scale

    Mean Rank    Cases
        45.25       56   - Ranks  (WSSCALE Lt HSSCALE)
        51.95       39   + Ranks  (WSSCALE Gt HSSCALE)
                     3     Ties   (WSSCALE Eq HSSCALE)
                   ---
                    98     Total
         Z =   -.9428            2-tailed P =  .3458
```

The Wald-Wolfowitz Runs Test

The runs test is a test of randomness. That is, given a sequence of observations, the runs test examines whether the value of one observation influences the values for later observations. If there is no influence (the observations are independent), the sequence is considered random.

A *run* is any sequence of like observations. For example, if a coin is tossed fifteen times and the outcomes recorded, the following sequence might result:

HHHTHHHHTTTTTTT

There are four runs in this sequence: HHH, T, HHHH, and TTTTTTT. The total number of runs is a measure of randomness, since too many runs, or too few, suggest dependence between observations. The **Wald-Wolfowitz runs test** converts the total number of runs into a *Z* statistic having approximately a normal distribution. The only requirement for this test is that the variable tested be dichotomous (have only two possible values).

Suppose, for example, that a weather forecaster records whether it snows for twenty days in February and obtains the following sequence (1=snow, 0=no snow):

01111111010111111100

To test the hypothesis that the occurrence or nonoccurrence of snow on one day has no effect on whether it snows on later days, the runs test is performed, resulting in the output in Figure 22.4.

Figure 22.4 Runs test

```
NPAR TESTS RUNS(1)=SNOW.

- - - - - Runs Test

     SNOW

          Runs:     7          Test Value = 1

          Cases:    5    Lt 1
                   15    Ge 1            Z =  -.6243
                   --
                   20    Total 2-tailed P =    .5324
```

Since the observed significance level is quite large (0.5324), the hypothesis of randomness is not rejected. It does not appear, from these data, that snowy (or nonsnowy) days affect the later occurrence of snow.

The Binomial Test

With data that are binomially distributed, the hypothesis that the probability p of a particular outcome is equal to some number is often of interest. For example, you might want to find out if a tossed coin was unbiased. To check this, you could test to see whether the probability of heads was equal to 1/2. The **binomial test** compares the observed frequencies in each category of a binomial distribution to the frequencies expected under a binomial distribution with the probability parameter p.

For instance, a nickel is tossed twenty times, with the following results (1=heads, 0=tails):

10011111101111011011

The output in Figure 22.5 shows a binomial test of the hypothesis that the probability of heads equals 1/2 for these data.

Figure 22.5 Binomial test

```
NPAR TESTS BINOMIAL=HEADS(0,1).

- - - - - Binomial Test

     HEADS

     Cases
                              Test Prop. =    .5000
          5    = 0            Obs. Prop. =    .2500
         15    = 1
         --                  Exact Binomial
         20    Total          2-tailed P =    .0414
```

The test proportion of cases for the first value (0) is 0.5000 and the observed proportion is 0.2500, that is, 1/4 of the actual tosses were tails. The small (0.0414) observed significance level indicates that it is not likely that p equals 1/2 and it appears that the coin is biased.

The Kolmogorov-Smirnov One-Sample Test

The **Kolmogorov-Smirnov test** is used to determine how well a random sample of data fits a particular distribution (uniform, normal, or Poisson). It is based on comparison of the sample cumulative distribution function to the hypothetical cumulative distribution function.

This test can be used with the beer data (see Chapter 6) to see whether it is reasonable to assume that the *ALCOHOL* variable is normally distributed. The Kolmogorov-Smirnov output in Figure 22.6 shows an observed significance level of 0.05, small enough to cast doubt on the assumption of normality.

Figure 22.6 Kolmogorov-Smirnov test

```
NPAR TESTS K-S(NORMAL)= ALCOHOL.

- - - - - Kolmogorov - Smirnov Goodness of Fit Test

     ALCOHOL   ALCOHOL BY VOLUME (IN %)

     Test Distribution  -  Normal              Mean:   4.577
                                  Standard Deviation:    .603

             Cases:  35

                Most Extreme Differences
          Absolute        Positive        Negative        K-S Z     2-tailed P
           0.22940        0.15585        -0.22940         1.357        0.050
```

The One-Sample Chi-Square Test

In Chapter 11, frequencies of deaths for the days of the week are examined. The FREQUENCIES output suggests that all days of the week are equally hazardous in regard to death. To test this conclusion, the one-sample chi-square test can be used. This nonparametric test requires only that the data be a random sample.

To calculate the one-sample chi-square statistic, the data are first classified into mutually exclusive categories of interest—days of the week in this example—and then expected frequencies for these categories are computed. Expected frequencies are the frequencies that would be expected if the null hypothesis is true. For the death data, the hypothesis to be tested is that the probability of death is the same for each day of the week. The day of death is known for 110 subjects. The hypothesis implies that the expected frequency of deaths for each weekday is $110/7$, or 15.71. Once the expected frequencies are obtained, the chi-square statistic is computed as

$$\chi^2 = \sum_{i=1}^{k} \frac{(O_i - E_i)^2}{E_i}$$

Equation 22.1

where O_i is the observed frequency for the ith category, E_i is the expected frequency for the ith category, and k is the number of categories.

If the null hypothesis is true, the chi-square statistic has approximately a chi-square distribution with $k - 1$ degrees of freedom. This statistic will be large if the observed and expected frequencies are substantially different. Figure 22.7 shows the output from the one-sample chi-square test for the death data. The observed chi-square value is 3.4, and the associated significance level is 0.757. Since the observed significance level is large, the hypothesis that deaths are evenly distributed over days of the week is not rejected.

Figure 22.7   One-sample chi-square test

```
NPAR TESTS   CHISQUARE=DAYOFWK.

- - - - - Chi-square Test

    DAYOFWK    DAY OF DEATH

                              Cases
                  Category  Observed  Expected  Residual

    SUNDAY            1        19      15.71      3.29
    MONDAY            2        11      15.71     -4.71
    TUESDAY           3        19      15.71      3.29
    WEDNSDAY          4        17      15.71      1.29
    THURSDAY          5        15      15.71      -.71
    FRIDAY            6        13      15.71     -2.71
    SATURDAY          7        16      15.71       .29
                              ---
                    Total    110

        Chi-Square          D.F.        Significance
          3.400              6              .757
```

The Friedman Test

The **Friedman test** is used to compare two or more related samples. (This is an extension of the tests for paired data.) The k variables to be compared are ranked from 1 to k for each case, and the mean ranks for the variables are calculated and compared, resulting in a test statistic with approximately a chi-square distribution.

The Friedman test can be used to analyze data from a psychology experiment concerned with memory. In this experiment, subjects were asked to memorize first a two-digit number, then a three-digit number, and finally a four-digit number. After each number was memorized, they were shown a single digit and asked if that digit was present in the number memorized. The times taken to reach a decision for the two-, three-, and four-digit numbers are the three related variables of interest.

Figure 22.8 shows the results of the Friedman test, examining the hypothesis that the number of digits memorized has no effect on the time taken to reach a decision. The observed significance level is extremely small, so it appears that the number of digits does affect decision time.

Figure 22.8   Friedman test

```
NPAR TESTS FRIEDMAN=P2DIGIT P3DIGIT P4DIGIT.

- - - - - Friedman Two-way ANOVA

    Mean Rank    Variable

        1.21    P2DIGIT
        2.13    P3DIGIT
        2.67    P4DIGIT

        Cases          Chi-Square        D.F.    Significance
          24             26.0833            2          .0000
```

Tests for Two or More Independent Samples

A variety of nonparametric tests involve comparisons between two or more independent samples. (The Mann-Whitney test is one such test.) In this respect, these tests resemble the *t* tests and one-way analyses of variance described in Chapter 16 and Chapter 17.

The Two-Sample Median Test

The two-sample median test is used to determine whether two populations have the same median. The two samples are combined and the median for the total distribution is calculated. The number of observations above this median, as well as the number of observations less than or equal to this median, is counted for each sample. The test statistic is based on these counts.

This test can be used to determine whether median sodium levels are the same for the highest-rated and lowest-rated beers in the beer data. The output in Figure 22.9 shows the largest possible *p* value, 1. Therefore, there is no reason to suspect different medians.

Figure 22.9   Median test of sodium by rating

```
NPAR TESTS MEDIAN=SODIUM BY RATING(3,1).

- - - - - Median Test

    SODIUM     SODIUM PER 12 FLUID OUNCES IN MG
  by RATING
```

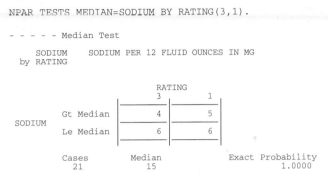

```
                           RATING
                             3          1

          Gt Median    |     4    |     5    |
  SODIUM               |----------|----------|
          Le Median    |     6    |     6    |

          Cases           Median          Exact Probability
           21               15                   1.0000
```

The Two-Sample Wald-Wolfowitz Runs Test

A runs test can be used to test the hypothesis that two samples come from populations with the same distributions. To perform this test, the two samples are combined and the values sorted. A run in this combined and sorted sample consists of a sequence of values belonging to the first sample or a sequence of values belonging to the second sample. If there are too few runs, it suggests that the two populations have different distributions.

The Wald-Wolfowitz test can be used with the beer data to compare calories for the highest-ranked and lowest-ranked beers. The output in Figure 22.10 shows an observed significance level of 0.0119. Since this is small, the distribution of calories for the highest-ranked beers appears to differ from the distribution of calories for the lowest-ranked beers.

Figure 22.10 Wald-Wolfowitz runs test

```
NPAR TESTS W-W=CALORIES BY RATING(3,1).

- - - - - Wald-Wolfowitz Runs Test

    CALORIES   CALORIES PER 12 FLUID OUNCES
  by RATING

        Cases

          10   RATING = 3   FAIR
          11   RATING = 1   VERY GOOD
          --
          21   Total
                                             Exact
                          Runs         Z    1-tailed P
  Minimum Possible:        6       -2.2335      .0119
  Maximum Possible:        6       -2.2335      .0119

  WARNING -- There are   1 Inter-group Ties involving    5 cases.
```

The Two-Sample Kolmogorov-Smirnov Test

The Kolmogorov-Smirnov test for two samples provides another method for testing whether two samples come from populations with the same distributions. It is based on a comparison of the distribution functions for the two samples.

This test can be used with the beer data to compare the alcohol content of the highest-ranked and lowest-ranked beers. Since the observed significance level in Figure 22.11 is small, the alcohol distributions do not appear to be the same. The approximation used to obtain the observed significance level may be inadequate in this case, however, because of the small sample size.

Figure 22.11 Kolmogorov-Smirnov two-sample test

```
NPAR TESTS K-S=ALCOHOL BY RATING(3,1).

- - - - - Kolmogorov - Smirnov 2-Sample Test

    ALCOHOL    ALCOHOL BY VOLUME (IN %)
  by RATING


      Cases

        10  RATING = 3  FAIR
        11  RATING = 1  VERY GOOD
        --
        21  Total

WARNING - Due to small sample size, probability tables should be consulted.
          Most Extreme Differences
      Absolute        Positive       Negative        K-S Z      2-tailed P
      0.60000           0.0          -0.60000        1.373        0.046
```

The *k*-Sample Median Test

An extension of the two-sample median test, the **k-sample median test** compares the medians of three or more independent samples. Figure 22.12 shows a *k*-sample median test comparing median prices for the highest-, middle-, and lowest-quality beers. The observed significance level is fairly large (.091), indicating no real difference in the median price of the three types of beer.

Figure 22.12 k-sample median test

```
NPAR TESTS MEDIAN=PRICE BY RATING(1,3).

- - - - - Median Test

     PRICE       PRICE PER 6-PACK
  by RATING

                                    RATING
                             1    |    2    |    3
                   ┌─────────┬─────────┬─────────┐
         Gt Median │    8    |    5    |    3
 PRICE             ├─────────┼─────────┼─────────┤
         Le Median │    3    |    9    |    7
                   └─────────┴─────────┴─────────┘

         Cases       Median    Chi-Square    D.F.   Significance
          35          2.65       4.7937        2        .0910
```

The Kruskal-Wallis Test

The experiment described at the beginning of this chapter investigates the effects of three diets on tumor development. The Mann-Whitney test was calculated to examine possible differences between saturated and unsaturated diets. To test for differences among all three diets, an extension of the Mann-Whitney test can be used. This test is known as the **Kruskal-Wallis one-way analysis of variance**.

The procedure for computing the Kruskal-Wallis test is similar to the procedure used in the Mann-Whitney test. All cases from the three groups are combined and ranked. Average ranks are assigned in the case of ties. For each group, the ranks are summed, and the Kruskal-Wallis H statistic is computed from these sums. The H statistic has approximately a chi-square distribution under the hypothesis that the three groups have the same distribution.

The output in Figure 22.13 shows that the third group, the low-fat-diet group, has the largest average rank. The value of the Kruskal-Wallis statistic is 11.1257. When the statistic is adjusted for the presence of ties, the value changes to 11.2608. The small observed significance level suggests that the time interval until development of a tumor is not the same for all three groups

Figure 22.13 Kruskal-Wallis one-way analysis of variance output

```
NPAR TESTS K-W=TUMOR BY DIET(0,2).

- - - - - Kruskal-Wallis 1-way ANOVA

     TUMOR
 by DIET

   Mean Rank   Cases

      34.12      30    DIET = 0    UNSATURATED
      43.50      29    DIET = 1    SATURATED
      56.24      29    DIET = 2    LOW-FAT
                 --
                 88    Total

                                          Corrected for Ties
       CASES   Chi-Square  Significance  Chi-Square  Significance
          88     11.1257        0.0038     11.2608        0.0036
```

Running Procedure NPAR TESTS

You can perform all of the nonparametric tests discussed in this chapter, and several more, with procedure NPAR TESTS. (See Siegel, 1956, for further information about these tests.) In addition to obtaining test statistics, you can request additional statistics, specify missing-value treatments, and use a random subsample of your data for NPAR TESTS. The tests available are summarized in Table 22.2.

Table 22.2   Nonparametric tests available in NPAR TESTS

Data organization	Nominal scale	Ordinal scale
One sample	Chi-square Runs Binomial	Kolmogorov-Smirnov
Two related samples	McNemar	Sign Wilcoxon
k related samples	Cochran's Q	Friedman Kendall
Two independent samples		Median Mann-Whitney Kolmogorov-Smirnov Wald-Wolfowitz Moses
k independent samples		Median Kruskal-Wallis

The general format for an NPAR TESTS command is

```
NPAR TESTS testname[(parameters)]=varlist
```

Each subcommand requests a specific test and lists the variables to be tested. The equals sign is optional. You can use keyword TO to refer to consecutive variables in the file. The form of the variable list depends on the type of test specified. More than one test can be requested on one NPAR TESTS command.

One-Sample Tests

The one-sample tests available in NPAR TESTS are the one-sample chi-square test, the Kolmogorov-Smirnov test, the runs test, and the binomial test.

The One-Sample Chi-Square Test

Use the CHISQUARE subcommand to obtain a one-sample chi-square test. The format is:

```
NPAR TESTS CHISQUARE=varlist[(lo,hi)]
```

The range following the variable list is optional. If it is not specified, each distinct value of the variable named is treated as a separate category. If the range is specified, noninteger values are truncated to integers, resulting in categories with only integer values. Cases with values outside the specified range are excluded from the analysis.

By default, the expected frequencies are assumed to be equal. You can specify other frequencies on the EXPECTED subcommand, which has the format

```
EXPECTED=f1,f2,...,fn
```

where $f1$ through fn are the expected frequencies. You must specify a frequency greater than 0 for each category of the variable. The values listed in EXPECTED are treated as proportions rather than actual numbers of cases expected. In other words, the values are summed, and each value is then divided by this sum to calculate the proportion of cases expected in the corresponding category. For example, the command

```
NPAR TESTS CHISQUARE=FLOWERS
  /EXPECTED=1,2,2,2,1.
```

specifies 1/8, 2/8, 2/8, 2/8, and 1/8 as the expected proportions for the values of *FLOWERS*.

The EXPECTED subcommand applies to all variables specified on the preceding CHISQUARE subcommand. If you want to specify different expected frequencies for each variable, use separate CHISQUARE and EXPECTED subcommands for each variable. Several CHISQUARE and EXPECTED subcommands can also be used to test different expected frequencies for the same variable.

The output in Figure 22.7 was produced with the command:

```
NPAR TESTS CHISQUARE=DAYOFWK.
```

For each chi-square test, the output includes the observed and expected numbers of cases in each category, the residual (observed minus expected) for each category, and the chi-square statistic with its degrees of freedom and observed significance level.

The Kolmogorov-Smirnov One-Sample Test

Use the K-S subcommand to obtain the Kolmogorov-Smirnov test for one sample. The distributions you can test against are the uniform, normal, and Poisson distributions.
    The K-S format is

```
NPAR TESTS K-S(distrib[parameters])=varlist
```

where *distrib* is one of the distribution keywords UNIFORM, NORMAL, or POISSON. Each of these keywords has optional parameters that are separated from the keyword and each other by commas:

UNIFORM   *Uniform distribution.* The optional parameters are the minimum and maximum values (in that order). By default, K-S uses the sample minimum and maximum values.

NORMAL   *Normal distribution.* The optional parameters are the mean and standard deviation (in that order). By default, K-S uses the sample mean and standard deviation.

POISSON   *Poisson distribution.* The one optional parameter is the mean. By default, K-S uses the sample mean. A word of caution about testing against a Poisson distribution: if the mean of the test distribution is large, evaluating the probabilities is a very time-consuming process. If a mean of 100,000 or larger is used, K-S uses a normal approximation to the Poisson distribution.

For example, the command

```
NPAR TESTS K-S(POISSON,5)=HORSKICK.
```

compares the sample distribution of *HORSKICK* with a Poisson distribution with a mean of 5. The output in Figure 22.6 was produced with the command:

```
NPAR TESTS K-S(NORMAL)=ALCOHOL.
```

The output for the Kolmogorov-Smirnov test includes the distribution used for the test, the most extreme positive, negative, and absolute differences, and the Kolmogorov-Smirnov Z with its observed significance level.
    The Kolmogorov-Smirnov test assumes that the parameters of the test distribution have been specified in advance (not calculated from the data). When the parameters are

estimated from the sample, the distribution of the test statistic changes. SPSS/PC+ makes no corrections for this.

The Runs Test

Use the RUNS subcommand to obtain the runs test. This subcommand has the general format

```
NPAR TESTS RUNS(cut point)=varlist
```

The cut point dichotomizes the variables in the variable list. Even if a variable is dichotomous to begin with, a cut point must be specified. For example, a variable that takes only the values 0 and 1 would have 1 for the cut point. For example, the command

```
NPAR TESTS RUNS(1)=SNOW.
```

produces the output in Figure 22.4. You can specify the observed mean, median, mode, or a value for the cut point.

MEAN   *Mean.* All values below the observed mean are in one category; all values greater than or equal to the mean make up the other category.

MEDIAN   *Median.* All values below the observed median are in one category; all values greater than or equal to the median are in the other category.

MODE   *Mode.* All values below the observed mode are in one category; all values greater than or equal to the mode are in the other category.

value   *Specified value.* All values below the specified value are in one category; all values greater than or equal to the specified value are in the other category.

The RUNS output shows the cut point, the number of runs, the number of cases below the cut point, the number of cases greater than or equal to the cut point, and the test statistic Z with its observed significance level.

The Binomial Test

Use the BINOMIAL subcommand to perform the binomial test. Its format is

```
NPAR TESTS BINOMIAL[(p)]=varlist(value or value1,value2)
```

where p is the proportion of cases expected in the *first* category. If p is not specified, a p of 0.5 is used. A two-tailed test is performed only when p is 0.5. When p is any other value, a one-tailed test is performed.

If no values are specified after the variable list, each variable named is assumed to have only two values. If one value follows the variable list, it is used as a cut point: all cases with values less than or equal to the cutting point are in the first category, and all other cases are in the second category. If two values follow the variable list, all cases with value 1 are in the first category and all cases with value 2 are in the second category. For example, the command

```
NPAR TESTS BINOMIAL=HEADS(0,1).
```

produces the output in Figure 22.5. If you specify two values and the variable is not a dichotomy, only cases with the two values specified are included in the analysis.

By default, the null hypothesis is that the data are from a binomial distribution with a probability of 0.5 for both values. You can change the probabilities by specifying a probability for the first value in parentheses after the subcommand BINOMIAL. For example, the command

```
NPAR TESTS BINOMIAL(.25)=RANK(2)
```

tests the null hypothesis that the data are from a binomial distribution with a probability of 0.25 for the first value and a probability of 0.75 for the second value.

The BINOMIAL output shows the value of each category, the number of cases in each category, the test proportion of cases, the observed proportion of cases, and the probability of the observed proportion.

Tests for Two Related Samples

The McNemar test, the sign test, and the Wilcoxon matched-pairs signed-ranks test are available for paired samples. The subcommands for requesting these tests have the general format

```
NPAR TESTS testname=varlist [WITH varlist]
```

When keyword WITH and the second variable list are specified, each variable in the first list is paired with each variable in the second list. For example, the command

```
NPAR TESTS SIGN=RATING1 WITH RATING2 RATING3.
```

requests two sign tests, one for *RATING1* with *RATING2* and one for *RATING1* with *RATING3*. Keyword WITH and the second variable list are optional. When only one variable list is specified, each variable in the list is paired with every other variable in the list. For example, the command

```
NPAR TESTS SIGN=RATING1 RATING2 RATING3.
```

produces three sign tests: *RATING1* with *RATING2*, *RATING1* with *RATING3*, and *RATING2* with *RATING3*.

You can also pair variables sequentially by specifying Option 3 on the OPTIONS subcommand. When Option 3 is specified with a single variable list, the first variable in the list is paired with the second, the second variable with the third, and so on. For example, the command

```
NPAR TESTS SIGN=RATING1 RATING2 RATING3
  /OPTIONS=3.
```

performs two sign tests: one for *RATING1* with *RATING2* and one for *RATING2* with *RATING3*. If Option 3 is specified with keyword WITH and two variable lists, the first variable in the first list is paired with the first variable in the second list, and so forth. For example, the command

```
NPAR TESTS SIGN=RATING1 RATING2 WITH RATING3 RATING4
  /OPTIONS=3.
```

requests sign tests for *RATING1* with *RATING3* and *RATING2* with *RATING4*.

The McNemar Test

The MCNEMAR subcommand requests the McNemar test for two correlated dichotomous variables. Pairs of variables being tested must have the same two values. Variables that are not dichotomous must be recoded before using NPAR TESTS. If fewer than ten cases have different values for the two variables, the binomial distribution is used to find the observed significance level. The output includes a 2×2 table and the observed significance level. If a chi-square statistic is calculated, it is also displayed.

The format for MCNEMAR is

```
NPAR TESTS MCNEMAR=varlist [WITH varlist]
```

For example, the command

```
NPAR TESTS MCNEMAR=CONTRCT1 CONTRCT2.
```

requests a McNemar test on the 2×2 table for *CONTRCT1* and *CONTRCT2*.

The Sign Test

The SIGN subcommand requests sign tests for paired variables. The format of SIGN is

```
NPAR TESTS SIGN=varlist [WITH varlist]
```

For example, the output in Figure 22.2 was produced by the command

```
NPAR TESTS SIGN=HSSCALE WITH WSSCALE.
```

If there are more than 25 cases, the observed significance level of the test statistic is based on a normal approximation. If there are 25 or fewer cases, the binomial distribution is used to compute the exact observed significance level.

The Wilcoxon Matched-Pairs Signed-Ranks Test

The WILCOXON subcommand requests the Wilcoxon test. Its format is

```
NPAR TESTS WILCOXON=varlist [WITH varlist]
```

For example, the output in Figure 22.3 was obtained with the command

```
NPAR TESTS WILCOXON=HSSCALE WITH WSSCALE.
```

The Wilcoxon output shows the mean rank for each variable, the number of positive, negative, and tied ranks, and the test statistic Z with its observed significance level.

Tests for *k*-Related Samples

Cochran's Q test, the Friedman test, and Kendall's coefficient of concordance W are tests for k-related samples. The general format for requesting these tests is

```
NPAR TESTS testname=varlist
```

Cochran's *Q*

The COCHRAN subcommand requests Cochran's Q and has the format

```
NPAR TESTS COCHRAN=varlist
```

The variables to be tested must be dichotomous and coded with the same two values. If they are not, they must be recoded. The output for COCHRAN includes the number of cases in each category for each variable and Cochran's Q with its degrees of freedom and observed significance level.

The Friedman Test

The Friedman test is requested with the FRIEDMAN subcommand, which has the format

```
NPAR TESTS FRIEDMAN=varlist
```

For example, the command

```
NPAR TESTS FRIEDMAN=P2DIGIT P3DIGIT P4DIGIT.
```

produces the output in Figure 22.8.

The output for Friedman shows the mean rank for each variable and a chi-square statistic with its degrees of freedom and its observed significance level.

Kendall's Coefficient of Concordance

The KENDALL subcommand requests Kendall's W and has the format

```
NPAR TESTS KENDALL=varlist
```

This test assumes that each case is a judge or rater. If you want to treat your variables as judges, you must transpose your data.

The output includes the number of cases, Kendall's W, and a chi-square statistic with its degrees of freedom and observed significance level.

Tests for Two Independent Samples

NPAR TESTS performs five tests for two independent samples: the two-sample median test, the Mann-Whitney U test, the Kolmogorov-Smirnov two-sample test, the Wald-Wolfowitz runs test, and the Moses test of extreme reactions. The general format for requesting these tests is

```
NPAR TESTS testname=varlist BY variable(value1,value2)
```

The variable specified after BY is used to group the cases. All cases with *value1* are in the first group and all cases with *value2* are in the second group.

The Two-Sample Median Test

The MEDIAN subcommand requests the two-sample median test. Its format is

```
NPAR TESTS MEDIAN [(value)]=varlist BY variable(value1,value2)
```

The value in parentheses after MEDIAN is the median to be used for the test. If a value is not specified, the sample median is used. The two values in parentheses following the variable named after BY specify the categories for the grouping variable. A two-sample median test is performed if the first value is greater than the second or if the second value equals the first value plus 1. If the second value is more than the first value plus 1, a k sample median test is performed (see "The k-Sample Median Test" on p. 383). For example, the command

```
NPAR TESTS MEDIAN=SODIUM BY RATING(3,1).
```

produces the output in Figure 22.9. The first group has value 3 for rating and the second has value 1.

The output shows a 2×2 table of cases greater than and less than or equal to the median, and the observed significance level. When the number of cases is more than 30, a chi-square statistic is displayed. When the number of cases is 30 or fewer, Fisher's exact test (one-tailed) is computed.

The Mann-Whitney *U* Test

The M-W subcommand requests the Mann-Whitney test and has the format

```
NPAR TESTS M-W=varlist BY variable(value1,value2)
```

For example, the command

```
NPAR TESTS M-W=TUMOR BY DIET(0,1).
```

produces the output in Figure 22.1.

The output produced by M-W includes the mean rank for each group, the Mann-Whitney U statistic, and the Wilcoxon W. For samples with fewer than 30 cases, the exact observed significance level (calculated using the algorithm of Dineen and Blakely, 1973) is displayed. For larger samples, a Z statistic with its (approximate) observed significance level is displayed.

The Kolmogorov-Smirnov Two-Sample Test

The K-S subcommand requests the Kolmogorov-Smirnov two-sample test and has the format

```
NPAR TESTS K-S=varlist BY variable(value1,value2)
```

For example, the command

```
NPAR TESTS K-S=ALCOHOL BY RATING(3,1).
```

produces the output in Figure 22.11.

The output shows the number of cases in each group, the most extreme positive, negative, and absolute differences, and the Kolmogorov-Smirnov Z with its observed significance level.

The Wald-Wolfowitz Test

The Wald-Wolfowitz runs test is obtained with the W-W subcommand, which has the format

```
NPAR TESTS W-W=varlist BY variable(value1,value2)
```

For example, the command

```
NPAR TESTS W-W=CALORIES BY RATING(3,1).
```

produces the output in Figure 22.10.

The output includes the number of cases in each group, the exact number of runs if there are no ties, and the observed significance level. If the sample size is 30 or fewer, the exact one-tailed observed significance level is calculated. Otherwise, a normal approximation is used to calculate the observed significance level.

The Moses Test of Extreme Reactions

The MOSES subcommand requests the Moses test of extreme reactions and has the format

```
NPAR TESTS MOSES[(n)]=varlist BY variable(value1,value2)
```

where n is the number of cases to be excluded from each end of the sorted data. This data trimming is sometimes needed to eliminate distortion due to outliers. If n is not specified, 5% of the cases are trimmed from each end of the range of the control group. Cases with the first value specified for the grouping variable are in the control group.

The output shows the number of cases in each group, the span of the control group with its observed significance level when all cases are included, and the span of the control group with its significance level after outliers have been removed.

Tests for *k* Independent Samples

Two tests for *k* samples are available: the *k*-sample median test and the Kruskal-Wallis one-way analysis of variance. The general format for requesting these tests is

```
NPAR TESTS testname=varlist BY variable(value1,value2)
```

The variable following keyword BY splits the cases into *k* groups, where *value1* and *value2* are the minimum and maximum values used to define groups. For example, the command

```
NPAR TESTS MEDIAN=POLRANK BY RACE(1,3).
```

groups the data into three categories corresponding to values 1, 2, and 3 for *RACE*.

The *k*-Sample Median Test

The *k*-sample median test is requested with the MEDIAN subcommand. The format is

```
NPAR TESTS MEDIAN [(value)] BY variable(value1,value2)
```

The value in parentheses after MEDIAN is the median to be used for the test. If no value is specified, the sample median is used. For a *k*-sample median test, *value2* must equal at least *value1* plus 2. For example, the command

```
NPAR TESTS MEDIAN=SOCATT BY RACE(1,3).
```

requests a three-sample median test for the groups defined by values 1, 2, and 3 for *RACE*. The command

```
NPAR TESTS MEDIAN=SOCATT BY RACE(3,1).
```

requests a two-sample median test for the groups defined by values 1 and 3 for *RACE*. The command

```
NPAR TESTS MEDIAN = PRICE BY RATING(1,3).
```

produces the output in Figure 22.12.

The output for the median test includes a 2×*k* table and the chi-square test with its degrees of freedom and observed significance level.

The Kruskal-Wallis One-Way Analysis of Variance

The K-W subcommand requests the Kruskal-Wallis test and has the format

```
NPAR TESTS K-W=varlist BY variable(value1,value2)
```

If the first grouping value is less than the second, every value in the range *value1* to *value2* defines a group. If the first value is greater than the second, two groups are formed, using the two values. For example, the output in Figure 22.13 was obtained with the command

```
NPAR TESTS K-W=TUMOR BY DIET(0,2).
```

The output includes the mean rank for each group, the number of cases in each group, the chi-square statistic with its observed significance level uncorrected for ties, and the chi-square statistic with its observed significance level corrected for ties.

Optional Statistics

You can obtain additional summary statistics for all variables specified on the NPAR TESTS command by specifying Statistics 1 or 2 on the STATISTICS subcommand. All cases with valid values for a variable are used to calculate the statistics for that variable. The following statistics are available:

Statistic 1   *Univariate statistics.* The mean, maximum, minimum, standard deviation, and count are displayed for each variable.

Statistic 2   *Quartiles and count.* The values corresponding to the 25th, 50th, and 75th percentiles are displayed for each variable.

Missing Values

By default, cases with missing values for any of the variables used in a particular test are excluded from calculations for that test only. You can request two alternative missing-value treatments with the OPTIONS subcommand.

Option 1   *Include cases with user-missing values.* Cases with user-missing values are included in all tests requested on the command.

Option 2   *Exclude cases with missing values listwise.* Cases with missing values for any variable named on any subcommand are excluded from all analyses.

Subsampling

Since many of the NPAR TESTS procedures are based on ranks, cases must be stored in memory. If you do not have enough computer memory to store all the cases, you will need to use Option 4 on the OPTIONS subcommand to select a random sample of cases for analysis.

Option 4   *Random sampling if there is insufficient memory.* This option is ignored when the RUNS subcommand is used.

23 Establishing Order: Procedure RANK

Ranks are sometimes the most natural way to collect data. Market researchers ask us to rank products from least favorite to most favorite; sportscasters give us their lists of the top twenty basketball or football teams. Ranks are also useful for interpreting measurements when we have reason to suspect that the underlying scale is not really interval. Registrars often convert grade-point averages to class ranks, perhaps suspecting that grades aren't really measured on a consistent interval scale. Similarly, when you have reason to suspect that your data are not measured on a nice interval scale or do not have the kind of distribution required for many statistical techniques, you might choose to analyze them using a nonparametric procedure that requires very limited assumptions about the underlying distribution. Many nonparametric procedures replace data values with ranks.

Computing Ranks

The basic idea of rank assignment is straightforward. Data values are ordered and then assign sequential integers, from 1 to the number of cases, to the ordered values. If the data values are sorted from smallest to largest—that is, the data are in ascending order—the smallest value receives the rank of 1. If the data are sorted in descending order, from largest to smallest, the largest value receives a rank of 1.

Difficulties with the assignment of ranks occur when there are tied values. For example, if the data values are 10, 10, 11, and 20, several different schemes can be used to assign ranks to the tied values of 10. The most frequently used method assigns the average of the ranks for which they are tied. If ranks are assigned based on ascending data values, the two cases with values of 10 are tied for ranks 1 and 2 and are assigned a rank of (1+2)/2, or 1.5. If there were three values of 10, each would receive a rank of (1+2+3)/3, or 2.

The RANK procedure offers several other options for treating ties. For example, in Figure 23.1, class ranks are assigned in descending order (the highest grade-point average receives rank 1). Students tied with the same grade-point average received the lower of the two ranks. Thus, the two students tied for second both receive rank 2.

Figure 23.1   Class ranks using descending order and low scores for ties

```
DATA LIST / NAME 1-24 (A) GPA 26-28 (2).
BEGIN DATA.
Mark Anderson            325
Andrew Brown             400
Yvonne Hirschfield       275
Harold Thompson          400
Sally Wilson             425
END DATA.
RANK GPA (D) /TIES=LOW.
SORT CASES BY RGPA.
LIST.


NAME                    GPA      RGPA

Sally Wilson            4.25     1.000
Andrew Brown            4.00     2.000
Harold Thompson         4.00     2.000
Mark Anderson           3.25     4.000
Yvonne Hirschfield      2.75     5.000
```

Ordering the Data into Categories

Cases can be assigned into several distinct groups based on their ranks. For example, they can be subdivided into quartiles, or four groups of approximately equal size based on the values of their ranks. You can subdivide the cases into as many groups as you like using the RANK procedure.

Figure 23.2 shows average weights of the men in the Western Electric Study (see Chapter 13) when they are grouped into quartiles based on their diastolic blood pressure. (Quartiles are determined by the RANK procedure and saved in the variable *NDBP58*, which is then used as the BY variable in the MEANS procedure.) You can see that the average weights increase across the quartiles. The four groups are not exactly the same size since there are many tied values for diastolic blood pressure (see the stem-and-leaf plots in Chapter 13). All tied values are assigned to the same quartile group.

Figure 23.2   Mean weight of subjects within quartiles

```
GET FILE='ELECTRIC.SYS'.
RANK VARIABLES=DBP58 /NTILES(4).
VALUE LABELS NDBP58 1 'First quartile of dbp58'
    2 'Second quartile' 3 'Third quartile' 4 'Fourth quartile'.
MEANS WT58 BY NDBP58.


Summaries of    WT58       BODY WEIGHT, 1958 -- LBS
By levels of    NDBP58     NTILES of DBP58


Variable       Value  Label              Mean      Std Dev   Cases

For Entire Population                     173.4812  24.7644    239

NDBP58           1  First quartile of db  167.0962  22.2994     52
NDBP58           2  Second quartile       171.8525  24.0720     61
NDBP58           3  Third quartile        176.4697  25.9847     66
NDBP58           4  Fourth quartile       177.3833  25.4313     60

   Total Cases =      240
Missing Cases =        1 OR    .4 PCT.
```

Programming Statistical Tests Based on Ranks

The SPSS/PC+ NPAR TESTS procedure contains most of the commonly used nonparametric tests. However, you may want to use a test that is not yet available in NPAR TESTS. Using the RANK procedure and some other simple SPSS/PC+ procedures, you should be able to implement most nonparametric tests.

Conover's Test for Equality of Variance

Conover (1980) describes a nonparametric test for the hypothesis that two samples come from populations with equal variance. He describes a food packaging company that wants to compare two methods for packaging cereal. Table 23.1 contains data for the two methods, designated as "present" and "new."

Table 23.1   Conover cereal packaging data

Amount in box	
Present	New
10.8	10.8
11.1	10.5
10.4	11.0
10.1	10.9
11.3	10.8
	10.7
	10.8
10.74	**10.79**

The test statistic for evaluating the null hypothesis of equal variances is

$$T = \frac{T_1 - n\bar{R}^2}{\sqrt{\dfrac{nm}{N(N-1)} \sum R_i^4 - \dfrac{nm}{(N-1)} (\bar{R}^2)^2}}$$

Equation 23.1

where T_1 is the sum of squared ranks for the smaller group, and n and m are the group sizes. In this test the ranks are based not on the original data but on the absolute value of the deviation from the group mean. To calculate the test statistic, we enter the data as two variables, one containing the measurements of amounts of cereal in the box and the other indicating the group for each measurement. A preliminary run of the MEANS procedure provides the means for each group. We then compute the absolute values of the differences from the group means, rank them, square the ranks and raise them to the fourth power. Descriptive statistics from the MEANS procedure for the new variables provide the information needed to compute the test statistic (see Figure 23.3).

From the numbers in Figure 23.3, we calculate:

$$T = \frac{462 - 5\,(54)}{\sqrt{\dfrac{5 \times 7}{12 \times 11} \times 60,660 - \dfrac{5 \times 7}{11} \times (54)^2}} = 2.3273 \qquad \text{Equation 23.2}$$

The observed significance level is obtained from tables available in Conover (1980). In this case, the observed significance level is less than 0.05, so we reject the null hypothesis that both methods have equal variability.

Figure 23.3   Calculating numbers for equality of variance test

```
IF (GROUP EQ 1) ABSDIF=ABS(AMOUNT-10.74).
IF (GROUP EQ 2) ABSDIF=ABS(AMOUNT-10.79).
RANK ABSDIF/RANK INTO R.
COMPUTE R2=R**2.
COMPUTE R4=R**4.
VARIABLE LABELS R2 'Squared ranks' r4 'Ranks to the fourth power'.
MEANS R2 R4 BY GROUP / OPTIONS 6 7.


Summaries of    R2          Squared ranks
By levels of    GROUP

Variable        Value  Label                  Sum        Mean      Cases

For Entire Population                       648.0000   54.0000      12

GROUP           1.00                        462.0000   92.4000       5
GROUP           2.00                        186.0000   26.5714       7

   Total Cases =       12



Summaries of    R4          Ranks to the fourth power
By levels of    GROUP

Variable        Value  Label                  Sum        Mean      Cases

For Entire Population                     60660.0000  5055.0000     12

GROUP           1.00                      52194.0000 10438.8000      5
GROUP           2.00                       8466.0000  1209.4286      7

   Total Cases =       12
```

Spearman Correlation Coefficient

The RANK procedure can also be used to calculate the Spearman rank correlation coefficient, a nonparametric correlation coefficient based on ranks. In fact, Spearman is just the usual Pearson correlation coefficient applied to ranks. For example, to calculate the Spearman correlation coefficient between diastolic blood pressure and weight in the Western Electric men, you can use the RANK procedure to rank the two variables and then calculate a correlation coefficient for the ranks (Figure 23.4).

Figure 23.4   Calculating the Spearman correlation coefficient

```
GET FILE='ELECTRIC.SYS'.
RANK VARIABLES=DBP58 WT58/RANK.
CORRELATION VARIABLES=RDBP58 RWT58 /OPTION 5.

Correlations:  RDBP58      RWT58

  RDBP58       1.0000       .1776
              (   36)      (   36)
               P=  .        P= .300

  RWT58         .1776      1.0000
              (   36)      (   36)
               P= .300      P=  .


(Coefficient / (Cases) / 2-tailed Significance)
" . " is printed if a coefficient cannot be computed
```

Normal Scores in Statistical Tests

When analyzing ranks, we ignore the actual distance between observations. For example, the values 1, 3, 9, and 10 or the values 1, 2, 70, and 100 are assigned the same set of ranks. Only the order of observations matters; the distance between them does not. There is a class of statistical tests that attempts to replace the ranks with other numbers that more closely resemble the observations from a particular distribution. For example, if you have five observations, instead of analyzing the ranks from 1 to 5, you can replace the ranks by quantiles from a particular distribution, usually the normal. That is, you find the five numbers that divide the area of a normal distribution into six equal parts and then analyze them. In this example, you would analyze the scores −0.9674, −0.4307, 0.0, 0.4307, and 0.9674. If you analyze the normal scores instead of the ranks, the resulting statistical tests will have, under certain conditions, somewhat better statistical properties, even if the population from which the sample is obtained is not normal.

The van der Waerden Test for Several Independent Samples

To see how normal scores can be used to test the null hypothesis that all population distributions are identical, consider the van der Waerden test for several independent samples. The test statistic is:

$$T = \frac{\sum n_i \overline{A}^2_i}{S^2}$$

Equation 23.3

where n_i is the number of cases in group i, $\overline{A}_i$ is the average normal score in group i, and S^2 is the variance of all of the normal scores. This statistic is computed by first computing the average score in each group, squaring these averages, multiplying them by the sample size in each group, and then summing them across all groups. Finally, this sum is divided by the variance of the scores.

Conover (1980) presents data for comparing four methods of growing corn. The SPSS/PC+ commands to calculate the van der Waerden test for the hypothesis that the four populations from which the samples were taken are identical are:

```
DATA LIST FREE/ GROUP YIELD.
BEGIN DATA.
1 83 1 91 1 94 1 89 1 89 1 96 1 91 1 92 1 90
2 91 2 90 2 81 2 83 2 84 2 83 2 88 2 91 2 89 2 84
3 101 3 100 3 91 3 93 3 96 3 95 3 94
4 78 4 82 4 81 4 77 4 79 4 81 4 80 4 81
END DATA.
FORMATS YIELD GROUP(F3.0).
RANK YIELD /RANK /NORMAL INTO VWSCORE /FRACTION VW.
LIST.
DESCRIPTIVES VARIABLES=VWSCORE /STATISTICS=6.
AGGREGATE OUTFILE=*/BREAK=GROUP
  /MEAN=MEAN(VWSCORE) /COUNT=N(VWSCORE).
COMPUTE PRODUCT=MEAN**2 * COUNT.
DESCRIPTIVES VARIABLES=PRODUCT /STATISTICS=12.
```

Figure 23.5 is the output from the LIST procedure, showing the data, the ranks, and the normal scores for all four methods. Figure 23.6 contains portions of the output from the two DESCRIPTIVES commands. The first gives the variance for all cases; the second gives the sum of the squared means multiplied by the sample sizes. Dividing that sum by the variance yields the test statistic:

$21.31 / 0.846 = 25.19$

The significance level is based on the chi-square distribution with degrees of freedom equal to one less than the number of groups. The observed significance level is less than 0.001, so the null hypothesis is rejected.

Figure 23.5   Data, ranks, and normal scores for Conover data

```
GROUP YIELD     RYIELD VWSCORE

  1     83      11.000  -.4837
  1     91      23.000   .4047
  1     94      28.500   .8938
  1     89      17.000  -.0358
  1     89      17.000  -.0358
  1     96      31.500  1.2816
  1     91      23.000   .4047
  1     92      26.000   .6522
  1     90      19.500   .1437
  2     91      23.000   .4047
  2     90      19.500   .1437
  2     81       6.500  -.8938
  2     83      11.000  -.4837
  2     84      13.500  -.2905
  2     83      11.000  -.4837
  2     88      15.000  -.1800
  2     91      23.000   .4047
  2     89      17.000  -.0358
  2     84      13.500  -.2905
  3    101      34.000  1.9022
  3    100      33.000  1.5792
  3     91      23.000   .4047
  3     93      27.000   .7436
  3     96      31.500  1.2816
  3     95      30.000  1.0676
  3     94      28.500   .8938
  4     78       2.000 -1.579
  4     82       9.000  -.6522
  4     81       6.500  -.8938
  4     77       1.000 -1.902
  4     79       3.000 -1.368
  4     81       6.500  -.8938
  4     80       4.000 -1.204
  4     81       6.500  -.8938
```

Figure 23.6   Output from DESCRIPTIVES

```
Variable     Variance Valid N   Label

VWSCORE          .85      34    NORMAL of YIELD using VW


Variable          Sum Valid N   Label

PRODUCT        21.31       4
```

Graphical Tests of Normality

Normal scores can also be used to examine the hypothesis that data come from a normal distribution. We can generate normal scores for each case based on its rank and then plot the observed values against the normal scores. If the underlying distribution is normal, the points should cluster around a straight line. Figure 23.7 is a plot of the observed diastolic blood pressures for the Western Electric men against the normal scores. (This example uses normal scores proposed by Blom, which result in scores that are somewhat closer to the exact expected values for the order statistics than the normal scores proposed by van der Waerden.) From this plot, we see that our observed distribution differs somewhat from normal. Similar normal probability plots can also be obtained with the EXAMINE procedure (see Chapter 13).

Figure 23.7   Normal probability plot

```
GET FILE='ELECTRIC.SYS'.
RANK VARIABLES=DBP58 /NORMAL INTO NORMAL.
PLOT PLOT=NORMAL WITH DBP58.
```

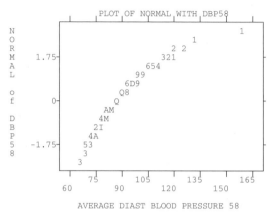

239 cases plotted.

Scores for an Exponential Distribution

If you have reason to believe that the data are a sample from an exponential distribution, you can compute scores based on the exponential distribution instead of normal scores. These scores are sometimes called Savage scores. (The length of time between consecutive events, when the events occur randomly in time, follows an exponential distribution.) To see whether a sample of data might originate from an exponential distribution, you can plot Savage scores against the observed values. Again, if the data are from an exponential distribution, the points should cluster around a straight line. Figure 23.8 is a plot of data values that appear to come from an exponential distribution.

Figure 23.8   Savage scores (Problem 5 from Conover, p. 367)

```
DATA LIST FREE/DISTANCE.
BEGIN DATA.
0.3 6.1 4.3 3.3 1.9 4.8 .3 1.2 .8 10.3 1.2 .1 10 1.6 27.6
12 14.2 19.7 15.5
END DATA.
RANK VARIABLES=DISTANCE /SAVAGE INTO SAVDIST.
PLOT PLOT=SAVDIST WITH DISTANCE.
```

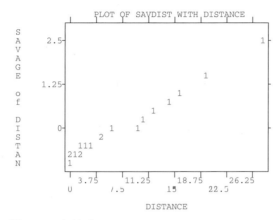

19 cases plotted.

Running Procedure RANK

RANK computes ranks, normal and Savage scores, and related statistics. It can also be used to classify cases into groups based on percentile values. Ranks, scores, and group memberships are saved as variables in the active file. The procedure does not require that the file be sorted.

Specifying the Variables

Variables for which ranks are to be computed are specified after the VARIABLES subcommand. For example,

```
RANK VARIABLES=INCOME.
```

creates a new variable, *RINCOME*, which contains ranks based on ascending values of *INCOME*. (Ascending order means that a rank of 1 goes to the case with the smallest value and a rank of *n*, where *n* is the number of cases, goes to the case with the largest value.)

To assign ranks in descending order, so that the case with the largest value is assigned a rank of 1, specify D in parentheses after the variable name. The command

```
RANK VARIABLES=INCOME(D).
```

assigns ranks based on descending values of the variable.

Specifying Groups

To classify cases into groups based on values of a factor variable and then rank cases within each group, specify the grouping variable following keyword BY. For example,

```
RANK VARIABLES=INCOME BY JOBCAT.
```

ranks the cases separately for each of the values of *JOBCAT*.

Treatment of Ties

By default, cases with the same values for a variable are assigned the average of the ranks for the tied values. The following optional treatments for ties can be specified on the TIES subcommand:

MEAN   *Assign the average rank to tied values.* This is the default.

LOW   *Assign the lowest rank assigned to tied values.*

HIGH   *Assign the highest rank assigned to tied values.*

CONDENSE   *Rank only distinct values of the variable.* Ranks are assigned from 1 to *D*, where *D* is the number of distinct values. Cases with the same value receive the same rank.

To understand these methods, consider a data set or six cases, with values 10, 15, 15, 15, 16, and 20. Table 23.2 shows the ranks assigned to the cases for each method.

Table 23.2   Options for handling ties in ranks

Case	Value	MEAN	LOW	HIGH	CONDENSE
1	10	1	1	1	1
2	15	3	2	4	2
3	15	3	2	4	2
4	15	3	2	4	2
5	16	5	5	5	3
6	20	6	6	6	4

For example, to rank values in descending order and assign the lowest rank to ties, specify:

```
RANK VARIABLES=INCOME(D)/TIES=LOW.
```

Computing Other Statistics

By default, the RANK procedure computes ranks for each variable listed on the VARIABLES subcommand. Other functions are also available. Each of the following keywords can be specified once:

RANK   *Assign ranks.*

RFRACTION *Divide each rank by the number of cases with valid values.* If the WEIGHT command is used, ranks are divided by the sum of weights.

PERCENT   *Divide each rank by the number of cases with valid values and multiply by 100.*

N   *Sum of case weights.* The value of the variable is a constant for all cases in the same group.

NTILES(n) *Percentile groups.* The new variable contains values from 1 to k, where k is the number of groups to be generated. Each case is assigned a group value, which is the integer part of $1+rk/(W+1)$, where r is the rank of the case, k is the number of groups specified on NTILES, and W is the sum of the case weights. Group values can be affected by the specification on TIES. There is no default for k.

PROPORTION *Proportion estimates.* The estimation method is specified by the FRACTION subcommand (see "Estimating the Cumulative Proportion" on p. 396). The default for FRACTION is BLOM.

NORMAL   *Normal scores* (Lehmann, 1975). The new variable contains the inverse of the standard normal cumulative distribution of the proportion estimate defined by the FRACTION subcommand (see "Estimating the Cumulative Proportion" on p. 396). The default for FRACTION is BLOM.

SAVAGE   *Scores based on an exponential distribution.*

Assigning Names to RANK Variables

By default, new variable names are created by adding the first letter of the function name to the first seven characters of the variable name. For example, the name *RINCOME* is used for the ranks and the name *NINCOME* for the normal scores of *INCOME*. If you are using several functions that start with the same letter (for example, PERCENT and PROPORTION), the first new variable is created by adding the first letter of the function to the variable name. Subsequent variables are named *XXXnnn*, where *XXX* is the first three letters of the function name and *nnn* is a sequence number assigned to the variable. For example, if PERCENT is specified first, the name *PINCOME* is assigned to the percent function and the name *PRO001* to the proportion function. If this naming scheme generates duplicate names, the duplicates are named *RNKXXnn*, where *XX* is the first two characters of the function and *nn* is a two-digit number starting with 01 and increased by 1 for each variable. Descriptive labels are assigned to each new variable, so it is easy to see what the resulting names are.

To assign your own variable names, use keyword INTO after each function. For example,

```
RANK VARIABLES=INCOME/RANK INTO RANKINC.
```

assigns the name *RANKINC* to the ranks of *INCOME*. Similarly,

```
RANK VARIABLES=INCOME/RANK INTO RANKINC/NORMAL INTO NORMINC.
```

also assigns the name *NORMINC* to the normal scores for *INCOME*.

Estimating the Cumulative Proportion

The functions NORMAL and PROPORTION require an estimate of the cumulative proportion corresponding to each rank. Four methods are available for estimating this cumulative proportion: BLOM, RANKIT, TUKEY, and VW. The default is BLOM. For a description of these methods, see RANK in the Syntax Reference.

Summary Table

By default, a summary table describing the newly created variables is displayed. Use the PRINT subcommand with the keyword NO to suppress this table.

Missing Values

By default, a case with a system-missing or user-missing value is assigned a rank of system-missing. To treat user-missing values as valid values, use the INCLUDE keyword on the MISSING subcommand. For example,

```
RANK VARIABLES=INCOME/MISSING=INCLUDE.
```

treats user-missing values as valid values. System-missing values are still assigned system-missing values for any variable created by the RANK procedure.

24 Reporting Results: Procedure REPORT

Case listings and descriptive statistics are basic tools for studying and presenting data. You can obtain case listings with LIST, frequency counts and descriptive statistics with FREQUENCIES and DESCRIPTIVES, and subpopulation statistics with MEANS. Each of these procedures uses a format designed to make the information clear, but if that format isn't what you need for presentation, there is little you can do to change it. REPORT gives you the control you need over data presentation.

REPORT is a formatting tool. It allows you to present case listings and summary statistics (including frequencies) in report format. Your report can be one page long, or it can be hundreds of pages long. With REPORT subcommands and keywords, you can specify the variables you want to summarize or list and organize them into subgroups. You can calculate summary statistics for the report variables and also calculate cross-variable statistics that are unavailable in other procedures, such as the ratio of two means.

Basic Report Concepts

This section introduces you to the two basic elements of a report: its contents, and the organization of those contents. To illustrate these concepts (and others in this chapter), we'll use information from a retail company's personnel file. The file contains data such as employee name, salary, employment grade, length of time in grade, overall length of employment, store branch and department, shift, and so forth.

Report Contents: Summaries and Listings

Reports contain summary statistics calculated for groups of cases, listings of individual cases, or a combination of both statistics and listings.

Summary Reports

Summary reports display summary statistics but not case listings. The summary information consists of the statistic or statistics you request for the **report variables** for subgroups defined by the **break variables.** Each statistic is displayed in a separate row on the report, referred to as a *summary line*. The cells within the summary line display the statistical values. Figure 24.1 shows a summary report presenting the mean of each report variable for each value of the break variable.

Figure 24.1   Summary personnel report

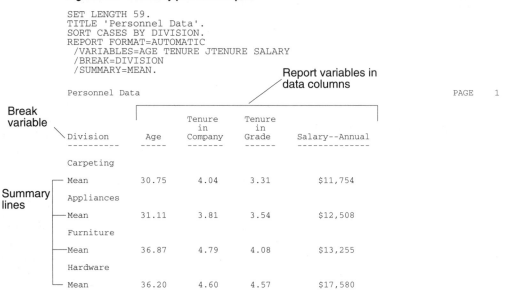

```
SET LENGTH 59.
TITLE 'Personnel Data'.
SORT CASES BY DIVISION.
REPORT FORMAT=AUTOMATIC
  /VARIABLES=AGE TENURE JTENURE SALARY
  /BREAK=DIVISION
  /SUMMARY=MEAN.
```

Report variables in
data columns

Personnel Data   PAGE   1

Break
variable

Division	Age	Tenure in Company	Tenure in Grade	Salary--Annual
Carpeting				
Mean	30.75	4.04	3.31	$11,754
Appliances				
Mean	31.11	3.81	3.54	$12,508
Furniture				
Mean	36.87	4.79	4.08	$13,255
Hardware				
Mean	36.20	4.60	4.57	$17,580

Summary
lines

Listing Reports

Listing reports list individual cases. The case listings can display the actual data values or the value labels defined for each of the report variables. The values for the report variables can be grouped according to the values of a break variables. Figure 24.2 presents a report that contains case listings for *AGE*, *TENURE*, *JTENURE*, *SALARY*, for subgroups defined by the break variable *DIVISION*.

Figure 24.2   Personnel report with case listings

```
SORT CASES BY DIVISION.
REPORT FORMAT=AUTOMATIC LIST
 /VARIABLES=AGE TENURE JTENURE SALARY
 /BREAK=DIVISION.
```

```
Personnel Data                                                  PAGE    1

                        Tenure     Tenure
                          in         in
Division       Age      Company     Grade     Salary--Annual
----------     -----    -------     ------     --------------

Carpeting      22.00     3.92        3.08        $10,900
               27.00     3.67        2.17         $9,200
               23.00     3.92        3.08        $10,900
               35.00     6.00        5.33        $19,500
               36.00     3.83        3.25        $10,000
               24.00     4.00        3.25        $10,000
               44.00     4.83        4.33        $15,690
               33.00     3.75        3.25        $10,000
               27.00     4.33        3.17        $10,000
               33.00     2.67        2.67         $9,335
               35.00     3.50        3.00        $15,520
               30.00     4.08        3.08        $10,000

Appliances     42.00     6.50        6.50        $18,000
               26.00     2.92        2.08         $8,000
               24.00     3.17        3.17         $8,975
               21.00     2.67        2.67         $8,700
               38.00     5.00        4.42        $28,300
               33.00     3.42        2.92         $8,900
               30.00     2.67        2.67         $7,500
               32.00     2.92        2.92         $8,900
               34.00     5.08        4.50        $15,300
```

Combined Reports

You can combine individual case listings and summary statistics in a single report, as in Figure 24.3.

Figure 24.3   Personnel report with case listings and summaries

```
SORT CASES BY DIVISION.
REPORT FORMAT=AUTOMATIC LIST
 /VARIABLES=AGE TENURE JTENURE SALARY
 /BREAK=DIVISION
 /SUMMARY=MEAN.
```

```
Personnel Data                                                          PAGE    1

                             Tenure       Tenure
                               in           in
           Division    Age   Company      Grade    Salary--Annual
           ----------  -----  -------      ------   --------------

           Carpeting  22.00    3.92        3.08       $10,900
                      27.00    3.67        2.17        $9,200
                      23.00    3.92        3.08       $10,900
                      35.00    6.00        5.33       $19,500
                      36.00    3.83        3.25       $10,000
                      24.00    4.00        3.25       $10,000
                      44.00    4.83        4.33       $15,690
                      33.00    3.75        3.25       $10,000
                      27.00    4.33        3.17       $10,000
                      33.00    2.67        2.67        $9,335
                      35.00    3.50        3.00       $15,520
                      30.00    4.08        3.08       $10,000

           Mean       30.75    4.04        3.31       $11,754

           Appliances 42.00    6.50        6.50       $18,000
                      26.00    2.92        2.08        $8,000
                      24.00    3.17        3.17        $8,975
                      21.00    2.67        2.67        $8,700
                      38.00    5.00        4.42       $28,300
                      33.00    3.42        2.92        $8,900
                      30.00    2.67        2.67        $7,500
                      32.00    2.92        2.92        $8,900
                      34.00    5.08        4.50       $15,300

           Mean       31.11    3.81        3.54       $12,508
```

Report Organization

A report is organized into columns and rows. Each column is defined by a variable. The columns on the left are the break variables (those whose values divide the report into subgroups). In Figure 24.1, Figure 24.2, and Figure 24.3, *DIVISION* is the break variable. The other columns, on the right, are the report variables (those whose values are listed or summarized). The order of the columns is the order in which you specify the variables.

The rows consist of case listings or summary statistics. The order of the rows is the order of the cases in the file. (See "Preparing Data for REPORT" on p. 405 for more information about the order of cases.)

Building the Report

Four basic subcommands determine the appearance of reports:

FORMAT   Determines the report's general layout and whether individual cases are listed. If it is specified, FORMAT precedes all other subcommands on the REPORT command.

VARIABLES   Specifies the *report variables* that are listed and/or summarized in columns in the report. The order in which you list variables on the VARIABLES subcommand determines the order in which columns appear on the report. The VARIABLES subcommand is required.

BREAK   Specifies the *break variables* that break the report rows into subgroups. Break variables always are displayed as the leftmost columns on the report.

SUMMARY   Names a statistic or set of statistics to be calculated.

The VARIABLES subcommand is required on every REPORT command. A listing report also requires the FORMAT subcommand with the LIST keyword, and a summary report requires the BREAK and SUMMARY subcommands.

Subcommands must be specified in the following order: FORMAT first, followed by VARIABLES, BREAK, and SUMMARY. You can specify multiple BREAK and SUMMARY subcommands.

REPORT has other subcommands, but the four above are the ones you'll use most often. They are described in more detail under "Refining the Report" on p. 406.

Choosing Formats and Obtaining Listings

Use the FORMAT subcommand to specify whether AUTOMATIC or MANUAL default formats are implemented. The AUTOMATIC keyword facilitates report design by implementing the basic format features you are most likely to use. MANUAL implements the defaults that were used in earlier versions of SPSS/PC+. MANUAL is the default. See REPORT in the Syntax Reference for a table that compares the default settings for AUTOMATIC and MANUAL.

The FORMAT subcommand also specifies whether a report contains summaries, listings, or both. Summaries are the default. To produce a listing report, as shown in Figure 24.2 and Figure 24.3, add keyword LIST to the FORMAT subcommand, as in:

```
REPORT FORMAT=AUTOMATIC LIST / VARIABLES=...
```

The keyword LIST applies to all variables named on the VARIABLES subcommand.

Specifying Report Variables

The required VARIABLES subcommand specifies the variables that appear in the report columns. The minimum VARIABLES specification is a list of variables. For example,

```
/VARIABLES=LNAME AGE TENURE JTENURE
```

instructs REPORT to list or summarize data for the variables *LNAME*, *AGE*, *TENURE*, and *JTENURE*.

Defining Break Groups

The BREAK subcommand specifies the variable whose values break the report rows into subgroups. For example, the REPORT subcommand

```
/BREAK=DIVISION
```

specifies a subgroup for each value of *DIVISION*.

The BREAK subcommand is required for all summary reports but is optional for listing reports. If you do not want to break a listing report into subgroups, omit the BREAK subcommand.

The REPORT command does not sort data. You must first use the SORT command to organize cases into the break groups you intend to specify on the BREAK subcommand (see "Preparing Data for REPORT" on p. 405).

Requesting Summary Statistics

To request statistics for subgroups of cases for either a summary or listing report, specify the statistic on a SUMMARY subcommand immediately after a BREAK subcommand. You cannot use a SUMMARY subcommand without a corresponding BREAK subcommand, and the BREAK subcommand must precede its associated SUMMARY subcommands. For example, the commands

```
SORT CASES BY DIVISION.
REPORT FORMAT=AUTOMATIC
       /VARS=AGE TENURE JTENURE SALARY
       /BREAK=DIVISION
       /SUMMARY=MEAN.
```

request the mean values for *AGE*, *TENURE*, *JTENURE*, and *SALARY* for each value of variable *DIVISION*, as shown in Figure 24.1.

To add more summaries, simply add more SUMMARY subcommands. For example, the following commands request the minimum and maximum values in addition to the means for variables *AGE*, *TENURE*, *JTENURE*, and *SALARY:*

```
SORT CASES BY DIVISION.
REPORT FORMAT=AUTOMATIC
        /VARS=AGE TENURE JTENURE SALARY
        /BREAK=DIVISION
        /SUMMARY=MEAN
        /SUMMARY=MIN
        /SUMMARY=MAX.
```

Each summary appears on its own line on the report. For a list of the summary statistics available in REPORT, see REPORT in the Syntax Reference.

Adding Break Levels

To subdivide the data into multiple break levels, adding break columns on the left of the report, specify multiple BREAK subcommands. Successive BREAK subcommands group the data within preceding BREAK subcommands. Before specifying a report with multiple break levels, use SORT CASES to sort the break variables into the order you intend to use them (see "Preparing Data for REPORT" on p. 405). Then specify successive BREAK subcommands.

When you specify a SUMMARY subcommand, REPORT calculates the statistic you request for the specified break level only. If you want the same statistic for multiple break levels, you must request it at each desired level, as in:

```
SORT CASES BY DIVISION STORE.
REPORT FORMAT=AUTOMATIC
        /VARS=AGE TENURE SALARY
        /BREAK=DIVISION
        /SUMMARY=MEAN
        /SUMMARY=VALIDN
        /BREAK=STORE
        /SUMMARY=MEAN.
```

Figure 24.4 shows a portion of the report. The *DIVISION* and *STORE* columns are defined by the break variables. Both means and the number of valid cases are shown for each division. Only the means are shown for each level of store branch within a division.

Figure 24.4   Personnel report with multiple breaks

```
Personnel Data                                                      PAGE    1

                                    Tenure
               Branch                 in
Division       Store        Age     Company    Salary--Annual
----------     --------     -----   -------    --------------

Carpeting      Suburban

               Mean         26.75    4.37        $12,625

               Downtown

               Mean         32.75    3.87        $11,318
Mean                        30.75    4.04        $11,754
N                              12      12              12
```

For a shorthand way of repeating summary specifications, see p. 421. If you don't want any summary statistics at a given break level, omit the SUMMARY subcommand at that level.

Breaks Defined by More than One Variable

To combine break groups in a single column, list multiple variables on the same BREAK subcommand. For example, the commands

```
SORT CASES BY DIVISION SHIFT.
REPORT FORMAT=AUTOMATIC
       /VARS=AGE TENURE SALARY
       /BREAK=DIVISION SHIFT 'Division' 'and' 'Shift'
       /SUMMARY=MEAN.
```

combine break variables *DIVISION* and *SHIFT* in the same column. By default, the heading is the first variable specified on the BREAK subcommand. A different heading can be specified in apostrophes (see "Column Headings" on p. 409).

As shown in Figure 24.5, REPORT displays the value labels of both break variables (*DIVISION* and *SHIFT*) in the same column, with the specified column heading, and calculates the mean for the report variables (*AGE, TENURE,* and *SALARY*) any time the value of any break variable changes. (Only two divisions are shown in Figure 24.5.) Note that REPORT does not calculate overall means for each division. To obtain means by division, specify *DIVISION* and *SHIFT* on separate BREAK subcommands (see "Adding Break Levels" on p. 403).

Figure 24.5   Report with stacked break variables

```
Personnel Data                                                    PAGE    1

Division             Tenure
and                    in
Shift          Age   Company   Salary--Annual
----------    -----  -------   --------------

Carpeting
First

Mean          30.57   3.80        $11,649

Carpeting
Second

Mean          24.00   4.00        $10,000

Carpeting
Weekend

Mean          32.75   4.48        $12,375

Appliances
First

Mean          31.17   3.75        $13,062

Appliances
Second

Mean          42.00   6.50        $18,000

Appliances
Weekend

Mean          25.50   2.67         $8,100
```

Preparing Data for REPORT

REPORT does not sort data as it reads the cases and computes the summaries. Instead, it simply reads cases in the order they reside in the file, listing them (if you request a listing) while keeping track of information requested for summaries.

For example, when REPORT calculates a statistic, it calculates it for the subgroup defined by the first value of the break variable. When the value of the break variable changes in the data, REPORT calculates and displays the statistics requested. It then displays the next value of the break variable and resumes reading cases until the value of the break variable changes again. It displays the requested summary statistics every time it reads a change in the value for the break variable.

Therefore, before you run REPORT, the data must be organized so that all cases with the same value for the break variable reside together. It doesn't matter if the values are in ascending, descending, or some other order—only that all the cases in the same group are together.

To organize data in the file, use the SORT command immediately before the REPORT command. For example, the command

```
SORT BY DIVISION.
```

organizes the data in Figure 24.1 by the subgroups Carpeting, Appliances, Furniture, and Hardware. To further subdivide the groups according to the values of other variables, name additional variables on the SORT command. For example, the command

```
SORT BY DIVISION STORE.
```

groups the data into Carpeting, Appliances, Furniture, and Hardware, and within each division according to the values of variable STORE, which are Suburban and Downtown.

Trial Runs

Because REPORT is so flexible and its output can have so many components, you may want to experiment with the layout before you run the final report. If you have a large data file, you can use a subset of the data until you obtain the desired format. To process a subset of the data, use one of the following techniques:

- Use the N command to limit the number of cases read to the first n cases. For example, if the file contains 10,000 cases and you specify 10 on the N command, REPORT reads only the first 10 cases.

- If the REPORT contains break variables and the labeling and spacing of breaks are important considerations, you can obtain a random sample of the entire file using the SAMPLE command.

Refining the Report

REPORT gives you the ability to refine various report components, including:

- Titles and footnotes.
- Margins and alignment.
- Column contents and labeling.
- Horizontal spacing.
- Summary statistics.
- String variables.
- Missing values.

These topics are discussed in the following sections.

Adding Titles and Footnotes

The optional TITLE and FOOTNOTE subcommands enable you to place titles and footnotes on each page of a report. Titles can be centered, left-justified, or right-justified.

Enclose each line of the title or footnote in apostrophes, separating lines by a comma or a space. To include an apostrophe in a title, use double apostrophes without an intervening space or enclose the string in quotation marks. For example,

```
SORT CASES BY DIVISION.
REPORT FORMAT=AUTOMATIC LIST
        /VARS=LNAME AGE TENURE SALARY
        /BREAK=DIVISION
        /SUMMARY=MEAN
        /TITLE= 'Personnel Report' "Employees' Profile".
```

specifies a two-line title. *Personnel Report* is displayed on the first title line, and *Employee's Profile* is displayed beneath it on the second line. The quotation marks enclosing the second line are used so that an apostrophe can be specified in the title.

If you don't specify a title, SPSS/PC+ uses its system title as long as there is enough room to display it. To specify a blank title line, type a space between apostrophes. There is no default footnote.

Use the following specifications to left-justify, right-justify, or center either titles or footnotes:

```
/TITLE=
    LEFT     'title'
    RIGHT    'title'
    CENTER   'title'

/FOOTNOTE=
    LEFT     'note'
    RIGHT    'note'
    CENTER   'note'
```

By default, titles and footnotes are centered. However, you must explicitly specify CENTER to center a title if you also specify LEFT or RIGHT on a subcommand. To specify multiple title and footnote lines in any given position, specify the positional keyword once followed by each line in apostrophes; do not repeat the positional keywords. For example,

```
/TITLE=LEFT  'Personnel Report' 'As of January 1, 1987'
       RIGHT 'ACME Products' '2201 LaSalle Park'
             'Chicago, Illinois 60611'
```

produces a two-line left title and a three-line right title. Note that LEFT, RIGHT, and CENTER are not separated by slashes.

Titles and footnotes are displayed on each page of a multiple-page report. The LEFT, RIGHT, and CENTER alignments are relative to the report's margins. If you specify a title or footnote that is wider than the report width, REPORT generates an error message.

You can specify titles and footnotes anywhere after the FORMAT subcommand (except between BREAK and SUMMARY). All title subcommands must precede all footnote subcommands. There is no fixed limit on the number of title or footnote lines you can define for a report.

Three special arguments are available in titles and footnotes:

)PAGE   *Print the page number right-justified in a five-character field.*

)DATE   *Print the current date in the form* dd/mmm/yy *right-adjusted in a nine-character field.*

)variable   *Print this variable's value label.*

You can use all three arguments in as many titles and footnotes as you like on a single report. The following are typical examples:

```
/TITLE=LEFT  'Personnel Report' 'Prepared on )DATE'
      RIGHT 'Page )PAGE'
/FOOTNOTE=RIGHT 'Regional Manager: )MGRNM'
```

The left title includes the current date, and the right title includes the current page numbers. The footnote includes the value label for *MGRNM*.

Each variable you specify with)variable must be defined in the active file but does not need to be a variable included as a column in the report. If you specify a variable that has no value label, the value itself will display, formatted according to its print format. You cannot specify a system variable or a variable created with the STRING subcommand (see "Using Strings" on p. 422).

One label or value from each variable specified in a)variable argument is displayed on every page of the report. The label that REPORT displays for each varies from page to page as follows:

- If a new page starts with a case listing, REPORT takes the label or value from the first case listed.

- If a new page starts with a BREAK line, REPORT takes the label or value from the first case of the break group.

- If a new page starts with a summary line, REPORT takes the label or value from the last case of the break group being summarized.

- If you specify the same variable in both a title and a footnote, REPORT takes the title label or value from the top case on the page and the footnote label or value from the last case on the page.

You cannot use variables named *DATE* or *PAGE* in the)variable argument because they will only display the current date or a page number. If you want to use a variable named *DATE* or *PAGE*, change the variable's name with the MODIFY VARIABLES command before you use it in the)variable argument.

Margins and Report Alignment

Report margins determine the maximum width allowed for a report. (The finished report may be narrower, however.) REPORT uses a default left margin of 1, and a default right margin equal to your system's defined width. To change the margins, use the MARGINS keyword on the FORMAT subcommand (see REPORT in the Syntax Reference).

Report alignment refers to a report's position relative to its defined margins. For example, report margins of (1,80) allow for an 80-character report. If the finished report is only 50 characters wide, the report's alignment refers to whether the report is left-justified against column 1, right-justified against column 80, or centered between columns 1 and 80. The default is left-justified. To change the default, use the ALIGNMENT keyword on the FORMAT subcommand (see REPORT in the Syntax Reference).

Column Contents and Labeling

The following sections discuss options for controlling the contents, layout, and labeling of columns.

Column Headings

Each column in a report has a heading. By default, REPORT uses the variable label for the heading. If there is no label, REPORT uses the variable name.

REPORT wraps default column headings within their column widths, using as many lines as necessary and attempting to split lines meaningfully at spaces. With AUTOMATIC format, REPORT centers each column heading within the width of its column. However, when value labels or string values exceed the width of the longest word in the heading, REPORT left-justifies the heading.

To specify a column heading, enclose the heading within apostrophes or quotation marks following the variable name on the VARIABLES or BREAK subcommand. With AUTOMATIC format, REPORT does not wrap a heading you specify; it displays the heading exactly as you arrange it in your specification. To display the heading on multiple lines, enclose each line within its own set of apostrophes or quotation marks. To include an apostrophe within the heading, use quotation marks around the heading. For example,

```
SORT CASES BY DIVISION
REPORT FORMAT=AUTOMATIC LIST
      /VARIABLES=LNAME 'Employee'
                  AGE "Employee's Age" TENURE JTENURE
      /BREAK=DIVISION 'Company' 'Division'
      /SUMMARY=MEAN
```

produces the report in Figure 24.6 (only the first few lines of the report are shown). Because *DIVISION* and *LNAME* are string variables with values wider than the longest word in the column heading, the column headings *Company Division* and *Employee* are left-justified. The remaining headings are centered.

Figure 24.6   Column headings

```
Personnel Data                                                    PAGE     1

                                              Tenure     Tenure
Company                                         in         in
Division      Employee      Employee's Age    Company    Grade
----------    -------------  --------------    -------    ------

Carpeting     Ford              27.00           3.67      2.17
              Cochran           22.00           3.92      3.08
              Hoawinski         23.00           3.92      3.08
              Gates             24.00           4.00      3.25
              Mulvihill         30.00           4.08      3.08
              Lavelle           27.00           4.33      3.17
              Mahr              33.00           2.67      2.67
```

Column Widths

When you don't specify a column width for a variable, REPORT determines a default width, using the *larger* of the following for each variable:

- The widest print format in the column, whether it is a variable print format or a summary print format.
- The width of any temporary variable you define with the STRING subcommand.
- If you assign a column heading, the length of the longest title line in that heading. For example,

```
VARS = TENURE 'Tenure in Company' 'Measured' 'in Months'
```

specifies *Tenure in Company* as the longest line in a three-line heading.

- When no column heading is specified, the length of the longest word in the variable label, or the length of the variable name. (If FORMAT=MANUAL, variable labels are not evaluated.)
- If you specify LABEL on VARIABLES (the default if FORMAT=AUTOMATIC), the length of the variable's longest value label. If FORMAT=MANUAL is in effect, 20 is the maximum value used for this criterion. REPORT reads value labels from the dictionary, so it's possible for you to exclude a value from your report, yet still have that value's label determine the width of a column.

To override the default, specify a column width in parentheses following the variable name on the VARIABLES or BREAK subcommand, as in:

```
REPORT FORMAT = AUTOMATIC
       /VARIABLES = LNAME (10) AGE
       /BREAK = DIVISION (5)
       /SUMMARY = MEAN.
```

Intercolumn Spacing and Automatic Fit

To determine intercolumn spacing, REPORT subtracts the combined column widths of the break and report variables from its margins. It then divides the result by the number of columns minus 1. It uses this value or 4, whichever is least, as the space between each column.

When these criteria result in a report that is too wide for the report margins, AUTO-MATIC format shrinks the report using the following steps, stopping as soon as the report fits within the margins:

- It reduces intercolumn spacing incrementally until it reaches a minimum intercolumn space of 1. It will never reduce it to 0.
- It shortens strings defined by the STRING subcommand, beginning with the longest string from a string variable at least 15 characters wide. It shortens the string as much as needed—up to 40% of its length. If necessary it repeats the step, using different string variables. It will not shorten the same string twice.

REPORT does not implement automatic fit criteria unless FORMAT=AUTOMATIC.

Labels versus Values

In a listing report you frequently want to see value labels for the report variables rather than the values themselves. For example, if you want to create a personnel report that includes an employee's sex, you would prefer to see the labels *Female* and *Male* rather than the values 1 and 2 on the report. By specifying the keyword LABEL in parentheses after the variable name on the VARIABLES subcommand, you instruct REPORT to display labels rather than values for that variable.

For example, to produce a listing report that shows the sex, age, job grade, and work shift for each employee, you would use the following commands:

```
SORT CASES BY LNAME
REPORT FORMAT=AUTOMATIC LIST
      /VARS=LNAME SEX(LABEL) AGE JOBGRADE(LABEL) SHIFT(LABEL)
```

LABEL generates a descriptive report, as shown in Figure 24.7.

Figure 24.7   Personnel report with keyword (LABEL)

```
Personnel Data                                                          PAGE    1

Last Name          Sex       Age     Job Grade            Shift
------------       ------     -----   -----------------    -------

     Baker         Male      42.00    Sales Staff          Weekend
     Blount        Male      41.00    Sales Staff          Weekend
     Carlyle       Female    40.00    Sales Staff          Weekend
     Cochran       Female    22.00    Sales Staff          First
     Cochran       Male      39.00    Sales Staff          Second
     Dan           Male      36.00    Sales Staff          Weekend
     Farkas        Male      37.00    Sales Staff          First
     Ford          Female    27.00    Support Staff        First
     Ford          Female    36.00    Sales Staff          Weekend
     Gates         Female    24.00    Sales Staff          Second
     Golden        Female    42.00    Sales Staff          First
     Gonzales      Female    42.00    Support Staff        First
     Hoawinski     Female    23.00    Sales Staff          First
     Jacobesen     Male      44.00    Supervisory Staff    Second
     Johnson       Female    42.00    Sales Staff          Second
```

If the variable list contains a set of inclusive variables implied by the keyword TO, LABEL applies to the entire set of variables in the list. However, LABEL cannot be implied for a set of variables named individually. For example, in

```
/VARIABLES=V1 TO V5(LABEL)
```

LABEL applies to all variables implied by V1 TO V5. However, in

```
/VARIABLES=V1 V2 V3 V4 V5(LABEL)
```

LABEL applies only to *V5*.

Stacking Report Variables

When FORMAT=LIST, you can stack report variables together in a single column by linking them with + signs on the VARIABLES subcommand. For example,

```
TITLE Personnel Data.
SORT CASES BY DIVISION LNAME.
REPORT FORMAT=AUTOMATIC LIST
       /VARS=LNAME
         TENURE + STORE(LABEL) 'Tenure' 'and' 'Location'
       /AGE SALARY
       /BREAK=DIVISION
       /SUMMARY=MEAN.
```

stacks the variables *TENURE* and *STORE* in a single column, as shown in Figure 24.8 (only one division is shown). *LNAME*, *AGE*, and *SALARY* are unaffected. The stacked variables each start a new line on the report and are listed in the order they are defined on the VARIABLES subcommand. REPORT will not split the values for a single case across page breaks in the report.

Figure 24.8   Report with stacked report variables

```
Personnel Data                                                    PAGE    1

                              Tenure
                              and
Division      Last Name       Location     Age    Salary--Annual
----------    -------------   --------     -----  --------------

Carpeting     Cochran             3.92     22.00      $10,900
                                Suburban
              Dan                 3.83     36.00      $10,000

              Ford                3.67     27.00       $9,200
                                Suburban
              Gates               4.00     24.00      $10,000
                                Downtown
              Hoawinski           3.92     23.00      $10,900
                                Suburban
              Jones               4.83     44.00      $15,690
                                Downtown
              Katz                3.75     33.00      $10,000
                                Downtown
              Lavelle             4.33     27.00      $10,000
                                Downtown
              Mahr                2.67     33.00       $9,335
                                Downtown
              McAndrews           3.50     35.00      $15,520
                                Downtown
              Mulvihill           4.08     30.00      $10,000
                                Downtown
              Tygielski           6.00     35.00      $19,500
                                Suburban
Mean                              4.04     30.75      $11,754
```

REPORT reads values from all the stacked variables which it determines column widths. However, it uses the default heading from the first stacked variable in the list (if a heading is not specified), and it uses values from the first variable in the list to calculate summaries.

Creating Empty Columns

You can add space between columns by creating a dummy variable on the VARIABLES subcommand. Since a dummy variable has no values, its column is blank. Specify a name for the dummy variable followed by the keyword DUMMY in parentheses between the names of the variables whose columns are to be separated by the blank column. For example,

```
/VARIABLES = AGE TENURE XX(DUMMY) (7)  ' '  SALARY
```

places a blank column between the columns for *TENURE* and *SALARY*. The blank column is seven spaces wide, and the blank title overrides the default column heading.

The space created by dummy variables is also useful for holding the results of composite functions (see "Composite Functions" on p. 419).

Adding Blank Lines

By default, there are no blank lines between cases in a listing report. You can specify an integer value in parentheses after keyword LIST on the FORMAT subcommand to add a blank line after every *n* cases. For example, LIST(1) produces a double-spaced listing, and LIST(3) lists cases in sets of three. The spacing option makes it easier to read reports with many cases. For example, the following commands generate the report shown in Figure 24.9 (only part of the report is shown):

```
SORT CASES BY LNAME.
REPORT FORMAT=AUTOMATIC LIST(3)
       /VARS=LNAME AGE TENURE JTENURE.
```

Figure 24.9   Personnel report with optional spacing

```
Personnel Data                                                    PAGE    1

                            Tenure      Tenure
                              in          in
            Last Name   Age  Company    Grade
            ----------- ----- -------    ------

            Baker       42.00  5.25      3.75
            Blount      41.00  5.25      3.75
            Carlyle     40.00  6.00      6.00

            Cochran     22.00  3.92      3.08
            Cochran     39.00  5.50      5.50
            Dan         36.00  3.83      3.25

            Farkas      37.00  4.42      3.67
            Ford        27.00  3.67      2.17
            Ford        36.00  4.50      3.67
```

To insert a blank line between two variables that are stacked in one column (see "Stacking Report Variables" on p. 412), either specify (DUMMY) after a nonexistent variable name or specify a blank space between two plus signs.

Other keywords in REPORT allow you to control spacing between titles and column headings, between headings and listings, between individual rows within the body of the report, and between the body of the report and footnotes. These keywords are listed in Table 24.1 at the end of this chapter and are described under REPORT in the Syntax Reference.

Summary Statistics

REPORT gives you precise control over the types of summaries to be displayed and their appearance on the report. The following sections describe summary specifications.

Selecting Variables for Statistics

A statistic specified on the SUMMARY subcommand is calculated for all variables specified on the VARIABLES subcommand. To calculate statistics only for selected report variables, specify the variables in parentheses on the SUMMARY subcommand, as in:

```
SORT CASES BY DIVISION.
REPORT FORMAT=AUTOMATIC LIST
        /VARIABLES=LNAME AGE TENURE JTENURE SALARY
        /BREAK=DIVISION
        /SUMMARY=MEAN(JTENURE, SALARY).
```

This command computes the mean for variables JTENURE and SALARY only. You cannot use keyword TO on SUMMARY to imply a set of variables.

Summaries across Break Groups (Report Totals)

Keyword TOTAL specified in parentheses on the BREAK subcommand calculates summary statistics for all the cases in the report. These totals are displayed at the end of the report. You can specify TOTAL for both listing and summary reports.

To generate a report that has break-level summaries plus total summaries, specify TOTAL in parentheses after the variable named on the BREAK subcommand that precedes the summary whose totals you want, as in:

```
SORT CASES BY STORE DIVISION.
REPORT FORMAT=AUTOMATIC
        /VARIABLES=AGE TENURE JTENURE SALARY
        /BREAK=STORE(TOTAL)
        /SUMMARY=VALIDN (AGE)
        /BREAK=DIVISION
        /SUMMARY=MEAN.
```

The first set of BREAK and SUMMARY subcommands calculates the number of employees who work at each branch store and the total number of employees who work for the company by counting those that have valid values for AGE. The second set calculates a mean for each division but does not calculate a mean for the entire company because TOTAL is not specified at this break level. Figure 24.10 shows the report.

Figure 24.10 Summary report with totals

```
Personnel Data                                                              PAGE      1

                                 Tenure       Tenure
Branch                              in           in
Store       Division      Age    Company       Grade    Salary--Annual
--------    ----------    -----  -------       ------    --------------

Suburban    Carpeting

            Mean          26.75   4.37          3.42        $12,625

            Appliances

            Mean          30.20   4.05          3.77        $14,395

            Furniture

            Mean          35.29   4.71          4.32        $12,975

            Hardware

            Mean          32.00   4.33          4.33        $22,500
N                           17

Downtown    Carpeting

            Mean          32.75   3.87          3.25        $11,318

            Appliances

            Mean          32.25   3.52          3.25        $10,150

            Furniture

            Mean          38.25   4.86          3.86        $13,500

            Hardware

            Mean          37.25   4.67          4.62        $16,350
N                           24

TOTAL

N                           41
```

When the statistics you want to calculate for the totals differ from those you want it to calculate at the various break levels or when you want to obtain totals for a listing report without break variables, specify TOTAL in parentheses on a BREAK subcommand but do not specify a variable; then use as many SUMMARY subcommands as you need to specify the summary totals you want to calculate. Specify the break variables on subsequent BREAK subcommands. For example, the commands

```
SORT CASES BY DIVISION.
REPORT FORMAT=AUTOMATIC
       /VARIABLES=AGE TENURE JTENURE SALARY
       /BREAK=(TOTAL)
       /SUMMARY=VALIDN (AGE)
       /BREAK=DIVISION
       /SUMMARY=MEAN.
```

calculate the total number of employees in the company but not the number of employees within each division. They calculate a mean for each division but not a mean for the entire company (see Figure 24.11).

Figure 24.11 Totals that differ from break level summaries

```
Personnel Data                                                    PAGE    1

                      Tenure     Tenure
                        in         in
Division      Age     Company     Grade     Salary--Annual
----------    -----   -------    ------     --------------

Carpeting

Mean          30.75    4.04       3.31        $11,754

Appliances

Mean          31.11    3.81       3.54        $12,508

Furniture

Mean          36.87    4.79       4.08        $13,255

Hardware

Mean          36.20    4.60       4.57        $17,580


N              41
```

The following commands obtain totals for a listing report that does not contain break levels:

```
SORT CASES BY LNAME.
REPORT FORMAT=AUTOMATIC LIST
        /VARIABLES=LNAME AGE TENURE JTENURE SALARY
        /BREAK=(TOTAL)
        /SUMMARY=MEAN
        /SUMMARY=VALIDN (JTENURE).
```

Each statistic specified on a SUMMARY subcommand is calculated for all the cases in the report. The SORT CASES is optional since the report has no break variables; it is specified to alphabetize the listing by *LNAME*.

Figure 24.12 shows the last lines of the report. The mean values are those for all 41 employees. The summary titles *Mean* and *N* begin in the left column and are left-justified. The values for each statistic display one row beneath their title, allowing you to specify a longer summary title if desired (see "Summary Titles" on p. 418).

Figure 24.12 Listing report with totals

```
Personnel Data                                                          PAGE    1

                          Tenure        Tenure
                            in            in
Last Name         Age     Company       Grade      Salary--Annual
-------------     -----   -------        ------     --------------
    .
    .
    .
Sedowski         30.00     2.67          2.67          $7,500
Shavilje         32.00     2.92          2.92          $8,900
Snolik           34.00     5.08          4.50         $15,300
Syms             32.00     4.33          4.33         $22,500
Totman           41.00     4.50          3.50         $13,300
Tygielski        35.00     6.00          5.33         $19,500
Wajda            26.00     3.17          3.17          $8,975
Washington       32.00     4.42          3.67         $14,400
White            25.00     3.92          3.33         $11,000
Wilson           36.00     4.42          3.75         $14,000

Mean
                 33.73     4.34          3.79         $13,179

N
                                          41
```

Summary Titles

By default, REPORT uses its own summary titles (listed in the Syntax Reference) on a report to identify each statistic you request on the SUMMARY subcommand. It displays the summary title in the column corresponding to the break being summarized, aligning the titles with the labels or values in the column. The title is displayed in mixed case or upper case, depending upon your system's default specifications.

You can change the default summary title by enclosing a one-line title in apostrophes or quotation marks, as in:

```
/SUMMARY=STDDEV 'Standard Deviation'
```

Use leading blanks to indent summary titles within the break column.

If you specify a summary title wider than its break column, the title extends into the break column to its right. If the width of the available break columns is insufficient to display the full summary title, the title is truncated.

REPORT allows you to move summary titles between break columns. Specify in parentheses the number of the break column in which you want the summary title to appear, counting the first specified BREAK subcommand as 1. For example, the commands

```
REPORT FORMAT=AUTOMATIC LIST
       /VARIABLES=LNAME AGE TENURE JTENURE SALARY
       /BREAK=STORE
       /SUMMARY=MEAN(JTENURE)
       /BREAK=DIVISION
       /SUMMARY=MEAN(SALARY) 'Average Salary' (1)
```

display the title *Average Salary* in the column for the first break (*STORE*) rather than in the column for *DIVISION*.

Although summary titles can only be one line long, when you use multiple SUMMA-RY subcommands you can continue a summary title from one summary line to another. For example,

```
/SUMMARY=SUM 'Sums and Averages'
/SUMMARY=MEAN 'Based on 1986 5% Sample'
```

produces a two-line summary with a title continuing from the first to the second line. You can also specify a blank title for any summary line.

Print Formats for Summary Statistics

Every summary function has a default display format. For example, the PERCENT function uses a width of 6, including one decimal place. For the default formats, see REPORT in the Syntax Reference.

You can specify COMMA and DOLLAR formats when they are not the default, or PLAIN to override those formats when they are the default. You can also specify an alternative number of decimal digits by enclosing the desired number in a separate set of parentheses. For example, the following SUMMARY subcommand displays the mean of *SALARY* without a dollar sign and with two decimal digits:

```
/SUMMARY = MEAN(SALARY(COMMA)(2))
```

If the column is not wide enough to display the specified decimal digits for a given function, REPORT displays fewer decimals. REPORT uses scientific notation or displays asterisks if the column is not wide enough to display the integer portion of the number.

Composite Functions

A composite function operates on simple aggregate statistics and their arguments to produce a single result. For example, suppose you want a listing report that shows average age, tenure, and salary of employees, and also reflects what the average salary will be when next year's 7% across-the-board salary increase takes effect. The following commands produce such a report:

```
SORT CASES BY DIVISION LNAME.
REPORT FORMAT=AUTOMATIC LIST
  /VARS=LNAME AGE TENURE SALARY
  /BREAK=DIVISION
  /SUMMARY=MEAN
  /SUMMARY=MULTIPLY(MEAN(SALARY)1.07) (SALARY(DOLLAR))
    '7% Raise'
```

The format specification (SALARY(DOLLAR)) and the summary title are specified after the function and its arguments. Figure 24.13 shows one division from the report. Note that the composite function produces only one result.

Figure 24.13 Report with composite function

```
Personnel Data                                                          PAGE    1


                                        Tenure
                                          in
Division        Last Name        Age    Company    Salary--Annual
----------      -------------    -----  -------    --------------

Carpeting       Cochran          22.00   3.92         $10,900
                Dan              36.00   3.83         $10,000
                Ford             27.00   3.67          $9,200
                Gates            24.00   4.00         $10,000
                Hoawinski        23.00   3.92         $10,900
                Jones            44.00   4.83         $15,690
                Katz             33.00   3.75         $10,000
                Lavelle          27.00   4.33         $10,000
                Mahr             33.00   2.67          $9,335
                McAndrews        35.00   3.50         $15,520
                Mulvihill        30.00   4.08         $10,900
                Tygielski        35.00   6.00         $19,500

Mean                             30.75   4.04         $11,754
7% Raise                                              $12,577
```

By default, REPORT displays the result of the composite function in the column defined by the first variable in the function that is also named on the VARIABLES subcommand. To move the result to another variable's column, specify that variable's name in parentheses after you define the composite function's argument. For example,

```
/SUMMARY=MULTIPLY(MEAN(SALARY)1.07) (LNAME)
```

places the result in the column defined by *LNAME*. Otherwise, this summary would appear in the column for *SALARY*. Unlike simple functions, the composite function result can be placed in any report column, including those defined by dummy variables or string variables.

It is often advisable to specify the format and number of decimal digits you want to display. Specify print formats for composites within parentheses following the name of the variable in whose column the result is to be displayed. For example, the subcommand

```
/SUMMARY=MULTIPLY(MEAN(SALARY)1.07) (SALARY(DOLLAR)(2))
```

displays increased average salary with 2 decimal places and DOLLAR format in the *SALARY* column.

You can use any numeric SPSS/PC+ variables, not just variables specified within REPORT, as arguments to composite functions. You cannot use a composite function as an argument to a composite function. You can only use simple functions, variables, and constants.

Composite functions are useful in the following situations:

1. To place a summary statistic in a column other than the one for which it is calculated. For example, the sum of *VARA* is normally displayed in the column corresponding to *VARA*. It can, however, be placed in any other column by using a composite such as

```
/SUMMARY=ADD(SUM(VARA)) (VARB)
```

which adds the sum of *VARA* to nothing and places it in the column for *VARB*. The SUBTRACT, GREAT, LEAST, and AVERAGE composite functions can achieve the same result.

2. To manipulate statistics and change the unit of analysis. Certain arithmetic operations between variables produce the same result at either the case level or the subpopulation level. You can subtract the sum of variable *A* from the sum of variable *B* and obtain the same answer as subtracting *A* from *B* for each case and summing the result. However, dividing the sum of *A* by the sum of *B* is not the same as dividing *A* by *B* for each case and averaging the results.

3. To manipulate variables not named on the VARIABLES subcommand so that these variables are not allocated a column in the report. For example, you might want to adjust dollar figures by some index when displaying means but do not want to display the index in the report.

For a complete list of the composite functions available in REPORT, see the Syntax Reference.

Repeating Summary Specifications

Keyword PREVIOUS on SUMMARY is used to repeat a set of SUMMARY subcommands defined for a previous BREAK subcommand. For example,

```
REPORT   FORMAT=LIST
         /VARIABLES=NAME AGE TENURE
         /BREAK=DIVISION
         /SUMMARY=MEAN
         /SUMMARY=VALIDN(AGE)
         /BREAK=STORE
         /SUMMARY=PREVIOUS.
```

displays means and the valid number of cases for *AGE* for each store within each division.

You can specify a number in parentheses on PREVIOUS to refer to a particular set of summaries. For example, PREVIOUS(1) copies all the SUMMARY subcommands applying to the first BREAK subcommand; PREVIOUS(2) copies SUMMARY specifications for the second BREAK subcommand. No other specification can be used on a SUMMARY subcommand with PREVIOUS.

Using Strings

The STRING subcommand enables you to link together SPSS/PC+ variables and constants to create new temporary variables you can use in REPORT. You can link together both alphanumeric and numeric variables. For example, the subcommand

```
/STRING= PHONE (AREA '/' EXCH '-' NUM)
```

creates a string variable named *PHONE*, which comprises three variables and two constants.

- The STRING subcommand must precede the VARIABLES subcommand.
- New STRING variables are temporary and available only in the REPORT procedure. The variable names you assign must be unique and must follow the usual SPSS/PC+ rules for variable names.
- You cannot use keyword TO on the STRING subcommand.

You can use STRING variables on both the VARIABLES and BREAK subcommands, specifying column headings for them as you do for any other variables.

An Example

One use of the STRING subcommand is to separate report columns with a column of special characters, such as asterisks or vertical bars. For example,

```
TITLE Personnel Data.
REPORT FORMAT=AUTOMATIC LIST
     /STRING=FILL ('*')
     /VARS=LNAME AGE TENURE FILL(1) ' ' SALARY.
```

defines a string variable *FILL* with the value * for each case. Specifying *FILL* between *TENURE* and *SALARY* on the VARIABLES subcommand displays a vertical column of asterisks between those two columns on a listing report. The (1) after *FILL* on VARIABLES specifies a column width of 1; the space between apostrophes specifies a blank column heading. Figure 24.14 shows the first few lines of the report.

Figure 24.14 Column of special characters

```
Personnel Data                                                    PAGE    1

                        Tenure
                          in
Last Name        Age    Company        Salary--Annual
-------------    -----  -------        --------------

Ford             27.00   3.67     *        $9,200
Cochran          22.00   3.92     *       $10,900
Hoawinski        23.00   3.92     *       $10,900
Gates            24.00   4.00     *       $10,000
Mulvihill        30.00   4.08     *       $10,000
Lavelle          27.00   4.33     *       $10,000
Mahr             33.00   2.67     *        $9,335
Katz             33.00   3.75     *       $10,000
Jones            44.00   4.83     *       $15,690
   .
   .
   .
```

Handling Missing Values

The MISSING subcommand controls the treatment of missing values. You can specify one MISSING subcommand per REPORT command. It must follow the VARIABLES subcommand and precede BREAK.

The MISSING subcommand has three options:

VAR	*Missing values are treated separately for each variable.* Missing values are displayed in case listings but are not included in the calculation of summary statistics on a function-by-function basis. This is the default.
LIST(varlist n)	*Cases with the specified number of missing values across the specified list of variables are not used.* The variable list and *n* are specified in parentheses. If *n* is not specified, the default is 1. If no variables are specified, all variables named on VARIABLES are assumed.
NONE	*Treat user-missing values as valid.* Keyword NONE applies to the entire set of variables named on the VARIABLES subcommand. It cannot be used to ignore missing-data indicators for some variables selectively.

For example, the subcommand

```
/MISSING=LIST (AGE TENURE SALARY 2)
```

deletes any case with missing values for two or more of the variables *AGE*, *TENURE*, or *SALARY* from case listings and from summaries. If a case has a missing value for just one or for none of the variables listed, it is not deleted from case listings but is deleted from summaries for those variables for which it is missing.

MISSING specifications apply to REPORT-generated strings, as well as to other variables. If one variable in a REPORT-generated string is missing, the string is missing.

Only variables named on the VARIABLES and SUMMARY subcommands are checked for missing values. Use a SELECT IF command to eliminate cases with missing values for break variables.

Changing the Missing-Value Indicator

By default, REPORT uses a period to indicate missing values in case listings, break values, and summary statistics. Use the MISSING keyword on FORMAT subcommand to specify any other character, including a blank, as the missing-value indicator. For example,

```
/FORMAT AUTOMATIC LIST MISSING 'm'
```

specifies m as the missing-value indicator.

Summary

REPORT has a full range of keywords that allow you to control the format and layout of a report. Table 24.1 will help you determine the subcommands and keywords to use to achieve the results you want. You can then consult REPORT in the Syntax Reference to quickly locate full descriptions of each.

Table 24.1   Summary of REPORT keywords

Function	Subcommand	Keyword
Adjusting margins	FORMAT	MARGINS(l,r)
Aligning columns	FORMAT	ALIGN(LEFT|CENTER|RIGHT)
Aligning report contents	VARIABLES, BREAK	(OFFSET(n|CENTER))
Determining column contents	FORMAT	LIST NOLIST
		MISSING ' '
	VARIABLES, BREAK	(VALUE|LABEL)
	BREAK	NAME NONAME
Moving summary titles	SUMMARY	( ) col number
Page lengths	FORMAT	LENGTH(*|TOP,BOTTOM)
	BREAK	(PAGE(RESET))
Page numbers	FORMAT	PAGE1(n)
Shifting column headings	FORMAT	CHALIGN(TOP|BOTTOM)
		TSPACE(n)
	VARIABLES, STRING, BREAK	literal
	VARIABLES, BREAK	(CENTER, LEFT, RIGHT)
Spacing between columns	FORMAT	COLSPACE (4 n)
	VARIABLES	(DUMMY)
Spacing between rows	FORMAT	TSPACE(n)
		CHDSPACE(n)
		LIST(n)
		BRKSPACE(n)
		SUMSPACE(n)
		FTSPACE(n)
	VARIABLES	(DUMMY)
	BREAK, SUMMARY	'SKIP(n))
Specifying column widths	VARIABLES, STRING, BREAK	(n) following varname
Totals on listing reports	BREAK	(TOTAL)
Underscores between listings and summaries	BREAK	UNDERSCORE
Underscoring column headings	FORMAT	UNDERSCORE(ON OFF)

SPSS

Syntax Reference

Universals

This part of the Syntax Reference discusses general topics pertinent to using SPSS/PC+ commands. The topics are divided into five sections:

- *SPSS/PC+ Commands* explains command syntax, including command specification and command order. In this section, you will learn how to read SPSS/PC+ syntax charts, which summarize command syntax in diagrams and provide an easy reference. Discussions of individual commands are found in an alphabetical reference following Universals.

- *Files* discusses the different types of files used by SPSS/PC+.

- *Variables* contains important information on general rules and conventions concerning variables and variable definition in SPSS/PC+, including information on variable names and variable formats.

- *Transformation Expressions* describes expressions that can be used in data transformations. In this section, you will find a complete list of available functions and operators.

SPSS/PC+ Commands

Commands are the instructions that you give SPSS/PC+ to initiate an action. For SPSS/PC+ to interpret your commands correctly, you must follow certain rules.

Syntax Diagrams

Each SPSS/PC+ command described in this Syntax Reference includes a diagram that shows all the subcommands, keywords, and specifications allowed for that command. By remembering the following rules, you can use the syntax diagram as a quick reference for each command.

- Elements in upper case are keywords.
- Elements in lower case describe specifications supplied by the user.
- Elements in boldface type are defaults. Some defaults are indicated with **.
- Parentheses, apostrophes, and quotation marks are required where indicated.
- Elements enclosed in square brackets ([ ]) are optional. When brackets would confuse the format, they are omitted. The command description explains which specifications are required or optional.
- Braces ({ }) indicate a choice between elements.
- Most abbreviations are obvious. For example, *varlist* stands for a list of variable names.
- The command terminator is not shown in syntax diagrams.

Command Specification

The following rules apply to all SPSS/PC+ commands:

- Commands begin with a keyword that is the name of the command and often have additional specifications, such as subcommands and user specifications. Refer to the discussion of each command to see which subcommands and additional specifications are required.

- Each command ends with a command terminator. The default command terminator is a period.

- The command terminator must be the last nonblank character in a line.

- Commands can begin in any column of a command line and continue for as many lines as needed. The exception is the END DATA command, which must begin in the first column of the first line after the end of data.

- The maximum length of any line in a command is 80 characters, including the prompt and the command terminator.

- Spaces can be added between specifications at any point where a single blank is allowed. In addition, lines can be broken at any point where a single blank is allowed. There are two exceptions: the END DATA command can have only one space between words, and specifications for the TITLE and SUBTITLE subcommands can be broken across two lines only by specifying a plus sign between string segments (see "String Values in Command Specifications" on p. 429).

- Commands and any command specifications can be entered in upper and lower case. Commands, subcommands, keywords, and variable names are translated to upper case before processing. All user specifications, including labels and data values, preserve upper and lower case.

- Each word in a command can be abbreviated to a minimum of three letters. For example, AGGREGATE can be abbreviated to AGG; ADD VAL LAB is a valid abbreviation for ADD VALUE LABELS; and EXA VAR=varlist is valid for EXAMINE VARIABLES=varlist.

- Most two-word commands—such as BEGIN DATA, SORT CASES, and VALUE LABELS—can be abbreviated to their first word. If the first specification on the command, such as a variable name, begins with the same three letters as the second word of a two-word command, you must enter the second word of the command explicitly before entering the specification. If two commands begin with the same three letters, such as DATE (in SPSS/PC+ Trends) and DATA LIST, you must specify the second word of the two-word command.

Subcommands

Many commands include additional specifications called *subcommands* for locating data, handling data, and formatting the output.

- Subcommands begin with a keyword that is the name of the subcommand. Some subcommands include additional specifications.

- A subcommand keyword is separated from its specifications, if any, by an equals sign. The equals sign is usually optional but is required where ambiguity is possible in the specification. To avoid ambiguity, it is best to use the equals signs as shown in the syntax diagrams in this manual.

- Most subcommands can be named in any order. However, some commands require a specific subcommand order. The description of each command includes a section on subcommand order.
- Subcommands are separated from one another by a slash.

Keywords

Keywords identify commands, subcommands, functions, operators, and other specifications in SPSS/PC+.

- Keywords, including commands and subcommands, can often be truncated to the first three characters of each word. An exception is keyword WITH, which must be spelled in full. See "Command Specification" on p. 428 for additional rules for three-character truncation of commands.
- Keywords identifying logical operators (AND, OR, and NOT), relational operators (EQ, GE, GT, LE, LT, and NE), and ALL, BY, TO, and WITH are reserved words and cannot be used as variable names.

Values in Command Specifications

Values specified in commands follow these rules:

- A single lowercase character in the syntax diagram, for example, n, w, or d, indicates a user-specified value.
- A number specified as an argument to a subcommand can be entered with or without leading zeros.
- The value can be an integer or a real number within a restricted range, as required by the specific command or subcommand. For exact restrictions, read the individual command description.

String Values in Command Specifications

The term **string** is used to refer to alphanumeric data or command specifications such as titles and labels. String values specified in commands follow these rules:

- Each string specified in a command should be enclosed in a set of apostrophes or quotation marks.
- To specify an apostrophe within a string, enclose the string in quotation marks, as in:
  ```
  "Client's Satisfaction"
  ```
- To specify quotation marks within a string, use apostrophes to enclose the string:
  ```
  'Categories Labeled "UNSTANDARD" in the Report'
  ```
- String specifications cannot be broken across command lines.
- Blanks within apostrophes or quotation marks are significant.

- String values in data files or entered between BEGIN DATA and END DATA do not need to be enclosed in special delimiters (see DATA LIST: Freefield Format for exceptions).

Delimiters

Delimiters are used to separate data values, keywords, arguments, and specifications.

- A blank is usually used to separate one specification from another, except when another delimiter serves the same purpose or when a comma is required.
- Commas are required to separate arguments to functions. Otherwise, blanks are generally valid substitutes for commas.
- Arithmetic operators (+, -, *, and /) serve as delimiters in expressions.
- Blanks can be used before and after operators or equals signs to improve readability, but commas cannot.
- Special delimiters include parentheses, apostrophes, quotation marks, the slash, and the equals sign. Blanks before and after special delimiters are optional.
- The slash is used primarily to separate subcommands and lists of variables. Although slashes are sometimes optional, it is a good practice to enter them as shown in the syntax diagrams.
- The equals sign is used between a subcommand and its specifications, as in STATISTICS= MEAN, and to show equivalence, as in COMPUTE target variable=expression. Equals signs following subcommands are frequently optional, but it is best to enter them for clarity.

Command Order

Command order in SPSS/PC+ is more often than not a matter of common sense and follows the following logical sequence: variable definition, data transformation, and statistical analysis. For example, you cannot label, transform, analyze, or use a variable in any way before it exists. The following general rules apply:

- Commands that define variables for a session (DATA LIST, GET, etc.) must precede commands that assign labels or missing values to those variables; they must also precede transformation and procedure commands that use those variables.
- Commands that are used to create variables must precede commands that assign labels or missing values to those variables, and they must also precede the procedures that use those variables.

In addition to observing the rules above, it is useful to distinguish between commands that cause the data to be read and those that do not. Table 1 shows the commands that cause the data to be read. Most of the remaining commands (those that do not cause the data to be read) do not take effect immediately; they are read by SPSS/PC+ but are not executed until a command that causes the data to be read is encountered in the command sequence. This avoids unnecessary passes through the data.

- Data transformation commands cause the data to be altered prior to processing data for a procedure. When these commands are entered prior to a procedure, the data are read twice: once to incorporate the instructions from the transformation commands, and then to perform the SPSS/PC+ procedure.

Table 1   Commands that cause the data to be read[*]

AGGREGATE	FREQUENCIES	PROBIT
ANOVA	HILOGLINEAR	QUICK CLUSTER
AUTORECODE	IMPORT	RANK
BEGIN DATA	JOIN	REGRESSION
CLUSTER	LIST	RELIABILITY
CORRELATIONS	LOGISTIC REGRESSION	REPORT
CROSSTABS	LOGLINEAR	SAVE
DESCRIPTIVES	MANOVA	SORT CASES
DSCRIMINANT	MEANS	SURVIVAL
EXAMINE	NLR	TRANSLATE
EXPORT	NPAR TESTS	T-TEST
FACTOR	ONEWAY	
FLIP	PLOT	

[*] This table shows the procedures in the SPSS/PC+ Base system and the Professional Statistics and Advanced Statistics options; it does not show commands in other SPSS/PC+ options, such as SPSS/PC+ Tables or SPSS/PC+ Trends.

Commands that alter the dictionary of the active file, such as MISSING VALUE, and commands that do not affect the data, such as SET, SHOW, and DISPLAY, take effect as soon as they are encountered in the command sequence, regardless of conditional statements that precede them. Table 2 lists commands that take effect immediately.

Table 2   Commands that take effect immediately

ADD VALUE LABELS	SET
DISPLAY	SHOW
FORMATS	VALUE LABELS
GSET	VARIABLE LABELS
GSHOW	WEIGHT
MISSING VALUE	

The order of transformations that take effect immediately in the command sequence can be misleading. Consider the following:

```
COMPUTE PROFIT=INCOME-EXPENSES.
MISSING VALUE INCOME EXPENSES (0).
LIST.
```

- COMPUTE precedes MISSING VALUE and is processed first; however, SPSS/PC+ delays its execution until the data are being read.
- MISSING VALUE takes effect as soon as it is encountered.
- LIST causes the data to be read; thus, SPSS/PC+ executes both COMPUTE and LIST during the same data pass. Because MISSING VALUE is already in effect by this time, all cases with the value 0 for either *INCOME* or *EXPENSES* return a missing value for *PROFIT*.

To prevent the MISSING VALUE command from taking effect before COMPUTE is executed, you must position MISSING VALUE after the LIST command.

Files

SPSS/PC+ uses a number of files in its operation. This section provides an overview of the types of files you can use, as well as a discussion of the active file.

The files that you can use in a session are:

active file *A file specially formatted for use by SPSS/PC+, containing the data and a dictionary that defines the data.* The active file is initially defined by the DATA LIST, GET, IMPORT, JOIN, or TRANSLATE command or within QED or SPSS Data Entry II. It is available until you replace it with a new active file or until you enter FINISH. Commands that can replace the active file are AGGREGATE, DATA LIST, GET, IMPORT, JOIN, TRANSLATE, QED, and DE. You can modify the data in the active file using transformations, analyze the data using procedures, and save the file with SAVE or EXPORT. The active file is stored in SPSS/PC+ workspace and in temporary files on disk, and it cannot be named.

command file *A file that contains SPSS/PC+ commands.* You can use the INCLUDE command to process the commands in a command file as an alternative to entering commands interactively, or you can submit a command file directly from Review.

data file *A file that contains only raw data.* The data in a raw data file must be defined on the DATA LIST command before they can be used by other procedures. Data files can be arranged in fixed or freefield format. In fixed format, the values of each variable for each case are recorded in the same location on each record. In freefield format, the values of each variable are recorded in the same order but not necessarily in the same location (see DATA LIST: Fixed Format and DATA LIST: Freefield Format).

listing file *A file containing output from SPSS/PC+ procedures.* Filenames for listing files can be specified on the SET command.

log file *A file created by SPSS/PC+ that contains a copy of all the commands that are executed during a session.* Filenames for log files can be specified on the SET command. You can use a log file as a command file in subsequent sessions.

portable file *An ASCII file specially formatted for transporting data and data definitions between computers with different versions of SPSS.* (To transport files between computers running DOS, use SPSS/PC+ system files.) Like the active file, a portable file contains data and a dictionary. A portable file can be created with the EXPORT command and read with the IMPORT command.

results file *A file that contains procedure output.* This file can contain a rectangular data set produced by the WRITE command, cell frequencies produced by CROSSTABS, survival table data records written by SURVIVAL, or matrix materials produced by CLUSTER, CORRELATION, DSCRIMINANT, FACTOR, MANOVA, ONEWAY, QUICK CLUSTER, or REGRESSION. Filenames for results files can be specified on the SET command.

scratch pad   *A file used by REVIEW as a work area for building commands.* The scratch pad is used as a command file.

system file   *A binary file that is a copy of the active file and is saved on disk for later use.* Like the active file, a system file contains both data and a data dictionary. Processing a system file is considerably more efficient than recreating the active file from raw data. You create system files with the SAVE command and read system files with the GET command.

- All filenames specified on SPSS/PC+ commands must be enclosed in apostrophes.

- Unless otherwise specified, file specifications default to the current drive and directory. When using a file on another drive or directory, you must explicitly specify the drive or path in the file specification.

- Command files, data files, and system files can be read from any drive and directory.

- System files, log files, and listing files can be written to any drive and directory.

- The results file cannot be written to a directory other than the current directory.

SPSS/PC+ Active File

When SPSS/PC+ processes data definition commands, it builds an internal file called the **active file.** The active file contains data and a data dictionary (stored in memory) of variable names, variable and value labels, missing-value flags, and format specifications (see "Variables" on p. 434). Data in the active file are stored in temporary files kept on the current default drive or on the drive specified on SET WORKDEV. The active file data can be altered by transformation commands and are used as input for SPSS/PC+ procedures.

- The active file is initially defined by a DATA LIST, GET, IMPORT, JOIN, or TRANSLATE command. It can also be defined in QED or SPSS Data Entry II.

- The active file can contain up to 500 variables.

- Each 8-character portion of a long string variable counts toward the system limit of 500 variables. For example, a 20-character string variable counts as 3 toward the system limit of 500 variables.

- The actual data associated with each variable for each case normally make up the bulk of the active file. Numeric values are stored in binary form for efficient processing and normally occupy eight bytes each. You can compress the data in the active file using the COMPRESS specification on the SET command (see SET).

- The active file is available for use with SPSS/PC+ commands until the FINISH command is entered or until a new active file is built.

- The N command limits the number of cases in the active file. The SELECT IF command limits the number of cases based upon some logical criteria. SELECT IF and N permanently affect the number of cases in the active file.

- The SAMPLE and PROCESS IF commands affect the number of cases only for the next procedure.

- The FORMATS, VALUE LABELS, VARIABLE LABELS, and MISSING VALUE commands affect the active file dictionary, not the data.

Variables

To prepare data for processing in SPSS/PC+, you must define variables by assigning variable names and formats. You can also specify variable labels, value labels, and missing values, but they are optional. All of these data definitions are stored in the dictionary of the SPSS/PC+ active file and in the dictionary of SPSS/PC+ system files.

Variable Names

Each variable must have a unique name. Variable names are stored in the dictionary of an SPSS/PC+ system file or active file. Observe the following rules when establishing variable names or referring to variables by their names on commands:

- Variable names have a maximum of eight characters. The first character must be a letter or the @ character.
- The period, underscore, and the characters $, #, and @ can be used *within* variable names. For example, *A._$@#1* is a valid variable name.
- A $ sign in the first position of a variable name indicates that the variable is a system variable (see "System Variables" on p. 437). The $ sign is not allowed as the initial character of a user-defined variable.
- Variable names ending with a period should be avoided, since the period may be interpreted as a command terminator.
- Variable names can be established on the DATA LIST, COMPUTE, COUNT, and IF commands. They can be changed with MODIFY VARS.
- Reserved keywords cannot be used as variable names. SPSS/PC+ reserved keywords are

ALL	AND	BY	EQ	GE	GT	LE
LT	NE	NOT	OR	TO	WITH	

Keyword TO

Keyword TO allows you to generate numerically consecutive names for a set of variables and to refer to a group of existing variables on a variety of commands.

To establish names for a set of variables with keyword TO, use a character prefix with numeric suffixes:

- The prefix can be any valid name. Both the beginning and ending variable must use the same prefix.
- The numeric suffixes can be any integers, but the first number must be smaller than the second. For example, ITEM1 TO ITEM5 establishes five variables named *ITEM1*, *ITEM2*, *ITEM3*, *ITEM4*, and *ITEM5*.
- Each variable name, including the number, must not exceed eight characters.
- Leading zeros used in numeric suffixes are included in the variable name. For example, V001 TO V100 establishes 100 variables, *V001, V002, V003, . . . V100*. V1 TO V100 establishes 100 variables, *V1, V2, V3, . . . V100*.

Keyword TO can also be used on procedures and other commands to refer to a group of consecutive variables in the active file. For example, AVAR TO VARB refers to the variables *AVAR* and all subsequent variables up to and including *VARB*.

- In most cases, the TO specification uses the order of variables in the active file. Use the DISPLAY command or the Variables menu ((Alt)-(V)) in Review to see the order of variables in the active file.

- On some subcommands, the order in which variables are named on a previous subcommand, usually the VARIABLES subcommand, is used to determine which variables are consecutive and therefore are implied by the TO specification. This is noted in the description of individual commands.

Variable and Value Labels

Variable labels are used in many SPSS/PC+ procedures to describe the meaning of variables. A variable label can be up to 60 characters long and can contain any printable ASCII character. Lowercase letters remain in lower case. Variable labels are defined on the VARIABLE LABELS command and are included in the active file dictionary.

Value labels are used in many SPSS/PC+ procedures to specify the meaning of coded values. A value label can be up to 60 characters long, although most SPSS/PC+ procedures use only the first 20 characters. (The TABLES procedure available in SPSS/PC+ Tables will display all 60 characters of a label.) Value labels can contain any printable ASCII character. Lowercase letters remain in lower case. Value labels are defined on the VALUE LABELS command and are included in the active file dictionary.

Missing Values

Each variable can have one value that is used to indicate missing information. These **user-missing values** are defined on the MISSING VALUE command and are included in the active file dictionary. Values declared as missing in this way are normally excluded from statistical analysis and reports. Typically the missing-value code represents "unknown" or "no answer." In addition, numeric variables can have values that are *system-missing,* which simply means that no value has been defined. You do not need to take any action to declare system-missing values. SPSS/PC+ represents system-missing values with a period.

Variable Formats

Variable formats determine how SPSS/PC+ reads raw data and how it displays and writes values out. The format of a variable in a raw data file is defined on the DATA LIST command. New variables created by IF, COUNT, or COMPUTE are assigned formats by SPSS/PC+.

Variable formats are stored in the dictionary of an SPSS/PC+ system file or active file. You can use the DISPLAY command with VARIABLES=ALL to see the format of all the variables in the active file. You can also see check variable formats wihin Review by pressing (Alt)-(V); when you then select a variable, its format is displayed. You can change the format of numeric variables with the FORMATS command. You cannot change the format of string variables.

Values are stored internally in double precision. The format specification does not affect the precision of data values stored in memory.

Variable formats have two components: variable type and variable width.

Variable Type

- Variables can be one of two types: numeric or string.
- By default, DATA LIST assumes variables are numeric. String variables are indicated by the A format specification.
- Variables created by COMPUTE or IF are assigned a format type based on the specifications in the assignment expression (see COMPUTE and IF). Variables created by COUNT are always numeric (see COUNT).
- Variables in a file translated from another computer program are assigned types by SPSS/PC+ (see TRANSLATE).

Numeric Variables

- Numeric variables can contain numbers, decimal points, and optional leading plus or minus signs. The system-missing value is assigned when the value of a numeric value contains any other characters.

String Variables

- The values of string variables can contain letters, numbers, and punctuation characters.
- String variables whose values contain 8 or fewer characters are referred to as *short string variables*. String variables that contain more than 8 characters are referred to as *long string variables*. The maximum number of characters in a long string is 255.
- Missing values cannot be generated for string variables read from a raw data file, since any character is a legal string value.
- Only short strings can be used in SPSS/PC+ transformation commands. To transform data based on the values of a long string variable, first use AUTORECODE to create a numeric variable from the long string variable.
- When a transformation of a string variable yields a missing or undefined result, a blank value is assigned. Blank is therefore defined as the user-missing value for string variables created by transformation commands. If you compute one string variable equal to another, user-missing values are converted to blanks and retain their user-missing status.

Variable Width

- Variables defined with DATA LIST FIXED use column specifications to calculate the maximum width of data values. If a decimal place is implied on DATA LIST, one column is added to the format to allow for the decimal point.
- Numeric variables read with DATA LIST FREE are assigned a display width of eight characters, including a decimal point and two decimal digits (format F8.2).

- String variables read with DATA LIST FREE are assigned a width of eight characters, unless you specify the maximum number of characters after the A format specification, as in NAME (A20).
- Numeric variables created with COMPUTE or IF are assigned a width of eight characters, including a decimal point and two decimal digits (format F8.2). String variables created with COMPUTE or IF are assigned a width based on the assignment expression. When the assignment expression creates a variable that is equal to an existing variable, the width of the new variable is equal to the width of the existing variable. When the assignment expression creates a new string variable by equating it to a string constant, the width of the new string variable equals the width of the string constant.
- New variables created with COUNT are always numeric and are assigned a width of eight characters, including a decimal point and two decimal digits (format F8.2).

System Variables

System variables are special variables created by SPSS/PC+ during a working session to keep system-required information, such as the number of cases read by the system, the system-missing value, and the current date. System variables can be used in data transformations but not in procedures.

- The names of system variables begin with a dollar sign ($).
- You cannot modify a system variable or alter its print or write format. Except for these restrictions, you can use system variables anywhere a normal variable is used in the transformation language.
- System variables cannot be named on a DATA LIST, GET, or IMPORT command.
- System variables cannot be named as target variables on COUNT, COMPUTE, and IF commands.

$DATE   *The date a case was read using the DATA LIST or IMPORT command or created in SPSS Data Entry II or QED.*

$CASENUM   *The sequence number of each case as it is read by SPSS/PC+ using a DATA LIST or IMPORT command or created using QED or SPSS Data Entry II. The value of $CASENUM remains unchanged, even after the SORT, SELECT IF, SAVE, and GET commands are used, so you can always identify the original case number.*

$WEIGHT   *Case weighting.* The initial value of *$WEIGHT* for each case is 1.00. The value of *$WEIGHT* is changed when you run a WEIGHT command.

- When a file is written using SAVE, the current values of each system variable are written to the file.
- When a file is written using EXPORT, *$WEIGHT* is the only system variable written to the file.
- When a file is written using WRITE, *$CASENUM* and *$WEIGHT* are written but *$DATE* is not.

Transformation Expressions

Transformation expressions are used in COMPUTE, IF, PROCESS IF, and SELECT IF commands. This section describes the operators and functions that can be used in transformation expressions.

Arithmetic Operators

Arithmetic operators are used with numeric variables in expressions on COMPUTE, IF, and SELECT IF commands. The following arithmetic operators are available in SPSS/PC+:

+   *Addition.*

-       *Subtraction.*

*   *Multiplication.*

/   *Division.*

**   *Exponentiation.*

- No two operators can appear consecutively.
- String variables and string constants cannot be used with arithmetic operators.
- Arithmetic operators cannot be implied. For example, (VAR1)(VAR2) is not a legal specification; you must specify VAR1*VAR2.
- Arithmetic operators and parentheses serve as delimiters. To improve readability, blanks (not commas) can be inserted before and after an operator.
- To form complex expressions, you can use variables, constants, and functions with arithmetic operators.
- The order of operations is exponentiation, then multiplication and division, and then addition and subtraction. Arithmetic operators are executed after functions.
- Operators at the same level are executed from left to right.
- To override the order of operation, use parentheses. Execution begins with the innermost set of parentheses and progresses out.
- Arithmetic operators cannot be entered before or after relational and logical operators (see "Logical Expressions" on p. 441).
- If any variables or values in an arithmetic expression are missing, the result is always system-missing.
- A negative number raised to a noninteger power and division by 0 is system-missing.

Functions

Functions can be used in expressions on the COMPUTE, IF, and SELECT IF commands. All functions can be used with numeric variables. Only the LAG function can be used with short string variables. Long string variables cannot be used in functions. For examples using functions, see COMPUTE, IF, and SELECT IF.

- The expression that is transformed by a function is called the *argument*. The argument to most functions is a variable name or a constant. Arguments are always enclosed in parentheses, as in SQRT(X), where the SQRT function takes the square root of variable X.
- Arguments can also be complex expressions that include arithmetic operators, numeric constants, and other functions. The expression (VARA+VARB) can be used as an argument by most functions. You can use sets of parentheses in complex expressions used as arguments.
- By default, functions are evaluated before arithmetic operators. The order of operations is functions first, then exponentiation, then multiplication and division, and then addition and subtraction.
- Operations at the same level are executed from left to right.
- Use parentheses to override the default order of operation. Execution begins with the innermost set of parentheses and progresses out.

Numeric Functions

- Numeric functions always return numbers (or the system-missing value whenever the result is indeterminate).
- All numeric functions take one argument enclosed in parentheses. The argument can be a variable name, a constant, or an expression, as in RND(A**2/B).

ABS(arg)   *Absolute value.* ABS(SCALE) is 4.7 when *SCALE* equals 4.7 or −4.7. The result is system-missing if the argument is missing.

RND(arg)   *Round the absolute value to an integer and reaffix the sign.* RND(SCALE) is −5 when SCALE equals −4.7. The result is system-missing if the argument is missing.

TRUNC(arg)   *Truncate to an integer.* TRUNC(SCALE) is −4 when *SCALE* equals -4.7. The result is system-missing if the argument is missing.

MOD10(arg)   *Remainder (modulus) when the argument is divided by 10.* MOD10(SCALE) is 8 when *SCALE* equals 8; MOD10(SCALE) is −8 when *SCALE* equals −8. The result is 0 if the argument is 0 and system-missing if the argument is missing.

SQRT(arg)   *Square root.* SQRT(SIBS) is 1.41 when *SIBS* equals 2. The result is system-missing if the argument is negative or missing.

EXP(arg)   *Exponential. e* is raised to the power of the argument. EXP(VARA) is 7.39 when *VARA* equals 2. The result is system-missing if the argument is missing or if the argument produces a result too large to be represented.

LG10(arg)   *Base 10 logarithm.* LG10(VARB) is 0.48 when *VARB* equals 3. The result is system-missing if the argument is negative, 0, or missing.

LN(arg)   *Natural or Naperian logarithm (base* e*).* LN(VARC) is 2.30 when *VARC* equals 10. The result is system-missing if the argument is negative, 0, or missing.

ARTAN(arg) *Arc tangent.* (Alias ATAN.) The result is given in radians. ARTAN(ANG2) is 0.79 when *ANG2* equals 1. The result is system-missing if the argument is missing.

SIN(arg) *Sine.* The argument must be specified in radians. SIN(VARD) is 0.84 when *VARD* equals 1. The result is system-missing if the argument is missing.

COS(arg) *Cosine.* The argument must be specified in radians. COS(VARE) is 0.54 when *VARE* equals 1. The result is system-missing if the argument is missing.

The arc sine function is not directly available but can be computed easily as the following:

```
COMPUTE ARCSINX = ARTAN(X/SQRT(1-X*X)).
```

This identity is valid only if X is greater than −1 and less than +1.

Missing-Value Functions

- Each missing-value function takes one variable name enclosed in parentheses as an argument.

VALUE(arg) *Ignore the missing-value status of user-defined missing values.* The value is treated as is. For example, if 999 was declared as a user-missing value for *VAR1*, the expression IF (VALUE(VAR1) EQ 999) is evaluated as *true* for cases where *VAR1* has that value; the expression IF (VAR1 EQ 999) is evaluated as *missing,* since this expression contains a variable with a missing value. Similarly, VALUE(VAR1) + 1 equals 1000, but VAR1 + 1 is missing.

MISSING(arg) *True or 1 if the value is user-missing or system-missing; false or 0 otherwise.*

SYSMIS(arg) *True or 1 if the value is system-missing; false or 0 otherwise.*

Cross-Case Function

LAG(arg) *The value of the variable one case before.* LAG(GNP) returns the value of GNP for the case before the current one. The argument can be a numeric or short string variable. The result is system-missing for the first case.

- When LAG is used with commands that select cases (for example, SELECT IF and SAMPLE), LAG counts cases after case selection, even if specified before these commands (see "Command Order" on p. 430).

Random-Number Functions

- The argument to a random-number function must be a numeric constant or variable name.
- The seed value used for random number functions can be changed using the SEED specification on the SET command.

UNIFORM(arg) *Return a uniform pseudo-random number with values varying between 0 and the value of the argument.* For example, SAMP1 = UNIFORM(150) assigns a value to *SAMP1* for each case in the file. All values are sampled from a uniform distribution between 0 and 150.

NORMAL(arg)   *Return a normal pseudo-random number with a mean of 0 and a standard deviation equal to the argument.* For example, SAMP2 = NORMAL(2.5) assigns a value to *SAMP2* for each case in the file. All values are sampled from a normal distribution with a mean of 0 and a standard deviation of 2.5. The result is system-missing if the argument is 0, negative, or missing.

Date Function

YRMODA(arg list)   *Convert year, month, and day to a day number.* Each argument is separated by a comma and the entire list of arguments is enclosed in parentheses. The number returned is the number of days since October 14, 1582 (day 0 of the Gregorian calendar).

- Arguments for YRMODA can be variables, constants, or any other type of numeric expression but must yield integers.
- Year, month, and day must be specified in that order.
- The first argument can be any year between 0 and 99, or between 1582 to 47516.
- If the first argument yields a number between 00 and 99, 1900 through 1999 is assumed.
- The month can range from 1 through 13. Month 13 with day 0 yields the last day of the year. For example, YRMODA(1990,13,0) produces the day number for December 31, 1990. Month 13 with any other day yields the day of the first month of the coming year; for example, YRMODA(1990,13,1) produces the day number for January 1, 1991.
- The day can range from 0 through 31. Day 0 is the last day of the previous month regardless of whether it is 28, 29, 30, or 31. For example, YRMODA(1990,3,0) yields 148791.00, the day number for February 28, 1990.
- The function returns the system-missing value if any of the three arguments is missing or if the arguments do not form a valid date *after* October 14, 1582.

Logical Expressions

Logical expressions can be specified on the IF, SELECT IF, and PROCESS IF commands. SPSS/PC+ evaluates a logical expression as true or false, or as missing if it is indeterminate. A logical expression returns 1 if the expression is true, 0 if it is false, or system-missing if it is missing. Thus, a logical expression can be any expression that yields this three-value logic.

- The simplest logical expression is a logical variable. A logical variable is any numeric variable that has values 1, 0, or system-missing. Logical variables cannot be strings.
- Logical expressions can be simple logical variables or relations, or they can be complex logical tests involving variables, constants, functions, relational operators, logical operators, and parentheses to control the order of evaluation. The complexity of a logical expression is limited by available memory.
- Logical expressions used with PROCESS IF can contain only relational operators, not logical operators.

- Parentheses enclosing a logical expression are required.
- Blanks (not commas) must be used to separate relational and logical operators from expressions.
- String values must be enclosed in apostrophes or quotation marks.
- Long string values cannot be used in logical expressions. Use AUTORECODE if necessary.
- On an IF command, a logical expression that is true causes the assignment expression to be executed. If the logical expression is false or missing, the assignment expression is not executed and the value of the target variable is not altered.
- On a SELECT IF command, a logical expression that is true causes the case to be selected. If the logical expression is false or missing, the case is not selected.
- On a PROCESS IF command, a logical expression that is true causes the case to be processed in the next procedure. If the logical expression is false or missing, the case is not processed.

Relational Operators

A relation is a logical expression that compares two values using a *relational operator*. In the command

```
IF (X EQ 0) Y=1
```

variable *X* and 0 are expressions that yield the values to be compared by the EQ relational operator. Relational operators are

EQ or =	*Equal to.*
NE or ~= or <>	*Not equal to.*
LT or <	*Less than.*
LE or <=	*Less than or equal to.*
GT or >	*Greater than.*
GE or >=	*Greater than or equal to.*

- The expressions in a relation can be variables, constants, or more complicated arithmetic expressions.
- Relational operators must compare one string variable to another or one numeric value to another. Only strings of the same length can be compared.

AND and OR Logical Operators

Two or more relations can be logically joined using the logical operators AND and OR. Logical operators combine relations according to the following rules:

- Only one logical operator can be used to combine two relations. However, multiple relations can be combined into a complex logical expression.
- Regardless of the number of relations and logical operators used to build a logical expression, the result is either true, false, or indeterminate because of missing values.

- Operators or expressions cannot be implied. For example, X EQ 1 OR 2 is illegal; you must specify X EQ 1 OR X EQ 2.

AND or &   *Both relations must be true for the logical expression to be true.*

OR or | *If either relation is true, the logical expression is true.*

NOT Logical Operator

The NOT logical operator reverses the true/false outcome of the expression that immediately follows. NOT affects only the expression that immediately follows, unless otherwise indicated by parentheses.

Order of Evaluation

- When arithmetic operators and functions are used in a logical expression, the order of operations is functions and arithmetic operations first, then relational operators, and then logical operators.
- When more than one logical operator is used, NOT is evaluated first, then AND, and then OR.
- Operators at the same level are executed from left to right.
- To change the order of evaluation, use parentheses. Execution begins with the innermost set of parentheses and progresses out.

Missing Values in Logical Expressions

In a simple relation, the logic is indeterminate if the expression on either side of the relational operator is missing. When two or more relations are joined by logical operators AND and OR, SPSS/PC+ always returns a missing value if all of the relations in the expression are missing. However, if any one of the relations can be determined, SPSS/PC+ tries to return true or false according to the logical outcomes shown in Table 3.

- When two relations are joined with the AND operator, the logical expression can never be true if one of the relations is indeterminate. The expression can, however, be false.
- When two relations are joined with the OR operator, the logical expression can never be false if one relation returns missing. The expression, however, can be true.

Table 3   Outcome for AND and OR combinations

Expression	Outcome	Expression	Outcome
true AND true	= true	true OR true	= true
true AND false	= false	true OR false	= true
false AND false	= false	false OR false	= false
true AND missing	= missing	true OR missing	= true
missing AND missing	= missing	missing OR missing	= missing
false AND missing	= false*	false OR missing	= missing

Commands

ADD VALUE LABELS

```
ADD VALUE LABELS varlist value 'label' value 'label'...[/varlist...]
```

Example:
```
ADD VALUE LABELS JOBGRADE 'P' 'Parttime Employee'
                          'C' 'Customer Support'.
```

Overview

ADD VALUE LABELS adds or alters value labels without affecting other value labels already defined for that variable. In contrast, VALUE LABELS adds or alters value labels but deletes all existing value labels for that variable when it does so.

Basic Specification

The basic specification is a variable name and individual values with associated labels.

Syntax Rules

- Labels can be assigned to values of any previously defined variable. It is not necessary to enter value labels for all of a variable's values.
- Each value label must be enclosed in apostrophes or quotation marks.
- When an apostrophe occurs as part of a label, enclose the label in quotation marks or enter the internal apostrophe twice with no intervening space.
- Value labels can contain any characters, including blanks.
- The same labels can be assigned to the same values of different variables by specifying a list of variable names. For string variables, the variables in the list must have the same defined width (for example, A8).
- Multiple sets of variable names and value labels can be specified on one ADD VALUE LABELS command as long as each set is separated from the previous one by a slash.

Operations

- ADD VALUE LABELS takes effect as soon as it is encountered in the command sequence.
- The added value labels are stored in the active file dictionary.

- ADD VALUE LABELS can be used for variables that have no previously assigned value labels.
- Adding labels to some values does not affect labels previously assigned to other values.

Limitations

- Value labels cannot exceed 60 characters. Most procedures display only 20 characters.

Example

```
ADD VALUE LABELS V1 TO V3 1 'Officials & Managers'
                          6 'Service Workers'
                /V4 'N' 'New Employee'.
```

- Labels are assigned to the values 1 and 6 of the variables between and including *V1* and *V3* on the active file.
- Following the required slash, a label for value N for variable *V4* is specified. N is a string value and must be enclosed in apostrophes or quotation marks.
- If labels already exist for these values, they are changed in the dictionary. If labels do not exist for these values, new labels are added to the dictionary.
- Existing labels for other values for these variables are not affected.

Value Labels for String Variables

- Value labels can be assigned to short string variables only. They cannot be assigned to long string variables.
- The values and the labels must be enclosed in apostrophes or quotation marks.
- If a specified value is longer than the defined width of the variable, SPSS/PC+ displays a warning and truncates the value. The added label will be associated with the truncated value.
- If a specified value is shorter than the defined width of the variable, SPSS/PC+ adds blanks to right-pad the value without warning. The added label will be associated with the padded value.
- If a single set of labels is to be assigned to a list of string variables, the variables must have the same defined width (for example, A8).

Example

```
ADD VALUE LABELS  STATE 'TEX' 'TEXAS' 'TEN' 'TENNESSEE'
                        'MIN' 'MINNESOTA'.
```

- ADD VALUE LABELS assigns labels to three values of variable *STATE*. Each value and each label is specified in apostrophes.
- Assuming variable *STATE* is defined as three characters wide, the labels *TEXAS*, *TENNESSEE*, and *MINNESOTA* will be associated with values TEX, TEN, and MIN. However, if *STATE* were defined as two characters wide, SPSS/PC+ would truncate the specified

values to two characters and would not be able to associate the labels correctly. Both TEX and TEN would be truncated to TE and would first be assigned label *TEXAS*.

Example

```
ADD VALUE LABELS=STATE REGION "U" "UNKNOWN".
```

- Label *UNKNOWN* is assigned to value U for both *STATE* and *REGION*.
- *STATE* and *REGION* must have the same defined width. If they do not, a separate specification must be made for each, as in:

```
ADD VALUE LABELS STATE "U" "UNKNOWN" / REGION "U" "UNKNOWN".
```

AGGREGATE

```
AGGREGATE OUTFILE={'filename'} [/MISSING=COLUMNWISE]
                  {*        }

[/PRESORTED] /BREAK=varlist[({A})][varlist...]
                            ({D})

/aggvar['label']aggvar['label']...=function(arguments)

[/aggvar ...]
```

Available functions:

SUM	Sum	MEAN	Mean
SD	Standard deviation	MAX	Maximum
MIN	Minimum	PGT	% of cases greater than value
PLT	% of cases less than value	PIN	% of cases between values
POUT	% of cases not in range	FGT	Fraction greater than value
FLT	Fraction less than value	FIN	Fraction between values
FOUT	Fraction not in range	N	Weighted number of cases
NU	Unweighted number of cases	NMISS	Weighted number of missing cases
NUMISS	Unweighted number of missing cases	FIRST	First nonmissing value
LAST	Last nonmissing value		

Example:

```
AGGREGATE OUTFILE=AGGEMP /BREAK=LOCATN DEPT /COUNT=N
  /AVGSAL AVGRAISE = MEAN(SALARY RAISE)
  /SUMSAL SUMRAISE = SUM(SALARY RAISE)
  /BLACKPCT 'Percentage Black' = PIN(RACE,1,1)
  /WHITEPCT 'Percentage White' = PIN(RACE,5,5).
```

Overview

AGGREGATE aggregates groups of cases in the active file into single cases and creates a new, aggregated file. The values of one or more variables in the active file define the case groups. These variables are called **break variables.** A set of cases with identical values for each break variable is called a **break group.** A series of aggregate functions are applied to **source variables** in the active file to create new, aggregated variables that have one value for each break group.

AGGREGATE is often used with JOIN MATCH to add variables with summary measures (sum, mean, etc.) to a file. Transformations performed on the combined file can create composite summary measures. In the REPORT procedure, the composite variables can be used to write reports with nested composite information.

Options

Aggregated File. You can produce either a system file or a new active file.

Sorting. By default, cases in the aggregated file are sorted in ascending order of the values of each break variable. Alternatively, you can specify descending order. If the active file is already sorted by the break variables, you can skip this final sorting pass through the file using the PRESORTED subcommand.

Aggregated Functions. You can create aggregated variables using any of 19 aggregate functions. Functions SUM, MEAN, and SD can aggregate only numeric variables. All other functions can use both numeric and string variables.

Labels and Formats. You can specify variable labels for the aggregated variables. Variables created with functions MAX, MIN, FIRST, and LAST assume the formats and value labels of their source variables. All other variables assume the default formats described under "Aggregate Functions" on p. 451.

Basic Specification

The basic specification is OUTFILE, BREAK, and at least one aggregate function and source variable. OUTFILE specifies a name for the aggregated file. BREAK names the case grouping (break) variables. The aggregate function creates a new aggregated variable based on the source variable.

Subcommand Order

- OUTFILE must be specified first.
- If specified, PRESORTED must precede BREAK. No other subcommand can be specified between these two subcommands.
- MISSING, if specified, must immediately follow OUTFILE.
- The aggregate functions must be specified last.

Operations

- When AGGREGATE produces a system file, the active file remains unchanged and is still available for analysis. When AGGREGATE creates a new active file, it replaces the old active file. Only the new active file is available for analysis.
- AGGREGATE places the new system file in the current DOS directory.
- The aggregated file contains the break variables plus the variables created by the aggregate functions.
- AGGREGATE excludes cases with missing values from all aggregate calculations except those involving functions N, NU, NMISS, and NUMISS.
- Unless otherwise specified, AGGREGATE sorts cases in the aggregated file in ascending order of the values of the grouping variables.
- If PRESORTED is specified, a new aggregate case is created each time a different value or combination of values is encountered for variables named on the BREAK subcommand.

Example

```
AGGREGATE OUTFILE='AGGEMP.SYS' /BREAK=LOCATN DEPT
 /COUNT=N
 /AVGSAL AVGRAISE = MEAN(SALARY RAISE)
 /SUMSAL SUMRAISE = SUM(SALARY RAISE)
 /BLACKPCT 'Percentage Black' = PIN(RACE,1,1)
 /WHITEPCT 'Percentage White' = PIN(RACE,5,5).
```

- AGGREGATE creates a new system file *AGGEMP.SYS*. *AGGEMP.SYS* contains two break variables (*LOCATN* and *DEPT*) and all the new aggregate variables (*COUNT*, *AVGSAL*, *AVGRAISE*, *SUMSAL*, *SUMRAISE*, *BLACKPCT*, and *WHITEPCT*).

- BREAK specifies *LOCATN* and *DEPT* as the break variables. In the aggregated file, cases are sorted in ascending order of *LOCATN* and in ascending order of *DEPT* within *LOCATN*. The active file remains unsorted.

- Variable *COUNT* is created as the weighted number of cases in each break group. *AVGSAL* is the mean of *SALARY* and *AVGRAISE* is the mean of *RAISE*. *SUMSAL* is the sum of *SALARY* and *SUMRAISE* is the sum of *RAISE*. *BLACKPCT* is the percentage of cases with value 1 for *RACE*. *WHITEPCT* is the percentage of cases with value 5 for *RACE*.

Example

```
GET FILE='HUBEMPL.SYS' /KEEP=LOCATN DEPT HOURLY RAISE SEX.
AGGREGATE OUTFILE='AGGFILE.SYS' /BREAK=LOCATN DEPT
 /AVGHOUR AVGRAISE=MEAN(HOURLY RAISE).
SORT CASES BY LOCATN DEPT.
JOIN MATCH TABLE='AGGFILE.SYS' /FILE=* /BY LOCATN DEPT
 /KEEP AVGHOUR AVGRAISE LOCATN DEPT SEX HOURLY RAISE /MAP.

COMPUTE HOURDIF=HOURLY/AVGHOUR.
COMPUTE RAISEDIF=RAISE/AVGRAISE.
LIST.
```

- GET reads the system file *HUBEMPL.SYS* and keeps a subset of variables.

- AGGREGATE creates a file aggregated by *LOCATN* and *DEPT* with the two new variables *AVGHOUR* and *AVGRAISE*, containing the means by location and department for *HOURLY* and *RAISE*. The aggregated file is saved as a system file named *AGGFILE.SYS*. Only the aggregated system file *AGGFILE.SYS* is sorted by *LOCATN* and *DEPT;* the active file remains unchanged.

- SORT CASES sorts the active file in ascending order of *LOCATN* and *DEPT,* the same variables used as AGGREGATE break variables.

- JOIN MATCH specifies a table lookup match with *AGGFILE.SYS* as the table file and the sorted active file as the case file.

- BY indicates that the keys for the match are *LOCATN* and *DEPT*.

- KEEP specifies the subset and order of variables to be retained in the resulting file.

- MAP provides a listing of the variables in the resulting file and the two input files.

- The COMPUTE commands calculate the ratios of each employee's hourly wage and raise to the department averages for wage and raise. The results are stored in variables *HOURDIF* and *RAISEDIF*.

- LIST displays the resulting file.

OUTFILE Subcommand

OUTFILE specifies a name for the file created by AGGREGATE. If an asterisk is specified on OUTFILE, the aggregated file replaces the active file. OUTFILE must be the first subcommand specified on AGGREGATE.

- If the aggregated file replaces the active file, the file is not automatically saved on disk. To save the file, use the SAVE command.

Example

```
AGGREGATE OUTFILE='AGGEMP.SYS'
 /BREAK=LOCATN
 /AVGSAL = MEAN(SALARY).
```

- OUTFILE creates a system file named *AGGEMP.SYS*. The active file remains unchanged and is available for further analysis.
- File *AGGEMP.SYS* contains two variables, LOCATN and AVGSAL.

BREAK Subcommand

BREAK lists the grouping variables, also called break variables. Each unique combination of values of the break variables defines one break group. A break group includes cases with identical values for the break variables.

- The variables named on BREAK can be any combination of variables in the active file.
- Unless PRESORTED is specified, AGGREGATE sorts cases after aggregating. By default, cases are sorted in ascending order of the values of the break variables. AGGREGATE sorts first in order of the first break variable, then in order of the second break variable within the groups created by the first, and so on.
- Sort order can be controlled by specifying an A (for ascending) or D (for descending) in parentheses after any break variables.
- The designations A and D apply to all preceding undesignated variables.
- Subcommand PRESORTED overrides all sorting specifications.

Example

```
AGGREGATE OUTFILE='AGGEMP.SYS'
 /BREAK=LOCATN DEPT (A) TENURE (D)
 /AVGSAL = MEAN(SALARY).
```

- BREAK names variables *LOCATN*, *DEPT*, and *TENURE* as the break variables.
- Cases in the aggregated file are sorted in ascending order of *LOCATN*, in ascending order of *DEPT* within *LOCATN*, and in descending order of *TENURE* within *LOCATN* and *DEPT*. For each group defined by these variables, *AVGSAL* is computed as the mean of salary.

PRESORTED Subcommand

PRESORTED indicates that cases in the active file are sorted according to the values of the break variables. This prevents AGGREGATE from sorting cases that have already been sorted and can save a considerable amount of processing time.

- If specified, PRESORTED must precede BREAK. The only specification is keyword PRESORTED. PRESORTED has no additional specifications.
- When PRESORTED is specified, SPSS/PC+ forms an aggregate case out of each group of *adjacent* cases with the same values for the break variables.
- If the active file is not sorted by the break variables in ascending order and PRESORTED is specified, a warning message is generated but the procedure is executed. Each group of adjacent cases with the same values for break variables forms a case in the aggregated file, which may produce multiple cases with the same values for the break variables.

Example

```
AGGREGATE OUTFILE='AGGEMP.SYS'
 /PRESORTED
 /BREAK=LOCATN DEPT
 /AVGSAL = MEAN(SALARY).
```

- PRESORTED indicates that cases are already sorted by variables *LOCATN* and *DEPT*.
- AGGREGATE does not make an extra data pass to sort the cases.

Aggregate Functions

An aggregated variable is created by applying an aggregate function to a variable in the active file. The variable in the active file is called the **source** variable, and the new aggregated variable is the **target** variable.

- The aggregate functions must be specified last on AGGREGATE.
- The simplest specification is a target variable list, followed by an equals sign, a function name, and a list of source variables.
- The number of target variables named must match the number of source variables.
- When several aggregate variables are defined at once, the first-named target variable is based on the first-named source variable, the second-named target is based on the second-named source, and so on.
- Only functions MAX, MIN, FIRST, and LAST copy complete dictionary information from the source variable. For all other functions, new variables do not have labels and are assigned default formats. The default format for a variable depends on the function used to create it (see list of functions below).
- You can provide a variable label for a new variable by specifying the label in apostrophes immediately following the new variable name. Value labels cannot be assigned in AGGREGATE.
- To change formats or add value labels to an active file created by AGGREGATE, use the FORMATS or VALUE LABELS commands. If the aggregated file is written to disk, first retrieve the file using GET, specify the new labels and formats, and resave the file.

The following is a list of available functions:

SUM(varlist)   *Sum across cases.* The default format is F8.2.

MEAN(varlist)   *Mean across cases.* The default format is F8.2.

SD(varlist)   *Standard deviation across cases.* The default format is F8.2.

MAX(varlist)   *Maximum value across cases.* Complete dictionary information is copied from the source variables to the target variables.

MIN(varlist)   *Minimum value across cases.* Complete dictionary information is copied from the source variables to the target variables.

PGT(varlist,value)   *Percentage of cases greater than the specified value.* The default format is F5.1.

PLT(varlist,value)   *Percentage of cases less than the specified value.* The default format is F5.1.

PIN(varlist,value1,value2)   *Percentage of cases between value1 and value2, inclusive.* The default format is F5.1.

POUT(varlist,value1,value2)   *Percentage of cases not between value1 and value2.* Cases where the source variable equals value1 or value2 are not counted. The default format is F5.1.

FGT(varlist,value)   *Fraction of cases greater than the specified value.* The default format is F5.3.

FLT(varlist,value)   *Fraction of cases less than the specified value.* The default format is F5.3.

FIN(varlist,value1,value2)   *Fraction of cases between value1 and value2, inclusive.* The default format is F5.3.

FOUT(varlist,value1,value2)   *Fraction of cases not between value1 and value2.* Cases where the source variable equals value1 or value2 are not counted. The default format is F5.3.

N(varlist)   *Weighted number of cases in break group.* The default format is F7.0 for unweighted files and F8.2 for weighted files.

NU(varlist)   *Unweighted number of cases in break group.* The default format is F7.0.

NMISS(varlist)   *Weighted number of missing cases.* The default format is F7.0 for unweighted files and F8.2 for weighted files.

NUMISS(varlist)   *Unweighted number of missing cases.* The default format is F7.0.

FIRST(varlist)   *First nonmissing observed value in break group.* Complete dictionary information is copied from the source variables to the target variables.

LAST(varlist)   *Last nonmissing observed value in break group.* Complete dictionary information is copied from the source variables to the target variables.

- Functions SUM, MEAN, and SD can be applied only to numeric source variables. All other functions can use short and long string variables as well as numeric ones.

- The N and NU functions do not require arguments. Without arguments, they return the number of weighted and unweighted valid cases in a break group. If you supply a variable list, they return the number of weighted and unweighted valid cases for the variables specified.

- For several functions, the argument includes values as well as a source variable designation. Either blanks or commas can be used to separate the components of an argument list.

- For PIN, POUT, FIN, and FOUT, the first value should be less than or equal to the second. If the first is greater, AGGREGATE automatically reverses them and prints a warning message. If the two values are equal, PIN and FIN calculate the percentages and fractions of values equal to the argument. POUT and FOUT calculate the percentages and fractions of values not equal to the argument.

- String values specified in an argument should be enclosed in apostrophes. They are evaluated in alphabetical order.

Example

```
AGGREGATE OUTFILE='AGGEMP.SYS' /BREAK=LOCATN
 /AVGSAL 'Average Salary' AVGRAISE = MEAN(SALARY RAISE).
```

- AGGREGATE defines two aggregate variables, *AVGSAL* and *AVGRAISE*.

- *AVGSAL* is the mean of *SALARY* for each break group and *AVGRAISE* is the mean of *RAISE*.

- The label *Average Salary* is assigned to *AVGSAL*.

Example

```
AGGREGATE OUTFILE=* /BREAK=DEPT
 /LOWVAC,LOWSICK = PLT (VACDAY SICKDAY,10).
```

- AGGREGATE creates two aggregated variables: *LOWVAC* and *LOWSICK*. *LOWVAC* is the percentage of cases with values less than 10 for *VACDAY* and *LOWSICK* is the percentage of cases with values less than 10 for *SICKDAY*.

Example

```
AGGREGATE OUTFILE='GROUPS.SYS' /BREAK=OCCGROUP
 /COLLEGE = FIN(EDUC,13,16).
```

- AGGREGATE creates variable *COLLEGE*, which is the fraction of cases with 13 to 16 years of education (variable *EDUC*).

Example

```
AGGREGATE OUTFILE=* /BREAK=CLASS
 /LOCAL = PIN(STATE,'IL','IO').
```

- AGGREGATE creates variable *LOCAL*, which is the percentage of cases in each break group whose two-letter state code represents Illinois, Indiana, or Iowa. (The abbreviation for Indiana, IN, is between IL and IO in an alphabetical sort sequence.)

MISSING Subcommand

By default, AGGREGATE uses all nonmissing values of the source variable to calculate aggregated variables. An aggregated variable will have a missing value only if the source variable is missing for every case in the break group. You can alter the default missing-value treatment by using the MISSING subcommand. You can also specify the inclusion of user-missing values on any function.

- MISSING must immediately follow OUTFILE.
- COLUMNWISE is the only specification available for MISSING.
- If COLUMNWISE is specified, the value of an aggregated variable is missing for a break group if the source variable is missing for any case in the group.
- COLUMNWISE does not affect the calculation of the N, NU, NMISS, or NUMISS functions.
- COLUMNWISE does not apply to break variables. If a break variable has a missing value, cases in that group are processed and the break variable is saved in the file with the missing value. Use SELECT IF to eliminate cases with missing values for break variables.

Including Missing Values

You can force a function to include user-missing values in its calculations by specifying a period after the function name.

- AGGREGATE ignores periods used with functions N, NU, NMISS, and NUMISS if these functions have no argument.
- User-missing values are treated as valid when these four functions are followed by a period and have a variable as an argument. NMISS.(AGE) treats the user-missing value for *AGE* as valid and gives the number of cases for which *AGE* has the system-missing value only.

The effect of specifying a period with N, NU, NMISS, and NUMISS is illustrated by the following:

N = N. = N(AGE) + NMISS(AGE) = N.(AGE) + NMISS.(AGE)
NU = NU. = NU(AGE) + NUMISS(AGE) = NU.(AGE) + NUMISS.(AGE)

- The function N (the same as N. with no argument) yields a value for each break group that equals the number of cases with valid values (N(AGE)) plus the number of cases with user- or system-missing values (NMISS(AGE)).
- This in turn equals the number of cases with either valid or user-missing values (N.(AGE)) plus the number with system-missing values (NMISS.(AGE)).
- The same identities hold for the NU, NMISS, and NUMISS functions.

Example

```
AGGREGATE OUTFILE-'AGGEMP.SYS' /MISSING=COLUMNWISE /BREAK=LOCATN
/AVGSAL = MEAN(SALARY).
```

- *AVGSAL* is missing for an aggregated case if *SALARY* is missing for any case in the break group.

Example

```
AGGREGATE OUTFILE=* /BREAK=DEPT
/LOVAC = PLT.(VACDAY,10).
```

- *LOVAC* is the percentage of cases within each break group with values less than 10 for *VACDAY*, even if one of those values is defined as user-missing.

Example

```
AGGREGATE OUTFILE='CLASS.AVG' /BREAK=GRADE
/FIRSTAGE = FIRST.(AGE).
```

- The first value of *AGE* in each break group is assigned to variable *FIRSTAGE*.
- If the first value of *AGE* in a break group is user-missing, that value will be assigned to *FIRSTAGE*. However, the value will retain its missing-value status, since variables created with FIRST take dictionary information from their source variables.

Comparing Missing-Value Treatments

Table 4 demonstrates the effects of specifying the MISSING subcommand and a period after the function name. Each entry in the table is the number of cases used to compute the specified function for variable *EDUC*, which has 10 nonmissing cases, 5 user-missing cases, and 2 system-missing cases for the group. Note that columnwise treatment produces the same results as the default for every function except the MEAN function.

Table 4 Default vs. columnwise missing-value treatments

Function	Default	Columnwise
N	17	17
N.	17	17
N(EDUC)	10	10
N.(EDUC)	15	15
MEAN(EDUC)	10	0
MEAN.(EDUC)	15	0
NMISS(EDUC)	7	7
NMISS.(EDUC)	2	2

ANOVA

```
ANOVA [VARIABLES=] varlist BY varlist(min,max) [WITH varlist]
      [/[VARIABLES=] varlist ...]

 [/OPTIONS=option numbers]

 [/STATISTICS={statistic numbers}]
             {ALL             }
```

Options:

1   Include user-missing values
2   Suppress labels
3   Suppress all interaction terms
4   Suppress three-way terms
5   Suppress four-way terms
6   Suppress five-way terms

7   Covariates with main effects
8   Covariates after main effects
9   Regression approach
10 Hierarchical approach
11 Narrow format

Statistics:

1   Multiple classification analysis (MCA) table
2   Unstandardized regression coefficients for covariates
3   Cell means and counts

Example:

```
ANOVA VARIABLES=YVAR1,YVAR2 BY XVAR(1,3) ZVAR1,ZVAR2(1,2)
/OPTIONS=4
/STATISTICS=3.
```

Overview

ANOVA performs analysis of variance for factorial designs. The default is the full factorial model if there are five or fewer factors. Analysis of variance tests the hypothesis that the group means of the dependent variable are equal. The dependent variable is interval level, and one or more categorical variables define the groups. These categorical variables are termed **factors**. ANOVA also allows you to include continuous explanatory variables, termed **covariates**. Other SPSS/PC+ procedures that perform analysis of variance are ONEWAY, MEANS, and MANOVA. To perform a comparison of two means, use TTEST.

Options

Specifying Covariates. You can introduce covariates into the model using keyword WITH on the VARIABLES subcommand.

Order of Entry of Covariates. You can control the order in which covariates and main effects are assessed using Options 7 and 8.

Suppressing Interaction Effects. You can suppress the effects of various orders of interaction using Options 3 through 6.

Methods for Decomposing Sums of Squares. By default, the classic experimental approach is used. You can request the regression or hierarchical approach using Option 9 or 10.

Statistics. Using the STATISTICS subcommand, you can request means and counts for each dependent variable for groups defined by each factor and each combination of factors up to the fifth level (Statistic 3). You also can request unstandardized regression coefficients for covariates (Statistic 2) and multiple classification analysis (MCA) results (Statistic 1). In the MCA table, effects are expressed as deviations from the grand mean. The table includes a listing of unadjusted category effects for each factor, category effects adjusted for other factors, category effects adjusted for all factors and covariates, and eta and beta values.

Formatting Options. You can suppress the display of variable labels in all tables and the display of value labels in the MCA table using Option 2. You can also force the table of cell means and counts to display in narrow format using Option 11.

Basic Specification

- The basic specification is a single VARIABLES subcommand with an analysis list. The minimum analysis list specifies a list of dependent variables, the keyword BY, a list of factor variables, and the minimum and maximum integer values of the factors in parentheses.
- By default, the model includes all interaction terms up to five-way interactions. In the default model, the sums of squares are decomposed using the classical experimental approach, in which covariates, main effects, and ascending orders of interaction are assessed separately in that order. The default display includes an analysis of variance table with variable labels, sums of squares, degrees of freedom, mean square, F, probability of F for each effect, and a count of valid and missing cases. By default, a case that has a missing value for any variable in an analysis list is omitted from the analysis.

Subcommand Order

- The analysis list must be first if keyword VARIABLES is omitted from the specification.

Operations

- A separate analysis of variance is performed for each dependent variable in an analysis list, using the same factors and covariates.
- All ANOVA output, except the table of cell means and counts (Statistic 3), fits in 80 columns. To limit the width of the means and counts table, use Option 11.

Limitations

- Maximum 5 analysis lists.
- Maximum 1 each STATISTICS and OPTIONS subcommands.

- Maximum 5 dependent variables per analysis list.
- Maximum 10 factors per analysis list.
- Maximum 10 covariates per analysis list.
- Maximum 5 interaction levels.
- Maximum 25 value labels per variable displayed in the MCA table.
- The combined number of categories for all factors in an analysis list plus the number of covariates must be less than the sample size.
- Memory requirements for ANOVA are roughly proportional to the square of the product of the number of values for each independent variable.
- The number of categories in each factor and the number of interaction terms included in the model will determine the amount of workspace required.

Example

```
ANOVA VARIABLES=PRESTIGE BY REGION(1,9) SEX, RACE(1,2)
 /OPTIONS=4
 /STATISTICS=3.
```

- VARIABLES specifies a three-way analysis of variance: *PRESTIGE* by *REGION*, *SEX*, and *RACE*.
- Variables *SEX* and *RACE* each have two categories with values 1 and 2 included in the analysis. *REGION* has nine categories valued 1 through 9.
- The OPTIONS subcommand pools the three-way interaction terms into the error sum of squares.
- The STATISTICS subcommand requests a table of means of *PRESTIGE* within the combined categories of *REGION*, *SEX*, and *RACE*.

Example

```
ANOVA VARIABLES=PRESTIGE BY REGION(1,9) SEX,RACE(1,2)
   /RINCOME BY SEX,RACE(1,2).
```

- ANOVA specifies a three-way analysis of variance of *PRESTIGE* by *REGION*, *SEX*, and *RACE*, and a two-way analysis of variance of *RINCOME* by *SEX* and *RACE*.

VARIABLES Subcommand

VARIABLES specifies the analysis list. The actual keyword VARIABLES can be omitted.

- More than one design can be specified on the same ANOVA command by separating the analysis lists with a slash.
- Variables named before keyword BY are dependent variables. Value ranges are not specified for dependent variables.
- Variables named after BY are factor (independent) variables.

- Every factor variable must have a value range indicating its minimum and maximum values. The values must be separated by a space or comma and enclosed in parentheses.
- Factor variables must have integer values. Noninteger values for factors are truncated.
- Cases with values outside the range specified for a factor are excluded from the analysis.
- If two or more factors have the same value range, you can specify the value range once following the last factor to which it applies. You can specify a single range that encompasses the ranges of all factors in the list. For example, if you have two factors, one with values 1 and 2 and the other with values 1 through 4, you can specify the range for both as 1,4. However, this may reduce performance and cause memory problems if the specified range is larger than some of the actual ranges.
- Variables named after keyword WITH are covariates.
- Each analysis list can include only one BY and one WITH keyword.

Suppressing Interaction Effects

By default, all interaction effects up to and including fifth-order interaction effects are tested. You can suppress any of these higher-order interactions and pool them into the error (residual) sums of squares by specifying Option 3, 4, 5, or 6. When you specify any of these options, cell means corresponding to suppressed interaction terms are not displayed.

Option 3   *Suppress all interaction terms.*

Option 4   *Suppress three-way and higher-order interaction terms.*

Option 5   *Suppress four-way and higher-order interaction terms.*

Option 6   *Suppress five-way and higher-order interaction terms.*

Order of Entry of Covariates

By default, covariates are assessed first and main effects are assessed after adjusting for the covariates. To change this order, use Option 7 or 8.

Option 7   *Process covariates concurrently with factor main effects.* Option 7 is ignored when the regression approach is used for decomposing sums of squares (Option 9).

Option 8   *Process covariates after factor main effects.* Option 8 is ignored when the regression approach is used for decomposing sums of squares (Option 9).

Decomposing Sums of Squares

By default, each type of effect is assessed separately in the following order (unless the order of entry of covariates has been changed using Option 7 or 8):

- Effects of covariates.
- Main effects of factors.
- Two-way interaction effects.
- Three-way interaction effects.
- Four-way interaction effects.
- Five-way interaction effects.

To change this order, specify Option 9 or 10.

Option 9   *Regression approach.* All effects are assessed simultaneously, with each effect adjusted for all other effects in the model. Option 9 overrides Options 7 and 8. The MCA table (Statistic 1) and cell means and counts (Statistic 3) are not available with Option 9.

Option 10   *Hierarchical approach.* Factor main effects and covariate effects are assessed hierarchically: factor main effects are adjusted only for factor main effects already assessed, and covariate effects are adjusted only for covariates already assessed. Factors are assessed in the order they are listed on the ANOVA command.

Table 5 shows how effects would be assessed under Options 9, 10, and the default for the following command:

```
ANOVA VARIABLES=Y BY A B C (0 3).
```

Table 5   Terms adjusted for under each option

Effect	Experimental (default)	Regression (Option 9)	Hierarchical (Option 10)
A	B,C	All others	None
B	A,C	All others	A
C	A,B	All others	A,B
AB	A,B,C,AC,BC	All others	A,B,C,AC,BC
AC	A,B,C,AB,BC	All others	A,B,C,AB,BC
BC	A,B,C,AB,AC	All others	A,B,C,AB,AC
ABC	A,B,C,AB,AC,BC	All others	A,B,C,AB,AC,BC

Summary of Analysis Methods

Table 6 describes the results obtained with various combinations of methods for controlling entry of covariates and decomposing the sums of squares.

Table 6   Summary of analysis methods

	Assessments between types of effects	Assessments within the same type of effect
Default	**Covariates** then **Factors** then **Interactions**	**Covariates:** adjust for all other covariates **Factors:** adjust for covariates and all other factors **Interactions**: adjust for covariates, factors, and all other interactions of the same and lower orders
Option 7	**Factors** and **Covariates** concurrently then **Interactions**	**Covariates**: adjust for factors and all other covariates **Factors**: adjust for covariates and all other factors **Interactions**: adjust for covariates, factors, and all other interactions of the same and lower orders
Option 8	**Factors** then **Covariates** then **Interactions**	**Factors**: adjust for all other factors **Covariates**: adjust for factors and all other covariates **Interactions**: adjust for covariates, factors, and all other interactions of the same and lower orders
Option 9	**Covariates, Factors,** and **Interactions** simultaneously	**Covariates**: adjust for factors, interactions, and all other covariates **Factors**: adjust for covariates, interactions, and all other factors **Interactions**: adjust for covariates, factors, and all other interactions
Option 10	**Covariates** then **Factors** then **Interactions**	**Covariates**: adjust for covariates that are preceding in the list **Factors**: adjust for covariates and factors preceding in the list **Interactions**: adjust for covariates, factors, and all other interactions of the same and lower orders
Options 7 and 10	**Factors** and **Covariates** concurrently then **Interactions**	**Factors**: adjust only for preceding factors **Covariates**: adjust for factors and preceding covariates **Interactions**: adjust for covariates, factors, and all other interactions of the same and lower orders

Table 6   Summary of analysis methods (Continued)

	Assessments between types of effects	Assessments within the same type of effect
Options 8 and 10	**Factors** then **Covariates** then **Interactions**	**Factors**: adjust only for preceding factors **Covariates**: adjust factors and preceding covariates **Interactions**: adjust for covariates, factors, and all other interactions of the same and lower orders

Statistical Display

You can request the following optional statistics on the STATISTICS subcommand:

Statistic 1   *Multiple classification analysis.* The MCA display is affected by the type of design specified with Options 7 through 10 (or their defaults). When covariates are specified, a complete MCA table can be obtained only in conjunction with Option 8, Options 8 and 10 together, or Options 7 and 10 together. In a model in which factors are not processed first, effects adjusted only for factors do not appear. The MCA table cannot be produced when Option 9 is in effect. See "Multiple Classification Analysis" below for more information on the MCA table.

Statistic 2   *Unstandardized regression coefficients for covariates.* The regression coefficients are computed when the covariates are entered into the equation. Thus, their values depend on the design you specify with Options 7 through 10 (or the defaults).

Statistic 3   *Cell means and counts for the dependent variable.* For each dependent variable, a separate table is displayed for each effect, showing the means and cell counts for each combination of values of the factors that define the effect, ignoring all other factors. Marginal means and counts and cell means and counts are displayed. Cells corresponding to the suppressed interaction terms (Options 3 through 6) are not displayed. Statistic 3 is not available when the regression approach (Option 9) is used.

ALL   *All statistics.* ALL includes display produced by Statistics 1, 2, and 3.

Multiple Classification Analysis

Multiple classification analysis is useful for displaying the results of analysis of variance when there are no significant interaction effects (see Andrews et al., 1973).

- For each category of each factor, the MCA table presents the unadjusted mean of the dependent variable expressed as a deviation from the grand mean; the deviation from the grand mean of the category mean adjusted for other factors; and the deviation from the grand mean of the category mean adjusted for both factors and covariates.

- For each factor, the complete MCA display includes the correlation ratio (eta) with the unadjusted deviations (the square of eta indicates the proportion of variance explained by all categories of the factor); a partial beta equivalent to the standardized partial regression coefficient that would be obtained by assigning the unadjusted deviations to each factor category and regressing the dependent variable on the resulting variables; the parallel partial betas from a regression that includes covariates in addition to factors, and the multiple R and R^2 from this regression.

Format

By default, ANOVA displays variable and value labels, and the table of cell means and counts (Statistic 3) uses the available width. To change these defaults, use the following options:

Option 2   *Suppress variable and value labels.*

Option 11   *Narrow format for the table of cell means and counts (Statistic 3).* The width of the table is restricted to narrow width regardless of the width defined on SET.

Missing Values

By default, a case that has a missing value for any variable named on an analysis list is omitted from all analyses requested by that list. You can change the treatment of missing values by specifying Option 1 on the OPTIONS subcommand:

Option 1   *Include cases with user-missing values.* Only cases with the system-missing value for a variable named on an analysis list is omitted from that analysis.

AUTORECODE

```
AUTORECODE VARIABLES=varlist

 /INTO new varlist

[/DESCENDING]

[/PRINT]
```

Example:

```
AUTORECODE VARIABLES=COMPANY /INTO RCOMPANY.
```

Overview

AUTORECODE recodes the values of string and numeric variables to consecutive integers and puts the recoded values into a new variable called a **target variable**. The value labels or values of the original variable are used as value labels for the target variable. AUTORECODE is useful for creating numeric independent (grouping) variables from string variables for procedures like ONEWAY, ANOVA, MANOVA, and DSCRIMINANT. AUTORECODE can recode the values of factor variables to consecutive integers, which is required by MANOVA and which reduces the amount of workspace needed by other procedures such as ANOVA. AUTORE-CODE is also useful with the TABLES procedure, where string values are truncated to eight characters but value labels can be displayed in full. (See the *SPSS/PC+ Tables* manual for more information.)

   AUTORECODE is similar to the RECODE command. The main difference is that AUTORE-CODE automatically generates the values. In RECODE, you must specify the new values.

Options

Displaying Recoded Variables. You can display the values of the original and recoded variables using the PRINT subcommand.

Ordering Values. By default, values are recoded in ascending order (lowest to highest). You can recode values in descending order (highest to lowest) using the DESCENDING subcommand.

Basic Specification

The basic specification is VARIABLES and INTO. VARIABLES specifies the variables to be recoded. INTO provides names for the target variables that store the new values. VARIABLES and INTO must name or imply the same number of variables.

Subcommand Order

- VARIABLES must be specified first.

- INTO must immediately follow VARIABLES.

Syntax Rules

A variable cannot be recoded into itself. More generally, target variable names cannot duplicate any variable names already in the active file.

Operations

- The values of each variable to be recoded are sorted and then assigned numeric values. By default, the values are assigned in ascending order: 1 is assigned to the lowest nonmissing value of the original variable, 2 to the second-lowest nonmissing value, and so on for each value of the original variable.
- Values of the original variables are unchanged.
- If a user-missing value is defined, it is recoded into a value higher than any nonmissing values. For example, if the original variable has 10 nonmissing values, the missing value is recoded as 11 and retains its user-missing status. System-missing values remain system-missing.
- AUTORECODE does not sort the cases in the active file. As a result, the consecutive numbers assigned to the target variables may not be in order in the file.
- Target variables are assigned the same variable labels as the original source variables. To change the variable labels, use the VARIABLE LABELS command after AUTORECODE.
- Value labels are automatically generated for each value of the target variables. If the original value had a label, that label is used for the corresponding new value. If the original value did not have a label, the old value itself is used as the value label for the new value. The defined print format of the old value is used to create the new value label.
- SELECT IF specifications are in effect for AUTORECODE.

Example

```
DATA LIST / COMPANY 1-21 (A) SALES 24-28.
BEGIN DATA
CATFOOD JOY            10000
OLD FASHIONED CATFOOD  11200
  . . .
PRIME CATFOOD          10900
CHOICE CATFOOD         14600
END DATA.

AUTORECODE VARIABLES=COMPANY /INTO=RCOMPANY /PRINT.

TABLES TABLE = SALES BY RCOMPANY
   /TTITLE='CATFOOD SALES BY COMPANY'.
```

- Because TABLES truncates string variables to eight characters, AUTORECODE is used to recode the string variable *COMPANY*, which contains the names of various hypothetical cat food companies.

- AUTORECODE recodes *COMPANY* into a numeric variable *RCOMPANY*. Values of *RCOM-PANY* are consecutive integers beginning with 1 and ending with the number of different values entered for *COMPANY*. The values of *COMPANY* are used as value labels for *RCOMPANY*'s numeric values. The *PRINT* subcommand displays a table of the original and recoded values.

- Variable *RCOMPANY* is used as the banner variable in the TABLES procedure to produce a table of sales figures for each cat food company. The value labels for *RCOMPANY* are used as column headings. Since TABLES does not truncate value labels, the full company names appear.

Example

```
AUTORECODE VARIABLES=REGION /INTO=RREGION /PRINT.
ANOVA Y BY RREGION (1,5).
```

- In statistical procedures, empty cells can reduce performance and increase memory requirements. In this example, assume factor *REGION* has only five nonempty categories, represented by the numeric codes 1, 4, 6, 14, and 20. AUTORECODE recodes those values into 1, 2, 3, 4, and 5 for target variable *RREGION*.

- Variable *RREGION* is used in ANOVA. If the original variable *REGION* were used, the amount of memory required by ANOVA would be 4429 bytes. Using variable *RREGION*, ANOVA requires only 449 bytes of memory.

Example

```
DATA LIST / RELIGION 1-8 (A) Y 10-13.
MISSING VALUE   RELIGION (' ').
BEGIN DATA
CATHOLIC 2013
PROTEST  3234
JEWISH   5169
NONE      714
OTHER    2321
  . . .
END DATA.
AUTORECODE VARIABLES=RELIGION /INTO=NRELIG /PRINT /DESCENDING.
MANOVA Y BY NRELIG(1,5).
```

- Because MANOVA requires consecutive integer values for factor levels, string variable *RE-LIGION* is recoded into a numeric variable. The five values for *RELIGION* are first sorted in descending order (Z to A) and are then assigned values 1, 2, 3, 4, and 5 in target variable *NRELIG*.

- Since a blank space is specified as the user-missing value for *RELIGION*, it is assigned the value 6. In the table produced by PRINT, value 6 is displayed as 6M for variable *NRELIG* to flag it as a user-missing value.

- The values of *RELIGION* are used as value labels for the corresponding new values in *NRELIG*.

- Target variable *NRELIG* is used as a factor variable in MANOVA.

VARIABLES Subcommand

VARIABLES specifies the variables to be recoded. VARIABLES is required and must be specified first. The actual keyword VARIABLES is optional.

- Values from the specified variables are recoded and stored in the target variables listed on INTO. Values of the original variables are unchanged.

INTO Subcommand

INTO provides names for the target variables that store the new values. INTO is required and must immediately follow VARIABLES.

- The number of target variables named or implied on INTO must equal the number of source variables listed on VARIABLES.

Example

```
AUTORECODE VARIABLES=V1 V2 V3 /INTO=NEWV1 TO NEWV3 /PRINT.
```

- AUTORECODE stores the recoded values of *V1*, *V2*, and *V3* into target variables named *NEWV1*, *NEWV2*, and *NEWV3*.

PRINT Subcommand

PRINT displays a correspondence table of the original values of the source variables and the new values of the target variables. The new value labels are also displayed.

- The only specification is keyword PRINT. There are no additional specifications.
- If the width is set to less than 132, the table is displayed in 80 columns. If the width has been previously set to 132 (by the SET WIDTH command), the table is displayed in 132 columns.
- Only the first 18 characters of the values of the source variables and the first 48 characters of the value labels of the target variables are displayed.

DESCENDING Subcommand

By default, values for the source variable are recoded in ascending order (from lowest to highest). DESCENDING assigns the values to new variables in descending order (from highest to lowest). The largest value is assigned 1, the second-largest 2, and so on.

- The only specification is keyword DESCENDING. There are no additional specifications.

BEGIN DATA—END DATA

```
BEGIN DATA
data records
END DATA
```

Example:

```
BEGIN DATA
1   3424   274 ABU DHABI 2
2 39932     86 AMSTERDAM 4
3  8889    232 ATHENS
4  3424    294 BOGOTA      3
END DATA.
```

Overview

BEGIN DATA and END DATA are used when data are entered within the command sequence (inline data). BEGIN DATA and END DATA are also used for inline matrix data. BEGIN DATA signals the beginning of data lines and END DATA signals the end of data lines.

Basic Specification

The basic specification is BEGIN DATA, the data lines, and END DATA. BEGIN DATA must be specified by itself on the line that immediately precedes the first data line. END DATA is specified by itself on the line that immediately follows the last data line.

Syntax Rules

- BEGIN DATA, the data, and END DATA must precede the first SPSS/PC+ procedure.
- The command terminator after BEGIN DATA is optional. It is best to leave it out so that SPSS/PC+ will treat inline data as one continuous specification.
- BEGIN DATA must be specified immediately before the first line of inline data.
- END DATA must begin in column 1 and must be specified immediately after the last line of data. It can have only one space between the words END and DATA. Procedures and additional transformations can follow the END DATA command.
- Data lines must *not* have a command terminator. For inline data formats, see DATA LIST.
- Inline data records are limited to a maximum of 80 columns. If data records exceed 80 columns, they must be stored in an external file that is specified on the FILE subcommand of the DATA LIST command.

Operations

- When SPSS/PC+ encounters BEGIN DATA, it begins to read and process data on the next input line. All preceding transformation commands are processed as the active file is built.
- SPSS/PC+ continues to evaluate input lines as data until it encounters END DATA, at which point it begins evaluating input lines as SPSS/PC+ commands.
- No other SPSS/PC+ commands are recognized between BEGIN DATA and END DATA.
- The INCLUDE command can specify a file that contains BEGIN DATA, data lines, and END DATA. The data in such a file are treated as inline data. Thus, the FILE subcommand should be omitted from the DATA LIST command.

Example

```
DATA LIST /XVAR 1 YVAR ZVAR 3-12 CVAR 14-22(A) JVAR 24.
BEGIN DATA
1   3424   274 ABU DHABI 2
2 39932    86 AMSTERDAM 4
3   8889   232 ATHENS
4   3424   294 BOCOTA      3
5 11323    332 HONG KONG 3
6    323   232 MANILA      1
7   3234   899 CHICAGO     4
8 78998   2344 VIENNA      3
9   8870   983 ZURICH      5
END DATA.
MEANS XVAR BY JVAR.
```

- DATA LIST defines the names and column locations of the variables. The FILE subcommand is omitted because the data are inline.
- There are nine cases in the inline data. Each line of data completes a case.
- END DATA signals the end of data lines. It begins in column 1 and has only a single space between END and DATA.

* (Comment)

```
* text
```

Overview

The comment facility inserts explanatory text within the command sequence. Comments are included among the commands printed back in the log file; they do not become part of the information saved in a system file.

Syntax Rules

- The first line of a comment must begin with an asterisk (*). The asterisk must be followed by a space.
- Comment text can contain any characters.
- Comment text can extend for multiple lines. Continuation comment lines can start in any column and do not begin with an asterisk.
- You cannot specify a continuation line if the preceding line ends with a period. Instead, start a new comment with an asterisk.
- Comments cannot be inserted within data lines or within lines of multiple-line commands.
- A command terminator must be placed at the end of a comment. If you omit the terminator, the first command following the comment is treated as a continuation of the comment.

Example

```
* Create a new variable as a combination of two old variables;
  the new variable is a scratch variable used later in the
  session; it will not be saved with the system file.

COMPUTE XYVAR=0.
IF (XVAR EQ 1 AND YVAR EQ 1) XYVAR=1.
```

- The three-line comment will be included in the log file but will not be part of the system file if the active file is saved.

COMPUTE

```
COMPUTE target variable=expression
```

Arithmetic operators:

+ Addition   - Subtraction
* Multiplication   / Division
** Exponentiation

Arithmetic functions:

ABS(arg)	Absolute value
RND(arg)	Round
TRUNC(arg)	Truncate
MOD10(arg)	Modulus
SQRT(arg)	Square root
EXP(arg)	Exponential
LG10(arg)	Base 10 logarithm
LN(arg)	Natural logarithm
ARTAN(arg)	Arctangent
SIN(arg)	Sine
COS(arg)	Cosine

Missing-value functions:

VALUE(varname)	Ignore user-missing
MISSING(varname)	True if missing
SYSMIS(varname)	True if system-missing

Cross-case function:

LAG(varname)	Value of variable one case before

Random-number functions:

UNIFORM(arg)	Uniform pseudo-random number between 0 and arg
NORMAL(arg)	Normal pseudo-random number with mean of 0 and standard deviation of arg

Date function:

YRMODA(yr,mo,da)	Convert year, month, day to day number

Example:

```
COMPUTE NEWVAR=RND((V1/V2)*100).
COMPUTE DEPT='PERSONNEL DEPARTMENT'.
```

Overview

COMPUTE creates new numeric variables or modifies the values of existing string or numeric variables. The variable named on the left of the equals sign is the **target variable**. The variables, constants, and functions on the right side of the equals sign form an **assignment expression**. For a complete discussion of functions, see "Transformation Expressions" on p. 438.

Numeric Transformations

Numeric variables can be created or modified with COMPUTE. The assignment expression for numeric transformations can include combinations of constants, variables, arithmetic operators, and functions.

String Transformations

You can create and modify short string variables with COMPUTE. A variable can be set equal to a string constant or to an existing string variable. The only function available for strings is the cross-case LAG function. All other functions are available for numeric transformations only.

Basic Specification

The basic specification is a target variable, an equals sign (required), and an assignment expression.

Syntax Rules

- The target variable must be named first, and the equals sign is required. Only one target variable is allowed per COMPUTE command.
- Numeric and string variables cannot be mixed in an expression. In addition, if the target variable is numeric, the expression must yield a numeric value; if the target variable is a string, the expression must yield a string value.
- Each function must specify an argument enclosed in parentheses. If a function has two or more arguments, the arguments must be separated by commas. For a complete discussion of the functions and their arguments, see "Transformation Expressions" on p. 438.

Numeric Variables

- Parentheses are used to indicate the order of execution and to set off the arguments to a function.
- To evaluate unary minus, you must enclose the minus sign and the variable or constant in parentheses.
- Numeric functions use simple or complex expressions as arguments. Expressions must be enclosed in parentheses.
- The arc sine function is not available directly but can be computed as shown in the example on p. 474.

String Variables

- Only short string variables, values, and constants can be used in an expression.
- String values and constants must be enclosed in apostrophes or quotation marks.
- LAG is the only function available for strings.

Operations

- If the target variable already exists, its values are replaced.
- If the target variable does not exist, SPSS/PC+ creates a new variable.
- COMPUTE is not executed if it contains invalid syntax. New variables are not created and existing target variables remain unchanged.

Numeric Variables

- New numeric variables created with COMPUTE are assigned a dictionary format of F8.2 and are initialized to the system-missing value for each case. Existing numeric variables transformed with COMPUTE retain their original dictionary formats. The format of a numeric variable can be changed with the FORMATS command.
- All expressions are evaluated in the following order: first functions, then exponentiation, then multiplication and division, and then addition and subtraction. The order of operations can be changed with parentheses.
- COMPUTE returns the system-missing value if a case has the system-missing value for any variable named in an assignment expression. However, you can include user-missing values on computations by using the VALUE function.

String Variables

- A new string variable created by setting a variable name equal to a string constant is assigned a format equal to the width of the string constant.
- A new string variable created by setting a variable name equal to an existing string variable has the same format as the existing variable.

- Existing string variables transformed with COMPUTE retain their original dictionary formats.
- The format of string variables cannot be changed.

Limitations

- The number of variables created with COMPUTE, COUNT, and IF plus the number defined on DATA LIST, IMPORT, and GET cannot exceed the system limit.

Numeric Examples

The following examples illustrate the use of COMPUTE with numeric variables. For a complete discussion of each function, see "Transformation Expressions" on p. 438.

Arithmetic Operations

```
COMPUTE XVAR=25.
COMPUTE YVAR1=(YVAR/XVAR)*100.
```

- *XVAR* is set to 25 for all cases.
- *YVAR1* is computed as the percentage *YVAR* is of *XVAR*.

Numeric Functions

```
COMPUTE WTCHANGE=ABS(WEIGHT1-WEIGHT2).
COMPUTE NEWVAR=RND((V1/V2)*100).
COMPUTE INCOME=TRUNC(INCOME).
COMPUTE ARCSINX=ARTAN(X/SQRT(1-X*X))

COMPUTE TEST = TRUNC(SQRT(X/Y)) * .5.
COMPUTE PARENS = TRUNC(SQRT(X/Y) * .5).
```

- *WTCHANGE* is the absolute value of *WEIGHT1* minus *WEIGHT2*.
- *NEWVAR* is the percentage of *V1* is of *V2*, rounded to an integer.
- *INCOME* is truncated to an integer.
- *ARCSINX* is computed as the arc sine of *X*, using the ARTAN and SQRT functions. This trigonometric identity is valid only if *X* is greater than −1 and less than +1.
- The last two examples illustrate the use of parentheses to control the order of execution. For a case with value 2 for *X* and *Y*, *TEST* equals 0.5, since 2 divided by 2 (X/Y) is 1, the square root of 1 is 1, truncating 1 returns 1, and 1 times 0.5 is 0.5. However, *PARENS* equals 0 for the same case, since SQRT(*X/Y*) is 1, 1 times 0.5 is 0.5, and truncating 0.5 returns 0.

Missing-Value Functions

```
MISSING VALUE V1 V2 V3 (0).
COMPUTE ALLVALID=V1 + V2 + V3.
COMPUTE UM=VALUE(V1) + VALUE(V2) + VALUE(V3).
COMPUTE SM=SYSMIS(V1) + SYSMIS(V2) + SYSMIS(V3).
COMPUTE M=MISSING(V1) + MISSING(V2) + MISSING(V3).
```

- The MISSING VALUE command declares value 0 as missing for *V1*, *V2*, and *V3*.

- *ALLVALID* is the sum of three variables only for cases with valid values for all three variables. *ALLVALID* is assigned the system-missing value for a case if any variable in the assignment expression has a system- or user-missing value.

- The VALUE function overrides user-missing value status. Thus, *UM* is the sum of *V1*, *V2*, and *V3* for each case, including cases with value 0 (the user-missing value) for any of the three variables. Cases with the system-missing value for *V1*, *V2*, and *V3* are system-missing.

- The SYSMIS function on the third COMPUTE returns value 1 if the variable is system-missing. Thus, *SM* ranges from 0 to 3 for each case, depending on whether variables *V1*, *V2*, and *V3* are system-missing for that case.

- The MISSING function on the fourth COMPUTE returns the value 1 if the variable named is system- or user-missing. Thus, *M* ranges from 0 to 3 for each case, depending on whether variables *V1*, *V2*, and *V3* are user- or system-missing for that case.

- Alternatively, you could use the COUNT command to create variables *SM* and *M*.

Example: Computing a Mean across Variables

Computation of the mean of several variables must take into account missing data. The following example illustrates a method of computing the mean of five variables:

```
RECODE V1 TO V5 (MISSING=999).
COUNT NMISS=V1 TO V5 (999).
COMPUTE MEAN15=((V1+V2+V3+V4+V5)-(999*NMISS))/(5-NMISS).
MISSING VALUE V1 TO V5 (999).
```

- To reduce missing values to a single numeric code, the RECODE command recodes the missing values for *V1* to *V5* to an arbitrary value outside the range of variables.

- The COUNT command counts the number of missing values for each case.

- The numerator for computing the mean is calculated by subtracting the total of the missing values from the sum of all the values.

- The denominator is calculated by subtracting the number of missing values from the number of variables included in the calculations.

- For use in further transformations and procedures, the recoded missing values are declared as missing.

- To limit the computation to only those cases with at least three valid values, a conditional command can be used in place of the COMPUTE command:

```
IF (NMISS LT 3) MEAN15=((V1+V2+V3+V4+V5)-(999*MISS))/(5-NMISS).
```

Cross-Case Function

```
COMPUTE LV1=LAG(V1).
COMPUTE LV2=LAG(LV1).
```

- *LV1* is the value of *V1* for the previous case.
- *LV2* is the value of *LV1* for the previous case. In effect, *LV2* is equal to the value of *V1* for two cases previous. This example illustrates the use of successive LAG transformations to perform multiple-case LAG operations.

Logical Functions

```
COMPUTE WORKERS=RANGE(AGE,18,65).
COMPUTE QSAME=ANY(Q1,Q2).
```

- *WORKERS* is 1 for cases where *AGE* is from 18 through 65, 0 for all other valid values of *AGE*, and system-missing for cases with a missing value for *AGE*.
- *QSAME* is 1 whenever *Q1* equals *Q2* and 0 whenever they are different.

Random-Number Functions

```
COMPUTE V1=UNIFORM(10).
COMPUTE V2=NORMAL(1.5).
```

- *V1* is a pseudo-random number from a distribution with values ranging between 0 and the specified value of 10.
- *V2* is a pseudo-random number from a distribution with a mean of 0 and a standard deviation of the specified value of 1.5.
- You can change the seed value of the pseudo-random-number generator with the SEED specification on SET.

Date Function

```
COMPUTE AGER=(YRMODA(1992,10,01)-
              YRMODA(YRBIRTH,MOBIRTH,DABIRTH))/365.25.
```

- The YRMODA function converts the current date (in this example, October 1, 1992) and birthdate to a number of days. Birthdate is subtracted from current date and the remainder is divided by the number of days in a year to yield age in years.

String Examples

The following examples illustrate the use of COMPUTE with string variables.

Equivalence

```
COMPUTE DEPT='Personnel Department'.
COMPUTE OLDVAR=NEWVAL.
```

- The first COMPUTE assigns the value Personnel Department to *DEPT* for each case.
- The second COMPUTE sets *OLDVAR* equal to *NEWVAL*. *NEWVAL* must be an existing string variable.

Cross-Case Function

```
COMPUTE NEIGHBOR=LAG(HSHOLDER).
```

- COMPUTE creates a new short string variable *NEIGHBOR* as the value of *HSHOLDER* for the previous case. The first case will have the system-missing value for *NEIGHBOR*.

CORRELATIONS

```
CORRELATIONS [VARIABLES=] {varlist} [WITH varlist] [/varlist ...]
                          {ALL    }

[/OPTIONS=option numbers]

[/STATISTICS={statistic numbers}]
             {ALL             }
```

Options:

1   Include user-missing values   4   Write count and correlation matrix
2   Exclude missing values pairwise   5   Display count and probability
3   One-tailed probability

Statistics:

1   Univariate mean, standard deviation, and count
2   Cross-product deviations and covariance

Example:

```
CORRELATIONS VARIABLES=WVAR XVAR YVAR
/VARIABLES=ZVAR1 TO ZVAR5 WITH ZVAR6 TO XVAR8
/OPTIONS=2 3
/STATISTICS=1.
```

Overview

CORRELATIONS produces Pearson product-moment correlations with two-tailed probabilities and, optionally, univariate statistics, covariances, and cross-product deviations. Other procedures that produce correlation matrices are DSCRIMINANT, FACTOR, and REGRESSION.

Options

Types of Matrices. A simple variable list on the VARIABLES subcommand produces a square matrix. You can also request a rectangular matrix of correlations between specific pairs of variables or between variable lists using the keyword WITH on VARIABLES.

Statistical Display. You can display counts and probabilities in the matrix of coefficients (Option 5), one-tailed probabilities (Option 3), univariate statistics for each variable (Statistic 1), and cross-product deviations and covariances for each pair of variables (Statistic 2).

Matrix Output. You can write out a square matrix containing correlation coefficients and the number of cases using Option 4. This matrix can be used as input to SPSS/PC+ procedures that read matrices.

Basic Specification

- The basic specification is the VARIABLES subcommand, which specifies the variables to be analyzed. The actual keyword VARIABLES can be omitted.
- By default, CORRELATIONS displays a matrix of correlation coefficients. An asterisk (*) indicates that a coefficient has a two-tailed probability of less than 0.01, and two asterisks (**) indicate a probability of less than 0.001. Cases that have missing values for any variable in the matrix are excluded.

Subcommand Order

- Subcommands can be specified in any order.

Operations

- The correlation of a variable with itself is displayed as 1.0000.
- A correlation that cannot be computed is displayed as a period (.).
- Correlation coefficients are displayed with four decimal places. Optional statistics are displayed with four decimal places where possible.
- CORRELATIONS does not execute if long or short string variables are specified on the variable list.
- The display uses the width set on the SET command.

Limitations

- Maximum 40 variable lists.
- Maximum 1 each OPTIONS and STATISTICS subcommands.
- Maximum 250 syntax elements. Each individual occurrence of a variable name, keyword, or special delimiter counts as 1 toward this total. Variables implied by the TO keyword do not count toward this total.
- The maximum number of variables that can be named on a CORRELATIONS command is the same as the system limit.

Example

```
CORRELATIONS VARIABLES=FOOD RENT PUBTRANS TEACHER COOK ENGINEER
    /VARIABLES=FOOD RENT WITH COOK TEACHER MANAGER ENGINEER
    /OPTIONS 2 3
    /STATISTIC=1.
```

- The first VARIABLES subcommand requests a square matrix of correlation coefficients among variables *FOOD*, *RENT*, *PUBTRANS*, *TEACHER*, *COOK*, and *ENGINEER*.

- The second VARIABLES subcommand requests a rectangular correlation matrix in which variables *FOOD* and *RENT* are the rows and *COOK*, *TEACHER*, *MANAGER*, and *ENGINEER* are the columns.
- Option 2 specifies pairwise deletion. All cases with valid values for the pair of variables used to compute a coefficient are included in the computation of that coefficient.
- Option 3 requests one-tailed probabilities.
- Statistic 1 requests univariate statistics for all variables named on the VARIABLES subcommands.

VARIABLES Subcommand

VARIABLES specifies the variable list. The actual keyword VARIABLES is optional.

- A simple variable list produces a square matrix of correlations of each variable with every other variable.
- A variable list that includes keyword WITH produces a rectangular correlation matrix. Variables before WITH define the rows of the matrix and variables after WITH define the columns.
- Keyword ALL can be used in the variable list to refer to all user-defined variables.
- You can specify multiple VARIABLES subcommands on a single CORRELATIONS command. The slash between the subcommands is required; the keyword VARIABLES is not.

Statistical Display

By default, the correlation matrix and number of valid cases on which the matrix is based are displayed. Two-tailed probabilities of less than 0.01 are indicated by an asterisk (*) and less than 0.001 by two asterisks (**). You can request the following on the OPTIONS and STATISTICS subcommands:

Option 3	*One-tailed probability.* An asterisk (*) indicates that a coefficient has a one-tailed probability of less than 0.01, and two asterisks (**) indicate a probability of less than 0.001. If Option 5 is also specified, the exact one-tailed probabilities are displayed.
Option 5	*Count and probability.* The number of cases used to compute each coefficient and exact probability are displayed.
Statistic 1	*Mean, standard deviation, and number of nonmissing cases for each variable.* Cases with missing values are excluded on a variable-by-variable basis regardless of the missing-value option in effect.
Statistic 2	*Cross-product deviations and covariance.*
ALL	*All statistics available with Statistics 1 and 2.* Specify ALL on the STATISTICS subcommand.

Writing Matrices

You can write matrices to the results file named on the SET command for use in other procedures by specifying Option 4.

- Any variable list that contains the keyword WITH is ignored when matrices are written.
- A matrix of coefficients followed by the number of cases is written for each variable list in the order in which the lists are specified.
- With listwise deletion of cases with missing values (the default), each correlation matrix is followed by a record containing the number of cases (n) used to compute all coefficients in the matrix. With pairwise deletion of cases with missing values (Option 2), each correlation matrix is followed by a matrix of n's used to compute the coefficients.
- Correlation matrices are written with F10.7 format.
- Matrices of n's are written with an F10.0 format.
- Each row of a matrix begins on a new record.
- Each record has a maximum of eight values.
- Option 4 sends the matrices to the results file, which by default is named *SPSS.PRC*. You can direct the output to a different file using SET RESULTS before CORRELATIONS (see SET).
- If a results file with the same name already exists, the matrices from CORRELATIONS replace the existing contents.

Option 4   *Write counts and correlation matrices to the results file named on SET.* A correlation matrix and number of cases is written for each variable list. Option 4 is ignored for variable lists that include keyword WITH.

Example

```
SET RESULTS='SAVINGS.MAT'.
DATA LIST FILE='SAVINGS.DAT'/ VAR1 TO VAR10 1-20.
CORRELATIONS VARIABLES=VAR1 TO VAR10
/OPTIONS=4.
```

- This example writes a matrix of correlations followed by a single n to file *SAVINGS.MAT*.

Missing Values

By default, a case with a user- or system-missing value for any variable in a matrix is excluded from that matrix. Alternatively, you can specify the following missing-value treatments on the OPTIONS subcommand:

Option 1   *Include cases with user-missing values.* User-missing values are treated as valid values.

Option 2   *Exclude missing values pairwise.* Cases with valid values for the variables used to compute a coefficient are included in the computation of that coefficient, even if those cases have missing values for other variables named on the variable list.

COUNT

```
COUNT varname=varlist(value list) varlist(value list) [/varname=...]
```

Keywords for numeric value lists:

LOWEST, LO, HIGHEST, HI, THRU, MISSING, SYSMIS

Example:

```
COUNT TARGET=V1 V2 V3 (2).
```

Overview

COUNT creates a numeric variable that, for each case, counts the occurrences of the same value (or list of values) across a list of variables. The new variable is called the **target** variable. The variables and values that are counted are the **criterion** variables and values. Criterion variables can be either numeric or string.

Basic Specification

The basic specification is the target variable, an equals sign, the criterion variable(s), and the criterion value(s) enclosed in parentheses.

Syntax Rules

- Use a slash to separate the specifications for each target variable.
- Each value in a list of criterion values must be separated by a comma or space. String values must be enclosed in apostrophes.
- Keywords THRU, LOWEST (LO), HIGHEST (HI), SYSMIS, and MISSING can only be used with numeric criterion variables.
- A variable can be specified in more than one criterion variable list.
- You can use keyword TO to specify consecutive criterion variables that have the same criterion value or values.
- You can specify multiple variable lists for a single target variable to count different values for different variables.
- The criterion variable list can include both string and numeric variables, provided they have separate value specifications.

Operations

- Target variables are always numeric and are initialized to 0 for each case. They are assigned a dictionary format of F8.2.
- If the target variable already exists, its previous values are replaced.

- COUNT ignores the missing-value status of user-missing values. It counts a value even if that value has been previously declared as missing.
- The target variable is never system-missing. To define missing values for target variables, use the RECODE or MISSING VALUE command.
- SYSMIS counts system-missing values for numeric variables.
- MISSING counts both user- and system-missing values for numeric variables.

Limitations

The number of variables created with COUNT combined with the number created with COMPUTE and IF and defined on DATA LIST, IMPORT, or GET cannot exceed the system limit.

Example

```
COUNT TARGET=V1 V2 V3 (2).
```

- The value of *TARGET* for each case will be either 0, 1, 2, or 3, depending on the number of times the value 2 occurs across the three variables for each case.
- *TARGET* is a numeric variable with an F8.2 format.

Example

```
COUNT QLOW=Q1 TO Q10 (LO THRU 0)
/QSYSMIS=Q1 TO Q10 (SYSMIS).
```

- Assuming there are 10 variables between and including *Q1* and *Q10* in the active file, *QLOW* ranges from 0 to 10, depending on the number of times a case has a negative or 0 value across variables *Q1* to *Q10*.
- *QSYSMIS* ranges from 0 to 10, depending on how many system-missing values are encountered for *Q1* to *Q10* for each case. User-missing values are not counted.
- Both *QLOW* and *QSYSMIS* are numeric variables and have F8.2 formats.

Example

```
COUNT SVAR=V1 V2 ('male  ') V3 V4 V5 ('female').
```

- *SVAR* ranges from 0 to 5, depending on the number of times a case has a value of male for *V1* and *V2* and a value of female for *V3*, *V4*, and *V5*.
- *SVAR* is a numeric variable with an F8.2 format.

CROSSTABS

General mode:

```
CROSSTABS [TABLES=]varlist BY varlist [BY...] [/varlist...]

 [/MISSING={TABLE**}]
          {INCLUDE}

 [/WRITE[={NONE**}]]
         {CELLS }
```

Integer mode:

```
CROSSTABS VARIABLES=varlist(min,max) [varlist...]

 /TABLES=varlist BY varlist [BY...] [/varlist...]

 [/MISSING={TABLE**}]
           {INCLUDE}
           {REPORT }

 [/WRITE[={NONE**}]]
         {CELLS }
         {ALL   }
```

Both modes:

```
[/FORMAT={LABELS**  }  {AVALUE**}  {NOINDEX**}  {TABLES** } {BOX**}]
         {NOLABELS  }  {DVALUE  }  {INDEX    }  {NOTABLES } {NOBOX }
         {NOVALLABS }

[/CELLS=[{COUNT**}]  [ROW    ]  [EXPECTED]  [SRESID ]]
         {NONE   }  [COLUMN]  [RESID   ]  [ASRESID]
                    [TOTAL  ]              [ALL    ]

[/STATISTICS=[CHISQ]  [LAMBDA]  [BTAU]  [GAMMA]  [ETA ]]
             [PHI  ]  [UC    ]  [CTAU]  [D    ]  [CORR]
             [CC   ]  [NONE  ]  [RISK]  [KAPPA]  [ALL ]
```

**Default if the subcommand is omitted.

Example:

```
CROSSTABS TABLES=FEAR BY SEX
 /CELLS=ROW COLUMN EXPECTED RESIDUALS
 /STATISTICS=CHISQ.
```

Overview

CROSSTABS produces contingency tables showing the joint distribution of two or more variables that have a limited number of distinct values. The frequency distribution of one variable is subdivided according to the values of one or more variables. The unique combination of values for two or more variables defines a cell. To analyze contingency tables using hierarchical log-linear models, use HILOGLINEAR; to analyze contingency tables using a general linear model approach, use LOGLINEAR (both in the SPSS/PC+ Advanced Statistics option).

CROSSTABS can operate in two different modes: *general* and *integer*. Integer mode builds some tables more efficiently but requires more specifications than general mode. Some subcommand specifications and statistics are available only in integer mode.

Options

Methods for Building Tables. To build tables in general mode, use the TABLES subcommand. Integer mode requires the TABLES and VARIABLES subcommands and minimum and maximum values for the variables.

Cell Contents. By default, CROSSTABS displays only the number of cases in each cell. You can request row, column, and total percentages, and also expected values and residuals using the CELLS subcommand.

Statistics. In addition to the tables, you can obtain measures of association and tests of hypotheses for each subtable using the STATISTICS subcommand.

Formatting Options. With the FORMAT subcommand you can control the order in which rows are displayed and suppress the display of variable labels, value labels, and the table itself. In addition, you can display a list of the tables produced by CROSSTABS with the page number where each table begins.

Writing and Reproducing Tables. You can write cell frequencies to an ASCII file with the WRITE subcommand.

Basic Specification

In general mode, the basic specification is TABLES with a table list. The actual keyword TABLES can be omitted. In integer mode, the minimum specification is the VARIABLES subcommand specifying the variables to be used and their value ranges, and the TABLES subcommand with a table list.

- The minimum table list specifies a list of row variables, the keyword BY, and a list of column variables.
- In integer mode, all variables must be numeric with integer values. In general mode, variables can be numeric (integer or noninteger) or string.
- The default table shows cell counts.

Subcommand Order

- In general mode, the table list must be first if keyword TABLES is omitted. If keyword TABLES is explicitly used, subcommands can be specified in any order.
- In integer mode, VARIABLES must precede TABLES. Keyword TABLES must be explicitly specified.

Operations

- Integer mode builds tables more quickly but requires more workspace if the table has many empty cells.
- If a long string variable is used in general mode, only the short-string portion (first eight characters) is tabulated.
- Statistics are calculated separately for each two-way table or two-way subtable. Missing values are reported for the table as a whole.
- If only percentages and/or cell counts are requested, percentages are displayed without a percent sign and zero values are displayed as blanks. If percentages and expected values or residuals are requested, the percent sign is used in percentages and zero values are displayed as zeros.
- Scientific notation is used for cell counts when necessary.
- The output uses the width defined on the SET command.
- The BOX subcommand on SET controls the characters used in the table display.
- In general mode, keyword TO on the TABLES subcommand refers to the order of variables in the active file. ALL refers to all variables in the active file. In integer mode, TO and ALL refer to the position and subset of variables specified on the VARIABLES subcommand.

Limitations

The following limitations apply to CROSSTABS in *general mode*:
- Maximum 200 variables named or implied on the TABLES subcommand.
- Maximum 250 nonempty rows or columns for each table.
- Maximum 20 table lists per CROSSTABS command.
- Maximum 10 dimensions (9 BY keywords) per table.
- Maximum 250 value labels displayed on any single table.

The following limitations apply to CROSSTABS in *integer mode*:
- Maximum 100 variables named or implied on the VARIABLES subcommand.
- Maximum 100 variables named or implied on the TABLES subcommand.
- Maximum 250 nonempty rows or columns for each table.
- Maximum 20 table lists per CROSSTABS command.
- Maximum 8 dimensions (7 BY keywords) per table.
- Maximum 20 rows or columns of missing values when REPORT is specified on MISSING.
- Minimum value that can be specified is –99,999.
- Maximum value that can be specified is 999,999.

Example

```
CROSSTABS TABLES=FEAR BY SEX
/CELLS=ROW COLUMN EXPECTED RESIDUALS
/STATISTICS=CHISQ.
```

- CROSSTABS generates a bivariate table. Variable *FEAR* defines the rows of the table and variable *SEX* defines the columns.
- CELLS requests row and column percentages, expected cell frequencies, and residuals.
- STATISTICS requests the chi-square statistic.

Example

```
CROSSTABS TABLES=JOBCAT BY EDCAT BY SEX BY INCOME3.
```

- This table list produces a subtable of *JOBCAT* by *EDCAT* for each combination of values of *SEX* and *INCOME3*.

VARIABLES Subcommand

The VARIABLES subcommand is required for integer mode. VARIABLES specifies a list of variables to be used in the crosstabulations and the lowest and highest values for each variable. Values are specified in parentheses and must be integers. Noninteger values are truncated.

- Variables can be specified in any order. However, the order in which they are named on VARIABLES determines their implied order on TABLES (see the TABLES subcommand on p. 488).
- A range must be specified for each variable. If several variables can have the same range, it can be specified once after the last variable to which it applies.
- CROSSTABS uses the specified ranges to allocate tables. One cell is allocated for each possible combination of values of the row and column variables before the data are read. Thus, if the specified ranges are larger than the actual ranges, workspace will be wasted.
- Cases with values outside the specified range are considered missing and are not used in the computation of the table. This allows you to select a subset of values within CROSSTABS.
- If the table is sparse because the variables do not have values throughout the specified range, consider using general mode or recoding the variables.

Example

```
CROSSTABS VARIABLES=FEAR SEX RACE (1,2) MOBILE16 (1,3)
/TABLES=FEAR BY SEX MOBILE16 BY RACE.
```

- VARIABLES defines values 1 and 2 for *FEAR*, *SEX*, and *RACE*, and values 1, 2, and 3 for *MOBILE16*.

TABLES Subcommand

TABLES specifies the table lists and is required in both integer and general mode. The following rules apply to both modes.

- You can specify multiple TABLES subcommands on a single CROSSTABS command. The slash between the subcommands is required; the keyword TABLES is required only in integer mode.

- Variables named before the first BY in a table list are row variables, and variables named after the first BY in a table list are column variables.

- When the table list specifies two dimensions (one BY keyword), the first variable before BY is crosstabulated with each variable after BY, then the second variable before BY with each variable after BY, and so forth.

- Each subsequent use of keyword BY in a table list adds a new dimension (or layer) to the tables requested. Variables named after the second (or subsequent) BY are control variables.

- When the table list specifies more than two dimensions, a two-way subtable is produced for each combination of values of control variables. The value of the last specified control variable changes the most slowly in determining the order in which tables are displayed.

- You can name more than one variable in each dimension.

General Mode

- The actual keyword TABLES can be omitted in general mode.

- In general mode, both numeric and string variables can be specified. Long strings are truncated to short strings for defining categories.

- Keywords ALL and TO can be specified in any dimension. In general mode, TO refers to the order of variables in the active file and ALL refers to all variables defined in the active file.

Example

```
CROSSTABS TABLES=FEAR BY SEX BY RACE.
```

- This example crosstabulates *FEAR* by *SEX* controlling for *RACE*. In each subtable, *FEAR* is the row variable and *SEX* is the column variable.

- A subtable is produced for each value of the control variable *RACE*.

Example

```
CROSSTABS TABLES=CONFINAN TO CONARMY BY SEX TO REGION.
```

- This command produces crosstabulations of all variables in the active file between and including *CONFINAN* and *CONARMY* by all variables between and including *SEX* and *REGION*.

Integer Mode

- In integer mode, variables specified on TABLES must be first named on VARIABLES.
- Keywords TO and ALL can be specified in any dimension. In integer mode, TO and ALL refer to the position and subset of variables specified on the VARIABLES subcommand, not to the variables in the active file.

Example

```
CROSSTABS VARIABLES=FEAR (1,2) MOBILE16 (1,3)
    /TABLES=FEAR BY MOBILE16.
```

- VARIABLES names two variables, *FEAR* and *MOBILE16*. Values 1 and 2 for *FEAR* are used in the tables, and values 1, 2, and 3 are used for variable *MOBILE16*.
- TABLES specifies a bivariate table with two rows (values 1 and 2 for *FEAR*) and three columns (values 1, 2, and 3 for *MOBILE16*). *FEAR* and *MOBILE16* can be named on TABLES because they were named on the previous VARIABLES subcommand.

Example

```
CROSSTABS  VARIABLES=FEAR SEX RACE DEGREE (1,2)
    /TABLES=FEAR BY SEX BY RACE BY DEGREE.
```

- This command produces four subtables. The first subtable crosstabulates *FEAR* by *SEX*, controlling for the first value of *RACE* and the first value of *DEGREE*; the second subtable controls for the second value of *RACE* and the first value of *DEGREE*; the third subtable controls for the first value of *RACE* and the second value of *DEGREE*; and the fourth subtable controls for the second value of *RACE* and the second value of *DEGREE*.

CELLS Subcommand

By default, CROSSTABS displays only the number of cases in each cell. Use CELLS to display row, column or total percentages, expected counts, or residuals. These are calculated separately for each bivariate table or subtable.

- CELLS specified without keywords displays cell counts plus row, column, and total percentages for each cell.
- If CELLS is specified with keywords, CROSSTABS displays only the requested cell information.
- The key located at the top left corner of each table describes the information contained in each cell.
- Scientific notation is used for cell contents when necessary.

COUNT	*Observed cell counts.* This is the default if CELLS is omitted.
ROW	*Row percentages.* The number of cases in each cell in a row is expressed as a percentage of all cases in that row.
COLUMN	*Column percentages.* The number of cases in each cell in a column is expressed as a percentage of all cases in that column.

TOTAL	*Two-way table total percentages.* The number of cases in each cell of a sub-table is expressed as a percentage of all cases in that subtable.
EXPECTED	*Expected counts.* Expected counts are the number of cases expected in each cell if the two variables in the subtable are statistically independent.
RESID	*Residuals.* Residuals are the difference between the observed and expected cell counts.
SRESID	*Standardized residuals* (Haberman, 1978).
ASRESID	*Adjusted standardized residuals* (Haberman, 1978).
ALL	*All cell information.* This includes cell counts; row, column and total percentages; expected counts; residuals; standardized residuals; and adjusted standardized residuals.
NONE	*No cell information.* Use NONE when you want to write tables to a results file without displaying them (see the WRITE subcommand on p. 492). This is the same as specifying NOTABLES on FORMAT.

STATISTICS Subcommand

STATISTICS requests measures of association and related statistics. By default, CROSSTABS does not display any additional statistics.

- STATISTICS without keywords displays the chi-square test.
- If STATISTICS is specified with keywords, CROSSTABS calculates only the requested statistics.
- In integer mode, values that are not included in the specified range are *not* used in the calculation of the statistics, even if these values exist in the data.
- If user-missing values are included with MISSING, cases with user-missing values are included in the calculation of statistics as well as in the tables.

CHISQ	*Chi-square.* Includes Pearson chi-square, likelihood-ratio chi-square, and Mantel-Haenszel chi-square. Mantel-Haenszel is valid only if both variables are numeric. For 2×2 tables, Fisher's exact test is computed when a table that does not result from missing rows or columns in a larger table has a cell with an expected frequency less than 5. Yates' corrected chi-square is computed for all other 2×2 tables. This is the default if STATISTICS is specified without keywords.
PHI	*Phi and Cramér's* V.
CC	*Contingency coefficient.*
LAMBDA	*Lambda (symmetric and asymmetric) and Goodman and Kruskal's tau.*
UC	*Uncertainty coefficient (symmetric and asymmetric).*
BTAU	*Kendall's tau*-b.
CTAU	*Kendall's tau*-c.

GAMMA   *Gamma*. Zero-order gammas are displayed for 2-way tables and conditional gammas are displayed for 3-way to 10-way tables in general mode and 3-way to 8-way tables in integer mode. Partial and zero-order gammas for 3-way to 8-way tables are available in integer mode only.

D   *Somers' d (symmetric and asymmetric).*

ETA   *Eta*. Available for numeric data only.

CORR   *Pearson's r and Spearman's correlation coefficient*. This is available for numeric data only.

KAPPA   *Kappa coefficient* (Kraemer, 1982). Kappa can be computed only for square tables in which the row and column values are identical. If there is a missing row or column, use integer mode to specify the square table, since a missing column or row in general mode would keep the table from being square.

RISK   *Relative risk* (Bishop et al., 1975). Relative risk can be calculated only for 2 × 2 tables.

ALL   *All statistics available.*

NONE   *No summary statistics*. This is the default if STATISTICS is omitted.

MISSING Subcommand

By default, CROSSTABS deletes cases with missing values on a table-by-table basis. Cases with missing values for any variable specified for a table are not used in the table or in the calculation of statistics. Use MISSING to specify alternative missing-value treatments.

- The only specification is a single keyword.
- The number of missing cases is always displayed at the end of the table, following the last subtable and any requested statistics.
- If the missing values are not included in the range specified on VARIABLES, they are excluded from the table regardless of the keyword you specify on MISSING.

TABLE   *Delete cases with missing values on a table-by-table basis*. When multiple table lists are specified, missing values are handled separately for each list. This is the default.

INCLUDE   *Include user-missing values.*

REPORT   *Report missing values in the tables*. This option includes missing values in tables but not in the calculation of percentages or statistics. The letter *M* is used to indicate that cases within a cell are missing. REPORT is available only in integer mode.

FORMAT Subcommand

By default, CROSSTABS displays tables and subtables with variable and value labels when they are available (only the first 16 characters of value labels are displayed). The values for the row variables are displayed in order from lowest to highest. Use FORMAT to modify the default table display.

LABELS   *Display both variable and value labels for each table.* This is the default.

NOLABELS   *Suppress variable and value labels.*

NOVALLABS   *Suppress value labels but display variable labels.*

AVALUE   *Display row variables from lowest to highest value.* This is the default.

DVALUE   *Display row variables from highest to lowest.*

NOINDEX   *Suppress the table index.* This is the default.

INDEX   *Display an index of tables.* The index follows the last page of tables. It lists all tables produced and the beginning page number of each table.

TABLES   *Display tables.* This is the default.

NOTABLES   *Suppress tables.* If STATISTICS is specified, only the statistics are displayed. If STATISTICS is omitted, no output is displayed. NOTABLES is useful when you want to write tables to a file without displaying them. This is the same as specifying NONE on CELLS.

BOX   *Use box characters around every cell.* This is the default.

NOBOX   *Suppress box characters around each cell.* The row and column headings are still separated from the table by box characters.

WRITE Subcommand

Use the WRITE subcommand to write cell frequencies to a file for subsequent use by SPSS/PC+ or another program. CROSSTABS can also use these cell frequencies as input to reproduce tables and compute statistics.

- The only specification is a single keyword.

- The WRITE subcommand sends output to the results file, which by default is named *SPSS.PRC.* You can direct the output to a different file using SET RESULTS before CROSSTABS (see SET).

- If a results file with the same name already exists, the cell frequencies from CROSSTABS replace the existing contents.

- If both CELLS and ALL are specified, CELLS is in effect and only the contents of nonempty cells are written to the file.

- If you include missing values with INCLUDE or REPORT on MISSING, no values are considered missing and all nonempty cells, including those with missing values, are written, even if CELLS is specified.

- If you exclude missing values on a table-by-table basis (the default), no records are written for combinations of values that include a missing value.

- If multiple tables are specified, the tables are written in the same order as they are displayed.

NONE   *Do not write cell counts to a file.* This is the default.

CELLS   *Write cell counts for nonempty and nonmissing cells to a file.* Combinations of values that include a missing value are not written to the file.

ALL   *Write cell counts for all cells to a file.* A record for each combination of values defined by VARIABLES and TABLES is written to the file. ALL is available only in integer mode.

The file contains one record for each cell. Each record contains the following:

Columns   Contents

1–4   *Split-file group number, which always equals 1.* This is written for compatibility with SPSS software on other operating systems.

5–8   *Table number.* Tables are defined by the TABLES subcommand.

9–16   *Cell frequency.* The number of times this combination of variable values occurred in the data, or, if case weights are used, the sum of case weights for cases having this combination of values.

17–24   *The value of the row variable* (the one named before the first BY).

25–32   *The value of the column variable* (the one named after the first BY).

33–40   *The value of the first control variable* (the one named after the second BY).

41–48   *The value of the second control variable* (the one named after the third BY).

49–56   *The value of the third control variable* (the one named after the fourth BY).

57–64   *The value of the fourth control variable* (the one named after the fifth BY).

65–72   *The value of the fifth control variable* (the one named after the sixth BY).

73–80   *The value of the sixth control variable* (the one named after the seventh BY).

- The split-file group number, table number, and frequency are written as integers.
- In integer mode, the values of variables are also written as integers. In general mode, the values are written according to the print format specified for each variable. Alphanumeric values are written at the left end of any field in which they occur.
- Within each table, records are written from one column of the table at a time, and the value of the last control variable changes most slowly.

Example

```
CROSSTABS VARIABLES=FEAR SEX (1,2)
 /TABLES=FEAR BY SEX
 /WRITE=ALL.
```

- CROSSTABS writes a record for each cell in the table *FEAR* by *SEX* to the file *SPSS.PRC*. Figure 1 shows the contents of the *SPSS.PRC* file.

Figure 1   Cell records

```
1   1      55      1      1
1   1     172      2      1
1   1     180      1      2
1   1      89      2      2
```

Example

```
SET RESULTS='CROSSTAB.DAT'.
CROSSTABS TABLES=V1 TO V3 BY V4 BY V10 TO V15
   /WRITE=CELLS.
```

- CROSSTABS writes a set of records for each table to file *CROSSTAB.DAT*.

- Records for the table *V1* by *V4* by *V10* are written first, followed by records for *V1* by *V4* by *V11*, and so forth. The records for *V3* by *V4* by *V15* are written last.

Reading a CROSSTABS Results File

You can use the file created by WRITE in a subsequent SPSS/PC+ session to reproduce a table and compute statistics for it. Each record in the file contains all the information used to build the original table. The cell frequency information can be used as a weight variable on the WEIGHT command to replicate the original cases.

Example

```
DATA LIST FILE='SPSS.PRC'
   /WGHT 9-16 FEAR 17-24 SEX 25-32.
VARIABLE LABELS FEAR 'AFRAID TO WALK AT NIGHT IN NEIGHBORHOODS'.
VALUE LABELS  FEAR 1 'YES' 2 'NO'/ SEX 1 'MALE' 2 'FEMALE'.
WEIGHT BY WGHT.
CROSSTABS TABLES=FEAR BY SEX
 /STATISTICS=ALL.
```

- DATA LIST reads the cell frequencies and row and column values from the *SPSS.PRC* file shown in Figure 1. The cell frequency is read as a weighting factor (variable *WGHT*). The values for the rows are read as *FEAR*, and the values for the columns as *SEX*, the two original variables.

- The WEIGHT command recreates the sample size by weighting each of the four cases (cells) by the cell frequency.

If you do not have the original data or the CROSSTABS results file, you can reproduce a crosstabulation and compute statistics by simply entering the values from the table:

```
DATA LIST  /FEAR 1 SEX 3 WGHT 5-7.
VARIABLE LABELS  FEAR 'AFRAID TO WALK AT NIGHT IN NEIGHBORHOOD'.
VALUE LABELS  FEAR 1 'YES' 2 'NO'/ SEX 1 'MALE' 2 'FEMALE'.
WEIGHT  BY WGHT.
BEGIN DATA.
1 1  55
2 1 172
1 2 180
2 2  89
END DATA.
CROSSTABS  TABLES=FEAR BY SEX
 /STATISTICS=ALL.
```

DATA LIST: Fixed Format

```
DATA LIST [FILE='filename'] [FIXED] [TABLE]

/varname columns [{(0)}] [varname columns ...]
                 {(n)}
                 {(A)}
  [/ ...] [/ ...]
```

Formats:

Format   Definition

(n)   Implied number of decimal places
       for numeric variables

(A)   String variable

Example:
```
DATA LIST FILE='MARCH.DAT'
  /ID 1-3 SEX 5 (A) AGE 7-8 OPINION1 TO OPINION5 10-14.
```

Overview

DATA LIST defines an ASCII data file (a file containing numbers and other alphanumeric characters) by assigning names and formats to each variable. The data can be inline (entered with SPSS/PC+ commands) or stored in an external file. By default, DATA LIST assumes the data are arranged in fixed format (keyword FIXED). In fixed format, the values for each variable are found in the same location on the same record for each case, and the DATA LIST command specifies record and column location in addition to variable names and formats. You can also use DATA LIST to define data in freefield format (see DATA LIST: Freefield Format) and to define matrix data (see DATA LIST: Matrix Materials).

DATA LIST is used only for ASCII data files. For information on reading system files created with the SAVE command or portable files created with the EXPORT command in SPSS/PC+ or SPSS, see GET and IMPORT.

Options

Data Source. You can read data from an external file using the FILE subcommand.

Data Formats. You can define string variables and specify implied decimal places for numeric variables.

Summary Table. You can display a table that summarizes the variable definitions using the TABLE keyword.

Basic Specification

- The basic specification for fixed format data is a slash followed by at least one variable name and its location.

- By default, all variables are assumed to be numeric without implied decimal places.
- Keyword FIXED is optional.
- If the data are in an external file, the FILE subcommand must be used.
- If the data are inline, the FILE subcommand is omitted and the data are specified between the BEGIN DATA and END DATA commands.

Syntax Rules

- Slashes are used only in the variable definition portion of DATA LIST to indicate the start of a new record. Do not use slashes to separate keywords.
- The FILE subcommand and keywords FIXED and TABLE must precede the first slash, which signals the beginning of variable definition.

Operations

- Variable names and formats are stored in the active file dictionary.
- The formats assigned on DATA LIST are used to display the values. You can use the FORMATS command to change formats of numeric variables.
- The order of the variables in the active file dictionary is the order in which they are defined on DATA LIST, not their sequence in the input data file. This order is important if you later use the TO keyword to refer to variables in the active file.
- Data stored in a command file that is included with the INCLUDE command are considered inline data. The included file must contain the BEGIN DATA and END DATA commands. The file is not specified on FILE subcommand on DATA LIST.
- By default, variables are assumed to be numeric. Alphabetical and special characters, except the decimal point and leading plus and minus signs, are not valid numeric values and are set to system-missing if encountered in the data.
- Blanks to the left or right of a number in the default format are ignored. Blanks within a number are not valid and the value is set to system-missing.
- The system-missing value is assigned to a completely blank field for numeric variables. The value assigned to blanks can be changed using SET BLANKS (see SET).

Limitations

- Maximum 500 variables can be defined on a DATA LIST command. Each 8-character portion of a long string variable counts as 1 toward the 500-variable limit (see "String Variables" on p. 436).
- The maximum length of an input record is 1024 characters.

Example

```
DATA LIST / ID 1-3 SEX 5 (A) AGE 7-8 OPINION1 TO OPINION5 10-14.
BEGIN DATA.
001 m 28 12212
002 f 29 21212
003 f 45 32145
  additional lines of data
128 m 17 11194
END DATA.
```

- The data are assumed to be inline because the FILE subcommand is not specified.
- The data are in fixed format (the default).
- Variable *ID* is a numeric variable located in columns 1 through 3.
- Variable *SEX* is a short string variable in column 5.
- *AGE* is a two-column numeric variable in columns 7 and 8.
- Variables *OPINION1*, *OPINION2*, *OPINION3*, *OPINION4*, and *OPINION5* are named using the TO convention (see "Keyword TO" on p. 434). Each is a one-column numeric variable, with *OPINION1* located in column 10 and *OPINION5* located in column 14.
- The BEGIN DATA and END DATA commands enclose the inline data. Since the values of *SEX* are lowercase, they must be specified as such on subsequent commands.

FILE Subcommand

FILE specifies the name of an ASCII file containing data. FILE is required when data are stored in an external data file. FILE cannot be used when the data are stored in a file that is included with the INCLUDE command or when the data are inline (see INCLUDE and BEGIN DATA—END DATA).

- The file specification must be enclosed in apostrophes.
- The file specification can be fully qualified, including drive, directory, filename, and extension.
- FILE must precede the first slash, which signals the beginning of variable definition.
- FILE must be separated from keywords FIXED and TABLE by at least one blank or comma.

Data on Diskette

If the data are contained on a diskette, include the drive specification on the FILE subcommand, as in

```
DATA LIST FILE='B:FLOPPY.DAT'. . .
```

Example

```
DATA LIST FILE='\INVENTORY\MARCH.DAT'
 / NUTS3 1-2 BOLTS35 3-5 NAILS3P 6-10.
```

- The FILE subcommand indicates the data are in file *MARCH.DAT* in the *INVENTORY* directory.

- Three numeric variables, *NUTS3*, *BOLTS35*, and *NAILS3P*, are defined.

TABLE Keyword

TABLE displays a table summarizing the variable definitions supplied on DATA LIST FIXED. For each variable, the table displays the variable name, record number, starting column, ending column, format, width, and number of decimal places. The table also includes the number of records per case.

- TABLE can be used only for fixed-format data.
- TABLE must precede the first slash, which signals the beginning of variable definition.
- TABLE must be separated from keyword FIXED and the FILE subcommand by at least one blank or comma.

Variable Definition

The variable definition portion of DATA LIST assigns names and formats to the variables in the data. The variable definition also specifies the record and column location of each variable in the data. The following sections describe record location, variable names, column location, and formats.

Record Location

- Records are indicated in the variable definition portion of DATA LIST by a slash. Each slash is followed by the variables defined from that record.
- Each slash indicates the beginning of a new record. The first slash indicates the first (or only) record. The second and any subsequent slashes tell SPSS/PC+ to go to a new record.
- To skip a record, specify a slash without any variables for that record.
- You must specify a slash for every record, even if no variables are being defined from that record.
- Variables from each record can be defined in any order, regardless of their sequence in the data file. You do not need to define all variables from a given record.
- All variables to be read from one record must be defined before you proceed to the next record.

Example

```
DATA LIST FILE='SOCSUR82.DAT'
  / ID 1-7 SEX 15 AGE 16-18
  / ANOMIA 15 LIKEPOL 17
  // OPIN1 76 OPIN2 77
  /.
```

- DATA LIST defines data from file *SOCSUR82.DAT* in the current directory. The data are in fixed format.
- Three variables, *ID*, *SEX*, and *AGE*, are defined from the first record.

- *ANOMIA* and *LIKEPOL* are defined from the second record.
- The third data record for each case is skipped; no variables are defined from that record.
- *OPIN1* and *OPIN2* are defined from the fourth record.
- The fifth record is skipped.
- The data file contains a total of five records per case. DATA LIST defines seven variables from three of these records.

Variable Names

- Variable names can contain up to eight characters.
- All variable names must begin with a letter or the @ character. System variables (beginning with a $) cannot be defined on DATA LIST.
- You can name a list of variables using the TO keyword (see "Keyword TO" on p. 434).
- For more information on variable-naming rules, see "Variable Names" on p. 434.

Column Location

- Each variable name is followed by its column location.
- If the variable is one column wide, specify the column number. Otherwise, specify the first column number followed by a dash (–) and the last column number.
- If several adjacent variables on the same record have the same width and format type, you can use one column specification after the last variable name. Specify the beginning column location of the first variable, a dash, and the ending column location of the last variable. SPSS/PC+ divides the total number of columns specified equally among the variables. If the number of columns does not divide equally, an error message is issued.
- The same column locations can be used to define multiple variables.

Example

```
DATA LIST FILE='AGES.DAT' TABLE / BIRTHDA 1-2 BIRTHMO 3-4
   BIRTHYR 5-8 BIRTHDAY 1-8 PRSNT1 TO PRSNT5 11-15
   CELEBRAT 65-68 CAKES 50-52 / WISHES 10-11.
```

- DATA LIST defines variables from the fixed-format file *AGES.DAT* in the current directory.
- TABLE generates a summary table of the names, formats, and locations of variables defined on the DATA LIST command.
- Three variables, *BIRTHDA*, *BIRTHMO*, and *BIRTHYR*, are read from columns 1 through 8 on the first record. Variable *BIRTHDAY* is read from columns 1 through 8 as one variable.
- Variables *PRSNT1*, *PRSNT2*, *PRSNT3*, *PRSNT4*, and *PRSNT5* are named using the TO keyword. Each of these variables is one column wide.
- Variable *CELEBRAT* is read from columns 65 through 68. *CAKES* is read from columns 50 through 52. The active file dictionary will contain these variables in the order they are defined on DATA LIST, even though they are in a different order in the data file.
- Variable *WISHES* is read from columns 10 and 11 on the second data record.

Example

```
DATA LIST / LINENUM 1 ID 2-6 V1 TO V7 7-13
   OPINREL OPINSEX OPINDRUG OPINRAR 15-18
   LOCATN76 TO LOCATN83 20-35.
```

- The DATA LIST command defines inline data in fixed format.
- Variables *V1*, *V2*, *V3*, *V4*, *V5*, *V6*, and *V7* are named using the TO keyword. Each variable is one column wide.
- Four variables, *OPINREL*, *OPINSEX*, *OPINDRUG*, and *OPINRAR*, are defined from columns 15 through 18. Each of these variables is one column wide.
- Eight variables are defined by the LOCATN76 TO LOCATN83 specification. Each of these variables is two columns wide.

Variable Formats

- By default, variables are assumed to be numeric, either signed or unsigned integer or real numbers.
- String (alphanumeric) variables are indicated by an A in parentheses following the column specification.
- If a value is encountered that cannot be read according to the format type specified, it is assigned the system-missing value and a warning message is issued.
- You can change the defined format of numeric variables using the FORMATS command.

Numeric Formats

- When a decimal point is not actually coded in real data, the number of implied decimal places can be indicated in parentheses following the column specification.
- A coded decimal point in the data overrides the number of implied decimal places indicated on the DATA LIST command.

Table 7 compares how values are interpreted for a four-column numeric variable when no decimal places are defined on DATA LIST and when two decimal places are defined.

Table 7   Interpretation of decimal places

Value in the data file	Default	Two defined decimal places
2001	2001	20.01
201	201	2.01
-201	-201	-2.01
2	2	.02
20	20	.20
2.2	2.2	2.2
.201	.201	.201
2 01	Undefined	Undefined

String Formats

- The values of string (alphanumeric) variables can contain any number, letter, or character, including special characters and embedded blanks. For further discussion of string variables, see "Variable Type" on p. 436.
- String variables whose values contain eight characters or less are called *short string variables*.
- String variables with values longer than eight characters and up to 255 characters are called *long string variables*.

Example

```
DATA LIST FILE='\SPSSDAT\FILEX.DAT' TABLE
  / XVAR 1 YVAR 10-15 ZVAR 3-9(2) /
  / AVAR 25-30(A) BVAR 31-45(A).
```

- The data are in file *FILEX.DAT* in directory *SPSSDAT* and are arranged in fixed format.
- TABLE generates a summary table of the variable names, formats, and locations defined in the DATA LIST command.
- *XVAR* is a numeric variable read from column 1 on the first record.
- *YVAR* is a numeric variable in columns 10 through 15.
- *ZVAR* is in columns 3 through 9 and contains two implied decimal places, indicated by (2).
- No variables are defined on the second record for each case.
- Two variables are defined from the third record for each case. *AVAR* is a six-column short string variable, and *BVAR* is a long string variable read from columns 31 through 45. *BVAR* counts as two variables toward the system limit.

DATA LIST: Freefield Format

```
DATA LIST [FILE='filename'] FREE

/variable [({A })] varlist
           {Aw}
```

Formats:

Format   Definition

(Aw)   String variable of width *w*

Example:

```
DATA LIST FILE='MYFILE.DAT' FREE / XVAR YVAR.
```

Overview

DATA LIST with keyword FREE defines data in freefield format. In freefield format, all variables are recorded in the same order for each case but not necessarily in the same column locations. Each value in the data file is separated by one or more blanks or by one comma. The data can be inline or read from an external file.

You can also use DATA LIST to define data in fixed format (see DATA LIST: Fixed Format) and to define matrix data (see DATA LIST: Matrix Materials).

Options

Data Source. You can read data from an external file using the FILE subcommand.

Data Formats. You can define string and numeric variables. You cannot specify implied decimal places for numeric variables.

Basic Specification

- The basic specification for freefield data is keyword FREE followed by a slash and at least one variable name.
- By default, all variables are assumed to be numeric.
- If the data are in an external file, the FILE subcommand must be used.
- If the data are inline, the FILE subcommand is omitted and the data are specified between the BEGIN DATA and END DATA commands.

Operations

- Variable names are stored in the active file dictionary.

- By default, variables are assumed to be numeric. Alphabetical and special characters, except the decimal point and leading plus and minus signs, are not valid numeric values and are set to the system-missing value.
- Data stored in a command file that is included with the INCLUDE command are considered inline data. The included file must contain the BEGIN DATA and END DATA commands. The file is not specified on FILE subcommand on DATA LIST.

Limitations

- Maximum 500 variables can be defined on a DATA LIST command. Each 8-character portion of a long string variable counts as 1 toward the 500-variable limit (see "String Variables" on p. 436).
- The maximum length of an input record is 1024 characters.
- Maximum 1200 syntax elements per DATA LIST command. Each individual occurrence of a variable name, keyword, or special delimiter counts as 1 toward this total. Variables implied by the TO keyword do not count toward this total.

Example

```
DATA LIST FREE / XVAR YVAR.
BEGIN DATA.
1 3 2 15 3 16 4
156
5 22 6 -3
END DATA.
```

- The DATA LIST command with keyword FREE specifies data in freefield format. The data are assumed to be inline because the FILE subcommand is not specified.
- Two variables, *XVAR* and *YVAR*, are defined.
- The first case has value 1 for variable *XVAR* and 3 for variable *YVAR*. The second case has value 2 for *XVAR* and 15 for *YVAR*. The third case has values 3 and 16, the fourth case has values 4 and 156, and so on.

FILE Subcommand

FILE specifies the name of an ASCII file containing data. FILE is required when data are stored in an external data file. FILE cannot be used when the data are stored in a file that is included with the INCLUDE command or when the data are inline (see INCLUDE and BEGIN DATA—END DATA).

- The file specification must be enclosed in apostrophes.
- The file specification can be fully qualified, including drive, directory, filename, and extension.
- FILE must precede the first slash, which signals the beginning of variable definition.
- FILE can be specified before or after keyword FREE and must be separated from keyword FREE by at least one blank or comma.

Example

```
DATA LIST FILE='MYFILE.DAT' FREE / XVAR YVAR.
```

- The data are in freefield format and are contained in file *MYFILE.DAT* in the current directory.
- Two numeric variables are defined.

Variable Definition

The variable definition portion of DATA LIST with keyword FREE specifies variable names and, for string variables, formats.

- Variables must be named in the order they are entered on the data file.
- There is no record or column specification for freefield format.

Variable Names

- Variable names can contain up to eight characters.
- All variable names must begin with a letter or the @ character. System variables (beginning with a $) cannot be defined on DATA LIST.
- You can name a list of variables using the TO keyword (see "Keyword TO" on p. 434).
- For more information on variable-naming rules, see "Variable Names" on p. 434.

Example

```
DATA LIST FREE / ID VAR1 TO VAR7.
```

- DATA LIST defines inline data (the default) in freefield format.
- Eight variables are defined: *ID*, *VAR1*, *VAR2*, *VAR3*, *VAR4*, *VAR5*, *VAR6*, and *VAR7*.

Variable Formats

- In freefield format, formats can be specified for string variables only.
- All numeric variables are automatically assigned print and write formats of F8.2. Use the FORMATS command to change the format for numeric variables.
- All numeric variable digits are read and stored by SPSS/PC+.
- Numeric values with decimal points in the data preserve the decimal point and decimal digits.
- String variables are indicated by an A in parentheses after the variable name.
- By default, all string variables are assigned formats of A8 (width of eight characters). You can assign a different width by specifying *A* and a width enclosed in parentheses, such as (A20).
- A format specification applies only to the variable immediately preceding it.
- If a string value in the data is longer than the specified length, the value is truncated and a warning message is displayed.

- If a string value in the data is shorter than the specified format, the value is right-padded with blanks and no warning message is displayed. If the value is specified in subsequent commands, the padded value must be used.

Example

```
DATA LIST FREE FILE='\MASTER\APRIL.DAT'
  / ID SEX (A1) NAME (A15) AGE TENURE ETHNIC (A).
FORMATS AGE (F2.0) TENURE (F3.1).
```

- The DATA LIST command defines data in freefield format from file *APRIL.DAT* in directory *\MASTER*.
- Six variables, *ID*, *SEX*, *NAME*, *AGE*, *TENURE*, and *ETHNIC*, are defined.
- *ID*, *AGE*, and *TENURE* are numeric variables and receive the default print and write format of F8.2.
- *SEX* is a one-column short string variable. *NAME* is a long string variable up to 15 columns wide. *ETHNIC* is a short string variable with an assumed width of eight columns.
- The FORMATS command changes the print and write formats of numeric variables *AGE* and *TENURE*.

Entering Freefield Data

- In freefield format, a single line of data can include values for more than one case, and the values for one case can be split across lines. Individual values cannot be split across lines.
- Values are read sequentially in the order variables are named.
- One data value is separated from another by any number of blanks or by a single comma. You can use both commas and blanks as delimiters within a single data file.
- Any number of consecutive blanks (except blanks specified within a string value) are interpreted as one delimiter.
- Two consecutive commas or commas separated by a blank indicate a system-missing numeric value or a blank string value.
- A blank field for a variable that is not delimited by commas causes values from that point on to be assigned to the wrong variable.
- You cannot use commas or blanks within numeric values.
- String values that contain imbedded blanks or commas must be delimited by apostrophes or quotation marks. The delimiters are not read as part of the string value.
- To include an apostrophe in a string value, delimit the value with quotation marks. To include quotation marks, delimit the value with apostrophes.
- If there are not enough values to complete the last case, a warning is issued and the incomplete case is dropped.

Example

```
DATA LIST FREE / AVAR BVAR STATE (A) MAYOR(A10).
BEGIN DATA.
7500000 20000000 'S DAKOTA' "O'LEARY" 22222000 55000000
'INDIANA' 'JONES' 120000000 56000000 'NEW YORK' 'ALDRIDGE'
-1.2 2222.223 'MAINE' 'BURNS'
END DATA.
FORMATS AVAR (COMMA15.2) BVAR(DOLLAR14.2).
DISPLAY VAR=ALL.
FREQ VAR=ALL.
LIST VAR=ALL.
```

- The DATA LIST command defines inline data (the default) in freefield format.

- *AVAR* and *BVAR* are numeric variables. *STATE* is a string variable with the default width of eight columns. *MAYOR* is a long string variable with a width of 10 columns (A10).

- The BEGIN DATA command indicates the beginning of data lines.

- The value of *AVAR* for the first case is 7500000. *BVAR* has the value 20000000. *STATE* has the value S DAKOTA enclosed in apostrophes to preserve the imbedded blank. The value O'LEARY is enclosed in quotation marks to preserve the imbedded apostrophe. The format for *MAYOR* indicates a width of 10 columns, so O'LEARY is right-padded with three blanks.

- The second case is split across two records. With freefield format, you can split cases but not individual values across records.

- The values for *AVAR* and *BVAR* for the fourth case include decimal places.

- The END DATA command indicates the end of inline data.

- The FORMATS command changes the print and write formats of numeric variables *AVAR* and *BVAR* from the default F8.2 format to the specified formats (see FORMATS).

- The DISPLAY command shows the current print and write formats of the variables.

- The FREQUENCIES procedure produces tables for each of the variables. Because FREQUENCIES uses the internal representation of values in tables, the DOLLAR and COMMA formats do not appear on these tables.

- The LIST procedure produces a listing of the values of each variable. The DOLLAR and COMMA formats are used in the listing.

Example

```
DATA LIST FREE / AVAR BVAR STATE (A) MAYOR(A10).
BEGIN DATA.
7500000,20000000,'S DAKOTA',"O'LEARY",22222000,,
'INDIANA','JONES',120000000,,,'ALDRIDGE'
-1.2 2222.223 'MAINE' 'BURNS'
END DATA.
```

- This example shows the use of both commas and blanks to separate values.

- The two commas at the end of the first record indicate missing information for *BVAR* for the second case.

- In the second line of data, the three commas after value 120000000 indicate missing values for *BVAR* and *STATE* for the third case. Blanks between the commas would also indicate missing information.

- The blanks after ALDRIDGE indicate the end of the value.

- The last line of data uses blanks as delimiters.

DATA LIST: Matrix Materials

```
DATA LIST [FILE='filename'] MATRIX [{FIXED}]
                                    {FREE }
        /varlist
```

Example:

```
DATA LIST MATRIX FILE='REG.MAT'/
   SUICIDE ANOMIE AGE.
N 488.
REG VAR=AGE SUICIDE ANOMIE
   /READ CORR
   /DEP=SUICIDE
   /METHOD=ENTER.
```

Overview

DATA LIST with keyword MATRIX defines matrix materials for use in CLUSTER, FACTOR, ONEWAY, REGRESSION, and MANOVA. (CLUSTER and FACTOR are contained in the SPSS/PC+ Professional Statistics option; MANOVA is in SPSS/PC+ Advanced Statistics.) The matrix materials can include correlation coefficients, covariance coefficients, a matrix of n's, or group distance measures. Matrix materials can be read in fixed or freefield format but must conform to the requirements of the individual procedures (see each procedure for details). Matrix input can be inline or read from an external file.

For information on reading individual casewise data, see DATA LIST: Fixed Format or DATA LIST: Freefield Format.

Basic Specification

- The basic specification is DATA LIST with keyword MATRIX followed by a slash and a list of variable names.
- By default, matrix materials are assumed to be in fixed format.
- If the data are in an external file, the FILE subcommand must be used.
- If the data are inline, the FILE subcommand is omitted and the data are specified between the BEGIN DATA and END DATA commands.

Syntax Rules

- Use keyword FREE to indicate that matrix materials are in freefield format. By default, matrix materials are assumed to be in fixed format (keyword FIXED).
- The file specification on FILE must be enclosed in apostrophes. You can specify files in directories other than the current directory by using fully qualified file specifications.
- The FILE subcommand and keywords FREE or FIXED can be specified before or after keyword MATRIX.
- The slash (/) before the variable names is required.

- Variable names must be eight characters or less and must begin with a letter or the @ character. For more information on variable-naming rules, see "Variable Names" on p. 434.
- You must supply names for all variables that will be used by the next procedure. If you specify more names on DATA LIST MATRIX than are specified for the procedure, the extra names are ignored.
- The order in which variables are named determines their order in the new active file but has no relation to the contents of the matrix.
- Format types are meaningless for matrix materials and cannot be specified.

Operations

- The format of a matrix to be read by SPSS/PC+ depends upon the procedure that will use it. Each procedure that reads matrix materials can accept its own matrix output in either fixed or freefield format. Matrices entered directly and matrices that will be processed by a procedure other than the one that created them should normally be read in freefield format.
- DATA LIST with keyword MATRIX cannot read individual casewise data.
- You cannot use DATA LIST MATRIX with procedures that expect casewise data.
- You cannot perform any SPSS/PC+ transformations on matrix materials.
- Data stored in a command file that is included with the INCLUDE command are considered inline data. The included file must contain the BEGIN DATA and END DATA commands. The file is not specified on FILE subcommand on DATA LIST.

Limitations

- Maximum 500 variables can be defined on a DATA LIST command. Each 8-character portion of a long string variable counts as 1 toward the 500-variable limit (see "String Variables" on p. 436).
- Maximum 1200 syntax elements per DATA LIST command. Each individual occurrence of a variable name, keyword, or special delimiter counts as 1 toward this total. Variables implied by the TO keyword do not count toward this total.

Example

```
DATA LIST MATRIX FILE='REG.MAT'/
   SUICIDE ANOMIE AGE.
N 488.
REG VAR=AGE SUICIDE ANOMIE
  /READ CORR
  /DEP=SUICIDE
  /METHOD=ENTER.
```

- DATA LIST reads matrix materials from file *REG.MAT* in the current directory. The matrix was written to this file by procedure CORRELATIONS in a previous SPSS/PC+ session.

- The matrix materials are read in fixed format (the default). CORRELATIONS writes matrices in the same format as does REGRESSION. This matrix could also be read in freefield format.
- The variables *SUICIDE*, *ANOMIE*, and *AGE* are defined for use in REGRESSION.
- The N command indicates that the matrix input is based on 488 cases. REGRESSION uses this information in computing significance tests.
- The VARIABLES subcommand on REGRESSION identifies the variables in the correlation matrix and their order.
- The READ subcommand on REGRESSION indicates that a correlation matrix will be read by the REGRESSION procedure.
- This example uses three-character truncation of keywords.

Example

```
DATA LIST FREE MATRIX / AGE SUICIDE ANOMIE.
BEGIN DATA.
1.0 .5555555 .3333333
0.555555  1.0       0.455555
0.333333  0.455555  1.0
488
END DATA.
REGRESSION VARIABLES=AGE SUICIDE ANOMIE
   /READ CORR N
   /DEPENDENT=SUICIDE
   /METHOD=ENTER.
```

- The DATA LIST command specifies matrix materials in freefield format.
- Because no file is specified on DATA LIST, the matrix data are assumed to be inline.
- The variable names *AGE*, *SUICIDE*, and *ANOMIE* are defined for use in the REGRESSION command.
- The matrix materials are entered between the BEGIN DATA and END DATA commands. Each row vector begins on a new line. The last line of data contains a single number indicating the number of cases.
- The READ subcommand on REGRESSION indicates that a correlation matrix followed by the number of cases (*n*) will be read.

Matrix Data

The SPSS/PC+ procedures CORRELATIONS, CLUSTER, ONEWAY, FACTOR, and REGRESSION write matrix materials in a fixed format that automatically conforms to the requirements of the various procedures that read matrix materials. Some matrix materials, such as factor matrices written by FACTOR and matrices written by ONEWAY and MANOVA, are specially formatted for a specific procedure.

If you enter your own matrix materials, they must conform to the following requirements:

- Matrix materials can be arranged in fixed or freefield format.

- A matrix written by an SPSS/PC+ procedure can always be read in fixed format by the same procedure.
- A matrix written by an SPSS/PC+ procedure can always be read in freefield format by any procedure that accepts that type of matrix. Factor matrices from FACTOR and matrix materials from ONEWAY and MANOVA are not accepted by other procedures.
- Each cell of the matrix must contain a value.
- Each element in a row in freefield format must be separated by at least one space or a comma.
- Each row of a matrix begins on a new line.
- Each type of matrix material begins on a new line.
- In fixed format, each procedure has a maximum number of elements that can be entered in a row (see individual procedures below). The format must conform to the requirements of the procedure that reads the matrix.
- If the elements for a vector do not fit in one row, the elements can be continued on the next row. Each row must be filled before continuing to the next in fixed format.
- Individual matrix elements cannot be split across input lines.
- Decimal points in the data must be entered explicitly. You cannot specify implied decimal places.
- You cannot use two commas in a row to indicate missing data.

Matrix Input for Procedure CLUSTER

- Procedure CLUSTER reads matrix materials in both fixed and freefield format.
- Fixed-format matrix materials for CLUSTER must be arranged so that each matrix cell is 16 columns wide with up to 5 decimal places. You can have only five elements of a vector in each row.
- Freefield-format matrix materials, such as a correlation matrix written by procedure COR-RELATIONS, must conform to the requirements described under "Matrix Data" on p. 509.

Example

```
DATA LIST MATRIX FREE/
   ABDEFECT ABHLTH ABNOMORE ABPOOR ABRAPE ABSINGLE.
BEGIN DATA.
 1.0000000   .6118418   .3936668   .3743177   .6284106   .3820830
  .6118418 1.0000000   .2870408   .3098805   .6097969   .2935045
  .3936668   .2870408 1.0000000   .7658386   .3806726   .7881280
  .3743177   .3098805   .7658386 1.0000000   .3847740   .7379326
  .6284106   .6097969   .3806726   .3847740 1.0000000   .3909586
  .3820830   .2935045   .7881280   .7379326   .3909586 1.0000000
END DATA.
CLUSTER ABDEFECT ABHLTH ABNOMORE ABPOOR ABRAPE ABSINGLE
   /READ=SIMILAR.
```

- The DATA LIST command specifies inline matrix materials in freefield format and defines six variables.
- The matrix is a correlation matrix. Each row vector begins on a new line.

- The READ subcommand on CLUSTER indicates that a square matrix based on a measure of similarity will be read (see CLUSTER in *SPSS/PC+ Professional Statistics*).

Example

```
DATA LIST MATRIX / CASE1 TO CASE19.
BEGIN DATA
       0.0           19062.00391    17697.00781    17545.00781    19038.00781
   19050.00781       17742.00781    17964.00781    19125.00391      111.99998
   19230.00391       18041.00781    17693.00781    19023.00781     9635.00781
    9860.00781        9899.00781     9901.00781    10028.00781
   19062.00391           0.0        18485.00000    17867.00000    17904.00000
   17890.00000       18484.00000    18508.00000       49.00000    18536.00391
     109.99998       18537.00000    18193.00000    18009.00000     9427.00000
    9228.00000        9657.00000     9885.00000     9726.00000
       :                 :              :              :              :
       :                 :              :              :              :
   10028.00781        9726.00000     9929.00000     9659.00000     9502.00000
    9435.99609        9589.99609     9737.99609     9537.00000     9730.00781
    9476.00000        9660.99609     9449.00000     9261.00000       87.00000
      46.00000          40.99998       52.99998        0.0
END DATA.
CLUSTER ALL
  /MISSING INCLUDE
  /READ.
```

- The DATA LIST command specifies inline matrix materials in fixed format (the default) and defines 19 variables.
- The distance matrix to be read was produced using procedure CLUSTER with the MISSING=INCLUDE and WRITE=DISTANCE subcommands. Here cases, not variables, are going to be clustered.
- The data are automatically arranged in the format required by CLUSTER. Each column vector is 16 characters wide with 5 decimal values. There are four rows for each vector. Only the first two and last vectors are shown.
- The READ subcommand on CLUSTER indicates that a distance matrix will be read (see CLUSTER in *SPSS/PC+ Professional Statistics*).

Matrix Input for Procedure FACTOR

- Procedure FACTOR can use matrix materials in either fixed or freefield format.
- Fixed-format matrix materials for FACTOR must be arranged so that each column vector entry is 10 columns wide with up to 3 decimal places. You can enter up to eight values in each row.
- Matrix materials in freefield format must conform to the requirements noted under "Matrix Data" on p. 509.

Example

```
DATA LIST MATRIX / X1 X2 X3 X4 X5.
N 100.
BEGIN DATA.
1.000
0.945     1.000
0.840     0.720     1.000
0.735     0.630     0.560     1.000
0.630     0.540     0.480     0.420     1.000
END DATA.
FACTOR READ=CORRELATION TRIANGLE
  /VARIABLES=X1 TO X5
  /ANALYSIS=X1 TO X5
  /PRINT=ALL
  /CRI=FAC(1)
  /EXT=ULS.
```

- The DATA LIST command specifies inline matrix materials in fixed format (the default) and defines five variables.

- The N command tells SPSS/PC+ that the matrix input is based on 100 cases.

- The matrix data conform to the fixed-format requirements of FACTOR. Each row vector starts on a new line and each column entry occupies 10 columns.

- The READ subcommand on FACTOR indicates that a lower-triangular correlation matrix will be read (see FACTOR in *SPSS/PC+ Professional Statistics*).

- This example uses three-character truncation of keywords.

Example

```
DATA LIST FREE MATRIX / X1 TO X5.
N 100.
BEGIN DATA.
1.000
0.945,1.000
0.840,0.720,1.000
0.735,0.630,0.560,1.000
0.630,0.540,0.480,0.420,1.000
END DATA.
FACTOR READ=CORRELATION TRIANGLE
  /VARIABLES=X1 TO X5
  /ANALYSIS=X1 TO X5
  /PRINT=ALL
  /CRI=FAC(1)
  /EXT=ULS.
```

- The DATA LIST command specifies inline matrix materials in freefield format and defines five variables (*X1*, *X2*, *X3*, *X4*, and *X5*).

- Each coefficient in the correlation matrix is separated by a comma.

- The READ subcommand on FACTOR indicates that a lower-triangular correlation matrix will be read (see FACTOR in *SPSS/PC+ Professional Statistics*).

Matrix Input for Procedure ONEWAY

- Procedure ONEWAY reads matrix materials in either fixed or freefield format.
- If you use matrix materials in fixed format, you must specify Option 7 on the ONEWAY command.
- Each matrix cell entry has a width of 10 columns with up to 4 decimal places. You can enter up to eight cells in each row.

Example

```
DATA LIST MATRIX / SCORE METHOD.
BEGIN DATA.
7         7         7
    4.4286    7.5714    6.7143
    1.2724    1.3973     .9512
END DATA.
ONEWAY SCORE BY METHOD(1,3)
  /OPTION 7.
```

- The DATA LIST command specifies inline matrix materials in the default fixed format and defines two variables, *SCORE* and *METHOD*.
- Each vector element occupies 10 columns and has four decimal places. The vector of counts does not require decimal places.
- Option 7 on ONEWAY indicates that a matrix with a vector of counts, a vector of means, and a vector of standard deviations will be read (see ONEWAY).

Example

```
DATA LIST FREE MATRIX / YVAR XVAR.
BEGIN DATA.
65 95 181 82 40 37
2.6462 2.7737 4.1796 4.5610 4.6625 5.2297
6.2699
494
END DATA.
ONEWAY VARIABLES=YVAR BY XVAR(1,6)
  /OPTIONS=8.
```

- The DATA LIST command specifies inline matrix materials in freefield format and defines two variables, *YVAR* and *XVAR*.
- The data are arranged to conform to the requirements of Option 8 in ONEWAY, with one row of counts, a row of means, an entry for the pooled variance estimate, and an entry for the degrees of freedom.
- Option 8 is specified on ONEWAY (see ONEWAY).

Matrix Input for Procedure REGRESSION

- Procedure REGRESSION reads matrix materials in either fixed or freefield format.
- Materials arranged in fixed format must have 10 columns for each vector entry with up to 7 decimal places. You can enter up to eight entries per line for each vector.

- Matrix materials in freefield format must conform to the requirements noted under "Matrix Data" on p. 509.

Example

```
DATA LIST MATRIX / AGE SUICIDE ANOMIE.
BEGIN DATA.
1.0        0.555555   0.333333
0.555555   1.0        0.455555
0.333333   0.455555   1.0
488
END DATA.
REGRESSION VARIABLES=AGE SUICIDE ANOMIE
  /READ CORR N
  /DEPENDENT=SUICIDE
  /METHOD=ENTER.
```

- DATA LIST specifies inline matrix materials in fixed format (the default) and defines three variables.

- The data are arranged to conform to the requirements of the REGRESSION procedure. Each row vector has 3 entries, each with a width of 10 columns. The last entry is the number of cases.

- The READ subcommand on REGRESSION reads the matrix of correlation coefficients and a value for the number of cases (see REGRESSION: Matrix Materials).

Example

```
DATA LIST MATRIX FREE / X1 X2 X3 X4 X5 Y.
BEGIN DATA.
35.0825 2.7315 40.9060 3.1405 25.0690 6.2550
5.8171 .4541 25.8985 9.6254 1.3138 .6543
33.8381250 .5079382 113.502300 51.9130250 2.5499079 2.7898921
 113.502300 2.1302800 670.734846 206.202997 1.7372853 15.7105368
51.9130250 1.0036676 206.202997 92.6479839 2.3183584 5.1585079
2.5499079 .2998858 1.7372853 2.3183584 1.7260832 .1064316
2.7898921 .0584658 15.7105368 5.1585079 .1064316 .4281316
20
END DATA.
VAR LABELS X1 'STAFF SALARIES PER PUPIL'
           X2 '6TH GRADE PER CENT WHITE-COLLAR FATHERS'
           X3 'SES COMPOSITE'
           X4 'MEAN TEACHER VERBAL TEST SCORE'
           X5 '6TH GRADE MEAN MOTHER EDUCATION'
           Y  'VERBAL MEAN TEST SCORE, ALL 6TH GRADERS'.
REGRESSION READ=COV MEAN STDDEV N
  /DES DEF
  /VAR=Y,X1 TO X5
  /CRI TOL(.0001)
  /STATS ALL
  /DEP Y
  /ENT.
```

- The DATA LIST command specifies inline matrix materials in freefield format and defines six variables.

- The data are arranged to conform to the requirements of the REGRESSION procedure. The first six rows form a covariance matrix, with each row starting on a new line. The seventh row forms a vector of means for each variable named. The eighth row is a vector of standard deviations. The last entry is the number of cases.

- The READ subcommand on REGRESSION specifies matrix materials with a covariance matrix, a vector of means, a vector of standard deviations, and the number of cases (see REGRESSION: Matrix Materials).

Matrix Input for Procedure MANOVA

- Procedure MANOVA reads matrix materials in either fixed or freefield format.
- For complete information on the contents and format of matrix materials used by MANOVA, see the WRITE subcommand under MANOVA in *SPSS/PC+ Advanced Statistics*.
- This procedure cannot use matrix materials written by another procedure, nor can another procedure use matrix materials written by MANOVA.

Example

```
DATA LIST MATRIX / Y1 Y2 Y3 EDUC SEX.
BEGIN DATA.
          6          54          2          3
      1          1
  2.09000000E+00  4.53000000E+00  3.56000000E+00
      1          2
  1.38000000E+00  4.17000000E+00  3.38000000E+00
      2          1
  2.12000000E+00  5.35000000E+00  3.59000000E+00
      2          2
  1.47000000D+00  4.90000000E+00  3.12000000E+00
      3          1
  2.13000000E+00  5.94000000E+00  3.51000000E+00
      3          2
  1.74000000E+00  5.37000000E+00  3.27000000E+00
          8          10          11          8          9          8
    1.00000
     .25689    1.00000
    -.07085     .13390    1.00000
  3.80000000E-01  6.30000000E-01  3.90000000E-01
END DATA.
MANOVA Y1 Y2 Y3 BY EDUC(1,3) SEX(1,2)
  /READ
  /ANALYSIS Y1 Y2 WITH Y3
  /DISCRIM
  /PRINT=ERROR(SSCP COR)
  /DESIGN.
```

- The DATA LIST command specifies inline matrix materials in fixed format (the default). The active file contains five variables (data from Tatsuoka, 1971).
- The matrix materials were produced by the WRITE subcommand in MANOVA, using the same variables specified on the MANOVA command that will read the matrix.
- The READ subcommand indicates that matrix materials should be read from the location specified or implied on DATA LIST MATRIX. In this example, the data are inline (the default).

DESCRIPTIVES

```
DESCRIPTIVES [VARIABLES=] {varlist}
                         {ALL    }

[/OPTIONS=option numbers]

[/STATISTICS={statistic numbers}]
            {ALL              }
```

Options:

1	Include user-missing values	6	Serial format
2	Suppress variable labels	7	Narrow format
3	Save *Z* scores in active file	8	Suppress variable names
5	Exclude missing values listwise		

Statistics:

1	Mean	9	Range
2	Standard error of mean	10	Minimum
5	Standard deviation	11	Maximum
6	Variance	12	Sum
7	Kurtosis	13	Mean, standard deviation, minimum, and maximum
8	Skewness		

Example:

```
DESCRIPTIVES VARIABLES=YVAR ZVAR, AVAR1 TO AVAR5,
                       BETATEST, IOTATEST
  /STATISTICS=6 13
  /OPTIONS=5.
```

Overview

DESCRIPTIVES computes univariate statistics, including the mean, standard deviation, minimum, and maximum, for numeric variables. Because it does not sort values into a frequency table, DESCRIPTIVES is an efficient means of computing descriptive statistics for continuous variables. Other procedures that display descriptive statistics include FREQUENCIES, MEANS, and EXAMINE.

Options

Statistical Display. Optional statistics available with the STATISTICS subcommand include the standard error of the mean, variance, kurtosis, skewness, range, and sum. DESCRIPTIVES does not compute the median or mode (see FREQUENCIES or EXAMINE).

Z Scores. You can create new variables that contain Z scores (standardized deviation scores from the mean) and add them to the active file by specifying Z-score names on the VARI-ABLES subcommand or by using Option 3.

Display Format. You can display statistics in serial format (Option 6) and restrict the width to narrow format regardless of the width defined on SET (Option 7). You can also control the display of variable labels and name (Options 2 and 8).

Basic Specification

- The basic specification is the VARIABLES subcommand with a list of variables. The actual keyword VARIABLES can be omitted.
- The default table displays the variable name, variable label, mean, standard deviation, minimum, maximum, and number of cases with valid value. All cases with valid values for a variable are included in the calculation of statistics for that variable.

Operations

- If a string variable is specified on the variable list, a warning is issued and no statistics are displayed for that variable.
- The available width and the statistics and options requested determine whether the statistics are displayed in tabular or serial form. If the width is insufficient to display the statistics requested, DESCRIPTIVES first truncates the variable label and then adopts serial format.
- If there is insufficient memory available to calculate statistics for all variables requested, DESCRIPTIVES truncates the variable list.
- Statistics that will fit within the allotted columns are displayed with two decimal places.

Limitations

- There is no fixed limit on the number of variables named or implied on DESCRIPTIVES.
- Maximum 1 each of the VARIABLES, OPTIONS, and STATISTICS subcommands.

Example

```
DESCRIPTIVES VARIABLES=YVAR ZVAR, AVAR1 TO AVAR5,
                      BETATEST, IOTATEST
  /STATISTICS=6 13
  /OPTIONS=5.
```

- This example requests statistics for *YVAR*, *ZVAR*, *BETATEST*, *IOTATEST*, and all variables between and including *AVAR1* and *AVAR5* in the active file.
- The STATISTICS subcommand requests the variance (Statistic 6) and the defaults (Statistic 13), which include the mean, standard deviation, minimum, and maximum.

- Option 5 specifies that cases with missing values for any variable in the variable list will be omitted from the calculation of statistics for all variables.

Example

```
DESCRIPTIVES VAR=RAGE RINC81.
```

- Because no STATISTICS subcommand is specified, only the mean, standard deviation, minimum, and maximum for *RAGE* and *RINC81* will be displayed.
- This example uses three-character truncation of keywords.

VARIABLES Subcommand

VARIABLES names the variables to be included in the table. The actual keyword VARIABLES can be omitted.

- You can use keyword ALL to refer to all user-defined variables in the active file.
- Variables named more than once appear in the display more than once.

Z Scores

The *Z*-score transformation standardizes variables to the same scale, producing new variables with a mean of 0 and a standard deviation of 1. These variables are added to the active file. There are two methods for requesting *Z* scores.

- To obtain *Z* scores for all specified variables, use Option 3.
- To obtain *Z* scores for a subset of variables, name the new variable in parentheses following the source variable on the VARIABLES subcommand. You must specify new names individually; a list in parentheses is not recognized.
- SPSS/PC+ creates variable labels for the new *Z*-score variables created with either method.
- Whenever *Z* scores are added to the file, a table is displayed showing the names of the new variables and of the original variables from which they were created.
- If you specify Option 3 and also enter variable names in parentheses for some variables, *Z* scores are calculated for all variables, using your names where you have supplied them and forming new names where you have not.
- If the new variables cause you to exceed the system limit, SPSS/PC+ displays an error message and does not process the DESCRIPTIVES command.

Option 3   *Add Z scores to the active file for all variables specified on DESCRIPTIVES.* SPSS/PC+ forms variable names for the new variables, using wherever possible the letter *Z* and the first seven characters of the old variable name.

Example

```
DESCRIPTIVES VAR1 VAR2 SCORE (STDSCORE) INCOME
  /OPTIONS 3.
```

- *Z* scores are produced for all four variables: *VAR1*, *VAR2*, *SCORE*, and *INCOME*.
- A name is specified for *SCORE*. The other variables are assigned names by SPSS/PC+.
- The variables *ZVAR1*, *ZVAR2*, *STDSCORE*, and *ZINCOME* are added to the end of the active file.

Display Format

By default, DESCRIPTIVES displays statistics and a 40-character variable label for each variable on one line. If the statistics requested do not fit within the available width, DESCRIPTIVES first truncates the variable label and then uses serial format.

You can request the following display options on the OPTIONS subcommand:

Option 2   *Suppress variable labels.*

Option 6   *Display statistics in serial format.* Statistics are displayed below the variable name, permitting larger field widths and more decimal digits for very large or very small numbers. DESCRIPTIVES automatically uses this format if the number of statistics requested does not fit in the column format

Option 7   *Use Narrow format.* The display width is restricted to 79 columns regardless of the width defined on SET.

Option 8   *Suppress variable names.* The variable name is displayed only if there is no variable label.

Statistical Display

By default, DESCRIPTIVES calculates the mean, standard deviation, minimum, and maximum. You can obtain additional statistics by specifying the following on the STATISTICS subcommand.

- If the STATISTICS subcommand is included, only statistics specifically requested are displayed.
- The valid count on which statistics are based is always displayed.

Statistic 1   *Mean.*

Statistic 2   *Standard error of mean.*

Statistic 5   *Standard deviation.*

Statistic 6   *Variance.*

Statistic 7   *Kurtosis and standard error of kurtosis.*

Statistic 8   *Skewness and standard error of skewness.*

Statistic 9   *Range.*

Statistic 10   *Minimum observed value.*

Statistic 11   *Maximum observed value.*

Statistic 12	*Sum.*
Statistic 13	*Mean, standard deviation, minimum, and maximum.* These are the default statistics.
ALL	*All statistics available in DESCRIPTIVES.*

Missing Values

By default, all cases with valid values for a variable are included in the calculation of statistics for that variable. You can alter the treatment of cases with missing values by specifying the following on the OPTIONS subcommand:

Option 1	*Include cases with user-missing values.* Cases with user-missing values will be included in the calculation of statistics for all variables specified on the command.
Option 5	*Exclude cases with missing values listwise.* Cases with a missing value for any variable specified on DESCRIPTIVES are excluded from the calculation of statistics for all variables. The valid count is reported for the table as a whole instead of for individual variables.

DISPLAY

```
DISPLAY [{varlist}]
        {ALL    }
```

Example:

```
DISPLAY AVAR TO FVAR.
```

Overview

DISPLAY exhibits information about variables in the active file.

Options

To display detailed information about some or all of the variables in the active file, specify a variable list (see "Variable List" below).

Basic Specification

- The basic specification is simply the command keyword, which displays a list of all variables in the active file and their variable labels.

Operations

- Information produced by DISPLAY is included with the output. By default, the output goes to the screen and the listing file *SPSS.LIS*. (See SET for information on output destinations.)

Example

```
GET 'WEATHER.SYS'.
DISPLAY.
```

- DISPLAY displays a list of variables in the system file *WEATHER.SYS* and their variable labels.

Variable List

You can obtain more detailed information on some or all of the variables in the active file by specifying either a list of variable names or keyword ALL.

- When a variable list or keyword ALL is specified, the information for each variable includes the variable name and label, value labels, missing-value flags, and variable type and width.

- Keyword ALL produces detailed information on all variables in the active file.
- Variable names can be separated by a comma or a space.

Example

```
DISPLAY ALL.
```

- DISPLAY exhibits detailed information on all variables in the active file.

EXAMINE

```
EXAMINE VARIABLES=varlist [[BY varlist] [varname BY varname]]

[/COMPARE={GROUPS**  }]
          {VARIABLES}

[/SCALE={PLOTWISE**}]
        {UNIFORM   }

[/ID={$CASENUM**}]
     {varname   }

[/FREQUENCIES [FROM(initial value)] [BY(increment)]]

[/PERCENTILES [[({5,10,25,50,75,90,95})=[{HAVERAGE }] [NONE]]
                {value list          }    {WAVERAGE }
                                          {ROUND    }
                                          {AEMPIRICAL}
                                          {EMPIRICAL }

[/PLOT=[STEMLEAF**] [BOXPLOT**] [NPPLOT] [SPREADLEVEL(n)] [HISTOGRAM]] [{ALL }]
                                                                       {NONE}

[/STATISTICS=[DESCRIPTIVES**] [EXTREME({5})] [{ALL }]]
                                      {n}    {NONE}

[/MESTIMATOR=[{NONE**}] [HUBER({1.339})] [ANDREW({1.34}]
             {ALL   }         {c    }           {c   }

          [HAMPEL({1.7,3.4,8.5})] [TUKEY({4.685})]]
                 {a  ,b  ,c    }         {c    }

[/MISSING=[{LISTWISE**}] [INCLUDE]]
          {PAIRWISE  }
          {REPORT    }
```

**Default if the subcommand is omitted.

Examples:

```
EXAMINE VARIABLES=ENGSIZE,COST.

EXAMINE VARIABLES=MIPERGAL BY MODEL,MODEL BY CYLINDERS.
```

Overview

EXAMINE provides stem-and-leaf plots, boxplots, robust estimates of location, tests of normality and other descriptive statistics and plots. Separate analyses can be obtained for subgroups of cases.

Options

Cells. You can subdivide cases into cells based on their values for grouping (factor) variables using the BY keyword on the VARIABLES subcommand.

Output. You can control the display of output using the COMPARE subcommand and the scale of plots using the SCALE subcommand. You can produce frequency tables and control their format with the FREQUENCIES subcommand. You can specify the computational method and break points for percentiles with the PERCENTILES subcommand, and you can assign a variable to be used for labeling outliers on the ID subcommand.

Plots. You can request stem-and-leaf plots, histograms, vertical boxplots, spread-and-level plots with the Levene test for homogeneity of variance, and normal and detrended probability plots with tests for normality. These plots are available through the PLOT subcommand.

Statistics. You can request univariate statistical output with the STATISTICS subcommand and robust maximum-likelihood estimators with the MESTIMATORS subcommand.

Basic Specification

- The basic specification is VARIABLES and at least one dependent variable.
- For each dependent variable named on VARIABLES, the default output includes univariate statistics (mean, median, standard deviation, standard error, variance, kurtosis, kurtosis standard error, skewness, skewness standard error, sum, interquartile range (IQR), range, minimum, maximum, and 5% trimmed mean), a vertical boxplot, and a stem-and-leaf plot. Outliers are labeled on the boxplot with the system variable *$CASENUM*.

Subcommand Order

Subcommands can be named in any order.

Limitations

When string variables are used as factors, only the first eight characters are used to form cells. String variables cannot be specified as dependent variables.

Example

```
EXAMINE VARIABLES=ENGSIZE,COST.
```

- *ENGSIZE* and *COST* are the dependent variables.
- EXAMINE produces univariate statistics, a vertical boxplot, and a stem-and-leaf plot for each dependent variable.

Example

```
EXAMINE VARIABLES=MIPERGAL BY MODEL,MODEL BY CYLINDERS.
```

- *MIPERGAL* is the dependent variable. The cell specification follows the first BY keyword. Cases are subdivided based on values of *MODEL* and also based on the combination of values of *MODEL* and *CYLINDERS*.
- Assuming there are three values for *MODEL* and two values for *CYLINDERS*, this example produces univariate statistics, boxplots, and stem-and-leaf plots for all cases considered

together, for the three cells defined by *MODEL*, and for the six cells defined by *MODEL* and *CYLINDERS* together.

VARIABLES Subcommand

VARIABLES specifies the dependent variables and the cells. The dependent variables are specified first, followed by keyword BY and the variables that define the cells.

- Only one VARIABLES subcommand can be specified.
- To create cells defined by the combination of values of two or more factors, specify the factor names separated by keyword BY.
- Each value of a factor produces at least one separate page of output. If factors are combined with keyword BY, each combination of values will also produce at least one page of output.

Caution. Large amounts of output can be produced if many cells are specified. If there are many factors or if the factors have many values, EXAMINE will produce a large number of separate analyses.

Example

```
EXAMINE VARIABLES=SALARY,YRSEDUC BY RACE,SEX,DEPT,RACE BY SEX.
```

- *SALARY* and *YRSEDUC* are dependent variables.
- Cells are formed first for the values of *RACE*, *SEX*, and *DEPT* individually and then by the combination of values for *RACE* and *SEX*.
- EXAMINE produces univariate statistics, a boxplot, and a stem-and-leaf plot for cases as a whole and for each cell specified. If *RACE* and *SEX* each have two possible values and *DEPT* has three possible values, this produces 1 set of output for cases as a whole, 2 sets for subgroups defined by *RACE*, 2 for *SEX*, 3 for *DEPT*, and 4 for *RACE* by *SEX*, for a total of 12 sets for each dependent variable, or 24 sets in all.

COMPARE Subcommand

COMPARE controls how boxplots are displayed. This subcommand is most useful if there is more than one dependent variable and at least one factor in the design.

GROUPS   *For each dependent variable, boxplots for all cells are displayed together.* With this display, comparisons across cells for a single dependent variable are easily made. This is the default.

VARIABLES   *For each cell, boxplots for all dependent variables are displayed together.* With this display, comparisons of several dependent variables are easily made. This is useful in situations where the dependent variables are repeated measures of the same variable (see the following example) or have similar scales, or when the dependent variable has very different values for different cells, and plotting all cells on the same scale would cause information to be lost.

Example

```
EXAMINE VARIABLES=GPA1 GPA2 GPA3 GPA4 BY MAJOR
/COMPARE=VARIABLES.
```

- The four GPA variables are summarized for each value of *MAJOR*.
- COMPARE=VARIABLES groups the boxplots for the four GPA variables together for each value of *MAJOR*.

Example

```
EXAMINE VARIABLES=GPA1 GPA2 GPA3 GPA4 BY MAJOR /COMPARE=GROUPS.
```

- COMPARE=GROUPS groups the boxplots for *GPA1* for all majors together, followed by boxplots for *GPA2* for all majors, and so on.

SCALE Subcommand

SCALE controls whether boxplots, stem-and-leaf plots, and histograms are constructed on the same scale for each cell in the analysis.

- EXAMINE does not use a uniform scale for boxplots of separate dependent variables unless they are plotted in the same plot with COMPARE=VARIABLES.

PLOTWISE   *Construct scales according to the values in each plot.* Boxplots for each cell are constructed on the basis of the values of the dependent variable for cases in that plot only. This is the default.

UNIFORM   *Display plots using a common scale.* Scales for boxplots and histograms are the same for each cell in the model. The common scale is constructed on the basis of the values of the dependent variable values of all cases.

Examples

```
EXAMINE VARIABLES=SALARY BY SEX
  /SCALE=UNIFORM.
```

- The stem-and-leaf plots for *SALARY* are plotted on the same scale for both values of *SEX*.

```
EXAMINE VARIABLES=SALARY BONUS BY SEX
  /COMPARE=VARIABLES
  /SCALE=UNIFORM.
```

- *SALARY* and *BONUS* are plotted in the same boxplot for each value of *SEX*. The scale is the same in each boxplot.

ID Subcommand

ID assigns a variable from the active file to identify the cases in the output. By default the system variable *$CASENUM* is used for labeling outliers and extreme cases in boxplots.

- The identification variable can be either string or numeric. If it is numeric, value labels are used to label cases. If no value labels exist, the values are used.
- Up to 25 characters of the identification variable are displayed.

- Only one identification variable can be specified.

Example

```
EXAMINE VARIABLES=SALARY BY RACE BY SEX /ID=LASTNAME.
```

- ID displays up to 25 characters of the value of *LASTNAME* for outliers and extreme cases in the boxplots.

FREQUENCIES Subcommand

The FREQUENCIES subcommand generates frequency tables. Two keywords are available:

FROM(value) *The lowest value for the frequency table.* Frequency tables are generated for values between the cutoff value and the maximum value for the dependent variable. All cases with values smaller than the cutoff value are reported as one group in the first row of the table. The default is the minimum value.

BY(increment) *The increment for frequency display.* The default increment is the same as that selected for stems in the stem-and-leaf plot. If the increment is 0, frequencies for each distinct value are produced.

- Each row in the frequency table is identified by its center value. All values below the cutoff value, if specified, are represented in the first row, which is identified with a less-than sign (<).
- The default statistics and plots (stem-and-leaf plot and boxplot) are displayed.

Example

```
EXAMINE VARIABLE=DEGREES
   /FREQUENCIES FROM (90) BY (10).
```

- FREQUENCIES produces a frequency table for the dependent variable *DEGREES*.
- The cutoff value for the frequency table is 90. If there are cases with values smaller than 90, they are reported as a group on the first row of the frequency table.
- BY specifies increments of 10. The first frequency bin contains all cases with values greater than or equal to 90 but less than 100. The center of the bin is 95. The next bin contains all cases with values greater than or equal to 100 but less than 110, with a center of 105.
- Frequencies continue in increments of 10 until the maximum value for *DEGREES* is included in a bin.

PERCENTILES Subcommand

PERCENTILES controls the method and break points for percentile computations. If PERCENTILES is omitted, no percentiles are produced. If PERCENTILES is specified without keywords, HAVERAGE is used with default break points of 5, 10, 25, 50, 75, 90, and 95.

- Values for break points are specified in parentheses following the subcommand.
- The method keywords follow the specifications for break points.

In the following formulas, cases are assumed to be ranked in ascending order. The following notation is used: w is the sum of the weights for all nonmissing cases, p is the specified percentile divided by 100, i is the rank of each case, and X_i is the value of the ith case.

HAVERAGE
Weighted average at $X_{(w+1)p}$. The percentile value is the weighted average of X_i and X_{i+1} using the formula $(1-f)X_i + fX_{i+1}$, where $(w+1)p$ is decomposed into an integer part i and a fractional part f. This is the default if PERCENTILES is specified without a keyword.

WAVERAGE
Weighted average at X_{wp}. The percentile value is the weighted average of X_i and $X_{(i+1)}$ using the formula $(1-f)X_i + fX_{i+1}$, where i is the integer part of wp and f is the fractional part of wp.

ROUND
Observation closest to wp. The percentile value is X_i, where i is the integer part of $(wp + 0.5)$.

EMPIRICAL
Empirical distribution function. The percentile value is X_i when the fractional part of wp is equal to 0. The percentile value is X_{i+1} when the fractional part of wp is greater than 0.

AEMPIRICAL
Empirical distribution with averaging. The percentile value is $(X_i + X_{i+1})/2$ when the fractional part of wp equals 0. The percentile value is X_{i+1} when the fractional part of wp is greater than 0.

NONE
Suppress percentile output. This is the default if PERCENTILES is omitted.

Example

```
EXAMINE VARIABLE=SALARY /PERCENTILES(10,50,90)=EMPIRICAL.
```

- PERCENTILES produces the 10th, 50th, and 90th percentiles for the dependent variable *SALARY* using the EMPIRICAL distribution function.

PLOT Subcommand

PLOT controls plot output. The default is a vertical boxplot and a stem-and-leaf plot for each dependent variable for each cell in the model.

- Spread-and-level plots can be produced only if there is at least one factor variable on the VARIABLES subcommand. If you request a spread-and-level plot and there are no factor variables, no spread-and-level plot is produced.
- If you specify the PLOT subcommand, only those plots explicitly requested are produced.

BOXPLOT
Vertical boxplot. The boundaries of the box are Tukey's hinges. The median is identified by an asterisk. The length of the box is the interquartile range (IQR) computed from Tukey's hinges. Values more than three IQR's from the end of a box are labeled as extreme (E). Values more than 1.5 IQR's but less than 3 IQR's from the end of the box are labeled as outliers (O).

STEMLEAF
Stem-and-leaf plot. In a stem-and-leaf plot, each observed value is divided into two components—leading digits (stem) and trailing digits (leaf).

HISTOGRAM	*Histogram.*
SPREADLEVEL(n)	*Spread-and-level plot.* This type of plot requires a factor variable (after keyword BY). If the keyword appears alone, the natural logs of the interquartile ranges are plotted against the natural logs of the medians for all cells. If a power for transforming the data (n) is given, the IQR and median of the transformed data are plotted. If 0 is specified for n, a natural log transformation of the data is done. The slope of the regression line and the Levene test for homogeneity of variance are also displayed. The Levene test is based on the original data if no transformation is specified and on the transformed data if a transformation is requested.
NPPLOT	*Normal probability and detrended probability plots.* NPPLOT calculates the Shapiro-Wilks statistic and a Kolmogorov-Smirnov statistic with a Lilliefors significance level for testing normality. Shapiro-Wilks is not calculated when the sample size exceeds 50.
ALL	*All available plots.*
NONE	*No plots.*

Example

```
EXAMINE VARIABLES=CYCLE BY TREATMNT /PLOT=NPPLOT.
```

- PLOT produces normal probability plots and detrended probability plots for each value of *TREATMNT*.

Example

```
EXAMINE VARIABLES=CYCLE BY TREATMNT /PLOT=SPREADLEVEL(.5).
```

- PLOT produces a spread-and-level plot of the medians and interquartile ranges of the square root of *CYCLE*. Each point on the plot represents one of the *TREATMNT* groups.

Example

```
EXAMINE VARIABLES=CYCLE BY TREATMNT /PLOT=SPREADLEVEL(0).
```

- PLOT generates a spread-and-level plot of the medians and interquartile ranges of the natural logs of *CYCLE* for each *TREATMENT* group.

Example

```
EXAMINE VARIABLES=CYCLE BY TREATMNT /PLOT=SPREADLEVEL.
```

- PLOT generates a spread-and-level plot of the natural logs of the medians and interquartile ranges of *CYCLE* for each *TREATMNT* group.

STATISTICS Subcommand

STATISTICS requests univariate statistics and determines how many extreme values are displayed. DESCRIPTIVES is the default. If you specify keywords on STATISTICS, only the requested statistics are displayed.

DESCRIPTIVES *Univariate statistics only.* This includes the mean, median, 5% trimmed mean, standard error, variance, standard deviation, minimum, maximum, range, interquartile range, skewness, skewness standard error, kurtosis, and kurtosis standard error. This is the default.

EXTREME(n) *The cases with the* n *largest and* n *smallest values.* If *n* is omitted, the five largest and five smallest values are displayed. Extreme cases are labeled with their values for the identification variable if the ID subcommand is used or with their values for the system variable *$CASENUM* if ID is not specified.

ALL *Univariate statistics and cases with the five largest and five smallest values.*

NONE *No univariate statistics or extreme values.*

Example

```
EXAMINE VARIABLE=FAILTIME /ID=BRAND
  /STATISTICS=EXTREME(10) /PLOT=NONE.
```

- STATISTICS identifies the cases with the 10 lowest and 10 highest values for *FAILTIME*. These cases are labeled with the first 15 characters of their values for variable *BRAND*. Univariate statistics are not displayed.

MESTIMATORS Subcommand

M-estimators are robust maximum-likelihood estimators of location. Four M-estimators are available. They differ in the weights they apply to the cases. MESTIMATORS with no keywords produces Huber's M-estimator with $c=1.339$; Andrew's wave with $c=1.34\pi$; Hampel's M-estimator with $a=1.7$, $b=3.4$, and $c=8.5$; and Tukey's biweight with $c=4.685$.

HUBER(c) *Huber's M-estimator.* The value of weighting constant c can be specified in parentheses following the keyword. The default is $c=1.339$.

ANDREW(c) *Andrew's wave estimator.* The value of weighting constant c can be specified in parentheses following the keyword. Constants are multiplied by π. The default constant is 1.34.

HAMPEL(a,b,c) *Hampel's M-estimator.* The values of weighting constants a, b, and c can be specified in order in parentheses following the keyword. The default values are $a=1.7$, $b=3.4$, and $c=8.5$.

TUKEY(c) *Tukey's biweight estimator.* The value of weighting constant c can be specified in parentheses following the keyword. The default is $c=4.685$.

ALL *All four above M-estimators.* This is the default when MESTIMATORS is specified with no keyword. The default values for weighting constants are used.

NONE   *No M-estimators.* This is the default if MESTIMATORS is omitted.

Example

```
EXAMINE VARIABLE=CASTTEST /MESTIMATORS.
```

- MESTIMATORS generates all four M-estimators computed with the default constants.

Example

```
EXAMINE VARIABLE=CASTTEST /MESTIMATORS=HAMPELS(2,4,8).
```

- MESTIMATOR produces Hampel's M-estimator with weighting constants $a=2$, $b=4$, and $c=8$.

MISSING Subcommand

MISSING controls the processing of missing values in the analysis. The default is LISTWISE.

- LISTWISE, PAIRWISE, and REPORT are alternatives and apply to all variables. They can be modified for dependent variables by INCLUDE.

LISTWISE   *Delete cases with missing values listwise.* A case with missing values for any dependent variable or any factor in the model specification is excluded from statistics and plots unless modified by INCLUDE. This is the default.

PAIRWISE   *Delete cases with missing values pairwise.* A case is deleted from the analysis only if it has a missing value for the dependent variable or factor being analyzed.

REPORT   *Include user- and system-missing values for factor variables.* User- and system-missing values for factors are treated as valid categories and arc labeled as missing. User- and system-missing values for dependent variables are reported in frequency output and excluded from statistical computations and graphs.

INCLUDE   *Include user-missing values.* Only system-missing values are excluded from the analysis.

Example

```
EXAMINE VARIABLES=RAINFALL MEANTEMP BY REGION.
```

- MISSING is not specified and the default is used. Any case with a user- or system-missing value for *RAINFALL*, *MEANTEMP*, or *REGION* is excluded from the analysis and display.

Example

```
EXAMINE VARIABLES=RAINFALL MEANTEMP BY REGION
  /MISSING=PAIRWISE.
```

- Only cases with missing values for *RAINFALL* are excluded from the analysis of *RAINFALL*, and only cases with missing values for *MEANTEMP* are excluded from the analysis of *MEANTEMP*. Missing values for *REGION* are not used.

EXECUTE

```
EXECUTE {path\filename}{.ext} ['parameters']
                       {.EXE}
        {DOS         }
```

Example:

```
EXECUTE '\SPSS\KERMIT.EXE'.
```

Overview

EXECUTE allows you to run other programs or execute DOS commands from within SPSS/PC+ and then resume your SPSS/PC+ session. This facility does not make SPSS/PC+ a regular operating environment: part of SPSS/PC+ remains in memory, which limits the memory available for other programs. Instead, EXECUTE lets you run other programs briefly or execute DOS commands without having to reload SPSS/PC+ and recreate your active file and SPSS/PC+ environment when you return.

SPSS/PC+ cannot control actions taken by other software that you invoke through EXECUTE and therefore cannot guarantee that any particular program will run safely.

Options

Parameters. You can pass command-line parameters to the other program as if you were running it from DOS (see "Parameters" on p. 534).

RAM. By default, the other program has approximately 128K of RAM in which to run. You can allocate more RAM for the program when you invoke SPSS/PC+ (see "Memory Considerations" on p. 536).

Basic Specification

- The basic specification is the name of an executable file with extension *.EXE* or *.COM*. The filename should be in apostrophes.
- If you do not specify a file extension, the extension *.EXE* is assumed.

Syntax Rules

- Parameters in apostrophes following the file specification are passed to the program you invoke. For example, you could pass a filename to an editor.
- The specification EXECUTE DOS or simply DOS is a synonym for COMMAND.COM, the DOS command processor. This provides access to any DOS command.
- To return from DOS to your SPSS/PC+ session, issue the DOS command EXIT.
- To return from any other program, issue the command normally used to leave that program.

Operations

- SPSS/PC+ passes control to the program named on the EXECUTE command. By default, that program has approximately 128K of RAM available (see "Memory Considerations" on p. 536).
- If you exit to SPSS/PC+ while printing, printing may be suspended but resumes either during or after the SPSS/PC+ session is ended.
- All files used by SPSS/PC+ are closed before control is passed to the other program.

Limitations

- The program you invoke must not leave anything resident in memory when you return to SPSS/PC+.
- The program must not attempt to redefine any of the interrupt vectors in low memory on the PC.
- The number of files that the program can open will be smaller than the FILES specification in *CONFIG.SYS* because some files remain allocated for use by SPSS/PC+.
- Temporary files used by SPSS/PC+ should not be deleted in the middle of a session. These include files named *SPSS.SY1* and *SPSS.SY2*, which hold the active file at various times.
- System files that have been read by the GET command should not be deleted unless data transformation or selection has created a new active file on disk.
- Entering some DOS commands will make it impossible to resume your session (such as erasing **SPSS/PC+** modules or a system file that will be needed by a subsequent procedure).

See "Problems" on p. 535 for further discussion of these limitations.

Example

```
DOS.
```

- This command is a synonym for EXECUTE DOS and executes the DOS command processor, *COMMAND.COM*.
- When you see the DOS command prompt (for example, C:\MYFILES>), you can issue any DOS command.
- To return to SPSS/PC+, issue the DOS EXIT command. You will again see the SPSSPC: prompt, and any active file you created earlier in your session will be available.

File Specification

To invoke a program from SPSS/PC+, specify an executable file with extension *.COM* or *.EXE*.

- You can omit the extension if it is *.EXE*.

- If the file is in a directory other than your current directory, you can include a path specification.
- Paths defined with the DOS PATH command are searched just as if you were naming the file from DOS.
- To execute a batch (.*BAT*) file, specify EXECUTE DOS and then invoke the batch file by name at the DOS prompt.
- Most programs can be invoked indirectly by specifying EXECUTE DOS and then running the program from DOS. This method slightly increases memory requirements and substantially increases the possibilities for confusion.

Example

```
EXECUTE '\SPSS\KERMIT.EXE'.
```

- This command runs KERMIT from within an SPSS/PC+ session. You can use KERMIT to log on to a mainframe and download a portable file created by the EXPORT command in SPSS.
- After logging off the mainframe and leaving KERMIT with the KERMIT EXIT or QUIT command, you can continue the SPSS/PC+ session and import the file you have downloaded.

Parameters

Any text following the file specification is passed to the program you invoke.

- Parameters specified after the file specification should be enclosed in apostrophes.
- If you execute the DOS PRINT command and printing stops when you specify EXIT to return to SPSS/PC+, printing will resume when you return to DOS.

Example

This example shows how to use the DOS PRINT command to begin printing a listing file and then continue with your SPSS/PC+ session. DOS and SPSS/PC+ prompts are in upper case and user commands are in lower case:

```
C:\MYFILES>print
NAME OF LIST DEVICE [PRN]:
RESIDENT PART OF PRINT INSTALLED
PRINT QUEUE IS EMPTY.

C:\MYFILES>spsspc

   ...beginning of SPSS/PC+ session...

SPSS/PC:get file='bigfile.sys'.
SPSS/PC:set listing 'freq.lis'.
SPSS/PC:frequencies all.
```

...output from FREQUENCIES procedure...

```
SPSS/PC:dos.

C:\MYFILES>print freq.lis

        C:FREQ     :LIS IS CURRENTLY BEING PRINTED

C:\MYFILES>exit

SPSS/PC:crosstabs ....
```

- The DOS PRINT command is issued before entering SPSS/PC+ to install the print driver (see "Programs Remaining in Memory" below). Since no file is specified, nothing is printed and DOS issues the message PRINT QUEUE IS EMPTY.
- In the SPSS/PC+ session, the GET command retrieves a system file. The SET command specifies a file (*FREQ.LIS*) for the output, and the FREQUENCIES command runs frequency distributions for all variables in the active file. If you had specified SET PRINTER ON, you would have to wait for the printing to finish before continuing your analysis.
- The SPSS/PC+ command DOS (an abbreviation for EXECUTE DOS) invokes the DOS command processor, which responds with its prompt (in this case, *C:\MYFILES>*).
- The DOS PRINT command prints the listing file *FREQ.LIS*.
- The DOS EXIT command returns to SPSS/PC+. If you exit before the printing is complete, printing may be suspended but will resume either during or after the SPSS/PC+ session.

Problems

The following types of programs may make it impossible to return to your SPSS/PC+ session.

Programs Remaining in Memory

A program that leaves anything in RAM after exiting will cause SPSS/PC+ to abort if that program is *first* invoked from an SPSS/PC+ session with the EXECUTE command. Among the programs that can cause this problem are:

- *The DOS PRINT command.* The first time you print a file, DOS loads a print driver into memory, where it remains. To use the DOS PRINT command during an SPSS/PC+ session, you must first specify PRINT with or without a filename prior to entering SPSS/PC+. This installs the print driver before SPSS/PC+ claims memory for its own use.
- *The DOS MODE command.* Certain uses of the MODE command, including those needed to configure a printer, cause additional code to be loaded into memory (see your DOS manual). Do not attempt to do this when you are executing DOS from within an SPSS/PC+ session.
- *Desk-accessory programs.* These programs remain in memory after being started and can be called up with a few keystrokes to perform notepad, calendar, communications, and other functions. You can use these programs within SPSS/PC+ but cannot use the EXECUTE command to start them or you will abort the SPSS/PC+ session.

- *Keyboard utilities.* You must run keyboard configuration utilities before entering SPSS/PC+, not from within a session.

If you do not know whether a particular program remains in memory, run it before entering SPSS/PC+. You should then be able to use EXECUTE safely for the remainder of the session.

Programs Altering the Interrupt Vectors

Any program that alters the interrupt vectors stored in low memory of the PC and does not restore them before exiting will make it impossible for SPSS/PC+ to resume. Commercially available software is unlikely to do this.

Memory Considerations

Normally, SPSS/PC+ uses all available memory (beyond that occupied by SPSS/PC+ itself) as workspace. Thus, only the 128K given up by SPSS/PC+ when you specify EXECUTE is available for use by another program.

If you intend to run a program that requires more than 128K, you must limit the amount of workspace SPSS/PC+ takes on a command-line switch.

- The switch is specified when you invoke SPSS/PC+ from DOS with the SPSSPC command.

- The switch is entered as /S=nnnK, where nnnK is the amount of workspace allocated to SPSS/PC+. A minimum of 20K is suggested for any productive work. For example, to free up as much memory as possible, specify SPSSPC /S=20K.

- If you specify a filename on the SPSSPC command, put the workspace switch after the filename, as in SPSSPC MYDATA.DEF /S=20K.

If you know that a program will require a certain amount of memory above 128K, you can maximize your SPSS/PC+ workspace by following these steps:

1. Run SPSS/PC+ without the /S switch, so that it will request the maximum possible workspace.

2. Use the SHOW command to find out how large this maximum workspace is (this amount will vary from one machine to another).

3. Run SPSS/PC+ again, using the /S switch to reduce the workspace sufficiently to leave the desired amount of memory free. Remember that your program will get about 128K of the SPSS/PC+ memory.

Example

To run a program requiring 192K with the EXECUTE command, you must reserve an additional 64K in addition to the 128K provided by SPSS/PC+. Suppose that the SHOW command reports a maximum workspace of 183K. To reduce this by 64K, specify a workspace of 119K (or a bit less to be safe):

```
SPSSPC /S=115K
```

This will allow you to run SPSS/PC+ while leaving 192K for another program.

EXPORT

```
EXPORT OUTFILE='filename'

  [/KEEP={ALL**  }] [/DROP=varlist]
          {varlist}

  [/RENAME=(old varnames=new varnames)...]

  [/MAP]

  [/DIGITS=n]
```

**Default if the subcommand is omitted.

Example:

```
EXPORT OUTFILE='NEWDATA.POR'/RENAME=(V1 TO V3=ID, SEX, AGE) /MAP.
```

Overview

EXPORT produces a portable data file from the active file. A portable data file is an ASCII file that contains all of the data and dictionary information stored in the active file from which it was created. A portable file can be read with the IMPORT command in SPSS/PC+ or in SPSS on a variety of computers and operating systems. You can upload portable files to a mainframe using KERMIT, provided that KERMIT is installed on both the personal computer and the receiving mainframe computer.

EXPORT is similar to the SAVE command. It can occur in the same position in the command sequence as the SAVE command and saves the active file. The file includes the results of all permanent transformations and any temporary transformations made just prior to the EXPORT command. The active file is unchanged after the EXPORT command.

Options

Variables. You can save a subset of variables from the active file and rename the variables using the DROP, KEEP, and RENAME subcommands. You can also produce a record of all variables and their names on the exported file with the MAP subcommand.

Precision. You can specify the number of decimal digits of precision for the values of all numeric variables on the DIGITS subcommand.

Basic Specification

The basic specification is the OUTFILE subcommand with a file specification. All variables from the active file are written to the portable file, with variable names, variable and value labels, missing-value flags, and print and write formats. The portable file also contains the originating computer (IBM PC), the name and release number of SPSS/PC+, and the date and time the portable file was created.

Subcommand Order

Subcommands can be named in any order.

Operations

- Portable files are written with 80-character record lengths.
- Portable files may contain some unprintable characters.
- The active file is still available for transformations and procedures after the portable file is created.
- The system variables $CASENUM$ and $DATE$ are assigned when the file is read by IMPORT.
- If the WEIGHT command is used before EXPORT, the portable file includes the values of $WEIGHT$ (see WEIGHT).

Example

```
EXPORT OUTFILE='NEWDATA.POR'/RENAME=(V1 TO V3=ID,SEX,AGE) /MAP.
```

- The portable file is written to *NEWDATA.POR* in the current directory.
- Variables *V1, V2,* and *V3* are renamed *ID, SEX,* and *AGE* in the portable file. Their names remain *V1, V2,* and *V3* in the active file. None of the other variables written to the portable file are renamed.
- MAP requests a display of the variables in the portable file.

OUTFILE Subcommand

OUTFILE specifies the portable file. OUTFILE is the only required subcommand on EXPORT.

- The filename must be enclosed in apostrophes.
- You can direct the portable file to another drive, including the *A:* or *B:* drive.

DROP and KEEP Subcommands

DROP and KEEP save a subset of variables in the portable file.

- DROP excludes a variable or list of variables from the portable file. All variables not named are included in the portable file.
- KEEP includes a variable or list of variables in the portable file. All variables not named are excluded.
- Variables can be specified on DROP and KEEP in any order. With the DROP subcommand, the order of variables in the portable file is the same as their order in the active file. With the KEEP subcommand, the order of variables in the portable file is the order they are named on KEEP. Thus, KEEP can be used to reorder variables in the portable file.

- Both DROP and KEEP can be used on the same EXPORT command, provided they do not name any of the same variables.

Example

```
EXPORT OUTFILE='NEWSUM.POR'/DROP=DEPT TO DIVISION.
```

- The portable file is written to file *NEWSUM.POR*. Variables between and including *DEPT* and *DIVISION* in the active file are excluded from the portable file.
- All other variables are saved in the portable file.

RENAME Subcommand

RENAME renames variables being written to the portable file. The renamed variables retain their original variable and value labels, missing-value flags, and print formats. The names of the variables are not changed in the active file.

- To rename a variable, specify the name of the variable in the active file, an equals sign, and the new name.
- A variable list can be specified on both sides of the equals sign. The number of variables on both sides must be the same, and the entire specification must be enclosed in parentheses.
- Keyword TO can be used for both variable lists (see "Keyword TO" on p. 434).
- If you specify a renamed variable on a subsequent DROP or KEEP subcommand, the new variable name must be used.

Example

```
EXPORT OUTFILE='NEWSUM.POR'/DROP=DEPT TO DIVISION
   /RENAME=(NAME,WAGE=LNAME,SALARY).
```

- RENAME renames *NAME* and *WAGE* to *LNAME* and *SALARY*.
- *LNAME* and *SALARY* retain the variable and value labels, missing-value flags, and print formats assigned to *NAME* and *WAGE*.

MAP Subcommand

MAP displays any changes that have been specified by the RENAME, DROP, or KEEP subcommands.

- MAP can be specified as often as desired.
- Each MAP subcommand maps the results of subcommands that precede it; results of subcommands that follow it are not mapped.When MAP is specified last, it also produces a description of the portable file.

Example

```
EXPORT OUTFILE='NEWSUM.POR'/DROP=DEPT TO DIVISION /MAP
   /RENAME NAME=LNAME WAGE=SALARY /MAP.
```

- The first MAP subcommand produces a listing of the variables in the file after DROP has dropped the specified variables.
- RENAME renames *NAME* and *WAGE*.
- The second MAP subcommand shows the variables in the file after renaming. Since this is the last subcommand, the listing will show the variables as they are written in the portable file.

DIGITS Subcommand

DIGITS specifies the degree of precision for all noninteger numeric values written to the portable file.

- DIGITS has the general form DIGITS=n, where n is the number of digits of precision.
- DIGITS applies to all numbers for which rounding is required.
- Different degrees of precision *cannot* be specified for different variables. Thus, DIGITS should be set according to the requirements of the variable that needs the most precision.

Example

```
EXPORT OUTFILE='NEWSUM.POR' /DROP=DEPT TO DIVISION /MAP /DIGITS=4.
```

- DIGITS guarantees the accuracy of values to four significant digits. For example, 12.34567890876 will be rounded to 12.35.

FINISH

```
FINISH
```

Overview

FINISH terminates an SPSS/PC+ session and returns control to DOS.

Basic Specification

- The basic specification is simply the command keyword. There are no additional specifications.
- The commands BYE, EXIT, and STOP are accepted as aliases for FINISH.

Operations

- FINISH causes SPSS/PC+ to stop reading commands.
- Any commands following FINISH in a command file specified on the INCLUDE command are ignored.

Example

```
DATA LIST FILE='NEW.DAT'/
   NAME 1-15(A) V1 TO V15 16-30.
LIST.
FINISH.
```

- The DATA LIST and LIST commands are executed.
- The FINISH command terminates the SPSS/PC+ session.

FLIP

```
FLIP [[VARIABLES=] {ALL     }]
                  {varlist }

  [/NEWNAMES=variable]
```

Example:
```
FLIP VARIABLES=WEEK1 TO WEEK52 /NEWNAMES=DEPT.
```

Overview

SPSS/PC+ requires a file structure in which the variables are the columns and observations (cases) are the rows. If a file is organized such that variables are in rows and observations are in columns, you need to use FLIP to reorganize it. FLIP transposes the rows and columns of the data in the active file so that, for example, row 1, column 2 becomes row 2, column 1, and so forth.

Options

Variable Subsets. You can transpose specific variables (columns) from the original file using the VARIABLES subcommand.

Variable Names. You can use the values of one of the variables from the original file as the variable names in the new file using the NEWNAMES subcommand.

Basic Specification

The basic specification is the command keyword FLIP, which transposes all rows and columns.

- By default, FLIP assigns variable names *VAR001* to *VARn* to the variables in the new file. It also creates the new variable *CASE_LBL*, whose values are the variable names that existed before transposition.

Subcommand Order

VARIABLES must precede NEWNAMES.

Operations

- FLIP replaces the active file with the transposed file and displays a list of variable names in the transposed file.

- FLIP discards any previous VARIABLE LABELS, VALUE LABELS, and WEIGHT settings. Values defined as user-missing in the original file are translated to system-missing in the transposed file.
- FLIP obeys any SELECT IF, N, and SAMPLE commands in effect.
- String variables in the original file are assigned system-missing values after transposition.
- Numeric variables are assigned a default format of F8.2 after transposition (with the exceptions of *CASE_LBL* and the variable specified on NEWNAMES).
- The variable *CASE_LBL* is created and added to the active file each time FLIP is executed.
- If *CASE_LBL* already exists as the result of a previous FLIP, its current values are used as the names of variables in the new file (if NEWNAMES is not specified).

Limitations

- The maximum number of variables (columns) is the same as the system limit; the maximum number of cases is one less than the system variable limit.
- FLIP will not execute if there is insufficient memory. The amount of memory required in bytes can be roughly calculated as (number of cases $\times$ number of variables $\times 8$) + (number of cases $\times 8$) + (number of variables $\times 8$). An active file with 200 variables and 199 cases requires about 314K.

Example

The following is the LIST output for a data file arranged in a typical spreadsheet format, with variables in rows and observations in columns:

```
A           B         C         D
Income    22.00     31.00     43.00
Price     34.00     29.00     50.00
Year    1970.00   1971.00   1972.00
```

The command

```
FLIP.
```

transposes all variables in the file. The LIST output for the transposed file is as follows:

```
CASE_LBL   VAR001    VAR002    VAR003
A            .         .         .
B          22.00     34.00    1970.00
C          31.00     29.00    1971.00
D          43.00     50.00    1972.00
```

- The values for the new variable *CASE_LBL* are the variable names from the original file.
- Case A has system-missing values, since variable *A* had the string values Income, Price, and Year.
- The names of the variables in the new file are *CASE_LBL, VAR001, VAR002, and VAR003*.

VARIABLES Subcommand

VARIABLES names one or more variables (columns) to be transposed. The specified variables become observations (rows) in the new active file.

- The VARIABLES subcommand is optional. If it is not used, all variables are transposed.
- The actual keyword VARIABLES can be omitted.
- If the VARIABLES subcommand is specified, variables that are not named are discarded.

Example

Using the untransposed file from the previous example, the command

```
FLIP VARIABLES=A TO C.
LIST.
```

transposes only variables *A* through *C*. Variable *D* is not transposed and is discarded from the active file.The LIST output for the transposed file is as follows:

```
CASE_LBL    VAR001    VAR002    VAR003

A              .         .         .
B            22.00     34.00   1970.00
C            31.00     29.00   1971.00
```

NEWNAMES Subcommand

NEWNAMES specifies a variable whose values are used as the new variable names.

- The NEWNAMES subcommand is optional. If it is not used, the new variable names are either *VAR001* to *VARn*, or the values of *CASE_LBL* if it exists.
- Only one variable can be specified on NEWNAMES.
- The variable specified on NEWNAMES does not become an observation (case) in the new active file, regardless of whether it is specified on the VARIABLES subcommand.
- If the variable specified is numeric, its values become a character string beginning with the letter *V*.
- If the variable specified is a long string, only the first eight characters are used.
- Lowercase character values of a string variable are converted to uppercase, and any bad character values, such as blank spaces, are replaced with underscore (_) characters.
- If the variable's values are not unique, a numeric extension *n* is added to the end of a value after its first occurrence, with *n* increasing by 1 at each subsequent occurrence.

Example

Using the untransposed file from the first example, the command

```
FLIP NEWNAMES=A.
LIST.
```

uses the values for variable *A* as variable names in the new file. The LIST output for the transposed file is as follows:

```
CASE_LBL    INCOME      PRICE       YEAR

B               22.00       34.00    1970.00
C               31.00       29.00    1971.00
D               43.00       50.00    1972.00
```

- Variable *A* does not become an observation in the new file. The string values for *A* are converted to upper case.

The following command transposes this file back to a form resembling its original structure:

```
FLIP.
```

The LIST output for the transposed file is as follows:

```
CASE_LBL        B           C           D

INCOME      22.00       31.00       43.00
PRICE       34.00       29.00       50.00
YEAR      1970.00     1971.00     1972.00
```

- Since the NEWNAMES subcommand is not used, the values of *CASE_LBL* from the previous FLIP (*B, C,* and *D*) are used as variable names in the new file.
- The values of *CASE_LBL* are now INCOME, PRICE, and YEAR.

FORMATS

```
FORMATS varlist (format) [varlist ...]
```

Formats:

Format	Definition
Fw.d	Numeric variable with width *w* and *d* decimal places
COMMAw.d	Numeric variable with commas and decimal places
DOLLARw.d	Numeric variable with dollar sign, commas, and decimal places

Examples:

```
FORMATS VARA (F4.2) VARB (DOLLAR9) VARC (COMMA7).
FORMATS VARD VARE VARF (F3.2).
```

Overview

FORMATS command allows you to change the print and write formats of numeric variables. You can change the display width, specify additional decimal digits, and add commas and dollar signs. These formats determine how values are displayed in SPSS/PC+ procedures and how data values are written using the WRITE command. The values used in computations by SPSS/PC+ are not affected by the FORMATS specification.

Basic Specification

The basic specification is a variable or variable list followed by a format in parentheses. All variables in the list receive the new format.

Syntax Rules

- You can specify more than one variable or variable list, followed by a format in parentheses. Only one format can be specified after each variable list. For clarity, each set of specifications can be separated by a slash.
- The available formats are Fw.d, COMMAw.d, and DOLLARw.d, where *w* is the total number of columns, including decimal point, commas, and dollar sign, and *d* is the number of decimal places. For example, to display the number 6543210 as $6,543,210, you must specify a dollar format of at least DOLLAR10. The *d* specification is optional.
- FORMATS cannot be used with string variables.
- You cannot change the variable type from string to numeric or vice versa.

Operations

- Variables not specified on FORMATS retain their current print and write formats in the active file. To see the current formats, use the DISPLAY command.
- The new formats are changed only in the active file and are in effect for the duration of the SPSS/PC+ session or until changed again with a FORMATS command. Formats in the original system file (if one exists) are not changed unless the file is resaved with the SAVE command.
- The FORMATS command changes only the print and write formats, not the internal representation, of a variable.
- If you do not allow enough room to display the values of a variable, SPSS/PC+ displays the value without decimal values, commas, or dollar signs. When the value cannot be reasonably represented in the width provided, SPSS/PC+ rounds it, uses scientific notation, or displays asterisks (**) in the available space.
- When a COMMA or DOLLAR format is incorrectly assigned, SPSS/PC+ attempts to display the value without commas or a dollar sign. If you have not allowed enough columns for a numeric value, SPSS/PC+ displays asterisks. The values in the active file are unchanged.
- Some procedures are unable to display values with wide formats.

Example

```
DATA LIST / VARA 1-4 (3) VARB 6-10 VARC 12-17.
BEGIN DATA.
155   10500  429813
4309  25000  389213
6256  18750  35946
END DATA.
LIST.
FORMATS VARA (F4.2) VARB (DOLLAR9) VARC (COMMA7).
LIST VAR=ALL.
```

- The DATA LIST command indicates inline fixed-format data and defines three variables. *VARA* is four columns wide with three implied decimal places. *VARB* is five columns wide, and *VARC* is six columns wide.
- The first LIST command displays all variables using the dictionary formats defined by the DATA LIST command. The results of the first LIST command are shown below:

```
VARA  VARB   VARC

 .155 10500  429813
4.309 25000  389213
6.256 18750   35946
```

- The FORMATS command defines new print formats for each variable. *VARA* is displayed in four columns (including decimal point) with two decimal digits. *VARB* is displayed in nine columns including dollar signs and commas. *VARC* is displayed in seven columns including commas.

- The second LIST command displays each of the variables using the new formats. The results of this LIST procedure are shown below:

```
VARA      VARB      VARC

 .15    $10,500  429,813
4.31    $25,000  389,213
6.26    $18,750   35,946
```

Example

```
DATA LIST FREE / VARA VARB VARC.
BEGIN DATA.
155 10500 429813 4309 25000 389213 6256 18750 35946
END DATA.
LIST.
FORMATS VARA (F4.0) VARB (DOLLAR11.2) VARC (COMMA9.1).
LIST VAR=ALL.
```

- The DATA LIST command identifies inline data in freefield format. By default, variables *VARA*, *VARB*, and *VARC* have print and write formats of eight columns with two decimal places (F8.2).

- The first LIST command shows the default formats of the three variables:

```
VARA       VARB       VARC

 155.00  10500.00  429813.0
4309.00  25000.00  389213.0
6256.00  18750.00   35946.00
```

- The FORMATS command specifies a print and write format of four columns with no decimal digits for *VARA*; eleven columns with a dollar sign, commas, and two decimal digits for *VARB*; and nine columns with commas and one decimal place for *VARC*.

- The LIST command uses the new formats. The results are shown below:

```
VARA       VARB       VARC

 155    $10,500.00  429,813.0
4309    $25,000.00  389,213.0
6256    $18,750.00   35,946.0
```

FREQUENCIES

```
FREQUENCIES [VARIABLES=]{varlist}
                        {ALL    }

[/FORMAT=[{CONDENSE}] [{NOTABLE }] [NOLABELS]
          {ONEPAGE }   {LIMIT(n)}

          [{AVALUE}] [DOUBLE] [NEWPAGE]]
           {DVALUE}
           {AFREQ }
           {DFREQ }

[/MISSING=INCLUDE]

[/BARCHART=[MINIMUM(n)] [MAXIMUM(n)] [{FREQ(n)   }]]
                                      {PERCENT(n)}

[/HISTOGRAM=[MINIMUM(n)] [MAXIMUM(n)] [{FREQ(n)   }]
                                       {PERCENT(n)}

          [{NONORMAL}] [INCREMENT(n)]]
           {NORMAL  }

[/HBAR=same as HISTOGRAM]

[/GROUPED=varlist [{(width)        }]]
                   {(boundary list)}

[/NTILES=n]

[/PERCENTILES=value list]

[/STATISTICS=[DEFAULT] [MEAN] [STDDEV] [MINIMUM] [MAXIMUM]
             [SEMEAN] [VARIANCE] [SKEWNESS] [SESKEW] [RANGE]
             [MODE] [KURTOSIS] [SEKURT] [MEDIAN] [SUM] [ALL]
             [NONE]]
```

Example:

```
FREQUENCIES VAR=RACE /STATISTICS=ALL.
```

Overview

FREQUENCIES produces tables of frequency counts and percentages of the values of individual variables. FREQUENCIES is used to obtain frequencies and statistics for categorical variables and to obtain statistics and graphical displays for continuous variables.

Options

Display Format. With the FORMAT subcommand you can condense, expand, or suppress tables and can start each table on a new page. You can also suppress value labels and can alter the order of values within tables.

Statistical Display. Percentiles and ntiles are available for numeric variables with the PERCENTILES and NTILES subcommands. The following statistics are available with the STATISTICS subcommand: mean, median, mode, standard deviation, range, minimum value, maximum value, variance, skewness, kurtosis, and sum.

Plots. Histograms can be specified for numeric variables on the HISTOGRAM subcommand. Bar charts can be specified for numeric or string variables on the BARCHART subcommand.

Input Data. On the GROUPED subcommand you can indicate whether the input data are grouped (or collapsed) so that a better estimate can be made of percentiles.

Basic Specification

The basic specification is the VARIABLES subcommand and the name of at least one variable. By default, FREQUENCIES produces a frequency table.

Subcommand Order

Subcommands can be named in any order.

Syntax Rules

- You can specify multiple NTILES and PERCENTILES subcommands. Multiple requests for the same percentiles are consolidated.
- VARIABLES, FORMAT, MISSING, and STATISTICS can be specified only once.
- BARCHART, HISTOGRAM, and HBAR are mutually exclusive. HBAR is used whenever any two of these subcommands are specified on the same FREQUENCIES command.
- FREQUENCIES operates in integer or general mode, depending on the VARIABLES specification.

Operations

- Variables are tabulated in the order they are mentioned on the VARIABLES subcommand. If a variable is mentioned more than once, it is tabulated more than once.
- If a requested ntile or percentile cannot be calculated, a period (.) is displayed.
- The display always uses narrow format regardless of the width defined on SET.

Limitations

- The maximum number of variables per FREQUENCIES command is the same as the system limit.
- The maximum number of unique observed values over all variables depends on available workspace and on available labels space (up to 5000 characters for all labels combined).

Example

```
FREQUENCIES VAR=RACE /STATISTICS=ALL.
```

- FREQUENCIES requests a frequency table and all statistics for the categorical variable *RACE*.

VARIABLES Subcommand

VARIABLES names the variables to be tabulated and is the only required subcommand.

- You can use keyword ALL to refer to all user-defined variables in the active file.

FORMAT Subcommand

FORMAT controls various features of the output, including frequency table format, order of categories, and suppression of tables.

- The minimum specification is a single keyword.

Table Formats

By default, FREQUENCIES displays as many single-spaced frequency tables with complete labeling information as fit within the page length.

CONDENSE	*Condensed format.* Counts are displayed in three columns without value labels and with valid and cumulative percentages rounded to integers. CONDENSE overrides ONEPAGE.
ONEPAGE	*Conditional condensed format.* Condensed format is used for tables that would otherwise require more than one page.
NEWPAGE	*Start each table on a new page.*
NOLABELS	*Suppress value labels.*
DOUBLE	*Double space frequency tables.*

Table Order

AVALUE	*Sort categories in ascending order of values (numeric variables) or in alphabetical order (string variables).* This is the default.
DVALUE	*Sort categories in descending order of values (numeric variables) or in reverse alphabetical order (string variables).* This is ignored when HISTOGRAM, HBAR, NTILES, or PERCENTILES is requested.
AFREQ	*Sort categories in ascending order of frequency.* This is ignored when HISTOGRAM, HBAR, NTILES, or PERCENTILES is requested.
DFREQ	*Sort categories in descending order of frequency.* This is ignored when HISTOGRAM, HBAR, NTILES, or PERCENTILES is requested.

Table Suppression

LIMIT(n)   *Suppress frequency tables with more than* n *categories.* The number of missing and valid cases and requested statistics are displayed for suppressed tables.

NOTABLE   *Suppress all frequency tables.* The number of missing and valid cases are displayed for suppressed tables. NOTABLE overrides LIMIT.

Example

```
FREQUENCIES VARIABLES=ALL /FORMAT=ONEPAGE.
```

• FREQUENCIES uses conditional condensed format.

BARCHART Subcommand

BARCHART produces a bar chart for each variable named on the VARIABLES subcommand. By default, the horizontal axis for each bar chart is scaled in frequencies, and the interval width is determined by the largest frequency count for the variable being plotted. Bar charts are labeled with value labels or with the value if no label is defined.

• The minimum specification is the keyword BARCHART, which generates default bar charts.

• BARCHART cannot be used with HISTOGRAM or HBAR. HBAR is used whenever any two of these subcommands appear on the same FREQUENCIES command.

MIN(n)   *Lower bound below which values are not plotted.*

MAX(n)   *Upper bound above which values are not plotted.*

PERCENT(n)   *Horizontal axis scaled in percentages, where optional* n *is the maximum.* If *n* is not specified or if it is too small, FREQUENCIES chooses 5, 10, 25, 50, or 100, depending on the frequency count for the largest category.

FREQ(n)   *Horizontal axis scaled in frequencies, where optional* n *is the maximum.* If *n* is not specified or if it is too small, FREQUENCIES chooses 5, 10, 20, 50, 100, 200, 500, 1000, 2000, and so forth, depending on the largest category. This is the default.

Example

```
FREQUENCIES VAR=RACE /BARCHART.
```

• FREQUENCIES produces a frequency table and the default bar chart for variable *RACE*.

Example

```
FREQUENCIES VAR=V1 V2 /BAR=MAX(10).
```

• FREQUENCIES produces a frequency table and bar chart with values through 10 for each of variables *V1* and *V2*.

HISTOGRAM Subcommand

HISTOGRAM displays a plot for each numeric variable named on the VARIABLES subcommand. By default, the horizontal axis of each histogram is scaled in frequencies and the interval width is determined by the largest frequency count of the variable being plotted.

- The minimum specification is the keyword HISTOGRAM, which generates default histograms.
- The HISTOGRAM subcommand on the SET command controls the character used to draw histograms.
- HISTOGRAM cannot be used with BARCHART or HBAR. HBAR is used whenever any two of these subcommands appear on the same FREQUENCIES command.

MIN(n)   *Lower bound below which values are not plotted.*

MAX(n)   *Upper bound above which values are not plotted.*

PERCENT(n)   *Horizontal axis scaled in percentages, where optional* n *is the maximum. If* n *is not specified or if it is too small, FREQUENCIES chooses 5, 10, 25, 50, or 100, depending on the largest category.*

FREQ(n)   *Horizontal axis scaled in frequencies, where optional* n *is the scale. If* n *is not specified or if it is too small, FREQUENCIES chooses 5, 10, 20, 50, 100, 200, 500, 1000, 2000, and so forth, depending on the largest category. This is the default.*

INCREMENT(n)   *Interval width, where* n *is the size of the interval.* This specification overrides the default number of intervals on the vertical axis, which depends on the system page length. For a variable that ranges from 1 to 100, INCREMENT(2) produces 50 intervals with 2 values each.

NORMAL   *Superimpose a normal curve.* The curve is based on all valid values for the variable, including values excluded by MIN and MAX.

NONORMAL   *Suppress the normal curve.* This is the default.

Example

```
FREQUENCIES VAR=V1 /HIST=NORMAL INCREMENT(4).
```

- FREQUENCIES requests a histogram with a superimposed normal curve and an interval width of 4.

HBAR Subcommand

HBAR produces a plot for each numeric and string variable named on the VARIABLES subcommand. For numeric variables, HBAR produces a bar chart if the number of categories fits within the page length (see SET). Otherwise, HBAR produces a histogram. For short string variables and for the short-string portion of long string variables, HBAR produces bar charts regardless of the number of values.

By default, the horizontal axis of each plot is scaled in frequencies and the interval is determined by the largest frequency count. All keyword specifications for HISTOGRAM and BARCHART work with HBAR.

GROUPED Subcommand

When the values of a variable represent grouped or collapsed data, it is possible to estimate percentiles for the original, ungrouped data from the grouped data. The GROUPED subcommand specifies which variables have been grouped. It affects only the output from the PERCENTILES and NTILES subcommands and the MEDIAN statistic from the STATISTICS subcommand.

- Multiple GROUPED subcommands can be used on a single FREQUENCIES command. Multiple variable lists, separated by slashes, can appear on a single GROUPED subcommand.

- The variables named on GROUPED must have been named on the VARIABLES subcommand.

- The value or value list in the parentheses is optional. When it is omitted, SPSS/PC+ treats the values of the variables listed on GROUPED as midpoints. If the values are not midpoints, they must first be recoded with the RECODE command.

- A single value in parentheses specifies the width of each grouped interval. The data values must be group midpoints, but there can be empty categories. For example, if you have data values of 10, 20, and 30 and specify an interval width of 5, the categories are 10 ± 2.5, 20 ± 2.5, and 30 ± 2.5. The categories 15 ± 2.5 and 25 ± 2.5 are empty.

- A value list in the parentheses specifies interval boundaries. The data values do not have to represent midpoints, but the lowest boundary must be lower than any value in the data. If any data values exceed the highest boundary specified (the last value within the parentheses), they will be assigned to an open-ended interval. In this case, some percentiles cannot be calculated.

Example

```
RECODE AGE  (1=15)  (2=25)  (3=35)  (4=45)  (5=55)
            (6=65)  (7=75)  (8=85)  (9=95)
    /INCOME (1=5)   (2=15)  (3=25)  (4=35)  (5=45)
            (6=55)  (7=65)  (8=75)  (9=100).

FREQUENCIES VARIABLES=AGE, SEX, RACE, INCOME
    /GROUPED=AGE, INCOME
    /PERCENTILES=5,25,50,75,95.
```

- The *AGE* and *INCOME* categories of 1, 2, 3, and so forth are recoded to category midpoints. Note that data can be recoded to category midpoints on any scale; here *AGE* is recoded in years, but *INCOME* is recoded in thousands of dollars.

- The GROUPED subcommand on FREQUENCIES allows more accurate estimates of the requested percentiles.

Example

```
FREQUENCIES VARIABLES=TEMP
  /GROUPED=TEMP (0.5)
  /NTILES=10.
```

- The values of *TEMP* (temperature) in this example were recorded using an inexpensive thermometer whose readings are precise only to the nearest half degree.
- The observed values of 97.5, 98, 98.5, 99, and so on, are treated as group midpoints, smoothing out the discrete distribution. This yields more accurate estimates of the deciles.

Example

```
FREQUENCIES VARIABLES=AGE
  /GROUPED=AGE (17.5, 22.5, 27.5, 32.5, 37.5, 42.5, 47.5
                52.5, 57.5, 62.5, 67.5, 72.5, 77.5, 82.5)
  /PERCENTILES=5, 10, 25, 50, 75, 90, 95.
```

- The values of *AGE* in this example have been estimated to the nearest five years. The first category is 17.5 to 22.5, the second is 22.5 to 27.5, and so forth. The artificial clustering of age estimates at multiples of five years is smoothed out by treating *AGE* as grouped data.
- It is not necessary to recode the ages to category midpoints, since the interval boundaries are explicitly given.

PERCENTILES Subcommand

PERCENTILES displays the value below which the specified percentage of cases falls. The desired percentiles must be explicitly requested. There are no defaults.

Example

```
FREQUENCIES VAR=V1 /PERCENTILES=10 25 33.3 66.7 75.
```

- FREQUENCIES requests the values for percentiles 10, 25, 33.3, 66.7, and 75 for *V1*.

NTILES Subcommand

NTILES calculates the percentages that divide the distribution into the specified number of categories and displays the values below which the requested percentages of cases fall. There are no default ntiles.

- Multiple NTILES subcommands are allowed. Each NTILES subcommand generates separate percentiles. Any duplicate percentiles generated by different NTILES subcommands are consolidated in the output.

Example

```
FREQUENCIES VARIABLE=V1 /NTILES=4.
```

- FREQUENCIES requests quartiles (percentiles 25, 50, and 75) for *V1*.

Example

```
FREQUENCIES VARIABLE=V1 /NTILES=4 /NTILES=10.
```

- The first NTILES subcommand requests percentiles 25, 50, and 75.
- The second NTILES subcommand requests percentiles 10 through 90 in increments of 10.
- The 50th percentile is produced by both specifications but is displayed only once in the output.

STATISTICS Subcommand

STATISTICS controls the display of statistics. By default, cases with missing values are excluded from the calculation of statistics.

- The minimum specification is the keyword STATISTICS, which generates the mean, standard deviation, minimum, and maximum (these statistics are also produced by keyword DEFAULT).
- If you specify STATISTICS without keywords, only the statistics requested are displayed.

MEAN	*Mean.*
SEMEAN	*Standard error of the mean.*
MEDIAN	*Median.* Ignored when AFREQ or DFREQ are specified on the FORMAT subcommand.
MODE	*Mode.* If there is more than one mode, only the first (lowest) mode is displayed.
STDDEV	*Standard deviation.*
VARIANCE	*Variance.*
SKEWNESS	*Skewness.*
SESKEW	*Standard error of the skewness statistic.*
KURTOSIS	*Kurtosis.*
SEKURT	*Standard error of the kurtosis statistic.*
RANGE	*Range.*
MINIMUM	*Minimum.*
MAXIMUM	*Maximum.*
SUM	*Sum.*
DEFAULT	*Mean, standard deviation, minimum, and maximum.*
ALL	*All available statistics.*
NONE	*No statistics.*

Example

```
FREQUENCIES VAR=AGE /STATS=MODE.
```

- STATISTICS requests the mode of *AGE*.

Example

```
FREQUENCIES VAR=AGE /STATS=DEF MODE.
```

- STATISTICS requests the default statistics (mean, standard deviation, minimum, and maximum) plus the mode of *AGE*.

MISSING Subcommand

By default, both user- and system-missing values are labeled as missing in the table but are not included in the valid and cumulative percentages, in the calculation of descriptive statistics, or in bar charts and histograms.

INCLUDE   *Include cases with user-missing values.* Cases with user-missing values are included in statistics and plots.

GET

```
GET [FILE={'SPSS.SYS'**}]
            {'filename'  }

  [/KEEP={ALL**   }] [/DROP=varlist]
         {varlist}

  [/RENAME=(old varnames=new varnames)...]
```

**Default if the subcommand is omitted.

Example:

```
GET FILE='EMPL'.
```

Overview

GET reads an SPSS/PC+ system file that was created by the SAVE command. A system file is in a format only SPSS/PC+ can read and contains data plus a dictionary. The dictionary contains a name for each variable in the system file, plus any assigned variable and value labels, missing-value flags, and variable print and write formats.

GET is used only for reading SPSS/PC+ system files. See DATA LIST for information on reading and defining data in an ASCII data file. See IMPORT for information on reading *portable files* created with EXPORT in SPSS or SPSS/PC+. See TRANSLATE for information on reading files created by other software programs.

Options

Variable Subsets and Order. You can read a subset of variables and reorder the variables that are copied into the active file using the DROP and KEEP subcommands.

Variable Names. You can rename variables as they are copied into the active file with the RE-NAME subcommand.

Basic Specification

- The basic specification is simply the command keyword.
- By default, GET copies all variables from the system file *SPSS.SYS* in the current directory. Variables in the active file are in the same order and have the same names as variables in the system file.

Subcommand Order

- FILE must be specified first.
- The remaining subcommands can be specified in any order.

Syntax Rules

- FILE can be specified only once.
- KEEP, DROP, and RENAME can be used as many times as needed.

Operations

- GET reads the dictionary of the system file.
- Data from the system file are copied into a separate active file on disk only if you use the DROP or KEEP subcommand or if you enter data transformation or selection commands. Otherwise, SPSS/PC+ will read data from the system file repeatedly when executing procedures.
- If KEEP is not specified, variables in the active file are in the same order as variables in the system file.
- A file saved with weighting in effect maintains the values of variable *$WEIGHT*. For a discussion of turning off weights, see WEIGHT.
- The order of cases in the active file is the same as their order in the system file. The values of *$CASENUM* are those from the original text data file before any selecting (see SELECT IF) or sorting (see SORT). The value of *$CASENUM* may differ from the actual number of a case after selecting or sorting.
- The variable counts displayed by GET treat each 8-character portion of a long string variable as one variable. For example, a 17-character long string counts as three variables.

FILE Subcommand

FILE specifies the system file to be read. FILE can be specified only once. It must be the first specification on GET.

- The only specification on FILE is the name of the file, which must be enclosed in apostrophes.
- You can specify files residing in other drives and directories by supplying a fully qualified filename.

Example

```
GET FILE='\KL\SALDATA.NOV'.
```

- The system file *SALDATA.NOV* is retrieved from directory *KL*.

DROP and KEEP Subcommands

DROP and KEEP are used to copy a subset of variables into the active file. DROP specifies variables that should not be copied into the active file. KEEP specifies variables that should be copied. Variables not specified on KEEP are dropped.

- Variables can be specified in any order. The order of variables on KEEP determines the order of variables in the active file. The order on DROP does not affect the order of variables in the active file.

- Keyword ALL on KEEP refers to all remaining variables not previously specified on KEEP. ALL must be the last specification on KEEP.

- If a variable is specified twice on the same subcommand, only the first mention is recognized.

- Multiple DROP and KEEP subcommands are allowed.

- Keyword TO can be used to specify a group of consecutive variables in the system file.

Example

```
GET FILE='D:HUBTEMP.SYS' /DROP=DEPT79 TO DEPT84 SALARY79.
```

- The active file is copied from system file *HUBTEMP.SYS*, which is in the current directory on the *D:* drive. All variables between and including *DEPT79* and *DEPT84*, as well as *SALARY79*, are excluded from the active file. All other variables are copied into the active file.

- Variables in the active file are in the same order as the variables in the *HUBTEMP* file.

Example

```
GET FILE='PRSNL.SYS' /DROP=GRADE STORE
                /KEEP=LNAME NAME TENURE JTENURE ALL.
```

- Variables *GRADE* and *STORE* are dropped when file *PRSNL.SYS* is copied into the active file.

- KEEP specifies that *LNAME*, *NAME*, *TENURE*, and *JTENURE* are the first four variables in the active file, followed by all remaining variables (except those dropped by the previous DROP). These remaining variables are copied into the active file in the same sequence in which they appear in the *PRSNL.SYS* file.

RENAME Subcommand

RENAME changes the names of variables as they are copied into the active file.

- The specification on RENAME is a list of old variable names followed by an equals sign and a list of new variable names. The same number of variables must be specified on both lists. Keyword TO can be used in the first list to refer to consecutive variables in the system file and in the second list to generate new variable names (see "Keyword TO" on p. 434). The entire specification must be enclosed in parentheses.

- Alternatively, you can specify each old variable name individually, followed by an equals sign and the new variable name. Multiple sets of variable specifications are allowed. The parentheses around each set of specifications are optional.

- Old variable names do not need to be specified according to their order in the system file.

- Name changes take place in one operation. Therefore, variable names can be exchanged between two variables.

- Multiple RENAME subcommands are allowed.

- On a subsequent DROP or KEEP subcommand, variables are referred to by their new names.

Example

```
GET FILE='EMPL88' /RENAME AGE=AGE88 JOBCAT=JOBCAT88.
```

- RENAME specifies two name changes for the active file. *AGE* is renamed to *AGE88* and *JOBCAT* is renamed to *JOBCAT88*.

Example

```
GET FILE='EMPL88' /RENAME (AGE JOBCAT=AGE88 JOBCAT88).
```

- The name changes are identical to those in the previous example. *AGE* is renamed to *AGE88* and *JOBCAT* is renamed to *JOBCAT88*. The parentheses are required with this method.

GSET

```
GSET [PACKAGE={SPSS}]   [optional specifications]
                {HG2 }
                {HG3 }
```

Optional specifications for SPSS/PC+ Graphics and Harvard Graphics with Trends:

```
[/HIGHRES={OFF        }]
          {'rootname'*}

[/LOWRES={AUTO}]
         {ON  }
         {OFF }

[/GINVOKE={YES}]
          {NO }
```

Optional specifications for SPSS/PC+ Graphics with GRAPH and Trends:

```
[/CYCLE={COLORS  }]
        {PATTERNS}
        {BOTH    }
```

* The root for filenames can be up to 5 characters long.

Examples:

```
GSET PACKAGE=SPSS
  /HIGHRES='grph'
  /CYCLE=BOTH.

GSET PACKAGE=HG2
  /HIGHRES='c:\spssfigs\gfile'
  /LOWRES=OFF.
```

Overview

GSET specifies a graphics package for producing the high-resolution charts generated by the SPSS/PC+ GRAPH command. GSET also allows you to specify SPSS/PC+ Graphics from TriMetrix or Harvard Graphics as the graphics package for use with SPSS/PC+ Trends. You can check the current GSET settings by running the GSHOW command.

Options

Graphics Package. In addition to the default SPSS/PC+ Graphics, you can specify Harvard Graphics version 3.0 or 2.3 on the PACKAGE subcommand.

Options for the GRAPH Command and SPSS/PC+ Trends. If the graphics package is SPSS/PC+ Graphics, you can specify whether elements in high-resolution graphics are differentiated by color, pattern, or both using the CYCLE subcommand.

Options for SPSS/PC+ Trends Only. You can control whether high-resolution or low-resolution graphics are generated by Trends using the HIGHRES and LOWRES subcommands. You can also control whether the graphics package is invoked automatically when Trends generates a high-resolution chart using the GINVOKE subcommand.

Basic Specification

- The basic specification is the PACKAGE subcommand and the keyword for one of the supported graphics programs.
- The default package is SPSS/PC+ Graphics. You do not need to specify PACKAGE=SPSS to use the optional specifications for SPSS/PC+ Graphics unless another package was specified on a previous GSET.

Subcommand Order

If specified, the PACKAGE subcommand must be the first specification on GSET.

Syntax Rules

- Only one graphics package can be specified.
- Slashes between subcommands are optional but recommended.
- The optional subcommands HIGHRES, LOWRES, and GINVOKE control graphics from SPSS/PC+ Trends procedures and do not affect the GRAPH command.
- The optional CYCLE subcommand is available only if PACKAGE is set to SPSS. CYCLE affects graphics produced by both Trends and the GRAPH command.

Operations

- GSET can be used more than once in an SPSS/PC+ session.
- The settings established with GSET are in effect until you enter another GSET command.
- Use GSHOW to display the current graphics package and other settings controlled by GSET.

PACKAGE Subcommand

PACKAGE specifies the graphics package and must be the first specification on GSET. Available options are:

SPSS   *SPSS/PC+ Graphics from TriMetrix.*

HG3   *Harvard Graphics version 3.0.*

HG2   *Harvard Graphics version 2.3.* HARVARD is an alias for HG2.

Example

```
GSET PACKAGE=HG3 .
```

• This example designates Harvard Graphics 3.0 as the default graphics package.

HIGHRES Subcommand

HIGHRES turns on high-resolution graphics output in SPSS/PC+ Trends and provides a *root-name* for the files used to send graphics instructions to SPSS/PC+ Graphics or Harvard Graphics. You can specify the keyword OFF instead of a rootname.

• If you specify a rootname on HIGHRES, high-resolution graphics are turned on. To suppress high-resolution graphics, specify HIGHRES=OFF. OFF is the default.

• The rootname is specified in apostrophes or quotation marks. It can have up to 5 letters and cannot include a file extension. If the package is Harvard Graphics, it can include a drive and path specification. It cannot include a drive and path if the package is SPSS/PC+ Graphics.

• The numbering of graphics instruction files restarts at 1 each time GSET HIGHRES is specified. Any existing files with the same names are overwritten.

• If the package is SPSS/PC+ Graphics, each graph produced by Trends generates two files: one in the subdirectory *HISTORY* and one in subdirectory *DATA*. The extensions for these files are *.HST* and *.DSF*, respectively (see "Example for SPSS/PC+ Graphics" on p. 565). You can specify other directories for SPSS/PC+ Graphics by selecting Setup/Paths within SPSS/PC+ Graphics.

• The default extension in Harvard Graphics is *.CHT*. In addition, a Harvard Graphics Show file with extension *.SHW* is written when there is more than one plot.

• This subcommand does not affect the GRAPH command. Use the OUTFILE subcommand on GRAPH to specify a filename for GRAPH output.

LOWRES Subcommand

LOWRES controls the display of low-resolution (character) graphics in SPSS/PC+ Trends and is independent of HIGHRES. The specification for LOWRES is ON, OFF, or AUTO.

AUTO   *Display low-resolution graphics whenever high-resolution graphics cannot be displayed.* AUTO is the default.

ON   *Display low-resolution graphics, even when high-resolution graphics are also generated.*

OFF   *Do not display low-resolution graphics.* Low-resolution graphics are used only where important statistics appear on the low-resolution graph, as in the ACF command.

GINVOKE Subcommand

GINVOKE determines whether SPSS/PC+ invokes SPSS/PC+ Graphics or Harvard Graphics immediately when SPSS/PC+ Trends generates high-resolution plots. The specification is YES or NO.

YES   *Invoke SPSS/PC+ Graphics or Harvard Graphics immediately when SPSS/PC+ Trends generates high-resolutions plots.* The SPSS/PC+ session resumes when you leave the graphics package. The names for the data files are generated from the rootname on the HIGHRES subcommand. The history files are named _SPSSn.HST, where *n* is the number from the associated data file. This is the default.

NO   *Do not invoke SPSS/PC+ Graphics or Harvard Graphics immediately.* You can later load the graphics instruction files into the graphics package and produce the charts. The names for both the history and the data files are generated from the root-name.

Example for SPSS/PC+ Graphics

```
GSET PACKAGE=SPSS
 /HIGHRES='FIG'
 /GINVOKE=NO.
```

- The HIGHRES subcommand causes SPSS/PC+ to generate high-resolution graphics instructions for SPSS/PC+ Graphics for the output from Trends procedures.

- If the Trends command generates three plots, the instructions for the first plot are written to *FIG1.HST* and *FIG1.DSF*; for the second plot to *FIG2.HST*, and *FIG2.DSF*; and for the third plot to *FIG3.HST* and *FIG3.DSF*. Existing files with these names are overwritten. If you then run another SPSS/PC+ Trends command that generates high-resolution graphics, the first history file is *FIG4.HST*, and the other files named accordingly.

- The GINVOKE=NO subcommand causes SPSS/PC+ not to invoke SPSS/PC+ Graphics automatically when a high-resolution plot is generated by Trends. To view the first set of plots later, start SPSS/PC+ Graphics with the filenames on the command line. You can also start SPSS/PC+ Graphics, select Data/History/Editor/Load/filename, and Execute the file.

Example for Harvard

```
GSET PACKAGE=HG3
 /HIGHRES='FIG'
 /GINVOKE=NO.
```

- The HIGHRES subcommand causes SPSS/PC+ to generate high-resolution graphics instructions for Harvard Graphics for the output from Trends procedures.

- Instructions for the first plot are written to *FIG1.CHT;* for the second plot to *FIG2.CHT;* and so on. A Harvard Graphics Show file *FIG1.SHW* is also written if there is more than one plot. Existing files with these names are overwritten. These files are written to the current directory.

- The GINVOKE=NO subcommand causes SPSS/PC+ not to invoke Harvard Graphics automatically when a high-resolution plot is generated by Trends. To view the plots later, start Harvard Graphics and view the slide show.

CYCLE Subcommand (SPSS/PC+ Graphics only)

CYCLE determines whether the elements in graphs produced in SPSS/PC+ Graphics will be differentiated by color, by pattern, or by both. It affects line charts, bar charts, pie charts, and scatterplots produced by GRAPH, as well as TSPLOT and CASEPLOT output in Trends. For example, bars in a bar chart can have different colors, different patterns, or a unique pattern as well as color.

COLORS   *Cycle through colors.* This is the default. Colors are easy to distinguish if you are viewing charts on the screen. Colors will be printed in various shades of gray on a monochrome printer.

PATTERNS   *Cycle through patterns.* The elements will be all one color, distinguished by fill patterns. Patterns are a good choice to distinguish elements if the charts are to be printed on a monochrome printer.

BOTH   *Cycle through patterns and colors simultaneously.* For pie charts, only patterns are used even if BOTH is specified.

Example

```
GSET CYCLE=BOTH.
GRAPH BAR=ORIGIN BY RATING.
```

- Each bar in the bar chart will have a different pattern and color from those surrounding it.

GSHOW

GSHOW

Overview

GSHOW displays the current settings of the GSET command, including the defaults.

Example

GSHOW.

- The GSHOW command lists a table similar to the one below of the current specifications on the GSET command.
- In this example, the settings are the default settings.

```
PACKAGE   SPSS
GINVOKE   ON
HIGHRES   OFF
LOWRES    AUTO
CYCLE     COLORS
```

IF

```
IF (logical expression) target variable=expression
```

The following relational operators can be used in logical expressions:

Symbol	Definition	Symbol	Definition
EQ or =	Equal to	NE or <> or ~=	Not equal to
LT or <	Less than	LE or <=	Less than or equal to
GT or >	Greater than	GE or >=	Greater than or equal to

The following logical operators can be used in logical expressions:

Symbol	Definition
AND or &	Both relations must be true
Or or |	Either relation can be true
Not or ~	Reverses the outcome of an expression

The following missing-value functions can be used in logical expressions:

Function	Definition
SYSMIS	True if value is system-missing
MISSING	True if value is system- or user-missing
VALUE	True if value meets stated criteria, ignoring user-missing value flags

Example:

```
IF (AGE > 20 AND SEX = 1) GROUP=2.
```

Overview

IF conditionally executes a single transformation command based upon logical conditions found in the data. The transformation can create a new variable or modify the values of an existing variable for each case in the active file. You can create or modify the values of both numeric and string variables.

IF has three components: a *logical expression* (see "Logical Expressions" on p. 441) that sets up the logical criteria, a *target variable* (the one to be modified or created), and an *assignment expression*. The target variable's values are modified according to the assignment expression.

IF is most efficient when used to execute a single, conditional, COMPUTE-like transformation. If you need multiple IF statements to define the condition, it is usually more efficient to use the RECODE command.

Basic Specification

The basic specification is a logical expression followed by a target variable, a required equals sign, and the assignment expression. The assignment is executed only if the logical expression is true.

Syntax Rules

- Logical expressions can be simple logical variables or relations, or complex logical tests involving variables, constants, functions, relational operators, and logical operators. Both the logical expression and the assignment expression can use any of the operators and functions allowed in COMPUTE transformations (see COMPUTE and "Functions" on p. 438). Relational and logical operators cannot be used in assignment expressions.
- The logical expression can contain short string variables, numeric variables, or both. To use a long string variable, you must convert it to numeric with the AUTORECODE command.
- Parentheses must be used to enclose the logical expression. Parentheses can also be used within the logical expression to specify the order of operations. Extra blanks or parentheses can be used to make the expression easier to read.
- A relation can compare variables, constants, or more complicated arithmetic expressions. Relations cannot be abbreviated. For example, (A EQ 2 OR A EQ 5) is valid, while (A EQ 2 OR 5) is not. Blanks (not commas) must be used to separate relational operators from the expressions being compared.
- At least one relation, SYSMIS function, or MISSING function must be included in the logical expression.
- A relation cannot compare a string variable to a numeric value or variable, or vice versa.
- To specify the condition that the value of a variable is system-missing, use IF (SYSMIS (var)). To specify the condition that the value of a variable is either system- or user-missing, use IF (MISSING·var)). You cannot specify IF (X=SYSMIS) or IF (X=MISSING).
- String values used in expressions must be specified in quotes and must include any leading or trailing blanks. Lowercase letters are considered distinct from uppercase letters.

Operations

- Each IF command is evaluated independently.
- The logical expression is evaluated as true, false, or missing. The assignment is executed only if the logical expression is true.
- If the logical expression is false or if one of the variables is system- or user-missing, the assignment is not made. Existing target variables remain unchanged; new numeric variables are assigned the system-missing value and new string variables are set to blanks. New string variables are assigned a width equal to the number of characters used in the initial assignment.
- Logical expressions are evaluated in the following order: numeric functions, followed by exponentiation, arithmetic operations, relations, and logical operators. When more than

one logical operator is used, NOT is evaluated first, followed by AND and then OR. You can change the order of operations using parentheses.

- Assignment expressions are evaluated in the following order: numeric functions, then exponentiation, and then arithmetic operators.

- In general, a logical expression is evaluated as missing if any one of the variables used in the logical expression is system- or user-missing. However, when relations are joined by the logical operators AND or OR, the expression can sometimes be evaluated as true or false even when variables have missing values (see "Missing Values and Logical Operators" below).

- Logical expressions are evaluated in the following order: string functions, then relations, then logical operators. When more than one logical operator is used, NOT is evaluated first, followed by AND and then OR. You can change the order of operations using parentheses.

- If the transformed value of a string variable exceeds the variable's defined width, the transformed value is truncated. If the transformed value is shorter than the defined width, the string is right-padded with blanks.

Missing Values and Logical Operators

When two or more relations are joined by logical operators AND or OR, SPSS always returns a missing value if all of the relations in the expression are missing. However, if any one of the relations can be determined, SPSS interprets the expression as true or false according to the logical outcomes shown in Table 8. The asterisk flags expressions where SPSS/PC+ can evaluate the outcome with incomplete information.

Table 8   Logical outcome

Expression	Outcome	Expression	Outcome
true AND true	= true	true OR true	= true
true AND false	= false	true OR false	= true
false AND false	= false	false OR false	= false
true AND missing	= missing	true OR missing	= true*
missing AND missing	= missing	missing OR missing	= missing
false AND missing	= false*	false OR missing	= missing

Example

```
IF (AGE > 20 AND SEX = 1) GROUP=2.
```

- Numeric variable *GROUP* is set to 2 for cases where *AGE* is greater than 20 *and SEX* is equal to 1.

- When the expression is false or missing, the value of *GROUP* remains unchanged. If *GROUP* has not been previously defined, it contains the system-missing value.

Example

```
IF (SEX EQ 'F') EEO=QUOTA+GAIN.
```

- The logical expression tests string variable *SEX* for the value F.
- When the expression is true (when *SEX* equals F), the value of numeric variable *EEO* is assigned the value of *QUOTA* plus *GAIN*. Both *QUOTA* and *GAIN* must be previously defined numeric variables.
- When the expression is false or missing (for example, if *SEX* equals f), the value of *EEO* remains unchanged. If *EEO* has not been previously defined, it contains the system-missing value.

Example

```
COMPUTE V3=0.
IF ((V1-V2) LE 7) V3=V1**2.
```

- COMPUTE assigns *V3* the value 0.
- The logical expression tests whether *V1* minus *V2* is less than or equal to 7. If it is, the value of *V3* is assigned the value of *V1* squared. Otherwise, the value of *V3* remains at 0.

Example

```
IF (ABS(A-C) LT 100) INT=100.
```

- IF tests whether the absolute value of variable *A* minus variable *C* is less than 100. If it is, *INT* is assigned the value 100. Otherwise, the value is unchanged. If *INT* has not been previously defined, it is system-missing.

Example

```
IF (SYSMIS(QVAR)) RVAR=0.
COMPUTE VALID=0.
IF (NOT(SYSMIS(VARA))) VALID=1.
```

- The first IF command tests whether *QVAR* is system-missing. If it is, *RVAR* is assigned the value 0. Otherwise *RVAR* is unchanged, or system-missing if *RVAR* has not been previously defined.
- COMPUTE assigns variable *VALID* a value of 0.
- The next IF command tests whether *VARA* is not system-missing. For each case where *VARA* contains a valid value (is not system-missing), the value of *VALID* is set to 1. For each case that contains a system-missing value for *VARA*, the value of *VALID* remains 0.

Example

```
IF (STATE EQ 'IL' AND CITY EQ 13) COST=1.07 * COST.
```

- The logical expression tests whether *STATE* equals IL and *CITY* equals 13.
- If the logical expression is true, numeric variable *COST* is increased by 7%.
- For any other value of *STATE* or *CITY*, the value of *COST* remains unchanged.

Example

```
IF (QVAR EQ 'ok') AVAR='fine'.
```

- The new string variable *AVAR* is set to fine when the value of *QVAR* is ok.
- *AVAR* has a width of four characters.
- When *QVAR* does not equal ok, *AVAR* is defined as a four-column blank field.

Example

```
IF (RECV GT DUE OR (REVNUES GE EXPNS AND BALNCE GT 0))
    STATUS='SOLVENT'
```

- First, SPSS/PC+ tests whether *REVNUES* is greater than or equal to *EXPNS* and whether *BALNCE* is greater than 0.
- Second, SPSS/PC+ evaluates if *RECV* is greater than *DUE*.
- If either of these expressions is true, *STATUS* is assigned the value SOLVENT.
- If both expressions are false, *STATUS* remains unchanged. If *STATUS* is not an existing string variable, it is defined as a seven-column blank field.

IMPORT

```
IMPORT FILE=file

 [/KEEP={ALL**  }] [/DROP=varlist]
         {varlist}

 [/RENAME=(old varnames=new varnames)...]

 [/MAP]
```

**Default if the subcommand is omitted.

Example:

```
IMPORT FILE='NEWDATA.POR' /RENAME=(V1 TO V3=ID, SEX, AGE) /MAP.
```

Overview

IMPORT reads portable data files created with the EXPORT command in SPSS or SPSS/PC+. A portable data file is an ASCII file that contains all of the data and dictionary information stored in the active file from which it was created. Portable files are used to transport data between SPSS/PC+ and SPSS on a variety of computers and operating systems. You can download portable files from a mainframe using KERMIT, provided that KERMIT is installed on both the personal computer and the receiving mainframe computer. For additional information on using portable files written by SPSS, see "SPSS Portable Files" on p. 576.

SPSS/PC+ can also read data files created by other software programs. See TRANSLATE for information on reading files created by spreadsheet and database programs such as dBASE, Lotus, and Multiplan.

Options

Variables. You can read a subset of variables from the active file with the DROP and KEEP subcommands. You can rename variables using RENAME. You can also produce a record of all variables and their names in the active file with the MAP subcommand.

Basic Specification

- The basic specification is the FILE subcommand with a file specification.
- By default, all variables from the portable file are copied into the active file with their original names, variable and value labels, missing-value flags, and print and write formats. The file also contains a message with the name, release, and version of the originating software, and the date and time the portable file was created. When the file originates from SPSS, it also includes the file label and the name of the originating installation.

Subcommand Order

- Subcommands can be specified in any order.

Operations

- The portable data file and dictionary become the active file and dictionary.
- SPSS/PC+ has a more restrictive dictionary than does SPSS. The SPSS/PC+ IMPORT command changes the dictionary to conform to SPSS/PC+ conventions (see "SPSS Portable Files" on p. 576).
- A file saved with weighting in effect (using the WEIGHT command) automatically uses the case weights when the file is read.

Limitations

- You may not have enough memory available on your PC to read data from a portable file produced by SPSS. When you produce portable files in SPSS for use in SPSS/PC+, you should include only the variables you need for a particular SPSS/PC+ session.
- The number of variables you can import is the same as the system limit.

Example

```
IMPORT FILE='NEWDATA.POR' /RENAME=(V1 TO V3=ID,SEX,AGE) /MAP.
```

- The active file is generated from the portable file *NEWDATA.POR*.
- Variables *V1*, *V2*, and *V3* are renamed *ID*, *SEX*, and *AGE* in the active file. Their names remain *V1*, *V2*, and *V3* in the portable file. None of the other variables copied into the active file are renamed.
- MAP requests a display of the variables in the active file.

FILE Subcommand

FILE specifies the portable file. FILE is the only required subcommand on IMPORT.
- The filename must be enclosed in apostrophes.
- You can specify a path on the IMPORT command.
- You can use a portable file stored on a floppy diskette.

DROP and KEEP Subcommands

DROP and KEEP are used to read a subset of variables from the portable file.
- DROP excludes a variable or list of variables from the active file. All variables not named are included in the file.
- KEEP includes a variable or list of variables in the active file. All variables not specified on KEEP are excluded.

- Variables can be specified in any order. The order of variables on KEEP determines the order of variables in the active file. The order on DROP does not affect the order of variables in the active file.
- If a variable is referred to twice on the same subcommand, only the first mention is recognized.
- Multiple DROP and KEEP subcommands are allowed, provided they do not name any of the same variables.
- Keyword TO can be used to specify a group of consecutive variables in the portable file.
- The portable file is not affected by DROP or KEEP.

Example

```
IMPORT FILE='NEWSUM.EXP' /DROP=DEPT TO DIVISION.
```

- The active file is generated from the portable file *NEWSUM.POR*. Variables between and including *DEPT* and *DIVISION* in the portable file are excluded from the active file.
- All other variables are copied into the active file.

RENAME Subcommand

RENAME renames variables being read from the portable file. The renamed variables retain the variable and value labels, missing-value flags, and print formats contained in the portable file.

- To rename a variable, specify the name of the variable in the portable file, a required equals sign, and the new name.
- A variable list can be specified on both sides of the equals sign. The number of variables on both sides must be the same, and the entire specification must be enclosed in parentheses.
- Keyword TO can be used for both variable lists (see "Keyword TO" on p. 434).
- Any DROP or KEEP subcommand after RENAME must use the new variable names.

Example

```
IMPORT FILE='NEWSUM.POR' /DROP=DEPT TO DIVISION
  /RENAME=(NAME,WAGE=LNAME,SALARY).
```

- RENAME renames *NAME* and *WAGE* to *LNAME* and *SALARY*.
- *LNAME* and *SALARY* retain the variable and value labels, missing-value flags, and print formats assigned to *NAME* and *WAGE*.

MAP Subcommand

MAP displays a list of variables in the active file, showing all changes that have been specified on the RENAME, DROP, or KEEP subcommands.

- MAP can be specified as often as desired.

- MAP confirms only the changes specified on the subcommands that precede the MAP request.

- When MAP is specified last, it also produces a description of the file.

Example

```
IMPORT FILE=NEWSUM /DROP=DEPT TO DIVISION /MAP
  /RENAME NAME=LNAME WAGE=SALARY /MAP.
```

- The first MAP subcommand produces a listing of the variables in the file after DROP has dropped the specified variables.

- RENAME renames *NAME* and *WAGE*.

- The second MAP subcommand shows the variables in the file after renaming.

SPSS Portable Files

EXPORT writes portable files that can be read by a number of mainframe and personal computers running SPSS as well as by personal computers running SPSS/PC+. SPSS/PC+ uses a more restrictive dictionary than SPSS. If you are creating a portable file in SPSS that will be read by SPSS/PC+, keep the following in mind:

- After reading 500 variables, SPSS/PC+ stops processing variables. You can avoid this problem by dropping variables when you create the portable file or by dropping variables as you read them into SPSS/PC+ with the IMPORT command.

- SPSS/PC+ allows one user-defined missing value per variable and accepts only the first value if multiple missing values have been defined in SPSS. You can override missing value declarations prior to creating the portable file with SPSS.

- SPSS/PC+ provides the following print and write formats: DOLLARw.d, COMMAw.d, Aw, or Fw.d. SPSS has many more formats, which SPSS/PC+ attempts to translate. You can change the translated format of variables with the FORMAT command.

INCLUDE

```
{INCLUDE 'filename'}
{@filename        }
```

Examples:
```
INCLUDE '\MASTER\SET.CMD'.
INCLUDE 'DEFINE.INC'.
@CODEBOOK.RUN.
```

Overview

INCLUDE allows you to execute SPSS/PC+ commands from a file. With INCLUDE, you can prepare an entire session with your editor and leave SPSS/PC+ to execute unattended, as in batch-type processing. You can also use INCLUDE to execute file definition commands (such as DATA LIST and labeling commands) and then execute analysis commands interactively.

Another use for INCLUDE is to execute a "profile" tailored to your computer. For example, you can create a file containing a SET command that specifies printer characters, a prompt, and page size, and then include that file in any SPSS/PC+ session. If you name a profile like this *SPSSPROF.INI* and save it in either your current directory (the one from which you work) or the directory in which the SPSS/PC+ system is saved, it will be executed automatically when you enter SPSS/PC+.

You can nest INCLUDE commands so that one set of included commands includes another set of commands. This "nesting" can go five levels deep.

Basic Specification

- The only specification for INCLUDE is a filename enclosed in apostrophes.
- The character @ is accepted as an alias for the INCLUDE command. When the @ character is used, the apostrophes around the filename are optional. The space between @ and the filename is also optional.

Syntax Rules

- You can include a file from another directory by using a fully qualified filename.
- You can use more than one INCLUDE command in a session, either in a series or nested.
- If you include a file of inline data, the first line of the data file must contain the BEGIN DATA command. The END DATA command can be specified as the last line of the included file or with your SPSS/PC+ commands.

Operations

- By default, each command from the included file is displayed on your screen as it is processed. You can suppress this display by specifying INCLUDE OFF on SET.

- Both the INCLUDE command and commands from the included file are copied to the log file. The INCLUDE command can be run from the log file; the commands from the included file are prefaced with an open bracket ([). These commands are treated as comments and are not executed. Thus, if you use the log file in a subsequent session, the INCLUDE command is read from the log file and the included commands are read from the original file. The included commands are executed only once.

- If an include file contains a FINISH command, the SPSS/PC+ session ends and you are returned to DOS. No subsequent SPSS/PC+ commands are processed.

Limitations

- SPSS/PC+ will process only up to five levels of nested included files at a time.

- The record length of command files cannot exceed 80 characters. To read data files with a record length exceeding 80 characters, use the FILE subcommand on DATA LIST.

Example

```
INCLUDE '\MASTER\SET.CMD'.
INCLUDE 'DEFINE.INC'.
@CODEBOOK.RUN.
```

- The first INCLUDE command processes the commands in file *SET.CMD* in directory *\MASTER*. The *SET.CMD* file contains the following commands:

```
SET LISTING=ON
 /LENGTH=59
 /BOXST='-|+'
 /BEEP OFF.
```

- The second INCLUDE command processes commands in file *DEFINE.INC* in the current directory. *DEFINE.INC* contains the following:

```
DATA LIST FILE='CURRENT.DAT' /
   MONTH 1-2 (A) DAY 3-4 TEMP 6-7 PRESSURE 8-12 (2) WINSPED 13-14.
MISSING VALUE DAY (99) / WINSPED (-1).
INCLUDE 'TRANSFOR.INC'.
```

- *DEFINE.INC* includes another INCLUDE command, which processes commands in file *TRANSFOR.INC* from the current directory. *TRANSFOR.INC* contains some data transformation commands. This is an example of a nested INCLUDE.

- The next command (@) is the abbreviated form of INCLUDE. Since the quotation marks and the space separating the command from the filename are optional with this form, they are omitted here. Commands are read from file *CODEBOOK.RUN* in the current directory. *CODEBOOK.RUN* contains the following commands:

```
FREQ VAR=ALL
 /HBAR.
DESC VAR=ALL.
```

JOIN

```
[JOIN]  {MATCH}
        {ADD  }

 /{FILE }={file specification}
  {TABLE} {*                 }

[/KEEP=varlist]

[/DROP=varlist]

[/RENAME (old varnames=new varnames) [(old varnames=...)]]

 /FILE=...
    ...

[/FILE=...  ]
    ...

[/BY=varlist]

[/MAP]
```

Example:

```
JOIN MATCH FILE='PART1.SYS'
  /RENAME (CASEID=ID)
  /FILE=*
  /BY ID.
```

Overview

JOIN allows you to combine two or more SPSS/PC+ system files. JOIN with keyword ADD is used to combine files containing the same variables but different cases. JOIN with keyword MATCH is generally used to combine files containing the same cases but different variables. With MATCH you can make parallel or nonparallel matches between different files or perform table lookups. **Parallel matches** combine files sequentially by case (they are sometimes referred to as **sequential matches**). **Nonparallel matches** combine files according to the values of one or more key variables. In a **table lookup**, JOIN MATCH looks up variables in one file and transfers those variables to a case file. A table lookup can be used with aggregation (see example on p. 809).

The files specified on JOIN can be SPSS/PC+ system files created by the SAVE command or the active file. The combined file created by JOIN replaces the existing active file. Statistical procedures following JOIN use this combined file unless you replace it by building another active file. You must use the SAVE command if you want to save the combined file as a system file.

Options

Variable Selection. You can specify which variables from each input file are included in the new active file using the DROP and KEEP subcommands.

Variable Names. You can rename variables in each input file before combining the files using the RENAME subcommand. This permits you to combine variables that are the same but whose names differ in different input files, or to separate variables that are different but have the same name.

Variable Map. You can request a map showing all variables in the new active file, their order, and the input files from which they came using the MAP subcommand.

Basic Specification

The basic specification is keyword MATCH or ADD and two or more FILE subcommands specifying the names of files to be joined.

- By default, all variables from all input files are included in the new active file.
- With keyword MATCH, BY is also required to specify the key variables for nonparallel matches. Both BY and TABLE are required for table lookups. The TABLE subcommand can be used instead of one of the FILE subcommands.

Subcommand Order

- The first specification must be either MATCH or ADD.
- RENAME, KEEP, and DROP apply only to variables in the file named on the immediately preceding FILE or TABLE subcommand.
- BY must follow all other subcommands except MAP.
- MAP can be specified anywhere.

Syntax Rules

- The command name JOIN is optional. MATCH is accepted as an alias for JOIN MATCH, and ADD is accepted as an alias for JOIN ADD.
- MATCH and ADD are alternatives. You cannot specify both on the same JOIN command.
- RENAME, KEEP, and DROP can be repeated after each FILE or TABLE subcommand.
- TABLE can be specified only once.
- BY can be specified only once.
- MAP can be repeated as often as desired.

Operations

- JOIN reads all files named on the FILE or TABLE subcommands and builds a new active file that replaces any active file created earlier in the session.
- If the active file is named as an input file, any N and SAMPLE commands that have been specified are applied to that file before files are combined.
- The PROCESS IF command has no effect on JOIN.

- JOIN creates only uncompressed active files.

Limitations

- Maximum 5 files total can be specified on the FILE and TABLE subcommands. Only 1 file can be specified per FILE or TABLE subcommand.
- Maximum 10 variables can be specified on the BY subcommand. Each 8-character portion of a long string variable counts as 1 toward this limit.

Keyword MATCH

In general, use MATCH to combine two or more files containing the same cases but different variables.

- The new active file will contain all cases that are in any of the input files named on the FILE subcommands.
- When two or more files have a variable with the same name, values in the resulting file are taken from the file named first on the JOIN command, even if they are missing in that file. Dictionary information for that variable is taken from the first file for which the variable has either value labels, a variable label, or a declared missing value.
- Cases that are absent from one of the input files are assigned missing values for variables that exist only in that file.
- If you do not specify a BY subcommand, SPSS/PC+ performs a parallel (sequential) match, combining the first case from each file, then the second case from each file, and so on, without regard to any identifying values that may be present.
- BY specifies that cases should be joined according to a common value on one or more key variables (a nonparallel match). All input files must be sorted in ascending order of the key variables.
- When you use the BY subcommand with MATCH, one of the input files can be specified on a TABLE subcommand to indicate that it is a table lookup file (see the TABLE subcommand on p. 584).

Example

```
MATCH FILE='PART1.SYS'
  /FILE='PART2.SYS'
  /FILE=*.
```

- MATCH is used here as an alias for JOIN MATCH.
- This example combines three files (the active file and two system files) in a parallel match. Cases are combined according to their order in each file.
- The new active file will contain as many cases as are contained in the largest of the three input files.
- If the same variable name is used in more than one input file, data are taken from the file specified first.

BY Subcommand with MATCH

When used with MATCH, the BY subcommand specifies one or more identification, or key, variables that determine which cases are to be combined. BY is required unless all input files are to be matched sequentially according to the order of cases.

- BY must be specified after all other file specifications. Only the MAP subcommand, which requests optional output, can follow BY.
- BY specifies the names of one or more key variables. The key variables must be present in all input files. The maximum is 10 keys.
- All input files must be sorted in ascending order of the key variables. If necessary, use SORT CASES before JOIN.
- Missing values for key variables are handled like any other values.
- String variables are permitted on the BY subcommand. Each 8-character portion of a long string variable counts as 1 toward the limit of 10 key variables. For example, a 17-character string counts as 3.
- Unmatched cases are assigned system-missing values (for numeric variables) or blanks (for string variables) for variables from the files that do not contain a match.
- If two or more cases from any input file have identical values for the key variables, SPSS/PC+ issues a message. Only one message is generated, regardless of the number of duplicates encountered, since duplicate keys are expected in many applications.

Duplicate Cases

Duplicate cases are those with the same values for the key variables named on the BY subcommand.

- Duplicate cases are permitted in any input files except table files.
- When there is no table file, the first duplicate case in each file is matched with the first matching case (if any) from the other files; the second duplicate case is matched with a second matching duplicate, if any; and so on. (In effect, a parallel match is performed within groups of duplicate cases.) Unmatched cases are assigned system-missing values (for numeric variables) or blanks (for string variables) for variables from files that do not contain a match.
- When a table file is specified, data from the table file are added to all cases in the other files with matching values for the BY variables. The table file itself cannot contain duplicate cases.

Keyword ADD

In general, use ADD to combine two or more files containing different cases but the same variables.

- Unless you specify the BY subcommand, the resulting file contains all cases from the first-named input file first, followed by all cases from the second input file, and so on.
- The number of cases in the new active file is the sum of the number of cases in all input files. No cases are combined.

- Cases in the new active file contain all variables that appear in any input files. Cases from files without all the variables will have system-missing values (numeric variables) or blanks (string variables) for the extra variables.
- You cannot use the TABLE subcommand to specify an input file for ADD.

Example

```
JOIN ADD FILE='JAN.SYS'
  /FILE='FEB.SYS'
  /FILE='MAR.SYS'
  /FILE=*.
```

- This example combines cases from three system files and from the active file.
- Cases from *JAN.SYS* are first in the new active file, followed by cases from *FEB.SYS*, then from *MAR.SYS*, and then from the file that was active prior to the JOIN command.

BY Subcommand with ADD

The BY subcommand can be used with keyword ADD to interleave cases from the different files according to the values of that variable.

- BY must be specified after all other file specifications. Only the MAP subcommand, which requests optional output, can follow BY.
- BY specifies the names of one or more key variables. The key variables must be present in all input files. The maximum is 10 keys. Each 8-character portion of a long string variable counts as 1 toward this limit.
- All input files must be sorted in ascending order of the key variables. If necessary, use SORT CASES before JOIN.
- If two or more cases from any input file have identical values for the key variables, SPSS/PC+ issues a message. Only one such message is generated, regardless of the number of duplicates encountered, since duplicate keys are expected in many applications.
- Cases with identical values for the key variables are arranged in the order you name their input files.

Example

```
ADD FILE='SAMPLE1.SYS'
  /FILE=*
  /BY DATE.
```

- This example uses ADD as an alias for JOIN ADD.
- Cases from the system file *SAMPLE1.SYS* are interleaved with cases from the active file in ascending order of their values for *DATE*.
- If cases have the same value for *DATE*, those from *SAMPLE1.SYS* will precede those from the active file.

FILE Subcommand

FILE identifies each input file (except table files) for a MATCH or ADD operation. A separate FILE subcommand must be used for each input file.

- A maximum of five files total can be specified on the FILE and TABLE subcommands.
- Specifications on the FILE subcommand consist of either a filename in apostrophes or an asterisk to refer to the active file.
- With MATCH, the order in which files are named on FILE subcommands determines the order of variables in the new active file. In addition, the order in which files are named determines which input file is used as the source for variables that can be taken from more than one input file (they are taken from the file named first).
- With ADD, the order in which files are named determines the order of cases in the new file (unless the BY subcommand is used).

TABLE Subcommand

TABLE can be used with keyword MATCH to specify a **table lookup** (or **keyed table**) file. A table file contributes variables but not cases to the new active file. Variables from the table file are added to all cases from other files that have matching values for the key variables. FILE specifies the files that supply the cases.

- Only one table file can be specified on any JOIN command.
- The BY subcommand is required when you specify a table file.
- Cases whose values for the key variables are not included in the table file will have system-missing values for numeric variables taken from the table and blanks for strings.
- A table file cannot contain duplicate cases (cases for which the key variables have identical values).

Example

```
JOIN MATCH FILE=*
  /TABLE='MASTER.SYS'
  /BY EMP_ID.
```

- This command adds variables from the system file *MASTER.SYS* to the current file, matching cases by the variable *EMP_ID*.
- No new cases are added to the current file as a result of the table lookup.
- Cases whose value for *EMP_ID* is not included in *MASTER.SYS* are assigned system-missing values for variables taken from the table file.

RENAME Subcommand

RENAME renames variables in the input files *before* they are processed by JOIN.

- RENAME applies only to the immediately preceding FILE or TABLE subcommand. To rename variables from more than one input file, specify a RENAME subcommand after each FILE or TABLE subcommand.

- Specifications for RENAME consist of a left parenthesis, a list of old variable names, an equals sign, a list of new variable names, and a right parenthesis. The two variable lists must have the same number of variables, and the new names must be unique within that input file.
- More than one rename specification on a single RENAME subcommand, each enclosed in its parentheses.
- You can specify more than one RENAME subcommand for a single input file. However, the effect is *not* cumulative: old variable names are always those in the input files, regardless of any previous RENAME subcommands for that file.
- RENAME takes effect immediately. Any KEEP and DROP subcommands entered prior to RENAME must use the old names, while any KEEP and DROP subcommands entered after RENAME must use the new names.
- All specifications within a single set of parentheses take effect simultaneously. For example, the specification RENAME (A,B = B,A) is legal and swaps the names of the two variables.
- The TO keyword cannot be used on the RENAME subcommand.
- Input system files are not changed on disk; only the copy of the file being joined is affected.

Example

```
JOIN MATCH FILE='UPDATE.SYS'
  /RENAME=(NEWPHONE,NEWID = PHONE,ID)
  /FILE='MASTER.SYS'
  /BY ID.
```

- This example matches a master system file (*MASTER.SYS*) with an update system file (*UPDATE.SYS*).
- Two variables in *UPDATE.SYS* are renamed prior to the match. *NEWPHONE* is renamed *PHONE* to combine it with variable *PHONE* in the master file. *NEWID* is renamed *ID* so that it will have the same name as the identification variable in the master file and can be used on the BY subcommand.
- The BY subcommand ensures that only cases with the same value for *ID* are joined.

Example

```
JOIN ADD FILE='SAMPLE1.SYS'
  /RENAME (SCALE=SCALE1)
  /FILE='SAMPLE2.SYS'
  /RENAME (SCALE=SCALE2)
  /FILE=*
  /RENAME (SCALE=SCALE3)
  /BY DATE.
```

- In this example, RENAME is used to give *different* names to variables that would otherwise be combined. Cases from *SAMPLE1.SYS* will have missing values for *SCALE2* and *SCALE3;* cases from *SAMPLE2.SYS* will have missing values for *SCALE1* and *SCALE3;* and cases from *SAMPLE3.SYS* will have missing values for *SCALE1* and *SCALE2*.
- The input files must be sorted by *DATE*. The new active file will also be sorted by *DATE*.

DROP and KEEP Subcommands

DROP and KEEP are used to include only a subset of variables in the new active file. DROP specifies a set of variables to exclude, and KEEP specifies a set of variables to retain.

- Specifications consist of a list of variables on the input file separated by spaces or commas.
- DROP and KEEP apply only to the immediately preceding FILE or TABLE subcommand.
- The TO keyword cannot be used on DROP or KEEP.
- DROP and KEEP do not affect the order of variables on the new active file. Variables retain their original order.

Example

```
MATCH FILE='THIS.SYS'
  /RENAME (ONE_VAR,TWO_VAR = VAR1,VAR2)
  /KEEP=ID,VAR1,VAR2
  /FILE='THAT.SYS'
  /KEEP=ID,ONE,TWO
  /RENAME (ONE,TWO = VAR1,VAR2)
  /BY ID.
```

- This example uses MATCH as an alias for JOIN MATCH.
- The KEEP subcommand that applies to the first file (*THIS.SYS*) follows RENAME and therefore uses the new names.
- The KEEP subcommand that applies to the second file (*THAT.SYS*) precedes RENAME and therefore uses the old names.
- After the RENAME subcommands, each input file has variables named *VAR1* and *VAR2*. These variables are combined, taking data from *THIS.SYS* for all cases present in that file and from *THAT.SYS* for cases absent in *THIS.SYS*.

MAP Subcommand

MAP produces a list of the variables in the new active file and the file or files from which they came.

- More than one MAP subcommand can be specified. Each MAP shows the current status of the active file and reflects only the subcommands that precede the MAP subcommand.
- To obtain a map of the new active file in its final state, specify MAP last.

LIST

```
LIST [[VARIABLES=] {ALL**  }] [/FORMAT=[{WRAP** }] [{UNNUMBERED**}] [WEIGHT]]
                  {varlist}              {SINGLE}   {NUMBERED   }

[/CASES=[FROM {1**}] [TO {eof**}] [BY {1**}]]
              {n  }      {n   }       {n  }
```

**Default if the subcommand is omitted.

Example:

```
LIST VARIABLES=V1 V2 /CASES=FROM 10 TO 100 BY 2.
```

Overview

LIST displays case values for variables in the active file.

Options

Selecting and Ordering Variables. You can specify the variables to list and their order with the VARIABLES subcommand.

Format. You can limit each case listing to a single line, and you can display the case number and weight for each listed case with the FORMAT subcommand.

Selecting Cases. You can limit the listing to a particular sequence of cases using the CASES subcommand.

Basic Specification

- The basic specification is simply LIST, which displays the values for all user-defined variables in the active file.
- By default, cases wrap to multiple lines if all the values do not fit within the page width (the page width is determined by the SET WIDTH command). Case numbers are not displayed for the listed cases.

Subcommand Order

All subcommands are optional and can be named in any order.

Operations

- If VARIABLES is not specified, variables are listed in the order in which they appear in the active file.
- System variables are not displayed unless specifically requested.

- LIST uses the print formats contained in the dictionary of the active file. Alternative formats cannot be specified on LIST. See FORMATS for information on changing print formats.
- LIST output uses the width specified on SET.
- If a numeric value is longer than its defined width, the decimal portion is rounded. If it is still too long, SPSS/PC+ displays asterisks.
- If a long string variable cannot be listed within the output width, it is truncated.
- Values of the variables listed for a case are always separated by at least one blank.
- System-missing values are displayed as a period for numeric variables and a blank for string variables.
- If cases fit on one line, the column width for each variable is determined by the length of the variable name or the format, whichever is greater. If the variable names do not fit on one line, they are printed vertically.
- If cases do not fit on one line within the output width specified on SET, they are wrapped. LIST displays a table illustrating the location of the variables in the output and prints the name of the first variable in each line at the beginning of the line.
- Each execution of LIST begins at the top of a new page.

Example

```
LIST.
```

- LIST by itself requests a display of the values for all variables in the active file.

Example

```
LIST VARIABLES=V1 V2 /CASES=FROM 10 TO 100 BY 2.
```

- LIST produces a list of every second case for variables *V1* and *V2*, starting with case 10 and stopping at case 100.

VARIABLES Subcommand

VARIABLES specifies the variables to be listed. The actual keyword VARIABLES can be omitted.

- The variables must already exist.
- If VARIABLES is used, only the specified variables are listed.
- Variables are listed in the order in which they are named on VARIABLES.
- If a variable is named more than once, it is listed more than once.
- Keyword ALL (the default) can be used to request all user-defined variables. ALL can also be used with a variable list (see example below).

ALL   *List all user-defined variables.* Variables are listed in the order in which they appear in the active file. This is the default if VARIABLES is omitted.

Example

```
LIST VARIABLES=V15 V31 ALL.
```

- VARIABLES is used to list values for *V15* and *V31* before all other variables. Keyword ALL then lists all variables, including *V15* and *V31*, in the order they appear in the active file. Values for *V15* and *V31* are therefore listed twice.

FORMAT Subcommand

FORMAT controls whether cases wrap if they cannot fit on a single line and whether the case number and weight is displayed for each listed case. The default display uses more than one line per case (if necessary) and does not number cases.

- The minimum specification is a single keyword.
- WRAP and SINGLE are alternatives, as are NUMBERED and UNNUMBERED. Only one of each pair can be specified.

WRAP   *Wrap cases if they do not fit on a single line.* Page width is determined by the SET WIDTH command. This is the default.

SINGLE   *Limit each case to one line.* If the variables requested do not fit on a single line, LIST is not executed.

UNNUMBERED   *Do not include the sequence number of each case.* This is the default.

NUMBERED   *Include the sequence number of each case.* The sequence number is displayed to the left of the listed values.

WEIGHT   *Include the value of the case's weight in the active file.*

CASES Subcommand

CASES limits the number of cases listed. By default, all cases in the active file are listed.

- Any or all of the keywords below can be used. Defaults that are not changed remain in effect.
- If LIST is preceded by a SAMPLE or SELECT IF command, case selections specified by CASES are taken from those cases that were selected by SAMPLE or SELECT IF.

FROM n   *Number of the first case to be listed.* The default is 1.

TO n   *Number of the last case to be listed.* The default is the end of the active file. CASES 100 is interpreted as CASES TO 100.

BY n   *Increment used to choose cases for listing.* The default is 1.

Example

```
LIST CASES BY 3 /FORMAT=NUMBERED.
```

- Every third case is listed for all variables in the active file. The listing begins with the first case and includes every third case up to the end of the file.

- FORMAT displays the case number of each listed case.

Example

```
LIST CASES FROM 10 TO 20.
```

- Cases from case 10 through case 20 are listed for all variables in the active file.

MEANS

```
MEANS [TABLES=] {varlist} BY varlist [BY varlist ...] [/varlist...]
                {ALL    }

[/OPTIONS=option numbers]

[/STATISTICS={statistic numbers}]
             {ALL              }
```

Options:

1   Include user-missing values
2   Exclude cases with user-missing dependent values
3   Suppress all labels

5   Suppress group counts
6   Display group sums
7   Suppress group standard deviations

8   Suppress value labels
9   Suppress independent variable names
10 Suppress independent variable values
11 Suppress group means
12 Display group variances

Statistics:

1   One-way analysis of variance
2   Test of linearity

Example:

```
MEANS TABLES=VAR1 TO VAR5 BY GROUP
  /OPTIONS=9
  /STATISTICS=1.
```

Overview

MEANS displays means, standard deviations, and group counts for a dependent variable within groups defined by one or more independent variables. Other SPSS/PC+ procedures that display univariate statistics are FREQUENCIES and DESCRIPTIVES.

Options

Format. You can suppress the display of all variable and value labels (Option 3), value labels only (Option 8), names of independent variables (Option 9), and values of independent variables (Option 10).

Cell Contents. You can display group sums (Option 6) and variances (Option 12) or suppress group counts (Option 5), group standard deviations (Option 7), and group means (Option 11).

Statistics. In addition to the statistics displayed for each cell of the table, you can obtain a one-way analysis of variance and a test of linearity with Statistics 1 and 2.

Basic Specification

- The basic specification is a TABLES subcommand with a table list. The actual keyword TABLES can be omitted.
- The minimum table list specifies a dependent variable, the keyword BY, and an independent variable.
- By default, MEANS displays means, standard deviations, and number of cases. The default table is labeled with the variable name and label of the dependent and independent variables. Groups are labeled with the variable name, variable label, values, and value labels of the independent variables.

Operations

- MEANS displays requested univariate statistics for the population as a whole and for each value of the first independent variable defined for the table in addition to statistics for groups.
- If an independent variable is a long string, only the short-string portion is used to identify groups in the analysis.
- If a string variable is specified as a dependent variable on any table list, the MEANS procedure stops executing.
- Statistics are displayed with four decimal places where possible.
- The output uses the width defined on the SET command. If the statistics requested cannot fit within the available width, the command is not executed. You can use the OPTIONS subcommand to tailor the output to fit within the defined width.

Limitations

- The number of variables allowed per MEANS command is the same as the system limit.
- Maximum 250 tables can be produced.
- Maximum 30 TABLES subcommands.
- Maximum 6 dimensions (5 BY keywords) per table.
- Maximum 200 value labels are displayed on any single table.
- Maximum 1 each OPTIONS and STATISTICS subcommands.

Example

```
MEANS TABLES=VAR1 TO VAR5 BY GROUP
   /OPTIONS=9
   /STATISTICS=1.
```

- The TABLES subcommand specifies *VAR1* through *VAR5* as the dependent variables. *GROUP* is the independent variable.

- Assuming variables *VAR2*, *VAR3*, and *VAR4* lie between *VAR1* and *VAR5* in the active file, five tables are produced: *VAR1* by *GROUP*, *VAR2* by *GROUP*, *VAR3* by *GROUP*, and so on.
- Option 9 suppresses the display of variable name *GROUP*.
- Statistic 1 requests one-way analysis of variance tables of *VAR1* through *VAR5* by *GROUP*.

Example

```
MEANS VARA BY VARB BY VARC / VAR1 VAR2 BY VAR3 VAR4 BY VAR5.
```

- This command contains two TABLES subcommands that omit the optional TABLES keyword.
- The first table list requests one table. Statistics are produced for *VARA* within groups defined by each combination of values of *VARB* and *VARC*.
- The second table list requests four tables: *VAR1* by *VAR3* by *VAR5*; *VAR1* by *VAR4* by *VAR5*; *VAR2* by *VAR3* by *VAR5*; and *VAR2* by *VAR4* by *VAR5*.

TABLES Subcommand

TABLES specifies the table list. The actual keyword TABLES can be omitted.

- You can specify multiple TABLES subcommands on a single MEANS command. The slash between the subcommands is required; the keyword is not.
- The dependent variable is named first and must be numeric. The independent variables follow the BY keyword and can be numeric or string.
- You can specify more than one dependent variable in a table list.
- Each use of the keyword BY in a table list adds a dimension to the tables requested.
- You can specify more than one independent variable in each dimension of a table list. Each combination of values of the independent variables defined for a table defines a group.
- A table is built for each dependent variable by each combination of independent variables across dimensions.
- The order in which independent variables are displayed is the same as the order in which they are named. The values of the first independent variable defined for the table appear in the leftmost column of the table and change most slowly in the definition of groups.
- You can use keyword ALL in each dimension to refer to all user-defined variables.

Format

By default, MEANS displays the variable names and variable labels of both independent and dependent variables at the beginning of each table. Within the table, groups defined by the independent variables are identified by variable name, values, and value labels. Specify the following on the OPTIONS subcommand to change these defaults:

Option 3   *Suppress all labels.* No variable or value labels are displayed for either the independent or dependent variables.

Option 8	*Suppress value labels.* No value labels are displayed for the independent variables.
Option 9	*Suppress independent variable names.*
Option 10	*Suppress independent variable values.*

Statistical Display

By default, MEANS displays means, standard deviations, and counts for each group and for the entire population. Specify the following on the OPTIONS and STATISTICS subcommands to change these defaults:

Option 5	*Suppress group counts.* The number of cases in each group is not displayed.
Option 6	*Display group sums.*
Option 7	*Suppress group standard deviations.*
Option 11	*Suppress group means.*
Option 12	*Display group variances.*
Statistic 1	*One-way analysis of variance including eta and eta^2.* The analysis of variance is performed for the first independent variable defined for the table only. For a one-way analysis of variance with multiple comparison tests, use procedure ONEWAY. To obtain two-way and higher analysis of variance, use procedure ANOVA.
Statistic 2	*Test of linearity.* Statistic 2 (alias ALL) produces a one-way analysis of variance in which the between-groups sum of squares is subdivided into linear and nonlinear components. Pearson's r and r^2 are displayed as part of the test of linearity. The analysis of variance is performed for the first independent variable defined for the table only, and the test of linearity is ignored if the independent variable is a string.
ALL	*Test of linearity.* Keyword ALL on the STATISTICS subcommand produces the same output as Statistic 2.

Example

```
MEANS TABLES=INCOME81 BY AGECAT BY SEX
  /STATISTICS=1.
```

- This example produces means and standard deviations for *INCOME81* for groups defined by values of *SEX* within *AGECAT*, as well as group counts.
- Statistic 1 requests an analysis of variance of *INCOME81* by *AGECAT*.

Missing Values

By default, MEANS excludes cases that have system- or user-missing values for any variables that define a table. You change the treatment of user-missing values by specifying the following on the OPTIONS subcommand:

Option 1   *Include cases with user-missing values.* Cases with user-missing values for the independent or dependent variable are included.

Option 2   *Exclude cases with user-missing dependent values only.* Cases with user-missing values for independent variables are included.

MISSING VALUE

```
MISSING VALUE  {varlist}([value]) [[/]varlist ...]
               {ALL    }
```

Example:
```
MISSING VALUE XVAR (8) / YVAR ZVAR (0) / AVAR ('     ').
```

Overview

MISSING VALUE declares values for numeric and short string variables as user-missing. These values can then be treated specially in data transformations, statistical calculations, and case selection. By default, user-missing values are treated the same as the system-missing values. System-missing values are assigned automatically when no legal value can be assigned, as when input data for a numeric field are blank or when an illegal calculation is requested.

Basic Specification

- The basic specification is a single variable followed by a value in parentheses. The specified value is treated as user-missing in any analysis.

Syntax Rules

- Each variable can have only one user-missing value.
- You can declare the same value as missing for more than one variable by specifying a variable list followed by the value in parentheses.
- The missing-value specification must correspond to the variable type (numeric or string).
- You can declare different values as missing for different variables by specifying separate variable lists for each value. The slash between different specifications is optional. Variable lists must have either all numeric or all string variables.
- You cannot assign missing values to long strings or system variables.
- Missing values for short string variables must be enclosed in apostrophes or quotation marks and must include any leading or trailing blanks (see "String Values in Command Specifications" on p. 429).
- A variable list followed by an empty set of parentheses ( ) deletes any missing-value declarations for those variables.
- Keyword ALL can be used to refer to all user-defined variables in the active file provided the variables are either all numeric or all string.
- Keyword TO can be used to refer to consecutive variables in the active file.
- More than one MISSING VALUE command can be specified per session.

Operations

- Missing-value specifications can be changed between procedures. New specifications replace previous ones. If a variable is mentioned more than once on one or more MISSING VALUE commands before a procedure, only the last specification is used.
- Missing-value specifications are saved in system files (see SAVE) and portable files (see EXPORT).

Example

```
MISSING VALUE XVAR (8) / YVAR ZVAR (0) / AVAR ().
```

- Value 8 is declared missing for numeric variable *XVAR*.
- Value 0 is missing for numeric variables *YVAR* and *ZVAR*.
- Any previously declared missing values for *AVAR* are deleted by the empty value specification.

Example

```
MIS VAL NAME1 TO NAME7 ('    ') / LIKE1 TO DLIKE7 (0).
```

- Blanks are declared missing for the variables between and including *NAME1* and *NAME7*. All of these variables must be string and must be four columns wide.
- The value 0 is declared missing for the variables between and including *LIKE1* and *DLIKE7*. All variables in this list must be numeric.

MODIFY VARS

```
MODIFY VARS [/REORDER=[{FORWARD**}] [{POSITIONAL**}] [{(varlist)}]]
                      {BACKWARD }   {ALPHA       }   {(ALL**) }

[/DROP=varlist] [/KEEP={varlist}]
                      {ALL**  }

[/RENAME (old varnames=new varnames) [(old varnames=...)]]

[/MAP]
```

**Default if the subcommand is omitted.

Example:
```
MODIFY VARS
  /RENAME (V1 TO V3 = ID GROUP AGE)
  /MAP.
```

Overview

MODIFY VARS lets you change the names or the order of the variables in the active file or drop variables from the active file. Reordering allows you to group related variables together so you can refer to them on other commands using the TO keyword. Reducing the number of variables in the active file speeds processing, saves the disk space used to hold the active file, and enables you to create additional variables without exceeding the system limit.

Basic Specification

- The basic specification is any one subcommand.

Subcommand Order

- Subcommands can be specified in any order.

Syntax Rules

- MAP is the only subcommand that can be specified more than once.
- Variable lists on all subcommands use the original variable names (before renaming) and the original variable order (before reordering).
- You cannot reorder, rename, or drop a system variable ($CASENUM$, $WEIGHT$, or $DATE$).
- You cannot specify both DROP and KEEP.

Operations

- MODIFY VARS reads the data if you specify DROP, KEEP, or REORDER. It does not read the data if you specify only RENAME.
- Reordered or renamed variables retain their original variable labels, value labels, and missing-value and format specifications.
- MODIFY VARS affects only the current active file. It does not affect any permanent disk file unless you use SAVE or some other command to write the file to disk.

Example

```
MODIFY VARS
  /RENAME (V1 TO V3 = ID GROUP AGE)
  /MAP.
```

- This example renames *V1* to *ID*, *V2* to *GROUP*, and *V3* to *AGE* and displays a map of the variable dictionary showing the changes.

REORDER Subcommand

REORDER changes the order of variables in the active file.

- You can specify the direction of ordering, the type of ordering, and the variables to be ordered.
- The direction of ordering is specified with keyword FORWARD or BACKWARD. The default is FORWARD.
- The type of ordering is specified with keyword POSITIONAL or ALPHA. The default is POSITIONAL.
- The variables to be reordered are specified in parentheses. Alternatively, you can specify ALL to reorder all variables.
- You can enter one, two, or all three types of specifications. If you specify more than one, you must specify the direction first, then type, and then the variables.
- After a variable list in parentheses, you can specify another direction and/or type of ordering and another variable list in parentheses, provided that the variable lists do not overlap. Variables named in the first set of parentheses precede those named in the second set of parentheses. Variables not named at all come at the end of the new active file.

FORWARD   *For type POSITIONAL, the current order of variables in the active file; for type ALPHA, alphabetical order.* This is the default.

BACKWARD   *For type POSITIONAL, the opposite of the current order of variables in the active file; for type ALPHA, reverse alphabetical order.*

POSITIONAL *The existing order of variables in the active file.* This is the default.

ALPHA   *Alphabetical order.* Variables are alphabetized according to their original names, even if RENAME precedes the REORDER subcommand. For variable names with numeric suffixes, such as *V1* to *V100*, ALPHA refers to the numeric order of the suffixes. For example, *V9* precedes *V10*.

(varlist)   *Reorder the specified variables.* The specified variables are placed at the beginning of the new active file according to the order indicated by the direction and type keywords (or the defaults). Variables not named are placed at the end of the new active file and retain their previous order.

ALL   *Reorder all variables.* This is the default.

Example

```
MODIFY VARS REORDER ALPHA (MAINE TO HAWAII).
```

- This example arranges all variables from *MAINE* to *HAWAII* into alphabetical order.

Example

```
MODIFY VARS REORDER (ID SSNUMBER) ALPHA (GROUP TO SALARY).
```

- *ID* and *SSNUMBER* are placed at the beginning of the new active file. Since the default direction and type are in effect, the variables appear according to their order in the original active file. In other words, whichever variable is first in the original file will be first in the new file.

- After *ID* and *SSNUMBER*, all variables from *GROUP* to *SALARY* are arranged in alphabetical order by variable name.

- Any other variables in the file are placed at the end of the new file, retaining their current order.

RENAME Subcommand

RENAME assigns new names to one or more variables in the active file.

- The specification on RENAME is a list of old variable names followed by an equals sign and a list of new variable names. The same number of variables must be specified on both lists. Keyword TO can be used in the first list to refer to consecutive variables in the active file and in the second list to generate new variable names (see "Keyword TO" on p. 434). The entire specification must be enclosed in parentheses.

- Alternatively, you can specify each old variable name individually, followed by an equals sign and the new variable name. Multiple sets of variable specifications are allowed.

- Name changes take place in one operation. Therefore, variable names can be exchanged between two variables.

- You can specify only one RENAME subcommand on a MODIFY VARS command.

Example

```
MODIFY VARS RENAME (PLAN,ALTERNAT = ALTERNAT,PLAN)
                   (TASKA TO TASKJ = OLDJOB1 TO OLDJOB10)
                   (ALT1 TO ALT10 = TASKA TASKB TASKC TASKD
                                    TASKE TASKF TASKG TASKH
                                    TASKI TASKJ)
    /MAP.
```

- The first specification switches the names of the two variables *PLAN* and *ALTERNAT*.
- Variables between and including TASKA to TASKJ in the original file are renamed *OLD-JOB1*, *OLDJOB2*, and so forth.
- Variables between and including *ALT1* to *ALT10* are renamed *TASKA*, *TASKB*, and so forth. Keyword TO cannot be used to generate the new variable names, since the new names do not have numeric suffixes.

DROP and KEEP Subcommands

DROP and KEEP allow you to reduce the number of variables in the active file. KEEP specifies variables to retain, and DROP specifies variables to drop.

- The specification on DROP or KEEP is the names of the variables you want to drop or retain.
- DROP and KEEP are alternatives. Use whichever is easier, but not both.
- Variables lists must use the original variable names, even if DROP or KEEP is specified after RENAME.
- You can use keyword TO to refer to consecutive variables in the active file.

MAP Subcommand

MAP displays a table showing the current names and order of variables in the active file along with their original names and order.

- More than one MAP subcommand can be specified. Each MAP shows the current status of the active file and reflects only the subcommands that precede the MAP subcommand.
- To obtain a map of the new active file in its final state, specify MAP last.

Example

```
MODIFY VARS DROP ERR_1 TO ERR_40
   /RENAME (VSCORE MSCORE = SCOREV SCOREM)
   /MAP.
MODIFY VARS
   /REORDER (ID DEPT) ALPHA (AREA TO SCOREV)
   /MAP.
```

- Variables between and including *ERR_1* and *ERR_40* are dropped from the active file.
- The two variables *VSCORE* and *MSCORE* are renamed *SCOREV* and *SCOREM*. MAP requests a table showing the results of the MODIFY VARS command.

- The second MODIFY VARS command places *ID* and *DEPT* at the beginning of the file, followed by the variables between and including *AREA* and *SCOREV* in alphabetical order, followed by any other variables in the file in their current order.
- MAP requests a table showing the names and order of variables in the new active file.
- Two MODIFY VARS commands were required to alphabetize the variables using their new names, since the REORDER subcommand uses the names as they existed prior to the MODIFY VARS command.

N

```
N n [ESTIMATED]
```

Example:
```
N 100.
```

Overview

N limits the number of cases in the active file to the first *n* cases. You can also use N with keyword ESTIMATED to provide information about the estimated number of cases in your data file. This allows SPSS/PC+ to optimize the allocation of memory for some procedures but does *not* limit the number of cases processed to the estimated number.

Basic Specification

The basic specification is N followed by at least one space and a positive integer. Cases in the active file are limited to the specified number.

Syntax Rules

- N can be entered at any point in an SPSS/PC+ session and can be used more than once.
- The keyword ESTIMATED can be specified after the integer estimate of the number of cases.

Operations

- N limits the number of cases analyzed by all subsequent procedures in the session.
- Without the N command, SPSS/PC+ processes all cases.
- N controls the building of cases, not the reading of individual data records.
- SPSS/PC+ stops reading data when N is reached. If keyword ESTIMATED is used, all data are read.
- Any SAMPLE, PROCESS IF, or SELECT IF commands are executed before cases are counted toward the limit specified on N.
- N limits the number of cases available for later procedures only if a new active file is created. (A new active file is created when a data transformation or data definition command is followed by a command that reads that data.) Otherwise, the "eliminated" cases are still in the active file and can be restored using an N command with a larger number.
- You cannot increase the size of the active file by specifying a value for N greater than the number of cases written to the active file.

Example

```
N 100.
```

- This example limits the number of cases in the active file to the first 100 cases.

Example

```
DATA LIST FILE='INVENT.DAT' / ITEM1 TO ITEM30 1-60.
N 400 ESTIMATED.
FREQ VAR=ITEM24.
N 23.
SELECT IF (ITEM11 EQ 8).
LIST VAR=ITEM1, ITEM12 TO ITEM18, ITEM24.
```

- DATA LIST defines 30 variables in the file *INVENT.DAT* in the current directory.
- The N command with keyword ESTIMATED tells SPSS/PC+ to allocate memory for processing approximately 400 cases.
- The FREQUENCIES procedure produces a frequency table for *ITEM24* and includes all cases.
- The second N command limits the number of cases in the active file to 23 after selecting cases that have value 8 for variable *ITEM11*, as specified on the subsequent SELECT IF command.
- The SELECT IF command causes a new active file to be created when the data are read for the LIST procedure. All cases other than the selected 23 cases are deleted from the active file and cannot be retrieved (unless the original active file is recreated with a new DATA LIST).
- LIST produces a listing of the values of *ITEM1*, *ITEM24*, and all variables between and including *ITEM12* and *ITEM18* for the remaining cases in the active file.

NPAR TESTS

```
NPAR TESTS [CHISQUARE=varlist[(lo,hi)]/] [/EXPECTED={EQUAL**    }]
                                                     {f1,f2,...fn}

[/K-S({UNIFORM [min,max]   })=varlist]
      {NORMAL [mean,stddev]}
      {POISSON [mean]       }

[/RUNS({MEAN  })=varlist]
       {MEDIAN}
       {MODE  }
       {value }

[/BINOMIAL[({.5})]=varlist[({value1,value2})]]]
           {p }           {value        }

[/MCNEMAR=varlist [WITH varlist]]

[/SIGN=varlist [WITH varlist]]

[/WILCOXON=varlist [WITH varlist]]

[/COCHRAN=varlist]

[/FRIEDMAN=varlist]

[/KENDALL=varlist]

[/M-W=varlist BY var (value1,value2)]

[/K-S=varlist BY var (value1,value2)]

[/W-W=varlist BY var (value1,value2)]

[/MOSES[(n)]=varlist BY var (value1,value2)]

[/K-W=varlist BY var (value1,value2)]

[/MEDIAN[(value)]=varlist BY var (value1,value2)]

[/OPTIONS=option numbers]

[/STATISTICS=statistic numbers]
```

**Default if the subcommand is omitted.

Options:

1   Include user-missing values

2   Exclude missing values listwise

3   Sequential pairing of variables for two related samples

4   Random sampling

Statistics:

1   Mean, maximum, minimum, standard deviation, and count
2   Quartiles and count

Example:

```
NPAR TESTS K-S(UNIFORM)=V1 /K-S(NORMAL,0,1)=V2.
```

Overview

NPAR TESTS is a collection of nonparametric tests. These tests make minimal assumptions about the underlying distribution of the data and are described in Siegel (1956). In addition to the nonparametric tests available in NPAR TESTS, the k-sample chi-square and Fisher's exact test are available in procedure CROSSTABS.

The tests available in NPAR TESTS can be grouped into three broad categories based on how the data are organized: one-sample tests, related-samples tests, and independent-samples tests. A one-sample test analyzes one variable. A test for related samples compares two or more variables for the same set of cases. An independent-samples test analyzes one variable grouped by categories of another variable.

The one-sample tests available in procedure NPAR TESTS are

- BINOMIAL.
- CHISQUARE.
- K-S (Kolmogorov-Smirnov).
- RUNS.

Tests for two related samples are
- MCNEMAR.
- SIGN.
- WILCOXON.

Tests for k related samples are
- COCHRAN.
- FRIEDMAN.
- KENDALL.

Tests for two independent samples are
- M-W (Mann-Whitney).
- K-S (Kolmogorov-Smirnov).
- W-W (Wald-Wolfowitz).
- MOSES.

Tests for k independent samples are
- K-W (Kruskal-Wallis).
- MEDIAN.

Tests are described below in alphabetical order.

Options

Statistical Display. In addition to the tests, you can request univariate statistics (Statistic 1), quartiles, and counts (Statistic 2) for all variables specified on the command. You can also control the pairing of variables in tests for two related samples (Option 3).

Random Sampling. NPAR TESTS must store cases in memory when computing tests that use ranks. You can use random sampling when there is not enough space to store all cases (Option 4).

Basic Specification

The basic specification is a single test subcommand and a list of variables to be tested. Some tests require additional specifications. CHISQUARE has an optional subcommand.

Subcommand Order

Subcommands can be used in any order.

Syntax Rules

- The OPTIONS and STATISTICS subcommands are optional. Each can be specified only once per NPAR TESTS command.
- You can request any or all tests, and you can specify a test subcommand more than once on a single NPAR TESTS command.
- Keyword ALL in any variable list refers to all user-defined variables in the active file.
- Keyword WITH controls pairing of variables in two-related-samples tests.
- Keyword BY introduces the grouping variable in two- and k-independent-samples tests.
- Option 3 can be used on the MCNEMAR, SIGN, and WILCOXON subcommands to obtain sequential pairing of variables for two related samples.

Operations

- The output always uses narrow format.
- If a string variable is specified on any subcommand, NPAR TESTS will stop executing.
- When ALL is used, requests for tests of variables with themselves are ignored and a warning is displayed.

Limitations

- The maximum number of variables that can be specified on NPAR TESTS is the same as the system limit.
- Maximum 100 subcommands.
- Maximum 200 values for subcommand CHISQUARE.
- Maximum 1 each OPTIONS and STATISTICS subcommands.

BINOMIAL Subcommand

```
NPAR TESTS BINOMIAL [({.5})]=varlist[({value,value})]
                       {p  }             {value        }
```

BINOMIAL tests whether the observed distribution of a dichotomous variable is the same as that expected from a specified binomial distribution. By default, each variable named is assumed to have only two values, and the distribution of each variable named is compared to a binomial distribution with p (the proportion of cases expected in the first category) equal to 0.5. The default output includes the number of valid cases in each group, the test proportion, and the two-tailed probability of the observed proportion.

Syntax

- The minimum specification is a list of variables to be tested.
- To change the default 0.5 test proportion, specify a value in parentheses immediately after keyword BINOMIAL.
- A single value in parentheses following the variable list is used as a cutting point. Cases with values equal to or less than the cutting point form the first category; the remaining cases form the second.
- If two values appear in parentheses after the variable list, cases with values equal to the first value form the first category, and cases with values equal to the second value form the second category.
- If no values are specified, the variables must be dichotomous.

Operations

- The proportion observed in the first category is compared to the test proportion. The probability of the observed proportion occurring given the test proportion and a binomial distribution is then computed. A test statistic is calculated for each variable specified.
- If the test proportion is the default (0.5), a two-tailed probability is displayed. For any other test proportion, a one-tailed probability is displayed. The direction of the one-tailed test depends on the observed proportion in the first category. If the observed proportion is more than the test proportion, the significance of observing that many or more in the first category is reported. If the observed proportion is less than the test proportion, the significance of observing that many or fewer in the first category is reported. In other words, the test is always done in the observed direction.

Example

```
NPAR TESTS BINOMIAL(.667)=V1(0,1).
```

- If more than 0.667 of the cases have value 0 for *V1*, BINOMIAL gives the probability of observing that many or more values of 0 in a binomial distribution with probability 0.667. If fewer than 0.667 of the cases are 0, the test will be of observing that many or fewer.

CHISQUARE Subcommand

```
NPAR TESTS CHISQUARE=varlist [(lo,hi)] [/EXPECTED={EQUAL**     }]
                                                  {f1,f2,... fn}
```

The CHISQUARE (alias CHI-SQUARE) one-sample test computes a chi-square statistic based on the differences between the observed and expected frequencies of categories of a variable. By default, equal frequencies are expected in each category. The output includes the frequency distribution, expected frequencies, residuals, chi-square, degrees of freedom, and probability.

Syntax

- The minimum specification is a list of variables to be tested. Optionally, you can specify a value range in parentheses following the variable list. You can also specify expected proportions with the EXPECTED subcommand.
- If you use the EXPECTED subcommand to specify unequal expected frequencies, you must specify a value greater than 0 for each observed category of the variable. The expected frequencies are specified in ascending order of category value. You can use the notation $n*f$ to indicate that frequency f is expected for n consecutive categories.
- Specifying keyword EQUAL on the EXPECTED subcommand has the same effect as omitting the EXPECTED subcommand.
- EXPECTED applies to all variables specified on the CHISQUARE subcommand. Use multiple CHISQUARE and EXPECTED subcommands to specify different expected proportions for variables.

Operations

- If no range is specified for the variables to be tested, each distinct value in the data defines a category.
- If a range is specified, integer-valued categories are established for each value within the range. Noninteger values are truncated before classification. Cases with values outside the specified range are excluded.
- Expected values are interpreted as proportions, not absolute values. Values are summed, and each value is divided by the total to calculate the proportion of cases expected in the corresponding category.
- A test statistic is calculated for each variable specified.

Example

```
NPAR TESTS CHISQUARE=V1 (1,5) /EXPECTED= 12, 3*16, 18.
```

- This example requests the chi-square test for values 1 through 5 of variable *V1*.
- The observed frequencies for variable *V1* are compared with the hypothetical distribution of 12/78 occurrences of value 1; 16/78 occurrences each of values 2, 3, and 4; and 18/78 occurrences of value 5.

COCHRAN Subcommand

```
NPAR TESTS COCHRAN=varlist
```

COCHRAN calculates Cochran's Q, which tests whether the distribution of values is the same for k related dichotomous variables. The output shows the frequency distribution for each variable, degrees of freedom, and probability.

Syntax

- The minimum specification is a list of two variables.
- The variables must be dichotomous and must be coded with the same two values.

Operations

- A $k \times 2$ contingency table (variables by categories) is constructed for dichotomous variables and the proportions for each variable are computed. A single test comparing all variables is calculated.
- Cochran's Q statistic has approximately a chi-square distribution.

Example

```
NPAR TESTS COCHRAN=RV1 TO RV3.
```

- This example tests whether the distribution of values 0 and 1 for *RV1*, *RV2*, and *RV3* is the same.

FRIEDMAN Subcommand

```
NPAR TESTS FRIEDMAN=varlist
```

FRIEDMAN tests whether k related samples have been drawn from the same population. The output shows the mean rank for each variable, number of valid cases, chi-square, degrees of freedom, and probability.

Syntax

- The minimum specification is a list of two variables.
- Variables should be at least at the ordinal level of measurement.

Operations

- The values of k variables are ranked from 1 to k for each case and the mean rank is calculated for each variable over all cases.

- The test statistic has approximately a chi-square distribution. A single test statistic comparing all variables is calculated.

Example

```
NPAR TESTS FRIEDMAN=V1 V2 V3
  /STATISTICS=1.
```

- This example tests variables *V1, V2,* and *V3*, and requests univariate statistics for all three.

K-S Subcommand (One-Sample)

```
NPAR TESTS K-S({NORMAL [mean,stddev]})=varlist
              {POISSON [mean]        }
              {UNIFORM [min,max]     }
```

The K-S (alias KOLMOGOROV-SMIRNOV) one-sample test compares the cumulative distribution function for a variable with a uniform, normal, or Poisson distribution, and it tests whether the distributions are homogeneous. The parameters of the test distribution can be specified; the defaults are the observed parameters. The output shows the number of valid cases, parameters of the test distribution, most-extreme absolute, positive, and negative differences, Kolmogorov-Smirnov Z, and two-tailed probability for each variable.

Syntax

The minimum specification is a distribution keyword and a list of variables. The distribution keywords are NORMAL, POISSON, and UNIFORM.

- The distribution keyword and its optional parameters must be enclosed within parentheses.
- The distribution keyword must be separated from its parameters by blanks or commas.

NORMAL [mean, stdev] *Normal distribution.* The default parameters are the observed mean and standard deviation.

POISSON [mean] *Poisson distribution.* The default parameter is the observed mean.

UNIFORM [min,max] *Uniform distribution.* The default parameters are the observed minimum and maximum values.

Operations

- The Kolmogorov-Smirnov Z is computed from the largest difference in absolute value between the observed and test distribution functions. A test statistic is calculated for each variable specified.
- The K-S probability levels assume that the test distribution is specified entirely in advance. The distribution of the test statistic and resulting probabilities are different when the parameters of the test distribution are estimated from the sample. No correction is made.

- For a mean of 100,000 or larger, a normal approximation to the Poisson distribution is used.

Example

```
NPAR TESTS K-S(UNIFORM)=V1 /K-S(NORMAL,0,1)=V2.
```

- The first K-S subcommand compares the distribution of *V1* with a uniform distribution that has the same range as *V1*.
- The second K-S subcommand compares the distribution of *V2* with a normal distribution that has a mean of 0 and a standard deviation of 1.

K-S Subcommand (Two-Sample)

```
NPAR TESTS K-S=varlist BY variable(value1,value2)
```

K-S (alias KOLMOGOROV-SMIRNOV) tests whether the distribution of a variable is the same in two independent samples defined by a grouping variable. The test is sensitive to any difference in median, dispersion, skewness, and so forth, between the two distributions. The output shows the valid number of cases in each group, the largest absolute, positive, and negative differences between the two groups, the Kolmogorov-Smirnov Z, and the two-tailed probability for each variable.

Syntax

- The minimum specification is a test variable, the keyword BY, a grouping variable, and a pair of values in parentheses.
- The test variable should be at least at the ordinal level of measurement.
- Cases with the first value form one group and cases with the second value form the other. The order in which values are specified determines which difference is the largest positive and which is the largest negative.

Operations

- The observed cumulative distributions for both groups are computed, as are the maximum positive, negative, and absolute differences. A test statistic is calculated for each variable named before BY.
- Cases with values other than those specified for the grouping variable are excluded.

Example

```
NPAR TESTS K-S=V1 V2 BY V3(0,1).
```

- This example specifies two tests. The first compares the distribution of *V1* for cases with value 0 for *V3* with the distribution of *V1* for cases with value 1 for *V3*.

- A parallel test is calculated for *V2*.

K-W Subcommand

```
NPAR TESTS K-W=varlist BY variable(value1,value2)
```

K-W (alias KRUSKAL-WALLIS) tests whether *k* independent samples defined by a grouping variable are from the same population. The output shows the number of valid cases, mean rank of the variable in each group, chi-square, probability, and chi-square and probability after correcting for ties.

Syntax

- The minimum specification is a test variable, the keyword BY, a grouping variable, and a pair of values in parentheses.
- Every value in the range defined by the pair of values for the grouping variable forms a group.

Operations

- Cases from the *k* groups are ranked in a single series, and the rank sum for each group is computed. A test statistic is calculated for each variable specified before BY.
- Kruskal Wallis *H* has approximately a chi-square distribution.
- Cases with values other than those in the range specified for the grouping variable are excluded.

Example

```
NPAR TESTS K-W=V1 BY V2(0,4).
```

- This example tests *V1* for groups defined by values 0 through 4 of *V2*.

KENDALL Subcommand

```
NPAR TESTS KENDALL=varlist
```

KENDALL tests whether *k* related samples are from the same population. *W* is a measure of agreement among judges or raters where each case is one judge's rating of several items (variables). The output includes the mean rank for each variable, valid number of cases, *W*, chi-square, degrees of freedom, and probability.

Syntax

The minimum specification is a list of two variables.

Operations

- The values of the k variables are ranked from 1 to k for each case and the mean rank is calculated for each variable over all cases. Kendall's W and a corresponding chi-square statistic are calculated, correcting for ties. A single test statistic is calculated for all variables.

- W ranges between 0 (no agreement) and 1 (complete agreement).

Example

```
DATA LIST /V1 TO V5 1-10.
BEGIN DATA
2 5 4 5 1
3 3 4 5 3
3 4 4 6 2
2 4 3 6 2
END DATA.
NPAR TESTS KENDALL=ALL.
```

- This example tests four judges (cases) on five items (variables *V1* through *V5*).

M-W Subcommand

```
NPAR TESTS M-W=varlist BY variable(value1,value2)
```

M-W (alias MANN-WHITNEY) tests whether two independent samples defined by a grouping variable are from the same population. The test statistic uses the rank of each case to test whether the groups are drawn from the same population. The output shows the mean rank of the variable within each group, valid number of cases for each group, Mann-Whitney U, Wilcoxon W (the rank sum of the smaller group), two-tailed probability of U (or W), Z statistic, and two-tailed probability of Z corrected for ties.

Syntax

- The minimum specification is a test variable, the keyword BY, a grouping variable, and a pair of values in parentheses.

- Cases with the first value form one group and cases with the second value form the other. The order in which the values are specified is unimportant.

Operations

- Cases are ranked in order of increasing size, and test statistic U (the number of times a score from group 1 precedes a score from group 2) is computed.

- An exact significance level is computed if there are 40 or fewer cases. For more than 40 cases, U is transformed into a normally distributed Z statistic and a normal approximation p value is computed.

- A test statistic is calculated for each variable named before BY.

- Cases with values other than those specified for the grouping variable are excluded.

Example

```
NPAR TESTS M-W=V1 BY V2(1,2).
```

- This example tests *V1* based on the two groups defined by values 1 and 2 of *V2*.

MCNEMAR Subcommand

```
NPAR TESTS MCNEMAR=varlist [WITH varlist] [/OPTIONS=3]
```

MCNEMAR tests whether combinations of values between two dichotomous variables are equally likely. The output shows the 2×2 contingency table, number of valid cases, and two-tailed probability for each pair of variables.

Syntax

- The minimum specification is a list of two variables. Variables must be dichotomous and must have the same two values.
- If keyword WITH is not specified, each variable is paired with every other variable in the list. If Option 3 is specified but WITH is not, the first variable is paired with the second, the second with the third, the third with the fourth, and so on.
- If WITH is specified, each variable before WITH is paired with each variable after WITH. If Option 3 is also specified, the first variable before WITH is paired with the first variable after WITH, the second variable before WITH with the second variable after WITH, and so on.
- With Option 3, the number of variables specified before and after WITH must be the same.

Operations

- A 2×2 table is constructed for each pair of dichotomous variables and a chi-square statistic is computed for cases with different values for the two variables. Only combinations for which the values for the two variables are different are considered.
- If fewer than 25 cases change values from the first variable to the second variable, the binomial distribution is used to compute the probability.

Example

```
NPAR TESTS MCNEMAR=V1 V2 V3.
```

- This example performs the MCNEMAR test on variable pairs *V1* and *V2*, *V1* and *V3*, and *V2* and *V3*.

MEDIAN Subcommand

```
NPAR TESTS MEDIAN [(value)]=varlist BY variable(value1,value2)
```

MEDIAN determines if *k* independent samples are drawn from populations with the same median. The independent samples are defined by a grouping variable. For each variable, the output shows a table of the number of cases greater than and less than or equal to the median in each category of the grouping variable, the median, chi-square, degrees of freedom, and probability.

Syntax

- The minimum specification is a single test variable, the keyword BY, a grouping variable, and two values in parentheses.
- If the first grouping value is less than the second, every value in the range defined by the pair of values forms a group and a *k*-sample test is performed.
- If the first value is greater than the second, two groups are formed using the two values and a two-sample test is performed.
- By default, the median is calculated from all cases included in the test. To override the default, specify a median value in parentheses following the MEDIAN subcommand keyword.

Operations

- A $2 \times k$ contingency table is constructed with counts of the number of cases greater than the median and less than or equal to the median for the *k* groups. A test statistic is calculated for each variable specified before BY.
- For more than 30 cases, a chi-square statistic is computed. For 30 or fewer cases, Fisher's exact procedure (two-tailed) is used instead of chi-square.
- For a two-sample test, cases with values other than the two specified are excluded.

Example

```
NPAR TESTS MEDIAN(8.4)=V1 BY V2(1,2) /MEDIAN=V1 BY V2(1,2)
  /MEDIAN=V1 BY V3(1,4) /MEDIAN=V1 BY V3(4,1).
```

- The first two MEDIAN subcommands test variable *V1* grouped by values 1 and 2 of variable *V2*. The first test specifies a median of 8.4 and the second uses the observed median.
- The third MEDIAN subcommand requests a four-samples test, dividing the sample into four groups based on values 1, 2, 3, and 4 of variable *V3*.
- The last MEDIAN subcommand requests a two-samples test, grouping cases based on values 1 and 4 of *V3* and ignoring all other cases.

MOSES Subcommand

```
NPAR TESTS MOSES[(n)]=varlist BY variable(value1,value2)
```

The MOSES test of extreme reactions tests whether the range of an ordinal variable is the same in a control group and a comparison group. The control and comparison groups are defined by a grouping variable. For each variable tested, the output includes the number of cases in each group, number of outliers removed, span of the control group before and after outliers are removed, and one-tailed probability of the span with and without outliers.

Syntax

- The minimum specification is a test variable, the keyword BY, a grouping variable, and two values in parentheses.
- The test variable must be at least at the ordinal level of measurement.
- The first value of the grouping variable defines the control group and the second value defines the comparison group.
- By default, 5% of the cases are trimmed from each end of the range of the control group to remove outliers. You can override the default by specifying a value in parentheses following the MOSES subcommand keyword. This value represents an actual number of cases, not a percentage.

Operations

- Values from the groups are arranged in a single ascending sequence. The span of the control group is computed as the number of cases in the sequence containing the lowest and highest control value.
- No adjustments are made for tied cases.
- Cases with values other than those specified for the grouping variable are excluded.
- A test statistic is calculated for each variable named before BY.

Example

```
NPAR TESTS MOSES=V1 BY V3(0,1) /MOSES=V1 BY V3(1,0).
```

- The first MOSES subcommand tests *V1* using value 0 of *V3* to define the control group and value 1 for the comparison group. The second MOSES subcommand reverses the comparison and control groups.

RUNS Subcommand

```
NPAR TESTS RUNS({MEAN   })=varlist
               {MEDIAN}
               {MODE  }
               {value }
```

RUNS tests whether the sequence of values of a dichotomized variable is random. The output includes the test value (cut point used to dichotomize the variable tested), number of runs, number of cases below the cut point, number of cases greater than or equal to the cut point, and test statistic Z with its two-tailed probability.

Syntax

- The minimum specification is a cut point in parentheses followed by a test variable.
- The cut point can be specified by an exact value or one of the keywords MEAN, MEDIAN, or MODE.

Operations

- All variables tested are treated as dichotomous: cases with values less than the cut point form one category, and cases with values greater than or equal to the cut point form the other category.
- A test statistic is calculated for each variable specified.

Example

```
NPAR TESTS RUNS(MEDIAN)=V2 /RUNS(24.5)=V2 /RUNS(1)=V3.
```

- This example performs three runs tests. The first tests variable *V2* using the median as the cut point. The second also tests *V2*, this time using 24.5 as the cut point. The third tests variable *V3* with value 1 specified as the cut point.

SIGN Subcommand

```
NPAR TESTS SIGN=varlist [WITH varlist] [/OPTIONS=3]
```

SIGN tests whether the distribution of two paired variables in a two-related-samples test is the same. The output includes the number of positive differences, number of negative differences, number of ties, and two-tailed binomial probability.

Syntax

- The minimum specification is a list of two variables.
- Variables should be at least at the ordinal level of measurement.
- If keyword WITH is not specified, each variable in the list is paired with every other variable in the list. If Option 3 is specified but WITH is not, the first variable is paired with the second, the second with the third, the third with the fourth, and so on.
- If WITH is specified, each variable before WITH is paired with each variable after WITH. If Option 3 is also specified, the first variable before WITH is paired with the first variable after WITH, the second variable before WITH with the second variable after WITH, and so on.

- With Option 3, the number of variables specified before and after WITH must be the same.

Operations

- The positive and negative differences between the pair of variables are counted. Ties are ignored.
- The probability is taken from the binomial distribution if 25 or fewer differences are observed. Otherwise, the probability comes from the Z distribution.
- Under the null hypothesis for large sample sizes, Z is approximately normally distributed with a mean of 0 and a variance of 1.

Example

```
NPAR TESTS SIGN=N1,M1 WITH N2,M2 /OPTIONS=3.
```

- *N1* is tested with *N2*, and *M1* is tested with *M2*.

W-W Subcommand

```
NPAR TESTS W-W=varlist BY variable(value1,value2)
```

W-W (alias WALD-WOLFOWITZ) tests whether the distribution of a variable is the same in two independent samples. A runs test is performed with group membership as the criterion. The output includes the number of valid cases in each group, number of runs, Z, and one-tailed probability of Z. If ties are present, the minimum and maximum number of ties possible, their Z statistics, and one-tailed probabilities are displayed.

Syntax

- The minimum specification is a single test variable, the keyword BY, a grouping variable, and two values in parentheses.
- Cases with the first value form one group and cases with the second value form the other. The order in which values are specified is unimportant.

Operations

- Cases are combined from both groups and ranked from lowest to highest, and a runs test is performed using group membership as the criterion. For ties involving cases from both groups, both the minimum and maximum number of runs possible are calculated. Test statistics are calculated for each variable specified before BY.
- For a sample size of 30 or less, the exact one-tailed probability is calculated. For a sample size greater than 30, the normal approximation is used.
- Cases with values other than those specified for the grouping variable are excluded.

Example

```
NPAR TESTS W-W=V1 BY V3(0,1).
```

- This example ranks cases from lowest to highest based on their values for *V1* and a runs test is performed. Cases with value 0 for *V3* form one group and cases with value 1 form the other.

WILCOXON Subcommand

```
NPAR TESTS WILCOXON=varlist [WITH varlist] [/OPTIONS=3]
```

WILCOXON tests whether the distribution of two paired variables in two related samples is the same. This test takes into account the magnitude of the differences between two paired variables. The output includes the number of positive and negative differences and their respective means, number of ties, valid number of cases, *Z*, and probability of *Z*.

Syntax

- The minimum specification is a list of two variables.
- If keyword WITH is not specified, each variable is paired with every other variable in the list. If Option 3 is specified but WITH is not, the first variable is paired with the second, the second with the third, the third with the fourth, and so on.
- If WITH is specified, each variable before WITH is paired with each variable after WITH. If Option 3 is also specified, the first variable before WITH is paired with the first variable after WITH, the second variable before WITH with the second variable after WITH, and so on.
- With Option 3, the number of variables specified before and after WITH must be the same.

Operations

- The differences between the pair of variables are counted, the absolute differences ranked, the positive and negative ranks summed, and the test statistic *Z* computed from the positive and negative rank sums.
- Under the null hypothesis for large sample sizes, *Z* is approximately normally distributed with a mean of 0 and a variance of 1.

Example

```
NPAR TESTS WILCOXON=A B WITH C D /OPTIONS=3.
```

- This example pairs *A* with *C* and *B* with *D*. If Option 3 were not specified, it would also pair *A* with *D* and *B* with *C*.

Statistical Display

The following optional statistics are available:

Statistic 1 *Univariate statistics.* The displayed statistics include the mean, maximum, minimum, standard deviation, and number of valid cases for each variable named on the command.

Statistic 2 *Quartiles and number of cases.* The 25th, 50th, and 75th percentiles are displayed for each variable named on the command.

Sequential Pairing

Option 3 requests sequential pairing of variables specified for two-related samples tests (MC-NEMAR, SIGN, and WILCOXON).

Option 3 *Sequential pairing of variables for two related samples.* If keyword WITH is not specified, the first variable is paired with the second, the second with the third, the third with the fourth, and so on. If WITH is specified, the first variable before WITH is paired with the first variable after WITH, the second variable before WITH with the second variable after WITH, and so on. The number of variables specified before and after WITH must be the same.

Random Sampling

NPAR TESTS must store cases in memory. Option 4 allows you to select a random sample of cases when there is not enough space on your computer to store all the cases.

Option 4 *Random sampling.* Option 4 is ignored with the RUNS subcommand.

Missing Values

By default, cases with user- or system-missing values for a variable used for a specific test are omitted from that test. On subcommands that specify several tests, each test is evaluated separately. Use the following to change these defaults.

Option 1 *Include user-missing values.* User-missing values are treated as valid values.

Option 2 *Exclude cases with missing values listwise.* Cases with missing values for any variable named on any subcommand are excluded from all analyses.

ONEWAY

```
ONEWAY  varlist BY varname(min,max)

[/POLYNOMIAL=n]  [/CONTRAST=coefficient list] [/CONTRAST=... ]

[/RANGES={LSD           {([{0.05}])] [/RANGES=...]
          {DUNCAN        {α    }
          {SNK           }
          {BTUKEY        }
          {TUKEY         }
          {MODLSD        }
          {SCHEFFE       }
          {range values}

[/OPTIONS=option numbers

[/STATISTICS={statistic numbers}]
             {ALL              }
```

Options:

1 Include user-missing values

2 Exclude missing values listwise

3 Suppress variable labels

4 Write matrix of counts, means, and standard deviations

6 Use value labels as group labels

7 Read matrix of counts, means, and standard deviations

8 Read matrix of counts, means, pooled variance, and degrees of freedom

10 Harmonic mean of all group sizes as sample sizes in range tests

Statistics:

1 Group descriptive statistics
2 Fixed- and random-effects statistics
3 Levene test for homogeneity of variance

Example:
```
ONEWAY VARIABLES=YVAR BY XVAR(1,4).
```

Overview

ONEWAY produces a one-way analysis of variance for an interval-level dependent variable by one numeric independent variable that defines the groups for the analysis. Other SPSS/PC+ procedures that perform analysis of variance are MEANS, ANOVA, and MANOVA (MANOVA is available in the SPSS/PC+ Advanced Statistics option). Some tests not included in the other procedures are available as options in ONEWAY.

Options

Trends, Contrasts, and Ranges. You can partition the between-groups sums of squares into linear, quadratic, cubic, and higher-order trend components using the POLYNOMIAL subcommand. You can specify up to 10 contrasts to be tested with the t statistic on the CONTRAST subcommand. You can also specify seven different range tests for comparisons of all possible pairs of group means, or multiple comparisons, using the RANGES subcommand.

Format. You can suppress the display of variable labels with Option 3. You can also label groups with the value labels of the independent variable using Option 6.

Statistics. In addition to the default output, you can obtain means, standard deviations, and other descriptive statistics for each group with Statistic 1. Fixed- and random-effects statistics (Statistic 2) as well as several tests for homogeneity of variance (Statistic 3) are also available. The harmonic mean of all group sizes can be used as the sample size for each group in range tests (Option 10).

Matrix Input and Output. You can write a matrix of group counts, means, and standard deviations for use in subsequent analyses using Option 4, and you can read such a matrix using Option 7. With Option 8 you can read matrix materials consisting of group counts, means, pooled variance, and degrees of freedom for the pooled variance.

Basic Specification

- The basic specification is the VARIABLES subcommand with a single analysis list.   The actual keyword VARIABLES can be omitted.
- The minimum analysis list specifies a dependent variable, the keyword BY, an independent variable, and the minimum and maximum values of the independent variable in parentheses.
- By default, ONEWAY produces a labeled table for each dependent variable by the independent variable. The table contains the between- and within- groups sums of squares, mean squares, and degrees of freedom. The F ratio and the probability of F for the test are displayed.

Subcommand Order

- The VARIABLES subcommand must be specified first.
- Other subcommands can be specified in any order.

Operations

- Noninteger values for the independent variable are truncated.
- Cases with values outside the range specified for the independent variable are omitted from the analysis.
- If a string variable is specified as an independent or dependent variable, ONEWAY is not executed.
- The output uses the width defined on SET.
- If SPSS/PC+ encounters more than one each of the POLYNOMIAL, OPTIONS, or STATISTICS subcommands, it uses the last one of each.

Limitations

- Maximum 100 dependent variables and 1 independent variable.
- The number of categories for the independent variable is limited only by available memory. However, contrasts tests are not performed if the range of values for the independent variable exceeds 50, and range tests are not performed if there are more than 50 nonempty categories.
- Range tests are not performed on less than 3 groups.
- Maximum 1 VARIABLES subcommand.
- Maximum 1 POLYNOMIAL subcommand.
- Maximum 10 CONTRAST subcommands.
- Maximum 10 RANGES subcommands.
- Maximum 1 OPTIONS subcommand.
- Maximum 1 STATISTICS subcommand.

Example

```
ONEWAY VARIABLES=YVAR BY XVAR(1,4).
```

- This example names *YVAR* as the dependent variable and *XVAR* as the independent variable with a minimum value of 1 and a maximum value of 4.

VARIABLES Subcommand

VARIABLES specifies the analysis list. The actual keyword VARIABLES can be omitted.

- An analysis list specifies a dependent variable list, the keyword BY, and an independent variable with its minimum and maximum values in parentheses.
- There can be only one VARIABLES subcommand, and it must be specified before any of the optional subcommands.
- All variables named must be numeric.
- The minimum and maximum values of the independent variable must be separated by a comma or a space and enclosed in parentheses. The values must be integers.

POLYNOMIAL Subcommand

POLYNOMIAL partitions the between-groups sums of squares into linear, cubic, quadratic, or higher-order trend components. The output is an expanded analysis of variance table that provides the degrees of freedom, sums of squares, mean square, F, and probability of F for each partition.

- The value specified on POLYNOMIAL indicates the highest-degree polynomial to be used.

- The polynomial value must be a positive integer less than or equal to 5. If the polynomial specified is greater than the number of groups, the highest-degree polynomial possible is assumed.
- With balanced designs, ONEWAY computes the sums of squares for each order polynomial from weighted polynomial contrasts, using the category of the independent variable as the metric. These contrasts are orthogonal.
- With unbalanced designs and equal spacing between groups, ONEWAY also computes sums of squares using the unweighted polynomial contrasts. These contrasts are not orthogonal.
- The deviation sums of squares are always calculated from the weighted sums of squares (Speed, 1976).
- Only one POLYNOMIAL subcommand can be specified per ONEWAY command. If more than one is used, the last one specified is in effect.

Example

```
ONEWAY VARIABLES=WELL BY EDUC6 (1,6)
  /POLYNOMIAL=2.
```

- This example requests an analysis of variance of *WELL* by EDUC6 with second-order (quadratic) polynomial contrasts.

CONTRAST Subcommand

CONTRAST specifies *a priori* contrasts to be tested by the t statistic. Contrasts are specified as a vector of coefficients, where each coefficient corresponds to a category of the independent variable. The output for each contrast list is the value of the contrast, the standard error of the contrast, the t statistic, and the degrees of freedom and the two-tailed probability of t. Both pooled- and separate-variance estimates are displayed.

- A contrast must be specified or implied for every group in the range specified for the independent variable, even if the group is empty. Trailing coefficients of 0 do not need to be specified. If the number of contrast values is less than the number of groups, contrast values of 0 are assumed for the remaining groups.
- The contrast coefficients for a set should sum to 0. If they do not, a warning is issued. ONEWAY will still give an estimate of this contrast.
- Coefficients are assigned to empty and nonempty groups defined by ascending integer values of the independent variable.
- Only one set of contrast coefficients can be specified per CONTRAST subcommand. Additional contrasts on a single CONTRAST subcommand are ignored.
- You can use the notation $n*c$ to indicate that coefficient c is repeated n times.

Example

```
ONEWAY VARIABLES=YVAR BY XVAR(1,4)
   /CONTRAST = -1 -1 1 1
   /CONTRAST = -1 0 0 1
   /CONTRAST = -1 0 .5 .5.
```

- The first CONTRAST subcommand contrasts the combination of the first two groups with the combination of the last two groups.
- The second CONTRAST subcommand contrasts the first group with the last group.
- The third CONTRAST subcommand contrasts the first group with the combination of the third and fourth groups.

Example

```
ONEWAY VARIABLES=YVAR BY XVAR(1,4)
   /CONTRAST = -1 1 2*0
   /CONTRAST = -1 1 0 0
   /CONTRAST = -1 1.
```

- All three CONTRAST subcommands specify the same contrast coefficients for a four-group analysis. The first group is contrasted with the second group in all three cases.
- The first CONTRAST uses the $n*c$ notation and the last CONTRAST omits the trailing zero coefficients.

RANGES Subcommand

RANGES specifies either a range test or explicit range values for multiple comparison. Seven range tests are available. The RANGES output always includes multiple comparisons between all groups. Nonempty group means are sorted in ascending order, with asterisks indicating significantly different groups. In addition, homogeneous subsets are calculated for balanced designs and for all designs when Option 10 is specified. The means of the groups included within a subset are not significantly different.

- By default, the range tests use sample sizes of the two groups being compared. This is equivalent to using the harmonic mean of the sample size of the two groups begin compared. You can use Option 10 to change this default.
- The default alpha for all tests is 0.05. For some tests, you can specify a different alpha.

The tests available on the RANGES subcommand are

LSD(α)   *Least-significant difference.* You can specify an alpha between 0 and 1. The default is 0.05.

DUNCAN(α)   *Multiple range test.* You can specify an alpha of 0.01, 0.05, and 0.10 only. The default is 0.05. DUNCAN uses 0.01 if the alpha specified is less than 0.05; 0.05 if the alpha specified is greater than or equal to 0.05 but less than 0.10; 0.10 if the alpha specified is greater than or equal to 0.10; and 0.05 if no alpha is specified.

SNK   *Student-Newman-Keuls.* Alpha is 0.05.

BTUKEY   *Tukey's alternate procedure.* Alpha is 0.05.

TUKEY   *Honestly significant difference.* Alpha is 0.05.

MODLSD(α)   *Modified LSD.* You can specify an alpha between 0 and 1. The default is 0.05.

SCHEFFE(α)   *Scheffé test.* You can specify an alpha between 0 and 1. The default is 0.05.

Alternatively, you can use any other type of range by specifying range values:

- The range values should be separated by commas or blanks.
- Up to k-1 range values can be specified in ascending order, where k is the number of groups and where the range value times the standard error of the combined subset is the critical value.
- If less than k-1 values are specified, the last value specified is used for the remaining range values.
- You can use the notation $n*r$ to indicate that the range r is repeated n times.
- To use a single critical value for all subsets, specify one range value.

Example

```
ONEWAY VARIABLES=WELL BY EDUC6 (1,6)
 /RANGES=SNK
 /RANGES=SCHEFFE (.01).
```

- This example requests two different range tests. The first uses the Student-Newman-Keuls test and the second uses Scheffé's test with an alpha of 0.01.

Example

```
ONEWAY VARIABLES=WELL BY EDUC (1,6)
 /RANGES=2.81, 3.34, 3.65, 3.88, 4.05.
```

- RANGES specifies five range values.

Harmonic Means

By default, range tests use the harmonic mean of the sizes of the two groups being compared. Use Option 10 on the OPTIONS subcommand to change this default.

Option 10   *Use the harmonic mean of all group sizes as the sample size for each group in range tests.* If Option 10 is used for unbalanced designs, ONEWAY determines homogeneous subsets for all range tests.

Format

By default, groups are identified in the output as *GRP1*, *GRP2*, and so forth, and variable labels are displayed. You can change these defaults by specifying the following on the OPTIONS subcommand:

Option 3   *Suppress variable labels.*

Option 6   *Use value labels for group labels.* The first eight characters from the value labels of the independent variable are used as group labels.

Statistical Display

By default, ONEWAY displays the between- and within-groups sums of squares, mean squares, degrees of freedom, *F* ratio, and probability of *F* for the test. It also calculates any statistics specified on the CONTRAST and RANGES subcommands. You can obtain additional statistics by specifying the following on the STATISTICS subcommand:

Statistic 1   *Group descriptive statistics.* The statistics include the number of cases, mean, standard deviation, standard error, minimum, maximum, and 95% confidence interval for each dependent variable for each group.

Statistic 2   *Fixed- and random-effects statistics.* The statistics include the standard deviation, standard error, and 95% confidence interval for the fixed-effects model, and the standard error, 95% confidence interval, and estimate of between-components variance for the random-effects model.

Statistic 3   *The Levene test for homogeneity of variance.* For each case it computes the absolute difference between the value for that case and its cell mean and then performs a one-way analysis of variance on these differences.

ALL   *All statistics.*

Missing Values

By default, cases with missing values for either the independent or dependent variable for a given analysis are excluded from that analysis. You can change the treatment of cases with missing values by specifying one or both of the following on the OPTIONS subcommand:

Option 1   *Include cases with user-missing values.* User-missing values are treated as valid values.

Option 2   *Exclude cases with missing values listwise.* Cases with missing values for any variables named in the analysis list are excluded from all analyses.

Matrix Output

ONEWAY writes matrix materials that it can read in subsequent analyses.

• To write matrix materials, specify Option 4 on the OPTIONS subcommand.

• Matrix materials are written to the results file named on the SET command (the default is *SPSS.PRC*). If the results file is not empty when Option 4 is executed, the contents of the file are overwritten. Use the SET command to specify a different results file.

• For each dependent variable, Option 4 writes a vector of group counts, followed by a vector of group means and a vector of group standard deviations.

• Vectors can contain 80 characters per line, with each vector beginning on a new line.

• The format for the counts vector is F10.2. The format for the means and standard deviation vectors is F10.4. There is thus a maximum of eight values per line.

Option 4   *Write a matrix containing vectors of counts, means, and standard deviations.*

Example

```
SET RESULTS='WELL.MAT'.
DATA LIST FILE='GSS80.DAT'
  /WELL 2-3 EDUC 4-5.
RECODE EDUC (0 THRU 8=1) (9 10 11=2) (12=3) (13 14 15=4)
  (16=5) (17 THRU 20=6).
ONEWAY VARIABLES=WELL BY EDUC (1,6)
  /OPTIONS=4.
```

- The SET command specifies file *WELL.MAT* in the current directory as the results file.
- Option 4 writes group counts, means, and standard deviations for *WELL* by *EDUC* to the results file using the format supplied by ONEWAY.

Matrix Input

You can read matrix materials in fixed or freefield format by specifying Option 7 or 8 on the OPTIONS subcommand. The general conventions for matrix materials are described in DATA LIST: Matrix Materials.

- If you specify Option 7 or 8 in ONEWAY, you must first use a DATA LIST command that defines matrix materials.
- All variables specified on the VARIABLES subcommand in ONEWAY must be defined on the DATA LIST command. In addition, the analysis list on the ONEWAY command must be the same as the analysis list that was used when the matrix was written.
- The matrix must include an entry for each group in the vectors of counts, means, and (with Option 7) standard deviations. Entries should be in ascending order of the values of the independent variable.
- Each vector must begin on a new line or record and can be entered in either fixed or freefield format.

Option 7   *Read matrix materials containing vectors of counts, means, and standard deviations.* ONEWAY expects a vector of group counts, followed by a vector of group means and a vector of group standard deviations like those written by Option 4.

Option 8   *Read matrix materials containing vectors of counts and means, followed by the pooled variance and the degrees of freedom.* ONEWAY expects a vector of group counts, followed by a vector of means, followed by a record containing the pooled variance (within-groups mean square) and another record containing the within-groups degrees of freedom for the pooled variance. If the degrees of freedom are omitted, then $n-k$ degrees of freedom are assumed, where n is the number of cases and k is the number of groups. Statistics 1, 2, and 3 and the separate variance estimate for contrasts named on the CONTRAST command are not available with Option 8.

Example

```
DATA LIST FREE MATRIX
  /WELL EDUC.
BEGIN DATA.
65 95 181 82 40 37
2.6462 2.7737 4.1796 4.5610 4.6625 5.2297
6.2699
494
END DATA.
ONEWAY VARIABLES=WELL BY EDUC(1,6)
  /OPTIONS=8.
```

- DATA LIST specifies matrix input in freefield format.

- Each vector to be read begins on a new line. The counts for the six analysis groups (the six categories of *EDUC*, in this example) are on the first line of the matrix, followed by the means for the six groups on the second line, the within-groups mean square on the third line, and the within-groups degrees of freedom on the fourth line.

- Option 8 reads matrix materials consisting of vectors of counts and means, plus the pooled variance and degrees of freedom.

PLOT

```
PLOT  [HSIZE={n}] [/VSIZE={n}]

[/CUTPOINT={EVERY(({1**}))}]
              {       {n }   }
              {value list    }

[/SYMBOLS={ALPHANUMERIC**                        }]
          {NUMERIC                               }
          {'symbols'[,'overplot symbols']        }
          {X'hexsymbs'[,'overplot hexsymbs']     }

[/MISSING=[{PLOTWISE**}] [INCLUDE]]
           {LISTWISE  }

[/FORMAT={DEFAULT**        }]
         {OVERLAY          }
         {CONTOUR[(({10}))] }
         {          {n }   }
         {REGRESSION       }

[/TITLE='title']

[/HORIZONTAL=['label'] [STANDARDIZE] [REFERENCE(value list)]
             [MIN(n)] [MAX(n)] [UNIFORM]]

[/VERTICAL=['label'] [STANDARDIZE] [REFERENCE(value list)]
           [MIN(n)] [MAX(n)] [UNIFORM]]

/PLOT={varlist} WITH varlist [(PAIR)] [BY varname] [;varlist...]
      {ALL    }

[/PLOT-...]
```

**Default if the subcommand is omitted.

Example:

```
PLOT FORMAT=OVERLAY /SYMBOLS='MD' /VSIZE=12 /HSIZE=60
  /TITLE='Marriage and Divorce Rates'
  /VERTICAL='Rates per 1000 population'
  /HORIZONTAL='Year' REFERENCE (1918, 1945) MIN (1880) MAX (2000)
  /PLOT=MARRATE DIVRATE WITH YEAR.
```

Overview

PLOT produces two-dimensional character-based plots, including simple bivariate scatter-plots, scatterplots with a control variable, contour plots, and overlay plots. You can also request bivariate regression statistics. You can choose from a variety of options for plot symbols, and you can add reference lines. You have control over size, labeling, and scaling of each axis, and you can constrain the axes to be uniform for a series of plots.

Options

Types of Plots. You can introduce a control variable for bivariate scatterplots and request regression plots with or without a control variable, contour plots, and overlay plots using the FORMAT subcommand.

Plot Tailoring. You can specify a title for the plot on the TITLE subcommand. You can scale and label the horizontal and vertical axes, request reference lines, and plot standardized variables using the VERTICAL and HORIZONTAL subcommands. You can control the plot size with the HSIZE and VSIZE subcommands, and you can specify plot symbols and the frequency they represent using the SYMBOL and CUTPOINT subcommands.

Basic Specification

The basic specification is a PLOT subcommand that names the variables for the vertical (y) axis, keyword WITH, and the variables for the horizontal (x) axis. By default, PLOT produces separate bivariate scatterplots for all combinations formed by each variable on the left side of WITH with each variable on the right.

Subcommand Order

- No subcommand can be specified after the last PLOT subcommand. Other than this, sub-commands can be specified in any order.

Syntax Rules

- The PLOT subcommand can be specified more than once.
- Subcommands MISSING, VSIZE, HSIZE, CUTPOINT, and SYMBOLS apply to all plots re-quested and can be specified only once.
- Subcommands HORIZONTAL, VERTICAL, FORMAT, and TITLE can be specified more than once and apply only to the following PLOT subcommand.

Operations

- The default plot size depends on the system page size, which is specified on SET. HSIZE and VSIZE override the default plot size.
- A longer page length can produce longer default plots within the same width. A wider page does not produce a wider default plot unless the page length is changed accordingly.

Limitations

There are no limitations on the number of plots requested or on the number of variables spec-ified on a PLOT command. The following limitations apply to the optional subcommands:

- Maximum 20 overlay plots per FORMAT subcommand.
- Maximum 1 control variable per PLOT subcommand.
- Maximum 60 characters for a title specified on TITLE.
- Maximum 36 symbols per SYMBOLS subcommand.
- Maximum 35 cut points per CUTPOINT subcommand.

- Maximum 10 reference points on each HORIZONTAL or VERTICAL subcommand.
- Maximum 40 characters per label on each HORIZONTAL or VERTICAL subcommand.
- Maximum 35 contour levels per contour plot.

Example

```
PLOT FORMAT=OVERLAY /SYMBOLS='MD' /VSIZE=12 /HSIZE=60
  /TITLE='Marriage and Divorce Rates'
  /VERTICAL='Rates per 1000 population'
  /HORIZONTAL='Year' REFERENCE (1918, 1945) MIN (1900) MAX (1983)
  /PLOT=MARRATE DIVRATE WITH YEAR.
```

- This example produces an overlay plot of marriage and divorce rates by year.
- SYMBOLS selects the symbols M and D, respectively, for the two plots.
- VSIZE and HSIZE limit the vertical and horizontal axes to 12 lines and 60 columns, respectively.
- TITLE specifies a plot title.
- VERTICAL provides a title for the vertical axis.
- HORIZONTAL provides a title for the horizontal axis. The REFERENCE keyword provides reference lines at values 1918 and 1945. MIN and MAX specify minimum and maximum scale values for the horizontal axis.

PLOT Subcommand

The PLOT subcommand names the variables to be plotted on each axis. PLOT can also name a control or contour variable.

- PLOT is the only required subcommand.
- Multiple PLOT subcommands are allowed.
- No other subcommands can follow the last PLOT subcommand.
- The basic specification on PLOT is a list of variables to be plotted on the vertical axis, keyword WITH, and a list of variables to be plotted on the horizontal axis.
- By default, PLOT creates a separate plot for each variable specified before WITH with each variable specified after WITH.
- To request special pairing of variables, specify keyword PAIR in parentheses following the second variable list. The first variable before WITH is plotted against the first variable after WITH, the second against the second, and so on.
- Use semicolons to separate multiple plot lists on a single PLOT subcommand.
- Keyword ALL can be used to refer to all user-defined variables.
- An optional control variable can be specified following keyword BY. Only one control variable can be specified on any plot list.
- If a control variable is specified for a bivariate scatterplot (the default), PLOT uses the first character of the control variable's value label as the plot symbol. If value labels have not

been specified, the first character of the value is used. The symbol $ indicates that more than one control value occurs at that position.

Example

```
PLOT PLOT=MARRATE WITH YEAR AGE;
        BIRTHS DEATHS WITH INCOME1 INCOME2 (PAIR);
        DIVRATE WITH AGE BY YEAR.
```

- The PLOT subcommand contains three plot lists. The first requests a plot of *MARRATE* with *YEAR* and of *MARRATE* with *AGE*.
- The second uses the keyword PAIR to request two plots: *BIRTHS* with *INCOME1* and *DEATHS* with *INCOME2*.
- The third requests a plot of *DIVRATE* with *AGE* using *YEAR* as a control variable. The first character of each value label (or the value itself if labels have not been defined) for *YEAR* as the plot symbol.

FORMAT Subcommand

FORMAT controls the type of plot produced.

- FORMAT can be specified once before each PLOT subcommand and applies only to plots requested on that PLOT subcommand.
- If FORMAT is not used or keyword DEFAULT is specified, bivariate scatterplots are displayed.
- Only one keyword can be specified on each FORMAT subcommand.

DEFAULT *Bivariate scatterplot.* When there is no control variable, each symbol represents the case count at that position. When a control variable is specified, each symbol represents the first character of the control variable's value label, or the first character of the value if no labels have been defined.

OVERLAY *Overlay plots.* All bivariate plots on the next PLOT subcommand appear in one plot frame. PLOT selects a unique symbol for each plot to be overlaid, plus a symbol to represent multiple plot points at one position (see "SYMBOLS Keywords" on p. 635).

CONTOUR(n) *Contour plot with* n *levels.* Contour plots use a continuous variable as the control variable and *n* successive symbols to represent the lowest to highest levels of the variable (see "SYMBOLS Keywords" on p. 635). The control variable is specified after BY on the PLOT subcommand and is recoded into *n* equal-width intervals. If *n* is omitted, the default of 10 is used; the maximum is 35. When more than one level of the contour variable occurs at the same position, PLOT displays the value of the highest level at that position.

REGRESSION *Regression of the* y *axis variable on the* x *axis variable.* The regression-line intercepts are marked with the letter *R*. When there is no control variable, each symbol represents the frequency of cases at that position. If a control variable is specified, regression statistics are pooled over all categories and each symbol represents the first character of the control variable's value label, or the first character of the value if no labels have been defined.

SYMBOLS and CUTPOINT Subcommands

A wide range of alphabetical, numeric, and hexadecimal characters are available for use as PLOT symbols. Two subcommands control the display of symbols: SYMBOLS controls the choice of plot symbols, and CUTPOINT controls the frequencies represented by a symbol.

SYMBOLS and CUTPOINT can each be specified only once and apply to all plots requested on a PLOT command. The operation of SYMBOLS and CUTPOINT depend on the specification on the FORMAT subcommand, as summarized below:

- DEFAULT or REGRESSION, with no control variable. Each symbol represents the frequency of cases and is controlled by SYMBOLS and CUTPOINT.

- DEFAULT or REGRESSION, with a control variable. Each symbol represents one value of the control variable. SYMBOLS and CUTPOINT do not apply. The plot symbol is the first character of the control variable's value label or the first character of the value if no value labels have been defined; the uniqueness of these symbols is not checked. The symbol $ indicates that more than one control value occurs at that position.

- OVERLAY. Each symbol represents one of the overlaid plots. SYMBOLS is applicable; CUTPOINT is not.

- CONTOUR. Each symbol represents one level of the contour variable. SYMBOLS is applicable; CUTPOINT is not.

SYMBOLS Keywords

SYMBOLS defines plot symbols for bivariate scatterplots, bivariate regression plots, overlay plots, and contour plots. Successive symbols represent increasing frequencies in scatterplots or regression plots, successive subplots in overlay plots, and successive intervals in contour plots.

- If the SYMBOLS subcommand is omitted, the default alphanumeric symbol set is used.

- A table defining the plot symbols is always displayed.

- Overprint symbols cannot be displayed on the screen. Overprinting will occur when the plot is printed.

ALPHANUMERIC	*Alphanumeric plot symbols.* Includes the characters 1 through 9, A through Z, and an asterisk (*). Thirty-six or more cases at a position are represented by an asterisk. This is the default.
NUMERIC	*Numeric plot symbols.* Includes the characters 1 through 9 and an asterisk (*). Ten or more cases at a plot position are represented by an asterisk.
'symbols'['ovprnt']	*List of plot symbols.* Up to 36 symbols can be specified. Symbols are specified without any intervening blanks or commas. Optionally, you can specify a list of overprinting symbols separated from the first list by a comma or space.

X'hexsym'[,'ovprnt']   *List of hexadecimal plot symbols.* Indicate hexadecimal symbols by specifying X before the hexadecimal representation list enclosed in apostrophes. Optionally, you can specify a list of overprinting symbols separated from the first list by a comma or space.

Example

```
PLOT CUTPOINTS=EVERY(5)/SYMBOLS='.+O','  X'
/PLOT=Y WITH X.
```

- This example uses a period (.) to represent 5 or fewer cases at one point, a plus sign (+) to represent 6 to 10 cases at the same position, and a symbol overprinting O and X to represent 11 or more cases at one position. Note the two leading blanks in the list of overprinting symbols.

CUTPOINT Keywords

By default, each frequency in a bivariate scatterplot or regression plot is represented by a different plot symbol, and successive plot symbols represent an interval width of 1. Use the CUTPOINT subcommand to alter the intervals or categories represented by plot symbols for these plots. Only one of the following keywords can be specified on CUTPOINT:

EVERY(n)   *Frequency intervals of width* n. Each plot symbol represents the specified frequency interval. The default is an interval width of 1. The last symbol specified represents all frequencies greater than those for the next-to-last symbol.

(value list)   *Each value defines a cut point.* Successive plot symbols are assigned to each cutpoint. Up to 35 cut points can be specified. Specify values separated by blanks or commas. The number of cutpoints is one less than the number of intervals.

Example

```
PLOT CUTPOINT=EVERY(2) /PLOT=Y WITH X.
PLOT CUTPOINT=(5,10,20) /PLOT=Y WITH X.
```

- In the first PLOT command, 1 or 2 cases at a position are represented by a 1; 3 or 4 cases by a 2; and so forth.
- In the second PLOT command, 1 to 5 cases at a position are represented by a 1; 6 to 10 cases by a 2; 11 to 20 cases by a 3; and 21 or more cases by a 4.

VSIZE and HSIZE Subcommands

VSIZE and HSIZE control length and width of the plot, respectively.

- VSIZE and HSIZE can each be used only once per PLOT command and apply to all plots requested.

- The default size of a plot depends on the system page size, which is controlled by the SET command. With a page width of 79 horizontal print positions and a page length (vertically) of 24 lines, the default plot size is 38 positions wide by 16 lines long.
- VSIZE and HSIZE each use a single integer as their only specification.
- The plot size specified on VSIZE and HSIZE does not include the plot frame itself or auxiliary information such as titles, axis scale numbers, regression statistics, or symbol table.
- If HSIZE is greater than SET WIDTH, the plot wraps.
- If VSIZE is greater than the length specified on SET LENGTH, VSIZE will override the length, but the symbol table and other information normally printed below a plot will appear on the following page.

VERTICAL and HORIZONTAL Subcommands

VERTICAL and HORIZONTAL control labeling and scaling for the vertical and horizontal axes.

- VERTICAL and HORIZONTAL can each be specified once before each PLOT subcommand and apply only to plots requested by that subcommand.
- If VERTICAL and HORIZONTAL are omitted, all defaults are in effect. If VERTICAL and HORIZONTAL are included, only those defaults explicitly altered are changed.

The following keywords are available for both VERTICAL and HORIZONTAL:

'label'	*Label for axis.* The label can contain up to 40 characters. A label that cannot fit in the frame is truncated. The default is the variable label for the variable plotted on that axis, or the variable name if no variable label has been specified.
MIN (n)	*Minimum axis value.* If you specify a minimum value greater than the observed minimum value, some points will not be included in the plot. The default is the minimum observed value.
MAX (n)	*Maximum axis value.* If you specify a maximum value less than the observed maximum value, some points will not be included in the plot. PLOT may extend the value slightly in order to display integer-scale values of equal width. The default is the maximum observed value.
UNIFORM	*Uniform values on axis.* All plots specified on that PLOT subcommand will have the same scale on that axis. A uniform scale is implied when both MIN and MAX are specified. If UNIFORM is specified, PLOT determines the minimum and maximum observed values across all variables on the PLOT subcommand.
REFERENCE(values)	*Reference lines.* The values at which reference lines should be drawn are separated by blanks or commas. The default is no reference lines.
STANDARDIZE	*Plot standardized variables.* Standardized variables are useful for overlay plots of variables with different scales. The default is to plot observed values.

TITLE Subcommand

TITLE provides titles for plots.

- TITLE can be specified once before each PLOT subcommand and applies to all plots named on that PLOT subcommand.
- The default title for a bivariate scatterplot or regression plot is the names of the variables in the plot. For other plots, the default is the plot type requested on FORMAT.
- The title can be up to 60 characters long and follows the usual rules for specifying strings (see "String Values in Command Specifications" on p. 429.)
- The title is truncated if it exceeds the width specified on the HSIZE subcommand.

MISSING Subcommand

MISSING controls the treatment of cases with missing values. By default, cases with system- or user-missing values for any variables in a plot are omitted from that plot.

- MISSING can be specified only once per PLOT command and applies to all plots requested.
- Keywords LISTWISE and PLOTWISE are alternatives. Either one can be specified with IN-CLUDE. The default is PLOTWISE.

PLOTWISE   *Delete cases with missing values plotwise.* Cases with missing values for any variable in a plot are not included in that plot. In overlay plots, PLOTWISE applies separately to each overlaid plot in the frame, not to the full list specified on the PLOT subcommand.

LISTWISE   *Delete cases with missing values listwise.* Cases with missing values for any variable named on the PLOT subcommand are deleted from all plots specified on that PLOT subcommand.

INCLUDE   *Treat user-missing values as valid values.* Only cases with system-missing values are excluded according to the missing-value treatment specified.

PROCESS IF

```
PROCESS IF [(]variable relational operator value[)]
```

The following relational operators can be used:

Symbol	Definition	Symbol	Definition
EQ or =	Equal to	NE or <> or ~=	Not equal to
LT or <	Less than	LE or <=	Less than or equal to
GT or >	Greater than	GE or >=	Greater than or equal to

Example:
```
PROCESS IF (TYPE EQ 1).
```

Overview

PROCESS IF temporarily designates cases for inclusion in the next procedure.

Basic Specification

The basic specification is a simple logical expression that can be evaluated as true or false. If the logical expression is true for a case, the case is included in the next procedure. See "Logical Expressions" on p. 441 for more information.

Syntax Rules

- Parentheses enclosing the logical expression are optional.
- The logical expression on PROCESS IF can use any one of the six logical operators (EQ, NE, LT, LE, GT, GE) or their symbolic forms (=, <> or ~=, <, <=, >, and >=).
- Logical operators cannot be used on PROCESS IF.
- Only numeric or short string variables can be specified. Long string variables cannot.
- String values must be enclosed in apostrophes or quotation marks and must match the length of the short string being tested.
- PROCESS IF can be entered anywhere in an SPSS/PC+ session, except between BEGIN DATA and END DATA.

Operations

- PROCESS IF temporarily designates cases for inclusion in the next procedure. If the logical expression is true, the case is processed. If it is false or missing, the case is not processed in the next procedure.

- If more than one PROCESS IF command is entered before a procedure, only the last one is in effect.
- PROCESS IF has no effect on SORT CASES and is ignored if SORT CASES is the next procedure.

Example

```
PROCESS IF (AGE GT 50).
```

- Only cases for which variable *AGE* is greater than 50 are included in the next procedure.

Example

```
PROCESS IF (SEX EQ 'MALE  ').
```

- *SEX* is a six-column left-justified variable. The trailing blanks must be included in the value specification.
- The next procedure uses cases in which the value of *SEX* is MALE with two trailing blanks.

QED

Overview

The QED command accesses QED, a data manipulation system within SPSS/PC+. It allows you to enter and edit data easily, in a format similar to a spreadsheet. QED creates, reads, and writes SPSS/PC+ system files.

Basic Specification

- To access QED, start SPSS/PC+ and run the QED command.
- Within QED, you use the mouse and/or function keys on your keyboard to perform QED functions. The use of the mouse, function keys, and other special keys is described on pp. 642–648. Starting on p. 648 is an overview of the menus and branches of the QED system.

Limitations

- The maximum number of variables allowed in QED is 500. Each 8-character portion of a long string variable counts as one variable toward the 500-variable limit.
- The number of cases is limited only by available memory.

Files in QED

QED reads and writes SPSS/PC+ system files, which contain data and a dictionary that describes the data. It can also work with the SPSS/PC+ active file.

- File functions are provided in QED on the Main Menu. See pp. 650–652 for a description of Main Menu functions.
- Before you can enter or edit data or modify a dictionary in QED you must define a new file or get an existing one, unless you brought the active file from SPSS/PC+. Use the Main Menu function key F2 to get an existing file, or F7 to define a new file
- To use QED to edit any other type of file that can be read by SPSS/PC+, first create an active file in SPSS/PC+ using DATA LIST, TRANSLATE, or IMPORT, and then go to QED to edit the active file.
- System files can be in either compressed or uncompressed form. Uncompressed files require 8 bytes of storage for every numeric value and a multiple of 8 bytes for every string value. Compressed files are usually smaller but require slightly more processing because small integers (from −99 to +155) occupy only one byte.
- Filenames must conform to DOS naming conventions. For a simple explanation of filenames and paths in DOS, see your DOS manual or Chapter 4 in this manual.
- The default extension for SPSS/PC and SPSS/PC+ system files is *.SYS*. You do not need to specify an extension to read or write a system file with the extension *.SYS*. You cannot read or write a file whose name has no extension.

- Do not enclose filenames in apostrophes or quotation marks.
- You can enter a path to specify a file in another directory. If you must specify a very long path, the entry window scrolls horizontally to accept it.
- If you enter QED directly from SPSS/PC+ and bring your active file with you, the phrase <active File> appears in windows where the filename ordinarily appears. To save such a file, you must give it a name.

The Mouse

In QED you can use the mouse. Table 9 lists mouse functions. Use the left mouse button unless the right button is indicated.

Table 9   Mouse functions in QED

Action	Mouse	Keyboard equivalent
Select a function from a menu	Click on the Function	Press a function key
Cancel an operation in progress	Click right mouse button	Esc
When menus are displayed, display Help menus	Click on Help	F1
Display help on a key listed in Help menu	Click on key description	Press a function key
Return to regular menus from Help menus	Click right mouse button	Esc
Display menus in Dictionary branch or Data branch	Click on bottom line of screen	F1
Hide menus in Dictionary branch or Data branch	Click anywhere outside menus	Space
Highlight an item in a list	Click on the item	↓ ↑
Select an item in a list	Double-click on the item	↓ ↑, ↵Enter
Move to a new position in the spreadsheet or data form	Click at the new position	→ ← ↓ ↑
Edit field (underscore cursor)	Double-click on the field	Ctrl-F8
Scroll the spreadsheet window left or right	Click on the arrows at the corners	Ctrl-→ Ctrl-←
Clear a QED message	Click within the message window	Space
Scroll a QED message that has arrows	Click on arrows	↓ ↑ PgUp PgDn
Accept an edited field and move to new field	Click on new field	↵Enter, ↓ ↑ → ←

Table 9   Mouse functions in QED (Continued)

Action	Mouse	Keyboard equivalent
Accept an edited field	Click	⏎Enter
Display variable definition window in Dictionary branch	Double-click on a variable	F3
Move to a new position in the Value Labels window	Click at the new position	⬇ ⬆
Exit from QED	Click on bottom line, then click on Exit	⇧Shift-F10

Function Keys

The function keys F1 through F10 invoke QED commands.

- Used alone, they perform the basic functions you need to define a file, enter data, and so forth. The command associated with each function key varies depending on whether you are at the Main Menu or in one of the two branches (Dictionary or Data). F1 always displays a menu showing what the function keys do. The use of function keys in each part of QED is described under "Menus and Branches" on p. 648.

- The up arrow to the left of each function key on the Main Menu indicates that you can execute Main Menu functions directly from the Data and Dictionary branches by holding down ⇧Shift while you press the function key, without having to press Esc to first return to the opening Main Menu display.

- Holding down Ctrl activates a group of useful functions that are available in both branches of QED. Ctrl is indicated on menus by the symbol ^. For example, you can always get dictionary information on any of your variables by pressing Ctrl F9, listed as ^F9 VarInfo on the Ctrl menu. Some of these functions apply to the field at which the cursor is placed and therefore work only when the cursor is on a field. For more information on these functions, see "Ctrl Menu" on p. 664.

The Cursor

The cursor marks the active spot on the screen. It appears in two forms:

- When you are typing or editing text on the screen, the cursor appears as a blinking *underscore* character. The cursor arrow keys move the cursor one character at a time.

- When you are moving among different fields on a selection menu, data-entry form, or spreadsheet, QED highlights an entire *field*. The cursor arrow keys move the cursor from one field to the next.

If you start typing when the cursor is in a highlighted field, any characters that were in that field are replaced by the text you type. If you want to edit just a few characters in a field rather than replace the entire field, switch to an underscore cursor by pressing Ctrl-F8.

Help

QED provides immediate online help at two levels, both reached through the function key ⓕ1. When you press ⓕ1 from anywhere within QED, the menus are displayed, as shown in Figure 2.

Figure 2   Data branch menus

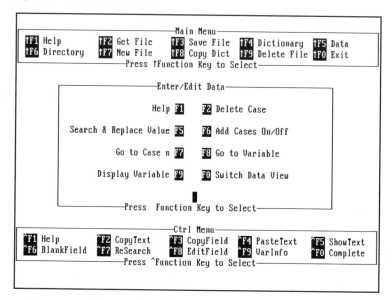

- The menu at the top shows how to move into another branch. The up arrow ⬆ preceding the function keys ⓕ1, ⓕ2, and so on, indicates that you must hold down ⇧Shift to issue these commands.

- The menu in the center shows the functions available in the current branch of QED (the Data branch is shown in Figure 2).

- The bottom menu shows the general-purpose functions available by using Ctrl with a function key. The caret ^ indicates the Ctrl key.

When the menus are on the screen, you can get help on any of the commands listed:

- Press ⓕ1 while the menu is on screen. The text at the bottom of the menu changes from Press Function Key to Select to Press Function Key for Help. Press the function key for which you want help.

- If you want help on more than one function key, clear the help message by pressing Space and then press the next function key for which you want help.

- To leave the help system, press Esc. The text on the menus changes back to Press Function Key to Select. You *must* press Esc to continue working with QED.

- To get help for a function in the other branch, shift to that branch before entering the help system.

Other Important Keys

In addition to function keys, QED uses some of the other keys on your keyboard in special ways.

Shift and Ctrl

The ⟨⇧Shift⟩ and ⟨Ctrl⟩ keys have no effect by themselves but modify the effect of other keys.

- ⟨⇧Shift⟩ and ⟨Ctrl⟩ modify the effect of function keys, as described in "Function Keys" on p. 643.
- ⟨⇧Shift⟩ produces capital letters and other shifted characters as indicated on the keyboard. On many keyboards it makes the cursor-movement keys function as a numeric keypad.
- ⟨Ctrl⟩ affects the action of cursor-movement keys (see "Cursor Movement" on p. 660).
- ⟨Ctrl⟩ is used with ⟨Break⟩ to interrupt QED (see "Break" on p. 645).

Other "control sequences" have no special meaning in QED.

Escape

⟨Esc⟩ cancels an operation in progress. Clicking the right mouse button is always equivalent to pressing ⟨Esc⟩.

- When QED displays a window for you to make a selection or enter information, ⟨Esc⟩ removes the window and cancels the command that opened the window.
- When you are editing a field, ⟨Esc⟩ cancels any changes you have made.
- When no operation is pending, ⟨Esc⟩ takes you out of your current branch to the Main Menu.

If the system does not respond to a command, you have probably forgotten about a pending operation. Pressing ⟨Esc⟩ will normally allow you to resume work.

Break

- If you hold down ⟨Ctrl⟩ and press ⟨Break⟩, you can interrupt any operation without leaving QED. This is equivalent to pressing ⟨Esc⟩, except that ⟨Ctrl⟩-⟨Break⟩ is recognized even when QED is not expecting you to type anything.
- Use ⟨Ctrl⟩-⟨Break⟩ to cancel operations that require a lot of processing, such as reading or writing a large file.

Text Editing Keys

QED uses the special text-editing keys on the PC keyboard in familiar ways.

Enter

- If you are filling in an entry window, ⏎Enter completes the current field and moves the cursor to the next field.

Delete

- Del deletes the character at the cursor position. The cursor remains where it is, and any text to the right shifts left.

CapsLock and NumLock

- CapsLock shifts all alphabetical characters into upper case.
- NumLock activates the numeric keypad.
- Neither CapsLock nor NumLock affects the function keys.
- The letters Num or Caps appear near the right corner of the status line (the last line on the screen) when NumLock or CapsLock is activated.

Insert Mode

Pressing Ins puts your keyboard into insert mode; pressing it again returns it to normal (over-strike) mode.

- In insert mode, characters you type are inserted at the cursor position. The character at the cursor position, and all characters to the right, shift to make room for them.
- Ins appears near the right corner of the status line whenever your keyboard is in insert mode.
- If NumLock is activated, Ins functions as the number 0 on many keyboards. You must de-activate NumLock before turning insert mode on or off.

Home and End

- Home moves the cursor to the "beginning" of the page or screen. End normally moves the cursor to the bottom left of a page. The specific effects of these keys in each branch are described in the sections on QED branches beginning on p. 652.
- Ctrl modifies the effect of Home and End. These combinations typically move you to the beginning or end of the entire file or form, rather than simply to the beginning or end of the page. Details are given in the discussion of each branch beginning on p. 652.
- On some keyboards, Home and End represent numerals when NumLock is activated.

Cursor Arrows

- When you are editing text and the cursor appears as a blinking underscore, the cursor arrows move the cursor from space to space.

- In spreadsheet mode in the Data branch, Ctrl-← moves to the beginning of the current line, and Ctrl-→ moves to the end of the current line.
- In the Data branch, the cursor keys normally move the cursor from field to field. You can use Ctrl-F8 (Edit Field) to use the cursor keys to move within a field in the Data or Dictionary branch.
- On many keyboards, the cursor arrows are numerals when NumLock is activated.

Tab

- Tab→ moves the cursor to the next "item," and ⇧Shift-Tab→ moves it to the previous item. The items vary between the two branches but are usually entry fields.

Windows

QED displays and accepts information in windows. In each branch you work from one or two **home windows**, which are used for the main work of that branch. On top of these, QED displays temporary windows as needed. These include

- **Information windows**, which may contain information you request, a description of a file QED has read or written, or an explanation of why a command cannot be executed. You can remove an information window by pressing Space.
- **Entry windows**, where you type information. After you type the required information, press ⏎Enter.
- **Selection menus**, where you choose among listed alternatives. After you make a selection, press ⏎Enter.

You can remove any temporary window by pressing Esc. Pressing Esc to remove an entry window or a selection menu cancels the command that caused QED to display the window.

Selection Menus

A selection menu displays a list of possibilities from which you can choose.

- On any selection menu, the current selection is highlighted or shown in reverse video. This is the cursor location within the selection menu. You can move from item to item with the cursor movement keys or the mouse.
- To select the item at the cursor position, press ⏎Enter or double-click on the item.

You can also use *incremental search* to move around a selection menu.

- Simply start typing the name of the item you want to select.
- The characters you type appear in the status line at the bottom left of the screen. The cursor moves to the first item (after the place where the cursor was when you first began to type) whose name matches the characters in the status line. You can search for additional items matching the same characters by pressing Ctrl-F7 (ReSearch).
- If you press ⏎Enter during an incremental search, you select the item at the cursor position.

- If you use one of the cursor movement keys, the cursor moves from its current position and the characters in the status line disappear.
- If you press ⟨←Backspace⟩, QED deletes characters from the status line.
- Incremental search will wrap around to the top of the menu but does not search past the place where it started.

The Status Line

QED uses the bottom line on the screen to report information about the status of your session.

- The middle of this line always shows which branch of the system you are in.
- The right side shows if ⟨Ins⟩, ⟨NumLock⟩, or ⟨CapsLock⟩ are activated.
- The left side occasionally displays brief messages.

Printing

You can also print the contents of any screen whenever you like by pressing ⟨PrintScreen⟩. The function depends on the formats that your printer will accept. The combination of ⟨Ctrl⟩ and ⟨PrintScreen⟩, which in some programs turns on continuous printing of screen contents, does not work in QED.

Leaving QED

- To leave QED, ⟨⇧Shift⟩-⟨F10⟩ at any point where QED will accept a command. If you have entered or changed information without saving, QED reminds you to save your work before leaving.
- If temporary windows are on screen, you first must remove them either by entering information and pressing ⟨←Enter⟩, by pressing ⟨Space⟩ (to remove an information window), or by pressing ⟨Esc⟩.
- When you return to SPSS/PC+ from QED, your QED file becomes the SPSS/PC+ active file. Remember to save the file before leaving SPSS/PC+.

Menus and Branches

QED is organized into a Main Menu and two branches: the Dictionary branch and the Data branch. QED also includes a Ctrl menu that provides global functions. The Main Menu is described on pp. 648–652; the Dictionary branch is described beginning on p. 652, and the Data branch begins on p. 659. The Ctrl menu is described on pp. 664–667.

Main Menu

The Main Menu gives you access to the two QED branches and provides functions that allow you to define a new file, read and write existing files, view a directory of available files on disk, or copy a dictionary from an existing file to a new file. Table 10 lists the Main Menu functions.

When you first enter QED with no active file, the Main Menu is displayed with the Ctrl menu. (If you enter QED with active file from SPSS/PC+, QED goes immediately to the Data branch). These are the *opening menus*, as shown in Figure 3. The Main Menu is also displayed at the top of the menu display in the Dictionary and Data branches.

Table 10   Main Menu function keys

Key	Function
F1	Help
F2	Get SPSS system file
F3	Save SPSS system file
F4	Go to Dictionary branch
F5	Go to Data branch
F6	Display directory information
F7	Define new file
F8	Copy Dictionary from an existing file to a new file
F9	Delete file
F10	Exit

Figure 0   Opening menus: Main and Ctrl

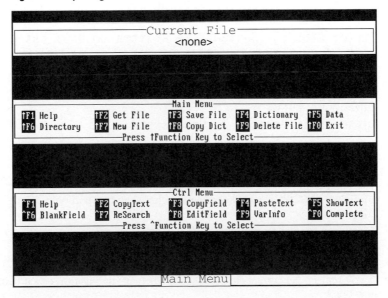

- To use Main Menu functions, press the indicated function key while holding down ⟨⇧Shift⟩. (When you are at the opening menus, pressing ⟨⇧Shift⟩ for Main Menu functions is optional.)
- Function keys ⟨⇧Shift⟩-⟨F4⟩ and ⟨⇧Shift⟩-⟨F5⟩ move you to one of the two QED branches.
- ⟨F1⟩ is the help key.
- ⟨⇧Shift⟩-⟨F10⟩ leaves the QED system.
- You can return to the opening menus from either branch of QED by pressing ⟨Esc⟩. If temporary windows are on the screen, you may have to press ⟨Esc⟩ more than once.

Home Window

When the opening windows are displayed, the home window simply names the current active file. You perform all functions by pressing the appropriate function key.

F2: Get File

Read a file from disk.

1. When you press ⟨F2⟩, an entry window asks you to type the name of the file. Type the filename and press ⟨↵Enter⟩.

2. After reading the dictionary of the file you specify, QED displays an information window (see Figure 4).

Figure 4   Information window

```
┌───────────────────────class.sys───────────────────────┐
│                                                        │
│  Title: SPSS/PC+ System File Written by Data Entry II  │
│  Date of Creation   :  9/21/92                         │
│  Time of Creation   : 10:39:18                         │
│  Number of Variables: 3 (6)                            │
│  Number of cases    : 5                                │
│  System File Version 2, Compressed                     │
│                                                        │
└──────────────────Press space to continue──────────────┘
```

- The number in parentheses following the number of variables is the variable count according to SPSS/PC+, which considers each 8-character portion of a long string as a separate variable.
- Press ⟨Space⟩ or ⟨Esc⟩ to remove the window and then proceed (normally by shifting to the Data or Dictionary branch).
- The file you specify replaces any file you have been working with.
- If you replace the current file, QED asks whether you wish to save it before getting the new one.

- QED does not read the data from the system file until it needs to display it and keeps only a portion of the data in memory; the rest of the file remains on disk. The system file must therefore be available as long as the file is active in QED.
- If you have SPSS/PC+ system files stored on diskette, you should copy them to the hard disk before using them with QED. This greatly speeds processing.

F3: Save File

Write the current file to disk.

1. When you press (F3), an entry window appears with the name of the current file. Press (←Enter) to save the file with that name, or type another name if you wish to save with another name. Press (Esc) to cancel the request.

2. An entry window asks whether to save the file in compressed or uncompressed form (see "Files in QED" on p. 641 for information on file compression). If the file was read from disk or if you brought an active file from SPSS/PC+, the default is the form of the input file.

3. After saving the file, QED displays a window giving information about the saved file. Press (Space) to clear the information window.

- QED holds only those cases in memory that you have modified. Unchanged cases are transferred directly from the input file.
- When saving a file under the same name as that with which it was read, QED does not delete the input file until it has written the output file. Thus, diskspace must be available for both the input and the output copies. This is a serious limitation for files on floppy diskettes. If possible, copy the file to the hard disk before getting it with QED.

F4: Dictionary

Shift to the Dictionary branch. The system displays the menus for the Dictionary branch (see "Dictionary Branch" on p. 652).

F5: Data

Shift to the Data branch. The system displays the menus for the Data branch (see "Dictionary Branch" on p. 652).

F6: Directory of Files

Display DOS directory information.

1. When you press (F6), an entry window appears for you to enter a file specification. Press (←Enter) to display all files in the current directory, or type in a file specification and then press (←Enter).

2. An information window containing the directory information is displayed. This window scrolls vertically if there are more files than will fit on the screen

- The file specification can include a path and may include DOS wildcard characters.

F7: New File

Define a new system file.

1. When you press (F7), an entry window asks you to supply a filename for the new file.

2. After you name the file, the usual next step is to press (F4) to go to the Dictionary branch and define the dictionary of the new file.

• If you give a filename that already exists on disk and later try to save the file by pressing (F3), you are asked if you want to replace the existing file.

• If you have an active file that you have changed in QED, a warning message reminds you that changes to the current file will be lost if you define a new file.

F8: Copy Dictionary

Create a new file just like an existing file, but with no data.

1. When you press (F8), QED asks you first for the name of the source file, which must be an existing system file on disk, and then for the name of the new file, which will become your active file.

2. If you have an active file, you are asked to confirm that you want to replace it.

• If the name you give for the new file exists on disk and you later try to save the file by pressing (F3), you are asked to confirm that you intend to replace it on disk.

• This function produces an active file with variable definitions and labels. The file contains no data.

F9: Delete File

Delete a file from disk.

1. When you press (F9), an entry window asks you to enter a file specification. Press (←Enter) after you have entered the specification.

• QED provides this function so that you can free diskspace to save your file.

• The file specification can include a path but not wildcard characters.

• You can delete only one file at a time.

• The filename must include an extension.

• You can delete any type of file, not just SPSS/PC+ system files.

• You cannot delete any file that QED needs, including the system file from which QED read the active file.

Dictionary Branch

The Dictionary branch allows you to define the variables in your file or to modify the variable definitions in an existing file. The Dictionary branch function keys are listed in Table 11 and are described on pp. 653–659.

- Within a single session, you cannot add or delete variables from the dictionary after adding or modifying data. To change the dictionary after modifying data, you must first save and then retrieve the file.

Changing the dictionary of an existing data file has the following consequences:

- New variables will have system-missing values for existing cases.
- If you delete variables, they will be removed from the form and spreadsheet in the Data branch.
- Changing the width of a variable affects the corresponding field on the form or spreadsheet.
- Where possible, QED warns you of the consequences of changing the dictionary.

Table 11   Dictionary branch function keys

Key	Function
F1	Help
F2	Define variable
F3	Edit variable
F4	Copy variable
F5	Edit value labels
F6	Copy value labels
F7	Delete variable

Home Window

The home window in the Dictionary branch is a selection menu that lists all variables in the file. If no variables are defined, the home window is blank.

- For most operations, you move the cursor to a particular variable in the menu and then press a function key to carry out the operation, or use the mouse to select a function. See "The Mouse" on p. 676 for mouse functions.
- Variables appear in the menu in alphabetical order.
- Pressing ⏎Enter from the home window has the same effect as F3 (see "F3: Edit Variable" on p. 656).

F2: Define Variable

Add a new variable to the dictionary. An entry window containing fields for variable definition is displayed (see Figure 5).

Figure 5   Entry window for variable definition

```
Variable Name      █████
Variable Label
Type of Variable  Numeric
Variable Length   1
Decimal Places    0
Display Mode      Edit
Missing
                          ─Press ^F10 to complete─────────
```

- Only the variable name is required.
- (⏎Enter) moves you from field to field. When you reach the bottom of the entry window, you return to the first field, Variable Name.
- To define the variable, you must press (Ctrl)-(F10) (Complete Function).
- Pressing (Esc) before completing the definition of a variable returns you to the home window. The variable definition is cancelled.
- If you have typed information in a field but have not pressed (⏎Enter), pressing (Esc) cancels what you have typed. Press (Esc) a second time to cancel the variable definition.
- Normally, anything you type replaces the previous contents of the highlighted field.
- To edit the existing contents of a field, press (Ctrl)-(F8) (Edit Field). An underscore cursor appears in the field, and you can edit it as needed. When you move to the next field by pressing (⏎Enter), the Edit Field function is no longer in effect.

Variable Name

- The variable name is the only attribute you must supply. Other attributes are optional or have default values.
- Variable names follow the usual SPSS/PC+ conventions (see "Variable Names" on p. 434).

Variable Label

- The variable label is optional.
- The variable label can contain up to 60 characters. The characters can be any printable ASCII characters.
- The label is used in SPSS/PC+ and on the data-entry form in QED.
- Do not enclose the label in apostrophes or quotation marks unless you want these characters to be part of the label.
- If you enter nothing, no label is defined.

- To enter a blank label for use in SPSS/PC+ Tables, type a space. To enter a null label, type two adjacent apostrophes. The apostrophes will be displayed in QED, but will be recognized as a null label by SPSS/PC+ Tables.

Type of Variable

- The choices are String and Numeric. For an explanation of these variable types, see "Variable Type" on p. 436.
- The current type (initially Numeric) is highlighted.
- Move the cursor to highlight the type you want to select and press ⏎Enter.
- String variables are treated simply as strings of printable characters. You cannot use them in calculations even if they are numeric characters.
- You must enter numeric variables in valid numeric format.
- The values of numeric variables can contain decimal points, but SPSS/PC+ and QED displays decimal values only if you specify them on the field for decimal places (see "Decimal Places" on p. 655).

Variable Length

- Specify the number of positions needed to display the longest possible values of the variable. The default is 1.
- The maximum length of a numeric variable is 20 characters. If you expect fractional or negative values, leave space for the decimal point and minus sign.
- The maximum length of a string variable is 255 characters. However, most procedures can tabulate only the first eight characters of string variables, and only REPORT can handle very long strings.
- The length of a string variable determines the amount of storage allocated and cannot be changed once the variable is defined.
- You can change the length of numeric variables.
- The length affects only the display of values in QED and SPSS/PC+ and the width of the field in which you enter values in forms and spreadsheets. Numeric values are always stored internally in full precision (technically, as 8-byte floating-point numbers), regardless of the display length you specify.
- Numeric values that are too long to be displayed in the specified length are rounded off for display, if possible, and otherwise are displayed as asterisks.

Decimal Places

- The specification is the number of decimal places to display. Decimals must also be entered in the data to be displayed.
- This specification is optional. If it is omitted, QED does not display decimal places, even if they are entered in the data.
- This specification affects neither the entry of values nor their internal representation.
- The variable length must be large enough to accommodate decimal places and the decimal point. Otherwise, the value is rounded for display.

Display Mode

The display mode is listed for your information. Variables created in QED are always in Edit mode. However, if you created or edited the file in SPSS Data Entry II, it may have a different mode (either Verify or Display). See the *SPSS Data Entry II* manual for more information.

Missing Value

- For each variable you can define a value that indicates missing information. For example, you might use the value 9 to indicate that a subject refused to answer a survey question and then define 9 as the missing value.

- Missing values are optional.

- Declaring a missing value does not affect data entry in QED.

- The missing value for numeric variables must be a number. The missing value can be longer than the variable length, but you will not be able to enter such values in QED unless you increase the variable length.

- For short string variables, the missing value must be a string. Long string variables (longer than 8 characters) cannot have missing values.

- The missing value for a string variable cannot exceed the variable length. If the value you specify is shorter than the variable length, it is right-padded with blanks.

F3: Edit Variable

Change the definition of an existing variable. This function allows you to edit the definition of the variable that is highlighted in the home window.

1. Select a variable and press F3 (or select a variable and press ⏎Enter).

2. The variable definition window is displayed, showing the current attributes of the variable (Figure 5). Press ⏎Enter to move from field to field, changing attributes as you like.

3. Press Ctrl F10 to complete the function or Esc to cancel your changes.

- You cannot change the variable name.

- You cannot change string variables to numeric or numeric variables to string.

- You cannot change the length of a string variable.

F4: Copy Variable

Create a new variable with the attributes of an existing variable. This function allows you to replicate a variable definition, changing selected attributes as needed.

1. Select a variable and press F4.

- The variable-definition window is displayed, showing the attributes of the selected variable but no variable name (Figure 5). You must specify a new variable name. You can change any of the other attributes as desired.

2. Press Ctrl-F10 to define the new variable or Esc to cancel the definition.

- You can change the variable type (from numeric to string or from string to numeric) immediately after making the copy.

- You can change the length of a copied string variable.
- To make editing changes within a field, press Ctrl-F8 (Edit Field). An underscore cursor appears within the selected field, and you can edit it as needed.
- This function also copies value labels, unless you change the variable type or the length of a string variable.
- If you change the variable type or if you change a a short string (8 characters or less) to a long string, any missing-value definition is discarded.
- If you reduce the length of a short string variable, the missing value is truncated to the new length.
- Once you press Ctrl-F10 to complete the definition, you can no longer change the variable type or the length of a string variable.

F5: Edit Value Labels

Add or revise value labels for existing variables. This function allows you to attach labels to the individual values of a variable for use within SPSS/PC+.

1. Select a variable and press F5.

2. A window appears for you to enter value labels (Figure 6). To assign a label to a value, enter the value, press ↵Enter, enter the label, and press ↵Enter again. To edit an existing label, press Ctrl-F8 (Edit Field). An underscore cursor appears within the selected field, and you can edit it as needed. To delete an existing label, press Del to erase either the value or the label.

3. Press Ctrl-F10 to save all the labels you have entered or Esc to cancel all additions you have made in the variable labels window.

Figure 6   Entry window for value labels

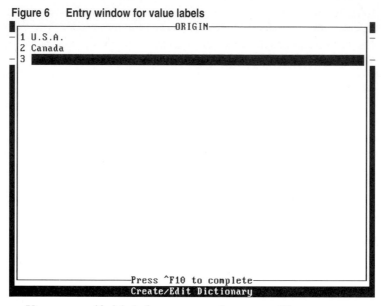

- You can specify labels for as many values as you like.
- You can use ⌈Ctrl⌉-⌈F2⌉ (Copy Text) and ⌈Ctrl⌉-⌈F4⌉ (Paste Text) to copy labels.
- A value label can be up to 60 characters long. However, most SPSS/PC+ procedures use only the first 20 characters.
- You can specify labels for the values of short string variables but not long string variables.
- Do not enclose string values in apostrophes or quotation marks.
- To specify a null label for use in SPSS/PC+ Tables, enter two apostrophes as the only characters in the label.
- The entry window sorts values, using the variable length and decimal places that are defined for the variable. For a variable with no decimal places defined, the values 5 and 5.1 will both appear as 5. You can change the number of decimal places to display in the variable definition window (press ⌈Esc⌉ and then ⌈F3⌉).
- You cannot assign a label to a numeric value that is longer than the length defined for the variable.

F6: Copy Value Labels

Copy all value labels from one variable to another.

1. First, move the cursor to highlight the variable whose labels you want to copy and press ⌈F6⌉. Copy labels to variable? appears in the status line.

2. Move the cursor to highlight the variable to which you want to copy the labels, and press ⌈↵Enter⌉. QED confirms the action by displaying the message labels copied in the status line.

- You can copy value labels only between numeric variables or between short string variables that have the same defined length.
- If you copy labels to a numeric variable whose defined length is too short to accommodate some of the copied values, those values will appear as asterisks in the value labels window for the new variable.

F7: Delete Variable

Delete a variable from the file.

1. Highlight the variable you want to delete and press F7.

2. QED will ask you for confirmation before deleting the variable.

- If the file contains data, the data for dropped variables will be dropped from the active file.

Data Branch

In the Data branch you can enter, change, and display data. The functions available in the Data branch are listed in Table 12 and are described on pp. 662–664.

- You cannot enter the Data branch unless you have defined a dictionary, either within QED or by getting a file previously saved on disk.
- You enter or edit data by typing it in and pressing ⏎Enter. What you type replaces the existing contents of the field, if any, and the cursor moves to the next field. At any time you can override the default entry order and move the cursor directly to any field (any variable of any case). See "Cursor Movement" on p. 660 for more information.
- To add cases to the file, press F6 (Add Cases). This moves you to the end of the file and allows you to enter new cases. The message <Add Cases On> appears in the status line until you press F6 again. You cannot add cases in the middle of the file.
- QED does not accept data under the following conditions: the data do not agree with the variable type (for example, letters in a numeric field), or the data are too long for the field.

Table 12   Data branch function keys

Key	Function
F1	Help
F2	Delete case
F5	Search & replace value
F6	Add cases on/off
F7	Go to case n
F8	Go to variable
F9	Display variable
F10	Switch data view (form or spreadsheet)

Cursor Movement

You can move the cursor in the Data branch by using the mouse or by using the following keys. See "The Mouse" on p. 642 for mouse functions.

- ⟨→⟩ moves to the next variable in the entry order or to the next case if the cursor is at the last variable.
- ⟨←⟩ moves to the previous variable in the entry order or to the previous case if cursor is at the first variable.
- ⟨↓⟩ moves to the next case.
- ⟨↑⟩ moves to the previous case.
- ⟨Tab→⟩ moves to the next variable in the entry order or to the next case if cursor is at the last variable.
- ⟨⇧Shift⟩-⟨Tab→⟩ moves to the previous variable in the entry order or to the previous case if cursor is at the first variable.
- ⟨Ctrl⟩-⟨→⟩ moves to the last variable of the current case.
- ⟨Ctrl⟩-⟨←⟩ moves to the first variable of the current case.
- ⟨Home⟩ moves to the first field on the page in forms mode or the top left of the page in spreadsheet mode.
- ⟨End⟩ moves to the last field on the page in forms mode or the bottom left of the page in spreadsheet mode.
- ⟨Ctrl⟩-⟨Home⟩ moves to the top of the file (first variable of the first case) in either mode.
- ⟨Ctrl⟩-⟨End⟩ moves to the first variable of the last case in either mode. (This is the bottom left of the file in spreadsheet mode.)
- ⟨PgDn⟩ moves down 20 cases in spreadsheet mode or to the next page of a case in form mode (if there is another page).
- ⟨PgUp⟩ moves up 20 cases in spreadsheet mode or the previous page in form mode (if there is another page).
- ⟨Ctrl⟩-⟨PgDn⟩ moves down 20 cases in spreadsheet mode.
- ⟨Ctrl⟩-⟨PgUp⟩ moves up 20 cases in spreadsheet mode.
- QED beeps and leaves the cursor where it is if you use a motion command that is inapplicable, such as ⟨PgUp⟩ on the first page of a form in forms mode.

Home Windows

The Data branch works in two different modes—form and spreadsheet—with a different home window for each. In *spreadsheet mode,* your data file appears as a rectangular array, much like a financial spreadsheet. Each case forms a row, and each variable forms a column (see Figure 7). In *form mode,* the screen looks like a form (see Figure 8). Only one case is visible at a time, showing variable names, variable labels, and data values. You can cycle through the cases by pressing ⟨↓⟩ or ⟨↑⟩.

- When you first enter the Data branch, you are in the spreadsheet window. Forms are displayed by default only if the data file exceeds the limits of the spreadsheet mode.
- You can switch between the two modes at any time by pressing ⟨F10⟩ (Switch Data View).

- The spreadsheet shows all variables in the order they exist in the file.
- The form shows the variable names in the first column in the order they exist in the file. The second column shows variable labels and values for one case. If there are more variables than can be listed on the screen, the remaining variables are listed on succeeding screens. You can go to these screens by pressing PgDn.
- A variable's width and display mode control its appearance both on a form and on the spreadsheet.
- When you switch between modes, the cursor remains on the same data value: the same variable for the same case.
- If you leave the Data branch and later return, the cursor remains on the same data value.

Figure 7   Form window

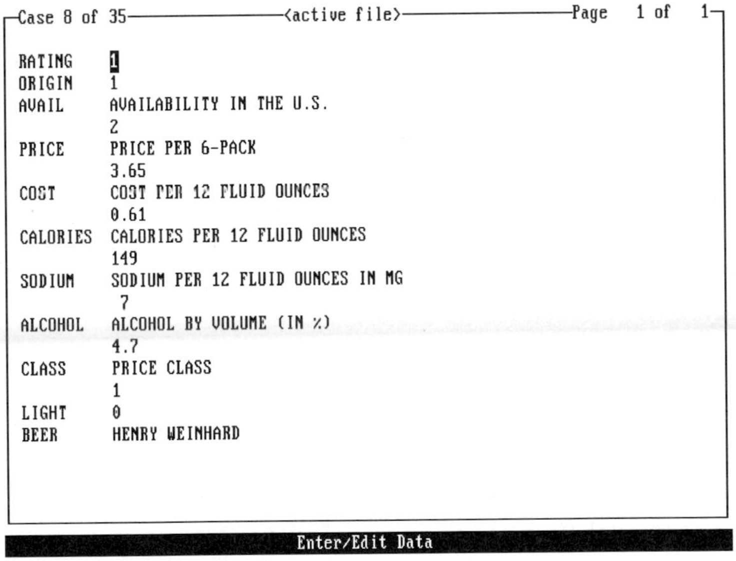

```
┌Case 8 of 35──────────────<active file>──────────Page   1 of   1─┐
│                                                                 │
│   RATING     ▌                                                  │
│   ORIGIN     1                                                  │
│   AVAIL      AVAILABILITY IN THE U.S.                           │
│              2                                                  │
│   PRICE      PRICE PER 6-PACK                                   │
│              3.65                                               │
│   COST       COST PER 12 FLUID OUNCES                           │
│              0.61                                               │
│   CALORIES   CALORIES PER 12 FLUID OUNCES                       │
│              149                                                │
│   SODIUM     SODIUM PER 12 FLUID OUNCES IN MG                   │
│              7                                                  │
│   ALCOHOL    ALCOHOL BY VOLUME (IN %)                           │
│              4.7                                                │
│   CLASS      PRICE CLASS                                        │
│              1                                                  │
│   LIGHT      0                                                  │
│   BEER       HENRY WEINHARD                                     │
│                                                                 │
│                                                                 │
│                                                                 │
└─────────────────────────────────────────────────────────────────┘
            ▐███████████████ Enter/Edit Data ███████████████▌
```

Figure 8   Spreadsheet window

```
                      ┌────────────beer.sys────────────────────┐
                      │RATING ORIGIN AVAIL PRICE COST CALORIES SODIUM ALCOHOL CLASS LIGH│
                        1      1     1   2.49 0.42    149      17     4.7     2
                        1      1     1   2.59 0.43    144      15     4.7     2
                        1      1     1   2.59 0.43    151      19     4.9     2
                        1      1     1   2.89 0.48    157      15     4.9     1
                        1      1     1   2.99 0.50    162      10     5.0     1
                        1      2     2   3.15 0.53    147      17     5.0     0
                        1      2     2   3.35 0.56    154      17     5.1     0
                        1      1     2   3.65 0.61    149       7     4.7     1
                        1      3     2   4.39 0.73    170       7     5.2     0
                        1      4     1   4.59 0.77    152      11     5.0     0
                        1      1     2   7.19 1.20    154      17     4.7     1
                        2      1     2   1.69 0.28    145      23     4.6     3
                        2      1     2   1.79 0.30    147       7     4.7     3
                        2      1     1   2.29 0.38    152       8     4.9     2
                        2      1     2   2.39 0.40    175      24     5.5     1
                        2      1     2   2.49 0.42    149      27     4.7     2
                        2      1     1   2.55 0.43     99      10     4.3     0
                        2      1     1   2.63 0.44    113       8     3.7     0
                        2      1     2   2.65 0.44    140      18     4.6     2
                        2      1     2   2.65 0.44    153      27     4.6     2
                      └──────────────Enter/Edit Data────────────┘
```

F2: Delete Case

Delete the current case.

- QED asks you to confirm this action before it deletes the case.
- After deletion, the cursor moves to the next case. (If you are at the last case, it moves to the previous case.)

F5: Search & Replace Value

Replace values for the variable on which the cursor is sitting.

1. Move the cursor to the variable where you want the search to start and press F5.

2. An entry window asks for the search value. Enter the value that you want to replace the first value.

3. A second window asks for the replacement value. Enter a replacement value.

4. A selection menu lets you specify the extent of the search (Figure 9).You have the option of searching and replacing the value for all cases, all cases following the current case, or the single next occurrence of the specified value. Controlled Replace shows you each occurrence of the specified value starting at the beginning of the file. At each occurrence, QED asks whether to make the replacement.

- This function will search only values of the variable marked by the cursor.

- The search is based in the actual value, including decimal places that may not be shown in the current format. For example, a value of 1.234 shown in F8.2 format as 1.23 will not be changed if you specify 1.23 as the search value. It will be changed if you specify 1.234.

Figure 9   Search and replace

```
                          ┌─────────────beer.sys─────────────┐
   35│AIL PRICE COST [CALORIES] SODIUM ALCOHOL CLASS LIGHT                    BEER│
  ┌──┼────────────────────────────────────────────────────────────────────────┐
  │ 1│  1  2.49 0.42    149     17    4.7     2     0 MILLER HIGH LIFE          │
  │ 2│  1  2.59 0.43    144     15    4.7     2     0 BUDWEISER                 │
  │ 3│  1  2.59 0.43    151     19    4.9     2     0 SCHLITZ                   │
  │ 4│  1  2.89 0.48    157     15    4.9     1     0 LOWENBRAU                 │
  │ 5│  1  2.99 0.50    162     10    5.0     1     0 MICHELOB                  │
  │ 6│  2  3.15 0.53    147     17    5.0     0     0 LABATTS                   │
  │ 7│  2  3.35 0.56    154     17    5.1     0     0 MOLSON                    │
  │ 8│  2  3.65 0.61    149      7    4.7     1     0 HENRY WEINHARD            │
  │ 9│  2  4.39 0.73    170      7    5.2     0     0 KRONENBOURG               │
  │10│  1  4.59 0.77   [152]    11    5.0     0     0 HEINEKEN                  │
  │11│  2  7.19 1.20    154     17    4.7     1     0 ANCHOR STEAM              │
  │12│  2  1.69 0.28    145     23    4.6     3     0 OLD MILWAUKEE             │
  │13│  2  1.79 0.30    147      7    4.7     3     0 SCHMIDTS                  │
  │14│  1  2.29 0.38    152      8    4.9     2     0 PABST BLUE RIBBON         │
  │15│  2  2.39 0.40    175     24    5.5     1     0 AUGSBERGER                │
  │16│  2  2.49 0.42   ┌──────Search mode──────┐    0 STROHS BOHEMIAN STYLE    │
  │17│  1  2.55 0.43   │This variable from beginning│ 1 MILLER LITE            │
  │18│  1  2.63 0.44   │This variable from here     │ 1 BUDWEISER LIGHT        │
  │19│  2  2.65 0.44   │Next occurrence in variable │ 0 COORS                  │
  │20│  2  2.65 0.44   │Controlled replace          │ 0 OLYMPIA                │
  └◄─┴────────────────└────────────────────────────┘─────────────────────────┘
                          Enter/Edit Data
```

F6: Add Cases On/Off

Add cases to the end of the file. This function turns Add Cases on and off.

1. When you press [F6] to turn the function on, the cursor moves to the last case. You can add cases to the end of the file by moving the cursor to an empty case. Press [↓], or enter a value for the last variable in the last case to move the cursor to a new case.

2. When you are entering data for the last case, turn this function off by pressing [F6] before you complete the case. Otherwise QED continues creating cases.

- When this function is on, the message Add Cases On appears in the status line.
- You can add cases only if the display mode of every variable in the file is Edit. If any variable is in Display or Verify mode, you cannot add cases. Variables can be in these modes only if you previously edited the file in SPSS Data Entry II.

F7: Go to Case n

Move the cursor to a specific case.

1. When you press [F7], an entry box requests the number of the case.

2. Type in a number and press [←Enter]. The cursor moves to that case.

- If you enter a number greater than the number of cases in the file, the cursor moves to the last case.
- The case number refers to the sequential position of the case within the file, not to the SPSS/PC+ system variable *$CASENUM*.

F8: Go to Variable

Move the cursor to a specific variable.

1. When you press F8, a selection menu appears showing all variables in the file.

2. Select a variable with the cursor arrows or with incremental search and press ⏎Enter.

3. The cursor moves to that variable within the current case.

F9: Display Variable

Show dictionary information for the field at the cursor location. This is a quick way of verifying which variable corresponds to a field.

- When you press F9, an information window displays the name, label, type, length, decimal places, display mode, and missing value for the variable associated with that field.
- QED displays the same information window as Ctrl-F9 from anywhere in the system.

F10: Switch Data View

Switch between the form and spreadsheet display. This function switches back and forth between the two displays.

- The cursor remains on the same data value when you switch the display.

Ctrl Menu

The Ctrl menu lists global functions, which work the same in both the Data and Dictionary branches. The functions are listed in Table 13.

- To use a Ctrl function, hold down Ctrl and press the appropriate function key.
- The Ctrl menu is displayed with the Main Menu when you first enter the system and also at the bottom of all branch menu displays.
- In the Ctrl menu the Ctrl key is represented by a caret (^).
- Functions Ctrl-F2 through Ctrl-F6 are for text and data editing.
- Functions Ctrl-F7 through Ctrl-F10 are general utilities.
- Ctrl-F10 (Complete Function) is required to complete operations wherever ⏎Enter is used to move the cursor.

Table 13   Ctrl Menu function keys

Key	Function
F1	Help
F2	Copy text
F3	Copy field
F4	Paste text
F5	Show text
F6	Blank field
F7	ReSearch
F8	Edit field
F9	Variable information
F10	Complete

Editing Functions

The editing functions on the Ctrl menu allow you to copy and paste text anywhere that you can type text.

- Text that you copy is kept in a **copy buffer**, a portion of memory reserved by the Ctrl editing functions.
- You can copy and paste any text that you can put the cursor on. This includes a filename; any element (or part of an element) of a variable definition in the Dictionary branch; or any data value (or part of one) in the Data branch.
- Text in the copy buffer is treated simply as a string of characters. QED will copy text without regard to any meaning it may have (for example, as a variable name or a data value).
- You can copy text between unrelated parts of the system.

F2: Copy Text

Copy text into the copy buffer. This function moves a rectangular block of text from anywhere on the screen into the copy buffer.

1. Move the cursor to one corner of the rectangle you want to copy.

2. Press Ctrl-F2. The character under the cursor changes to reverse video.

3. Move the cursor to the opposite corner of the rectangle you want to copy. As you move, a reverse-video rectangle appears on the screen.

4. When the rectangle contains the text you want to copy, press ↵Enter and the screen returns to normal.

5. The text in the rectangle has been copied to the copy buffer.

F3: Copy Field

Copy the contents of an input or editing field into the buffer. A *field* is an entry area in the Data branch or in an entry window. This command is a shorthand way of copying the entire contents of a field without having to mark the field using [Ctrl]-[F2].

1. Place the cursor anywhere on the field and press [Ctrl]-[F3].

2. The text in the field is copied to the copy buffer.

F4: Paste Text

Place the contents of the copy buffer at the position of the cursor.

1. Place the cursor where you want to paste the text and press [Ctrl]-[F4].

2. Depending on whether you are in insert mode, the text in the copy buffer either is inserted or replaces existing text, starting at the cursor location. (See "Insert Mode" on p. 646.)

- You can paste only as much of the rectangle as will fit in the field.

- You can paste only text where you can type text.

- The paste function can paste into a single field at a time only. You cannot, for example, paste into more than one cell in the spreadsheet.

F5: Show Text

Display the contents of the copy buffer. When you press [Ctrl]-[F5], an information window displays the contents of the copy buffer. You can remove the window with [Space].

F6: Blank Field

Blank out the contents of an input or editing field.

1. Place the cursor anywhere in the field and press [Ctrl]-[F6].

2. QED replaces the field with blanks.

- The Data branch interprets a blank numeric field as system-missing.

Utility Functions

Function keys [F7] through [F10] are general-purpose utilities. The function [Ctrl]-[F10] (Complete Function) is required when you are defining variables. The others are optional, but sometimes handy.

F7: ReSearch

Search again for the same characters in a selection menu. This function applies to incremental search. Each character you type moves the cursor to the first occurrence of the characters typed so far. To search for subsequent occurrences of the same characters, press [Ctrl]-[F7].

F8: Edit Field

Editing within a highlighted field. When an entire entry field is highlighted, anything you type replaces the entire contents of the field. If you press Ctrl-F8, an underscore cursor appears and you can move about within the field to edit individual characters.

F9: Var Info

Display dictionary information about variables in the active file.

1. When you press Ctrl-F9, a selection menu appears showing all variables in the active file, in alphabetical order.

2. Move the cursor to any variable and press ↵Enter. The variable definition window appears as an information window.

3. Press Space to remove the information window and return to the selection menu. Press Esc to return to the home window from which you came.

F10: Complete Function

Complete the function in progress. This is equivalent to pressing ↵Enter whenever ↵Enter confirms an entry or selection. In the following circumstances, ↵Enter is used to move the cursor and you must use Ctrl-F10 to complete a function:

- When defining or editing a variable in the variable definition window in the Dictionary branch.
- When entering or editing value labels in the Dictionary branch.

RANK

```
RANK [VARIABLES=] varlist [({A**})] [BY varlist]
                           {D   }

   [/TIES={MEAN**  }]
          {LOW     }
          {HIGH    }
          {CONDENSE}

   [/FRACTION={BLOM** }]
             {TUKEY  }
             {VW     }
             {RANKIT }

   [/PRINT={YES**}]
          {NO   }

   [/MISSING={EXCLUDE**}]
            {INCLUDE  }
```

The following function subcommands can each be specified once:

```
[/RANK**] [/NTILES(k)] [/NORMAL] [/PERCENT]

[/RFRACTION] [/PROPORTION] [/N] [/SAVAGE]
```

The following keyword can be used with any function subcommand:

```
[INTO varname]
```

**Default if the subcommand is omitted.

Example:
```
RANK VARIABLES=SALARY JOBTIME.
```

Overview

RANK produces new variables containing ranks, normal scores, and Savage and related scores for numeric variables.

Options

Methods. You can rank variables in ascending or descending order by specifying A or D on the VARIABLES subcommand. You can compute different rank functions and also name the new variables using the function subcommands. You can specify the method for handling ties on the TIES subcommand, and you can specify how the proportion estimate is computed for the NORMAL and PROPORTIONAL functions on the FRACTION subcommand.

Format. You can suppress the display of the summary table that lists the ranked variables and their associated new variables in the active file using the PRINT subcommand.

Basic Specification

The basic specification is VARIABLES and at least one variable from the active file. By default, the ranking function is RANK. Direction is ascending, and ties are handled by assigning the mean rank to tied values. A summary table that lists the ranked variables and the new variables into which computed ranks have been stored is displayed.

Subcommand Order

- VARIABLES must be specified first.
- The remaining subcommands can be specified in any order.

Operations

- RANK does not change the way the active file is sorted.
- If new variable names are not specified with the INTO keyword on the function subcommand, RANK creates default names. (See the INTO keyword on p. 671.)
- RANK automatically assigns variable labels to the new variables. The labels identify the source variables. For example, the label for a new variable with the default name *RSALARY* is *RANK of SALARY*.

Example

```
RANK VARIABLES=SALARY JOBTIME.
```

- RANK ranks *SALARY* and *JOBTIME* and creates two new variables in the active file, *RSALARY* and *RJOBTIME*, which contain the ranks.

VARIABLES Subcommand

VARIABLES specifies the variables to be ranked. Keyword VARIABLES can be omitted.

- VARIABLES is required and must be the first specification on RANK. The minimum specification is a single numeric variable. To rank more than one variable, specify a variable list.
- After the variable list, you can specify the direction for ranking in parentheses. Specify A for ascending (smallest value gets smallest rank) or D for descending (largest value gets smallest rank). A is the default.
- To rank some variables in ascending order and others in descending order, use both A and D in the same variable list. A or D applies to all preceding variables in the list up to the previous A or D specification.
- To assign ranks within subgroups, specify keyword BY followed by the variable whose values determine the subgroups. The active file does not have to be sorted by this variable.

- String variables cannot be specified. Use AUTORECODE to recode string variables for ranking.

Example

```
RANK VARIABLES=MURDERS ROBBERY (D).
```

- RANK ranks *MURDERS* and *ROBBERY* and creates two new variables in the active file: *RMURDERS* and *RROBBERY*.
- D specifies descending order of rank. D applies to both *MURDERS* and *ROBBERY*.

Example

```
RANK VARIABLES=MURDERS (D) ROBBERY (A) BY ETHNIC.
```

- Ranks are computed within each group defined by *ETHNIC*. *MURDERS* is ranked in descending order and *ROBBERY* in ascending order within each group of *ETHNIC*. The active file does not have to be sorted by *ETHNIC*.

Function Subcommands

The optional function subcommands specify different rank functions. RANK is the default function.

- Any combination of function subcommands can be specified for a RANK procedure, but each function can be specified only once.
- Each function subcommand must be preceded by a slash.
- The functions assign default names to the new variables unless keyword INTO is specified (see the INTO keyword on p. 671).

RANK — *Simple ranks.* The values for the new variable are the ranks. Rank can either be ascending or descending, as indicated on the VARIABLES subcommand. Rank values can be affected by the specification on the TIES subcommand.

RFRACTION — *Fractional ranks.* The values for the new variable equal the ranks divided by the sum of the weights of the nonmissing cases. If HIGH is specified on TIES, fractional rank values are an empirical cumulative distribution.

NORMAL — *Normal scores* (Lehmann, 1975). The new variable contains the inverse of the standard normal cumulative distribution of the proportion estimate defined by the FRACTION subcommand. The default for FRACTION is BLOM.

PERCENT — *Fractional ranks as a percentage.* The new variable contains fractional ranks multiplied by 100.

PROPORTION — *Proportion estimates.* The estimation method is specified by the FRACTION subcommand. The default for FRACTION is BLOM.

N — *Sum of case weights.* The new variable is a constant.

SAVAGE — *Savage scores* (Lehmann, 1975). The new variable contains Savage (exponential) scores.

NTILES(k)   *Percentile groups.* The new variable contains values from 1 to k, where k is the number of groups to be generated. Each case is assigned a group value, which is the integer part of $1+rk/(W+1)$, where r is the rank of the case, k is the number of groups specified on NTILES, and W is the sum of the case weights. Group values can be affected by the specification on TIES. There is no default for k.

INTO Keyword

INTO specifies variable names for the new variable(s) added to the active file. INTO can be used with any of the function subcommands.

- INTO must follow a function subcommand. You must specify the INTO subcommand to assign names to the new variables created by the function.
- You can specify multiple variable names on INTO. The names are assigned to the new variables in the order they are created (the order the variables are specified on the VARI-ABLES subcommand).
- If you specify fewer names than the new variables, default names are used for the remaining new variables. If you specify more names, SPSS/PC+ issues a message and the command is not executed.

If INTO is not specified on a function, RANK creates default names for the new variables according to the following rules:

- The first letter of the ranking function is added to the first seven characters of the original variable name.
- New variable names cannot duplicate variable names in the active file or names specified after INTO or generated by default.
- If a new default name is a duplicate, the scheme *XXXnnn* is used, where *XXX* represents the first three characters of the function and *nnn* is a three-digit number starting with 001 and increased by 1 for each variable. (If the ranking function is N, *XXX* is simply *N*.) If this naming scheme generates duplicate names, the duplicates are named *RNKXXnn*, where *XX* is the first two characters of the function and *nn* is a two-digit number starting with 01 and increased by 1 for each variable.
- If it is not possible to generate unique names, an error results.

Example

```
RANK VARIABLES=SALARY
 /NORMAL INTO SALNORM
 /SAVAGE INTO SALSAV
 /NTILES(4) INTO SALQUART.
```

- RANK generates three new variables from variable *SALARY*.
- NORMAL produces the new variable *SALNORM*. *SALNORM* contains normal scores for *SALARY* computed with the default formula BLOM.
- SAVAGE produces the new variable *SALSAV*. *SALSAV* contains Savage scores for *SALARY*.

- NTILES(4) produces the new variable *SALQUART*. *SALQUART* contains the value 1, 2, 3, or 4 to represent one of the four percentile groups of *SALARY*.

TIES Subcommand

TIES determines the way tied values are handled. The default method is MEAN.

MEAN   *Mean rank of tied values is used for ties.* This is the default.

LOW   *Lowest rank of tied values is used for ties.*

HIGH   *Highest rank of tied values is used for ties.*

CONDENSE   *Consecutive ranks with ties sharing the same value.* Each distinct value of the ranked variable is assigned a consecutive rank. Ties share the same rank.

Example

```
RANK VARIABLES=BURGLARY /RANK INTO RMEAN /TIES=MEAN.
RANK VARIABLES=BURGLARY /RANK INTO RCONDS /TIES=CONDENSE.
RANK VARIABLES=BURGLARY /RANK INTO RHIGH /TIES=HIGH.
RANK VARIABLES=BURGLARY /RANK INTO RLOW /TIES=LOW.
```

- The values of *BURGLARY* and the four new ranking variables are shown below:

```
BURGLARY   RMEAN    RCONDS   RHIGH    RLOW

    0        3        1        5        1
    0        3        1        5        1
    0        3        1        5        1
    0        3        1        5        1
    0        3        1        5        1
    1        6.5      2        7        6
    1        6.5      2        7        6
    3        8        3        8        8
```

FRACTION Subcommand

FRACTION specifies the way to compute a proportion estimate *P* for the NORMAL and PROPORTION rank functions.

- FRACTION can be used only with function subcommands NORMAL or PROPORTION. If it is used with other function subcommands, FRACTION is ignored and a warning message is displayed.

- Only one formula can be specified for each RANK procedure. If more than one is specified, an error results.

In the following formulas, *r* is the rank and *w* is the sum of case weights ranging from 1 to *w*.

BLOM   *Blom's transformation, defined by the formula $(r - 3/8) / (W + 1/4)$* (Blom, 1958). This is the default.

RANKIT   *The formula is $(r - 1/2) / W$* (Chambers et al., 1983).

TUKEY   *Tukey's transformation, defined by the formula $(r - 1/3) / (W + 1/3)$* (Tukey, 1962).

VW   *Van der Waerden's transformation, defined by the formula r / (W +1)* (Lehmann, 1975).

Example

```
RANK VARIABLES=MORTGAGE VALUE /FRACTION=BLOM
  /NORMAL INTO MORTNORM VALNORM.
```

- RANK generates new variables *MORTNORM* and *VALNORM*. *MORTNORM* contains normal scores for *MORTGAGE*, and *VALNORM* contains normal scores for *VALUE*.

PRINT Subcommand

PRINT determines whether the summary tables are displayed. The summary table lists the ranked variables and their associated new variables in the active file.

YES   *Display the summary tables.* This is the default.

NO   *Suppress the summary tables.*

MISSING Subcommand

MISSING controls the treatment of user-missing values.

INCLUDE *Include user-missing values.* User-missing values are treated as valid values.

EXCLUDE *Exclude all missing values.* User-missing values are treated as missing. This is the default.

Example

```
MISSING VALUE SALARY (0).
RANK VARIABLES=SALARY /RANK INTO SALRANK /MISSING=INCLUDE.
```

- RANK generates the new variable *SALRANK*.
- INCLUDE causes user-missing value 0 to be included in the ranking process.

RECODE

For numeric variables:

```
RECODE varlist (value list=value)...(value list=value)
       [/varlist...]
```

Input keywords:

LO, LOWEST, HI, HIGHEST, THRU, MISSING, SYSMIS, ELSE

Output keywords:

SYSMIS

For string variables:

```
RECODE varlist [('string',['string'...]='string')]
       [/varlist...]
```

Input keywords:

ELSE

Examples:

```
RECODE V1 TO V3 (0=1) (1=0) (2,3=-1) (9=9) (ELSE=SYSMIS).
 RECODE STRNGVAR ('A','B','C'='A')('D','E','F'='B')(ELSE=' ').
```

Overview

RECODE changes, rearranges, or consolidates the values of an existing numeric or string variable. RECODE can be executed on a value-by-value basis or for a range of values. Where it can be used, RECODE is much more efficient than the series of IF commands that produce the same transformation.

With RECODE, you must specify the new values. Use AUTORECODE to automatically recode the values of string or numeric variables to consecutive integers.

Basic Specification

The basic specification is a variable name and, within parentheses, the original values followed by a required equals sign and a new value. RECODE changes the values on the left of the equals sign into the single value on the right of the equals sign.

Syntax Rules

- The variables to be recoded must already exist and must be specified before the value specifications.

- Value specifications are enclosed in parentheses. The original value or values must be specified to the left of an equals sign. A single new value is specified to the right of the equals sign.
- Multiple values can be consolidated into a single recoded value by specifying, to the left of the equals sign, a list of values separated by blanks or commas. Only one recoded value per set is allowed to the right of the equals sign.
- Multiple sets of value specifications are permitted. Each set must be enclosed in parentheses and can result in only one new value.
- To recode multiple variables using the same set of value specifications, specify a variable list before the value specifications. Each variable in the list is recoded identically.
- To recode variables using different value specifications, separate each variable (or variable list) and its specifications from the others by a slash.
- Original values that are not mentioned remain unchanged unless keyword ELSE is used. ELSE refers to all original values not previously mentioned, including the system-missing value. ELSE should be the last specification for the variable.

Numeric Variables

- Keywords that can be used in the list of original values are LO (or LOWEST), HI (or HIGHEST), THRU, MISSING, SYSMIS, and ELSE. The only keyword that can be used in place of a new value is SYSMIS.
- THRU specifies a value range and includes the specified end values.
- LOWEST and HIGHEST (LO and HI) specify the lowest and highest values encountered in the data. LOWEST and HIGHEST include user-missing values but not the system-missing value.
- MISSING specifies user- and system-missing values for recoding. MISSING can be used in the list of original values only.
- SYSMIS specifies the system-missing value and can be used as both an original value and a new value.
- ELSE refers to all original values not previously mentioned, including the system-missing value.

String Variables

- Only short string variables can be recoded.
- Values must be enclosed in apostrophes or quotation marks.
- Blanks are significant characters.
- Input and output values must be specified according to the defined width of the variable.
- ELSE can be used as an input value to refer to all original values not previously mentioned, including the system-missing value.

Operations

- Value specifications are scanned left to right.
- A value is recoded only once per RECODE command.
- Invalid specifications on a RECODE command that result in errors stop all processing of that RECODE command. No variables are recoded.

Numeric Variables

- Blank fields for numeric variables are handled according to the SET BLANKS specification prior to recoding.
- When you recode a value that was previously defined as user-missing on the MISSING VALUE command, the new value is not missing.

String Variables

- If the original or new value specified is longer or shorter than the width defined for the variable, SPSS/PC+ issues an error message and RECODE is not executed.

Limitations

- You can recode (and count using the COUNT command) approximately 400 values.

Example

```
RECODE V1 TO V3 (0=1) (1=0) (2,3=-1) (9=9) (ELSE=SYSMIS)
   /QVAR(1 THRU 5=1)(6 THRU 10=2)(11 THRU HI=3)(ELSE=0).
```

- The numeric variables between and including *V1* and *V3* are recoded: original values 0 and 1 are switched respectively to 1 and 0; 2 and 3 are changed to -1; 9 remains 9; and any other value is changed to the system-missing value.
- Variable *QVAR* is also recoded: original values 1 through 5 are changed to 1; 6 through 10 are changed to 2; 11 through the highest value in the data are changed to 3; and any other value, including system-missing, is changed to 0.

Example

```
RECODE STRNGVAR ('A','B','C'='A')('D','E','F'='B')(ELSE=' ').
RECODE PET ('IGUANA', 'SNAKE ' = 'WILD  ').
```

- Values A, B, and C are changed to value A. Values D, E, and F are changed to value B. All other values are changed to a blank.
- Values IGUANA and SNAKE are changed to value WILD. The defined width of variable *PET* is 6. Thus, values SNAKE and WILD include trailing blanks for a total of six characters. If blanks are not specified, an error results and RECODE is not executed.
- Each string value is enclosed within apostrophes.

REGRESSION

```
REGRESSION [/VARIABLES={varlist    }]
                      {(COLLECT)**}
                      {ALL        }

  [/DESCRIPTIVES=[DEFAULTS] [MEAN] [STDDEV] [CORR] [COV]
                 [VARIANCE] [XPROD] [SIG] [N] [BADCORR]
                 [ALL] [NONE**]]

  [/SELECT={varname relation value}]

  [/MISSING=[{LISTWISE**       }] [INCLUDE]]
            {PAIRWISE         }
            {MEANSUBSTITUTION }

  [/WIDTH={value on SET**}]
          [n             }

  [/REGWGT=varname]

  [/STATISTICS=[DEFAULTS**] [R**] [COEFF**] [ANOVA**] [OUTS**]
               [ZPP] [CHA] [CI] [F] [BCOV] [SES] [LINE] [HISTORY]
               [XTX] [COLLIN] [END] [TOL] [SELECTION] [ALL]]

  [/CRITERIA=[DEFAULTS**] [TOLERANCE({0.0001**})] [MAXSTEPS(n)]
                                    {value   }

             [PIN[({0.05**})]] [POUT[({0.10**})]]
                  {value  }         {value  }

             [FIN[({3.84 })]] [FOUT[({2.71 })]]
                  {value}          {value}

             [CIN[({ 95**})]]]
                  {value}

  [/{NOORIGIN**}]
    {ORIGIN   }

  /DEPENDENT=varlist

  /[METHOD=]{STEPWISE [varlist]        }  [/[METHOD=]...]
            {FORWARD [varlist]         }
            {BACKWARD [varlist]        }
            {ENTER [varlist]           }
            {REMOVE varlist            }
            {TEST(varlist)(varlist)... }
```

**Default if the subcommand is omitted.

Example:

```
REGRESSION VARIABLES=POP15,POP75,INCOME,GROWTH,SAVINGS
 /DEPENDENT=SAVINGS
 /METHOD=ENTER POP15,POP75,INCOME
 /METHOD=ENTER GROWTH.
```

Overview

REGRESSION calculates multiple regression equations and associated statistics and plots.
REGRESSION also calculates collinearity diagnostics, predicted values, residuals, measures

of fit and influence, and several statistics based on these measures (see REGRESSION: Residuals).

Options

Global-Control Subcommands. These optional subcommands can be specified only once and apply to the entire REGRESSION command. DESCRIPTIVES requests descriptive statistics on the variables in the analysis. SELECT estimates the model based on a subset of cases. REGWGT specifies a weight variable for estimating weighted least-squares models. MISSING specifies the treatment of cases with missing values.

Equation-Control Subcommands. These optional subcommands control the calculation and display of statistics for each equation. STATISTICS controls the statistics displayed, CRITERIA specifies the criteria used by the variable selection method, and ORIGIN specifies whether regression is through the origin.

Format. The WIDTH subcommand controls the width of the output for REGRESSION only. It applies to all output from the REGRESSION command.

Analysis of Residuals, Fit, and Influence. The optional subcommands that analyze and plot residuals and add new variables to the active file containing predicted values, residuals, measures of fit and influence, or related information, are described in REGRESSION: Residuals. These subcommands apply to the final equation.

Matrix Input and Output. The optional subcommands that read and write matrix materials are described in REGRESSION: Matrix Materials. These subcommands are global.

Basic Specification

The basic specification is DEPENDENT, which initiates the equation(s) and defines at least one dependent variable, and METHOD, which specifies the method for selecting independent variables.

- By default, all variables named on DEPENDENT and METHOD are used in the analysis.

- For each block of variables selected, the default display includes summary statistics for the goodness of fit of the model (including R^2 and analysis of variance), coefficients and related statistics for variables in the equation, and statistics for the variables not yet in the equation.

- By default, all cases in the active file with valid values for all selected variables are used to compute the correlation matrix on which the regression equations are based. The default equations include a constant (intercept).

Subcommand Order

The standard subcommand order for REGRESSION is:

```
REGRESSION /VARIABLES=...
    /DESCRIPTIVES=...
    /SELECT=...
    /MISSING=...
    /WIDTH=...
    /REGWGT=...
    /READ=...
    /WRITE=...
```

Equation Block(s)

```
/STATISTICS=...
/CRITERIA=...
/ORIGIN
/DEPENDENT=...
```

Method Block(s)

```
    /METHOD-...
    [/METHOD...]...
```

```
/RESIDUALS=...
/SAVE=...
/CASEWISE ...
/SCATTERPLOT=...
/PARTIALPLOT=...
```

- Subcommands listed outside the equation and method blocks apply to all analyses performed by the REGRESSION command. Subcommands listed within the equation block apply to all methods used in estimating that equation.

- A REGRESSION command can include multiple equation blocks, and each equation block can contain multiple METHOD subcommands. These methods are applied, one after the other, to the estimation of the equations for that equation block.

- Each DEPENDENT subcommand must be followed immediately by one or more METHOD subcommands.

- If used, VARIABLES must be specified before the DEPENDENT and METHOD subcommands.

- The DESCRIPTIVES, SELECT, and MISSING subcommands can be entered anywhere except between a DEPENDENT subcommand and the immediately following METHOD subcommands.

- The WIDTH subcommand can be specified anywhere.

- The STATISTICS, CRITERIA, ORIGIN/NOORIGIN, and REGWT subcommands must precede the DEPENDENT subcommand for the equation to which they apply.

- The READ and WRITE subcommands can be specified anywhere except between DEPENDENT and METHOD.

- The RESIDUALS, CASEWISE, SCATTERPLOT, SAVE, and PARTIALPLOT subcommands must follow the last METHOD subcommand in an equation block and apply only to the final equation after all METHOD subcommands have been processed.

Syntax Rules

- VARIABLES can be specified only once. If omitted, VARIABLES defaults to COLLECT.
- More than one variable can be specified on the DEPENDENT subcommand. An equation is estimated for each.
- If no variables are specified on METHOD, all variables named on VARIABLES but not on DEPENDENT are considered for selection.
- If more than one DESCRIPTIVES, SELECT, MISSING, or WIDTH subcommand is specified, the last one of each type is in effect for the entire REGRESSION command.
- CRITERIA, STATISTICS, and ORIGIN remain in effect for all subsequent equations until replaced.

Operations

- REGRESSION calculates a correlation matrix that includes all variables named on VARIABLES. All equations requested on the REGRESSION command are calculated from the same correlation matrix.
- The MISSING, DESCRIPTIVES, and SELECT subcommands control the calculation of the correlation matrix and associated displays.
- The METHOD subcommands control the building of an equation for each variable named on the preceding DEPENDENT subcommand. The equation generated for each variable specified on a DEPENDENT subcommand uses the same independent variables and methods.
- If multiple METHOD subcommands are specified, they operate in sequence on the equations defined by the preceding DEPENDENT subcommand.
- Only independent variables that pass the tolerance criterion are candidates for entry into the equation (see the CRITERIA subcommand on p. 686).
- If the specified width is less than 132, some statistics requested may not be displayed. Use the WIDTH subcommand within REGRESSION to increase the output width and obtain all requested statistics.

Limitations

- The number of variables that can be named on the VARIABLES subcommand depends on available memory.

Example

```
REGRESSION VARIABLES=POP15,POP75,INCOME,GROWTH,SAVINGS
 /DEPENDENT=SAVINGS
 /METHOD=ENTER POP15,POP75,INCOME
 /METHOD=ENTER GROWTH.
```

- VARIABLES calculates a correlation matrix of five variables for use by REGRESSION.
- DEPENDENT defines a single equation, with *SAVINGS* as the dependent variable.
- The first METHOD subcommand enters *POP15, POP75*, and *INCOME* into the equation.
- The second METHOD subcommand adds *GROWTH* to the equation containing *POP15* to *INCOME*.

VARIABLES Subcommand

VARIABLES names all the variables to be used in the analysis.

- The minimum specification is a list of two variables or the keyword ALL or COLLECT. COLLECT, which must be specified in parentheses, is the default.
- Only one VARIABLES subcommand is allowed and it must precede any DEPENDENT or METHOD subcommands.
- You can use keyword TO to refer to consecutive variables in the active file.
- The order of variables in the correlation matrix constructed by REGRESSION is the same as their order on VARIABLES. If COLLECT is used (explicitly or by default), the order of variables in the correlation matrix is the order in which they are first listed on the DEPENDENT and METHOD subcommands.

ALL   *Include all user-defined variables in the active file.*

(COLLECT)   *Include all variables named on the DEPENDENT and METHOD subcommands.* COLLECT *is the default if the* VARIABLES *subcommand is omitted.* COLLECT *must be specified in parentheses. If* COLLECT *is used (explicitly or by default), the* METHOD *subcommands must specify variable lists.*

Example

```
REGRESSION VARIABLES=(COLLECT)
 /DEPENDENT=SAVINGS
 /METHOD=STEP POP15 POP75 INCOME
 /METHOD=ENTER GROWTH
 /DEPENDENT=GROWTH
 /METHOD=ENTER INCOME.
```

- COLLECT requests that the correlation matrix include *SAVINGS, POP15, POP75, INCOME,* and *GROWTH*. Since COLLECT is the default, the VARIABLES subcommand could have been omitted.
- The first DEPENDENT subcommand defines a single equation in which *SAVINGS* is the dependent variable.
- The first METHOD subcommand requests that the block of variables *POP15, POP75,* and *INCOME* be considered for inclusion using a stepwise procedure.

- The second METHOD subcommand adds variable *GROWTH* to the equation.
- A second DEPENDENT subcommand requests an equation in which *GROWTH* is the dependent variable.
- *INCOME* is entered into this equation as specified by the last METHOD subcommand.

DEPENDENT Subcommand

DEPENDENT specifies a list of variables and requests that an equation be built for each. DEPENDENT is required.

- The minimum specification is a single variable. There is no default variable list.
- More than one DEPENDENT subcommand can be specified. Each must be followed by at least one METHOD subcommand.
- Keyword TO on a DEPENDENT subcommand refers to the order in which variables are specified on the VARIABLES subcommand. If VARIABLES=(COLLECT) or if VARIABLES is not specified, TO refers to the order of variables in the active file.
- If DEPENDENT names more than one variable, an equation is built for each using the same independent variables and methods specified on the associated METHOD subcommands.
- No variable named on the DEPENDENT subcommand can be specified as an independent variable on associated METHOD subcommands.

METHOD Subcommand

METHOD specifies a variable selection method and names a block of variables to be evaluated using that method. METHOD is required.

- The minimum specification is a method keyword and, for some methods, a list of variables. The actual keyword METHOD can be omitted.
- At least one METHOD subcommand must follow each DEPENDENT subcommand.
- When more than one METHOD subcommand is specified for a single DEPENDENT subcommand, each METHOD subcommand is applied to the equation that resulted from the previous METHOD subcommands.
- The default variable list for methods FORWARD, BACKWARD, STEPWISE, and ENTER consists of all variables named on VARIABLES that are not named on the preceding DEPENDENT subcommand. If VARIABLES=(COLLECT) or if VARIABLES is not specified, the variables must be specified for these methods.
- There is no default variable list for the REMOVE and TEST methods.
- Keyword TO in a variable list on METHOD refers to the order in which variables are specified on the VARIABLES subcommand. If VARIABLES=(COLLECT) or if VARIABLES is not specified, TO refers to the order of variables in the active file.

The available stepwise methods are as follows:

BACKWARD [varlist]   *Backward elimination.* Variables in the block are considered for removal. At each step, the variable with the largest probability-of-*F* value is removed, provided that the value is larger than POUT (see the

CRITERIA subcommand on p. 686). If no variables are in the equation when BACKWARD is specified, all independent variables in the block are first entered.

FORWARD [varlist]   *Forward entry.* Variables in the block are added to the equation one at a time. At each step, the variable not in the equation with the smallest probability of F is entered if the value is smaller than PIN (see the CRITERIA subcommand on p. 686).

STEPWISE [varlist]   *Stepwise selection.* If there are independent variables already in the equation, the variable with the largest probability of F is removed if the value is larger than POUT. The equation is recomputed without the variable and the process is repeated until no more independent variables can be removed. Then, the independent variable not in the equation with the smallest probability of F is entered if the value is smaller than PIN. All variables in the equation are again examined for removal. This process continues until no variables in the equation can be removed and no variables not in the equation are eligible for entry, or until the maximum number of steps has been reached (see the CRITERIA subcommand on p. 686).

The methods that enter or remove the entire variable block in a single step are as follows:

ENTER [varlist]   *Forced entry.* All variables specified are entered in a single step in order of decreasing tolerance. You can control the order in which variables are entered by specifying the variables on multiple METHOD=ENTER subcommands.

REMOVE varlist   *Forced removal.* All variables specified are removed in a single step. REMOVE requires a variable list.

TEST (varlist) (varlist) R^2 *change and its significance for sets of independent variables.* This method first adds all variables specified on TEST to the current equation. It then removes in turn each subset from the equation and displays requested statistics. Specify test subsets in parentheses. A variable can be used in more than one subset, and each subset can include any number of variables. Variables named on TEST remain in the equation when the method is completed.

Example

```
REGRESSION VARIABLES=POP15 TO GROWTH, SAVINGS
 /DEPENDENT=SAVINGS
 /METHOD=STEPWISE
 /METHOD=ENTER.
```

- STEPWISE applies the stepwise procedure to variables *POP15* to *GROWTH*.
- All variables not in the equation when the STEPWISE method is completed will be forced into the equation with ENTER.

Example

```
REGRESSION VARIABLES=(COLLECT)
 /DEPENDENT=SAVINGS
 /METHOD=TEST(MEASURE3 TO MEASURE9)(MEASURE3,INCOME)
 /METHOD=ENTER GROWTH.
```

- The VARIABLES=(COLLECT) specification assembles a correlation matrix that includes all variables named on the DEPENDENT and METHOD subcommands.

- REGRESSION first builds the full equation of all the variables named on the first METHOD subcommand: *SAVINGS* regressed on *MEASURE3* to *MEASURE9* and *INCOME*. For each set of test variables (MEASURE3 to MEASURE9, and MEASURE3 and INCOME), the R^2 change, F, probability, sums of squares, and degrees of freedom are displayed.

- *GROWTH* is added to the equation by the second METHOD subcommand. Variables *MEASURE3* to *MEASURE9* and *INCOME* are still in the equation when this subcommand is executed.

STATISTICS Subcommand

STATISTICS controls the display of statistics for the equation and for the independent variables.

- If STATISTICS is omitted or if it is specified without keywords, R, ANOVA, COEFF, and OUTS are displayed (see below).

- If any statistics are specified on STATISTICS, only those statistics specifically requested are displayed.

- STATISTICS applies to any equations that are subsequently defined and remains in effect until overridden by another STATISTICS subcommand.

- A STATISTICS subcommand cannot be placed between the DEPENDENT and METHOD subcommands.

- If the output width is set to less than 132, some requested statistics may not be displayed. Use the WIDTH subcommand in REGRESSION to increase the width (see p. 692).

Global Statistics

DEFAULTS   *R, ANOVA, COEFF, and OUTS.* These are displayed if STATISTICS is omitted or if it is specified without keywords.

ALL   *All statistics except F, LINE, and END.*

Equation Statistics

R   *Multiple R.* R includes R^2, adjusted R^2, and standard error of the estimate.

ANOVA   *Analysis of variance table.* This option includes regression and residual sums of squares, mean square, F, and probability of F.

CHA	*Change in R^2.* This option includes the change in R^2 between steps, F at the end of each step and its probability, and F for the equation and its probability. For stepwise methods (BACKWARD, FORWARD, and STEPWISE), these statistics are displayed at the end of each step. For other methods, the statistics are displayed for the independent variables in that method block.
BCOV	*Variance-covariance matrix for unstandardized regression coefficients.* The matrix has covariances below the diagonal, correlations above the diagonal, and variances on the diagonal.
XTX	*Swept correlation matrix.*
COLLIN	*Collinearity diagnostics.* COLLIN includes the variance-inflation factors (VIF), the eigenvalues of the scaled and uncentered cross-products matrix, condition indexes, and variance-decomposition proportions (Belsley et al., 1980).
SELECTION	*Selection statistics.* This option includes Akaike's information criterion (AIK), Ameniya's prediction criterion (PC), Mallow's conditional mean squared error of prediction criterion (C_p), and the Schwarz Bayesian criterion (SBC) (Judge et al., 1980).

Statistics for the Independent Variables

COEFF	*Regression coefficients.* This option includes regression coefficients (B), standard errors of the coefficients, standardized regression coefficients (beta), t, and two-tailed probability of t.
OUTS	*Statistics for variables not yet in the equation that have been named on METHOD subcommands for the equation.* OUTS displays beta, t, two-tailed probability of t, and minimum tolerance of the variable if it were the only variable entered next.
ZPP	*Zero-order, part, and partial correlation.*
CI	*95% confidence interval for the unstandardized regression coefficients.*
SES	*Approximate standard error of the standardized regression coefficients* (Meyer & Younger, 1976).
TOL	*Tolerance.* This option displays tolerance for variables in the equation and, for variables not entered but specified on the METHOD subcommand for the equation, the tolerance each variable would have if it were the only variable entered next.
F	F *value for* B *and its probability.* This is displayed instead of the t value.

Step Summary Statistics

The full summary line displayed by keywords LINE, END, and HISTORY includes R, R^2, adjusted R^2, F, probability of F, R^2 change, F of the change, probability of R^2 change, and statistics on variables added or removed. For stepwise methods (BACKWARD, FORWARD, and STEPWISE), the statistics refer to each step. For other methods (ENTER, REMOVE, and

TEST), the statistics refer to independent variables in the method block. The summary line may not be produced for a block that does not involve steps if other statistics are requested.

LINE   *A single summary line for each step for stepwise methods only.* LINE does not affect direct methods. The default or requested statistics are displayed at the end of each method block for all methods.

END   *The same summary line produced by LINE after each step for stepwise methods and after each variable in the method block for other methods.* For TEST, the summary line is displayed only if the equation changes. Other default or requested statistics are displayed at the completion of the last METHOD subcommand for the equation.

HISTORY   *Final summary report.* HISTORY can be requested in addition to LINE or END. For stepwise methods, the report includes a summary line for each step. For ENTER and REMOVE, the report includes a summary line for each method. For TEST, the summary line is displayed only if the equation changes. If HISTORY is the only statistic requested, COEFF is also displayed for the final equation.

CRITERIA Subcommand

CRITERIA controls the statistical criteria used to build the regression equations. The way in which these criteria are used depends on the method specified on METHOD. The default criteria are noted in the description of each CRITERIA keyword below.

- The minimum specification is a criterion keyword and its arguments, if any.
- If CRITERIA is omitted or included without specifications, the default criteria are in effect.
- A CRITERIA subcommand affects any subsequent DEPENDENT and METHOD subcommands and remains in effect until overridden by another CRITERIA subcommand.
- CRITERIA cannot be placed between the DEPENDENT subcommand and its METHOD subcommands.

Tolerance and Minimum Tolerance Tests

Variables must pass both tolerance and minimum tolerance tests in order to enter and remain in a regression equation. Tolerance is the proportion of the variance of a variable in the equation that is not accounted for by other independent variables in the equation. The minimum tolerance of a variable not in the equation is the smallest tolerance any variable already in the equation would have if the variable being considered were included in the analysis.

If a variable passes the tolerance criteria, it is eligible for inclusion based on the method in effect.

Criteria for Variable Selection

- The ENTER, REMOVE, and TEST methods use only the TOLERANCE criterion.
- BACKWARD removes variables according to the probability of F-to-remove (keyword POUT). Specify FOUT to use F-to-remove instead.

- FORWARD enters variables according to the probability of *F*-to-enter (keyword PIN). Specify FIN to use *F*-to-enter instead.
- STEPWISE uses both PIN and POUT (or FIN and FOUT) as criteria. If the criterion for entry (PIN or FIN) is less stringent than the criterion for removal (POUT or FOUT), the same variable can cycle in and out until the maximum number of steps is reached. Therefore, if PIN is larger than POUT or FIN is smaller than FOUT, REGRESSION adjusts POUT or FOUT and issues a warning.
- The values for these criteria are specified in parentheses. If a value is not specified, the default values are used.

DEFAULTS	*PIN(0.05), POUT(0.10), and TOLERANCE(0.0001)*. These are the defaults if CRITERIA is omitted. If criteria have been changed, DEFAULTS restores these defaults.
PIN[(value)]	*Probability of* F-*to-enter*. The default value is 0.05. Either PIN or FIN can be specified. If more than one is used, the last one specified is in effect.
FIN[(value)]	F-*to-enter*. The default value is 3.84. Either PIN or FIN can be specified. If more than one is used, the last one specified is in effect.
POUT[(value)]	*Probability of* F-*to-remove*. The default value is 0.10. Either POUT or FOUT can be specified. If more than one is used, the last one specified is in effect.
FOUT[(value)]	F-*to-remove*. The default value is 2.71. Either POUT or FOUT can be specified. If more than one is used, the last one specified is in effect.
TOLERANCE[(value)]	*Tolerance*. The default value is 0.0001. If the specified tolerance is very low, REGRESSION issues a warning.
MAXSTEPS[(n)]	*Maximum number of steps*. The value of MAXSTEPS is the sum of the maximum number of steps for each method for the equation. The default values are, for the BACKWARD or FORWARD methods, the number of variables meeting PIN/POUT or FIN/FOUT criteria, and for the STEPWISE method, twice the number of independent variables.

Confidence Intervals

CIN[(value)]	*Reset the value of the percent for confidence intervals*. The default is 95, indicating 95%. The specified value sets the percentage interval used in the computation of temporary variable types MCIN and ICIN. (See the list of temporary variable types on p. 698.)

Example

```
REGRESSION VARIABLES=POP15 TO GROWTH, SAVINGS
 /CRITERIA=PIN(.1) POUT(.15)
 /DEPENDENT=SAVINGS
 /METHOD=FORWARD
 /CRITERIA=DEFAULTS
 /DEPENDENT=SAVINGS
 /METHOD=STEPWISE.
```

- The first CRITERIA subcommand relaxes the default criteria for entry and removal while the FORWARD method is used. Note that the specified PIN is less than POUT.

- The second CRITERIA subcommand reestablishes the defaults for the second equation.

ORIGIN and NOORIGIN Subcommands

ORIGIN and NOORIGIN control whether or not the constant is suppressed. By default, the constant is included in the model (NOORIGIN).

- The specification is either the ORIGIN or NOORIGIN subcommand. There are no additional specifications.

- ORIGIN and NOORIGIN must be specified before the DEPENDENT and METHOD subcommands they modify.

- ORIGIN requests regression through the origin. The constant term is suppressed.

- Once specified, ORIGIN remains in effect until NOORIGIN is requested.

- If you specify ORIGIN, statistics requested on the DESCRIPTIVES subcommand are computed as if the mean were 0.

- ORIGIN and NOORIGIN affect the way the correlation matrix is built. If matrix materials are used as input to REGRESSION, the keyword that was in effect when the matrix was written should be in effect when that matrix is read.

Example

```
REGRESSION VAR=(COL)
 /DEP=HOMICIDE
 /METHOD=ENTER POVPCT
 /ORIGIN
 /DEP=HOMICIDE
 /METHOD=ENTER POVPCT
 /NOORIGIN
 /DEP=POVPCT
 /METHOD=ENTER SOUTHPCT.
```

- The subcommand VAR=(COL) builds a correlation matrix that includes *HOMICIDE*, *POVPCT*, and *SOUTHPCT*.

- The REGRESSION command requests three equations. The first regresses *HOMICIDE* on *POVPCT* and includes a constant term because the default (NOORIGIN) is in effect. The second regresses *HOMICIDE* on *POVPCT* and suppresses the constant (ORIGIN). The third regresses *POVPCT* on *SOUTHPCT* and includes a constant term because NOORIGIN has been specified.

REGWGT Subcommand

The only specification on REGWGT is the name of the variable containing the weights to be used in estimating a weighted least-squares model. With REGWGT, the default display is the usual REGRESSION display.

- REGWGT is a global subcommand.
- If more than one REGWGT subcommand is specified on a REGRESSION procedure, only the last one is in effect.
- REGWGT can be used with the WRITE subcommand but not with READ.
- Residuals saved from equations using the REGWGT command are not weighted. To obtain weighted residuals, multiply the residuals created with SAVE by the square root of the weighting variable in a COMPUTE statement.
- REGWGT is in effect for all equations and affects the way the correlation matrix is built. Thus, if REGWGT is specified on a REGRESSION procedure that writes matrix materials to a file, subsequent REGRESSION procedures using that file will be automatically weighted.

Example

```
REGRESSION VARIABLES=GRADE GPA STARTLEV TREATMNT
 /DEPENDENT=GRADE
 /METHOD=ENTER
 /SAVE PRED(P).
COMPUTE WEIGHT=1/(P*(1-P)).
REGRESSION VAR=GRADE GPA STARTLEV TREATMNT
 /REGWGT=WEIGHT
 /DEP=GRADE
 /METHOD=ENTER.
```

- VARIABLES builds a correlation matrix that includes *GRADE*, *GPA*, *STARTLEV*, and *TREATMNT*.
- DEPENDENT identifies *GRADE* as the dependent variable.
- METHOD regresses *GRADE* on *GPA*, *STARTLEV*, and *TREATMNT*.
- SAVE saves the predicted values from the regression equation as variable *P* in the active file (see the SAVE subcommand on p. 704).
- COMPUTE creates the variable *WEIGHT* as a transformation of *P*.
- The second REGRESSION procedure performs a weighted regression analysis on the same set of variables using *WEIGHT* as the weighting variable.

Example

```
REGRESSION VAR=GRADE GPA STARTLEV TREATMNT
 /REGWGT=WEIGHT
 /DEP=GRADE
 /METHOD=ENTER
 /SAVE RESID(RGRADE).
COMPUTE WRGRADE=RGRADE * SQRT(WEIGHT).
```

- This example illustrates the use of COMPUTE with SAVE to weight residuals.

- REGRESSION performs a weighted regression analysis of *GRADE* on *GPA*, *STARTLEV*, and *TREATMNT*, using *WEIGHT* as the weighting variable.
- SAVE saves the residuals as *RGRADE* (see the SAVE subcommand on p. 704). These residuals are not weighted.
- COMPUTE creates variable *WRGRADE*, which contains the weighted residuals.

DESCRIPTIVES Subcommand

DESCRIPTIVES requests the display of correlations and descriptive statistics. By default, descriptive statistics are not displayed.

- The minimum specification is simply the subcommand keyword DESCRIPTIVES, which obtains MEAN, STDDEV, and CORR.
- If DESCRIPTIVES is specified with keywords, only those statistics specifically requested are displayed.
- Descriptive statistics are displayed only once for all variables named or implied on VARIABLES.
- Descriptive statistics are based on all valid cases for each variable if PAIRWISE or MEAN-SUBSTITUTION has been specified on MISSING. Otherwise, only cases with valid values for all variables named or implied on the VARIABLES subcommand are included in the calculation of descriptive statistics.
- If regression through the origin has been requested (subcommand ORIGIN), statistics are computed as if the mean were 0.

NONE	*No descriptive statistics.* This is the default if the subcommand is omitted.
DEFAULTS	*MEAN, STDDEV, and CORR.* This is the same as specifying DESCRIPTIVES without specifications.
MEAN	*Variable means.*
STDDEV	*Variable standard deviations.*
VARIANCE	*Variable variances.*
CORR	*Correlation matrix.*
SIG	*One-tailed probabilities of the correlation coefficients.*
BADCORR	*The correlation matrix only if some coefficients cannot be computed.*
COV	*Covariance matrix.*
XPROD	*Cross-product deviations from the mean.*
N	*Numbers of cases used to compute correlation coefficients.*
ALL	*All descriptive statistics.*

Example

```
REGRESSION DESCRIPTIVES=DEFAULTS SIG COV
 /VARIABLES=AGE,FEMALE,YRS_JOB,STARTPAY,SALARY
 /DEPENDENT=SALARY
 /METHOD=ENTER STARTPAY
 /METHOD=ENTER YRS_JOB.
```

- The variable means, variable standard deviations, correlation matrix, one-tailed probabilities of the correlation coefficients, and covariance matrix are displayed.
- Statistics are displayed for all variables named on VARIABLES, even though only variables *SALARY, STARTPAY*, and *YRS_JOB* are used to build the equations.
- *STARTPAY* is entered into the equation by the first METHOD subcommand. *YRS_JOB* is entered by the second METHOD subcommand.

SELECT Subcommand

By default, all cases in the active file are considered for inclusion in REGRESSION. Use SELECT to include a subset of cases in the correlation matrix and resulting regression statistics.

- The minimum specification is a logical expression.
- The variable named on SELECT should not be specified on the VARIABLE3 subcommand.
- The logical expression on SELECT is of the form

```
/SELECT=varname relation value
```

where the relation can be EQ, NE, LT, LE, GT, or GE.

- Only cases for which the logical expression on SELECT is true are included in the calculation of the correlation matrix and regression statistics. All other cases, including those with missing values for the variable named on SELECT, are not included in the computations.
- By default, residuals and predicted values are calculated and reported separately for both selected and unselected cases (see the RESIDUALS subcommand on p. 700).
- Cases deleted from the active file with SELECT IF, PROCESS IF, or SAMPLE are not passed to REGRESSION and are not included among either the selected or unselected cases.
- The display of the values of the variable named on SELECT is controlled by the variable's format (see DATA LIST: Fixed Format).

Example

```
REGRESSION SELECT SEX EQ 'M'
 /VARIABLES=AGE,STARTPAY,YRS_JOB,SALARY
 /DEPENDENT=SALARY
 /METHOD=STEP
 /RESIDUALS=NORMPROB.
```

- Only cases with the value M for *SEX* are included in the correlation matrix calculated by REGRESSION.
- Separate normal probability plots are displayed for cases with *SEX* equal to M and for other cases (see the RESIDUALS subcommand on p. 700).

MISSING Subcommand

MISSING controls the treatment of cases with missing values. By default, a case that has a user- or system-missing value for any variable named or implied on VARIABLES is omitted from the computation of the correlation matrix on which all analyses are based.

- The minimum specification is a keyword specifying a missing-value treatment.

LISTWISE   *Delete cases with missing values listwise.* Only cases with valid values for all variables named on the current VARIABLES subcommand are used. If INCLUDE is also specified, only cases with system-missing values are deleted listwise. LISTWISE is the default if the MISSING subcommand is omitted.

PAIRWISE   *Delete cases with missing values pairwise.* Each correlation coefficient is computed using cases with complete data for the pair of variables correlated. If INCLUDE is also specified, only cases with system-missing values are deleted pairwise.

MEANSUBSTITUTION   *Replace missing values with the variable mean.* All cases are included and the substitutions are treated as valid observations. If INCLUDE is also specified, user-missing values are treated as valid and are included in the computation of the means.

INCLUDE   *Includes cases with user-missing values.* All user-missing values are treated as valid values. This keyword can be specified along with the methods LISTWISE, PAIRWISE, or MEANSUBSTITUTION.

Example

```
REGRESSION  VARIABLES=POP15,POP75,INCOME,GROWTH,SAVINGS
 /DEPENDENT=SAVINGS
 /METHOD=STEP
 /MISSING=MEANSUBSTITUTION.
```

- System- and user-missing values are replaced with the means of the variables when the correlation matrix is calculated.

WIDTH Subcommand

WIDTH controls the width of the output within the REGRESSION procedure.

- The minimum specification is an integer between 72 and 132.
- The default display uses the width specified on SET. The width specified on the WIDTH subcommand within REGRESSION overrides the width specified on SET for the REGRESSION output only.
- The WIDTH subcommand can be specified anywhere.
- If more than one WIDTH subcommand is specified, the last one is in effect.
- If the width is less than 132, some statistics may not be displayed.

REGRESSION: Matrix Materials

```
REGRESSION [READ=[DEFAULTS] [MEAN] [STDDEV]

          [VARIANCE] {CORR} [N]]
                     {COV }

 [/WRITE=[DEFAULTS] [MEAN] [STDDEV]

         [VARIANCE] [CORR] [COV]

         [N] [NONE**]]

 /VARIABLES=varlist /DEPENDENT=varlist /METHOD=method
```

**Default if the subcommand is omitted.

Example:

```
REGRESSION  VARIABLES=AGE TO SUICIDE
  /DESCRIPTIVES
  /WRITE
  /DEP=SUICIDE
  /METHOD=ENTER
  /RESIDUALS.
```

Overview

REGRESSION can both read and write matrix materials. It can read matrix materials written by REGRESSION or other SPSS/PC+ procedures such as CORRELATIONS, and it can read matrices from other sources provided that the appropriate keyword specifications are used. Matrix materials read by REGRESSION can be in either fixed or freefield format but must conform to certain format and record specifications (see DATA LIST: Matrix Materials).

The subcommands for writing and reading matrix materials can be used in addition to the subcommands described for REGRESSION.

WRITE Subcommand

Use WRITE to write the matrix materials used in REGRESSION computations to an external file.

- WRITE can be specified anywhere except between the DEPENDENT subcommand and its associated METHOD subcommands.
- If WRITE is specified without keywords, REGRESSION writes a vector of means, a vector of standard deviations, a correlation matrix, and the number of cases. If any keywords are specified, only requested materials are written.
- Each type of matrix material written begins on a new record. Each record can contain eight 10-column fields.
- Matrix materials are written for all variables named on the VARIABLES subcommand.
- The order of variables in vectors and matrices is the order in which variables are named on the VARIABLES subcommand. If VARIABLES=(COLLECT) or if VARIABLES is not spec-

ified, the order of the variables is the order in which they are first named on REGRES-SION. You can use keyword CORRELATION on the DESCRIPTIVES subcommand to display the matrix you write.

- REGRESSION displays a table describing the contents and format of the file it has written.

- If more than one WRITE subcommand is specified on the REGRESSION command, only the last one is in effect.

- The VARIABLES, SELECT, ORIGIN/NOORIGIN, MISSING, and REGWGT subcommands affect the matrix materials that are written.

- Matrix materials are written to the results file named on the SET command (by default, *SPSS.PRC*). If the results file named on SET is not empty when the WRITE subcommand is executed, the contents of the file will be overwritten. Use SET to specify a different results file.

The following keywords can be specified on WRITE. These keywords should be specified in the order they are listed below.

DEFAULTS   *MEAN, STDDEV, CORR, and N.* This is the default if the WRITE subcommand is used without specifications.

MEAN   *Write a vector of means.*

STDDEV   *Vector of standard deviations.*

VARIANCE   *Vector of variances.*

CORR   *Correlation matrix.*

COV   *Covariance matrix.*

N   *Numbers of cases used to compute correlation coefficients.* When MISS-ING=LISTWISE is in effect, the number of cases is written as one item on the last record. When PAIRWISE or MEANSUBSTITUTION is specified on MISS-ING, a matrix of *n*'s is written.

NONE   *No matrix output.* This is the default if WRITE is not specified.

Example

```
SET RESULTS='GSS82.MAT'.
DATA LIST FILE='GSS82.DAT'/AGE 5-6 INCOME 7-13
  ANOMIE1 TO ANOMIE7 14-20 SUICIDE 21.
REGRESSION  VARIABLES=AGE TO SUICIDE
  /DESCRIPTIVES
  /WRITE
  /DEP=SUICIDE
  /METHOD=ENTER
  /RESIDUALS.
```

- The SET command specifies *GSS82.MAT* in the current directory as the results file.

- The DATA LIST command specifies variable names and column locations for the data in file *GSS82.DAT*.

- The VARIABLES subcommand includes all variables in the active file between and including *AGE* and *SUICIDE* in the computation of the correlation matrix for the regression.

- The DESCRIPTIVES subcommand requests descriptive statistics for all variables in the analysis.
- The WRITE subcommand writes default matrix materials to *GSS82.MAT*. The file will contain a vector of means, a vector of standard deviations, a correlation matrix, and the number of cases, in that order. All variables from *AGE* to *SUICIDE* will be included in the matrix materials.
- A regression of *SUICIDE* on all other variables implied by the VARIABLES subcommand is computed (see REGRESSION).
- The RESIDUALS subcommand displays a histogram of standardized residuals, a normal probability plot of standardized residuals, the Durbin-Watson test statistic, and a listing of the 10 worst outliers based on the absolute value of the standardized residuals (see REGRESSION: Residuals).

READ Subcommand

Use READ to read matrix materials.

- READ can be specified only once.
- READ cannot be specified between the DEPENDENT subcommand and its associated METHOD subcommands.
- If READ is specified without keywords, REGRESSION assumes that the matrix materials include a vector of means, a vector of standard deviations, a correlation matrix, and the number of cases, in that order.
- If any keywords are used, READ expects only the specified matrix materials.
- The matrix materials must include either a correlation or covariance matrix.
- When you use READ on REGRESSION, you must first specify a DATA LIST MATRIX command that points to the file containing the matrix materials and names the variables that will be read (see DATA LIST: Matrix Materials).
- The matrix materials to be read must be contained in a single input file.
- The order in which variables are named on the VARIABLES subcommand must be the order of the variables in each vector or matrix that is read.
- If a correlation matrix is the only matrix material to be read, an N command specifying the number of cases must be used prior to REGRESSION. Only standardized coefficients will be available.
- If *n* is read from the matrix file and *n* is specified on the N command, the *n* in the matrix file is used.
- If the input file includes more than one type of matrix material, they must be arranged in the following order: the vector of means, the vector of standard deviations, the vector of variances, the correlation or covariance matrix, and the number of cases.
- If you read a matrix written by a previous REGRESSION command, the specifications on the MISSING and ORIGIN/NOORIGIN subcommands must agree with the options that were in effect when the matrix was written.

- The RESIDUALS, CASEWISE, SCATTERPLOT, PARTIALPLOT, and SAVE subcommands and the COLLECT keyword on the VARIABLES subcommand are not available when matrix materials are read.
- The descriptive statistics available with the DESCRIPTIVES subcommand depend on which matrix materials are read.

DEFAULTS   *MEAN, STDDEV, CORR, and N.* This is the default if you specify READ without keywords. Matrix materials written by REGRESSION are in this format by default.

MEAN   *The matrix is preceded by a vector of means.*

STDDEV   *The matrix is preceded by a vector of standard deviations.*

VARIANCE   *The matrix is preceded by a vector of variances.*

CORR   *Correlation matrix.* CORR is an alternative to COV.

COV   *Covariance matrix.* COV is an alternative to CORR. A covariance matrix cannot be used with pairwise deletion of missing values.

N   *The number of cases used to compute correlation coefficients follows the matrix.* If the MISSING subcommand specifies MEANSUBSTITUTION or PAIRWISE, a symmetric matrix of *n*'s is expected. If MISSING specifies LISTWISE (either explicitly or by default), all coefficients are based on the same number of cases and a single *n* is expected. If a single number of cases is expected, it will be read from the first 10 columns of the last record of the matrix file. If the number of cases is not included in the matrix file, the *n* specified on the N command is used.

Example
```
DATA LIST FIXED MATRIX FILE='GSS82.MAT'
  /AGE INCOME ANOMIE1 TO ANOMIE7 SUICIDE.
REGRESSION  READ
  /VARIABLES=AGE INCOME ANOMIE1 TO ANOMIE7 SUICIDE
  /DEPENDENT=SUICIDE
  /METHOD=ENTER ANOMIE1 TO ANOMIE7.
```

- The DATA LIST command reads matrix input from the file *GSS82.MAT* and names the variables in the file.
- The READ subcommand on REGRESSION indicates that matrix materials will be read in the default format. REGRESSION therefore expects a vector of means, a vector of standard deviations, a correlation matrix, and the number of cases. Because listwise missing-value treatment (the default) is in effect for this command, the number of cases must be a single *n*.
- The VARIABLES subcommand names the variables in the order in which they appear in the vectors and matrix to be read.
- The DEPENDENT subcommand defines an equation in which *SUICIDE* is the dependent variable.
- The METHOD subcommand enters variables *ANOMIE1* to *ANOMIE7* into the equation using the ENTER method.
- The variables *AGE* and *INCOME* are not used in the equation but must be named on the VARIABLES subcommand so that the locations of all variables in the matrix file are identified accurately.

REGRESSION: Residuals

```
REGRESSION VARIABLES=varlist /DEPENDENT=varname /METHOD=method

[/RESIDUALS=[DEFAULTS] [DURBIN] [OUTLIERS({ZRESID })] [ID (varname)]
                                         {tempvars}

    [NORMPROB({ZRESID })] [HISTOGRAM({ZRESID })]
             {tempvars}             {tempvars}

    [SIZE({SMALL})] [{SEPARATE}]]
          {LARGE}    {POOLED  }

[/CASEWISE=[DEFAULTS]  [{OUTLIERS({3    })}] [PLOT({ZRESID })]
                       {         {value}  }        {tempvar}
                       {ALL                }

    [{DEPENDENT PRED RESID}]]
     {tempvars            }

[/SCATTERPLOT=(varname,varname)...  [SIZE({SMALL})]]
                                          {LARGE}

[/PARTIALPLOT=[{ALL    }]  [SIZE({SMALL})]]
               {varlist}         {LARGE}

[/SAVE tempvar[(newname)]  [tempvar[(newname)],..]  [FITS]]
```

Temporary residual variables are:

PRED, ADJPRED, SRESID, MAHAL, RESID, ZPRED, SDRESID, COOK, DRESID, ZRESID,
SEPRED, LEVER, DFBETA, SDBETA, DFFIT, SDFFIT, COVRATIO, MCIN, ICIN

SAVE FITS saves:

DFFIT, SDFIT, DFBETA, SDBETA, COVRATIO

Example:

```
REGRESSION VARIABLES=SAVINGS INCOME POP15 POP75
    /WIDTH=132
    /DEPENDENT=SAVINGS
    /METHOD=ENTER
    /RESIDUALS
    /CASEWISE
    /SCATTERPLOT (*ZRESID *ZPRED)
    /PARTIALPLOT
    /SAVE ZRESID(STDRES) ZPRED(STDPRED).
```

Overview

REGRESSION creates temporary variables containing predicted values, residuals, measures of fit and influence, and several statistics based on these measures. These temporary variables can be analyzed within REGRESSION using casewise plots (available with the CASEWISE subcommand), scatterplots (SCATTERPLOT subcommand), histograms and normal probability plots (RESIDUALS subcommand), and partial residual plots (PARTIALPLOT subcommand). Any of the residuals subcommands can be specified to obtain descriptive statistics for the predicted values, residuals, and their standardized versions. Any of the temporary variables can be added to the active file with the SAVE subcommand.

Basic Specification

All residuals analysis subcommands are optional. Most have defaults that can be requested by including the subcommand without any further specifications. These defaults are described in the discussion of each subcommand below.

Subcommand Order

- The residuals subcommands RESIDUALS, CASEWISE, SCATTERPLOT, PARTIALPLOT, and SAVE follow the last METHOD subcommand of any equation for which residuals analysis is requested. Statistics are based on this final equation.
- The residuals subcommands themselves can be specified in any order.

Syntax Rules

- If you specify more than one equation (more than one DEPENDENT subcommand), residuals analysis can be requested for each.
- Residuals subcommands cannot be specified if matrix input (the READ subcommand) is used.

Operations

- Residuals subcommands affect only the equation they follow.
- The temporary variables *PRED*, *RESID*, *ZPRED*, and *ZRESID* are calculated and descriptive statistics are displayed whenever any RESIDUALS or SCATTERPLOT subcommand is specified. If any of the other temporary variables are referred to on the REGRESSION command (or if DEPENDENT is specified on CASEWISE), they are also calculated.
- Predicted values and statistics based on predicted values are calculated for every observation that has valid values for all variables in the equation. Residuals and statistics based on residuals are calculated for all observations that have a valid predicted value and a valid value for the dependent variable. The missing-values option therefore affects the calculation of residuals and predicted values.
- The amount of information displayed in a casewise plot is limited by the output width. Use the WIDTH subcommand (see p. 692) to increase the width within REGRESSION. The widest page allows a maximum of eight variables in a casewise plot.
- No residuals or predictors are generated for cases deleted from the active file with SELECT IF, PROCESS IF, or SAMPLE.
- All variables are standardized before plotting. If the unstandardized version of a variable is requested, the standardized version is plotted.

For each analysis, REGRESSION can calculate the following types of temporary variables:

PRED	*Unstandardized predicted values.*
RESID	*Unstandardized residuals.*

DRESID	*Deleted residuals.*
ADJPRED	*Adjusted predicted values.*
ZPRED	*Standardized predicted values.*
ZRESID	*Standardized residuals.*
SRESID	*Studentized residuals.*
SDRESID	*Studentized deleted residuals.* (See Hoaglin & Welsch, 1978.)
SEPRED	*Standard errors of the predicted values.*
MAHAL	*Mahalanobis distances.*
COOK	*Cook's distances.* (See Cook, 1977.)
LEVER	*Centered leverage values.* (See Velleman & Welsch, 1981.)
DFBETA	*Change in the regression coefficient that results from the deletion of the ith case.* A DFBETA value is computed for each case for each regression coefficient generated by a model. (See Belsley et al., 1980.)
SDBETA	*Standardized DFBETA.* An SDBETA value is computed for each case for each regression coefficient generated by a model. (See Belsley et al., 1980.)
DFFIT	*Change in the predicted value when the ith case is deleted.* (See Belsley et al., 1980.)
SDFIT	*Standardized DFFIT.* (See Belsley et al., 1980.)
COVRATIO	*Ratio of the determinant of the covariance matrix with the ith case deleted to the determinant of the covariance matrix with all cases included.* (See Belsley et al., 1980.)
MCIN	*Lower and upper bounds for the prediction interval of the mean predicted response.* A lowerbound *LMCI_n* and an upperbound *UMCI_n* are generated. The default confidence interval is 95%. The confidence interval can be reset with the CIN subcommand. (See Dillon & Goldstein, 1984.)
ICIN	*Lower and upper bounds for the prediction interval for a single observation.* A lowerbound *LICI_n* and an upperbound *UICI_n* are generated. The default confidence interval is 95%. The confidence interval can be reset with the CIN subcommand. (See Dillon & Goldstein, 1984.)

Limitations

If there is not enough memory available to assemble the requested plots, a warning is displayed. Small plots are displayed and some plots may be deleted.

Example

```
REGRESSION VARIABLES=SAVINGS INCOME POP15 POP75
  /WIDTH=132
  /DEPENDENT=SAVINGS
  /METHOD=ENTER
  /RESIDUALS
  /CASEWISE
  /SCATTERPLOT (*ZRESID *ZPRED)
  /PARTIALPLOT
  /SAVE ZRESID(STDRES) ZPRED(STDPRED).
```

- REGRESSION requests a single equation in which *SAVINGS* is the dependent variable and *INCOME*, *POP15*, and *POP75* are independent variables.
- RESIDUALS requests the default residuals output.
- CASEWISE requests a default casewise plot of *ZRESID* for cases for which the absolute value of *ZRESID* is greater than 3. Values of the dependent variable, predicted value, and residual are listed for each case.
- SCATTERPLOT requests a small plot of the standardized predicted value and the standardized residual.
- PARTIALPLOT requests small partial residual plots for all independent variables.
- SAVE adds the standardized residual and the standardized predicted value to the active file as new variables named *STDRES* and *STDPRED*.
- Because residuals processing has been requested, statistics for predicted values, residuals, and standardized versions of predicted values and residuals are displayed.

RESIDUALS Subcommand

RESIDUALS controls the display and labeling of summary information on outliers as well as the display of the Durbin-Watson statistic and histograms and normal probability plots for the temporary variables.

- If RESIDUALS is specified without keywords, it displays a histogram of standardized residuals, a normal probability plot of standardized residuals, the values of *$CASENUM* and *ZRESID* for the ten cases with the largest absolute value of *ZRESID*, and the Durbin-Watson test statistic. The default size of both plots is small when no size specifications are given.
- If any keywords are specified on RESIDUALS, only the requested information and plots are displayed.

DEFAULTS   *DURBIN, NORMPROB(ZRESID), HISTOGRAM(ZRESID), OUTLIERS (ZRESID).* These are the defaults if RESIDUALS is used without specifications.

SIZE(plot size)   *Plot sizes.* The plot size can be SMALL or LARGE. The default is SMALL. Four small histograms or normal probability plots can be displayed on a single page if the width is 132 and the page length is 59.

HISTOGRAM(tempvars)   *Histogram of the standardized temporary variable or variables.* The default is *ZRESID.* You can request histograms for *PRED, RESID, ZPRED, DRESID, SRESID, SDRESID,* and *ADJPRED.* The specification of any other temporary variable will result in an error. Histograms are always displayed in standardized form; therefore, when *PRED, RESID, DRESID,* or *ADJPRED* is requested, the standardized equivalent is displayed.

NORMPROB(tempvars)   *Normal probability (P-P) plot.* The default is *ZRESID.* The other temporary variables for which normal probability plots are available are *PRED, RESID, ZPRED, DRESID, SRESID, SDRESID,* and *ADJPRED.* The specification of any other temporary variable will result in an error. Normal probability plots are always displayed in standardized form; therefore, when *PRED, RESID, DRESID,* or *ADJPRED* is requested, the standardized equivalent is displayed.

OUTLIERS(tempvars)   *The ten cases with the largest absolute values of the specified temporary variables.* The default is *ZRESID.* The output includes the values of *$CASENUM* and of the temporary variables for the ten cases. The other temporary variables available for OUTLIERS are *RESID, SRESID, SDRESID, DRESID, MAHAL,* and *COOK.* The specification of any temporary variable other than these will result in an error.

DURBIN   *Durbin-Watson test statistic.*

ID(varname)   *Case identifier for outlier plots.* Any variable in the active file can be named. ID also labels the list of cases produced by CASEWISE.

POOLED   *Pooled plots and statistics using all cases in the active file when the SELECT subcommand is in effect.* (See the SELECT subcommand on p. 691.)

SEPARATE   *Separate reporting of residuals statistics and plots for selected and unselected cases.* This is an alternative to POOLED and is the default.

Example

```
/RESID=DEFAULT ID(SVAR)
```

- DEFAULT produces the default residuals statistics: Durbin-Watson statistic, a normal probability plot and histogram of *ZRESID,* and an outlier listing for *ZRESID.*
- Descriptive statistics for *ZRESID, RESID, PRED,* and *ZPRED* are automatically displayed.
- *SVAR* is specified as the case identifier on the outlier output.

CASEWISE Subcommand

CASEWISE requests a casewise plot of residuals. You can specify a temporary residual variable for casewise plotting (PLOT) and control the selection of cases for plotting (OUTLIERS or ALL). You can also specify variables to be listed next to the plot entry for each case.

- If CASEWISE is used without any additional specifications, it displays a casewise plot of *ZRESID* for cases whose absolute value of *ZRESID* is at least 3. By default, the values of the case sequence number, *DEPENDENT*, *PRED*, and *RESID* are listed next to the plot entry for each case. To label each case with a case identifier, use the ID keyword on the RESIDUALS subcommand.

- Defaults remain in effect unless specifically altered.

DEFAULTS *OUTLIERS(3), PLOT(ZRESID), DEPENDENT, PRED, and RESID.* These are the defaults if the subcommand is used without specifications.

OUTLIERS(value) *Plot only cases for which the absolute standardized value of the plotted variable is at least as large as the specified value.* The default value is 3. Keyword OUTLIERS is ignored if keyword ALL is also specified.

ALL *Include all cases in the casewise plot.* ALL is the alternative to keyword OUTLIERS.

PLOT(tempvar) *Plot the values of the temporary variable in the casewise plot.* The default temporary variable is *ZRESID*. Other variables that can be plotted are *RESID*, *DRESID*, *SRESID*, and *SDRESID*. The specification of any temporary variable other than these will result in an error. When requested, *RESID* is standardized and *DRESID* is studentized in the output.

tempvars *Display the values of these variables next to the casewise plot entry for each case.* The default variables are *DEPENDENT* (the dependent variable), *PRED*, and *RESID*. Any of the other temporary variables can be specified. If an ID variable is specified on RESIDUALS, the ID variable is also listed instead of the case sequence number if the width is sufficient.

Example

```
/CASEWISE=DEFAULT ALL SRE MAH COOK SDR
```

- This example requests a casewise plot of the standardized residuals for all cases.
- The dependent variable and the temporary variables *PRED*, *RESID*, *SRESID*, *MAHAL*, *COOK*, and *SDRESID* are listed next to the plot entry for all cases.

SCATTERPLOT Subcommand

SCATTERPLOT names pairs of variables for scatterplots and controls the size of the plots.

- The minimum specification for SCATTERPLOT is a pair of variables in parentheses. There are no default specifications.
- You can specify as many pairs of variables in parentheses as you want.
- The first variable named in each set of parentheses is plotted along the vertical axis, and the second variable is plotted along the horizontal axis.
- Plotting symbols are used to represent multiple points occurring at the same position.
- Specify an asterisk before temporary variable names to distinguish them from user-defined variables. For example, use *PRED* to specify *PRED*.
- All scatterplots are standardized. For example, *RESID* is the same as *ZRESID*, *PRED* is the same as *ZPRED*, and *DRESID* is the same as *SDRESID*.

(varname,varname)	*Plot the pairs of specified variables.* You can specify *PRED, RESID, ZPRED, ZRESID, DRESID, SRESID, SDRESID,* and *ADJPRED.* The specification of any other temporary variables will result in an error. However, you can specify any variable named on the VARIABLES subcommand.
SIZE(plotsize)	*Plot size.* The plot size can be either SMALL or LARGE. The default is small. Four small scatterplots can be displayed on a single page if the width is at least 120 (see the WIDTH subcommand on p. 692) and the page length is at least 57 (see SET).

Example

```
/SCATTERPLOT (*RES,*PRE)(*RES,SAVINGS)
```

- This example specifies two scatterplots: residuals against predicted values and residuals against the values of variable *SAVINGS*.

PARTIALPLOT Subcommand

PARTIALPLOT requests partial residual plots and controls the size of the plots. Partial residual plots are scatterplots of the residuals of the dependent variable and an independent variable when both of these variables are regressed on the rest of the independent variables.

- If PARTIALPLOT is included without any additional specifications, it produces a partial residual plot for every independent variable in the equation.
- If variables are specified on PARTIALPLOT, only the requested plots are displayed.
- At least two independent variables must be in the equation for partial residual plots to be produced.
- All plots are standardized.

varlist	*Plot the specified variables.* Any variable entered into the equation can be specified. The default is every independent variable in the equation. You can request the default with keyword ALL.
SIZE(plot size)	*Plot size.* The plot size can be either SMALL or LARGE. The default is SMALL. Four small partial plots can be displayed on a single page if the width is at least 120 (see the WIDTH subcommand on p. 692) and the page length is at least 57 (see SET).

Example

```
REGRESSION VARS=PLOT15 TO SAVINGS
  /DEP=SAVINGS
  /METH=ENTER
  /RESID=DEFAULTS
  /PARTIAL.
```

- A partial residual plot is produced for every independent variable in the equation.

SAVE Subcommand

Use SAVE to add one or more residual or fit variables to the active file.

- The specification on SAVE is one or more of the temporary variable types listed on pp. 698–699, each followed by an optional name in parentheses for the new variable.
- New variable names must be unique.
- If new names are not specified, REGRESSION generates a rootname using a shortened form of the temporary variable name with a suffix to identify its creation sequence.
- If you specify DFBETA or SDBETA on the SAVE subcommand, the number of new variables saved is the total number of independent variables in the equation plus one variable for the intercept.

FITS   *Save all influence statistics.* FITS saves *DFFIT, SDFIT, DFBETA, SDBETA,* and *COV-RATIO.* You cannot specify new variable names when using this keyword. Default names are generated.

Example

```
/SAVE=PRED(PREDVAL) RESID(RESIDUAL) COOK(CDISTANC)
```

- This subcommand adds three variables to the end of the active file: *PREDVAL*, containing the unstandardized predicted value for each case; *RESIDUAL*, containing the unstandardized residual; and *CDISTANC*, containing Cook's distance.

Example

```
/SAVE=PRED RESID
```

- This subcommand adds two variables named *PRE_1* and *RES_1* to the end of the active file.

Example

```
REGRESSION DEPENDENT=Y
 /METHOD=ENTER X1 X2
 /SAVE DFBETA(DFBVAR).
```

- The SAVE subcommand creates and saves three new variables with the names *DFBVAR0*, *DFBVAR1*, and *DFBVAR2*.

Example

```
REGRESSION VARIABLES=SAVINGS INCOME POP15 POP75 GROWTH
 /DEPENDENT=SAVINGS
 /METHOD=ENTER INCOME POP15 POP75
 /SAVE=PRED(PREDV) SDBETA(BETA) ICIN.
```

- The SAVE subcommand adds seven variables to the end of the file: *PREDV*, containing the unstandardized predicted value for the case; *BETA0*, the standardized *SDBETA* for the intercept; *BETA1*, *BETA2*, and *BETA3*, the standardized *SDBETA*'s for the three independent variables in the model; *LICI_1*, the lower bound for the prediction interval for an individual case; and *UICI_1*, the upper bound for the prediction interval for an individual case.

REPORT

```
REPORT  [/FORMAT=[{MANUAL    }] [{NOLIST    }] [ALIGN({LEFT  })] [TSPACE({1})]
                  {AUTOMATIC}    {LIST[(n)]}          {CENTER}          {n}
                                                      {RIGHT }

        [CHDSPACE({1})] [FTSPACE({1})] [SUMSPACE({1})] [COLSPACE({4})]
                  {n}             {n}             {n}             {n}

        [BRKSPACE({ 1 })][LENGTH({1,length})] [MARGINS({1,width})]
                  { n }          {t,b    }            {l,r    }
                  {-1†}          {*,*    }            {*,*    }

        [CHALIGN({TOP    })] [UNDERSCORE({OFF})] [PAGE1({1})] [MISSING {'.'}]]
                 {BOTTOM†}                {ON† }        {n}           {'s'}

[/OUTFILE=file]

[/STRING=stringname (varname[(width)]) [(BLANK)] ['literal'])

/VARIABLES=varname ({VALUE}) [+ varname({VALUE})] ['col head'] [option list]
                    {LABEL}              {LABEL}
                    {DUMMY}              {DUMMY}

    where option list can contain any of the following:
        (width)    (OFFSET({0     })) ({LEFT   })
                           {n     }    {CENTER†}
                           {CENTER†}   {RIGHT  }

[/MISSING={VAR                      }]
          {NONE                     }
          {LIST[([varlist][{1}])]}
                            {n}

[       /TITLE='line1' 'line2'...]      [     /FOOTNOTE='line1' 'line2'...]
        or                                    or
[/TITLE=LEFT 'line1' 'line2'...]        [/FOOTNOTE=LEFT 'line1' 'line2'...]
[       CENTER 'line1' 'line2'...]      [        CENTER 'line1' 'line2'...]
[       RIGHT 'line1' 'line2'...]       [        RIGHT 'line1' 'line2'...]

              [)PAGE]    [)DATE]    [)var]

[/BREAK=varlist ['col head'] [option list]]

    where option list can contain any of the following:
        (width)    ({VALUE }) ({NOTOTAL}) (SKIP({1})) (PAGE[(RESET)])
                    {LABEL†}   {TOTAL  }        {n}

        (OFFSET({0     })) (UNDERSCORE[(varlist)]) ({LEFT   }) ({NONAME})
                {n     }                            {CENTER†}   {NAME  }
                {CENTER†}                           {RIGHT  }

[/SUMMARY=function...['summary title'][(break col #)] [SKIP({0})]]
                                                            {n}
    or
[/SUMMARY=PREVIOUS[({1})]]
                   {n}

    where function is
aggregate [(varname[({PLAIN })][(d)][varname...])]
                     {DOLLAR}
                     {COMMA }
    or
composite(arguments)[(report col[({PLAIN })][(d)])]
                                  {DOLLAR}
                                  {COMMA }
```

†Default if FORMAT=AUTOMATIC.

Aggregate functions:

VALIDN	VARIANCE	PLT(n)
SUM	KURTOSIS	PIN(min,max)
MIN	SKEWNESS	FREQUENCY(min,max)
MAX	MEDIAN(min,max)	PERCENT(min,max)
MEAN	MODE(min,max)	
STDDEV	PGT(n)	

Composite functions:

$DIVIDE(arg_1\ arg_2\ [factor])$
$MULTIPLY(arg_1...arg_n)$
$PCT(arg_1\ arg_2)$
$SUBTRACT(arg_1\ arg_2)$
$ADD(arg_1...arg_n)$
$GREAT(arg_1...arg_n)$
$LEAST(arg_1...arg_n)$
$AVERAGE(arg_1...arg_n)$

where arg is either one of the aggregate functions or a constant

Example:

```
REPORT FORMAT=LIST
  /VARIABLES=PRODUCT (LABEL) ' ' 'Retail' 'Products'
          SALES 'Annual' 'Sales' '1981'
  /BREAK=DEPT 'Department' (LABEL)
  /SUMMARY=VALIDN (PRODUCT) MEAN (SALES).
```

Overview

REPORT produces case listings and summary statistics and gives you considerable control over the appearance of the output. REPORT calculates all the univariate statistics available in DESCRIPTIVES and the statistics and subpopulation means available in MEANS. In addition, REPORT calculates statistics not directly available in any other SPSS/PC+ procedure, such as computations involving aggregated statistics.

REPORT provides complete report format defaults but also lets you customize a variety of table elements, including column widths, titles, footnotes, and spacing. Because REPORT is so flexible and the output has so many components, it is often efficient to preview report output using a small number of cases until you find the format that best suits your needs.

Defaults

Column Heads. REPORT uses variable labels as default column heads; if no variable labels have been specified, variable names are used.

Missing Values. By default, cases with user-missing values are excluded from the calculation of report statistics, and missing-value indicators are ignored for variables named on BREAK.

Column Widths. Default column widths are determined by REPORT, using the maximum of the following for each column:

- The widest print format in the column, whether it is a variable print format or a summary print format.
- The width of any temporary variable defined with the STRING subcommand.
- The length of the longest title line in the heading, if a column heading is assigned.
- When no column heading is specified, the length of the longest word in the variable label, or the length of the variable name. If FORMAT=MANUAL is in effect, variable labels are not evaluated.
- If you specify LABEL on VARIABLES, the length of the variable's longest value label. If FORMAT=MANUAL is in effect, 20 is the maximum value used for this criterion.

Intercolumn Spacing. Intercolumn spacing adjusts automatically, using a minimum of one and a maximum of four spaces between columns.

Automatic Fit. When the above criteria for column width result in a report that is too wide for the report margins, FORMAT=AUTOMATIC shrinks the report. AUTOMATIC performs the following two steps sequentially, stopping as soon as the report fits within the margins:

1. AUTOMATIC reduces intercolumn spacing incrementally until it reaches a minimum intercolumn space of 1. It will never reduce it to 0.

2. AUTOMATIC shortens widths for strings specified on the STRING subcommand. It begins with the longest string if that string is at least 15 characters wide and shortens the column width as much as needed (up to 40% of its length), wrapping the string within the new width. If necessary it repeats the step, using different defined strings. It will not shorten the column width of the same string twice.

REPORT does *not* implement the automatic fit unless AUTOMATIC is specified on the FORMAT subcommand.

AUTOMATIC vs. MANUAL Defaults. Many default settings depend on whether you specify AUTOMATIC or MANUAL on FORMAT. Table 14 shows the defaults according to both specifications.

Table 14   Keyword default settings

Subcommand	Keyword	Default for AUTOMATIC	Default for MANUAL
FORMAT	ALIGN	left	left
	BRKSPACE		
	summary report	1	1
	listing report	-1	1
	CHALIGN	bottom	top
	CHDSPACE	1	1
	COLSPACE	4	4

Table 14   Keyword default settings (Continued)

Subcommand	Keyword	Default for AUTOMATIC	Default for MANUAL
	FTSPACE	1	1
	LENGTH	1,system length	1,system length
	LIST|NOLIST	NOLIST	NOLIST
	MARGINS	1,system length	1,system length
	MISSING	.	.
	PAGE1	1	1
	SUMSPACE	1	1
	TSPACE	1	1
	UNDERSCORE	on	off
VARIABLES	LABEL|VALUE|DUMMY	VALUE	VALUE
	LEFT|CENTER|RIGHT	CENTER	RIGHT for numbers LEFT for strings
	OFFSET	CENTER	0
BREAK	LABEL|VALUE	LABEL	VALUE
	LEFT|CENTER|RIGHT	CENTER	RIGHT for numbers LEFT for strings
	NAME|NONAME	NONAME	NONAME
	OFFSET	CENTER	0
	PAGE	off	off
	SKIP	1	1
	TOTAL|NOTOTAL	NOTOTAL	NOTOTAL
	UNDERSCORE	off	off
SUMMARY	PREVIOUS	1	1
	SKIP	0	0

Options

Format. REPORT provides full format defaults and offers you optional control over page length, vertical spacing, margin and column widths, page titles, footnotes, and labels for statistics. The maximum width and length of the report are controlled by specifications on the SET command. The FORMAT subcommand on REPORT controls how the report is laid out on a page and whether case listings are displayed. The VARIABLES subcommand specifies the variables that are listed or summarized in the report (**report variables**) and controls the titles, width, and contents of report columns. The BREAK subcommand specifies the variables that define groups (**break variables**) and controls the titles, width, and contents of break columns. SUMMARY specifies statistics and controls the titles and spacing of summary lines. The TITLE and FOOTNOTE subcommands control the specification and placement of multiple-line titles and footnotes. STRING concatenates variables to create temporary variables that can be specified on VARIABLES or BREAK.

Output File. You can direct reports to a file separate from the listing file using the OUTFILE subcommand.

Statistical Display. The statistical display is controlled by the SUMMARY subcommand. Statistics can be calculated for each category of a break variable and for the group as a whole. Available statistics include mean, variance, standard deviation, skewness, kurtosis, sum, minimum, maximum, mode, median, and percentages. Composite functions perform arithmetic operations using two or more summary statistics calculated on single variables.

Missing Values. You can include user-missing values in report statistics and listings with the MISSING subcommand. You can also use FORMAT to define a missing-value symbol to represent missing data.

Basic Specification

The basic specification depends on whether you want a listing report or a summary report. A listing report without subgroup classification requires FORMAT and VARIABLES. A listing report with subgroup classification requires FORMAT, VARIABLES, and BREAK. A summary report requires VARIABLES, BREAK, and SUMMARY.

Listing Reports. FORMAT=LIST and VARIABLES with a variable list are required. Case listings are displayed for each variable named on VARIABLES. There are no break groups or summary statistics unless BREAK or SUMMARY are specified.

Summary Reports. VARIABLES, BREAK, and SUMMARY are required. The report is organized according to the values of the variable named on BREAK. The variable named on BREAK must be named on a preceding SORT CASES command. Specified statistics are computed for the variables specified on VARIABLES for each subgroup defined by the break variables.

Subcommand Order

The following order must be observed among subcommands when they are used:

- FORMAT must precede all other subcommands.
- VARIABLES must precede BREAK.
- Each SUMMARY subcommand must immediately follow its associated BREAK. Multiple SUMMARY subcommands associated with the same BREAK must be specified consecutively.
- TITLE and FOOTNOTE can appear anywhere after FORMAT except between BREAK and SUMMARY.
- MISSING must follow VARIABLES and precede the first BREAK.
- STRING must precede VARIABLES.

Syntax Rules

- Only one each of the FORMAT, STRING, VARIABLES, and MISSING subcommands is allowed.
- To obtain multiple break groups, use multiple BREAK subcommands.
- To obtain multiple summaries for a break level, specify multiple SUMMARY subcommands for the associated BREAK.
- Keywords on REPORT subcommands have default specifications that are in effect if the keyword is not specified. Specify keywords only when you wish to change a default.
- Keywords are enclosed in parentheses if the subcommand takes variable names as arguments.

Operations

- REPORT processes cases sequentially. When the value of a break variable changes, REPORT displays a statistical summary for cases processed since the last set of summary statistics was displayed. Thus, the file must be sorted in order on the break variable or variables.
- The maximum width and page length of the report are determined by the SET command.
- If a column is not wide enough to display numeric values, REPORT first rounds decimal digits, then converts to scientific notation if possible, and then displays asterisks. String variables that are wider than the column are wrapped.
- The format used to display values in case listings is controlled by the dictionary format of the variable. Each statistical function in REPORT has a default format.

Limitations

- The maximum number of variables per VARIABLES subcommand is the same as the system limit.
- Maximum 10 dummy variables per VARIABLES subcommand.
- Maximum 20 MODE and MEDIAN requests per SUMMARY subcommand.
- Maximum 20 PGT, PLT, and PIN requests per SUMMARY subcommand.
- Maximum 50 strings per STRING subcommand.
- The length of titles and footnotes cannot exceed the report width.
- The length of string variables created on STRING cannot exceed the page width.
- There is no fixed limit on the number of BREAK and SUMMARY subcommands. However, the page width limits the number of variables that can be displayed and thereby limits the number of break variables. The limit of 10 variables on SORT CASES can limit the number of break variables.
- The maximum margin of a report is 255 characters.
- The number of report variables that can be specified depends upon the width of the report, the width of the variable columns, and the number of BREAK subcommands.

- Maximum 50 variables for the FREQUENCY or PERCENT functions.
- Memory requirements significantly increase if FREQUENCY, PERCENT, MEDIAN, or MODE is requested for variables with a wide range of values. The amount of workspace required is $20 + 8*(max-min +1)$ bytes per variable per function per break. If the same range is used for different statistics for the same variable, only one set of cells is collected. For example, FREQUENCY(1,100)(VARA) PERCENT(1,100)(VARA) requires only 820 bytes.
- If TOTAL is in effect, workspace requirements are almost doubled.
- Memory requirements also increase if value labels are displayed for variables with many value labels. The amount of workspace required is $4 + 24*n$ bytes per variable, where n is the number of value labels specified for the variable.

Example

```
SORT CASES BY DEPT.
REPORT FORMAT=LIST
   /VARIABLES=PRODUCT (LABEL) ' ' 'Retail' 'Products'
          SALES 'Annual' 'Sales' '1981'
   /BREAK=DEPT 'Department' (LABEL)
   /SUMMARY=VALIDN (PRODUCT) MEAN (SALES) 'No.Sold,Mean Sales'.
```

- This report is a listing of products and sales by department. A summary of the total number of products sold and the average sales by department is also produced.
- Cases are first sorted by *DEPT* so that cases are grouped by department for the case listing and for the calculation of statistics.
- FORMAT requests a report that lists individual cases within each break group.
- VARIABLES specifies *PRODUCT* and *SALES* as the report variables. Keyword LABEL requests that the case listings for *PRODUCT* display value labels instead of values. Three-line column headings are provided for each report column. The first line of the column heading is blank for the variable *PRODUCT*.
- BREAK identifies *DEPT* as the break variable and provides a one-line column title for the break column. LABEL displays the value label instead of the value itself.
- SUMMARY calculates the valid number of cases for *PRODUCT* and the mean of *SALES* for each value of *DEPT*. A title is provided for the summary line to override the default title, *VALIDN*.

FORMAT Subcommand

FORMAT controls the overall width and length of the report and vertical spacing. Keywords and their arguments can be specified in any order.

- MANUAL and AUTOMATIC are alternatives. The default is MANUAL.
- LIST and NOLIST are alternatives. The default is NOLIST.

MANUAL   *Default settings for manual format.* MANUAL displays values for break variables, right-justifies numeric values and their column headings, left-justifies value labels and string values and their column headings, top-aligns and does not underscore column headings, extends column widths to accommodate the variable's longest value label (but not the longest word in the variable label) up to a width of 20, and generates an error message when a report is too wide for its margins. MANUAL is the default.

AUTOMATIC   *Default settings for automatic format.* AUTOMATIC displays labels for break variables, centers all data, centers column headings but left-justifies column headings if value labels or string values exceed the width of the longest word in the heading, bottom-aligns and underscores column headings, extends column widths to accommodate the longest word in a variable label or the variable's longest value label, and shrinks a report that is too wide for its margins.

LIST(n)   *Individual case listing.* The values of all variables named on VARIABLES are displayed for each case. The optional *n* inserts a blank line after each *n* cases. By default, no blank lines are inserted. Values for cases are listed using the default formats for the variables.

NOLIST   *No case listing.* This is the default.

PAGE(n)   *Page number for the first page of the report.* The default is 1.

LENGTH(t,b)   *Top and bottom line numbers of the report.* You can specify any numbers to define the report page length. By default, the top of the report begins at line 1, and the bottom of the report is the last line of the system page. You can use an asterisk for *t* or *b* to indicate a default value. The value for *b* cannot exceed the system page length. The system page length is controlled by SET.

MARGINS(l,r)   *Columns for the left and right margins.* By default, the left margin is display column 1 and the right margin is the rightmost display column of the system page, which is controlled by SET. You can use an asterisk for *l* or *r* to indicate a default value.

ALIGN   *Placement of the report relative to its margins.* LEFT, CENTER, or RIGHT can be specified in the parentheses following the keyword. LEFT left-justifies the report. CENTER centers the report between its margins. RIGHT right-justifies the report. The default is LEFT.

COLSPACE(n)   *Number of spaces between each column.* The default is 4 or the average number of spaces that will fit within report margins, whichever is less. When AUTOMATIC is in effect, REPORT overrides the specified column spacing if necessary to fit the report between its margins.

CHALIGN   *Alignment of column headings.* Either TOP or BOTTOM can be specified in the parentheses following the keyword. TOP aligns all column headings with the first, or top, line of multiple-line headings. BOTTOM aligns headings with the last, or bottom, line of multiple-line headings. When AUTOMATIC is in effect, the default is BOTTOM; when MANUAL is in effect, the default is TOP.

UNDERSCORE   *Underscores for column headings.* Either ON or OFF can be specified in the parentheses following the keyword. ON underscores the bottom line of each column heading for the full width of the column. OFF does not underscore column headings. The default is ON when AUTOMATIC is in effect and OFF when MANUAL is in effect.

TSPACE(n)   *Number of blank lines between the report title and the column heads.* The default is 1.

CHDSPACE(n)   *Number of blank lines beneath the longest column head.* The default is 1.

BRKSPACE(n)   *Number of blank lines between the break head and the next line.* The next line is a case if LIST is in effect or the first summary line if NOLIST is in effect. BRKSPACE(-1) places the first summary statistic or the first case listing on the same line as the break value. When a summary line is placed on the same line as the break value, the summary title is suppressed. When AUTOMATIC is in effect, the default is −1; when MANUAL is in effect, it is 1.

SUMSPACE(n)   *Number of blank lines between the last summary line at the lower break level and the first summary line at the higher break level when they break simultaneously.* SUMSPACE also controls spacing between the last listed case and the first summary line if LIST is in effect. The default is 1.

FTSPACE(n)   *Minimum number of blank lines between the last listing on the page and the footnote.* The default is 1.

MISSING 's'   *Missing-value symbol.* The symbol can be only one character and represents both system- and user-missing values. The default is a period.

Example

```
FORMAT=AUTOMATIC LIST MARGINS(1,60) LENGTH(5,30) MISSING ('*')
```

- FORMAT requests a case listing, defines a new page size smaller than the system page size, and specifies an asterisk as the missing-value symbol.

Page Layout

Figure 7 shows the complete page layout and subcommand specifications used to control the basic format of the report.

OUTFILE Subcommand

OUTFILE directs the report to a file separate from the SPSS/PC+ listing file. This allows you to print the report without having to delete the extraneous material that would be present in the listing file.

- OUTFILE must follow FORMAT.
- Specifications on OUTFILE consist of a filename in apostrophes.
- You can send the report to a directory or drive other than your current defaults by specifying an appropriate DOS file specification.
- You can print the report with the DOS PRINT command at the end of your session.
- The report does not appear on your screen when you specify OUTFILE.

Figure 7   Page layout for REPORT

```
----------------------------------------------- top of page -----------------------------------------------
```

		COLUMN	COLUMN	COLUMN	COLUMN	
***************	TITLE	***************				◄—— LENGTH
						◄—— TSPACE
BREAK HEAD	BREAK HEAD	COLUMN HEAD (VAR)	COLUMN HEAD (VAR)	COLUMN HEAD (VAR)	COLUMN HEAD (VAR)	
						◄—— CHDSPACE
BREAK A VALUE 1	BREAK B VALUE 1					◄—— BRKSPACE
		VALUE VALUE	VALUE VALUE	VALUE VALUE	VALUE VALUE	◄—— LIST
		VALUE VALUE	VALUE VALUE	VALUE VALUE	VALUE VALUE	
						◄—— SUMSPACE
	SUMMARY TITLE	AGG	AGG	AGG	AGG	◄—— SKIP w/ SUMMARY
	SUMMARY TITLE	AGG	AGG	AGG	AGG	◄—— SKIP w/ BREAK
	BREAK B VALUE 2					◄—— BRKSPACE
		VALUE VALUE	VALUE VALUE	VALUE VALUE	VALUE VALUE	◄—— LIST
		VALUE VALUE	VALUE VALUE	VALUE VALUE	VALUE VALUE	
						◄—— SUMSPACE
	SUMMARY TITLE	AGG	AGG	AGG	AGG	◄—— stats for B=2, A=1
	SUMMARY TITLE	AGG	AGG	AGG	AGG	
SUMMARY TITLE		AGG	AGG	AGG	AGG	◄—— SUMSPACE stats for A=1
SUMMARY TITLE		AGG	AGG	AGG	AGG	
BREAK A VALUE 2	BREAK B VALUE 1					◄—— SKIP w/ BREAK
		VALUE VALUE	VALUE VALUE	VALUE VALUE	VALUE VALUE	◄—— BRKSPACE
		VALUE VALUE	VALUE VALUE	VALUE VALUE	VALUE VALUE	◄—— LIST
						◄—— SUMSPACE
	SUMMARY TITLE	AGG	AGG	AGG	AGG	◄—— SKIP w/ SUMMARY
	SUMMARY TITLE	AGG	AGG	AGG	AGG	◄—— SKIP w/ BREAK
	BREAK B VALUE 2					◄—— BRKSPACE
		VALUE VALUE	VALUE VALUE	VALUE VALUE	VALUE VALUE	◄—— LIST
		VALUE VALUE	VALUE VALUE	VALUE VALUE	VALUE VALUE	
	SUMMARY TITLE	AGG	AGG	AGG	AGG	
	SUMMARY TITLE	AGG	AGG	AGG	AGG	◄—— SUMSPACE
SUMMARY TITLE		AGG	AGG	AGG	AGG	
SUMMARY TITLE		AGG	AGG	AGG	AGG	◄—— FTSPACE
						◄—— LENGTH

```
*************** FOOTNOTE ***************
--------------------------------------- bottom of page ---------------------------------------
|                                                                                          |
```

Left margin   Right margin

Example

```
REPORT FORMAT=AUTOMATIC LIST
   /OUTFILE=PRSNLRPT
   /VARIABLES=LNAME AGE TENURE JTENURE SALARY
   /BREAK=DIVISION
   /SUMMARY=MEAN.

REPORT FORMAT=AUTOMATIC
   /OUTFILE=PRSNLRPT
   /VARIABLES=LNAME AGE TENURE JTENURE SALARY
   /BREAK=DIVISION
   /SUMMARY=MEAN
   /SUMMARY=MIN
   /SUMMARY=MAX.
```

- Both a listing report and a summary report are written to file *PRSNLRPT*.

VARIABLES Subcommand

The required VARIABLES subcommand names the variables to be listed and summarized in the report. You can also use VARIABLES to control column titles, column widths, and the contents of report columns.

- The minimum specification on VARIABLES is a list of report variables. The number of variables that can be specified is limited by the system page width.

- Each report variable defines a report column. The value of the variable or an aggregate statistic calculated for the variable is displayed in that variable's report column.

- Variables are assigned to columns in the order in which they are named on VARIABLES.

- Variables named on BREAK can also be named in VARIABLES.

- When FORMAT=LIST, variables can be stacked in a single column by linking them with plus signs (+) on the VARIABLES subcommand. If no column heading is specified, REPORT uses the default heading from the first variable in the list. Only values from the first variable in the column are used to calculate summaries.

- Optional specifications apply only to the immediately preceding variable or list of variables implied by the TO keyword. Options can be specified in any order.

- All optional specifications except column headings must be enclosed in parentheses; headings must be enclosed in apostrophes or quotes.

Column Contents

The following options can be used to specify the contents of the report column for each variable:

(VALUE)   *Display the values of the variable.* This is the default.

(LABEL)   *Display value labels.* If value labels are not defined, values are displayed.

(DUMMY)   *Display blank spaces.* DUMMY defines a report column for a variable that does not exist in the active file. Dummy variables are used to control spacing or to reserve space for statistics computed for other variables. Do not name an existing SPSS/PC+ variable as a dummy variable.

- These three options are alternatives; the default is VALUE.

- VALUE and LABEL have no effect unless LIST has been specified on the FORMAT subcommand.

- When AUTOMATIC is in effect, value labels or string values are centered in the column based on the length of the longest string or label; numeric values are centered based on the width of the widest value or summary format. When MANUAL is in effect, value labels or string values are left-justified in the column and numeric values are right-justified. (See the OFFSET keyword on p. 717 for information on adjusting the position of column contents.)

Column Heading

The following option can be used to specify a heading for the report column:

'column heading'   *Column heading for the preceding variable.* The heading must be enclosed in apostrophes or quotes. If no column heading is specified, the default is the variable label or, if no variable label has been specified, the variable name.

- To specify multiple-line headings, enclose each line in a set of apostrophes or quotes, using the conventions for strings (see "String Values in Command Specifications" on p. 429). The specifications for title lines should be separated by at least one blank.

- Default column headings wrap for as many lines as are required to display the entire label. If AUTOMATIC is in effect, user-specified column headings appear exactly as specified, even if the column width must be extended. If MANUAL is in effect, user-specified titles wrap to fit within the column width.

Column Heading Alignment

The following options can be used to specify how column headings are aligned:

(LEFT)   *Left-aligned column heading.*

(CENTER)   *Centered column heading.*

(RIGHT)   *Right-aligned column heading.*

- These three options are alternatives. The default depends on whether AUTOMATIC or MANUAL is in effect.

- If AUTOMATIC is in effect, column headings are centered within their columns by default. If value labels or string values exceed the width of the longest word in the heading, the heading is left-justified.

- If MANUAL is in effect, column headings are left-justified for value labels or string values and right-justified for numeric values by default.

Column Format

The following options can be used to specify column width and adjust the position of the column contents:

(width)   *Width for the report column.* If no width is specified for a variable, REPORT determines a default width using the criteria described under "Defaults" on p. 706. If you specify a width that is not wide enough to display numeric values, REPORT first rounds decimal digits, then converts to scientific notation if possible, and then displays asterisks. Value labels or string values that exceed the width are wrapped.

(OFFSET)   *Position of the report column contents.* The specification is either *n* or CENTER specified in parentheses. OFFSET(*n*) indicates the number of spaces to offset the contents from the left for value labels or string values, and from the right for numeric values. OFFSET(CENTER) centers contents within the center of the column. If AUTOMATIC is in effect, the default is CENTER. If MANUAL is in effect, the default is 0: value labels and string values are left-justified and numeric values are right-justified.

Example

```
/VARIABLES=V1 TO V3(LABEL) (15)
  V4 V5 (LABEL)(OFFSET (2))(10)
  SEP1 (DUMMY) (2) ''
  V6 'Results using' "Lieben's Method" 'of Calculation'
```

- The width of the columns for variables *V1* through *V3* is 15 each. Value labels are displayed for these variables in the case listing.

- The column for variable *V4* uses the default width. Values are listed in the case listing.

- Value labels are displayed for variable *V5*. The column width is 10. Column contents are offset two spaces from the left.

- *SEP1* is a dummy variable. The column width is 2, and there is at least one space on each side of *SEP1*. Thus, there are at least four blanks between the columns for *V5* and *V6*. *SEP1* is given a null title to override the default column title *SEP1*.

- *V6* has a three-line title. Its column uses the default width, and values are listed in the case listing.

STRING Subcommand

STRING creates temporary string variables by concatenating variables and user-specified strings. These variables exist only within the REPORT procedure.

- The minimum specification is a name for the string variable followed by a variable name or a user-specified string enclosed in parentheses.

- The name assigned to the string variable must be unique.

- Any combination of string variables, numeric variables, and user-specified strings can be used in the parentheses to define the string.

- Keyword TO cannot be used within the parentheses to imply a variable list.

- More than one string variable can be defined on STRING.
- If a case has a missing value for a variable within the parentheses, the variable passes the missing value to the temporary variable without affecting other elements specified. The string has the system-missing value for that case and the missing-value symbol is used for that value in case listings.
- A string variable defined in REPORT cannot exceed the system page width.
- String variables defined on STRING can be used on VARIABLES or BREAK.

The following options can be used to specify how components are to be concatenated:

(width) *Width of the preceding variable within the string.* The default is the dictionary width of the variable. The maximum width for numeric variables within the string definition is 16. The maximum width for a string variable is the system page width. If the width specified is less than that required by the value, numeric values are displayed as asterisks and string values are truncated. If the width exceeds the width of a value, numeric values are padded with zeros on the left and string values are padded with blanks on the right.

(BLANK) *Left-pad values of the preceding numeric variable with blanks.* The default is to left-pad values of numeric variables with zeros. If a numeric variable has a dollar or comma format, it is automatically left-padded with blanks.

'literal' *User-specified string.* Any combination of characters can be specified within apostrophes or quotes.

Example

```
/STRING=JOB1(AVAR NVAR)
       JOB2(AVAR(2) NVAR(3))
       JOB3(AVAR(2) NVAR(BLANK) (4))
```

- STRING defines three string variables to be used within the report.
- Assume that *AVAR* is a string variable read from a four-column field using keyword FIXED on DATA LIST and that *NVAR* is a computed numeric variable with the default format of eight columns with two implied decimal places.
- If a case has value KJ for *AVAR* and value 241 for *NVAR*, *JOB1* displays the value KJ 00241.00, *JOB2* the value KJ241, and *JOB3* the value KJ 241. If *NVAR* has the system-missing value for a case, the value KJ. is displayed for *JOB1*.

Example

```
/STRING=SOCSEC(S1 '-' S2 '-' S3)
```

- STRING concatenates the three variables *S1*, *S2*, and *S3*, each of which contains a segment of the social security number.
- Hyphens are inserted between the segments when the values of *SOCSEC* are displayed.
- This example assumes that the variables *S1*, *S2*, and *S3* were read from three-column, two-column, and four-column fields respectively, using the keyword FIXED on DATA LIST. These variables would then have default format widths of 3, 2, and 4 columns and would not be left-padded with zeros.

BREAK Subcommand

BREAK specifies the variables that define the subgroups for the report, or it specifies summary totals for reports with no subgroups. BREAK also allows you to control the titles, width, and contents of break columns and to begin a new page for each level of the break variable.

- A break occurs when any one of the variables named on BREAK changes value. Cases must be sorted by the values of all BREAK variables on all BREAK subcommands.
- The BREAK subcommand must precede the SUMMARY subcommand that defines the summary line for the break.
- A break column is reserved for each BREAK subcommand.
- To obtain multiple break levels, specify multiple break variables on a BREAK subcommand.
- If more than one variable is specified on a BREAK subcommand, a single break column is used. The value or value label for each variable is displayed on a separate line in the order in which the variables are specified on BREAK. The first variable specified changes most slowly. The default column width is the longest of the default widths for any of the break variables.
- To obtain summary totals without any break levels, use keyword TOTAL on BREAK without listing any variables. TOTAL must be specified on the first BREAK subcommand.
- Optional specifications apply to all variables in the break column and to the break column as a whole. Options can be specified in any order following the last variable named.
- All optional specifications except column headings must be enclosed in parentheses; column headings must be enclosed in apostrophes.

Column Contents

The following can be used to specify the contents of the break column:

(VALUE)   *Display values of the break variables.*

(LABEL)   *Display value labels.* If no value labels have been defined, values are displayed.

- The value or label is displayed only once for each break change and is not repeated at the top of the page in a multiple-page break group.
- These two options are alternatives. The default depends on whether AUTOMATIC or MANUAL is in effect.
- When AUTOMATIC is in effect, the default is LABEL; when MANUAL is in effect, the default is VALUE.
- When AUTOMATIC is in effect, the value or label is centered in the column. When MANUAL is in effect, value labels and string values are left-justified and numeric values are right-justified. (See the OFFSET keyword on p. 721 for information on adjusting the position of column contents.)

Column Heading

The following option specifies headings used for the break column:

'column heading'   *Column heading for the break column.* The heading must be included in apostrophes or quotes. The default heading is the variable label of the break variable or, if no label has been defined, the variable name. If the break column is defined by more than one variable, the label or name of the first variable is used.

- To specify multiple-line headings, enclose each line in a set of apostrophes or quotes, following the conventions for strings (see "String Values in Command Specifications" on p. 429). Separate the specifications for heading lines with at least one blank.

- Default column headings wrap for as many lines as are required to display the entire label. When AUTOMATIC is in effect, user-specified column headings appear exactly as specified, even if the column width must be extended.

Column Heading Alignment

The following options can be used to specify how column headings are aligned:

(LEFT)   *Left-aligned column heading.*

(CENTER) *Centered column heading.*

(RIGHT)   *Right-aligned column heading.*

- These three options are alternatives. The default depends on whether AUTOMATIC or MANUAL is in effect.

- When AUTOMATIC is in effect, column headings are centered within their columns by default. If value labels or string values exceed the width of the longest word in the heading, the heading is left-justified.

- When MANUAL is in effect, column headings are left-justified for value labels or string values and right-justified for numeric values.

Column Format

The following options can be used to format break columns.

- TOTAL and NOTOTAL are alternatives. The default is NOTOTAL.
- SKIP and PAGE are alternatives. The default is SKIP(1).
- NAME and NONAME are alternatives. The default is NONAME.

(width)   *Column width for the break column.* If no width is specified for a variable, REPORT determines a default width using the criteria described under "Defaults" on p. 706. If you specify a width that is not wide enough to display numeric values, REPORT first rounds decimal digits, then converts them to scientific notation if possible, and then displays asterisks. Value labels or string values that exceed the width are wrapped.

(OFFSET)   *Position of the break column contents.* The specification is either *n* or CEN-TER specified in parentheses. OFFSET(*n*) indicates the number of spaces to offset the contents from the left for value labels or string values, and from the right for numeric values. OFFSET(CENTER) centers contents within the column. If AUTOMATIC is in effect, the default is CENTER. If MANUAL is in effect, the default is 0: value labels and string values are left-justified and numeric values are right-justified.

(UNDERSCORE)   *Use underscores below case listings.* Case listing columns produced by FORMAT LIST are underscored before summary statistics are displayed. You can optionally specify the names of one or more report variables in parentheses after UNDERSCORE, as in (UNDERSCORE(PRICE)). Only the specified columns are underscored.

(TOTAL)   *Display the summary statistics requested on the next SUMMARY subcommand for all the cases in the report.* TOTAL must be specified on the first BREAK subcommand and applies only to the next SUMMARY subcommand specified.

(NOTOTAL)   *Display summary statistics only for each break.* This is the default.

(SKIP(n))   *Skip* n *lines after the last summary line for a break before beginning the next break.* The default for *n* is 1.

(PAGE)   *Begin each break on a new page.* If (RESET) is also specified on PAGE, the page counter resets to the PAGE1 setting on the FORMAT subcommand every time the break value changes for the specified variable. PAGE(RESET) cannot be specified for listing reports with no break levels.

(NAME)   *Display the name of the break variable next to each value or value label of the break variable.* NAME requires 10 spaces (the maximum eight-character width of SPSS/PC+ variable names plus a colon and a blank space) in addition to the space needed to display break values or value labels. NAME is ignored if the break-column width is insufficient.

(NONAME)   *Suppress the display of break variable names.* This is the default.

Example

```
SORT DIVISION BRANCH DEPT.
REPORT FORMAT=AUTOMATIC MARGINS (1,70) BRKSPACE(-1)

  /VARIABLES=SPACE(DUMMY) ' ' (4)
            SALES 'Annual' 'Sales' '1981' (15) (OFFSET(2))
            EXPENSES 'Annual' 'Expenses' '1981' (15) (OFFSET(2))

  /BREAK=DIVISION
        BRANCH (10) (TOTAL) (OFFSET(1))
  /SUMMARY=MEAN

  /BREAK=DEPT 'Department' (10)
  /SUMMARY=MEAN.
```

- This example creates a report with three break variables. *BRANCH* breaks within values of *DIVISION*, and *DEPT* breaks within values of *BRANCH*.

- FORMAT sets margins to a maximum of 70 columns and requests that summary lines be displayed on the same line as break values. Because LIST is not specified on FORMAT, only summary statistics are displayed.
- VARIABLES defines three report columns, each occupied by a report variable: *SPACE*, *SALES*, and *EXPENSES*.
- The variable *SPACE* is a dummy variable that exists only within REPORT. It has a null heading and a width of 4. It is used as a space holder to separate the break columns from the report columns.
- *SALES* has a three-line heading and a width of 15. The values of *SALES* are offset two spaces from the right.
- *EXPENSES* is the third report variable and has the same width and offset specifications as *SALES*.
- The leftmost column in the report is reserved for the first two break variables, *DIVISION* and *BRANCH*. Value labels are displayed, since this is the default for AUTOMATIC. The break column has a width of 10 and the value labels are offset one space from the left. Value labels more than nine characters long are wrapped. The default column heading is used. TOTAL requests a summary line at the end of the report showing the mean of all cases in the report.
- The first SUMMARY subcommand displays the mean of each report variable in its report column. This line is displayed each time the value of *DIVISION* or *BRANCH* changes.
- The third break variable, *DEPT*, occupies the second column from the left in the report. The break column has a width of 10 and has a one-line heading. The first ten characters of the value labels are displayed in the break column.
- The second SUMMARY subcommand displays the mean for each report variable when the value of *DEPT* changes.

SUMMARY Subcommand

SUMMARY calculates a wide range of aggregate and composite statistics.

- SUMMARY must be specified if LIST is not specified on FORMAT.
- The minimum specification is an aggregate or a composite function and its arguments. This must be the first specification on SUMMARY.
- Each SUMMARY subcommand following a BREAK subcommand specifies a new summary line.
- The default location of the summary title is the column of the break variable to which the summary applies. When more than one function is named on SUMMARY, the default summary title is that of the function named first. Both the title and its default column location can be altered (see "Summary Titles" on p. 726).
- The default format can be altered for any function (see "Summary Print Formats" on p. 727).
- SUMMARY subcommands apply only to the preceding BREAK subcommand. If there is no SUMMARY subcommand after a BREAK subcommand, no statistics are displayed for that break level.

- To use the summary specifications from a previous BREAK subcommand for the current BREAK subcommand, specify keyword PREVIOUS on SUMMARY. (See "Other Summary Keywords" on p. 729.)
- Summary statistics are displayed in report columns. With aggregate functions you can compute summary statistics for all report variables or for a subset (see "Aggregate Functions" below).With composite functions you can compute summaries for all or a subset of report variables and you have additional control over the placement of summary statistics in particular report columns (see "Composite Functions" on p. 725).
- Multiple summary statistics requested on one SUMMARY subcommand are all displayed on the same line. More than one function can be specified on SUMMARY as long as you do not attempt to place two results in the same report column (REPORT will not be executed if you do). To place results of more than one function in the same report column, use multiple SUMMARY subcommands.
- Any composite and aggregate functions (except FREQUENCY and PERCENT) can be specified on the same summary line for different variables.
- To insert blank lines between summaries when more than one summary line is requested for a break, use keyword SKIP followed by the number of lines to skip in parentheses. The default is 0. (See "Other Summary Keywords" on p. 729.)

Aggregate Functions

Use the aggregate functions to request descriptive statistics for report variables.

- If no variable names are specified as arguments to an aggregate function, the statistic is calculated for all variables named on VARIABLES (all report variables).
- To request an aggregate function for a subset of report variables, specify the variables in parentheses after the function keyword.
- All variables specified for an aggregate function must have been named on VARIABLES.
- Keyword TO cannot be used to specify a list of variables for an aggregate function.
- The result of an aggregate function is always displayed in the report column reserved for the variable for which the function was calculated.
- To use several aggregate functions for the same report variable, specify multiple SUMMARY subcommands. The results are displayed on different summary lines.
- The aggregate functions FREQUENCY and PERCENT have special display formats and cannot be placed on the same summary line with other aggregate or composite functions. They can be specified only once per SUMMARY subcommand.
- Aggregate functions use only cases with valid values.

VALIDN	*Valid number of cases.* This is the only function available for string variables.
SUM	*Sum of values.*
MIN	*Minimum value.*
MAX	*Maximum value.*
MEAN	*Mean.*

STDDEV	*Standard deviation.* Aliases are SD and STDEV.
VARIANCE	*Variance.*
KURTOSIS	*Kurtosis.*
SKEWNESS	*Skewness.*
MEDIAN(min,max)	*Median value for values within the range.* MEDIAN sets up integer-valued bins for counting all values in the specified range. Noninteger values are truncated when the median is calculated.
MODE(min,max)	*Modal value for values within the range.* MODE sets up integer-valued bins for counting all values in the specified range. Noninteger values are truncated when the mode is calculated.
PGT(n)	*Percentage of cases with values greater than* n. Alias PCGT.
PLT(n)	*Percentage of cases with values less than* n. Alias PCLT.
PIN(min,max)	*Percentage of cases within the inclusive value range specified.* Alias PCIN.
FREQUENCY(min,max)	*Frequency counts for values within the inclusive range.* FREQUENCY sets up integer-valued bins for counting all values in the specified range. Noninteger values are truncated when the frequency is computed. FREQUENCY cannot be mixed with other aggregate statistics on a summary line.
PERCENT(min,max)	*Percentages for values within the inclusive range.* PERCENT sets up integer-valued bins for counting all values in the specified range. Noninteger values are truncated when the percentages are computed. PERCENT cannot be mixed with other aggregate statistics on a summary line.

Example

```
SORT CASES BY BVAR AVAR.
REPORT FORMAT=AUTOMATIC LIST /VARIABLES=XVAR YVAR ZVAR

  /BREAK=BVAR
    /SUMMARY=SUM
    /SUMMARY=MEAN (XVAR YVAR ZVAR)
    /SUMMARY=VALIDN(XVAR)

  /BREAK=AVAR
    /SUMMARY=PREVIOUS.
```

- FORMAT requests a case listing, and VARIABLES establishes a report column for variables *XVAR*, *YVAR*, and *ZVAR*. The report columns have default widths and titles.
- Both break variables, *BVAR* and *AVAR*, have default widths and headings.
- Every time the value of *BVAR* changes, three summary lines are displayed. The first line contains the sums for variables *XVAR, YVAR*, and *ZVAR*. The second line contains the means of all three variables. The third line displays the number of valid cases for *XVAR* in the report column for *XVAR*.

- Every time the value of *AVAR* changes within each value of *BVAR*, the three summary lines requested for *BVAR* are displayed. These summary lines are based on cases with the current values of *BVAR* and *AVAR*.

Example

```
SORT CASES BY DEPT.
REPORT FORMAT=AUTOMATIC
  /VARIABLES=WAGE BONUS TENURE
  /BREAK=DEPT (23)
  /SUMMARY=SUM(WAGE BONUS) MEAN(TENURE) 'Sum Income: Mean Tenure'.
```

- SUMMARY defines a summary line consisting of the sums of *WAGE* and *BONUS* and the mean of TENURE. The result of each aggregate function is displayed in the report column of the variable for which the function is calculated.

- A title is assigned to the summary line. A width of 23 is defined for the break column to accommodate the title for the summary line.

Composite Functions

Use composite functions to obtain statistics based on aggregated statistics, to place a summary statistic in a column other than that of the report variable for which it was calculated, or to manipulate variables not named on VARIABLES.

- Composite functions can be computed for the following aggregate functions: VALIDN, SUM, MIN, MAX, MEAN, STDEV, VARIANCE, KURTOSIS, and SKEWNESS. Constants can also be arguments to composite functions.

- When used within composite functions, aggregate functions can have only one variable as an argument.

- A composite function and its arguments cannot be separated by other SUMMARY specifications.

- The result of a composite function can be placed in any report column, including columns of dummy or string variables, by specifying a target column. To specify a target column, enclose the variable name of the column in parentheses after the composite function and its arguments. By default, the results of a composite function are placed in the report column of the first variable specified on the composite function that is also specified on VARIABLES.

- The format for the result of a composite function can be specified in parentheses after the name of the column location, within the parentheses that enclose the column-location specification.

DIVIDE(arg$_1$ arg$_2$ [factor])	*Divide the first argument by the second and then multiply the result by the factor if it is specified.*
MULTIPLY(arg$_1$ ... arg$_n$)	*Multiply the arguments.*
PCT(arg$_1$ arg$_2$)	*The percentage of the first argument over the second.*
SUBTRACT(arg$_1$ arg$_2$)	*Subtract the second argument from the first.*
ADD(arg$_1$ ... arg$_n$)	*Add the arguments.*

GREAT(arg₁ ... argₙ)   *The maximum of the arguments.*

LEAST(arg₁ ... argₙ)   *The minimum of the arguments.*

AVERAGE(arg₁ ... argₙ)   *The average of the arguments.*

Example

```
SORT CASES BY DEPT.
REPORT FORMAT=AUTOMATIC BRKSPACE(-1)
  /VARIABLES=WAGE BONUS SPACE1 (DUMMY) ''
            BNFT1 BNFT2 SPACE2 (DUMMY)''
  /BREAK=DEPT

  /SUMMARY=MEAN(WAGE BONUS BNFT1 BNFT2)
      ADD(VALIDN(WAGE)) (SPACE2)

  /SUMMARY=ADD(SUM(WAGE) SUM(BONUS))
      ADD(SUM(BNFT1) SUM(BNFT2)) 'Totals' SKIP(1)

  /SUMMARY=DIVIDE(MEAN(WAGE) MEAN(BONUS)) (SPACE1 (COMMA)(2))
      DIVIDE(MEAN(BNFT1) MEAN(BNFT2)) (SPACE2 (COMMA)(2)) 'Ratios'
      SKIP(1).
```

- VARIABLES defines six report columns. The columns for *WAGE, BONUS, BNFT1,* and *BNFT2* contain aggregate statistics based on those variables. The variables *SPACE1* and *SPACE2* are dummy variables that are created for use as space holders; each is given a blank heading to suppress the default column heading.

- The first SUMMARY computes the means of the variables *WAGE, BONUS, BNFT1,* and *BNFT2.* Because BRKSPACE=-1, this summary line will be placed on the same line as the break value and will have no summary title. The means are displayed in the report column for each variable. SUMMARY also computes the valid number of cases for *WAGE* and places the result in the *SPACE2* column.

- The second SUMMARY adds the sum of *WAGE* to the sum of *BONUS.* Since no location is specified, the result is displayed in the *WAGE* column. In addition, the sum of *BNFT1* is added to the sum of *BNFT2* and the result is placed in the *BNFT1* column. The title for the summary line is *Totals.* One line is skipped before the summary line requested by this SUMMARY subcommand is displayed.

- The third summary line divides the mean of *WAGE* by the mean of *BONUS* and places the result in *SPACE1.* The ratio of the mean of *BNFT1* to the mean of *BNFT2* is displayed in the *SPACE2* column. The results are displayed with commas and two decimal places. The title for the summary line is *Ratios.* One line is skipped before the summary line requested by this SUMMARY subcommand is displayed.

Summary Titles

- You can specify a summary title enclosed in apostrophes or quotes, following the conventions for strings (see "String Values in Command Specifications" on p. 429). Table 15 shows the default titles.

- The summary title cannot separate any function from its arguments and cannot be the first specification on SUMMARY.

- A summary title can be only one line long.
- A summary title wider than the break column extends into the next break column to the right. If the title is wider than all of the available break columns, it is truncated.
- Only one summary title can be specified per summary line. If more than one is specified, the last is used.
- The summary title is left- or right-justified depending upon whether the break title is left- or right-justified.
- The default location for the summary title is the column of the BREAK variable to which the summary applies. With multiple breaks, you can override the default placement of the title by specifying, in parentheses following the title, the number of the break column in which you want the summary title to be displayed.
- In a report with no break levels, REPORT displays the summary title above the summary line at the left margin.

Table 15   Default title for summary lines

Function	Title
VALIDN	N
VARIANCE	Variance
SUM	Sum
MEAN	Mean
STDDEV	StdDev
MIN	Minimum
MAX	Maximum
SKEWNESS	Skewness
KURTOSIS	Kurtosis
PGT(n)	>n
PLT(n)	<n
PIN(min,max)	In n_1 to n_2
FREQUENCY(min,max)	Total
PERCENT(min,max)	Total
MEDIAN(min,max)	Median
MODE(min,max)	Mode

Summary Print Formats

All functions have default formats that are used to display results (see Table 16). You can override these defaults by specifying a format keyword and/or the number of decimal places.

- Format specifications must be enclosed in parentheses.
- For aggregate functions, the format and/or number of decimal places is specified after the variable name, within the parentheses that enclose the variable name. The variable must be explicitly named as an argument.

- For composite functions, the format and/or number of decimal places is specified after the variable name of the column location, within the parentheses that enclose the variable name. The column location must be explicitly specified.
- If the report column is wide enough, SUM, MEAN, STDDEV, MIN, MAX, MEDIAN, MODE, and VARIANCE use DOLLAR or COMMA format, if a DOLLAR or COMMA format has been declared for the variable on the FORMATS command.
- If the column is not wide enough to display the decimal digits for a given function, RE-PORT displays fewer decimal places. If the column is not wide enough to display the integer portion of the number, REPORT uses scientific notation if possible, or, if not, displays asterisks.
- An exact value of 0 is displayed with one 0 to the left of the decimal point and as many 0 digits to the right as specified by the format. A number less than 1 in absolute value is displayed without a 0 to the left of the decimal point, except with DOLLAR and COMMA formats.

(PLAIN)   *Override DOLLAR or COMMA dictionary formats.* PLAIN is the default for all functions except SUM, MEAN, STDDEV, MIN, MAX, MEDIAN, MODE, and VARIANCE. For these functions, the default is the dictionary format of the variable for which the function is computed.

(COMMA)   *Display the value using COMMA format.*

(DOLLAR)   *Display the value using DOLLAR format.*

(d)   *Number of decimal places.*

Example

```
/SUMMARY=MEAN(INCOME (DOLLAR)(2))
        ADD(SUM(INCOME)SUM(WEALTH)) (WEALTH(DOLLLAR(2))
```

- SUMMARY displays the mean of *INCOME* with dollar format and two decimal places. The result is displayed in the *INCOME* column.
- The sums of *INCOME* and *WEALTH* are added, and the result is displayed in the *WEALTH* column with dollar format and two decimal places.

Table 16   Default print formats for functions

Function	Width	Decimal places
VALIDN	5	0
SUM	Dictionary + 2	Dictionary
MEAN	Dictionary	Dictionary
STDDEV	Dictionary	Dictionary
VARIANCE	Dictionary	Dictionary
MIN	Dictionary	Dictionary
MAX	Dictionary	Dictionary
SKEWNESS	5	2
KURTOSIS	5	2

Table 16   Default print formats for functions (Continued)

Function	Width	Decimal places
PGT	6	1
PLT	6	1
PIN	6	1
MEDIAN	Dictionary	Dictionary
MODE	Dictionary	Dictionary
PERCENT	6	1
FREQUENCY	5	0
DIVIDE	Dictionary	0
PCT	6	2
SUBTRACT	Dictionary	0
ADD	Dictionary	0
GREAT	Dictionary	0
LEAST	Dictionary	0
AVERAGE	Dictionary	0
MULTIPLY	Dictionary	0

Other Summary Keywords

The following additional keywords can be specified on SUMMARY. These keywords are not enclosed in parentheses.

SKIP(n)   *Blank lines before the summary line.* The default is 0. If SKIP is specified for the first SUMMARY subcommand for a BREAK, it skips the specified lines after skipping the number of lines specified for BRKSPACE on FORMAT. Similarly, with case listings SKIP skips *n* lines after the blank line at the end of the listing.

PREVIOUS(n)   *Use the SUMMARY subcommands specified for the* n*th BREAK.* If *n* is not specified, PREVIOUS refers to the set of SUMMARY subcommands for the previous BREAK. If an integer is specified, the SUMMARY subcommands from the *n*th BREAK are used. If PREVIOUS is specified, no other specification can be used on that SUMMARY subcommand.

TITLE and FOOTNOTE Subcommands

TITLE and FOOTNOTE provide titles and footnotes for the report.

- TITLE and FOOTNOTE are optional and can be placed anywhere after FORMAT except between the BREAK and SUMMARY subcommands.
- The specification on TITLE or FOOTNOTE is the title or footnote in apostrophes or quotes. To specify a multiple-line title or footnote, enclose each line in apostrophes or quotes and separate the specifications for each line by at least one blank.

- The default REPORT title is the title specified on the TITLE command. If there is no TITLE command specified in your SPSS/PC+ session, the default REPORT title is the first line of the SPSS/PC+ header.
- Titles begin on the first line of the report page. Footnotes end on the last line of the report page.
- Titles and footnotes are repeated on each page of a multiple-page report.
- The positional keywords LEFT, CENTER, and RIGHT can each be specified once. The default is CENTER.
- If the total width needed for the combined titles or footnotes for a line exceeds the page width, REPORT generates an error message.

LEFT   *Left-justify titles or footnotes within the report page margins.*

RIGHT   *Right-justify titles or footnotes within the report page margins.*

CENTER   *Center titles and footnotes within the report page width.*

The following can be specified as part of the title or footnote.

)PAGE   *Display the page number right-justified in a five-character field.*

)DATE   *Display the current date in the form* dd/mmm/yy, *right-justified in a nine-character field.*

)var   *Display this variable's value label at this position.* If you specify a variable that has no value label, the value is displayed, formatted according to its print format. You cannot specify a scratch or system variable or a variable created with the STRING subcommand. If you want to use a variable named *DATE* or *PAGE* in the file, change the variable's name with the RENAME VARIABLES command before you use it on the TITLE or FOOTNOTE subcommands, to avoid confusion with the)PAGE and)DATE keywords.

-)PAGE and)DATE must be specified in upper case.
-)PAGE,)DATE, and)var are specified within apostrophes or quotes and can be mixed with string segments within the apostrophes or quotes.
- A variable specified on TITLE or FOOTNOTE must be defined in the active file but does not need to be included as a column on the report.
- One label or value from each variable specified on TITLE or FOOTNOTE is displayed on every page of the report. If a new page starts with a case listing, REPORT takes the value label from the first case listed. If a new page starts with a BREAK line, REPORT takes the value label from the first case of the new break group. If a new page starts with a summary line, REPORT takes the value label from the last case of the break group being summarized.
- If you specify the same variable in both a title and footnote, REPORT takes the title and footnote values from the top case on the page.

Example

```
/TITLE=LEFT 'Personnel Report' 'Prepared on )DATE'
    RIGHT 'Page: )PAGE'
```

- TITLE specifies a two-line left-justified title and a one-line right-justified title. These titles are displayed at the top of each page of the report.
- The second line of the left-justified title contains the date on which the report was processed.
- The right-justified title displays the page number following the string *Page:* on the same line as the first line of the left-justified title.

MISSING Subcommand

MISSING controls the treatment of cases with missing values.

- MISSING specifications apply to variables named on VARIABLES and SUMMARY and to strings created with the STRING subcommand. Use a SELECT IF command to eliminate cases with missing values for break variables.
- The character used to indicate missing values is controlled by the FORMAT subcommand.

VAR	*Missing values are treated separately for each variable.* Missing values are displayed in case listings but are not included in the calculation of summary statistics on a function-by-function basis. This is the default.
NONE	*User-missing values are treated as valid values.* This applies to all variables named on VARIABLES.
LIST[([varlist][n])]	*Cases with the specified number of missing values across the specified list of variables are not used.* The variable list and *n* are specified in parentheses. If *n* is not specified, the default is 1. If no variables are specified, all variables named on VARIABLES are assumed.

Example

```
/MISSING= LIST (XVAR,YVAR,ZVAR 2)
```

- Any case with two or more missing values across the variables *XVAR*, *YVAR*, and *ZVAR* is omitted from the report.

REVIEW

```
REVIEW [ { SCRATCH                    } ]
         { LISTING                    }
         { LOG                        }
         { BOTH                       }
         { 'filename' ['filename']    }
```

Example:

```
REVIEW.
```

Overview

The REVIEW command places you in Review, a full-screen editing environment complete with the SPSS/PC+ Menu and Help system. Review is specifically designed for editing SPSS/PC+ scratch pad and listing files. You can use Review to build SPSS commands in the scratch pad, browse and edit the listing file, and then return to the scratch pad to edit and submit revised command lines directly to SPSS/PC+ for execution. Since Review allows you to look at two files at once in separate windows, it's easy to check your commands against the output they produce.

In Review, you can build your SPSS/PC+ commands in any combination of the following three ways: by selecting them from the Menu and Help windows; by browsing the menus and then typing commands or parts of commands yourself; or by clearing the menus and typing complete commands in the scratch pad. Review's editing commands are issued by selecting options from mini-menus called up with the function keys on your keyboard. For example, pressing F4 calls up a mini-menu from which you can insert, delete, or undelete lines.

Many functions in Review and in the Menu and Help system can be accomplished using the mouse. See "The Mouse" on p. 741 for more information.

Options

You can edit any file or pair of files that consist of legible characters (see "Limitations" on p. 734). On color monitors, you can choose colors for the two editing windows and frame. You can also turn color off.

Basic Specification

- The basic specification is simply the command keyword REVIEW followed by the command terminator.
- By default, REVIEW initiates an editing session of the current scratch pad and listing files. The scratch pad is displayed in the bottom window, and the Menu and Help windows initially cover up the listing file in the upper window (press Alt-M to reveal the listing file). On color monitors, Review uses a default color scheme of 1,2,4 for lower-window (or only window) background color, upper-window background color, and frame color, respectively. See the manual for your monitor for the colors that correspond to these numbers. The default selection for each mini-menu is highlighted when the menu is called up.

Syntax Rules

- Only one keyword (SCRATCH, LISTING, LOG, or BOTH) can be specified.
- Use SCRATCH to edit your SPSS/PC+ scratch pad file.
- Use LISTING to edit your SPSS/PC+ listing file.
- Use LOG to edit your SPSS/PC+ log file.
- Use BOTH to edit both the log and listing files simultaneously.
- If you do not use a keyword, you can specify one or two filenames within apostrophes to edit files other than your scratch pad, listing, and log files.
- To set nondefault colors, specify the SET RCOLOR command before entering Review (see SET).
- To turn color off, specify SET COLOR OFF before entering Review.
- As an alternative to using the mini-menus, you can perform some editing functions by using the (Alt) key in combination with various other keys.
- Some commands cause Review to prompt for additional information, such as a filename, at the bottom of the screen. To cancel such commands when the prompt appears, press (Esc).

Operations

- You can enter Review from SPSS/PC+ or directly from DOS.
- If you edit two files at once, Review divides your screen into upper and lower windows. The file named first occupies the upper window and the file named second occupies the lower window. At first, the Menu and Help windows cover the upper window. You can clear the menus (or recall them) with (Alt)-(M).
- When you first enter Review and the menus are on screen, the system searches the menu for a match to every character you type. The cursor moves to the first menu entry that matches what you've typed. This is called *incremental search.* To direct your keystrokes to the other window while keeping the menus up, press (Alt)-(E). To return to incremental search in the menus, press (Esc).
- At the beginning of a session, Review displays the *last* lines in the files and reads additional lines as required.
- Editing occurs at the current line and character as determined by the position of the cursor.
- There are two editing modes: insert mode and overtype mode. In *insert mode,* the text you type is inserted to the left of the current character. In *overtype mode,* text replaces existing text.
- A two-digit number in the lower-right corner of the screen displays the column location of the cursor.
- To enter extended ASCII characters in the Edit window, activate (Num Lock) and use (Alt) with the numeric keypad. If (Num Lock) is not activated, the keypad controls cursor movement, and when used with (Alt) scrolls the Help window.

Limitations

- You can edit only ASCII files with Review. Do not attempt to edit formatted text created by spreadsheet, word-processing, or other software. If the listing of a file that results from a DOS TYPE command is meaningful, the file is probably an ASCII file.
- Review displays only the first 80 characters of any line. Use the Split Line command to view lines longer than 80 characters.
- Files used by Review are held in memory. You may not be able to edit very large files.

Example

```
REVIEW 'A:PLOT.INC' 'PLOT.LIS'.
```

Entering Review from DOS

To enter Review directly from DOS, specify:

```
SPSSPC/RE filename1 [filename2] [/La] [/Ub] [/Fc] [/B]
```

- Specify the names of the files you want to edit in place of filename1 and filename2.
- If you want to edit only one file, omit the second filename.
- The /La, /Ub, and /Fc options allow you to change the colors used for the lower (or only) window, upper window, and frame, respectively. Specify integers from 0 to 6 in place of a, b, and c. See the manual for your monitor for the colors that correspond to numbers 0 through 6.
- To turn off color, specify /B.

If you plan to use Review frequently from outside SPSS/PC+ with nondefault colors, create a batch file (a file with a *.BAT* extension) that contains the following single line:

```
SPSSPC /REVIEW /La /Ub /Fc %1 %2
```

- Specify the desired color numbers in place of a, b, and c.
- The batch file should be in the directory that holds your SPSS/PC+ program files.
- After you create the batch file, you can enter Review by typing the name of the batch file followed by the names of the files you want to edit. The colors you have specified in the batch file will take effect automatically.

Setting and Information Commands

Commands flagged with an asterisk (*) are mini-menu items that can be selected by highlighting the item with the cursor arrows and pressing ⏎Enter.

Command Name	Key Combination/Function
Review help*	F1 followed by R (or Alt-R) reveals the Help screen for Review function keys and Menu system commands. Pressing F1 again reveals the

Help screen for motion commands. When pressed in response to a prompt, F1 provides a short message explaining the prompt.

Menus* F1 followed by M (or Alt-M) brings up the SPSS/PC+ Menu and Help system.

Glossary* F1 followed by G (or Alt-G) calls up the online glossary. You are prompted for the term to look up; press ⏎Enter to look up the term currently under the cursor, or enter another term before pressing ⏎Enter. The glossary displays the closest alphabetic match.

Filelist* F1 followed by F (or Alt-F) switches the Files menu on and off. The Files menu displays all (or a specified subset of) the files in your current directory. When you need a filename to execute an SPSS/PC+ command, you can select the name from this menu. Esc also clears the menu.

Varlist* F1 followed by V (or Alt-V) switches the Variables menu on and off. The Variables menu displays all the variables in the active file. You can select variable names from this menu. Esc also clears the menu.

Switch windows* F2 followed by S (or Alt-S) switches windows.

Change window size* F2 followed by C allows you to change the relative sizes of the two windows.

Menu Commands

Commands flagged with an asterisk (*) are mini-menu items that can be selected by highlighting the item with the cursor arrows and pressing ⏎Enter.

Command Name	Key Combination/Function
menu Hlp on*	F1 followed by H (or Alt-H) switches the Help window on and off. The Help window contains an explanation of the currently highlighted menu item.
Incremental Search	When the Menu and Help windows are displayed, the cursor automatically moves to the first item on the menu that matches what you type. If you type an *s*, the cursor moves to the first item that begins with *s*. If you then type an *e*, the cursor moves to the first item that begins with *se*.
Get Typing Window	Alt-T opens a narrow window at the bottom of the Menu and Help system window, where you can type anything you want. When you press ⏎Enter the contents of this typing window are pasted in the Edit window.
Down Menu	↓ moves the cursor down one item on the menu.
Up Menu	↑ moves the cursor up one item on the menu.
Bottom of Menu	End moves the cursor to the bottom of the menu.

Top of Menu
(Home) moves the cursor to the top of the menu.

Down Help Window
(Alt)-(↓) moves you down one line in the Help window. (Alt)-(PgDn) moves you down one page in the Help window.

Up Help Window
(Alt)-(↑) moves you up one line in the Help window. (Alt)-(PgUp) moves you up one page in the Help window.

Bottom of Help Window
(Alt)-(End) moves you to the bottom of the Help window.

Top of Help Window
(Alt)-(Home) moves you to the top of the Help window.

**Paste Menu Item,
Descend Menus**
(←Enter) pastes the highlighted menu item into the Edit window and descends to a lower-level menu (if any). If the menu item is followed by empty parentheses or apostrophes, you'll be prompted to fill in the space before descending to a lower menu, unless lower menu selections fill in the space.

Browse Menus
(→) or (Tab→) selects the highlighted menu item without pasting the item in the Edit window. This allows you to browse through lower-level menus before deciding what to paste into your Edit window. Your selections are stored in a memory buffer so you can later paste them. You can climb back out of the menus and clear the buffer with either (←) or (Esc).

Clear Memory Buffer
(Alt)-(K) clears ("kills") the memory buffer. When you browse through menus without pasting items into the Edit window, your selections are stored in a memory buffer. If you had already typed part of a command, for example, and you wanted to paste just one keyword instead of a complete command, you would first clear the buffer and then paste the keyword you need.

**Remove Window,
Ascend Menus**
(Esc) either returns you to the Main Menu or brings you one step closer to the Main Menu. (Esc) removes the Variables and Files menus and the typing window. If you've descended several levels into the menus, (Esc) brings you up one level at a time. If you're typing in the Edit window, (Esc) returns you to the Menu and Help window.

Jump to Main Menu
(Alt)-(Esc) returns you to the Main Menu from any level in the Menu and Help system.

**Standard/Extended
Menus**
(Alt)-(X) switches you back and forth between standard and extended menus. The *standard menus* contain the procedures and operations that you will use most of the time. The *extended menus* contain keywords that you probably will not need as often. STD or EXT appears at the bottom of the screen indicating which menus are displayed.

File Commands

Commands flagged with an asterisk (*) are mini-menu items that can be selected by high-lighting the item with the cursor arrows and pressing ⏎Enter.

Command Name	Key Combination/Function
write Marked area*	F9 followed by M writes the current marked area to a file using a name you specify. The default filename is *REVIEW.TMP*.
write Whole file*	F9 followed by W (or Alt-W) saves the current file using a name you specify. The default is the current name. The original copy is renamed with the extension of *.BAK*.
Delete file on disk*	F9 followed by D allows you to delete any file from a DOS directory.
Insert File*	F3 followed by I inserts the contents of a DOS file into the current file below the current line.
Edit different file*	F3 followed by E replaces the file in the current window.
run marked Area*	F10 followed by A (or Alt-A) submits a marked area to SPSS/PC+ for execution. This command is available only if Review was entered from SPSS/PC+. If unsaved changes have been made in either window, you are prompted to save or abandon the changes.
run from Cursor*	F10 followed by C (or Alt-C) submits commands to SPSS/PC+ for execution, beginning with the command containing the cursor and continuing to the end of the file. This command is available only if Review was entered from SPSS/PC+. If unsaved changes have been made in either window, you are prompted to save or abandon the changes.
Exit to prompt*	F10 followed by E exits Review and returns you to the SPSS/PC+ prompt. If unsaved changes have been made in either window, you are prompted to save or abandon the changes.

Editing Commands

Commands flagged with an asterisk (*) are mini-menu items that can be selected by high-lighting the item with the cursor arrows and pressing ⏎Enter.

Command Name	Key Combination/Function
Change Edit Mode	Ins changes the editing mode from overtype to insert and from insert to overtype.
Insert after*	F4 followed by I (or Alt-I) inserts a blank line after the current line. The blank line becomes the current line.
insert Before*	F4 followed by B (or Alt-B) inserts a blank line before the current line. The blank line becomes the current line.

Delete*	F4 followed by D deletes the current line. The line below becomes the current line.
Undelete*	F4 followed by U restores the most recently deleted line and places it immediately above the current line. You can restore only the single most recently deleted line.
Split Line	⏎Enter in insert mode splits the current line at the current character. In overtype mode, it moves the cursor to the next line.
Join Line	Del joins the next line to the current line if the cursor is at the end of a line.
Delete Current Character	Del deletes the current character. The text to the right of the cursor moves left one space.
Delete Previous Character	⟵Backspace deletes the character to the left of the cursor. The cursor and text to the right move left.
fOrward change*	F5 followed by O replaces one character string with another following the current cursor position. At each occurrence you can press C to change the occurrence and move to the next one, A to change all occurrences without individual prompting, N to move to the next occurrence without changing the current one, S to stop the search, or X to change the occurrence and then stop the search. The previous search-and-replace strings are the defaults but you can type in new ones. Upper and lower case are distinguished in searches. To identify only those occurrences of the string that begin in column 1, place a tilde (~) at the beginning of the search string. You cannot change a character string that begins with a tilde.
bAckward change*	F5 followed by A works the same as fOrward change except that it moves backward through the file to the earliest line in memory.

The following commands deal with marking or unmarking areas:

Command Name	Key Combination/Function
Lines*	F7 followed by L marks an area of lines for subsequent action. Press F7 followed by L at the first or last line of an area and F7 again at the opposite border to mark the area. Press F7 a third time to unmark the area. Areas of lines consist of *whole* lines.
Rectangle*	F7 followed by R marks any rectangle for subsequent action. Press F7 followed by R at one corner of the rectangle, and F7 again at the other corner. Press F7 a third time to unmark the area. A rectangle consists of a given number of lines of the marked width, which may be shorter than the width of the longest line. When you copy or move a rectangular area, place the cursor at the top left of the area to which you want to copy or move it.

Command*	F7 followed by C marks the current command for subsequent execution. Place the cursor anywhere within the command and press F7 followed by C. Press F7 again to unmark the command.

The following commands apply to marked areas:

Command Name	Key Combination/Function
Copy*	F8 followed by C copies a marked area to the line below the current line; it copies a marked rectangle to the right of and below the cursor. In insert mode, a rectangle pushes existing text to the right; in overtype mode, a rectangle replaces existing text. Marked lines, commands, and rectangles can be copied between windows.
Move*	F8 followed by M moves a marked area to the line below the current line; it moves a marked rectangle to the right of and below the cursor. In insert mode, a rectangle pushes existing text to the right; in overtype mode, a rectangle replaces existing text. Marked lines, commands, and rectangles can be moved between windows.
Delete*	F10 followed by D deletes a marked area or rectangle.
Round*	F7 followed by R rounds all numeric values in the marked area or rectangle to a specified number of decimal places. When you press F7 followed by R, Review prompts you for the desired number of decimal places. There is no way to reverse this command after execution; you should save important files before you round them in case the results are not what you expected. To round columns of numbers that are adjacent to one another, mark and round each column separately as a rectangle. Do not try to round numbers with imbedded commas (Review will round each group of three digits) or numbers in scientific notation.

Motion Commands

Commands flagged with an asterisk (*) are mini-menu items that can be selected by highlighting the item with the cursor arrows and pressing ⏎Enter.

Command Name	Key Combination/Function
Left	← moves the cursor left one space.
Right	→ moves the cursor right one space.
Up	↑ moves the cursor up one line.
Down	↓ moves the cursor down one line.
Start of Line	Ctrl-← moves the cursor to the first character of the current line.
End of Line	Ctrl-→ moves the cursor to the last character of the current line.

Tab Forward	(Tab→) moves the cursor eight characters to the right.
Tab Backward	(⇧Shift)-(Tab→) moves the cursor eight characters to the left.
Previous Page	(PgUp) moves the cursor to the last line of the preceding page.
Next Page	(PgDn) moves the cursor to the first line of the following page.
Top of Page	(Home) moves the cursor to the start of the first line in the window.
Bottom of Page	(End) moves the cursor to the end of the last line in the window.
Top of File	(Ctrl)-(Home) moves the cursor to the first line of the file.
Bottom of File	(Ctrl)-(End) moves the cursor to the last line of the file.
Top of Memory	(Ctrl)-(PgUp) moves the cursor to the first line of the portion of the file currently in memory.
Put Line at Top	(Ctrl)-(PgDn) moves the current line to the top of the window.
Start of Next Line	(←Enter) moves the cursor to the first character of the next line in over-type mode.
Forward search*	(F5) followed by (F) moves the cursor to the first occurrence of a specified character string on or below the current line. Upper and lower case are not distinguished in searches. The search continues to the end of the file, and the search string defaults to the last specified string. To locate the string only when it appears at the beginning of a line, specify a tilde (~) at the beginning of the search string. You cannot search for a string that begins with a tilde.
Backward search*	(F5) followed by (B) works the same as Forward search, moving backward through the file to the earliest line in memory.

The following commands tell the cursor to go to the indicated location:

Command Name	Key Combination/Function
Marked area*	(F6) followed by (M) moves the cursor to the top left corner of the marked area. If the cursor is already at the top left corner, this command moves it to the bottom right corner. If you are editing two files, this command may switch the cursor from one window to the other.
after executed Line*	(F6) followed by (L) (or (Alt)-(L)) moves the cursor to the line below the last one executed.
Error line*	(F6) followed by (E) moves the cursor to the line below the first one that caused an error when the commands where executed.
Output page*	(F6) followed by (O) moves the cursor to a specified page in the listing file. Review prompts you for the page number. The cursor must be located in the listing file when you use this command. Some types of

output are not saved in listing files; thus, some page numbers may be missing.

The Mouse

If a mouse is installed in your system, you can use it in place of keyboard strokes to perform many functions. Many actions you can perform are listed in Table 17 through Table 19. If you have a multiple-button mouse, the left button is assumed where the instruction "click" appears in the tables unless the right button is specifically named. Pressing the right mouse button is equivalent to pressing [Esc]. For a description of mouse functions in QED, see QED.

Table 17   Mouse functions with the mini-menu, Review help, and Glossary

Action	Mouse	Keyboard equivalent
Move the cursor to the non-active window	Click in the non-active window	[F2] [S]
Display the mini-menu for Help	Click in the status line	[F1]
Highlight an item in the mini-menu	Click on the item	[→] [←]
Select from the mini-menu	Double-click on selection	Type uppercase letter or use [→] to highlight selection and press [↵Enter]
In Review help, select action from Guide to Review Function Keys or Guide to Menu Commands	Click anywhere in the row	Press the key or key combination listed for the row
Close a window (for example, the Variables window)	Click the right mouse button	[Esc]
Leave Review help and return to the Menu and Help system	Click the right mouse button	[Esc]
In the glossary, move back one definition	Click on PgUp	[Ctrl]-[PgUp]
In the glossary, move forward one definition	Click on PgDn	[Ctrl]-[PgDn]
In the glossary, scroll the definition	Click on arrows at the right	[PgUp] [PgDn]

Table 18   Mouse functions in the Menu and Help window

Action	Mouse	Keyboard equivalent
Highlight a menu item	Click on the item	⬇ ⬆
Select and paste a menu item	Double-click on the item	⬇ ⬆, ↵Enter
Back up one level in the menus	Click the right mouse button	Esc
Paste information from the typing window	Click	↵Enter
Display listing window	Click in the Help window of the Menu and Help system	Alt-M
Scroll the menu or help window	Click on the up or down arrows at the edge of the window	Alt-⬇ or Alt-⬆
Close the help window	Click in the help window	Alt-H
Restore the closed help window	Click on the menu status	F2
Activate the menus when they are inactive	Click on the menu window	Alt-E

Table 19   Mouse functions in the scratch pad, variables menu, files menu, and output

Action	Mouse	Keyboard equivalent
Move the cursor	Click on the new position	➡ ⬅ ⬇ ⬆
Run commands from the cursor	Position the cursor somewhere on the command line and press the left and right mouse buttons simultaneously	F10 ↵Enter
Shift the focus from the menu to the scratch pad	Click in the scratch pad	Alt-E
Shift the focus from the scratch pad to the menu	Click the right mouse button	Alt-E
Highlight a variable in the Variables menu	Click on the variable	➡ ⬅ ⬇ ⬆
Highlight a filename in the Files menu	Click on the filename	➡ ⬅ ⬇ ⬆

Table 19   **Mouse functions in the scratch pad, variables menu, files menu, and output**

Action	Mouse	Keyboard equivalent
Paste a variable from the Variables menu into the scratch pad at the cursor	Double-click on the variable	Highlight the variable and press ⏎Enter
Paste a filename from the Files menu into the scratch pad, at the cursor	Double-click on the filename	Highlight the filename and press ⏎Enter
Scroll up and down in the Variables or Files menu	Click on arrows at right side of menu	Alt-↓ Alt-↑ PgUp PgDn
Advance to next screen of output	Click	Press any key

SAMPLE

```
SAMPLE {decimal value}
       {n FROM m      }
```

Example:
```
SAMPLE .25.
```

Overview

SAMPLE temporarily draws a random sample of cases for processing in the next procedure.

Basic Specification

The basic specification is either a decimal value between 0 and 1 or the sample size followed by keyword FROM and the size of the active file.

- To select an approximate percentage of cases, specify a decimal value between 0 and 1.
- To select an exact-size random sample, specify a positive integer less than the file size, followed by keyword FROM and the file size.

Operations

- SAMPLE is a temporary transformation.
- Sampling is based on a pseudo-random-number generator that depends on a seed value. By default, the initial seed value is randomly assigned. Use the SEED subcommand on SET to assign a specific seed value.
- To obtain the same sample for different procedures in the same session or in different sessions, use the SET command specifying the same seed value before entering the SAMPLE command.
- A proportional sample (a sample based on a decimal value) usually does not produce the exact proportion specified.
- If the number specified for *m* following FROM is less than the actual file size, the sample is drawn only from the first *m* cases.
- If the number following FROM is greater than the actual file size, SPSS/PC+ samples an equivalent proportion of cases from the active file (see the example on p. 745).
- If SAMPLE follows SELECT IF or PROCESS IF, it samples only cases selected by SELECT IF or PROCESS IF.
- If SAMPLE precedes SELECT IF or PROCESS IF, cases are selected from the sample.
- SAMPLE does not affect SORT CASES and is ignored if SORT CASES is the next procedure.
- If more than one SAMPLE is specified before a procedure, only the last SAMPLE command is executed.

Example

```
SAMPLE .25.
```

- This command samples approximately 25% of the cases in the active file.

Example

```
SAMPLE 500 FROM 3420.
```

- The active file must have 3420 cases or more to obtain a random sample of exactly 500 cases.
- If the file contains fewer than 3420 cases, proportionally fewer cases are sampled.
- If the file contains more than 3420 cases, a random sample of 500 cases is drawn from the first 3420 cases.

SAVE

```
SAVE [OUTFILE={'SPSS.SYS'**}]
              {'filename'  }

 [/KEEP={ALL**  }] [/DROP=varlist]
        {varlist}

 [/RENAME=(old varnames=new varnames)...]

 [/{COMPRESSED  }]
   {UNCOMPRESSED}
   {QUICK       }
```

**Default if the subcommand is omitted.

Example:

```
SAVE OUTFILE='EMPL.SYS'  /RENAME=(AGE=AGE88) (JOBCAT=JOBCAT88).
```

Overview

SAVE produces an SPSS/PC+ system file. A system file is in a format only SPSS/PC+ or SPSS for Windows can read and contains data plus a dictionary. The dictionary contains a name for each variable in the system file plus any assigned variable and value labels, missing-value flags, and variable print formats. See TRANSLATE for information on saving files that can be used by other programs.

Options

Variable Subsets and Order. You can save a subset of variables and reorder the variables that are saved using the DROP and KEEP subcommands.

Variable Names. You can rename variables as they are copied into the system file using the RENAME subcommand.

Data Compression. You can write the system file in compressed or uncompressed form using the COMPRESSED, UNCOMPRESSED, or QUICK subcommand.

Basic Specification

- The basic specification is simply the command keyword.
- By default, SAVE writes all variables in the active file to the file *SPSS.SYS* in the current directory. The system file is written in compressed form if the active file is compressed (COMPRESSED=ON has been specified on SET) or in uncompressed form if the active file is uncompressed.

Subcommand Order

- Subcommands can be specified in any order.

Syntax Rules

- OUTFILE can be specified only once.
- KEEP, DROP, and RENAME can each be used as many times as needed.
- Only one of the subcommands COMPRESSED, UNCOMPRESSED, or QUICK can be specified per SAVE command.

Operations

- SAVE is executed immediately and causes the data to be read.
- The new system file dictionary is arranged in the same order as the active file dictionary, unless variables are reordered with the KEEP subcommand.
- New variables created by transformations and procedures previous to the SAVE command are included in the new system file, and variables altered by transformations are saved in their modified form.
- The system file created by SAVE includes the system variables $CASENUM$, $DATE$, and $WEIGHT$.
- System files are binary files designed to be read and written by SPSS/PC+ only and cannot be edited. Use JOIN to combine system files.
- The active file is still available for SPSS/PC+ transformations and procedures after SAVE is executed.
- SAVE processes the dictionary first and displays a message that indicates how many variables will be saved (each eight-character portion of a long string variable counts as one variable). Once the data are written, SAVE indicates how many cases were saved. If the second message does not appear, the file was probably not completely written.

Example

```
GET FILE='HUBEMPL.SYS'.
SAVE OUTFILE='EMPL88.SYS' /RENAME=(AGE=AGE88) (JOBCAT=JOBCAT88).
```

- The GET command retrieves the system file *HUBEMPL.SYS*.
- The RENAME subcommand renames variable *AGE* to *AGE88* and variable *JOBCAT* to *JOBCAT88*.
- SAVE causes the data to be read and saves a new system file with filename *EMPL88.SYS*. The original system file *HUBEMPL* is not changed.

OUTFILE Subcommand

OUTFILE specifies a name for the system file to be saved. By default, the file is saved as *SPSS.SYS*.

- OUTFILE can be specified only once.
- The only specification on OUTFILE is the name of the file.
- The file specification must be enclosed in apostrophes.
- You can save a system file in another directory or on a drive other than the default by specifying a fully qualified filename.

DROP and KEEP Subcommands

DROP and KEEP are used to save a subset of variables. DROP specifies the variables not to save in the new system file; KEEP specifies the variables to save in the new system file; variables not named on KEEP are dropped.

- Variables can be specified in any order. The order of variables on KEEP determines the order of variables in the system file. The order on DROP does not affect the order of variables in the system file.
- Keyword ALL on KEEP refers to all remaining variables not previously specified on KEEP. ALL must be the last specification on KEEP.
- If a variable is specified twice on the same subcommand, only the first mention is recognized.
- Multiple DROP and KEEP subcommands are allowed.
- Keyword TO can be used to specify a group of consecutive variables in the active file.

Example

```
GET FILE='PRSNL.SYS'
COMPUTE TENURE=(12-CMONTH +(12*(88-CYEAR)))/12.
COMPUTE JTENURE=(12-JMONTH +(12*(88-JYEAR)))/12.
VARIABLE LABELS        TENURE 'Tenure in Company'
                       JTENURE 'Tenure in Grade'.
SAVE OUTFILE='PRSNL88.SYS' /DROP=GRADE STORE
  /KEEP=LNAME NAME TENURE JTENURE ALL.
```

- Variables *TENURE* and *JTENURE* are created by COMPUTE commands and assigned variable labels by the VARIABLE LABELS command. *TENURE* and *JTENURE* are added to the end of the active file.
- DROP excludes variables *GRADE* and *STORE* from file *PRSNL88.SYS*. KEEP specifies that *LNAME, NAME, TENURE*, and *JTENURE* are the first four variables in *PRSNL88.SYS*, followed by all remaining variables not specified on DROP. These remaining variables are saved in the same sequence as they appear in the original file.

RENAME Subcommand

RENAME changes the names of variables as they are copied into the new system file.

- The specification on RENAME is a list of old variable names followed by an equals sign and a list of new variable names. The same number of variables must be specified on both lists. Keyword TO can be used in the first list to refer to consecutive variables in the active file and in the second list to generate new variable names (see "Keyword TO" on p. 434). The entire specification must be enclosed in parentheses.

- Alternatively, you can specify each old variable name individually, followed by an equals sign and the new variable name. Multiple sets of variable specifications are allowed. The parentheses around each set of specifications are required.

- RENAME does not affect the active file. If RENAME precedes DROP or KEEP, variables must be referred to by their old names on DROP or KEEP.

- Old variable names do not need to be specified according to their order in the active file.

- Name changes take place in one operation. Therefore, variable names can be exchanged between two variables.

- Multiple RENAME subcommands are allowed.

Example

```
SAVE OUTFILE='EMPL88.SYS' /RENAME (AGE=AGE88) (JOBCAT=JOBCAT88).
```

- RENAME specifies two name changes for file *EMPL88.SYS*: variable *AGE* is renamed to *AGE88* and variable *JOBCAT* is renamed to *JOBCAT88*.

Example

```
SAVE OUTFILE='EMPL88.SYS' /RENAME (AGE JOBCAT=AGE88 JOBCAT88).
```

- The name changes are identical to those in the previous example: *AGE* is renamed to *AGE88* and *JOBCAT* is renamed to *JOBCAT88*.

COMPRESSED, UNCOMPRESSED, and QUICK Subcommands

COMPRESSED saves the system file in compressed form. UNCOMPRESSED saves the file in uncompressed form. QUICK saves the file in the same form as that of the active file.

- The only specification is the keyword COMPRESSED, UNCOMPRESSED, or QUICK. There are no additional specifications.

- QUICK is the default. If the active file is uncompressed, the system file is saved in uncompressed form. If the active file is compressed, the system file is saved in compressed form.

- In a compressed file, small integers (from −99 to 155) are stored in one byte instead of the eight bytes used in an uncompressed file.

- Compressed system files occupy less disk space than do uncompressed files.

- Use the SET COMPRESS command at any time during an SPSS/PC+ session to set the active file to either compressed or uncompressed form. The default for SET COMPRESS is OFF.

SELECT IF

```
SELECT IF (logical expression)
```

The following relational operators can be used:

Symbol	Definition	Symbol	Definition
EQ or =	Equal to	NE or <> or ~=	Not equal to
LT or <	Less than	LE or <=	Less than or equal to
GT or >	Greater than	GE or >=	Greater than or equal to

The following logical operators can be used in logical expressions:

Symbol	Definition
AND or &	Both relations must be true
Or or |	Either relation can be true
Not or ~	Reverses the outcome of an expression

The following missing-value functions can be used in logical expressions:

Function	Definition
SYSMIS	True if value is system-missing
MISSING	True if value is system- or user-missing
VALUE	True if value meets stated criteria, ignoring user-missing value flags

Example:

```
SELECT IF (SEX EQ 'MALE').
```

Overview

SELECT IF permanently selects cases for analysis based upon logical conditions found in the data. These conditions are specified in a *logical expression*. The logical expression can contain relational operators, logical operators, missing-value functions, arithmetic operations, and any functions allowed in COMPUTE transformations (see COMPUTE, and "Transformation Expressions" on p. 438). For temporary case selection, use PROCESS IF.

Basic Specification

The basic specification is simply a logical expression.

Syntax Rules

- Logical expressions can be simple logical variables or relations, or complex logical tests involving variables, constants, functions, relational operators, and logical operators. The logical expression can use any of the functions allowed in COMPUTE transformations (see COMPUTE).
- Parentheses must be used to enclose the logical expression. Parentheses can also be used within the logical expression to specify the order of operations. Extra blanks or parentheses can be used to make the expression easier to read.
- At least one relation, SYSMIS function, or MISSING function must be included in the logical expression.
- A relation can compare variables, constants, or more complicated arithmetic expressions.
- Relations cannot be abbreviated. For example, (A EQ 2 OR A EQ 5) is valid while (A EQ 2 OR 5) is not. Blanks (not commas) must be used to separate relational operators from the expressions being compared.
- A relation cannot compare a string variable to a numeric value or variable, or vice versa.
- To specify the condition that the value of a variable is system-missing, use SELECT IF (SYSMIS (var)). To specify the condition that the value of a variable is either system- or user-missing, use SELECT IF (MISSING(var)). You cannot specify SELECT IF (X=SYSMIS) or SELECT IF (X=MISSING).
- A relation cannot compare the result of the logical functions SYSMIS or MISSING to a number.
- String values used in expressions must be specified in quotes and must include any leading or trailing blanks. Lowercase letters are considered distinct from uppercase letters.
- Long string variables cannot be used on SELECT IF.

Operations

- SELECT IF permanently selects cases. Cases not selected are dropped from the active file.
- The logical expression is evaluated as true, false, or missing. If a logical expression is true, the case is selected; if it is false or missing, the case is not selected.
- Multiple SELECT IF commands issued prior to a procedure command must all be true for a case to be selected.
- SELECT IF should be placed before other transformations for efficiency considerations.
- Logical expressions are evaluated in the following order: first numeric functions, then exponentiation, then arithmetic operators, then relational operators, and last logical operators. Use parentheses to change the order of evaluation.
- If N is used with SELECT IF, SPSS/PC+ reads as many records as required to build the specified n cases. It makes no difference whether the N precedes or follows the SELECT IF.

Missing Values

- If the logical expression is indeterminate because of missing values, the case is not selected. In a simple relational expression, a logical expression is indeterminate if the expression on either side of the relational operator has a missing value.
- If a compound expression is used in which relations are joined by the logical operator OR, the case is selected if either relation is true, even if the other is missing.
- To select cases with missing values for the variables within the expression, use the missing-value functions. To include cases with values that have been declared user-missing along with other cases, use the VALUE function (see p. 440).

Limitations

The complexity of logical expressions is limited by available memory.

Example

```
SELECT IF (SEX EQ 'MALE').
```

- All subsequent procedures will use only cases in which the value of *SEX* is MALE.
- Since upper and lower case are treated differently in comparisons of string variables, cases for which the value of *SEX* is male are not selected.

Example

```
SELECT IF (INCOME GT 75000 OR INCOME LE 10000).
```

- The logical expression tests whether a case has a value either greater than 75,000 or less than or equal to 10,000. If either relation is true, the case is used in subsequent analyses.

Example

```
SELECT IF (V1 GE V2).
```

- This example selects cases where variable *V1* is greater than or equal to *V2*. If either *V1* or *V2* is missing, the logical expression is indeterminate and the case is not selected.

Example

```
SELECT IF (SEX = 'F' & INCOME <= 10000).
```

- The logical expression tests whether string variable *SEX* is equal to F and if numeric variable *INCOME* is less than or equal to 10,000. Cases that meet both conditions are included in subsequent analyses. If either *SEX* or *INCOME* is missing for a case, the case is not selected.

Example

```
SELECT IF (SYSMIS(V1)).
```

- The logical expression tests whether *V1* is system-missing. If it is, the case is selected for subsequent analyses.

Example

```
SELECT IF (VALUE(V1) GT 0).
```

- Cases are selected if *V1* is greater than 0, even if the value of *V1* has been declared user-missing.

Example

```
SELECT IF (V1 GT 0).
```

- Cases are not selected if *V1* is user-missing, even if the user-missing value is greater than 0.

Example

```
SELECT IF (RECEIV GT DUE AND (REVNUS GE EXPNS OR BALNCE GT 0)).
```

- By default, AND is executed before OR. This expression uses parentheses to change the order of evaluation.
- SPSS/PC+ first tests whether variable *REVNUS* is greater than or equal to variable *EXPNS*, or variable *BALNCE* is greater than 0. Second, SPSS/PC+ tests whether *RECEIV* is greater than *DUE*. If one of these expressions is true and *RECEIV* is greater than *DUE*, the case is selected.
- Without the inner set of parentheses, SPSS/PC+ would first test whether *RECEIV* is greater than *DUE* and *REVNUS* is greater than or equal to *EXPNS*. Second, SPSS/PC+ would test whether *BALNCE* is greater than 0. If the first two expressions are true *or* if the third expression is true, the case is selected.

Example

```
SELECT IF ((V1-15) LE (V2*(-0.001))).
```

- The logical expression compares whether *V1* minus 15 is less than or equal to *V2* multiplied by −0.001. If it is, the case is selected.

Example

```
SELECT IF ((YRMODA(88,13,0) - YRMODA(YVAR,MVAR,DVAR)) LE 30).
```

- The logical expression subtracts the number of days representing the date *(YVAR, MVAR, and DVAR)* from the number of days representing the last day in 1988. If the difference is less than or equal to 30, the case is selected.

SET

```
SET [SCREEN={ON }]  [PRINTER={OFF}]  [LISTING={'SPSS.LIS'}]
            {OFF}             {ON }            {ON       }
                                               {OFF      }
                                               {'filename'}

    [LENGTH={24}]  [WIDTH={79    }]  [EJECT={OFF}]  [VIEWLENGTH={MINIMUM}]
            {n }          {132   }          {ON }               {MEDIUM }
                          {n     }                              {MAXIMUM}
                          {NARROW}                              {number }
                          {WIDE  }

    [RUNREVIEW={AUTO  }]  [AUTOMENU={ON }]  [RLINES={ON }]
              {MANUAL}              {OFF}          {OFF}

    [MENUS={STANDARD}]  [HELPWINDOWS={ON }]  [ERRORBREAK={ON }
           {EXTENDED}                {OFF}               {OFF}

    [LOG={'SPSS.LOG'}]  [RESULTS={'SPSS.PRC'}]
         {ON        }           {'filename' }
         {OFF       }
         {'filename'}

    [HISTOGRAM={'■'       }]  [BLOCK={'■'       }]
              {'character'}         {'character'}

    [BOXSTRING={'|┴└┘┐H┬┤'      }]  [PTRANSLATE={ON }]
              {'11 characters'}                {OFF}
              {' 3 characters'}

    [INCLUDE={ON }]  [ECHO={ON }]
            {OFF}          {OFF}

    [PROMPT={'SPSS/PC:'}]  [CPROMPT={'     :'}]  [MORE={ON }]
           {'string'  }            {'string'}          {OFF}

    [ENDCMD={'.'      }]  [NULLINE={ON }]
           {'character'}           {OFF}

    [BEEP={ON }]
          {OFF}

    [COLOR={(15,1,1) }]  [RCOLOR={(1,2,4)}]
           {ON       }           {(a,b,c)}
           {OFF      }
           {(a,b[,c])}

    [COMPRESS={ON }]  [WORKDEV=drive]  [WKSPACE={384}]
             {OFF}                             {n  }

    [BLANKS={'.'}]  [SEED={RANDOM}]
            {n  }         {n     }

    [CPI={6    }]  [LPI={10   }]
         {chars}        {lines}
```

When SCREEN is OFF, the following defaults are in effect:

```
LENGTH=59   EJECT=ON
BOXSTRING='-|+++++++++'   HISTOGRAM='X'   BLOCK='X'
```

Example:

```
SET MORE=OFF /ECHO=ON /LENGTH=59 /EJECT=ON.
```

Overview

Many of the running options in SPSS/PC+ can be tailored to your own preferences with the SET command. To display the current settings, use the SHOW command.

Options

Output Destination. You can send your output to multiple destinations (screen, disk, and printer), and you can change destinations throughout the course of an SPSS/PC+ session using the SCREEN, LISTING, and PRINTER subcommands.

Output Format and Layout. You can change the length and width of output using LENGTH and WIDTH. Additionally, you can include carriage-control characters for page ejects in the listing file using EJECT. If you have an EGA or VGA adapter, you can also control the number of lines shown in the screen using VIEWLENGTH.

Log Files. You can specify a name for the file that contains the SPSS/PC+ commands issued during a session and you can suppress this file with LOG.

Data and Matrix Output Files. You can write data from the WRITE procedure or matrix materials from REGRESSION, CORRELATION, CLUSTER, ONEWAY, and FACTOR to a file of your choice using the RESULTS subcommand.

Environment. You can control the default SPSS/PC+ environment (command prompt, Review with the Menu and Help system, or Review alone) with RUNREVIEW and AUTOMENU. If you do use the Menu and Help system, you can suppress Help windows with HELPWINDOWS, and you can control whether extended or standard menus are displayed with MENUS. If you use two-byte character sets, you can suppress high-order ASCII characters using RLINES.

Error Processing. You can direct SPSS/PC+ to try to continue processing commands after a command causes an error using ERRORBREAK.

Special Characters and Character Translation. You can change the characters SPSS/PC+ uses to print crosstabulation grids as well as the symbols used in histograms and icicle plots with the BOXSTRING, HISTOGRAM, and BLOCK subcommands. SPSS/PC+ automatically translates special characters to simpler ones in output going directly to a printer. If you have a printer that can handle special characters, you can suppress this translation with PTRANSLATE.

Command Printback. You can control whether SPSS/PC+ commands are printed back in your output using ECHO. You can also control whether commands included with the INCLUDE command are displayed on the screen using the INCLUDE subcommand.

Prompts. You can specify your own command prompt and continuation prompt using PROMPT and CPROMPT. You can turn off the prompt that appears by default after each screen of output using MORE.

Command Terminators. You can change the default command terminator from a period to a character of your choice with ENDCMD, and you can control whether a blank line is interpreted as a command terminator with NULLINE.

Sound and Color. You can suppress the paging and error-message beeps with BEEP. On a color monitor, you can choose colors for screen text, background, and border using COLOR and RCOLOR.

Active and Scratch Files. You can specify the disk drive location of the active and scratch files with WORKDEV, and you can control whether the active file is compressed or uncompressed using COMPRESS.

Numeric Blanks. You can specify the value that SPSS/PC+ uses when it encounters a blank field for numeric variables using BLANKS. All numeric blanks are translated to this value.

Random Number Seed. You can change the initial seed value to a particular number or to a random number using SEED.

Plots for SPSS/PC+ Categories. You can specify the number of characters per inch and lines per inch needed to produce square plots from the SPSS/PC+ Categories option with CPI and LPI.

Basic Specification

The basic specification is at least one subcommand.

Subcommand Order

- Subcommands can be specified in any order.

Syntax Rules

- The slash between subcommands is optional.
- Only one keyword or argument can be specified for each subcommand.
- SET can be used more than once in an SPSS/PC+ session. Each time it is used, only the specified settings are affected. All others remain at their previous settings or the default.
- YES is accepted as an alias for keyword ON.
- NO is accepted as an alias for keyword OFF.

Operations

- SET takes effect immediately.
- The default character settings use graphics characters that may not be available on your printer.
- *SPSS.LIS* and *SPSS.LOG* are erased at the beginning of each SPSS/PC+ session. If you want to preserve their contents, use the DOS RENAME command to rename them before restarting SPSS/PC+.

- If you use multiple log, listing, or results files, you should not start with one file, go to another file, and then return to the first file. SPSS/PC+ will not append new information to the first file but will write over the previous contents.
- The results file can be directed only to the current directory. The log and listing files can be sent to any directory.

Limitations

- A screen display length of 35 or 43 lines can only be used with an EGA or VGA adapter. A length of 43 may not be compatible with an *ANSI.SYS* file.

Example

```
SET MORE=OFF /ECHO=ON /LENGTH=59 /EJECT=ON.
```

- MORE=OFF sends output to the screen continuously without pausing to give the MORE prompt when the screen fills.
- ECHO=ON includes all commands in the listing file. This is independent of whether commands are written to a log file.
- LENGTH=59 specifies a page length of 59 for output sent to the screen and listing file.
- EJECT=ON inserts a page-eject carriage-control character in the listing file after each 59 lines of output and suppresses the dashed line between pages.

Output Destination

By default, SPSS/PC+ directs output both to the screen and to a listing file named *SPSS.LIS* in the current directory. You can also direct output directly to a printer or suppress any of these three output destinations. You can also change the name of the listing file.

SCREEN   *Screen output.* You can specify ON or OFF. ON is the default. You can suppress screen output by specifying SCREEN=OFF and then restart screen output by specifying SCREEN=ON.

PRINTER   *Printer output.* You can specify ON or OFF. OFF is the default. With PRINTER=ON, output is sent directly to your printer in addition to any other destinations. Your printer must be turned on if you specify PRINTER=ON. You can stop sending output to the printer by specifying PRINTER=OFF. This specification does not work when your computer is connected to a network printer.

LISTING   *Disk output.* You can specify ON or OFF or a filename for the listing file. ON is the default, and the default file is *SPSS.LIS* in the current directory. You can stop sending output to a disk file by specifying LISTING=OFF, or you can direct the output to another file in a directory of your choice by specifying a filename enclosed in apostrophes. The keyword DISK is accepted as an alias for LISTING.

- When SCREEN=ON is in effect, the output is, by default, formatted especially for screen-by-screen displays and includes special graphics characters that are available only on the screen.

- If you turn screen output off, SPSS/PC+ uses different defaults for output. The defaults for SCREEN=ON and SCREEN=OFF are listed in Table 20. You can change these options with other SET subcommands.

- When you direct output to both the screen and printer or listing file, you must specify format options that are compatible with your printer.

- The keywords ON and OFF on subcommand LISTING apply to the current listing file, regardless of its name. You can suspend sending output to a file and then resume sending output to the same file as long as you do not specify a different listing file in the interim. If you specify a different file in the interim, SPSS/PC+ will write over the first file. It cannot append output to a file once another file has been named.

- The output from different procedures can be directed to different disk files by naming a different file on the LISTING subcommand prior to a procedure command.

Example

```
GET FILE='MARCH.SYS'.
LIST VAR=V1 TO V10.
SET LISTING='MEANS.LIS'
MEANS V1 TO V5 BY V7.
SET LISTING=OFF.
FREQ VAR=V1,V3,V4
   /HISTOGRAM.
SET LISTING=ON
   /HISTOGRAM='X'.
FREQ VAR=V3
   /HISTOGRAM.
FINISH.
```

- GET reads the SPSS/PC+ system file *MARCH.SYS* from the current directory.

- Output from LIST is directed to the screen and to the default listing file *SPSS.LIS*.

- The second SET command directs output to the file *MEANS.LIS* in the current directory.

- Output from MEANS is directed to *MEANS.LIS* and to the screen.

- The next SET command suspends sending output to the file *MEANS.LIS*. Output continues to go to the screen.

- FREQUENCIES requests frequency tables and histograms for three variables. The histograms use the default histogram characters for the screen.

- The next SET command resumes sending output to the file *MEANS.LIS*. The character used in any histogram on the screen and in the listing file is X.

- FREQUENCIES produces a table and histogram for the variable *V3*. Output is directed to both the screen and to the listing file.

- FINISH ends the SPSS/PC+ session.

- The file *SPSS.LIS* contains the results from the LIST procedure. The file *MEANS.LIS* contains output from the MEANS procedure and from the last FREQUENCIES procedure.

Output Format and Layout

You can change the defaults for output format and layout with the LENGTH, VIEWLENGTH, WIDTH, and EJECT subcommands. The defaults depend on whether SCREEN=ON or SCREEN=OFF (see Table 20).

LENGTH
Page length. The specification is a positive integer. When SCREEN=ON, the default is 24. LENGTH is normally set to one line less than VIEWLENGTH. If you intend to print your output, you may want to set LENGTH to a suitable value for your printer. A standard printer page length is 59 lines.

VIEWLENGTH
Number of lines shown on the screen. The specification is MINIMUM, MEDIUM, MAXIMUM, or a number. The default is MINIMUM (25 lines). Available settings depend upon your display adapter. MDA and CGA allow only MINIMUM. EGA allows 25, 35, and 43 line displays. VGA also accepts all three keywords, with 50 lines displayed for MAXIMUM. If you specify an inappropriate number, SPSS/PC+ rounds it to the nearest available number.

WIDTH
Page width. The specification is an integer or keywords NARROW (79 characters) or WIDE (130 characters). The default is 79. Most SPSS/PC+ output fits in a page width of 79 characters.

EJECT
Carriage control for page ejects for output sent to the printer or listing file. The specification is ON or OFF. When SCREEN=ON, the default is EJECT= OFF. With EJECT=OFF, output sent to the printer and/or to a listing file contains a dotted line indicating page breaks. With EJECT=ON, no dotted line is printed, and SPSS/PC+ inserts margins between each page.

- LENGTH controls the page length for the screen, printer, and listing file. On the screen, the MORE prompt appears between pages. In output sent to the printer or listing file, a dotted line is printed or a page eject occurs at the end of each page, depending on the specification on EJECT.

- VIEWLENGTH controls the display of lines on the screen. PC's with EGA or VGA adapters can display more than 25 lines at a time by making the lines appear smaller. PC's that do not have these adapters will display only MINIMUM (25 lines).

- If the *CONFIG.SYS* file contains the specification DEVICE=ANSI.SYS, a VIEWLENGTH of 43 may not work.

- WIDTH controls width for the screen, printer, and listing file.

- The screen allows a width of only 79 characters. Lines longer than 79 characters are normally wrapped onto two lines. However, some SPSS/PC+ output will not wrap. To examine such output, you will need to either print the listing file or use an editor that wraps or allows horizontal scrolling. Alternatively, you can specify SET WIDTH 79 prior to running the procedure to ensure that the output can be viewed on the screen.

- Output sent to the printer or listing file can contain lines longer than 79 characters. However, to print long lines (from 80 to 132 characters), use the DOS MODE command to reduce the size of characters on your printer.

- EJECT affects only output sent to the printer or listing file. If LENGTH=59 and EJECT=ON, insert printer paper so that there is a half-inch margin at the top; SPSS/PC+ will print each page with skips over subsequent perforations.

Table 20   Defaults for SCREEN settings

SCREEN	LENGTH	BOXSTRING	HISTOGRAM	BLOCK	EJECT
ON	24	├┴└┌┐├┤┴	■	▮	OFF
OFF	59	-┤++++++++	X	X	ON

Example

```
SET LISTING='REG.LIS' /VIEWLENGTH=MAXIMUM
   /LENGTH=59 /WIDTH=130 /EJECT=ON.
 REG VAR=SAVINGS POP15 POP75 INCOME GROWTH
   /SELECT IN2 NE 1
   /DEP SAVINGS /ENTER POP15 /RES SEPARATE
   /CASEWISE DEP OUTLIER (3) ALL PLOT (RESID)
   /DEP SAVINGS /ENTER INCOME /RES POOLED.
```

• The SET command directs output to the screen and to the file *REG.LIS*. The screen will display the maximum number of lines possible for the display adapter. The output is formatted with 59 lines for each page with an eject after each page. Thus, if *REG.LIS* is printed, each page includes top and bottom margins to skip over the perforations. The width of each page is 130 characters.

• The REGRESSION procedure uses up to 130 characters on each line of the output.

Log Files

By default, SPSS/PC+ copies all the commands you enter into log file *SPSS.LOG* in the current directory. Use the LOG subcommand to change these defaults.

LOG   *Log file.* The specification is ON or OFF or a filename for the file. ON is the default, and the default file is *SPSS.LOG* in the current directory. You can stop sending commands to a log file by specifying LOG=OFF, or you can direct the commands to another file in a directory of your choice by specifying a filename enclosed in apostrophes.

• You can resume sending commands to the file *SPSS.LOG* or to the log file last specified by specifying LOG=ON. Any existing contents of that file will be overwritten.

• The log file contains each command processed during a session.

• If you enter a command with errors, the log file contains a comment line after that command describing the error.

• The log file can be edited for use as a command file (see INCLUDE). Review allows you to do this without leaving SPSS/PC+.

• When you use a log file from a completed session as a command file, you must initially send the log file to a file other than *SPSS.LOG* or rename the log file using the DOS RENAME command, since *SPSS.LOG* is initialized at the start of each session.

When you use INCLUDE in your session, the commands from the included command file are preceded by a square bracket ([) in the log file. If this log file is then used as a command file in a subsequent session, only the INCLUDE command is processed, not the commands preceded by the square bracket. This avoids double processing of commands. You cannot enter the square bracket yourself in interactive sessions.

Example

```
SET LOG='DATADEF.FIL'.
DATA LIST FILE='MARCH.DAT' / OP1 TO OP7 1-14.
VARIABLE LABELS OP1 'Opinion on sex' /
                OP2 'Opinion on religion' /
                OP7 'Opinion on divorce'.
VALUE LABELS OP1 TO OP7 1 'Agree' 2 'Disagree'.
MISSING VALUE OP1 TO OP7(9).
INCLUDE 'DES.INC'.
FIN.
```

- SET directs the log file to *DATADEF.FIL* in the current directory.

- DATA LIST, VARIABLE LABELS, VALUE LABELS, MISSING VALUE, and INCLUDE and their specifications are copied to the file. Each command processed from file *DES.INC* is copied to the log file preceded by a square bracket.

- The file *DATADEF.FIL* can be used as a command file in a subsequent SPSS/PC+ session.

Data and Matrix Output Files

Some SPSS/PC+ procedures produce data that can be used in other sessions. WRITE produces a rectangular data file of individual values. Procedures CORRELATIONS, ONEWAY, REGRESSION, CLUSTER, FACTOR, MANOVA, SURVIVAL, and QUICK CLUSTER produce summary data in the form of matrix materials. By default, SPSS/PC+ writes these materials to the file *SPSS.PRC* in the current directory. You can direct these materials to other files using the RESULTS subcommand.

RESULTS   *Data and matrix output file.* The specification is a filename enclosed in apostrophes. The results file is always written to the current directory.

- The results file can later be specified as an input file on DATA LIST or, after editing, on the INCLUDE command (see INCLUDE for information on including data files).

- SPSS/PC+ does *not* append data to the results file. If two procedures write results to the same file, the second set of data will overwrite the first set.

Example

```
SET LISTING 'NEWDAT.LIS'
  /RESULTS='NEWDAT.DAT'.
GET FILE='INVENT.SYS'.
COMPUTE TOTCOST=V1+V7+V9.
SELECT IF (V3 LT 7).
WRITE VARIABLES=ID TO V15, TOTCOST.
FINISH.
```

- SET sends output from procedures to *NEWDAT.LIS* and matrix data to *NEWDAT.DAT*. Both files are written to the current directory.

- GET reads the system file *INVENT.SYS* from the current directory.

- COMPUTE computes variable *TOTCOST*.
- SELECT IF selects cases in which the value of variable *V3* is less than 7.
- WRITE writes the values of variable *TOTCOST* and variables between and including *ID* and *V15* (provided the value of *V3* is less than 7). The data are written to *NEWDAT.DAT*.

Environment

SPSS/PC+ provides three environments in which to enter commands: the Menu and Help system within Review; the Review text editor alone; and the command prompt. The default environment when you enter SPSS/PC+ is the Menu and Help system within Review (both AUTOMENU=ON and RUNREVIEW=AUTO). You can make one of the other environments the default, and you can alter the default settings of the Menu and Help system environment.

RUNREVIEW   *Automatic Review.* The specification is AUTO or MANUAL. With keyword AUTO (the default), the default environment when you enter SPSS/PC+ is Review. To make the default environment the SPSS/PC+ command prompt, specify MANUAL. To get into Review from the command prompt, use the RE-VIEW command.

AUTOMENU   *Automatic Menu and Help system.* The specification is ON or OFF. With keyword ON (the default), the Menu and Help system is displayed whenever you enter Review. To enter the Review text editor without the Menu and Help system, specify OFF. You can still call up the menus whenever you like by pressing Alt-M.

MENUS   *Extended or standard menus.* The specification is STANDARD or EXTENDED. With keyword STANDARD (the default), the default menus omit seldom-used keywords. To automatically display menus with all possible keywords, use EXTENDED. You can switch between standard and extended menus at any time by pressing Alt-X.

HELPWINDOWS   *Help windows.* The specification is ON or OFF. With keyword ON (the default), menus are displayed with Help windows that annotate each menu selection. To display menus without Help windows specify OFF. This speeds up the display of menus on slow machines. You can bring back the Help windows at any time by pressing Alt-H.

RLINES   *Line-drawing characters in the Review menus.* The specification is ON or OFF. With keyword ON, the menus use high-order ASCII characters to draw lines. In some versions of SPSS/PC+ that use two-byte character sets, you should suppress these line-drawing characters by specifying OFF. ON is the default.

Example

```
SET RUNREVIEW MANUAL.
```

- The default environment is the SPSS/PC+ command prompt. If commands are entered and run from Review, the system returns to the command prompt after commands are processed, not to Review.

Example

```
SET MENUS=EXTENDED
  /HELPWINDOWS=OFF.
```

- All keywords are included in the menus, but Help windows do not appear.

Error Processing

You can control whether SPSS/PC+ continues processing commands after a command causes an error. This is useful when initial commands are not essential for the processing of subsequent commands.

ERRORBREAK   The specification is ON or OFF. With keyword ON (the default), SPSS/PC+ stops processing commands when it encounters an error. To continue command processing even if errors occur, specify OFF.

- Regardless of the setting of ERRORBREAK, when SPSS/PC+ returns to Review after processing commands that caused errors, the cursor is always positioned at the first command that caused an error.

Example

```
SET ERRORBREAK=OFF.
VRIABLE LABELS OP1 'Opinion on sex' /
               OP2 'Opinion on religion' /
               OP7 'Opinion on divorce'.
LIST.
```

- SET directs the system to continue processing even if errors are encountered.
- VARIABLE LABELS is misspelled as VRIABLE LABELS and causes an error.
- Because ERRORBREAK is set to OFF, LIST is processed even though the preceding command caused an error. However, the listing does not include these variable labels.

Special Characters

By default, SPSS/PC+ uses special graphic characters in tables and plots. These graphic characters appear on the screen but may not print correctly, depending upon the type of printer you are using. Three subcommands, HISTOGRAM, BLOCK, and BOXSTRING, are used to specify other characters.

HISTOGRAM   *Character used in histograms and bar charts.* The specification is a single character in apostrophes. If output is directed to the screen (SCREEN=ON), the default is a lower-half solid block (ASCII decimal 220). If output is not directed to the screen, X is the default.

BLOCK   *Character used in icicle plots.* The specification is a single character in apostrophes. If output is directed to the screen (SCREEN=ON), the default is a full solid block (ASCII decimal 219). If output is not directed to the screen, the default is X.

BOXSTRING   *Box-building characters.* The specification is the characters used to build boxes enclosed in apostrophes. You can specify a set of three characters or a full set of eleven. A set of three characters represents the horizontal bar, vertical bar, and intersection characters, in that order. The intersection character is used for all types of intersections. A set of eleven characters represents the following characters: horizontal bar, vertical bar, intersection, lower-left corner, upper-left corner, lower-right corner, upper-right corner, left T, right T, top T, bottom T. The characters must be specified in this order. If output is directed to the screen (SCREEN=ON), the defaults are the eleven single-stroke graphics characters listed in Table 21. If output is not directed to the screen, the default BOXSTRING characters are - |+++++++++.

- At the command prompt and in Review, you can enter special characters by holding down (Alt) and entering the ASCII decimal value for the character desired on the numeric keypad on the right side of the keyboard. For example, to enter the light-intensity block, press (Alt) and hold it down while entering 176. Then release (Alt).

- A complete list of characters and their ASCII decimal values is available in the DOS BASIC manual. Table 21 lists some of the more useful characters and their ASCII decimal codes.

Table 21   Special characters

Character	ASCII value	Character	ASCII value
Single-stroke horizontal bar	196	Double-stroke horizontal bar	205
Single-stroke vertical bar	179	Double-stroke vertical bar	186
Single-stroke intersection	197	Double-stroke intersection	206
Single-stroke lower-left corner	192	Double-stroke lower-left corner	200
Single-stroke upper-left corner	218	Double-stroke upper-left corner	201
Single-stroke lower-right corner	217	Double-stroke lower-right corner	188
Single-stroke upper-right corner	191	Double-stroke upper-right corner	187
Single-stroke left T	195	Double-stroke left T	204
Single-stroke right T	180	Double-stroke right T	185
Single-stroke top T	194	Double-stroke top T	203
Single-stroke bottom T	193	Double-stroke bottom T	202
Light-intensity block	176	Lower-half solid block	220
Medium-intensity block	177	Upper-half solid block	223
Heavy-intensity block	178	Left-half solid block	221
Solid block	219	Right-half solid block	222
Small solid block	254		

Character Translation

Many printers cannot print the special characters used by SPSS/PC+ for histograms, plots, and tables. By default, SPSS/PC+ translates these characters to simpler ones when output is sent directly to a printer (PRINTER=ON). If your printer can print special characters, you may want to turn off this translation.

PTRANSLATE   *Character translation for output directed to the printer.* The specification is ON or OFF. ON (the default) translates special characters to simpler ones when PRINTER=ON. OFF prevents this translation.

Example

```
SET PTRANSLATE=OFF.
```

- Special characters are not translated to simpler ones when output is directed to the printer.

Command Printback

SPSS/PC+ provides two options for printing back commands on the screen or in listing files.

- If you don't want to see SPSS/PC+ commands from an INCLUDE file on your screen, specify INCLUDE=OFF prior to using the INCLUDE command.
- If you do not want SPSS/PC+ commands copied to your listing file, specify ECHO=OFF.

ECHO   *Printback of commands in output sent to the printer and listing files.* The specification is ON or OFF. ON (the default) sends SPSS/PC+ commands (from whatever source) to printer and listing files along with results of statistical and reporting procedures. Specify OFF if you want only results of statistical and reporting procedures sent to the listing file and printer. ECHO does not affect screen output.

INCLUDE   *Printback of commands from included command files on the screen.* The specification is ON or OFF. ON (the default) displays commands from any included command file on your screen, even if SCREEN=OFF. Inline data from included files is never displayed on the screen.

Example

```
SET ECHO=OFF.
GET FILE='MYFILE.SYS'.
CROSSTABS TABLES=AVAR BY BVAR BY CVAR.
SET SCREEN=OFF.
INCLUDE 'REG.INC'.
FIN.
```

- The first SET command specifies that commands should not be included in the listing file.
- The second SET command stops sending output to the screen. Output is still sent to the listing file.
- The INCLUDE command processes commands from file *REG.INC* in the current directory. By default, all commands from *REG.INC* are displayed on the screen as they are processed. If INCLUDE=OFF is specified in *REG.INC*, subsequent commands from that file are not displayed on the screen as they are processed.

Prompts

SPSS/PC+ uses two types of prompts for command input: a command prompt, which prompts for a new command, and a continuation prompt, which prompts for the next line of a command. The continuation prompt is always issued if a command terminator has not been used on the previous input. You can specify the characters used for these prompts with PROMPT and CPROMPT.

By default, SPSS/PC+ pauses after each screen of output and displays the MORE prompt. To go to the next screen of output you must press a key. The MORE subcommand lets you eliminate the pause and prompt between screens of output.

PROMPT   *Command prompt.* Specify a string of up to 8 characters in apostrophes. You can specify special characters. The default is SPSS/PC: .

CPROMPT   *Continuation prompt.* Specify a string of up to 8 characters in apostrophes. You can specify special characters. The default is   : .

MORE   *Full screen prompt.* Specify ON or OFF. ON (the default) causes SPSS/PC+ to pause between screens of output and display the MORE prompt. OFF eliminates the prompt, and output is displayed continuously across the screen.

Example

```
SET PROMPT='===> '
   /CPROMPT='done?'
   /MORE=OFF.
```

- The command prompt is changed to ===> .
- The continuation prompt is done?.
- SPSS/PC+ will not pause between screens of output.

Command Terminators

Every SPSS/PC+ command must end with a command terminator. By default, the terminator is a period, but you can change it with the ENDCMD. SPSS/PC+ continues to read lines as part of the current command until it encounters the command terminator. By default, a completely empty input line is accepted as an alternative command terminator. You can change this default using NULLINE.

ENDCMD   *Command terminator.* The specification is a character in apostrophes. The default is a period. The character should be printable and should not be any character that may be the last character in any variable names nor any character with special syntactic meaning in SPSS/PC+ (such as a slash).

NULLINE   *Blank lines as alternative command terminator.* The specification is ON or OFF. When ON (the default) is in effect, a blank line is accepted as a command terminator. If OFF is specified, you must enter the character specified for ENDCMD to end a command.

Example

```
SET ENDCMD='!'
   /NULLINE=OFF.
```

- The command terminator is set to !.
- A blank line will not be accepted as a command terminator.

Sound and Color

By default, SPSS/PC+ beeps to signal the next screen of output and errors. A high-pitched beep reminds you to go to the next screen of output, and a low-pitched beep is sounded when an error occurs. The BEEP subcommand allows you to suppress the beep.

The COLOR subcommand controls the text, background, and border colors on color monitors. RCOLOR allows you to set the background colors in Review, the SPSS/PC+ text editor.

BEEP *Beep.* The specification is ON or OFF. To suppress the beep, specify OFF. To turn it on (the default), specify ON.

COLOR *Color.* The specification is a set of two or three integers in parentheses or ON or OFF. ON is the default and turns color on. OFF eliminates all color. A set of three integers represents text color, background color, and border color, in that order. An asterisk in place of an integer retains the existing color. If you specify the first two integers only, the border color is assumed to be the same as the background color. The default colors are (15,1,1), which on many color monitors corresponds to white text on a blue background with a blue border. Check your monitor manual for the colors available on your monitor and the integers that represent these colors. Colors for the standard IBM color monitor are shown in Table 22. The high-intensity colors 8–15 can only be used for the first (text) color.

RCOLOR *Color in Review.* The specification is a set of three integers in parentheses, representing background color in the lower (or only) window, background color in the upper window (when present), and frame color, in that order. The three integers must be between 0 and 6. An asterisk in place of an integer retains the existing color. The default colors are (1,2,4). Text is always white in Review. The keywords OFF and ON are not available for RCOLOR. However, if you specify COLOR OFF, Review will use a monochrome display.

- On some monochrome monitors, colors may be interpreted as patterns and shading. The manual for your monitor will tell you how to control these patterns. To eliminate these patterns and shades, specify COLOR=OFF.
- COLOR=OFF affects Review as well as the SPSS/PC+ command environment; however, the colors used by Review when COLOR=ON are determined by RCOLOR.
- COLOR=ON returns to the color patterns that were in effect before color was turned off.

Table 22   Colors on standard IBM color monitors

0	Black	8	Gray
1	Blue	9	Light blue
2	Green	10	Light green
3	Cyan	11	Light cyan
4	Red	12	Light red
5	Magenta	13	Light magenta
6	Brown	14	Yellow
7	White	15	High-intensity white

Example

```
SET BEEP=OFF.
GET FILE='AUTO.SYS'.
SET COLOR=(6,1,3).
FREQUENCIES VARIABLES=COSTCAT,SIZE,POWER.
SET COLOR OFF.
CROSSTABS TABLES=MANUFACT BY POWER.
SET COLOR ON.
FREQUENCIES VARIABLES=COSTCAT.
FINISH.
```

- The first SET command turns off beeps for this session.
- Prior to the second SET command, the default color pattern (15,1,1) is in effect.
- The second SET command sets the text color to 6, the background color to 1, and the border color to 3.
- The third SET command turns color off, creating a monochrome display.
- The fourth SET command restores the text, background, and border colors to their previous values of 6, 1, and 3.

Active and Scratch Files

COMPRESS controls whether the active file for an SPSS/PC+ session is kept in compressed or uncompressed form. WORKDEV allows you to direct the active and scratch files to a specific disk drive.

COMPRESS   *Compression of active file.* The specification is ON or OFF. ON keeps the active file in compressed form, and OFF keeps it in uncompressed form. ON is the default.

WORKDEV   *Location of active and scratch files.* The specification is a letter that corresponds to one of your disk drives. The active file and most scratch files for the session will be kept on that drive. The drive is that of the current directory. Once an active file has been written during the session, you cannot specify WORKDEV.

- A compressed active file occupies less space in your directory than does an uncompressed active file. However, a compressed active file takes longer to access when you run a procedure.

- When you perform transformations during a session, SPSS/PC+ creates a new active file but both the new and old active files exist simultaneously. Thus, the space you save by keeping your active file compressed doubles if you do any transformations during an SPSS/PC+ session.

Example

```
SET COMPRESS=ON
  /WORKDEV=B.
```

- The active file for this session will be kept in compressed form.

- The active file and other scratch files will be kept on the B: drive. If an active file has already been written during the session, WORKDEV will generate an error message.

Working Memory (Applies Only to Extended Memory)

If extended memory is installed on your computer, you can dynamically change the amount of working memory available. Working memory is used to store intermediate results. Unless SPSS/PC+ tells you that there is insufficient memory to run a procedure, increasing the working memory allocation is usually not recommended, since this can actually decrease performance (make your computer slower) under some circumstances.

- Insufficient memory is most likely to occur when the procedure you are running uses a large number of variables.

- The allocation of working memory takes effect immediately.

- If you request more working memory than is available, the allocation is not changed and a warning is displayed.

- Working memory is not constrained by the amount of actual memory installed on your computer but is constrained by the available disk space.

- You can allocate up to 15000K (15 megabytes) of virtual memory for working memory. The maximum allocation available on your system depends on its configuration.

- The amount of working memory is limited by parameters which can be set in the *SPSSPC.VMC* file. (See the installation instructions.)

WKSPACE=n   *Amount of working memory available.* The specification is a number of kilobytes. The default is 384K, which is sufficient for most purposes.

Example

```
SET WKSPACE=1500.
```

- The new amount of working memory is 1500K (1.5 megabytes).

- The next procedure executed will be able to take advantage of the new working memory.

Treatment of Numeric Blanks

By default, SPSS/PC+ translates blank fields for numeric variables to the system-missing value. You can use the BLANKS subcommand to specify some other value.

BLANKS   *Treatment of blanks for numeric variables.* The specification is any number. Blanks are translated to this number. The number is not automatically defined as missing. The default is the system-missing value.

- BLANKS affects only numeric variables. If a blank field is read with an A format, the resulting value is a blank.

- BLANKS controls the treatment of blanks for all numeric variables. You cannot have different treatments for different variables.

- BLANKS must be specified before data are read. Otherwise, blanks in numeric fields are converted to system-missing as they are read.

Example

```
SET BLANKS=-1.
```

- BLANKS translates all blanks encountered for numeric variables to the value −1.

Random Number Seed

SPSS/PC+ has a random number generator used by the SAMPLE command and the NORMAL and UNIFORM functions. By default, the seed is a random seed generated from the clock. Optionally, you can specify a seed on the SEED subcommand.

SEED   *Random number seed.* Specify a positive integer or keyword RANDOM. The default is RANDOM. If you specify an integer, it cannot exceed 2147483647.

- You can change the random number seed any number of times within a session.

- To replicate samples across sessions or procedures, specify the same seed each time.

Example

```
SET SEED=200000000.
```

- The random number seed is set to the value 200000000.

Plots for SPSS/PC+ Categories

The optimal-scaling procedures in the SPSS/PC+ Categories option compute square plots. Square plots (as opposed to rectangular ones) are easier to interpret geometrically. Occasionally, certain printers might make the plots appear rectangular because their print density is different than what SPSS/PC+ expects. If your printer is producing rectangular ones, you need to specify the characters-per-inch and lines-per-inch parameters. CPI and LPI specify the characters-per-inch and lines-per-inch, respectively. You can use the SHOW command to see what the current settings are.

The correct CPI and LPI values can be found in the manual for your printer or can easily be calculated with a ruler and some output. The CPI is simply the number of characters per inch moving horizontally across the page. The LPI is the number of lines per inch moving vertically down the page. SPSS/PC+ uses these values only when plotting output from ANA-COR, HOMALS, PRINCALS, and OVERALS. Plots from other procedures are unaffected.

CPI   *Characters per inch horizontally.* The default is 6.

LPI   *Lines per inch vertically.* The default is 10.

SHOW

```
SHOW
```

Overview

SHOW displays a table of all the current specifications on the SET command, plus information about memory and disk space.

Basic Specification

- The basic specification is simply the command keyword. SHOW has no additional specifications.

Operations

- SHOW is executed immediately.
- SHOW lists every current SET specification, including the default settings.
- If you have extended memory, SHOW displays the total amount of extended memory available. There is no corresponding subcommand on the SET command. With some memory managers, this will not be equal to the total amount of extended memory installed on your computer, since the amount of extended memory *available* depends on how your system allocates memory.
- If you have SPSS/PC+ (640K version) the table does not show extended memory.

Limitations

- The graphics characters on BOXSTRING and HISTOGRAM may not be printable on non-graphics printers.

Example

```
SHOW.
```

- SHOW produces a table similar to the one in Figure 8 of the current specifications on SET.
- In this example, the settings shown are the default settings for SPSS/PC+ with extended memory.
- *Extended Memory* displays the total amount of extended memory available to SPSS/PC+.

Figure 8   Output from SHOW

```
SPSS/PC+ V5.0 (02- 0)      Workspace:  384.0K
        Serial Number: 123456        Free disk space: 41332K
        Extended Memory: 2048K    Work Device C:   41332K
        Current directory:  C:\SPSS\DATA
        SPSS/PC+ directory:  C:\SPSS

        LISTING   SPSS.LIS         SCREEN     ON      INCLUDE   ON
        LOG       SPSS.LOG         PRINTER    OFF     BEEP      OFF
        RESULTS   SPSS.PRC         PTRANSL    ON      MORE      ON
        NULLINE   ON               ECHO       ON      EJECT     OFF

        PROMPT    SPSS/PC:         LENGTH     24      WIDTH     79
        CPROMPT        :           BLOCK              BOX
        ENDCMD    .                HIST               SEED      600350385
        COLOR     (15, 1, 1)       CPI      10.00     LPI       6.00
        WEIGHT    OFF              COMPRESS   ON      BLANKS
                                   ERRORBREAK ON      VIEWLENGTH  25
        _____ Review Settings _____

        AUTOMENU  OFF              HELPWINDOWS ON     MENUS     EXTENDED
        RCOLOR    ( 1, 2, 4)       RLINES      ON     RUNREVIEW AUTO
```

SORT CASES

```
SORT CASES [BY] varlist[({A})] [varlist...]
                       {D}
```

Example:
```
SORT CASES BY DIVISION (A) STORE (D).
```

Overview

SORT CASES reorders the sequence of cases in the active file based on the values of one or more variables. You can sort cases in ascending or descending order, or use combinations of ascending and descending order for different variables.

Basic Specification

The basic specification is a variable or list of variables that are used as sort keys. By default, cases are sorted in ascending order of each variable, starting with the first variable named. For each subsequent variable, cases are sorted in ascending order within categories of the previously named variables.

Syntax Rules

- Keyword BY is optional.
- BY variables can be numeric or string.
- You can explicitly request the default sort order (ascending) by specifying A or UP in parentheses after the variable name. To sort cases in descending order, specify D or DOWN.
- An order specification (A or D) applies to all variables in the list up to the previous order specification. If you combine ascending and descending order on the same SORT CASES command, you may need to specify the default A explicitly.

Operations

- SORT CASES first sorts the file according to the first variable named. For subsequent variables, cases are sorted within categories of the previously named variables.
- The sort sequence of string variables is the ASCII collating sequence. An ascending sort order places numeric characters first, followed by uppercase alphabetical characters and then lowercase alphabetical characters. Descending order does the reverse.
- The values of system variable $CASENUM are not changed from their original values as the file is sorted. You can use the variable $CASENUM as a sorting key to restore the original order.

SORT CASES with Other Commands

- For the REPORT procedure, the file should be sorted in order of the break variable or variables. Specify the SORT CASES command before the REPORT command, and list the break variables in the same order on each.
- In AGGREGATE, cases are sorted in order of the break variable or variables. You do not have to use SORT CASES prior to running AGGREGATE, since the procedure does its own sorting.
- You can use SORT CASES in conjunction with the BY keyword in JOIN ADD to interleave cases with the same variables but from different files. With JOIN MATCH, cases must be sorted in the same order for all files you combine.
- The temporary transformations SAMPLE and PROCESS IF are ignored by SORT CASES.

Example

```
SORT CASES BY DIVISION (A) STORE (D).
```

- Cases are sorted in ascending order of variable *DIVISION*. Cases are further sorted in descending order of *STORE* within categories of *DIVISION*. A must be specified so that D applies to *STORE* only.

Example

```
SORT DIVISION STORE (A) AGE (D).
```

- Cases are sorted in ascending order of *DIVISION*. Keyword BY is not used in this example.
- Cases are further sorted in ascending order of *STORE* within values of *DIVISION*. Specification A applies to both *DIVISION* and *STORE*.
- Cases are further sorted in descending order of *AGE* within values of *STORE* and *DIVISION*.

Example

```
SORT CASES BY EDUC SEX.
REPORT VARS=SCORE1 TO SCORE5
  /BREAK=EDUC
  /SUMMARY= MEAN
  /BREAK=SEX
  /SUMMARY=MEAN.
```

- Each variable named on a BREAK subcommand in REPORT is first named on SORT CASES. Variables are named on SORT CASES in the order in which they will be used in REPORT.

SUBTITLE

```
SUBTITLE [{'}]text[{'}]
         {"}      {"}
```

Example:
```
SUBTITLE  "Children's Training Shoes Only".
```

Overview

SUBTITLE inserts a left-justified subtitle on the second line from the top of each page of the output. By default, there is no subtitle.

Basic Specification

The only specification is the subtitle itself.

Syntax Rules

- The subtitle can include any characters.
- The subtitle can be up to 64 characters long. Subtitles longer than 64 characters are truncated.
- The apostrophes or quotation marks enclosing the subtitle are optional; using them allows you to include apostrophes, quotation marks, and lowercase text in the subtitle.
- A subtitle that is not enclosed in apostrophes or quotation marks is converted to upper case.
- If the subtitle is enclosed in apostrophes, quotation marks are valid characters but apostrophes must be specified as double apostrophes. If the subtitle is enclosed in quotation marks, apostrophes are valid characters but quotation marks must be specified as double quotation marks.
- More than one SUBTITLE command is allowed in a single session.
- A subtitle cannot be placed between a procedure command and BEGIN DATA—END DATA or within data records when the data are inline.

Operations

- Each SUBTITLE command overrides the previous one and takes effect on the next output page.
- SUBTITLE is independent of TITLE and each can be changed separately.

Example

```
TITLE 'Running Shoe Study from Runner''s World Data'.
SUBTITLE  "Children's Training Shoes Only".
```

- The title is enclosed in apostrophes, so the apostrophe in *Runner's* must be specified as a double apostrophe.
- The subtitle is enclosed in quotation marks, so the apostrophe in *Children's* is simply specified as an apostrophe.

SYSFILE INFO

```
SYSFILE INFO [FILE=] 'file specification'
```

Example:
```
SYSFILE INFO FILE='PERSNL.SYS'.
```

Overview

SYSFILE INFO displays dictionary information for all variables in an SPSS/PC+ system file. You do not have to retrieve the file with GET to use SYSFILE INFO. If the file has already been retrieved, use DISPLAY to display dictionary information.

Basic Specification

- The basic specification is the command keyword and a file specification enclosed in apostrophes.

Syntax Rules

- Only one file specification is allowed per command. To display dictionary information for more than one system file, use multiple SYSFILE INFO commands.
- The file extension, if there is one, must be specified.
- The subcommand keyword FILE is optional.
- The specification can include a drive and/or a path.

Operations

- No procedure is needed to execute SYSFILE INFO, since SYSFILE INFO obtains information from the dictionary alone.
- SYSFILE INFO displays the following: filename, creation date and time; file title; number of cases and variables; case weight information; whether the file is compressed; whether the file contains special information for use by Data Entry II; the names and variable labels of all user-defined variables in the file.

Example

```
SYSFILE INFO FILE='PERSNL.SYS'.
```

- SPSS/PC+ displays dictionary information for all variables in the *PERSNL.SYS* system file.

TITLE

```
TITLE [{'}]text[{'}]
      {"}       {"}
```

Example:

```
TITLE "Running Shoe Study from Runner's World Data".
```

Overview

TITLE inserts a left-justified title on the top line of each page of SPSS/PC+ output. The default title contains the date, SPSS/PC+, and the display page number.

Basic Specification

The only specification is the title.

Syntax Rules

- The title can include any characters. To specify a blank title, enclose a blank between apostrophes.
- The title can be up to 58 characters long. Titles longer than 58 characters are truncated.
- The apostrophes or quotation marks enclosing the title are optional; using them allows you to include apostrophes, quotation marks, and lowercase text in the title.
- A title that is not enclosed in apostrophes or quotation marks is converted to upper case.
- If the title is enclosed in apostrophes, quotation marks are valid characters but apostrophes must be specified as double apostrophes. If the subtitle is enclosed in quotation marks, apostrophes are valid characters but quotation marks must be specified as double quotation marks.
- More than one TITLE command is allowed in a single session.
- A title cannot be placed between a procedure command and BEGIN DATA—END DATA or within data records when the data are inline.

Operations

- The title is displayed as part of the output heading, which also includes the date and page number.
- Each TITLE command overrides the previous one and takes effect on the next output page.
- Only the title portion of the heading changes. The date and page number are still displayed.
- TITLE is independent of SUBTITLE and each can be changed separately.

Example

```
TITLE "Running Shoe Study from Runner's World Data".
SUBTITLE 'Children''s Training Shoes Only'.
```

- The title is enclosed in quotations to allow the apostrophe in *Runner's* and to preserve upper and lower case.
- The subtitle is enclosed in apostrophes, so the apostrophe in *Children's* must be specified as a double apostrophe.

TRANSLATE

```
TRANSLATE {FROM = 'filename.ext'} [/RANGE={name        }]*
          {TO   = 'filename.ext'}         {start..stop}
                                          {start:stop }
    [/TYPE={WKS}]
           {WK1}
           {WK3}
           {WRK}
           {WR1}
           {SLK}
           {DBF}
           {DB2}
           {DB3}
           {DB4}

    [/REPLACE]

    [/DROP=variable list]  [/KEEP={variable list}]
                                  {ALL          }

    [/FIELDNAMES]**

    [/MAP]
```

*RANGE is available only for translating from spreadsheet files.
**FIELDNAMES is available only for spreadsheet files.

Keyword	Type of file
WKS	1-2-3 Release 1A
WK1	1-2-3 Release 2.0, 2.01, 2.2
WK3	1-2-3 Release 3
WRK	Symphony 1.0, 1.01
WR1	Symphony 1.1, 1.2, 2.0
SLK	Multiplan, Excel (symbolic format only)
DBF	all dBASE (with FROM)
DB2	dBASE II (with TO)
DB3	dBASE III, dBASE III PLUS (with TO)
DB4	dBASE IV (with TO)

Examples:

```
TRANSLATE FROM='PROJECT.WKS'
  /FIELDNAMES
  /RANGE=D3..J279.

TRANSLATE FROM='ANNUAL.DBF'
  /DROP=JANUARY TO MARCH
  /MAP.

TRANSLATE TO='SALESREP.SLK'
  /KEEP=SALES, UNITS, MONTHS, PRICE1 TO PRICE20
  /FIELDNAMES
  /MAP.
```

Overview

TRANSLATE either creates an active file from a file produced by another software application (subcommand FROM) or translates the SPSS/PC+ active file into a file that can be used by another software application (subcommand TO). Supported formats are 1-2-3 (1A through 3.0), Symphony, Excel, Multiplan, dBASE II, dBASE III, dBASE III PLUS, and dBASE IV. Excel and Multiplan are supported via the symbolic (SYLK) format.

Options

Variable Subsets. You can use the DROP and KEEP subcommands to specify variables to omit or retain in the resulting file.

Variable Map. To confirm the names and order of the variables in the resulting file, use the MAP subcommand. MAP displays the variables in the original file and their corresponding names in the resulting file.

Spreadsheet Files. You can use the RANGE subcommand to translate a subset of cells from a spreadsheet file. You can use the FIELDNAMES subcommand to translate field names in the spreadsheet file to SPSS/PC+ variable names or to translate SPSS/PC+ variable names to field names.

Basic Specification

- The basic specification is subcommand FROM or TO with an associated filename. FROM or TO must precede any other specifications.
- The file specification is enclosed in apostrophes and can be fully qualified, including drive, directory, filename, and extension.
- By default, all data are translated from the input file into the resulting file.
- The TYPE subcommand is required for translating from the SPSS/PC+ active file to a dBASE file, since the file extension *DBF* is shared by all dBASE database files. For all other translations, the format of the input or output file can be inferred from the file extension.

Syntax Rules

- The RANGE subcommand can be used only for translating spreadsheet files into SPSS/PC+ active files.
- The FIELDNAMES subcommand is available for spreadsheet files only.

Operations

- TRANSLATE FROM replaces an existing active file. If TRANSLATE FROM is not successful, the current active file is not changed and is still available.

- After TRANSLATE TO is executed, the active file remains available for SPSS/PC+ transformations and procedures.
- TRANSLATE TO will *not* overwrite an existing file with the same name unless you use the REPLACE subcommand.
- Commands N, SAMPLE, PROCESS IF, SELECT IF, and any transformations are executed prior to TRANSLATE TO.

Limitations

- The number of variables translated into the active file is limited by the source file. You cannot retrieve more than 256 columns from a 1-2-3, Symphony, or SYLK file. You cannot retrieve more than 32 variables from dBASE II, 128 variables from dBASE III, and 255 variables from dBASE IV.
- Maximum 2048 cases can be translated to 1-2-3 Release 1A; maximum 8192 cases to 1-2-3 Release 2.0, 3.0, or Symphony; and maximum 16,384 cases to SYLK files.
- Maximum 32 variables and 65,535 cases can be translated to dBASE II; maximum 128 variables and 1 billion cases (subject to diskspace availability) to dBASE III or dBASE III PLUS; and maximum 255 variables and 1 billion cases (subject to diskspace availability) to dBASE IV.

FROM Subcommand

TRANSLATE FROM reads a file from another application and translates it into the SPSS/PC+ active file. The only required specification on FROM is the name of the file from the other application enclosed in apostrophes.

Spreadsheets

A spreadsheet file suitable for SPSS/PC+ should be arranged so that each row represents a case and columns indicate variables.

- By default, the new active file contains all rows and up to 256 columns from 1-2-3, Symphony, and SYLK (Excel or Multiplan) files.
- Only one worksheet at a time can be translated from a *WK3* (1-2-3 Release 3) file. By default, the first (A:) worksheet is translated.
- By default, TRANSLATE FROM uses the column letters as variable names in the active file.
- The first row of a spreadsheet or specified range may contain field labels immediately followed by rows of data. These names can be transferred as SPSS/PC+ variable names (see the FIELDNAMES subcommand).
- The current value of a formula is translated to the active file.
- Blank, ERR, and NA values in 1-2-3 and Symphony are translated as system-missing in the SPSS/PC+ active file.
- Hidden columns and cells in 1-2-3 and Symphony files are translated into the SPSS/PC+ active file.

- Column width and format type are transferred to the active file dictionary.
- The format type is assigned from values in the first data row. By default, the first data row is row 1. If RANGE is specified, the first data row is the first row in the range. If FIELD-NAMES is specified, the first data row follows immediately after the single row containing field names.
- If a cell in the first data row is empty, the variable is assigned the global default format from the spreadsheet.

The formats from 1-2-3, Symphony, and Multiplan are translated by default as follows:

123/ Symphony	Multiplan	SPSS/PC+
Fixed	Fixed	Number
	Integer	Number
Scientific	Exponent	Number
Currency	$ (dollar)	Dollar
,(comma)		Comma
General	General	Number
+/-	* (bargraph)	Number
Percent	Percent	Number
Date		String
Time		String
Text		Number
Label	Alpha	String

- If a string is encountered in a column with numeric format, it is converted to the system-missing value in the SPSS/PC+ active file.
- If a numeric value is encountered in a column with string format, it is converted to a blank in the SPSS/PC+ active file.
- TRANSLATE FROM creates string variables for 1-2-3 and Symphony variables with DATE format. The SPSS/PC+ variable is in the form mm/dd/yy if the spreadsheet column has a width of 9 or less. If the width of the spreadsheet column is greater than 9, the SPSS/PC+ variable is in the form mm/dd/yyyy.
- Values with the Percent format in 1-2-3 files earlier than *WK3* and in Symphony files are multiplied by 100 so that the value in the SPSS/PC+ active file is the same as the value displayed in the spreadsheet. This is not done in translating from *WK3* files.
- Values longer than 255 characters in label cells from *WK3* files are truncated to 255 characters.
- Blank lines are translated as cases containing the system-missing value for numeric variables and blanks for string variables.
- 1-2-3 and Symphony date and time indicators (shown at the bottom of the screen) are not transferred from *WKS*, *WK1*, *WK3*, or *WRK* files. The values for system variables *$CASE-*

NUM, *$WEIGHT*, and *$DATE* are assigned by TRANSLATE as each case is written to the active file.

Example

```
TRANSLATE FROM='PROJECT.WKS'.
```

- TRANSLATE creates an active file from the 1-2-3 Release 1A spreadsheet with the name *PROJECT.WKS*.
- The active file contains all rows and uses the column letters as variable names.
- The format for each variable is determined by the format of the value in the first row of each column.

Databases

Database files are logically very similar to SPSS/PC+ data files.

- By default, all fields and records from dBASE II, dBASE III, or dBASE IV files are included in the SPSS/PC+ active file.
- Field names are automatically translated to SPSS/PC+ variable names.
- If the FIELDNAMES subcommand is used with database files, it is ignored.
- Field names to be translated should comply with SPSS/PC+ variable-naming conventions. Field names longer than eight characters are first truncated; if duplicate names result, the final characters of the name are modified to produce unique names.
- Colons used in dBASE II field names are translated to underscores.
- Records in dBASE II, dBASE III, or dBASE IV that have been marked for deletion but that have not actually been purged are included in the active file. To differentiate these cases, TRANSLATE creates a new string variable *D_R*, which contains an asterisk for cases marked for deletion. Other cases contain a blank for *D_R*.
- Character and numeric fields are transferred directly to SPSS/PC+ variables. Date and logical fields are converted into string variables. Memo fields are ignored.

The following table shows how dBASE formats are translated to SPSS/PC+:

dBASE	SPSS/PC+
Character	String
Logical	String
Date	String
Numeric	Number
Float	Number
Memo	Ignored

Example

```
TRANSLATE FROM='ANNUAL.DBF'.
```

- TRANSLATE creates an active file from the database file *ANNUAL.DBF*.

- All cases are translated and each field becomes a variable in the active file.

TO Subcommand

TRANSLATE TO converts an SPSS/PC+ active file to a file that can be used by another application. The only required specification on TO is the name to be used for the new file.

- User-missing values are transferred as the actual values.
- The three system variables *$DATE*, *$WEIGHT*, and *$CASENUM* are translated only if they are specified explicitly on the KEEP subcommand. *$DATE* is translated as a short string value with an A8 format; *$WEIGHT* and *$CASENUM* are translated as numeric values with formats of *F8.2* and *F8.0*.

Spreadsheets

Variables in the active file become columns and cases become rows in the spreadsheet file.

- If you specify FIELDNAMES, variable names become the first row and indicate field names.
- String variable values are left-justified and numeric variable values are right-justified.
- The resulting spreadsheet file is given the range name of SPSSPC.
- System-missing values are translated to NA in spreadsheet files.

SPSS/PC+ formats are translated as follows:

SPSS/PC+	1-2-3 /Symphony	Multiplan
Number	Fixed	Fixed
Comma	Comma	Fixed
Dollar	Currency	$ (dollar)
String	Label	Alpha
$DATE	Date	Alpha

Example

```
TRANSLATE TO='STAFF.WRK'.
```

- TRANSLATE TO creates a Symphony spreadsheet file containing all variables in the active file. The variable names are not transferred to the Symphony file.

Databases

Variables in the active file become fields and cases become records in the database file.

- You must use the TYPE subcommand with keyword DB2, DB3, or DB4 when translating from SPSS/PC+ to a dBASE file.

- Characters that are allowed in SPSS/PC+ variable names but are not allowed in dBASE field names are translated to colons in dBASE II and underscores in dBASE III or dBASE IV. If requested, the system variables *$CASENUM*, *$WEIGHT*, and *$DATE* are translated to fields *PC:CASENUM*, etc., for dBASE II and *PC_CASENUM*, etc., for dBASE III and dBASE IV.
- SPSS/PC+ numeric variables containing the system-missing value are translated to **** in dBASE III or dBASE IV, and to 0 in dBASE II.

SPSS/PC+ variable formats are translated to dBASE formats as follows:

SPSS/PC+	dBASE
Number	Numeric
String	Character
Dollar	Numeric
Comma	Numeric
$DATE	Date

Example

```
TRANSLATE TO='STAFF.DBF'
   /TYPE=DB3.
```

- TRANSLATE TO creates a dBASE III file called *STAFF.DBF*. The TYPE subcommand is required.

TYPE Subcommand

TYPE indicates the format of the other application's file.

- You can use the TYPE subcommand with both FROM and TO subcommands.
- The TYPE subcommand can be omitted for translating to and from spreadsheet files if the file extension named on the TO or FROM subcommand corresponds to the format keyword.
- The TYPE subcommand with keyword DB2, DB3, or DB4 is required for translating the SPSS/PC+ active file into a dBASE file. TYPE is optional for translating dBASE files into SPSS/PC+ if the file extension named on FROM is DBF.
- The TYPE subcommand takes precedence over the file extension.
- You can create a Lotus format file in Multiplan and translate it to an SPSS/PC+ active file with TYPE=WKS.

Available keywords on TYPE are:

WKS   *1-2-3 Release 1A.*

WK1   *1-2-3 Release 2.0, 2.01, 2.2.*

WK3   *1-2-3 Release 3.*

WRK   *Symphony Release 1.0, 1.01.*

WR1   *Symphony Release 1.1, 1.2, 2.0.*

SLK   *Symbolic format for use with Excel or Multiplan.*

DBF   *dBASE files.* Use DBF as the file extension or specify it on the TYPE subcommand when translating any dBASE file into an SPSS/PC+ active file.

DB2   *dBASE II.* Specify DB2 on TYPE when translating to a dBASE II file.

DB3   *dBASE III.* Specify DB3 on TYPE when translating to a dBASE III or dBASE III PLUS file.

DB4   *dBASE IV.* Specify DB2 on TYPE when translating to a dBASE IV file.

Example

```
TRANSLATE FROM='PROJECT.OCT'
   /TYPE=SLK.
```

- TRANSLATE creates an active file from the Multiplan spreadsheet *PROJECT.OCT*.

FIELDNAMES Subcommand

When used with the FROM subcommand, the optional FIELDNAMES subcommand translates spreadsheet field names into SPSS/PC+ variable names. When used with TO, FIELDNAMES translates SPSS/PC+ variable names into field names in the spreadsheet.

- FIELDNAMES can be used with spreadsheets only. FIELDNAMES is ignored when used with database files.
- SPSS/PC+ variable names are transferred to the first row of the spreadsheet file.
- For translating spreadsheet field names to SPSS/PC+, each cell in the first row of the spreadsheet file or range must contain a field name. If a column does not contain a name, the column is dropped.
- Field names to be translated into SPSS/PC+ should conform to the SPSS/PC+ variable-naming conventions.
- Variable names that exceed eight characters are truncated.
- If duplicate variable names occur, the final characters of the name are modified to produce unique names.
- If two or more columns in the spreadsheet have the same field name, new unique variable names are assigned to the second and subsequent columns.
- Illegal characters in field names are changed to underscores in SPSS/PC+.
- If the spreadsheet file uses SPSS/PC+ reserved words (ALL, AND, BY, EQ, GE, GT, LE, LT, NE, NOT, OR, TO, or WITH) as field names, TRANSLATE FROM appends a dollar sign ($) to the variable name. For example, 1-2-3 columns named *GE*, *GT*, *EQ*, and *BY* are named *GE$*, *GT$*, *EQ$*, and *BY$* in the SPSS/PC+ active file.

Example

```
TRANSLATE TO='STAFF.WRK'
   /FIELDNAMES.
```

- TRANSLATE TO creates a Symphony spreadsheet file containing all variables in the active file. Variable names are transferred to the Symphony file.

Example
```
TRANSLATE FROM='MONTHLY.WRK'
  /FIELDNAMES.
```

- TRANSLATE creates an active file from a Symphony spreadsheet. The first row in the spreadsheet contains field names that are used as variable names in the active file.

RANGE Subcommand

RANGE translates a specified set of cells from a spreadsheet file.

- RANGE cannot be used with subcommand TO or for translating from database files.
- For 1-2-3 or Symphony, specify the beginning of the range with a column letter and row number, two periods, and the end of the range with a column letter and row number, as in A1..K14.
- For 1-2-3 Release 3 files of type WK3, you can specify a range of cells in a worksheet other than the first by including a worksheet specification separated from the column speci fication by a colon (see the example below). The entire range must be within a single worksheet. If the second worksheet specification differs from the first, the entire range is taken from the worksheet specified first.
- For Multiplan spreadsheets, specify the beginning and ending cells of the range separated by a colon, as in R1C1:R14C11.
- You can also specify the range using range names supplied in Symphony, 1-2-3, or Multiplan.
- If you specify FIELDNAMES with RANGE, the first row of the range must contain field names. If you do not, it must contain data.

Example
```
TRANSLATE FROM='PROJECT.WKS'
  /FIELDNAMES
  /RANGE=D3..J279.
```

- TRANSLATE FROM creates an active file from the 1-2-3 Release 1A file *PROJECT.WKS*.
- Field names in the first row of the range (row 3) are used as variable names.
- Data from cells D4 through J279 are transferred to the active file.

Example
```
TRANSLATE FROM='PROJECT.WK3'
  /FIELDNAMES
  /RANGE=C:D3..C:J279.
```

- This example takes the same range as above from the third worksheet of the 1-2-3 Release 3 file *PROJECT.WK3*.

DROP and KEEP Subcommands

DROP and KEEP are used to include only a subset of variables in the resulting file. DROP specifies a set of variables to exclude, and KEEP specifies a set of variables to retain.

- DROP and KEEP can be used with TO or FROM.
- The specification on DROP or KEEP is a list of variable, column, or field names separated by commas or spaces. When SPSS/PC+ alters field names to form valid and unique variable names, use the SPSS/PC+ variable names on the DROP and KEEP subcommands.
- You can use TO to refer to adjacent variables or columns.
- You can use keyword ALL on KEEP to specify all user-defined (not system) variables. KEEP=ALL is equivalent to omitting the KEEP subcommand.
- Variables can be specified in any order. Neither DROP nor KEEP affects the order of variables in the resulting file. Variables are kept in their original order.
- If FIELDNAMES is specified when translating from a spreadsheet, the DROP and KEEP subcommands must refer to the field names, not the default column letters.
- If you specify both RANGE and KEEP, the resulting file contains only variables that are both within the range and named on KEEP.
- If you specify both RANGE and DROP, the resulting file contains only variables that are within the range and not named on DROP.

Example

```
TRANSLATE FROM='ADDRESS.DBF'
  /DROP=PHONENO, ENTRY.
```

- TRANSLATE creates an active file from the dBASE file *ADDRESS.DBF*, omitting the fields named *PHONENO* and *ENTRY*.

Example

```
TRANSLATE FROM='PROJECT.OCT'
  /TYPE=WK1
  /FIELDNAMES
  /KEEP=NETINC, REP, QUANTITY, REGION, MONTH, DAY, YEAR.
```

- TRANSLATE creates an active file from the 1-2-3 Release 2.0 file called *PROJECT.OCT*.
- FIELDNAMES indicates that the first row of the spreadsheet contains field names, which will be translated into variable names in the active file.
- KEEP translates columns with the field names *NETINC*, *REP*, *QUANTITY*, *REGION*, *MONTH*, *DAY*, and *YEAR* to the active file.

REPLACE Subcommand

You can replace an existing spreadsheet or database file by specifying the REPLACE subcommand. This subcommand should be used with caution.

Example

```
TRANSLATE TO='WEEKLY.WK1'
  /REPLACE.
```

- If *WEEKLY.WK1* already exists, it is replaced without warning.

MAP Subcommand

MAP displays a list of the variables transferred from or to a file.

- The list displays the names of the variables, the variable type (string or numeric), the width of the variable, and the number of decimal places.
- If TRANSLATE has changed the name of a variable, the original name (up to 10 characters) is also displayed.
- MAP can be specified anywhere on the TRANSLATE command.

Example

```
TRANSLATE TO='STAFF.DBF'
  /TYPE=DB3
  /MAP.
```

- MAP requests a list of the variables translated to the dBASE III database.

T-TEST

Independent-samples tests:

```
T-TEST GROUPS=varname ({1,2**    }) /VARIABLES=varlist
                       {value     }
                       {value,value}
```

Paired-samples tests:

```
T-TEST PAIRS=varlist [WITH varlist [(PAIRED)]] [/varlist ...]
```

Both types of tests:

```
[/MISSING={ANALYSIS**}   [INCLUDE]]
          {LISTWISE  }

 [/FORMAT={LABELS** }]
          {NOLABELS}

 [/CRITERIA=CI [{( 0.95)}]
               {(value) }
```

**Default if the subcommand is omitted.

Examples:

```
T-TEST GROUPS=WORLD(1,3) /VARIABLES=NTCPRI NTCSAL NTCPUR.

T-TEST PAIRS=TEACHER CONSTRUC MANAGER.
```

Overview

T-TEST compares population means by calculating Student's *t* and displays the two-tailed probability of the difference between the means. Statistics are available for either independent samples (different groups of cases) or paired samples (different variables). Other procedures that compare group means are ANOVA, ONEWAY, and MANOVA (MANOVA is available in the SPSS/PC+ Advanced Statistics option).

Options

Format. You can suppress the display of variable labels using the FORMAT subcommand.

Statistics. You can control which variables are paired in paired-samples tests using the PAIRED keyword. There are no optional statistics. All statistics available are displayed by default.

Confidence Level. You can change the level of the confidence interval with the CRITERIA subcommand. The default level is 95%.

Basic Specification

The basic specification depends on whether you want an independent-samples test or a paired-samples test. For both types of tests, T-TEST displays Student's *t*, degrees of freedom, and two-tailed probabilities, as well as the mean, standard deviation, standard error, and count for each group or variable.

- To request an independent-samples test, use the GROUPS and VARIABLES subcommands. Both equal-variance (pooled) and unequal-variance (separate) estimates are calculated, along with Levene's test for homogeneity of variance and its probability. The two-tailed probability is displayed for each *t* value, as is the confidence interval.
- To request a paired-samples test, use the PAIRS subcommand. The default output includes the difference between the means, two-tailed probability level for a test of the difference, correlation coefficient for the two variables, the two-tailed probability level for a test of the coefficient, and the confidence interval.
- To request both independent- and paired-samples tests, specify GROUPS, VARIABLES, and PAIRS.

Subcommand Order

Subcommands can be named in any order.

Operations

- If a variable specified on GROUPS is a long string, only the short-string portion is used to identify groups in the analysis.
- Probability levels are two-tailed. To obtain the one-tailed probability, divide the two-tailed probability by 2.
- The BOXSTRING subcommand on SET controls the characters used in the table display (see SET).

Limitations

Maximum 1 GROUPS and 1 VARIABLES subcommand per T-TEST command.

Example

```
T-TEST GROUPS=WORLD(1,3) /VARIABLES=NTCPRI NTCSAL NTCPUR.
```

- This independent-samples *t* test compares the means of the two groups defined by values 1 and 3 of *WORLD* for variables *NTCPRI*, *NTCSAL*, and *NTCPUR*.

Example

```
T-TEST PAIRS=TEACHER CONSTRUC MANAGER.
```

- This paired-samples *t* test compares the means of *TEACHER* with *CONSTRUC*, *TEACHER* with *MANAGER*, and *CONSTRUC* with *MANAGER*.

GROUPS and VARIABLES Subcommands

GROUPS and VARIABLES are used to request independent-samples *t* tests. GROUPS specifies a variable used to group cases. VARIABLES specifies the dependent variables.

- GROUPS can specify only one variable, which can be numeric or string.
- VARIABLES can specify multiple variables, all of which must be numeric.

Any one of three methods can be used to define the two groups for the variable specified on GROUPS:

- Specify a single value in parentheses to group all cases with a value equal to or greater than the specified value into one group and the remaining cases into the other group.
- Specify two values in parentheses to include cases with the first value in one group and cases with the second value in the other group. Cases with other values are excluded.
- If no values are specified on GROUP, T-TEST uses 1 and 2 as default values for numeric variables. There is no default for string variables.

PAIRS Subcommand

PAIRS requests paired-samples *t* tests.

- The minimum specification for a paired-samples test is PAIRS with an analysis list. Only numeric variables can be specified on the analysis list. The minimum analysis list is two variables.
- If keyword WITH is not specified, each variable in the list is compared with every other variable in the list.
- If keyword WITH is specified, every variable to the left of WITH is compared with every variable to the right of WITH. WITH can be used with keyword PAIRED to obtain special pairing.
- To specify multiple analysis lists, use multiple PAIRS subcommands, each separated by a slash. Keyword PAIRS is required only for the first analysis list; a slash can be used to separate each additional analysis list.

(PAIRED)   *Special pairing for paired-samples test.* PAIRED must be enclosed in parentheses and must be used with keyword WITH. When PAIRED is specified, the first variable before WITH is compared with the first variable after WITH, the second variable before WITH is compared with the second variable after WITH, and so forth. The same number of variables must be specified before and after WITH. PAIRED generates an error message if keyword WITH is not specified on PAIRS.

Example

```
T-TEST PAIRS=TEACHER CONSTRUC MANAGER.
T-TEST PAIRS=TEACHER MANAGER WITH CONSTRUC ENGINEER.
T-TEST PAIRS=TEACHER MANAGER WITH CONSTRUC ENGINEER (PAIRED).
```

- The first T-TEST compares *TEACHER* with *CONSTRUC, TEACHER* with *MANAGER*, and *CONSTRUC* with *MANAGER*.
- The second T-TEST compares *TEACHER* with *CONSTRUC, TEACHER* with *ENGINEER*, *MANAGER* with *CONSTRUC*, and *MANAGER* with *ENGINEER. TEACHER* is not compared with *MANAGER*, and *CONSTRUC* is not compared with *ENGINEER*.
- The third T-TEST compares *TEACHER* with *CONSTRUC* and *MANAGER* with *ENGINEER*.

Example

```
T-TEST PAIRS=WCLOTHES MCLOTHES / NTCPRI WITH NTCPUR NTCSAL.
```

- Two paired analysis lists are specified.

FORMAT Subcommand

FORMAT allows you to suppress variable labels. By default, T-TEST prints variable labels.

LABELS   *Print variable labels.* This is the default.

NOLABELS   *Suppress variable labels.*

Example

```
GET FILE='CITY'.
T-TEST    PAIRS=WCLOTHES MCLOTHES
 /FORMAT=NOLABELS.
```

- FORMAT suppresses variable labels.

MISSING Subcommand

MISSING controls the treatment of missing values. The default is ANALYSIS.

- ANALYSIS and LISTWISE are alternatives; however, each can be specified with INCLUDE.

ANALYSIS   *Delete cases with missing values on an analysis-by-analysis or pair-by-pair basis.* For independent-samples tests, cases with missing values for either the grouping variable or the dependent variable are excluded from the analysis of that dependent variable. For paired-samples tests, a case with a missing value for either of the variables in a given pair is excluded from the analysis of that pair. This is the default.

LISTWISE   *Exclude cases with missing values listwise.* A case with a missing value for any variable specified on either GROUPS or VARIABLES is excluded from any independent-samples test. A case with a missing value for any variable specified on PAIRS is excluded from any paired-samples test.

IINCLUDE   *Include user-missing values.* User-missing values are treated as valid values.

CRITERIA Subcommand

CRITERIA controls the level of the confidence interval.

CI(n)   *Reset the confidence level.* You can specify a value between zero and one in parentheses. If you do not use the parentheses, the level is restored to the default 0.95, indicating a 95% confidence interval.

VALUE LABELS

```
VALUE LABELS varlist value 'label' value 'label'... [/varlist...]
```

Example:
```
VALUE LABELS JOBGRADE 'P' 'Parttime Employee'
                      'C' 'Customer Support'.
```

Overview

VALUE LABELS deletes all existing value labels for the specified variable(s) and assigns new value labels. ADD VALUE LABELS can be used to add new labels or alter labels for specified values without deleting other existing labels.

Basic Specification

The basic specification is a variable name and the individual values with their assigned labels.

Syntax Rules

- Labels can be assigned to any previously defined variables except long string variables.
- It is not necessary to enter value labels for all values for a variable.
- Each value label must be enclosed in apostrophes or quotation marks. For short string variables, the values themselves must also be enclosed in apostrophes or quotation marks.
- Value labels can contain any characters, including blanks. To enter an apostrophe as part of a label, enclose the label in quotation marks.
- The values of string variables must be specified with the correct width, including any leading or trailing blanks.
- Each value label can be up to 60 characters long, although most procedures display only 20 characters. The TABLES procedure (available in SPSS/PC+ Tables) will display all 60 characters of a label.
- The same labels can be assigned to the values of different variables by specifying a list of variable names. For string variables, the variables specified must be of equal length.
- Multiple sets of variable names and value labels can be specified on one VALUE LABELS command as long as the sets are separated by slashes.

Operations

- VALUE LABELS takes effect as soon as it is encountered in the command sequence.
- VALUE LABELS deletes all previously assigned value labels for the specified variables.

- The value labels assigned are stored in the dictionary of the active file and are automatically displayed on the output from many procedures.
- If a specified value is longer than the format of the variable, SPSS/PC+ will be unable to read the full value and may not be able to assign the value label correctly.

Example

```
VALUE LABELS V1 TO V3 1 'Officials & Managers'
                      6 'Service Workers'
                    /V4 'N' 'New Employee'.
```

- Labels are assigned to the values 1 and 6 for the variables between and including *V1* and *V3* in the active file.
- Following the required slash, a label for value N of *V4* is specified. N is a string value and must be enclosed in apostrophes or quotes.
- If labels exist for values 1 and 6 on *V1* to *V3* and value N on *V4*, they are changed in the dictionary of the active file. If labels do not exist for these values, new labels are added to the dictionary.
- Existing labels for values other than 1 and 6 on *V1* to *V3* and value N on *V4* are deleted.

Example

```
VALUE LABELS=STATE REGION 'U' "UNKNOWN".
```

- Label *UNKNOWN* is assigned to value U for both *STATE* and *REGION*.
- *STATE* and *REGION* must be string variables of equal length. If *STATE* and *REGION* have unequal lengths, a separate specification must be made for each, as in

```
VALUE LABELS STATE 'U' "UNKNOWN" / REGION 'U' "UNKNOWN".
```

Example

```
DATA LIST / CITY 1-8(A) STATE 10-12(A).
VALUE LABELS  STATE 'TEX' "TEXAS" 'TEN' "TENNESSEE"
                    'MIN' "MINNESOTA".
BEGIN DATA
AUSTIN    TEX
MEMPHIS   TEN
ST. PAUL MIN
END DATA.
FREQUENCIES VARIABLES=STATE.
```

- The DATA LIST command defines two variables. *CITY* is eight characters wide and *STATE* is three characters. The values are included between the BEGIN DATA and END DATA commands.
- The VALUE LABELS command assigns labels to three values of variable *STATE*. Each value and each label is specified in either apostrophes or quotation marks.
- The format for variable *STATE* must be at least three characters wide, because the specified values, TEX, TEN, and MIN, are three characters. If the format for *STATE* were two characters, SPSS/PC+ would issue a warning. This would occur even though the values named on VALUE LABELS and the values after BEGIN DATA agree.

VARIABLE LABELS

```
VARIABLE LABELS varname 'label' [/varname...]
```

Example:
```
VARIABLE LABELS YRHIRED 'YEAR OF FIRST HIRING'.
```

Overview

VARIABLE LABELS assigns descriptive labels to variables in the active file.

Basic Specification

The basic specification is a variable name and the associated label in apostrophes or quotes.

Syntax Rules

- Labels can be added to any previously defined variable. It is not necessary to enter labels for all variables in the active file.
- Each variable label must be enclosed in apostrophes or quotation marks.
- Variable labels can contain any characters, including blanks. To enter an apostrophe as part of a label, enclose the label in quotation marks.
- Each variable label can be up to 60 characters long, although only the TABLES procedure (available in SPSS/PC+ Tables) will display all 60 characters. Most procedures display only 40, and some procedures display fewer than 40 characters.
- Multiple variables can be assigned labels on a single VARIABLE LABELS command. Only one label can be assigned to each variable.
- Individual variable labels cannot be split across lines.

Operations

- VARIABLE LABELS takes effect as soon as it is encountered in the command sequence.
- Variable labels are automatically displayed in the output from many procedures and are stored in the dictionary of the active file.
- VARIABLE LABELS can be used for variables that have no previously assigned variable labels. If a variable has a previously assigned variable label, the new label replaces the old label.

Example

```
VARIABLE LABELS  YRHIRED 'YEAR OF FIRST HIRING'
  DEPT88 'DEPARTMENT OF EMPLOYMENT IN 1988'
  SALARY88 'YEARLY SALARY IN 1988'
  JOBCAT 'JOB CATEGORIES'.
```

- Variable labels are assigned to the variables *YRHIRED*, *DEPT88*, *SALARY88*, and *JOBCAT*.

WEIGHT

```
WEIGHT {BY varname}
       {OFF     }
```

Example:
```
WEIGHT BY V1.
FREQUENCIES VAR=V2.
```

Overview

WEIGHT weights cases differentially for analysis. WEIGHT can be used to obtain population estimates when you have a sample from a population for which some subgroup has been over- or undersampled. WEIGHT can also be used to weight a sample up to population size for reporting purposes or to replicate an example from a table or other aggregated data (see p. 494 for an example). With WEIGHT, you can arithmetically alter the sample size or its distribution.

Basic Specification

The basic specification is keyword BY followed by the name of the weight variable. Cases are weighted according to the values of the specified variable.

Syntax Rules

- Only one numeric variable can be specified.
- WEIGHT OFF turns weighting off. You cannot weight the file by a variable named *OFF*.

Operations

- WEIGHT takes effect as soon as it is encountered in the command sequence.
- Weighting is permanent during a session changed by another WEIGHT command or turned off with the WEIGHT OFF specification.
- Each WEIGHT command overrides the previous one.
- The default value of *$WEIGHT* for each case is 1.0.
- WEIGHT uses the value of the specified variable to arithmetically replicate cases for subsequent procedures. Cases are not physically replicated. For example, if you use a weighted file with CROSSTABS, the counts in the cells are actually the sums of the case weights. CROSSTABS then rounds cell counts when displaying the tables.
- Weight values do not need to be integer.
- Cases with missing or nonpositive values for the weighting variable are treated as having a weight of 0 and are thus invisible to statistical procedures.

- A file saved when weighting is in effect maintains the weighting.
- If the weighted number of cases exceeds the sample size, tests of significance are inflated; if it is smaller, they are deflated.

Example

```
WEIGHT BY V1.
FREQ VAR=V2.
```

- The frequency counts for the values of variable *V2* will be weighted by the values of variable *V1*.

Example

```
COMPUTE WVAR=1.
IF (GROUP EQ 1) WVAR=.5.
WEIGHT BY WVAR.
```

- Variable *WVAR* is initialized to 1 with the COMPUTE command. The IF command changes the value of *WVAR* to 0.5 for cases where *GROUP* equals 1.
- Subsequent procedures will use a case base in which cases from group 1 count only half as much as other cases.

Example

```
GET FILE 'CITY'.
WEIGHT BY POP87.
DESCRIPTIVES ALL.
WEIGHT BY POP88.
DESCRIPTIVES ALL.
```

- The first DESCRIPTIVES command computes summary statistics based on cases weighted by *POP87*. The second DESCRIPTIVES command computes summary statistics based on cases weighted by *POP88*.

WRITE

```
WRITE [VARIABLES={ALL**  }]
                 {varlist}

  [/CASES=[FROM {1**}] [TO {eof**}]
               {n  }      {n    }

        [BY {1**}]]]
            {n  }

  [/FORMAT=[{UNNUMBERED**}] [{WRAP**}] [WEIGHT]]
           {NUMBERED    }   {SINGLE}
```

**Default if the subcommand is omitted.

Example:

```
WRITE VARIABLES=XVAR AVAR
  /CASES=FROM 10 TO 100 BY 2.
```

Overview

WRITE writes cases to an ASCII file. The cases are written to the results file specified on SET (by default, *SPSS.PRC*). The format of the file is automatically determined by SPSS/PC+ using the dictionary formats of the variables and a record length of 80. In addition to writing the file, WRITE also displays a table showing the names and the record and column locations of the variables on the written file.

Options

Selecting and Ordering Variables. You can limit the written file to specified variables using the VARIABLES subcommand.

Format. You can limit each case to a single record, and you can include the case weight and sequence number with the FORMAT subcommand.

Selecting Cases. You can limit the file to a particular sequence of cases using the CASES subcommand.

Basic Specification

- The basic specification is simply WRITE, which writes the values of all user-defined variables for all cases in the file. Each case is written on as many records as are needed.

Subcommand Order

- All subcommands are optional and can be specified in any order.

Syntax Rules

- A subcommand or its abbreviation may not be recognized if a variable name is identical to it, unless the subcommand is followed by an equals sign.
- The VARIABLES, FORMAT, and CASES subcommands can each be specified only once.

Operations

- WRITE uses the dictionary print formats (see "Variable Formats" on p. 435). If a value is longer than the format allows, asterisks (*) are written.
- The record length is 80 characters regardless of the width defined on SET.
- If VARIABLES is not specified, variables are listed in the order in which they appear in the active file.
- If a long string variable cannot be written within the record length of 80, it is truncated.
- Records are always written with a single blank between variables.
- System-missing values are written as blanks.
- System variables are written only when explicitly requested.
- Records are written to the results file specified on SET. The default is *SPSS.PRC*. If you write to the same file more than once in the same session, the file will contain only the results of the last procedure. Use the SET command to change the results file if you write output more than once in a session.

Example

```
DATA LIST FILE='EMPLOYEE.DAT'
  / XVAR 1 YVAR 10-15 ZVAR 3-9(2)
  / AVAR 25-30(A).
WRITE VARIABLES=XVAR AVAR
  /CASES=FROM 10 TO 100 BY 2.
```

- This example writes an ASCII file containing data for every other case starting with Case 10 and stopping at 100 for variables *XVAR* and *AVAR*.
- The records are written to the default results file *SPSS.PRC*.
- A display table describing the format of the file is sent to the screen and to the default listing file *SPSS.LIS*.

VARIABLES Subcommand

VARIABLES specifies the variables to write. The actual keyword VARIABLES can be omitted.

- If VARIABLES is used, only the specified variables are written.
- The variables must already exist.
- Variables are written in the order in which they are named on VARIABLES.
- If a variable is named more than once it is written more than once.

- Keyword ALL (the default) can be used to request all variables. ALL can also be used with a variable list. For example, you can specify VARIABLES=$CASENUM ALL.

- ALL does not include the system variables *$CASENUM*, *$WEIGHT*, and *$DATE*. You must request them explicitly to write them, as in VARIABLES=$CASENUM ALL.

ALL   *Write all user-defined variables.* Variables are written in the order in which they appear in the active file. This is the default if the VARIABLES subcommand is omitted.

FORMAT Subcommand

FORMAT controls whether the file includes the case weight or sequence number for each case, and whether cases are limited to a single line. By default, the case weight and sequence number of not included, and cases that do not fit on a single line are wrapped.

- If the FORMAT subcommand is omitted or if it is included without specifications, the defaults are in effect.

- Defaults that are not changed remain in effect.

- WRAP and SINGLE are alternatives, as are NUMBERED and UNNUMBERED. Only one of each pair can be specified.

NUMBERED   *Include the sequence number of the case.* The sequence number is the first item written for each case and is labeled *Case#* in the display table.

UNNUMBERED   *Do not include the sequence number of each case.* This is the default.

SINGLE   *Limit each case to one record.* If variables requested cannot be written on a single record, WRITE is not executed.

WRAP   *Wrap cases if they do not fit on a single line.* Page width is determined by the SET WIDTH command. This is the default.

WEIGHT   *Write the value of the case's weight in the active file.*

CASES Subcommand

CASES limits the number and pattern of cases written. By default, all cases in the active file are written.

- Any or all of the keywords below can be specified. Defaults that are not changed remain in effect.

- If WRITE is preceded by a SAMPLE, SELECT IF, or N command, case selections are taken from those cases that were selected by SAMPLE, SELECT IF, or N.

FROM n   *The case number of the first case to be written.* The default is 1.

TO n   *Case number of the last case to be written.* The default is the end of the active file. CASES 100 is interpreted as CASES TO 100.

BY n   *Increment used to choose cases for writing.* The default is 1.

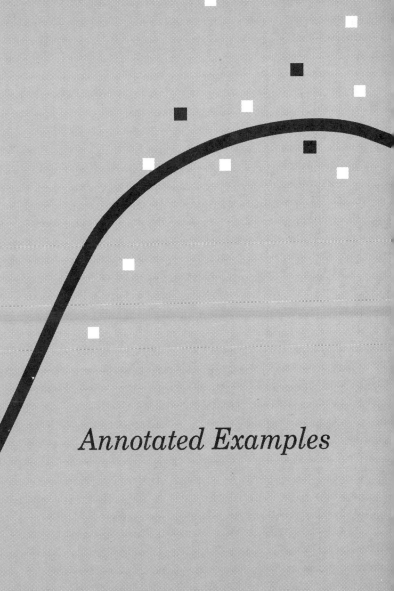

SPSS

Annotated Examples

Annotated Examples

AGGREGATE and JOIN

This example creates a file that can be used to produce a report of product sales by different sales representatives. The file contains data on the individual sales of each product by each representative, the average and total sales for each product, and the performance of each representative relative to the product average and total. There are two system files containing data on individual sales by each representative, one for the first quarter and one for the second quarter. The variables are:

- *SALESREP*—the name of the sales representative who closed a sale.
- *PRODUCT*—the product, coded 1=Primo, 2=Mocha, 3=Blend, and 4=Special.
- *NUMBER*—the quantity sold of each product.
- *MONTH*—the month of a sale, coded as a number with a value label
- *DAY*—the day of a sale, coded as a number.
- *YEAR*—the year of a sale.

The two system files first are combined. The resulting active file is sorted and aggregated to produce variables summarizing the sales of each product. The summary variables are appended to the individual sales data so that variables can be computed for the sales of each representative in comparison to the summarized sales. Finally, the REPORT command produces the report. The SPSS/PC+ commands are:

```
GET FILE='FSTQTR.SYS'.
SORT CASES BY PRODUCT MONTH.
SAVE OUTFILE='FSTQTRSO.SYS'.

GET FILE='SECQTR.SYS'.
SORT CASES BY PRODUCT MONTH.

JOIN ADD FILE='FSTQTRSO.SYS'/FILE=*
  /BY PRODUCT MONTH/MAP.

AGGREGATE OUTFILE='AGGSALES.SYS'/BREAK=PRODUCT
  /TOTAL=SUM(NUMBER)
  /AVSALES=MEAN(NUMBER).

JOIN MATCH FILE=*/TABLE='AGGSALES.SYS'/BY PRODUCT/MAP.

SORT BY PRODUCT SALESREP.

COMPUTE CONTRIB=NUMBER/TOTAL*100.
COMPUTE DIFF=RND(NUMBER-AVSALES).
FORMATS DIFF(F4.0).
```

```
REPORT FORMAT=MANUAL LIST BRKSPACE(-1)
  /TITLE 'Mid Year Sales Report'
  /VARIABLES=NUMBER 'Number of' 'Units Sold' (10)
             MONTH (label) 'Month' (5)
             DIFF 'Deviation' (9)
             CONTRIB '% of Total' (10)
  /BREAK=PRODUCT (label) 'Product' 'Name' (12)
  /SUMMARY=SUM '   Total' (NUMBER CONTRIB)
  /SUMMARY=MEAN '  Average' (NUMBER)
  /BREAK=SALESREP 'Sales' 'Rep' (SKIP(0)).
```

- The first GET command retrieves the system file *FSTQTR.SYS*. The cases are ordered according to months within product categories, as specified on the SORT command. The SAVE command saves a copy of the sorted system file, named *FSTQTRSO.SYS*.

- The second GET command retrieves the system file *SECQTR.SYS*, and SORT again orders the cases by months within product categories. The sorted system file is the active file.

- ADD (alias for JOIN ADD) combines cases from *FSTQTRSO.SYS* and the active file, interleaving the cases according to the values of *PRODUCT* and *MONTH*. The MAP subcommand produces a listing of the variables contained on the resulting active file (Figure 1).

- AGGREGATE writes an aggregated system file called *AGGSALES.SYS*. The file contains one case for each category of variable *PRODUCT*, which is specified on the BREAK subcommand. Each case contains a value for *PRODUCT*; a value for *TOTAL*, representing the sum of variable *NUMBER* for each break group; and a value for *AVSALES*, representing the mean of *NUMBER* for each break group. Figure 2 shows the variables in the system file *AGGSALES.SYS*.

- MATCH (a synonym for JOIN MATCH) combines variables from the active file and from the aggregated file, which is a table file. Cases with matching values for *PRODUCT* are joined. The MAP subcommand requests a listing of the variables that are in the resulting active file (Figure 2).

- SORT orders the file according to *SALESREP* within categories of *PRODUCT*. The subsequent REPORT command requires that the input file be sorted on each variable named on a BREAK subcommand.

- The two COMPUTE commands create two new variables, *CONTRIB* and *DIFF*, based on variables from the combined files. The FORMATS command assigns four columns for *DIFF*.

- REPORT requests a case listing of variables *SALESREP*, *NUMBER*, *MONTH*, *DIFF*, and *CONTRIB* for each category of product. For each category, two summary measures are computed. Figure 3 shows the report.

The exact appearance of the output depends on the characters available on your printer.

Figure 1   MAP output

```
RESULT          FSTQTRSO.SYS  *
------------    ------------  ------------
SALESREP        SALESREP      SALESREP
PRODUCT         PRODUCT       PRODUCT
NUMBER          NUMBER        NUMBER
MONTH           MONTH         MONTH
DAY             DAY           DAY
YEAR            YEAR          YEAR
```

Figure 2 Table look-up MAP output

```
RESULT         *            AGGSALES.SYS
-----------    -----------  -----------
SALESREP       SALESREP
PRODUCT        PRODUCT      PRODUCT
NUMBER         NUMBER
MONTH          MONTH
DAY            DAY
YEAR           YEAR
TOTAL                       TOTAL
AVSALES                     AVSALES
```

Figure 3   REPORT output

Mid Year Sales Report

Product Name	Sales Rep	Number of Units Sold	Month	Deviation	% of Total
Primo	Brennan	6	Feb	-3	23.08
		1	Jun	-8	3.85
	Walsh	19	Feb	10	73.08
Total		26			100.00
Average		8.67			
Mocha	Curtis	6	Feb	-9	5.08
		6	Mar	-9	5.08
		14	May	-1	11.86
		26	Jun	11	22.03
	Feyerherd	11	Feb	-4	9.32
		3	Jun	-12	2.54
	Sullivan	24	Mar	9	20.34
	Walsh	28	May	13	23.73
Total		118			100.00
Average		14.75			
Blend	Brennan	5	Feb	-6	6.58
		13	Jun	2	17.11
	Curtis	11	Feb	0	14.47
		10	May	-1	13.16
	Feyerherd	1	Jun	-10	1.32
	James	18	Jan	7	23.68
	Schultz	18	Jan	7	23.68
Total		76			100.00
Average		10.86			
Special	Brennan	6	Apr	-6	7.06
	James	10	Mar	-2	11.76
		9	Jun	-3	10.59
	Schultz	5	Jan	-7	5.88
		12	May	0	14.12
	Sullivan	29	Jun	17	34.12
	Walsh	14	Mar	2	16.47
Total		85			100.00
Average		12.14			

ANOVA

This example is a three-way analysis of variance with one covariate. The data are 500 cases from the 1980 General Social Survey. The variables are:

- *PRESTIGE*—the respondent's occupational prestige scale score. *PRESTIGE* is the dependent variable.
- *EDUC*—the respondent's education in years.
- RACE—the respondent's race, coded 1=*WHITE*, 2=*BLACK*, and 3=*OTHER*.
- SEX—the respondent's sex, coded 1=*MALE* and 2=*FEMALE*.
- *REGION*—the respondent's residence, coded as one of nine regions.

The task is twofold: determine the degree to which the American occupations across race, sex, and region; and measure the effect of the respondent's educational level. The data are in an external file named *AANOVA.DAT*. The SPSS/PC+ commands are:

```
DATA LIST FILE='AANOVA.DAT'
   /PRESTIGE 1-2 EDUC 3-4 RACE 5 SEX 6 REGION 7.
VARIABLE LABELS PRESTIGE "Resp's Occupational Prestige Score"
                EDUC 'Highest Year School Completed'
                REGION 'Region of Interview'.
ANOVA PRESTIGE BY REGION(1,9) SEX,RACE(1,2) WITH EDUC
   /STATISTICS 2
   /OPTIONS 10,11.
FINISH.
```

- DATA LIST assigns variable names and gives column locations for the variables in the analysis.
- VARIABLE LABELS labels for the variables.
- ANOVA names *PRESTIGE* as the dependent variable; *REGION*, *SEX*, and *RACE* as the factors; and *EDUC* as the covariate. The minimum and maximum values for *REGION* are 1 and 9, and the minimum and maximum values for both *SEX* and *RACE* are 1 and 2. Although variable *RACE* actually has values 1, 2, and 3, cases with value 3 are eliminated from the model.
- Statistic 2 requests the regression coefficient for the covariate *EDUC*.
- Option 10 requests the hierarchical approach for decomposing sums of squares. First, the covariate *EDUC* is assessed to establish statistical control. Then the effect of *REGION* is assessed. Next, the effect of *SEX* is adjusted for *REGION*; then the effect of *RACE* is adjusted for *REGION* and *SEX*. Finally, each of the interaction effects is assessed.
- Option 11 requests that the output be displayed using narrow width.

The output is shown in Figure 4. The exact appearance of the output depends on the characters available on your printer.

Figure 4   ANOVA output

```
        PRESTIGE  Resp's Occupational Prestige Score
BY      REGION    Region of Interview
        SEX
        RACE
WITH    EDUC      Highest Year School Completed
```

Source of Variation	Sum of Squares	DF	Mean Square	F	Signif of F
Covariates	23715.522	1	23715.522	191.701	0.000
EDUC	23715.522	1	23715.522	191.701	0.000
Main Effects	2708.380	10	270.838	2.189	0.018
REGION	1260.552	8	157.569	1.274	0.255
SEX	22.413	1	22.413	0.181	0.671
RACE	1425.415	1	1425.415	11.522	0.001
2-way Interactions	3144.833	17	184.990	1.495	0.092
REGION SEX	1349.220	8	168.653	1.363	0.211
REGION RACE	1138.839	8	142.355	1.151	0.328
SEX RACE	534.154	1	534.154	4.318	0.038
3-way Interactions	1663.399	6	277.233	2.241	0.039
REGION SEX RACE	1663.399	6	277.233	2.241	0.039
Explained	31232.135	34	918.592	7.425	0.0
Residual	52205.957	422	123.711		
Total	83438.092	456	182.978		

```
Covariate    Raw Regression Coefficient

EDUC              2.331


500 Cases were processed.
 43 Cases (  8.6 PCT) were missing.
```

CORRELATIONS

This example analyzes 1979 prices and earnings in 45 cities around the world, compiled by the Union Bank of Switzerland. The variables are:

- *FOOD*—the average net cost of 39 food and beverage items in the city, expressed as a percentage above or below that of Zurich, where Zurich equals 100%.

- *RENT*—the average gross monthly rent in the city, expressed as a percentage above or below that of Zurich, where Zurich equals 100%.

- *SERVICE*—the average cost of 28 different goods and services in the city, expressed as a percentage above or below that of Zurich, where Zurich equals 100%.

- *PUBTRANS*—the average cost of a three-mile taxi ride within city limits, expressed as a percentage above or below that of Zurich, where Zurich equals 100%.

- *TEACHER, COOK, ENGINEER, MECHANIC, BUS*—the average gross annual earnings of primary-grade teachers in public schools, cooks, electrical engineers, automobile mechanics, and municipal bus drivers, each working from 5 to 10 years in their respective occupations. Each of these variables is expressed as a percentage above or below those of Zurich, where Zurich equals 100%.

This example analyzes the degree to which variation in the costs of goods and services in a city is related to variation in earnings in several occupations. CORRELATIONS is used to compute correlations between the average costs of various goods and services and the average gross earnings in five different occupations. The data are in a file named *ACORR.DAT*. The SPSS/PC+ commands are:

```
DATA LIST FILE='ACORR.DAT'
   /FOOD 2-4 RENT 6-8 PUBTRANS 10-12 TEACHER 14-16 COOK 18-20
     ENGINEER 22-24 SERVICE 26-28 MECHANIC 30-32 BUS 34-36.
CORRELATIONS VARIABLES=FOOD RENT PUBTRANS TEACHER COOK ENGINEER
             /SERVICE PUBTRANS WITH MECHANIC BUS
   /STATISTICS=1,2.
FINISH.
```

- DATA LIST assigns variable names and gives column locations for the variables in the analysis.

- CORRELATIONS requests two correlation matrices. The first variable list produces correlation coefficients for each variable with every other variable. The second variable list produces four coefficients, pairing *SERVICE* with *MECHANIC* and *BUS*, and *PUBTRANS* with *MECHANIC* and *BUS*.

- The STATISTICS subcommand requests the mean, standard deviation, and number of nonmissing cases for each variable, and the cross-product deviations and covariance for each pair of variables. The statistics for all the variable lists precede all the correlation matrices in the CORRELATIONS output.

The output is shown in Figure 5 and Figure 6. The exact appearance of the output depends on the characters available on your printer.

Figure 5   Statistics from CORRELATIONS

Variable	Cases	Mean	Std Dev
FOOD	43	70.9767	18.8319
RENT	43	122.2558	95.7054
PUBTRANS	43	48.8837	24.9258
TEACHER	43	38.3023	25.4797
COOK	43	64.9767	30.5626
ENGINEER	43	60.1163	26.4802
SERVICE	43	73.5116	18.9892
MECHANIC	43	50.4884	31.0762
BUS	43	42.9535	27.3652

Variables		Cases	Cross-Prod Dev	Variance-Covar
FOOD	RENT	43	18459.2558	439.5061
FOOD	PUBTRANS	43	11121.8837	264.8068
FOOD	TEACHER	43	11244.3023	267.7215
FOOD	COOK	43	9574.9767	227.9756
FOOD	ENGINEER	43	10106.1163	240.6218
RENT	PUBTRANS	43	-3527.7209	-83.9934
RENT	TEACHER	43	-2515.3256	-59.8887
RENT	COOK	43	17443.2558	415.3156
RENT	ENGINEER	43	26859.7209	639.5172
PUBTRANS	TEACHER	43	18659.5116	444.2741
PUBTRANS	COOK	43	19394.8837	461.7829
PUBTRANS	ENGINEER	43	17621.5814	419.5615
TEACHER	COOK	43	20326.3023	483.9596
TEACHER	ENGINEER	43	18627.4884	443.5116
COOK	ENGINEER	43	25524.1163	607.7171

Variables		Cases	Cross-Prod Dev	Variance-Covar
SERVICE	MECHANIC	43	11965.2558	284.8870
SERVICE	BUS	43	12806.0233	304.9053
PUBTRANS	MECHANIC	43	23496.4186	559.4385
PUBTRANS	BUS	43	21561.6744	513.3732

Figure 6   Correlation matrices

Correlations:	FOOD	RENT	PUBTRANS	TEACHER	COOK	ENGINEER
FOOD	1.0000	.2439	.5641**	.5579**	.3961*	.4825*
RENT	.2439	1.0000	-.0352	-.0246	.1420	.2523
PUBTRANS	.5641**	-.0352	1.0000	.6995**	.6062**	.6357**
TEACHER	.5579**	-.0246	.6995**	1.0000	.6215**	.6573**
COOK	.3961*	.1420	.6062**	.6215**	1.0000	.7509**
ENGINEER	.4825*	.2523	.6357**	.6573**	.7509**	1.0000

N of cases: 43   2-tailed Signif: * - .01   ** - .001

" . " is printed if a coefficient cannot be computed

Correlations:	MECHANIC	BUS
SERVICE	.4828*	.5868**
PUBTRANS	.7487**	.7802**

N of cases: 43   2-tailed Signif: * - .01   ** - .001

" . " is printed if a coefficient cannot be computed

CROSSTABS

This example examines how respondents in different age groups answer a question on alcohol-drinking habits. The data are from a 500-case sample drawn from the 1980 General Social Survey. The variables are:

- *AGE*—the respondent's age recoded to four categories.

- *DRUNK*—the response to the question, Did you ever drink too much?

The raw data are stored in a file named *AXTABS.DAT*. The SPSS/PC+ commands are:

```
DATA LIST FILE='AXTABS.DAT'
 /DRUNK 1 AGE 2-3.
RECODE AGE (LOW THRU 29=1) (29 THRU 40=2) (40 THRU 58=3)
           (58 THRU HI=4) /DRUNK (1=1) (2=2) (ELSE=8).
MISSING VALUE DRUNK(8).
VARIABLE LABELS AGE 'Age in Four Categories'
 /DRUNK 'Ever Drink Too Much'.
VALUE LABELS AGE 1 'YoungestQuarter' 4 'Oldest  Quarter'
 /DRUNK 1 'Yes' 2 'No' 8 "Don't Drink/NA".
CROSSTABS TABLES=DRUNK BY AGE
 /CELLS=COUNT, ROW, COLUMN
 /STATISTICS=CHISQ, LAMBDA, BTAU, CTAU, GAMMA, D.
```

- DATA LIST identifies the data file and gives the names and locations of the variables to be analyzed.

- RECODE recodes variable *AGE* into four categories and recodes all missing values for variable DRUNK to one missing value.

- VARIABLE LABELS, VALUE LABELS, and MISSING VALUE add variable and value labels and specify 8 as the missing value for *DRUNK*. Since each value label breaks after eight characters in a CROSSTABS column, the label *YoungestQuarter* is specified with no blanks between the words, and the label *Oldest Quarter* has two blanks separating the words.

- CROSSTABS requests a table with *DRUNK* as the row variable and *AGE* as the column variable.

- The CELLS subcommand requests row and column percentages.

- The STATISTICS subcommand requests chi-square, lambda, Kendall's tau-*b*, Kendall's tau-*c*, gamma, and Somers' *d*.

The output is shown in Figure 7. The exact appearance of the output depends on the characters available on your printer.

Figure 7 CROSSTABS output

DRUNK Ever Drink Too Much by AGE Age in Four Categories

```
                   AGE                                 Page 1 of 1
           Count
           Row Pct  Youngest                Oldest
           Col Pct  Quarter                 Quarter      Row
                      1        2        3      4        Total
DRUNK
            1        62       33       36      16        147
  Yes              42.2     22.4     24.5    10.9       38.5
                   57.9     34.7     37.9    18.8

            2        45       62       59      69        235
  No               19.1     26.4     25.1    29.4       61.5
                   42.1     65.3     62.1    81.2

          Column    107       95       95      85        382
          Total     28.0     24.9     24.9    22.3      100.0
```

Chi-Square	Value	DF	Significance
Pearson	31.57230	3	.00000
Likelihood Ratio	32.49043	3	.00000
Mantel-Haenszel test for linear association	26.54495	1	.00000

Minimum Expected Frequency   32.709

Statistic	Value	ASE1	T-value	Approximate Significance
Lambda :				
symmetric	.09716	.04043	2.34152	
with DRUNK dependent	.11565	.06617	1.64929	
with AGE dependent	.08727	.03709	2.26282	
Goodman & Kruskal Tau :				
with DRUNK dependent	.08265	.02707		.00000 *2
with AGE dependent	.02808	.00970		.00000 *2

Page 4	SPSS/PC+			7/17/92

Statistic	Value	ASE1	T-value	Approximate Significance
Kendall's Tau-b	.24165	.04394	5.46443	
Kendall's Tau-c	.28768	.05265	5.46443	
Gamma	.39632	.06875	5.46443	
Somers' D :				
symmetric	.23546	.04281	5.46443	
with DRUNK dependent	.19222	.03519	5.46443	
with AGE dependent	.30381	.05511	5.46443	

*2 Based on chi-square approximation

Number of Missing Observations: 119

DESCRIPTIVES

This example analyzes 1979 prices and earnings in 45 cities around the world, compiled by the Union Bank of Switzerland. The variables are:

- *NTCPUR*—the city's net purchasing power, calculated as the ratio of labor expended (measured in number of working hours) to the cost of more than 100 goods and services, weighted by consumer habits. NTCPUR is expressed as a percentage above or below that of Zurich, where Zurich equals 100%.

- *FOOD*—the average net cost of 39 food and beverage items in the city, expressed as a percentage above or below that of Zurich, where Zurich equals 100%.

- *RENT*—the average gross monthly rent in the city, expressed as a percentage above or below that of Zurich, where Zurich equals 100%.

- *APPL*—the average cost of six different household appliances, expressed as a percentage above or below that of Zurich, where Zurich equals 100%.

- *SERVICE*—the average cost of 28 goods and services in the city, expressed as a percentage above or below that of Zurich, where Zurich equals 100%.

- *WCLOTHES*—the cost of medium-priced women's clothes, expressed as a percentage above or below that of Zurich, where Zurich equals 100%.

- *MCLOTHES*—the cost of medium-priced men's clothes, expressed as a percentage above or below that of Zurich, where Zurich equals 100%.

This example produces univariate summary statistics for purchasing power and the costs of various goods and services in cities. The data are in a file named *ADESC.DAT*. The SPSS/PC+ commands are:

```
DATA LIST FILE='ADESC.DAT'
 /NTCPUR 1-3 FOOD 12-14 RENT 23-25 APPL 34-36
 SERVICE 45-47 WCLOTHES 56-58 MCLOTHES 67-69.
 VARIABLE LABLES NTCPUR 'Net Purchasing Level'
 /FOOD 'Avg Food Prices'
 /RENT 'Normal Rent'
 /APPL 'Price of Appliances'
 /SERVICE 'Price for Services'
 /WCLOTHES "MediumPriced Woman's Clothes"
 /MCLOTHES "MediumPriced Men's Clothes".
COMPUTE CLOTHES=(WCLOTHES + MCLOTHES)/2.
VARIABLE LABELS CLOTHES 'Ave. Cost of W and M Clothes'.
DESCRIPTIVES VARIABLES=NTCPUR, FOOD, RENT TO SERVICE, WCLOTHES,
 MCLOTHES, CLOTHES
 /STATISTICS=1,5,9
 /OPTIONS=5.
```

- DATA LIST defines the names and locations of the variables to be analyzed.

- VARIABLE LABELS adds variable labels.

- COMPUTE creates the variable CLOTHES by adding the values for *WCLOTHES* and *MCLOTHES* and dividing by 2.

- VARIABLE LABELS assigns a label to the new variable *CLOTHES*.

- DESCRIPTIVES requests statistics for the variables named.

- The STATISTICS subcommand requests the mean, standard deviation, and range for each variable in the analysis.
- Option 5 specifies listwise deletion of missing values. A case with a missing value for any variable specified on the DESCRIPTIVES command is excluded from the computation of statistics for all variables.
- Because the default width of 79 is used, DESCRIPTIVES displays the statistics and variable labels for each variable on one line using only 79 columns.

The output is shown in Figure 8. The exact appearance of the output depends on the characters available on your printer.

Figure 8   DESCRIPTIVES output

```
Number of Valid Observations (Listwise) =        44.00

Variable      Mean     Std Dev      Range   Label

NTCPUR        58.70     28.81      100.00   Net Purchasing Level
FOOD          71.00     18.61       90.00   Avg Food Prices
RENT         121.75     94.65      413.00   Normal Rent
APPL          78.70     22.23      111.00   Price of Appliances
SERVICE       73.68     18.80       71.00   Price for Services
WCLOTHES      81.20     30.36      153.00   Medium-Priced Woman's Clothes
MCLOTHES      87.86     25.91      125.00   Medium-Priced Men's Clothes
CLOTHES       84.53     26.75      139.00   Ave. Cost of W and M Clothes
```

EXAMINE

This example compares salaries and bonuses among male and female bank employees. The variables are:

- *SALNOW*—The current salary for each employee.
- *JOBCAT*—The job category for each employee. The value labels for variable *JOBCAT* are 1=*Clerical Staff;* 2=*Office Trainee;* 3=*Security Officer;* 4=*College Trainee;* 5=*Exempt Employee;* 6=*MBA Trainee;* 7=*Technical Staff.*
- *SEX*—The employee's sex. The value labels for variable *SEX* in the data are 0=*Male* and 1=*Female.*

The SPSS/PC+ commands are:

```
GET FILE='BANK.SYS'.
SET WIDTH=132 /LENGTH=60.
EXAMINE VARIABLES = SALNOW BY JOBCAT
  /STATISTICS=ALL /PLOT=BOXPLOT /ID=SEX.
```

- GET reads an existing SPSS/PC+ system file, which includes data and a data dictionary.
- SET increases the page width to 132 and the page length to 60 for larger and more readable plots. Long lines will wrap on the screen, but the listing file will show the larger plots when printed on a suitable printer.
- EXAMINE specifies one dependent variable (*SALNOW*) and one independent variable (*JOBCAT*). The STATISTICS subcommand requests all statistics available on EXAMINE. The PLOT subcommand requests boxplots. EXAMINE will display the statistics and plots for all employee salaries, followed by separate statistics and boxplots for salaries within each job category. The ID subcommand specifies that extreme values and outliers in the salary ranges will be identified by employee sex.
- Figure 9 shows the statistics for overall salaries. The extreme values indicate that the five bank employees with the highest salaries all are male, and the five employees with the lowest salaries all are female.
- Figure 10 shows the boxplot for overall salaries. Again, you can see that the extreme values and higher outliers all are males. Figure 11 shows the footnote that prints on the page following the boxplot. The footnote explains that the outlier at the salary range of about $24,000 (this outlier is indicated by *note 1* in the plot) represents one male and one female employee.
- Figure 12 shows the statistics for three of the job categories: clerical staff, office trainees, and security officers. Comparing mean, median, and 5% trim values for clerical staff and office trainees, you can see there is very little difference in the salaries offered by each job category. Among clerical staff, the highest salaries are mixed between males and females; the lowest salaries are all females. Among office trainees, all the highest salaries are paid to men and all the lowest salaries to women.
- Among security officers, all the highest and all the lowest salaries are paid to males, suggesting that all the security officers might be males. (This might prompt you to run a crosstabulation of *JOBCAT* by *SEX* to see the distribution of males and females in each job category.) Note the small interquartile range ($480) for security officers. Because the $47,700 range in salary imposes a broad scale on the vertical axis, an interquartile range

of only $480 causes the boxplot that displays for security officers (value 3 along the horizontal axis) to collapse into one spot (Figure 13). All you can see are the lower corners of the box.

- Looking at the number of cases in each job category (see Figure 13), you can see that there are a high number of clerical workers and office trainees, a small number of security officers, college trainees, and exempt employees, and very few MBA trainees and technical staff members.

Figure 9   Overall statistics for variable SALNOW

```
     SALNOW     Current Salary

Valid cases:        474.0   Missing cases:        .0   Percent missing:        .0


Mean        13767.83   Std Err    313.7244   Min      6300.000   Skewness    2.1246
Median      11550.00   Variance   46652514   Max      54000.00   S E Skew     .1122
5% Trim     12982.08   Std Dev    6830.265   Range    47700.00   Kurtosis    5.3778
                                             IQR      5265.000   S E Kurt     .2238

                                    Extreme Values
                                    ======= ======

     5    Highest    SEX              5    Lowest     SEX

              54000    Males                    6300    Females
              44250    Males                    6360    Females
              41500    Males                    6480    Females
              41400    Males                    6540    Females
              40000    Males                    6600    Females
     SALNOW     Current Salary

Valid cases:        474.0   Missing cases:        .0   Percent missing:        .0
```

Figure 10   Boxplot for overall salaries

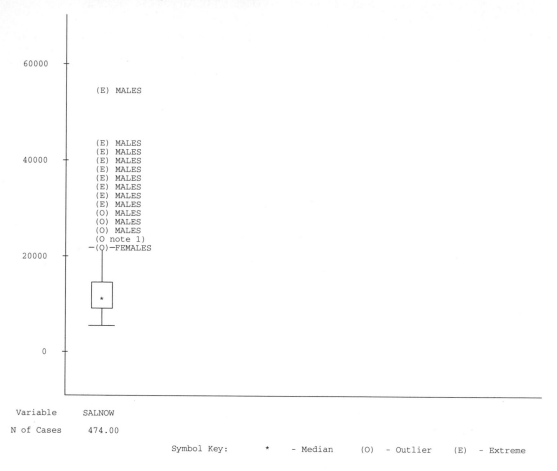

Variable	SALNOW
N of Cases	474.00

Symbol Key: *   - Median   (O) - Outlier   (E) - Extreme

Figure 11   Footnote on the first page following the boxplots

Boxplot footnotes denote the following:

1)   Female, Male

Figure 12   Salary statistics broken down by job category

```
        SALNOW      Current Salary
By      JOBCAT    1            Clerical

Valid cases:         227.0   Missing cases:        .0   Percent missing:      .0


Mean       11134.82   Std Err    212.1638   Min     6300.000   Skewness    1.2922
Median     10500.00   Variance   10218056   Max     26750.00   S E Skew     .1615
5% Trim    10903.13   Std Dev    3196.569   Range   20450.00   Kurtosis    2.7254
                                            IQR     3660.000   S E Kurt     .3217

                              Extreme Values
                              ------- ------

     5   Highest    SEX              5   Lowest     SEX

         26750      Males                6300      Females
         21600      Females              6360      Females
         21060      Males                6480      Females
         20400      Females              6540      Females
         20220      Males                6600      Females


        SALNOW      Current Salary
By      JOBCAT    2            Office Trainee

Valid cases:         136.0   Missing cases:        .0   Percent missing:      .0


Mean       11136.41   Std Err    234.3188   Min     7260.000   Skewness     3.5272
Median     10950.00   Variance   7467119    Max     32000.00   S E Skew      .2078
5% Trim    10913.92   Std Dev    2732.603   Range   24740.00   Kurtosis    24.2175
                                            IQR     3075.000   S E Kurt      .4127

                              Extreme Values
                              ----- ------

     5   Highest    SEX              5   Lowest     SEX

         32000      Males                7260      Females
         17364      Males                7600      Females
         16800      Males                7860      Females
         15960      Males                8040      Females
         15660      Males                8160      Females


        SALNOW      Current Salary
By      JOBCAT    3            Security Officer

Valid cases:          27.0   Missing cases:        .0   Percent missing:      .0


Mean       12375.56   Std Err    162.7832   Min     9720.000   Skewness    -.3680
Median     12300.00   Variance   715456.4   Max     14100.00   S E Skew     .4479
5% Trim    12403.09   Std Dev    845.8466   Range   4380.000   Kurtosis    3.6515
                                            IQR     480.0000   S E Kurt     .8721

                              Extreme Values
                              ------- ------

     5   Highest    SEX              5   Lowest     SEX

         14100      Males                9720      Males
         13800      Males               11400      Males
         13500      Males               11820      Males
         12780      Males               12000      Males
         12480      Males               12120      Males
```

Figure 13   Salary boxplots broken down by job category

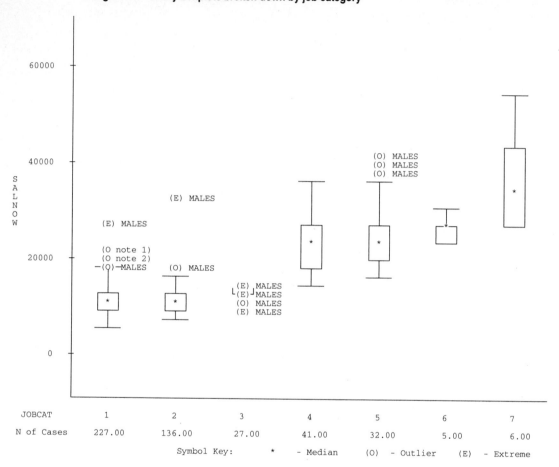

FREQUENCIES

The following example demonstrates the use of FREQUENCIES to do some preliminary checks on a newly defined file. The file is based on employment data from Hubbard Consultants Inc. The variables include: date employee was hired, employee's department, salary, job category, name, age, and sex, as well as salary increases from 1980 to 1982. The data are in a file named *AFREQ.DAT*. The SPSS/PC+ commands are:

```
DATA LIST FILE='AFREQ.DAT'
 / MOHIRED YRHIRED 12-15 DEPT79 TO DEPT82 SEX 16-20
 / SALARY79 TO SALARY82 6-25
 AGE 54-55 RAISE80 TO RAISE82 56-70
 /JOBCAT 6 EMPNAME 25-48 (A).
MISSING VALUE    SALARY79 TO SALARY82 AGE (0)
 JOBCAT (9).
VARIABLE LABELS   SALARY79 'Salary in 1979'
 SALARY80 'Salary in 1980'
 SALARY81 'Salary in 1981'
 SALARY82 'Salary in 1982'
 JOBCAT 'Job Categories'.
VALUE LABELS   SEX 1 'Male' 2 'Female'
 /JOBCAT 1 'Officials & Managers' 2 'Professionals'
 3 'Technicians' 4 'Office & Clerical' 5 'Craftsmen'
 6 'Service Workers'.
FREQUENCIES   VARIABLES=SALARY79 TO SALARY82 SEX AGE JOBCAT
 /FORMAT=LIMIT(10)
 /STATISTICS=DEFAULT MEDIAN.
```

- DATA LIST assigns variable names and gives column locations for the variables in the analysis.
- MISSING VALUE defines 0 as missing for *SALARY 79* to *SALARY 82* and *AGE*. VARIABLE LABELS and VALUE LABELS define variable and value labels.
- FREQUENCIES displays frequency tables for variables having 10 or fewer categories and default statistics and the median for all variables. The default statistics are the mean, standard deviation, minimum, and maximum.
- The output uses the default format of 79 characters.

The output is shown in Figure 14 and Figure 15. The exact appearance of the output depends on the characters available on your printer.

Figure 14   FREQUENCIES output

SALARY79 Salary in 1979

Mean	12247.323	Median	10140.000	Std Dev	6665.182
Minimum	6337.000	Maximum	45500.000		

Valid Cases   158   Missing Cases   117

- -

SALARY80 Salary in 1980

Mean	12123.725	Median	10400.000	Std Dev	6316.356
Minimum	5720.000	Maximum	48100.000		

Valid Cases   273   Missing Cases   2

- -

SALARY81 Salary in 1981

Mean	15096.212	Median	12359.500	Std Dev	8074.387
Minimum	7605.000	Maximum	52000.000		

Valid Cases   160   Missing Cases   115

- -

SALARY82 Salary in 1982

Mean	17161.552	Median	15132.000	Std Dev	8695.734
Minimum	5830.000	Maximum	50700.000		

Valid Cases   145   Missing Cases   130

- -

SEX

Value Label	Value	Frequency	Percent	Valid Percent	Cum Percent
Male	1	83	30.2	30.2	30.2
Female	2	192	69.8	69.8	100.0
		-------	-------	-------	
	TOTAL	275	100.0	100.0	

Mean	1.698	Median	2.000	Std Dev	.460
Minimum	1.000	Maximum	2.000		

Valid Cases   275   Missing Cases   0

Figure 15   FREQUENCIES output (continued)

AGE

Mean	37.158	Median	34.000	Std Dev	11.335
Minimum	20.000	Maximum	69.000		

Valid Cases   272   Missing Cases   3

- -

JOBCAT   Job Categories

Value Label	Value	Frequency	Percent	Valid Percent	Cum Percent
Officials & Managers	1	48	17.5	17.5	17.5
Professionals	2	62	22.5	22.5	40.0
Technicians	3	98	35.6	35.6	75.6
Office & Clerical	4	67	24.4	24.4	100.0
		-------	-------	-------	
	TOTAL	275	100.0	100.0	

Mean	2.669	Median	3.000	Std Dev	1.030
Minimum	1.000	Maximum	4.000		

Valid Cases   275   Missing Cases   0

LIST

This example demonstrates the use of LIST to display values of selected cases in a newly defined file. The file is based on employment data from Hubbard Consultants Inc. The variables include date employee was hired, employee's department, salary, job category, name, age, and sex, as well as salary increases from 1979 to 1982. The data are contained in a file named *ALIST.DAT*. The SPSS/PC+ commands are:

```
SET WIDTH=WIDE.
DATA LIST FILE='ALIST.DAT'
 /EMPLOYID 1-5 MOHIRED YRHIRED 12-15 DEPT79 TO DEPT82
  SEX 16-20
 /SALARY79 TO SALARY82 6-25
  HOURLY81 HOURLY82 40-53(2) PROMO81 72
  AGE 54-55 RAISE82 66-70
 /JOBCAT 6 NAME 25-48 (A).
LIST VARIABLES=MOHIRED YRHIRED DEPT82 SALARY79 TO SALARY82 NAME
 /CASES FROM 50 TO 100 BY 5/ FORMAT=SINGLE,NUMBERED.
```

- SET requests a width of 132 (WIDE) so the column titles will all be horizontal.

- DATA LIST assigns variable names and gives column locations for the variables in the analysis. Variable *NAME* is defined as a string variable.

- LIST displays values for variables *MOHIRED*, *YRHIRED*, *DEPT82*, *SALARY79* to *SALARY 82*, and *NAME*. Every 5th case is listed, starting with the 50th case. The output will include the sequence number and will use one line per case.

The output is shown in Figure 16. The exact appearance of the output depends on the characters available on your printer.

Figure 16   LIST output

```
Cas MOHIRED YRHIRED DEPT82 SALARY79 SALARY80 SALARY81 SALARY82 NAME

 50     1      79      0     14300    14300    15730        0  EVA ELDER
 55     6      79      0         0    15600        0        0  EDWARD GREEN
 60    12      79      0         0     8840     9503        0  LOVEY E. HUDSON
 65     5      80      0         0    13520        0        0  PATRICIA SMITH
 70     8      79      0         0     8255        0        0  HELEN D. SMITH
 75    10      70      4     14300    18850    21450    26182  MONICA C. RIVERS
 80     1      79      0         0     7442        0        0  THOMAS P. JOHNSON
 85     4      80      3         0    18200    18395    19682  ANN JOHNSON
 90    10      79      0         0     5720        0        0  CHRISTINA P. NORRIS
 95     5      79      0      7670     9490        0        0  M. ELLIOT KRAFT
100     2      70      3     11830    12545    13799    18083  FANNIE SMITH

Number of cases read =    100   Number of cases listed =     11
```

MEANS

This example uses MEANS to analyze personnel data from Hubbard Consultants Inc. Salaries from 1981 are analyzed by sex within department and grade. The data are in a file named *AMEANS.DAT*. The SPSS/PC+ commands are:

```
DATA LIST FILE='AMEANS.DAT'
 /SALARY81 1-5 DEPT81 6 GRADE81 7-8 SEX 9.
VARIABLE LABELS SALARY81 'Yearly Salary in 1981'
 /DEPT81 'Department Code in 1981'
 /SEX "Employee's Sex".
VALUE LABELS DEPT81 1 'Admin' 2 'Project Directors'
 3 'Chicago Operations' 4 'St Louis Operations'
 /SEX 1 'Male' 2 'Female'.
COMPUTE GRADE81S=GRADE81.
RECODE GRADE81S (1 THRU 4=1) (5 THRU 7=2) (8 THRU 15=3)
 (ELSE=0).
VALUE LABELS GRADE81S 1 'Grades 1-4'
 2 'Grades 5-7' 3 'Grades 8-15'.
MISSING VALUE GRADE81S(0).
MEANS TABLES=SALARY81 BY DEPT81 BY GRADE81S BY SEX
 /OPTIONS=6,9,10,12.
```

- DATA LIST assigns variable names and gives the column locations of the four variables used in the analysis.
- VARIABLE LABELS and VALUE LABELS provide variable and value labels.
- COMPUTE creates variable *GRADE81S* as a copy of *GRADE81*.
- RECODE recodes variable *GRADE81S* into three values that represent the 15 valid values of *GRADE81*. Other values of *GRADE81S* are recoded to value 0.
- VALUE LABELS provide value labels for the new variable *GRADE81S*. MISSING VALUE defines 0 as missing.
- MEANS specifies a three-way breakdown of salaries with *SALARY81* as the dependent variable.
- Since no missing-value option is specified, MEANS does not use cases with missing values on a tablewide basis.
- The OPTIONS subcommand requests group sums and variances and suppresses the display of independent variable names and values so that the output will fit within the default width of 79 columns.

The output is shown in Figure 17. The exact appearance of the output depends on the characters available on your printer.

Figure 17   MEANS output

```
Summaries of     SALARY81    Yearly Salary in 1981
By levels of     DEPT81      Department Code in 1981
                 GRADE81S
                 SEX         Employee's Sex
```

Label	Sum	Mean	Std Dev	Variance	Cases
For Entire Population	2415394.00	15096.2125	8074.3872	65195729.2	160
Admin	590438.000	15537.8421	9810.5522	96246934.7	38
Grades 1-4	120922.000	10076.8333	1685.2658	2840120.70	12
Male	111172.000	10106.5455	1764.2221	3112479.67	11
Female	9750.0000	9750.0000	0.0	0.0	1
Grades 5-7	179291.000	11952.7333	2019.7453	4079371.07	15
Male	13910.0000	13910.0000	0.0	0.0	1
Female	165381.000	11812.9286	2019.2662	4077435.92	14
Grades 8-15	290225.000	26384.0909	12759.5664	162806534	11
Male	170625.000	34125.0000	15498.1047	240191250	5
Female	119600.000	19933.3333	4858.3605	23603666.7	6
Project Directors	428804.000	15314.4286	8146.9522	66372830.5	28
Grades 1-4	181449.000	11340.5625	1999.6042	3998416.80	16
Male	105839.000	10583.9000	1143.2161	1306942.99	10
Female	75610.0000	12601.6667	2566.9469	6589216.27	6
Grades 5-7	38480.0000	12826.6667	2015.3494	4061633.33	3
Female	38480.0000	12826.6667	2015.3494	4061633.33	3
Grades 8-15	208875.000	23208.3333	10558.8272	111488831	9
Male	143065.000	28613.0000	11587.9159	134279795	5
Female	65810.0000	16452.5000	2953.7674	8724741.67	4
Chicago Operations	940294.000	14925.3016	7705.3167	59371905.9	63
Grades 1-4	168677.000	9922.1765	1536.2349	2360017.78	17
Male	20917.0000	10458.5000	836.5073	699744.500	2
Female	147760.000	9850.6667	1612.6409	2600610.67	15
Grades 5-7	197356.000	12334.7500	2190.5735	4798612.47	16
Male	40924.0000	13641.3333	3333.0827	11109440.3	3
Female	156432.000	12033.2308	1903.0008	3621412.19	13
Grades 8-15	574261.000	19142.0333	9294.0232	86378866.9	30
Male	142090.000	28418.0000	15680.5949	245881058	5
Female	432171.000	17286.8400	6471.7384	41883398.6	25
St Louis Operations	455858.000	14705.0968	6624.5319	43884422.6	31
Grades 1-4	66118.0000	9445.4286	680.5620	463164.619	7
Male	18395.0000	9197.5000	873.2769	762612.500	2
Female	47723.0000	9544.6000	679.0183	461065.800	5
Grades 5-7	160420.000	12340.0000	1925.6254	3708033.33	13
Male	35100.0000	11700.0000	1357.2398	1842100.00	3
Female	125320.000	12532.0000	2087.3897	4357195.56	10
Grades 8-15	229320.000	20847.2727	7667.4707	58790106.8	11
Male	21775.0000	21775.0000	0.0	0.0	1
Female	207545.000	20754.5000	8075.7134	65217146.9	10

```
Total Cases  =     275
Missing Cases =    115 OR  41.8 PCT.
```

NPAR TESTS

This example requests two chi-square tests for data that are inline. The SPSS/PC+ commands are:

```
TITLE   'CHISQUARE TEST, SIEGEL, P. 45'.
DATA LIST   /POSTPOS 1-2 NWINS 4-5.
BEGIN DATA
 2 19
 7 15
 4 25
 5 17
 8 11
 3 18
 6 10
 1 29
END DATA.
VAR LABELS  POSTPOS 'POST POSITION'.
WEIGHT   BY NWINS.
NPAR TESTS   CHISQUARE=POSTPOS
  /CHISQUARE=POSTPOS
  /EXPECTED=22,20,4*18,16,14.
```

- TITLE prints a title on each page of the output.
- DATA LIST defines two variables, *POSTPOS* and *NWINS*. Because the FILE subcommand is omitted, the data must be inline.
- The data are specified between the BEGIN DATA and END DATA commands.
- VARIABLE LABELS assigns a label to variable *POSTPOS*.
- WEIGHT weights cases according to the values of variable *NWINS*.
- NPAR TESTS requests two chi-square tests. The first test assumes equal expected frequencies because the EXPECTED subcommand is omitted. The second test uses the proportions specified on EXPECTED.

The output is shown in Figure 18. For each test, the output shows the number of observed cases and expected cases in each category of variable *POSTPOS*; the residual (observed minus expected) for each category; and the chi-square statistic, degrees of freedom, and significance of the chi-square.

Figure 18   One-sample chi-square test

```
- - - - - Chi-Square Test

 POSTPOS    POST POSITION

                Cases
  Category   Observed   Expected   Residual

       1        29       18.00      11.00
       2        19       18.00       1.00
       3        18       18.00        .00
       4        25       18.00       7.00
       5        17       18.00      -1.00
       6        10       18.00      -8.00
       7        15       18.00      -3.00
       8        11       18.00      -7.00
                ---
    Total      144

      Chi-Square           D.F.        Significance
       16.333               7              .022

- - - - - Chi-Square Test

 POSTPOS    POST POSITION

                Cases
  Category   Observed   Expected   Residual

       1        29       22.00       7.00
       2        19       20.00      -1.00
       3        18       18.00        .00
       4        25       18.00       7.00
       5        17       18.00      -1.00
       6        10       18.00      -8.00
       7        15       16.00      -1.00
       8        11       14.00      -3.00
                ---
    Total      144

      Chi-Square           D.F.        Significance
        9.316               7              .231
```

ONEWAY

This example examines the degree to which sense of well-being differs across educational levels using a 500-case sample from the 1980 General Social Survey. The variables are:

- *WELL*—the respondent's score on a scale measuring sense of well-being. *WELL* is the dependent variable, computed from measures of happiness, health, life, helpfulness of others, trust of others, and satisfaction with city, hobbies, family life and friendships.

- *EDUC*—the respondent's education in six categories, where the original codes are years of education completed.

The data are in a file named *AONE.DAT*. The SPSS/PC+ are:

```
DATA LIST FILE='AONE.DAT'/
    EDUC 1-2 HAPPY 3 HEALTH 4 LIFE 5 HELPFUL 6 TRUST 7 SATCITY 8
    SATHOBBY 9 SATFAM 10 SATFRND 11.
COUNT   X1=HAPPY HEALTH LIFE HELPFUL TRUST SATCITY SATHOBBY
            SATFAM SATFRND(1).
COUNT   X2=HAPPY HEALTH SATCITY SATHOBBY SATFAM SATFRND(2).
COUNT   X3=HEALTH HELPFUL TRUST (3).
COUNT   X4=SATCITY SATHOBBY SATFAM SATFRND(6).
COUNT   X5=HAPPY LIFE (3).
COUNT   X6=SATCITY SATHOBBY SATFAM SATFRND(7).
COMPUTE WELL=X1 + X2* .5 - X3* .5 - X4* .5 - X5 - X6.
VAR LABELS  WELL 'Sense of Well-Being Scale'.
COMPUTE EDUC6=EDUC.
RECODE  EDUC6 (0 THRU 8=1)(9,10,11=2)(12=3)(13,14,15-4)
            (16=5)(17,18,19,20=6).
VAR LABELS  EDUC6 'Education in 6 Categories'.
VALUE LABELS  EDUC6 1 'Grade School or Less'
                    2 'Some High School'
                    3 'High Sch Grad' 4 'Some College'
                    5 'College Grad' 6 'Grad Sch'.
ONEWAY  VARIABLES=WELL BY EDUC6 (1,6)
    /POLYNOMIAL=2
    /CONTRAST= 2* -1, 2* 1
    /CONTRAST=2* 0,2* -1,2* 1
    /CONTRAST=2* -1,2* 0,2* 1
    /RANGES=SNK
    /RANGES=SCHEFFE(.01)
    /STATISTICS=ALL.
FINISH.
```

- DATA LIST names the file that contains the data and specifies variable names and the column locations of the variables in the analysis.

- COUNT and COMPUTE create variable *WELL* by counting the number of *satisfied* responses for each variable on the scale and computing a weighted sum of these responses.

- A copy of *EDUC* is created with COMPUTE and is then recoded into six categories with RECODE.

- VARIABLE LABELS and VALUE LABELS assign labels to the new variables *WELL* and *EDUC6*.

- ONEWAY specifies *WELL* as the dependent variable and *EDUC6* as the independent variable. The minimum and maximum values for *EDUC6* are 1 and 6.

- The POLYNOMIAL subcommand specifies second-order polynomial contrasts. The sum of squares using the unweighted polynomial contrasts is calculated because the design is unbalanced (see Figure 19).
- The CONTRAST subcommands request three different contrasts (see Figure 20).
- The RANGES subcommands calculate multiple comparisons between means using the Student-Newman-Keuls and Scheffé tests (see Figure 21).
- The STATISTICS subcommand requests all optional statistics, including the Levene test for homogeneity of variances (see Figure 22).

The output is shown in Figure 19 through Figure 22. The exact appearance of the output depends on your printer and the LENGTH and WIDTH specifications on SET. This example uses the default settings.

Figure 19   ONEWAY polynomial contrasts

```
       Variable   WELL       Sense of Well-Being Scale
    By Variable   EDUC6      Education in 6 Categories

                              Analysis of Variance

                            Sum of       Mean          F      F
         Source        D.F.  Squares      Squares      Ratio  Prob.

Between Groups          5    361.3217     72.2643     11.5255  .0000

  Unweighted  Linear Term  1   257.3422    257.3422    41.0439  .0000
    Weighted  Linear Term  1   307.2051    307.2051    48.9966  .0000
  Deviation from  Linear   4    54.1166     13.5291     2.1578  .0727

  Unweighted  Quad. Term   1     6.6073      6.6073     1.0538  .3051
    Weighted  Quad. Term   1    16.6406     16.6406     2.6540  .1039
  Deviation from   Quad.   3    37.4759     12.4920     1.9924  .1142

Within Groups          494   3097.3463      6.2699

Total                  499   3458.6680
```

Figure 20   ONEWAY contrasts

```
        Variable  WELL        Sense of Well-Being Scale
     By Variable  EDUC6       Education in 6 Categories

Contrast Coefficient Matrix

            Grp 1        Grp 3        Grp 5
                 Grp 2        Grp 4        Grp 6

Contrast  1  -1.0  -1.0   1.0   1.0   0.0   0.0

Contrast  2   0.0   0.0  -1.0  -1.0   1.0   1.0

Contrast  3  -1.0  -1.0   0.0   0.0   1.0   1.0


                                    Pooled Variance Estimate
                    Value    S. Error    T Value    D.F.      T Prob.

Contrast  1        3.3207     0.5230      6.349    494.0       0.000

Contrast  2        1.1517     0.6613      1.742    494.0       0.082

Contrast  3        4.4724     0.6990      6.398    494.0       0.000


                                    Separate Variance Estimate
                    Value    S. Error    T Value    D.F.      T Prob.

Contrast  1        3.3207     0.5401      6.148    252.5       0.000

Contrast  2        1.1517     0.6108      1.886    123.2       0.062

Contrast  3        4.4724     0.6984      6.404    172.7       0.000
```

Figure 21 ONEWAY multiple comparisons

```
        Variable   WELL          Sense of Well-Being Scale
     By Variable   EDUC6         Education in 6 Categories


Multiple Range Test


Student-Newman-Keuls Procedure
Ranges for the 0.050 level -

         2.81    3.34    3.65    3.88    4.05

The ranges above are table ranges.
The value actually compared with Mean(J)-Mean(I) is..
        1.7706 * Range * Sqrt(1/N(I) + 1/N(J))


  (*) Denotes pairs of groups significantly different at the 0.050 level

        Variable   WELL          Sense of Well-Being Scale
        (Continued)


                                G G G G G
                                r r r r r
                                p p p p p
      Mean        Group         1 2 3 4 5 6

      2.6462      Grp 1
      2.7737      Grp 2
      4.1796      Grp 3         * *
      4.5610      Grp 4         * *
      4.6625      Grp 5         * *
      5.2297      Grp 6         * *

        Variable   WELL          Sense of Well-Being Scale
     By Variable   EDUC6         Education in 6 Categories


Multiple Range Test


Scheffe Procedure
Ranges for the 0.010 level -

         5.53    5.53    5.53    5.53    5.53

The ranges above are table ranges.
The value actually compared with Mean(J)-Mean(I) is..
        1.7706 * Range * Sqrt(1/N(I) + 1/N(J))


  (*) Denotes pairs of groups significantly different at the 0.010 level

        Variable   WELL          Sense of Well-Being Scale
        (Continued)


                                G G G G G
                                r r r r r
                                p p p p p
      Mean        Group         1 2 3 4 5 6

      2.6462      Grp 1
      2.7737      Grp 2
      4.1796      Grp 3         * *
      4.5610      Grp 4         * *
      4.6625      Grp 5         * *
      5.2297      Grp 6         * *
```

Figure 22   ONEWAY statistics

Group	Count	Mean	Standard Deviation	Standard Error	95 Pct Conf Int for Mean		
Grp 1	65	2.6462	2.7539	.3416	1.9638	To	3.3285
Grp 2	95	2.7737	2.8674	.2942	2.1896	To	3.3578
Grp 3	181	4.1796	2.4220	.1800	3.8243	To	4.5348
Grp 4	82	4.5610	2.1450	.2369	4.0897	To	5.0323
Grp 5	40	4.6625	2.3490	.3714	3.9113	To	5.4137
Grp 6	37	5.2297	2.3291	.3829	4.4532	To	6.0063
Total	500	3.8920	2.6327	.1177	3.6607	To	4.1233
Fixed Effects Model			2.5040	.1120	3.6720	To	4.1120
Random Effects Model				.4492	2.7374	To	5.0466

Random Effects Model - Estimate of Between Component Variance   0.8491

Group	Minimum	Maximum
Grp 1	-4.0000	8.5000
Grp 2	-5.0000	8.5000
Grp 3	-4.0000	9.0000
Grp 4	-.5000	9.0000
Grp 5	-1.0000	8.0000
Grp 6	-1.5000	9.0000
Total	-5.0000	9.0000

Levene Test for Homogeneity of Variances

Statistic	df1	df2	2-tail Sig.
1.3897	5	494	.227

PLOT

Example 1: An Overlay Plot

Overlay plots are useful when several variables represent the same type of measurement or when the same variable is measured at different times. This example overlays two time series: marriage and divorce rates from 1900–1981. The data are drawn from the 1983 *Information Please Almanac*. Rates are specified for five-year periods for 1900–1940 and annually after 1943. The variables are

- *MARRATE*—Marriage rate per 1,000 population, excluding armed forces overseas.
- *DIVRATE*—Divorce rate (including annulments) per 1,000 population. (The rates for 1941-1946 include armed forces overseas.)

The data are in a file named *APLOT1.DAT*. The SPSS/PC+ commands are:

```
DATA LIST FILE='APLOT1.DAT'
 / YEAR 1-4 MARRATE 6-9 (1) DIVRATE 11-13 (1).
PLOT SYMBOLS='MD'
 /VSIZE=30 /HSIZE=70
 /FORMAT=OVERLAY
 /TITLE 'MARRIAGE AND DIVORCE RATES  1900-1981'
 /VERTICAL='RATES PER 1000 POPULATION'
 /HORIZONTAL='YEAR' REFERENCE (1918,1945) MIN (1900) MAX (1983)
 /PLOT=MARRATE DIVRATE WITH YEAR.
```

- DATA LIST defines the variables to be used in the overlay plot.
- The SYMBOLS subcommand specifies the symbol *M* for the plot of marriage rate with year and *D* for the plot of divorce rate by year.
- The VSIZE and HSIZE subcommands on PLOT specify a plot frame size of 30 lines high and 70 columns wide.
- The FORMAT subcommand requests an overlay plot of the variables specified on the PLOT subcommand.
- The VERTICAL subcommand supplies a label for the vertical axis.
- The HORIZONTAL subcommand supplies a label for the horizontal axis. The REFERENCE keyword requests reference lines to be drawn at the dates on which World War I and World War II ended. The MIN and MAX keywords specify the horizontal scale. SPSS/PC+ automatically divides the scale into equal-width intervals.
- The PLOT subcommand requests two bivariate plots: marriage rate by year and divorce rate by year.

The output is shown in Figure 23. The exact appearance of the output depends on the characters available on your printer.

Figure 23   Overlay plot

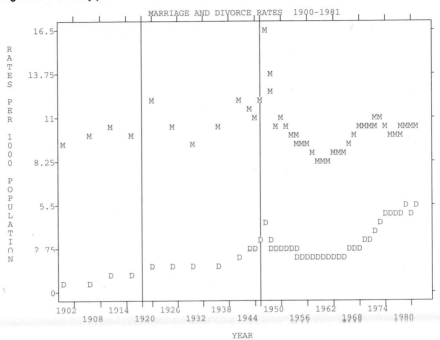

Example 2: A Regression Plot

Regression plots display a set of basic regression statistics below your plot and mark the regression-line intercepts on each axis. The statistics include the correlation coefficient, slope and intercept values, standard errors, and significance level.

This example examines the relationship of beginning salary to current salary as a first step in an analysis of salary differences between race and sex groups. The data are drawn from bank employees hired between 1969 and 1971. The variables are:

- *SALBEG*—annual starting salary of bank employees.
- *SALNOW*—current annual salary.

The data are in a file named A*PLOT2.DAT*. The SPSS/PC+ commands are:

```
DATA LIST FILE='APLOT2.DAT'
 /SALNOW 1-5 SALBEG 6-10.
PLOT   HSIZE=40/ VSIZE=40
 /CUTPOINT=EVERY (4)
 /SYMBOLS='+X*'
 /TITLE='SALARY REGRESSION'
 /VERTICAL='CURRENT ANNUAL SALARY'
 /HORIZONTAL= 'ANNUAL STARTING SALARY'MIN(0) MAX(32000)
 /FORMAT=REGRESSION
 /PLOT=SALNOW WITH SALBEG.
```

- DATA LIST defines the variables to be used in the regression plot.
- The VSIZE and HSIZE subcommands on PLOT specify a plot frame size of 40 lines high and 40 columns wide.
- The CUTPOINT subcommand requests that each successive symbol represent accumulated frequency intervals of 4. The SYMBOLS subcommand specifies the actual symbols. Thus, the symbol + represents positions with 4 or fewer cases; *X* represents positions with 5 to 8 cases; and * represents positions with 9 or more cases.
- The TITLE subcommand supplies a plot title.The title contains fewer than 35 characters because of the HSIZE specification.
- The VERTICAL subcommand supplies a label for the vertical axis. The HORIZONTAL subcommand supplies a label for the horizontal axis and adjusts the scale by specifying the minimum and maximum values.
- The FORMAT subcommand requests a regression plot and regression statistics. The regression intercepts for the regression of *SALNOW* on *SALBEG* are marked by the letter *R*.
- The PLOT subcommand specifies the variables to be plotted.

The output is shown in Figure 24. The exact appearance of the output depends on the characters available on your printer.

Figure 24 Regression plot

Frequencies and symbols used (not applicable for control or overlay plots)

```
 4 - +
 8 - X
12 - *
```

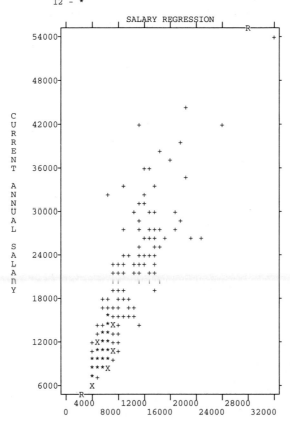

474 cases plotted. Regression statistics of SALNOW on SALBEG:
Correlation .88012 R Squared .77461 S.E. of Est 3246.14226 Sig. .0000
Intercept(S.E.) 771.28230(355.47195) Slope(S.E.) 1.90945(.04741)

REGRESSION

The example attempts to predict the average aggregate personal savings rate of a country as a function of the age distribution of the population, the average level of real per capita disposable income, and the average percentage growth rate of real per capita disposable income. The data are 50 cases taken from an example in Belsley, Kuh, and Welsch (1980). The variables are:

- *COUNTRY*—the country.
- *SAVINGS*—the average aggregate personal savings rate in the country over the period 1960–1970.
- *POP15*—the average percentage of the population under 15 years of age over the period 1960–1970.
- *POP75*—the average percentage of the population over 75 years of age over the period 1960–1970.
- *INCOME*—the average level of real per capita disposable income in the country over the period 1960–1970, measured in United States dollars.
- *GROWTH*—the average percentage growth rate of *INCOME* over the period 1960–1970.

The data are in a file named *AREG.DAT*. The SPSS/PC+ commands are:

```
DATA LIST FILE='AREG.DAT'
   /COUNTRY 1-8(A) SAVINGS POP15 POP75
   INCOME GROWTH 11-60.
VAR LABELS     SAVINGS 'Avg Agg Personal Savings Rate'
               POP15 'Avg % Pop Under 15 Years Old'
               POP75 'Avg % Pop Over 75 Years Old'
               INCOME 'Avg Level Real Per-Cap Disposable Inc'
               GROWTH 'Avg % Growth Rate of DPI'.
REGRESSION   VARIABLES=SAVINGS TO GROWTH
   /DEP=SAVINGS
   /ENTER
   /RESID=DEFAULT SIZE(SMALL) ID(COUNTRY)
   /SCATTERPLOT (*RES,*PRE).
```

- DATA LIST specifies the file that contains the data and gives variable names and column locations for the variables.
- VAR LABELS assigns labels to the variables.
- REGRESSION requests a direct-entry regression analysis with variable *SAVINGS* as the dependent variable.
- The RESIDUALS subcommand requests the default residuals output. The SIZE(SMALL) keyword overrides the default plot sizes so that small plots are displayed. ID(COUNTRY) specifies that the values for variable *COUNTRY* are to be used to label outlier plots. Figure 25 shows the residuals statistics and outliers. Figure 26 displays the histogram of the standardized residual and the normal probability plot.
- The SCATTERPLOT subcommand requests a plot of residuals against predicted values. Since *RES* is specified first, it is plotted along the vertical axis (see Figure 27).

The output is shown in Figure 25 through Figure 27. The exact appearance of the output depends on your printer used and the LENGTH and WIDTH specifications on SET. This example uses the default settings.

Figure 25   REGRESSION residual statistics and outliers

```
Residuals Statistics:

                    MIN         MAX     MEAN  STD DEV    N

*PRED            5.5874     15.8185   9.6710   2.6066   50
*RESID          -8.2422      9.7509    .0000   3.6441   50
*ZPRED          -1.5666      2.3584   -.0000   1.0000   50
*ZRESID         -2.1675      2.5642    .0000    .9583   50

Total Cases =       50


Durbin-Watson Test =    1.68579


Outliers - Standardized Residual

    Case #   COUNTRY        *ZRESID

        50   Zambia         2.56423
         7   Chile         -2.16749
        36   Philippi       1.75534
        35   Peru           1.71969
        18   Iceland       -1.63321
        34   Paraguay      -1.61093
        24   Korea         -1.60598
        10   Denmark        1.42014
        23   Tๅๅ๓๓         1.38890
         9   Costa Ri       1.34776
```

Figure 26   REGRESSION histogram and normal probability plot

```
Histogram - Standardized Residual

NExp N        (* = 1 Cases,     . : = Normal Curve)
0  .04   Out
0  .08  3.00
1  .20  2.67 *
0  .45  2.33
0  .91  2.00 .
2 1.67  1.67 *:
3 2.74  1.33 **:
3 4.03  1.00 ***.
7 5.31   .67 ****:**
4 6.26   .33 **** .
6 6.62  0.0  ******.
8 6.26  -.33 *****:**
9 5.31  -.67 ****:****
3 4.03 -1.00 ***.
0 2.74 -1.33    .
3 1.67 -1.67 *:*
0  .91 -2.00 .
1  .45 -2.33 *
0  .20 -2.67
0  .08 -3.00
0  .04   Out
```

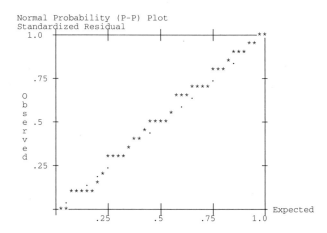

Figure 27   Residuals against predicted values

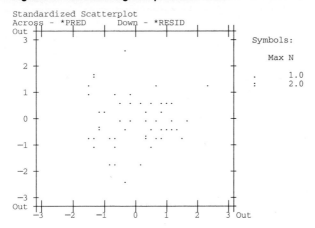

REPORT

Example 1: A Report with Summaries

This example produces a report that summarizes information from a retail company's personnel file. It reports summary statistics for employees in each division of the company within each store. The variables are:

- *AGE*—age of employee in years.
- *TENURE*—length of employment at the company in months.
- *JTENURE*—length of employment in job grade in months.
- *SALARY*—annual salary in dollars.

The data are in a file named *AREPORT.DAT*. The SPSS/PC+ commands are:

```
DATA LIST FILE='AREPORT.DAT'
 /AGE 4-8 TENURE 13-16 JTENURE 21-24 SALARY 25-29
   STORE 30 DIVISION 31.
VARIABLE LABELS TENURE 'Tenure in Company'
 JTENURE 'Tenure in Grade'
 DIVISION 'Product Division'
 SALARY 'Annual Salary'
 STORE 'BRANCH STORE' age 'Age'.
VALUE LABELS DIVISION  1  'CARPETING'  2  'APPLIANCES'
 3  'FURNITURE' 4  'HARDWARE'
 /STORE 1 'SUBURBAN' 2 'DOWNTOWN'.
FORMATS AGE (F2.0) TENURE JTENURE (F3.1).
SORT CASES  BY STORE DIVISION.
REPORT FORMAT=AUTOMATIC  MARGINS(1,72) LENGTH(1,24) BRKSPACE(-1)
 /VARIABLES=AGE TENURE JTENURE SPACE(DUMMY)' '(4) SALARY
 /TITLE='Chicago Home Furnishing'
 /FOOTNOTE=LEFT 'Tenure measured in months'
 /BREAK=STORE
 /SUMMARY=MEAN 'AVERAGE:' (2)
 /SUMMARY=VALIDN (AGE) '  Count:' (2)
 /BREAK=DIVISION (SKIP(0))
 /SUMMARY=MEAN.
```

- **DATA LIST** assigns variable names and gives column locations for the variables, which are in the file *AREPORT.DAT*.
- **VARIABLE LABELS** defines labels for the variables. These labels appear as column headings in the report if headings are not specified.
- **VALUE LABELS** defines labels for the values of the break variables. These labels will be displayed in upper case, since they are specified in upper case.
- **FORMATS** overrides the default print formats.
- **SORT CASES** sorts the file into the breaks required for REPORT.
- The **FORMAT** subcommand on REPORT implements the automatic settings, sets the left margin at column 1 and the right margin at column 72, sets the top of the report page on the first line and the last line of the page as line 24, and places the label for the break group on the first line of summary statistics.

- The VARIABLES subcommand defines five columns in the body of the report. *AGE*, *TEN-URE*, *JTENURE*, and *SALARY* are SPSS/PC+ variables. *SPACE* is a four-column dummy variable with a blank column heading for spacing purposes.
- The TITLE subcommand defines a one-line centered title.
- The FOOTNOTE subcommand defines a left-justified one-line footnote.
- The first BREAK subcommand defines the major break in this two-break report. Variable *STORE* breaks the file into two categories: the downtown store and the suburban store.
- The first two SUMMARY subcommands display two lines of summary statistics for each store. The first SUMMARY subcommand computes means for *AGE*, *TENURE*, *JTENURE*, and *SALARY*. The second SUMMARY subcommand computes the number of employees in each store. Titles are specified for each summary line.
- The second BREAK subcommand breaks the file into divisions within each store. The SKIP specification suppresses blank lines between the summary for each division.
- The last SUMMARY subcommand computes means for the report variables for each division.

The output is shown in Figure 28.

Figure 28   Summary report

```
                        Chicago Home Furnishing

                                   Tenure    Tenure
                                     in        in
BRANCH      Product                Company    Grade       Annual
STORE       Division      Age                             Salary
--------    ----------    -----    -------    ------      ------

SUBURBAN    CARPETING      40        2.4        2.4        20869
            APPLIANCES     35        2.3        2.3        16105
            FURNITURE      38        2.4        2.4        18821
            HARDWARE       35        2.3        2.4        15234

            AVERAGE:       36        2.3        2.4        17011
            Count:         97

DOWNTOWN    CARPETING      37        2.3        2.4        14207
            APPLIANCES     37        2.3        2.4        14130
            FURNITURE      38        2.3        2.4        14403
            HARDWARE       37        2.3        2.4        14469

            AVERAGE:       37        2.3        2.4        14307
            Count:        153

Tenure measured in months
```

Example 2: A Report Using LIST

This example produces a report using data from the October 1980 issue of *Runner's World* magazine. It lists the top-rated shoes in the survey, organized by manufacturer, and reports the measures used by raters to determine an overall evaluation. The data are in a file named *AREPT.DAT*. The SPSS/PC+ commands are:

```
SET WIDTH=110 /LENGTH=45.
DATA LIST FILE='AREPT.DAT' FIXED
 /TYPE 1 MAKER 2-3 QUALITY 5-9
  REARIMP FOREIMP FLEX SOLEWEAR 10-29
  REARCONT SOLETRAC 31-40 WEIGHT 42-46 LASTYEAR 48
  PREFER 50-53 STARS 55 NAME 57-72 (A).
VARIABLE LABELS NAME 'SHOE' STARS 'RATING'
  REARIMP 'REARFOOT IMPACT'
  FOREIMP 'FOREFOOT IMPACT'
  SOLEWEAR 'SOLE WEAR' REARCONT 'REARFOOT CONTROL'
  SOLETRAC 'SOLE TRACTION' LASTYEAR '1979 STARS'
  PREFER 'READER PREFERENCE'.
VALUE LABELS MAKER 1 'ADIDAS' 2 'AUTRY' 3 'BROOKFIELD'
  4 'BROOKS' 5 'CONVERSE'  6 'REEBOK'  7 'NEW BALANCE'  8 'PUMA'
  9 'OSAG' 10 'PONY'  11 'ETONIC'  12 'NIKE'  13 'SAUCONY'
  14 'WILSON-BATA'  15 'VOL SHOE CORP'
  16 'SPECS INTERNATIONAL'  17 'POWER SPORT'
  18 'THOM MCAN JOX'  19 'REGAL SHOES'  20 'SHOE CORP'
  21 'ASICS'  22 'INTL FOOTWEAR'  23 'EB SPORT INTL'
  24 'VAN DOREN'
  /TYPE 1 'MALE'  2 'FEMALE'
  /STARS 6 '******'  5 '*****'.
FORMATS  QUALITY (F5.3)/REARIMP FOREIMP SOLEWEAR (F4.1)
  /FLEX SOLETRAC (F4.2)/REARCONT WEIGHT (F5.1)
  /PREFER (F4.3).
SELECT IF (STARS GE 5).
SORT CASES MAKER STARS(D).
REPORT  FORMAT=AUTOMATIC LIST MISSING ' '
 /VARIABLES=TYPE(LABEL)(6) 'TYPE'
  NAME (16)' ' 'SHOE'  STARS(LABEL) (6)' ' 'RATING'
  SEP1(DUMMY)(1)' '
  REARIMP(6)'REAR' 'FOOT' 'IMPACT'
  FOREIMP(6)'FORE' 'FOOT' 'IMPACT'
  FLEX(6)' ' 'FLEXI-' 'BILITY'
  SOLEWEAR(4)' ' 'SOLE' 'WEAR'
  REARCONT(7)'REAR' 'FOOT' 'CONTROL'
  SOLETRAC(5)'SOLE ' 'TRAC-' 'TION'
  WEIGHT(6)' ' ' ' 'WEIGHT'
  LASTYEAR(5)' ' '1979' 'STARS'
  PREFER(6)'READER' 'PREFE-' 'RENCE'
 /TITLE='RATINGS OF TRAINING SHOES'
  "RUNNER'S WORLD MAGAZINE - OCTOBER, 1980"
 /FOOTNOTE=LEFT '****** HIGHLY RECOMMENDED'
  '***** RECOMMENDED'
 /RIGHT ' ' 'PAGE )PAGE'
 /BREAK=MAKER(LABEL)'MANUFACTURER'(12).
```

- Because there are many variables, the SET command sets the width to 110 characters and the length to 45 lines. The maximum width is 132 characters. The width can be specified to accommodate your page and font sizes.

- DATA LIST assigns variable names and gives column locations for the variables in the analysis.

- VARIABLE LABELS defines labels for the variables. These labels appear as column headings in the report if headings are not specified.

- VALUE LABELS supplies value labels for the manufacturer, type of shoe, and rating. These labels are used in the report.
- FORMATS overrides the default print formats.
- SELECT IF selects shoes with the top two ratings.
- SORT CASES sorts cases in descending order of ranking for each manufacturer. They are sorted by manufacturer so that the report can group them by manufacturer.
- The FORMAT subcommand on REPORT implements the automatic settings and specifies a case listing. In a listing report, AUTOMATIC places the first case for each break on the same line as the break value, so BRKSPACE(-1) is not needed. The MISSING keyword displays a blank in place of a period for variables with missing values.
- The VARIABLES subcommand names all the variables to be listed as well as a dummy column (variable *SEP1*) to separate the measurements from the rating. Value labels are displayed in place of values for variables *TYPE* and *STAR*. The number of columns for each variable is specified in parentheses after the variable name. The column headings for *FLEXIBILITY*, *SOLETRAK*, and *PREFER* are hyphenated so that the name fits into the size of the column.
- The TITLE subcommand displays a two-line centered title.
- The FOOTNOTE subcommand displays a two-line left-justified footnote and a two-line right-justified footnote in which the first line is blank and the second line uses keyword)PAGE to display page numbers.
- The BREAK subcommand groups the shoes by manufacturer.

The report produced by these commands is shown in Figure 29 and Figure 30.

Figure 29 Report on running shoe data, page 1

```
                          RATINGS OF TRAINING SHOES
                  RUNNER'S WORLD MAGAZINE - OCTOBER, 1980
```

MANUFACTURER	TYPE	SHOE	RATING	REAR FOOT IMPACT	FORE FOOT IMPACT	FLEXI-BILITY	SOLE WEAR	REAR FOOT CONTROL	SOLE TRAC-TION	WEIGHT	1979 STARS	READER PREFE-RENCE
SAUCONY	MALE	TC84	******	9.3	15.1	1.56	6.5	5.2	.85	278.0	0	.02₹
	MALE	HORNET 84	******	9.9	13.1	2.65	7.6	3.0	.68	265.0	4	.09₹
	FEMALE	MS TRAINER	******	10.2	13.3	1.58	6.4	22.4	.86	237.7	5	.05₹
	MALE	JAZZ	*****	8.9	12.7	2.04	7.6	-7.0	.64	270.8	0	
	MALE	TRAINER 80	*****	10.5	14.5	2.18	4.1	11.5	.82	307.6	5	.23₹
	FEMALE	JAZZ	*****	9.0	12.2	1.86	6.1	-7.5	.63	223.0	0	.01₹
	FEMALE	TC 84	*****	9.3	14.6	1.46	7.5	1.3	.77	231.1	0	
	FEMALE	MS HORNET	*****	9.8	13.2	2.59	6.4	6.5	.67	224.0	4	.04₹
NIKE	MALE	DAYBREAK	******	10.8	15.4	2.17	3.7	7.8	.54	304.2	5	.60₹
	MALE	YANKEE	*****	10.9	13.7	1.93	2.0	9.8	.66	276.6	0	
	FEMALE	LIBERATOR	*****	10.6	14.7	2.20	5.8	6.5	.52	254.2	5	.50₹
ETONIC	MALE	ECLIPSE TRAINER	******	10.0	12.9	1.65	10.0	-2.6	.51	237.4	0	
	FEMALE	ECLIPSE TRAINER	******	9.6	12.8	1.78	10.0	1.4	.57	204.1	0	
	MALE	STABILIZER	*****	10.3	15.5	2.25	1.2	-.6	.53	283.1	4	.23₹
	MALE	STREETFIGHTER	*****	10.8	15.5	2.28	1.4	-.4	.61	266.1	4	.22₹
	FEMALE	STREETFIGHTER	*****	10.7	15.5	1.66	.7	-7.7	.70	214.1	4	.34₹
	FEMALE	STABILIZER	*****	10.8	14.4	2.09	2.6	-6.9	.67	235.3	4	.29₹
PONY	MALE	TARGA FLEX	******	9.6	14.3	1.32	2.5	-22.7	.86	253.0	3	
	MALE	SHADOW	*****	9.9	13.8	1.53	2.5	-17.9	.77	270.2	0	
	FEMALE	LADY SHADOW	*****	10.6	17.4	.91	3.0	-7.1	.90	211.8	0	
OSAG	MALE	FAST RIDER	*****	10.5	14.0	2.48	4.9	1.9	.66	296.7	5	.02₹
	FEMALE	KT-26	*****	10.7	17.3	1.66	5.5	8.1	.60	223.1	2	
NEW BALANCE	MALE	420	*****	9.8	14.8	2.09	1.8	-17.7	.46	267.9	0	.51₹
	MALE	620	*****	12.0	14.6	2.73	1.1	-3.5	.41	242.0	5	.47₹
	FEMALE	420	*****	9.9	13.9	1.94	1.6	-.7	.46	219.3	0	.41₹
REEBOK	MALE	AZTEC	******	10.9	12.6	2.07	2.5	3.7	.65	260.8	5	.06₹
	MALE	SHADOW I	*****	10.7	13.1	1.79	1.9	-8.7	.63	253.0	0	
	FEMALE	SHADOW III	*****	10.2	12.9	1.63	2.4	-24.6	.66	212.8	0	
	FEMALE	AZTEC PRINCESS	*****	10.2	12.8	2.18	5.9	-20.3	.70	221.3	5	.03₹

```
****** HIGHLY RECOMMENDED
***** RECOMMENDED
```

Figure 30 Report on running shoe data, page 2

RATINGS OF TRAINING SHOES
RUNNER'S WORLD MAGAZINE - OCTOBER, 1980

MANUFACTURER	TYPE	SHOE	RATING	REAR FOOT IMPACT	FORE FOOT IMPACT	FLEXI- BILITY	SOLE WEAR	REAR FOOT CONTROL	SOLE TRAC- TION	WEIGHT	1979 STARS	READER PREFE- RENCE
CONVERSE	MALE	ARIZONA 84	*****	10.1	13.6	1.90	6.6	-5.1	.55	302.9	4	.006
	FEMALE	WORLD CLASS 84	*****	9.4	14.0	2.19	4.3	-.3	.65	234.7	3	.020
BROOKS	MALE	VANTAGE	******	8.3	11.0	1.33	10.0	-13.6	.55	232.4	5	.531
	MALE	VANTAGE SUPREME	******	8.5	10.9	1.31	10.0	-16.5	.58	239.1	5	
	MALE	HUGGER GT	******	8.5	11.2	1.32	9.4	-11.7	.60	234.5	5	.488
	MALE	NIGHTHAWK	******	8.7	13.5	1.57	3.1	-8.6	.45	216.7	0	
	MALE	SUPER VILLANOVA	******	10.0	14.1	1.07	10.0	14.4	.61	238.7	5	.155
	FEMALE	VANTAGE	******	8.1	11.0	1.27	10.0	-13.1	.58	199.9	5	.563
	FEMALE	HUGGER GT	******	8.2	11.1	1.28	10.0	-12.7	.60	203.8	0	.126
	FEMALE	VANTAGE SUPREME	******	8.2	11.1	1.34	10.0	.6	.62	201.4	3	.205
	FEMALE	SUPER VILLANOVA	******	9.0	13.4	1.01	10.0	11.9	.62	195.1	5	.298
	FEMALE	NIGHTHAWK	*****	8.6	13.1	1.54	2.4	-9.3	.45	189.0	0	
BROOKFIELD	MALE	COLT	*****	12.4	17.4	2.31	3.5	21.5	1.13	289.3	4	
AUTRY	MALE	MACH III	*****	8.7	13.0	2.13	3.0	-37.6	.66	250.2	4	
	MALE	NEW JET	*****	9.1	14.5	1.88	4.0	-37.9	.69	242.4	4	
	MALE	CONCORDE	*****	9.2	13.2	2.41	2.0	-33.9	.61	261.7	5	.023
	FEMALE	CLOUD 9	*****	9.4	17.6	1.79	2.3	-27.3	.63	198.6	3	
ADIDAS	MALE	TRX TRAINER	*****	10.5	16.8	2.07	2.1	-.6	.72	309.0	5	.143
	MALE	MARATHON TRAINER	*****	13.0	17.2	2.75	10.0	14.5	.63	302.3	5	.315
	FEMALE	MARATHON TRAINER	*****	11.7	16.5	2.14	10.0	17.5	.58	243.6	5	.298

****** HIGHLY RECOMMENDED
***** RECOMMENDED

T-TEST

This example analyzes 1979 prices and earnings in 45 cities around the world, compiled by the Union Bank of Switzerland. The variables are:

- *WORLD*—the economic class of the country in which the city is located. The 45 cities are divided into three groups: cities in economically developed nations such as the United States and most European nations; cities in nations that are members of OPEC; and cities in underdeveloped countries. These groups are coded from 1 to 3 and are labeled *1st World*, *Petro World*, and *3rd World*, respectively.

- *NTCPRI*—the city's net price level, based on more than 100 goods and services weighted by consumer habits. *NTCPRI* is expressed as the percentage above or below that of Zurich, where Zurich equals 100%.

- *NTCSAL*—the city's net salary level, calculated from average net hourly earnings in 12 occupations. *NTCSAL* is expressed as a percentage above or below that of Zurich, where Zurich equals 100%.

- *NTCPUR*—the city's net purchasing power, calculated as the ratio of labor expended (measured in number of working hours) to the cost of more than 100 goods and services, weighted by consumer habits. *NTCPUR* is expressed as a percentage above or below that of Zurich, where Zurich equals 100%.

- *WCLOTHES*—the cost of medium-priced women's clothes, expressed as the percentage above or below that of Zurich, where Zurich equals 100%.

- *MCLOTHES*—the cost of medium-priced men's clothes, expressed as the percentage above or below that of Zurich, where Zurich equals 100%.

This example compares mean price, salary and purchasing power for cities grouped by economic class. It also compares the mean costs of women's and men's clothes. The data are in a file named *ATTEST.DAT*. The SPSS/PC+ commands are:

```
DATA LIST FILE='ATTEST.DAT'
   /NTCPRI 9-11 NTCSAL 20-22 NTCPUR 31-33 WCLOTHES 42-44
    MCLOTHES 53-55 WORLD 66.
VARIABLE LABELS NTCPRI 'Net Price Level'/
                NTCSAL 'Net Salary Level'/
                NTCPUR 'Net Purchasing Level'/
                WCLOTHES "Medium-Priced Women's Clothes"/
                MCLOTHES "Medium-Priced Men's Clothes"/.
VALUE LABELS WORLD 1 '1st World' 2 'Petro World' 3 '3rd World'.
T-TEST GROUPS=WORLD(1,3)
   /VARIABLES=NTCPRI NTCSAL NTCPUR
   /PAIRS=WCLOTHES MCLOTHES/
    NTCPRI WITH NTCPUR NTCSAL.
FINISH.
```

- DATA LIST command assigns variable names and gives the column locations of the variables to be analyzed.

- VARIABLE LABELS provides variable labels. VALUE LABELS assigns labels to the values of *WORLD*.

- The T-TEST command requests an independent-samples and a paired-samples test. For the independent-samples test, the variable *WORLD* specifies a grouping criterion that compares cities in *1st World* countries to cities in *3rd World* countries. Cities in *Petro World* countries are not included.

- By default, the output is formatted within 79 columns.

The output is shown in Figure 31 through Figure 34. The exact appearance of the output depends on the characters available on your printer.

Figure 31   T-TEST output for NTCPRI

```
t-tests for independent samples of  WORLD

                                  Number
               Variable          of Cases    Mean        SD      SE of Mean

               NTCPRI  Net Price Level

               1st World             25      83.8400    13.309      2.662
               3rd World             13      67.3077    14.773      4.097


               Mean Difference = 16.5323

               Levene's Test for Equality of Variances: F= .066   P= .799


             t-test for Equality of Means                            95%
   Variances  t-value    df     2-Tail Sig    SE of Diff      CI for Diff

   Equal       3.50      36        .001         4.724       (6.950, 26.115)
   Unequal     3.38      22.28      .003         4.886       (6.397, 26.668)
```

Figure 32   T-TEST output for NTCSAL

t-tests for independent samples of   WORLD

Variable	Number of Cases	Mean	SD	SE of Mean
NTCSAL Net Salary Level				
1st World	25	64.4000	19.026	3.805
3rd World	12	25.6667	13.241	3.822

Mean Difference = 38.7333

Levene's Test for Equality of Variances: F= .595   P= .446

Variances	t-test for Equality of Means t-value	df	2-Tail Sig	SE of Diff	95% CI for Diff
Equal	6.33	35	.000	6.116	(26.313, 51.153)
Unequal	7.18	30.07	.000	5.394	(27.716, 49.751)

Figure 33   T-TEST output for NTCPUR

t-tests for independent samples of   WORLD

Variable	Number of Cases	Mean	SD	SE of Mean
NTCPUR Net Purchasing Level				
1st World	25	76.7600	21.491	4.298
3rd World	12	31.9167	17.573	5.073

Mean Difference = 44.8433

Levene's Test for Equality of Variances: F= .888   P= .352

Variances	t-test for Equality of Means t-value	df	2-Tail Sig	SE of Diff	95% CI for Diff
Equal	6.28	35	.000	7.144	(30.338, 59.349)
Unequal	6.74	26.26	.000	6.649	(31.173, 58.514)

Figure 34   T-TEST output for paired samples

```
               - - - t-tests for paired samples - - -

                    Number of          2-tail
Variable              pairs    Corr    Sig       Mean      SD     SE of Mean

WCLOTHES  Medium-Priced Woman's Clothe          80.7111   30.195    4.501
                         45      .807    .000
MCLOTHES  Medium-Priced Men's Clothes           87.0444   26.192    3.905
```

```
          Paired Differences               |
Mean         SD       SE of Mean           |   t-value    df   2-tail Sig

-6.3333    17.916       2.671               |    -2.37     44      .022
95% CI (-11.717, -.949)                     |
```

```
               - - - t-tests for paired samples - - -

                    Number of          2-tail
Variable              pairs    Corr    Sig       Mean      SD     SE of Mean

NTCPRI    Net Price Level                       82.1591   19.773    2.981
                         44      .098    .528
NTCPUR    Net Purchasing Level                  58.7045   28.806    4.343
```

```
          Paired Differences               |
Mean         SD       SE of Mean           |   t-value    df   2-tail Sig

23.4545    33.310       5.022               |    4.67      43      .000
95% CI (13.325, 33.584)                     |
```

```
               - - - t-tests for paired samples - - -

                    Number of          2-tail
Variable              pairs    Corr    Sig       Mean      SD     SE of Mean

NTCPRI    Net Price Level                       82.1591   19.773    2.981
                         44      .482    .001
NTCSAL    Net Salary Level                      50.3409   24.295    3.663
```

```
          Paired Differences               |
Mean         SD       SE of Mean           |   t-value    df   2-tail Sig

31.8182    22.753       3.430               |    9.28      43      .000
95% CI (24.899, 38.737)                     |
```

Appendix A
Using SPSS/PC+ with RAM Disks

If your PC has an extended or expanded memory board and RAM-disk software—that is, software that makes some of your memory (RAM) appear to be an extremely fast disk drive—you can put the RAM disk to good use in SPSS/PC+.

- You should not use a RAM disk in regular DOS memory (below 640K). Such memory is best used directly by SPSS/PC+.

- The following examples assume that the RAM disk is drive D and that SPSS/PC+ is installed into its default location (the *SPSS* directory) on your default drive.

If you have expanded memory, you can use the RAM disk for your active file, for Review, or for both.

The Active File

Whenever you read a raw data file or transform your active file, SPSS/PC+ writes the data in binary format to a scratch file, called the **active file**. You can control the location of these scratch files with the SPSS/PC+ command SET WORKDEV. When you are going to be processing a file large enough so that reading the data occupies substantial time, begin your session with the SPSS/PC+ command:

```
SET WORKDEV=D:.
```

SPSS/PC+ will write one and perhaps two copies of the active file to the RAM disk. Be certain that they will fit before giving this command. You cannot set the work device after the active file has been created in a session.

You may want to put the SET WORKDEV command in your automatic SPSS/PC+ profile, *SPSSPROF.INI*.

Review

This section applies only to SPSS/PC+ (640K version). It does *not* apply to SPSS/PC+ using the DOS extender.

You can also put Review onto a RAM disk. If you go in and out of Review frequently (for example, using the default RUNREVIEW AUTO setting), you can speed up the automatic return to Review considerably. Use the DOS command SET SPSSR=path and place Review on a RAM disk. Here is a sample batch file to place Review on drive D:

```
ECHO OFF
IF EXIST D:SPSREV.EXE GOTO RUN
COPY C:\SPSS\SPSREV.EXE D:
:RUN
SET SPSSR=D:\
SPSSPC %1 %2 %3 %4 %5
SET SPSSR=
```

- The IF command checks whether Review has already been copied to the RAM disk. (If you had executed this batch file earlier in the same session, it would already be there.)

- The COPY command places Review on the RAM disk, if it is not already there. Review occupies approximately 180,000 bytes of space on the RAM disk. *Do not* invoke Review by the name of this *.EXE* file. To invoke Review from DOS, use the command:

```
SPSSPC/RE file1 [file2]
```

- The SET SPSSR command sets a DOS environment variable so that SPSS/PC+ will know that Review is in drive D.

- The SPSSPC command invokes SPSS/PC+, passing any parameters that you may have used when calling the batch file (such as the name of a command file).

- The second SET SPSSR command deletes the string SPSSR from the DOS environment area. There should be nothing—not even a blank space—after the equals sign.

Cautions

SPSS Inc. does not distribute or support any RAM-disk software.

Neither of the two applications suggested above places anything on the RAM disk that needs to be copied to a physical disk at the end of your session. Nevertheless, if you use a RAM disk:

- Use reliable RAM-disk software and be aware of its limitations.

- Be sure that your RAM disk has enough room for the application. If you place your active file on the RAM disk, you need enough room for two copies of the data in binary form. If you place Review on the RAM disk, you need enough room to hold the file *SPSSREV.EXE*.

Appendix B
Files Created by Other Software

SPSS/PC+ reads and writes several types of files. This section discusses the use of these files with other text editors typically used in the personal computing environment. You probably will use an editor to prepare command files and data files. The Review editor that is part of SPSS/PC+ allows you to prepare these files, but many other editors are available as well.

You may also want to analyze data stored in a database or spreadsheet program. SPSS/PC+ has the ability to translate files produced by several popular spreadsheet or database packages into its own active file format—and the ability to translate files into formats used by the same packages. SPSS/PC+ can do this with one command: TRANSLATE. See TRANSLATE in the Syntax Reference section for a description of this command and a list of the database and spreadsheet packages supported.

Editors

An editor is software used to create or modify files containing text or data. SPSS/PC+ processes command and data files created with editors.

SPSS/PC+ itself contains a text editor called Review. However, you can use another editor to create SPSS/PC+ command and data files, as long as you produce an ASCII file that conforms to the following criteria:

- Each line in the file must end with a carriage-return line-feed sequence. (This is typical of most DOS files.)

- The file must end with a Ctrl-Z for SPSS/PC+ to read the last line correctly. (This is typical of most DOS files.)

- The file must not contain special format codes or other information specific to the program from which it was created. (An example of this is the use of control characters to indicate special document formatting options, such as Ctrl-B for boldface.)

- The maximum line length for files containing SPSS/PC+ commands and inline data is 80 characters. Anything past column 80 is ignored.

- The maximum line length for data files named on the DATA LIST command is 1,024 characters.

The Review Editor

The Review editor (see Chapter 3) allows you to edit the ASCII files produced by SPSS/PC+ and to produce data and command files that can be read by SPSS/PC+. If you use Review for editing related to SPSS/PC+, you don't have to worry about problems of compatibility between SPSS/PC+ and the editor.

You can use Review as your general-purpose editor, creating and modifying text files for other applications.

Other Editors

Some editors store files in a special format that combines text with escape sequences and/or control characters. The escape sequences and control characters are usually used to perform font shifts when printing, or to format text for display. For example, the editor might add a special character to the end of every line, paragraph, and page. Editors designed for word processing are more likely to use such special formats than are editors designed for programming. If you INCLUDE a file created with an editor that inserts escape sequences, SPSS/PC+ reads the escape sequences literally and cannot interpret them. Fortunately, these types of editors usually have a special mode or translate program to produce files readable by programs such as SPSS/PC+. For example, WordStar™ has a "non-document" mode for creating files. Other word processors typically let you specify ASCII or "text" format when you save a file.

Another potential problem is the requirement for a carriage-return line-feed sequence at the end of the line. If an editor has an automatic word-wrap procedure that automatically creates a new line while you continue typing, it may not insert the end-of-line sequence required by SPSS/PC+. To obtain the carriage-return line-feed sequence required by SPSS/PC+, you may need to use the enter key after typing in each line. Some editors may not even wrap to start a new line but appear to do so because they are displaying a line longer than 80 characters in an 80-character window. In general, you should avoid using the word-wrap facilities of your editor when preparing files to read with SPSS/PC+ unless your editor explicitly documents that it inserts the carriage-return line-feed sequence. If your editor's documentation provides special instructions for preparing files for use with other applications such as language compilers, follow them.

How do you find out whether your favorite editor is going to work with SPSS/PC+? Use the DOS TYPE command to type a file created with your editor. If the file does not look the same when typed as when viewed within the editor, then it probably cannot be read correctly by SPSS/PC+. Beware of special symbols that are not directly available on the keyboard. The one exception to this rule is the use of tabs. If your editor permits tabs, and it places an ASCII 09 character into the file, SPSS/PC+ interprets it as *one* blank. Although the file does not look the same when echoed by SPSS/PC+ (since the interpretation of tabs is always context specific), it is interpreted correctly.

With the exception of forms control for listing files, ASCII files written by SPSS/PC+ do not contain special escape sequences, tabs, etc., and are generally readable and editable by most editors. The one exception is a file produced by SPSS/PC+ that does not contain a Ctrl-Z at the end because a session was not ended normally. Some editors can read such a file (although they might issue a read error warning); other editors have great difficulty. If you terminate an SPSS/PC+ session normally, you should be able to TYPE, PRINT, or otherwise display listing and log files written by SPSS/PC+. Follow your editor's discussion for editing "foreign" files.

Communications Programs

Communications programs such as CROSSTALK™ and PC-TALK III can be used to transfer ASCII files read and written by SPSS/PC+. However, they should not be used with SPSS/PC+ system files or portable system files. ASCII files containing special graphics characters used in SPSS/PC+ output cannot be transferred correctly to mainframes or to other types of personal computers.

Glossary

active default. Options that are in effect when an optional subcommand is included but is not followed by any keywords. For example, in REGRESSION, including the subcommand DESCRIPTIVES without any modifying keywords requests the active defaults MEAN, STDDEV, and CORR. See also *passive default*.

active file. The file defined in a session by a DATA LIST command or called by a GET or IMPORT command. Consists of the data and a dictionary, and it is the file that you modify using transformations and analyze using any of the procedures.

active window. In Review, the portion of the screen that accepts file modifications. Two windows of different sizes can be accessed, but only the active window can be modified.

alias. A keyword that is a synonym for another SPSS/PC+ keyword. For example, XTABS is an alias for CROSSTABS.

alphanumeric variable. A variable whose values are stored as characters and are not available for arithmetic operations. The values may contain letters or special characters as well as numbers. Also known as *string variable*. Compare *numeric variable*.

analysis list. Portion of an SPSS/PC+ command that requests an analysis (such as a correlation matrix) or a set of related analyses (such as a set of crosstabs that use the same variables).

argument. An expression (usually within parentheses) following a function or another SPSS/PC+ keyword that is the object of the operation. For arithmetic function SQRT(X), variable X is the argument. For REPORT function PCGT(150), the value 150 is the argument.

arithmetic operators. Graphic symbols used in a variable transformation to represent arithmetic functions such as addition (+), subtraction (−), multiplication (*), division (/), and exponentiation (**).

ASCII file. A data or command file containing characters conforming to the American Standard Code for Information Interchange standards. These files contain a carriage-return line-feed sequence at the end of each line and a Ctrl-Z at the end of the file. SPSS/PC+ reads and writes ASCII files.

assignment expression.   The expression following the equals sign in the COMPUTE and IF commands that assigns a value for each case to the target variable. See also *target variable*.

batch processing.   Using the INCLUDE command to process SPSS/PC+ commands stored in a file. While SPSS/PC+ is processing the commands from the file, you cannot change any of the specifications given on the commands in the file. See also *interactive operation*.

case identifier.   Unique code assigned to each case.

case, observation.   Basic unit of analysis for which measurements are taken.

categorical variable.   A variable that has a limited number of values that form categories of cases. See also *continuous variable*.

code.   A numeric or alphabetical value that represents the status of a case on a variable.

codebook.   Document that describes each variable, its name, label, values and value labels, formats, and missing values. Also known as a *coding form*.

command.   A specific instruction that controls the execution of SPSS/PC+.

command file.   A file that contains SPSS/PC+ commands and sometimes includes data. Use the INCLUDE command to process command files. See also *batch processing*.

command line.   A line of specifications for one SPSS/PC+ command. It may take more than one line to enter all of the instructions for a single command (see *continuation line*).

conditional transformation.   Changing the values of a variable contingent upon logical conditions found in the data; e.g., altering variables one way for one subset of cases and other ways for other subsets. See the IF command in the Syntax Reference section.

constant.   A value that is the same for every case. For example, in the expression $B = A + 12$, 12 is a constant. Constants can be either numeric or string values.

contingency table.   A table containing the joint frequency distribution of two or more variables. See the CROSSTABS command in the Syntax Reference section.

continuation line.   The second or any subsequent line of specifications for one SPSS/PC+ command.

continuous variable.   A variable that does not have a fixed number of values. For example, the variable *INCOME*, measured in dollars, can take on many different values.

control variable.   The variable whose values are used to separate cases into subgroups. In a crosstabulation, the variable whose values form subtables.

CPU.   The abbreviation for central processing unit. The CPU performs tasks based on instructions from SPSS/PC+ commands.

current character.   The character highlighted by the cursor.

current line. The line containing the cursor.

cursor. The highlighted symbol on the screen indicating the current location.

data. Information organized for analysis.

data line. A line of information for a single case recorded on a disk. It may take more than one line to enter all the data for a case.

default. Instruction assumed when no other specification is stated.

delimiter. A symbol or a blank used by SPSS/PC+ to detect when one specification on a command ends and another one begins (blanks between keywords, commas between arguments, slashes between subcommands, and so on).

dictionary. Descriptive information about variables in the active file. Includes variable names and labels, print formats, value labels, missing-value flags, and a positional index.

directory (DOS). The type of structure used for storing files. Your personal computer uses a tree structure of directories. The primary level is the root directory. SPSS/PC+ is loaded into the directory \SPSS. This is a subdirectory under the root. See "Using Tree-Structured Directories" in your DOS manual.

discrete variable. A variable that has a limited number of values. The values can have nominal or ordinal properties. For example, *INCOME* with values high, medium, and low is a discrete variable. Compare *continuous variable*.

disk. Oxide-coated plastic disk that stores data magnetically. See also *hard disk, diskette*.

diskette. A flexible disk (5 1/4 inches in diameter for the IBM PC) that can be removed from the drive.

drive. A device for reading data or commands from a disk or diskette. The floppy disk drive is usually called the A drive. The hard disk drive is usually called the C drive.

editor. A program that allows you to enter text or data from your keyboard into the computer, to edit text or data, and to save files on disk. A text editor named Review is integrated into the SPSS/PC+ system. Another text editor, EDLIN or EDIT, is supplied with DOS.

external file. A file residing on the hard disk that can be called in during an SPSS/PC+ session. SPSS/PC+ can read external files that contain data or commands. The term is generally not used in this manual to refer to system files or portable files.

file. A physical organization of records, usually stored on a disk. See Universals in the Syntax Reference section for files used by SPSS/PC+.

file definition. Description of file characteristics. Points SPSS/PC+ to the data file and indicates the format of the file and the number of records SPSS/PC+ should read per case from fixed-format data files. See also *variable definition*.

floppy disk.   A flexible disk.

format.   The way values of a variable are represented to the computer and the way these values are displayed. The DATA LIST and FORMATS commands assign formats that SPSS/PC+ uses to write or display values. The components of a format are the variable type (string or numeric), the variable width, and the number of decimal places.

fully qualified name.   A filename that includes the drive, directory, and name of a file.

hard disk.   Rigid, oxide-coated plastic disk that stores data magnetically. Generally holds more information than a floppy.

implied decimal places.   The number of digits that are placed to the right of a decimal point in the stored value for a value that contains no decimal places when it is read. Implied decimal places are declared on the DATA LIST command when fixed-format data are read.

include file.   A file of SPSS/PC+ commands and/or data to be processed in an SPSS/PC+ session via the INCLUDE command. See also *batch processing*.

incremental search.   Typing the initial characterr(s) of a an item on a menu in order to move the cursor to the item.

initialization.   The assignment of a value to a new variable before a data transformation assigns a computed value. New numeric variables are initialized with the system-missing value. New string variables are initialized with blanks. See the IF and COMPUTE commands in the Syntax Reference section.

inline data.   Data included as lines in a command file or entered from the terminal during a session. The BEGIN DATA command precedes the first data line and the END DATA command follows the last data line.

input.   Information entered into the computer.

input data file.   Contains data in almost any format stored on a disk. This file can be included within an SPSS/PC+ command file as inline data, or it can be a separate file defined on the DATA LIST command.

interactive operation.   Entering commands (and sometimes data) directly into SPSS/PC+, as opposed to entering a file of SPSS/PC+ commands using the INCLUDE command. See also *batch processing*.

keyword.   A word already defined by SPSS/PC+ to identify a command, subcommand, or specification. See Universals in the Syntax Reference section for rules for using keywords.

label.   A string that contains an extended description associated with a file, a variable, or a value of a variable. See also *dictionary*.

line.   A line of SPSS/PC+ command text or a line of data. See *command line, continuation line, data line* (or *record*).

listing file. A file that contains the statistical and tabular output from SPSS/PC+ procedures, diagnostic information, and messages about the session. The default listing file is *SPSS.LIS*. This default can be changed with the SET command.

listwise deletion. Cases that have missing values for any of the variables named are omitted from the analysis.

literal. The value of a string variable or a label, enclosed within apostrophes or quotation marks. See also *string*.

log file. A file that contains all commands entered and processed by SPSS/PC+. The default log file is *SPSS.LOG*. This default can be changed using the SET command.

logical expression. Expression composed of logical operators and relations comparing two or more variables, or a compound expression. Results in assignment as true or false (or missing).

logical operator. Symbol that joins two or more relations logically in a conditional transformation. The SPSS/PC+ logical operators are AND (both relations must be true) and OR (either relation can be true). The NOT logical operator reverses the outcome of the expression that immediately follows.

logical variable. A numeric variable whose values are 0 (false), 1 (true), or missing.

long string variable. A string variable that has more than 8 and up to 255 alphanumeric characters.

map. Lists variable names from the active-file dictionary, showing the result of the IMPORT or EXPORT command.

matrix materials. Summary data used as input to procedures CLUSTER, FACTOR, ONEWAY, and REGRESSION. The data can contain correlation coefficients, covariance coefficients, standard deviations, distance measures, counts, means, standard deviations, as well as other summary measures. See these commands and DATA LIST: Matrix Materials in the Syntax Reference section for more information.

memory. The internal storage area of the CPU where SPSS/PC+ operates and where calculations are performed. See also *workspace*.

missing value. A code that indicates that the true value of the variable could not be obtained, or a code that you would like to have ignored during statistical calculations. These values are defined on the MISSING VALUE command and are then flagged in the dictionary of the active file. The SPSS/PC+ statistical procedures and transformation commands recognize this flag. See also *user-missing value, system-missing value*.

module. A portion of SPSS/PC+ software. SPSS/PC+ is stored on the hard disk as a set of modules. Each module contains different parts of the whole system.

narrow format. The default width, 79 characters, of SPSS/PC+ display. Narrow format is designed to fit on your screen. Compare *wide format*.

numeric expression. An expression consisting of numeric variables, constants, and operators.

numeric function. A function that operates on a numeric expression and returns a number or system-missing value. The expression to be transformed by a function is called an *argument* and usually consists of a variable name or a list of variable names.

numeric variable. A variable whose values are numbers. Compare *string* (or *alphanumeric*) *variable*.

operating system. A collection of programs that supervise the operation of the computer and handle files and sessions. SPSS/PC+ uses MSDOS.

option numbers. Numbers used on the OPTIONS subcommand to request that options be in effect for a procedure.

output. Results produced by a computer from specific input. SPSS/PC+ produces several types of output (statistics, tables, reports, plots, data, matrices, and so forth). The output destination is controlled by the SET command.

output file. Contains data formatted to be read by a computer. Some procedures create output files containing matrix or other materials. The WRITE command produces a rectangular file to your specifications. SAVE produces a system file that can be read by SPSS/PC+. EXPORT produces a portable file that can be read by SPSS/PC+ or SPSS.

pairwise deletion. Cases that have valid values on both variables used in a calculation are included in the calculation. Other cases are deleted.

passive default. Options that are in effect when an optional subcommand is omitted. Passive defaults are indicated by two asterisks (**) in the syntax diagrams. For example, in REGRESSION, when the optional subcommand STATISTICS is omitted, the passive defaults R, COEFF, ANOVA, ZPP, and OUTS are requested. See also *active default*.

portable file. An ASCII file produced by SPSS/PC+ or SPSS EXPORT. Portable files contain data and a dictionary of labels and variable formats. See also *system file*.

print format. Format used for displaying and printing the values of a variable. Controlled by the DATA LIST and FORMATS commands. See also *dictionary*.

procedure. Any SPSS/PC+ command that reads data from the active file. Procedures cause preceding transformations to be executed. Most SPSS/PC+ procedures produce statistical results.

prompt. The string that SPSS/PC+ displays to indicate that it is ready to receive your commands. The default prompt is SPSS/PC: for the first line of a command and : for a continuation line. You can change the prompts by using the SET command.

record. Line of machine-readable information.

rectangular data file. A file in which each case contains only one value for each variable and in which each case is the same type of unit of analysis throughout the entire file. The variables are in the same order for each case.

relational operator.	Symbol that compares two values of a logical expression in a conditional transformation such as EQ (equal to), LT (less than), LE (less than or equal to), and so forth.
reserved keyword.	Keywords that cannot be used as variable names since they can appear in variable lists (e.g., TO, EQ, WITH, BY).
scientific notation.	Expression of a number as a fractional part and a power of ten. 350,000,000 can be expressed as 0.3500E9 or 3.5000E8.
scratch file.	A file used by SPSS/PC+ to hold intermediate results from transformation and procedure commands. You cannot directly access this file.
scrolling.	The phenomenon of watching your results fly by on your screen when you set the page length too long.
session.	An SPSS/PC+ session begins with the SPSSPC command given in response to the DOS prompt, and ends with the SPSS/PC+ FINISH command.
short string variable.	A string variable with a width of 8 or fewer alphanumeric characters.
specifications.	Instructions added to a command. May include subcommands, keywords, numbers, strings, arithmetic operators, variable names, special delimiters, and spacing as needed to separate these elements. Specifications begin at least one space after the command keyword and continue for as many lines as necessary.
statistic number.	A number that is included on the STATISTICS subcommand to request optional statistics from a procedure.
status area.	The area in the upper right corner of your screen that contains messages about what SPSS/PC+ is doing. The status area informs you when modules are swapped and when data are read into memory.
string.	One or more alphanumeric characters. Strings are specified in apostrophes or quotation marks in SPSS/PC+ commands. See also *alphanumeric variable, string variable, literal.*
string variable.	A variable whose values contain letters or special characters (as well as numbers). Also known as *alphanumeric variable.* Compare *numeric variable.*
subcommand.	Additional instructions that further specify SPSS/PC+ commands. A command may contain one or more subcommands, each with specifications to that subcommand. See Universals in the Syntax Reference section for more information.
syntax.	General rules for the structure of the SPSS/PC+ language.
system-missing value.	Value assigned by SPSS/PC+ when a value in your data is undefined according to the format type that you have specified, when a numeric field is blank for the default format type, or when a value resulting from a transformation command is undefined. See also *user-missing value.*

system file. A binary file specially formatted for use by SPSS/PC+, containing both data and the dictionary that is written by the SPSS/PC+ SAVE command. See also *portable file*.

system variable. Special variables assigned by SPSS/PC+ that determine the number of cases read by the system, compare the system-missing value, obtain the current date, and so forth. System variable names begin with a dollar sign. You cannot modify system variables or use them in most procedures, but you can use them in transformations.

table list. The portion of an SPSS/PC+ command that requests tables using a subset of variables.

tabulation. Counting, arranging, or listing values and cases in table format.

target variable. A variable that contains the result of a transformation. See the IF, COMPUTE, and COUNT commands in the Syntax Reference section. See also *assignment expression*.

terminator. The character used to indicate the end of an SPSS/PC+ command. The default terminator is a period.

transformation. Changing the values of a variable to correct coding errors, modify the coding scheme, create new variables, or construct an index.

truncation. The convention that allows you to enter only the first three characters of an SPSS/PC+ keyword.

unary operator. The algebraic operation of using the minus sign before a numeric variable or value to reverse the sign, or using the plus sign, which does not produce a reversal.

user-missing value. A value that indicates missing information. Defined on the MISSING VALUE command. See also *system-missing value*.

valid. Not missing (having neither the system-missing value nor a value defined as missing).

value. A numeric or alphabetical code that represents the status of a case on a variable.

variable. Observable entity that can take on more than one value or characteristic.

variable definition. The portion of the DATA LIST command that assigns a name to each variable you intend to analyze and provides information about the location and format of the variables in the data file.

variable name. A name assigned to a variable. The name can be up to 8 characters in length. It must begin with a letter (A–Z) or the character @. The remaining characters in the name can be any letter, any digit, a period (.), an underscore (_), and the symbols @, #, or $. See also *reserved keyword*.

wide format. The display is 132 columns wide. Usually for printed output. See also *narrow format*.

window.   A portion of the screen used for displaying parts of a file. Review allows access to two windows for displaying two files.

workspace.   The amount of memory available to SPSS/PC+ to perform procedures and transformations. You can change the workspace by using the SET command.

Bibliography

Anderson, R., and S. Nida. 1978. Effect of physical attractiveness on opposite and same-sex evaluations. *Journal of Personality*, 46:3, 401–413.

Andrews, F., J. Morgan, J. Sonquist, and L. Klein. 1973. *Multiple classification analysis*. 2nd ed. Ann Arbor: University of Michigan Press.

Beard, C. M., V. Fuster, and L. R. Elveback. 1982. Daily and seasonal variation in sudden cardiac death, Rochester, Minnesota, 1950–1975. *Mayo Clinic Proceedings*, 57: 704–706.

Belsley, D. A., E. Kuh, and R. E. Welsch. 1980. *Regression diagnostics: Identifying influential data and sources of collinearity*. New York: John Wiley and Sons.

Berk, K. N. 1977. Tolerance and condition in regression computation. *Journal of the American Statistical Association*, 72: 863–866.

_____. 1978. Comparing subset regression procedures. *Technometrics:* 20: 1–6.

Bishop, Y. M. M., S. E. Fienberg, and P. W. Holland. 1975. *Discrete multivariate analysis: Theory and practice*. Cambridge, Mass.: MIT Press.

Blalock, H. M. 1979. *Social statistics*. New York: McGraw-Hill.

Blom, G. 1958. *Statistical estimates and transformed beta variables*. New York: John Wiley and Sons.

Bock, R. D. 1975. *Multivariate statistical methods in behavioral research*. New York: McGraw-Hill.

Borgatta, E. F., and G. W. Bohrnstedt. 1980. Level of measurement once over again. *Sociological Methods and Research*, 9:2, 147–160.

Cedercreutz, C. 1978. Hypnotic treatment of 100 cases of migraine. In: *Hypnosis at Its Bicentennial*, F. H. Frankel and H. S. Zamansky, eds. New York: Plenum.

Chambers, J. M., W. S. Cleveland, B. Kleiner, and P. A. Tukey. 1983. *Graphical methods for data analysis*. Belmont, Calif.: Wadsworth International Group; Boston: Duxbury Press.

Churchill, G. A., Jr. 1979. *Marketing research: Methodological foundations*. Hinsdale, Ill.: Dryden Press.

Cleveland, W. S., and R. McGill. 1984. The many faces of a scatterplot. *Journal of the American Statistical Association*, 79: 807–822.

Cohen, J. 1960. A coefficient of agreement for nominal scales. *Educational and Psychological Measurement*, 20: 37–46.

Conover, W. J. 1974. Some reasons for not using the Yates continuity correction on 2×2 contingency tables. *Journal of the American Statistical Association*, 69: 374–376.

_____. 1980. *Practical nonparametric statistics*. 2nd ed. New York: John Wiley and Sons.

Cook, R. D. 1977. Detection of influential observations in linear regression. *Technometrics*, 19: 15–18.

Daniel, C., and F. Wood. 1980. *Fitting Equations to Data*. Rev. ed. New York: John Wiley and Sons.

Davis, H., and E. Ragsdale. 1983. Unpublished working paper. Chicago: University of Chicago, Graduate School of Business.

Davis, J. A., T. W. Smith. 1991. *General social surveys, 1972–1991: Cumulative codebook.* Chicago: National Opinion Research Center.

Dillon, W. R., and M. Goldstein. 1984. *Multivariate analysis: Methods and applications.* New York: John Wiley and Sons.

Dineen, L. C., and B. C. Blakesley. 1973. Algorithm AS 62: A generator for the sampling distribution of the Mann-Whitney U statistic. *Applied Statistics,* 22: 269–273.

Draper, N. R., and H. Smith. 1981. *Applied regression analysis.* New York: John Wiley and Sons.

Duncan, O. D. 1966. Path analysis: Sociological examples. *American Journal of Sociology,* 72: 1–16.

Fisher, R. A. 1973. *Statistical methods for research workers.* 14th ed. New York: Hafner Press.

Fox, J. 1984. *Linear statistical models and related methods.* New York: John Wiley and Sons.

Frane, J. W. 1976. Some simple procedures for handling missing data in multivariate analysis. *Psychometrika,* 41: 409–415.

_____. 1977. A note on checking tolerance in matrix inversion and regression. *Technometrics,* 19: 513–514.

Frigge, M., D. C. Hoaglin, and B. Iglewicz. 1987. Some implementations of the boxplot. In: *Computer Science and Statistics Proceedings of the 19th Symposium on the Interface,* R. M. Heiberger and M. Martin, eds. Alexandria, Va.: American Statistical Association.

Goodman, L. A., and W. H. Kruskal. 1954. Measures of association for cross-classification. *Journal of the American Statistical Association,* 49: 732–764.

Haberman, S. J. 1978. *Analysis of qualitative data.* Vol. 1. New York: Academic Press.

Hansson, R. O., and K. M. Slade. 1977. Altruism toward a deviant in city and small town. *Journal of Applied Social Psychology,* 7:3, 272–279.

Hoaglin, D. C., and R. E. Welsch. 1978. The hat matrix in regression and ANOVA. *American Statistician,* 32: 17–22.

Hoaglin, D. C., F. Mosteller, and J. W. Tukey. 1983. *Understanding robust and exploratory data analysis.* New York: John Wiley and Sons.

_____. 1985. *Exploring data tables, trends, and shapes.* New York: John Wiley and Sons.

Hocking, R. R. 1976. The analysis and selection of variables in linear regression. *Biometrics,* 32: 1–49.

Hogg, R. V. 1979. An introduction to robust estimation. *Robustness in Statistics,* 1–18.

Judge, G. G., W. E. Griffiths, R. C. Hill, H. Lutkepohl, and T. C. Lee. 1985. *The theory and practice of econometrics.* 2nd ed. New York: John Wiley and Sons.

Kendall, M. G., and A. Stuart. 1973. *The advanced theory of statistics.* Vol. 2. New York: Hafner Press.

King, M. M., et al. 1979. Incidence and growth of mammary tumors induced by 7,12-dimethylbenz(a) anthracene as related to the dietary content of fat and antioxident. *Journal of the National Cancer Institute,* 63:3, 657–663.

Kleinbaum, D. G., and L. L. Kupper. 1978. *Applied regression analysis and other multivariable methods.* North Scituate, Mass.: Duxbury Press.

Kleinbaum, D. G., L. L. Kupper, and H. Morgenstern. 1982. *Epidemiological research: Principles and quantitative methods.* Belmont, Calif.: Wadsworth, Inc.

Kraemer, H. C. 1982. Kappa coefficient. In: *Encyclopedia of statistical sciences*, S. Kotz and N. L. Johnson, eds. New York: John Wiley and Sons.

Lehmann, E. L. 1975. *Nonparametrics: Statistical methods based on ranks.* San Francisco: Holden-Day.

Loether, H. J., and D. G. McTavish. 1976. *Descriptive and inferential statistics: An introduction.* Boston: Allyn and Bacon.

Lord, F. M., and M. R. Novick. 1968. *Statistical theories of mental test scores.* Reading, Mass.: Addison-Wesley.

Mantel, N. 1974. Comment and a suggestion on the Yates continuity correction. *Journal of the American Statistical Association*, 69: 378–380.

Mantel, N., and W. Haenszel. 1959. Statistical aspects of the analysis of data from retrospective studies of disease. *Journal of the National Cancer Institute*, 22: 719–748.

Meyer, L. S., and M. S. Younger. 1976. Estimation of standardized coefficients. *Journal of the American Statistical Association*, 71: 154–157.

Morrison, D. F. 1967. *Multivariate statistical methods.* New York: McGraw-Hill.

Neter, J., W. Wasserman, and R. Kutner. 1985. *Applied linear statistical models.* 2nd ed. Homewood, Ill.: Richard D. Irwin, Inc.

Nunnally, J. 1978. *Psychometric theory.* 2nd ed. New York: McGraw-Hill.

Paul, O., et al. 1963. A longitudinal study of coronary heart disease. *Circulation*, 28: 20–31.

Rabkin, S. W., F. A. Mathewson, and R. B. Tate. 1980. Chronobiology of cardiac sudden death in men. *Journal of the American Medical Association*, 244:12, 1357–1358.

Roberts, H. V. 1979. *An analysis of employee compensation.* Report 7946, Center for Mathematical Studies in Business and Economics, University of Chicago, October.

———. 1980. Statistical bases in the measurement of employment discrimination. In: *Comparable worth: Issues and alternatives*, E. Robert Livernash, ed. Washington, D.C.: Equal Employment Advisory Council, 173–195.

Siegel, S. 1956. *Nonparametric statistics for the behavioral sciences.* New York: McGraw-Hill.

Sigall, H., and N. Ostrove. 1975. Beautiful but dangerous: Effects of offender attractiveness and nature of the crime on juridic judgment. *Journal of Personality and Social Psychology*, 31: 410–414.

Smirnov, N. V. 1948. Table for estimating the goodness of fit of empirical distributions. *Annals of Mathematical Statistics*, 19: 279–281.

Snedecor, G. W., and W. G. Cochran. 1967. *Statistical methods.* Ames, Iowa: Iowa State University Press.

Somers, R. H. 1962. A new symmetric measure of association for ordinal variables. *American Sociological Review*, 27: 799–811.

Speed, M. F. 1976. Response curves in the one way classification with unequal numbers of observations per cell. *Proceedings of the Statistical Computing Section*, American Statistical Association.

SPSS Inc. 1991. *SPSS statistical algorithms.* 2nd ed. Chicago: SPSS Inc.

Stevens, S. S. 1946. On the theory of scales of measurement. *Science*, 103: 677–680.

Tatsuoka, M. M. 1971. *Multivariate analysis.* New York: John Wiley and Sons.

Theil, H. 1967. *Economics and information theory.* Chicago: Rand McNally.

Tukey, J. W. 1962. The future of data analysis. *Annals of Mathematical Statistics*, 33: 22.

———. 1977. *Exploratory data analysis.* Reading, Mass.: Addison-Wesley.

Velleman, P. F., and D. C. Hoaglin. 1981. *Applications, basics, and computing of exploratory data analysis.* Boston: Suxbury Press.

Velleman, P. F., and R. E. Welsch. 1981. Efficient computing of regression diagnostics. *American Statistician*, 35: 234–242.

Winer, B. J., D. R. Brown, and K. M. Michels. 1991. *Statistical principles in experimental design*. 3rd ed. New York: McGraw-Hill.

Wright, S. 1960. Path coefficients and path regressions: Alternative or complementary concepts? *Biometrics*, 16: 189–202.

Wynder, E. L. 1976. Nutrition and cancer. *Federal Proceedings*, 35: 1309–1315.

Wyner, G. A. 1980. Response errors in self-reported number of arrests. *Sociological Methods and Research*, 9:2, 161–177.

Index